Shaping North America

Shaping North America

From Exploration to the American Revolution

Volume 1: A–E

JAMES E. SEELYE JR. AND
SHAWN SELBY, EDITORS
CHRISTINE EISEL, ASSISTANT EDITOR

ABC-CLIO™

An Imprint of ABC-CLIO, LLC
Santa Barbara, California • Denver, Colorado

Library of Congress Cataloging-in-Publication Data

Names: Seelye, James E., editor. | Selby, Shawn, editor. | Eisel, Christine, editor.
Title: Shaping North America : from exploration to the American Revolution / James E. Seelye Jr. and Shawn Selby, editors ; Christine Eisel, assistant editor.
Description: Santa Barbara, California : ABC-CLIO, LLC, [2018] | Includes bibliographical references and index.
Identifiers: LCCN 2017055421 (print) | LCCN 2018013246 (ebook) | ISBN 9781440836695 (eBook) | ISBN 9781440836688 (set : alk. paper) | ISBN 9781440848742 (volume 1 : alk. paper) | ISBN 9781440848759 (volume 2 : alk. paper) | ISBN 9781440848766 (volume 3 : alk. paper)
Subjects: LCSH: United States—History—Encyclopedias. | United States—Discovery and exploration—Encyclopedias. | North America—Discovery and exploration—Encyclopedias.
Classification: LCC E174 (ebook) | LCC E174 .S54 2018 (print) | DDC 973.03—dc23
LC record available at https://lccn.loc.gov/2017055421

ISBN: 978-1-4408-3668-8 (set)
978-1-4408-4874-2 (vol. 1)
978-1-4408-4875-9 (vol. 2)
978-1-4408-4876-6 (vol. 3)
978-1-4408-3669-5 (ebook)

22 21 20 19 18 1 2 3 4 5

This book is also available as an eBook.

ABC-CLIO
An Imprint of ABC-CLIO, LLC

ABC-CLIO, LLC
130 Cremona Drive, P.O. Box 1911
Santa Barbara, California 93116-1911
www.abc-clio.com

This book is printed on acid-free paper ♾

Manufactured in the United States of America

Contents

List of Entries

Guide to Related Topics

COLONIAL ADMINISTRATION AND POLITICS

Acadians, Deportation of the
Albany Congress
Brent, Margaret Reed
Burke, Edmund
Calvert, George
Calvert, Leonard
Carolina Constitution
Carteret, Philip
Carteret, Sir George
Clarke, John
Colonial Charters
Colonial Government and Politics
Encomienda
George III
Goose Creek Men
Headrights
Hutchinson, Thomas
Hyde, Edward, Viscount Cornbury
Loyalists
Mason, George
Patroonship
Penn, William
Raleigh, Sir Walter
Salutary Neglect
Seeds of Change
Sons of Liberty
Stamp Act Congress
Williams, Roger
Wythe, George

COLONIAL CULTURE AND SOCIETY

American Architecture
American Philosophical Society
Banneker, Benjamin
Bartram, John
Black Legend
Books and Reading
Bradford, William
Bundling
Church, Benjamin
College of William and Mary
Colonial Sports
Contraception
Craftsmen/Artisans
Deference
Drinking and Tavern Culture
English Ballads
Franklin, Benjamin
Fraunces Tavern
Hammon, Jupiter
Harvard College
Holidays
Households
Limners
Literacy
Little Commonwealths
Locke, John
Lotteries
Midwives
Milton, John
Mortality Rates
Punishments
Republicanism
Salutary Neglect
Scotch-Irish
Seeds of Change
Tobacco Brides
Warren, Mercy Otis
Wheatley, Phillis
Widows
Witchcraft
Women

COLONIES AND EUROPEAN POWERS

Chesapeake Bay
Connecticut
Delaware
England
Florida
France
Georgia
Jamestown
Maryland
Massachusetts Bay
Netherlands
New France
New Hampshire
New Haven
New Jersey
New Spain
New York
North Carolina
Pennsylvania
Plymouth
Portugal
Rhode Island
Roanoke, Lost Colony of
South Carolina
Spain
Virginia

ECONOMICS, TRADE, AND LABOR

Agriculture
Apprenticeships
Atlantic Slave Trade
Beaver Trade
Boston Tea Party
Cacao
Charleston
Colonial Economy
Company of One Hundred Associates
Consumer Goods
Craftsmen/Artisans
Disease
Dutch Slave Trade
Fisheries
Fort Michilimackinac
Fur Trade
Gendered Labor
Gun Trade
Hudson's Bay Company
Indentured Servants
Limners
Mercantilism
Middle Passage
Midwives
Navigation Acts
Ohio Company of Virginia
Planters
Redemptioners
Repartimiento
Rice Cultivation
Slavery and Race
Starving Time
Tea
Tobacco Cultivation
Trade
Wampum

EXPLORERS AND CONQUISTADORS

Balboa, Vasco Núñez
Cabeza de Vaca, Alvar Núñez
Cabot, John and Sebastian
Champlain, Samuel de
Clark, George Rogers
Columbian Exchange
Columbus, Christopher
Coronado, Francisco Vasquez de
Cortés, Hernán
Disease
Doctrine of Discovery/Conquest
Hakluyt, Richard
Hudson, Henry
La Salle, Robert
Las Casas, Bartolomé de
Leon, Juan Ponce de
Magellan, Ferdinand
Marquette, Jacques
Oñate, Juan de
Pizarro, Francisco
Prince Henry the Navigator
Soto, Hernando de
Vespucci, Amerigo

INDEPENDENCE

Adams, Abigail
Adams, John
Adams, Samuel
Anti-Federalists
Articles of Confederation
Bill of Rights
Boston Tea Party
Committee of Detail
Committee of Style and Arrangement
Committees of Correspondence
Congress of Confederation
Connecticut Compromise
Constitutional Convention
Continental Congresses
Declaration of Independence
Federal Hall
Federalist Papers
Federalists
Franklin, Benjamin
George III
Hamilton, Alexander
Hancock, John
Henry, Patrick
Independence Hall
Jefferson, Thomas
Madison, James
New Jersey Plan
Paine, Thomas
Randolph, Peyton
Ratification
Three-Fifths Compromise
Virginia Plan
Washington, George

NATIVE PEOPLES AND CONTACT

Aleuts
Algonquin
Atahualpa
Aztec
Brant, Joseph
Columbian Exchange
Cuauhtémoc
Cuzco
Disease
Inca
Iroquois Confederacy
Maya
Mesoamerica
Montezuma II
Natchez Revolt
Native Music and Dancing
Opechancanough
Pequot
Pontiac
Pontiac's Rebellion
Powhatan
Powhatan Confederacy
Pueblo Revolt
Squanto
Tenochtitlán
Wampanoag

RELIGION

Alexander VI
Anglicans
Antinomianism
Baptists
Calvinism
Catholicism
Congregational Church
Cotton, John
Dominicans
Dyer, Mary
Franciscans
German Reformed Church
Gorton, Samuel
Great Awakening
Half-Way Covenant
Holidays
Hooker, Thomas
Hutchinson, Anne
Jesuits
Little Commonwealths
Marquette, Jacques
Mather, Cotton
Mather, Increase
Penn, William
Presbyterianism
Puritan Dissenters

Puritanism
Quakers
Selpúlvada, Juan Ginés de
Slave Religion
Toleration Acts
Virgin of Guadalupe
Whitefield, George
Winthrop, John
Witchcraft

TREATIES AND DOCTRINES

Doctrine of Discovery/Conquest
Treaty of Alliance
Treaty of Fort Stanwix
Treaty of Paris, 1763
Treaty of Paris, 1783
Treaty of Tordesillas

WARFARE, CONFLICTS, AND REVOLTS

Acadians, Deportation of the
Anglo-Dutch Wars
Arnold, Benedict
Bacon's Rebellion
Beaver Wars
Boston Massacre
Braddock, Edward
Brandywine, Battle of
Bunker Hill, Battle of
Camden, Battle of
Chesapeake, Battle of the
Clinton, Sir Henry
Comte de Grasse, François-Joseph Paul
Comte de Rochambeau
Cornwallis, Lord Charles
Cowpens, Battle of
Culpeper's Rebellion
Deerfield Massacre
Disease
Drake, Francis
Dunmore's War
Dutch-Indian Wars
English Civil War
Fort Detroit
Fort Ticonderoga
Fox-French Wars
Gage, Thomas
Gaspee Affair
Gates, Horatio
Goose Creek Men
Greene, Nathanael
Guilford Courthouse, Battle of
Jones, John Paul
King Philip's War
Knox, Henry
Kościuszko, Thaddeus
Lafayette, Marquis de
Lee, Richard Henry
Lexington and Concord
Lincoln, Benjamin
Long Island, Battle of
Militias
Minutemen
Monmouth, Battle of
New York Conspiracy of 1741
Newburgh Conspiracy
Plains of Abraham, Battle of the
Pontiac's Rebellion
Pueblo Revolt
Queen Anne's War
Revere, Paul
Saratoga, Battle of
Seven Years' War
Shays' Rebellion
Steuben, Baron Friedrich von
Stono Rebellion
Trenton, Battle of
Uprising of 1622
Valley Forge
Warfare
Washington, George
Yorktown, Battle of

WESTWARD EXPANSION

Preface

There are many resources available to those interested in learning more about the earliest days of the American continents. Scholars devote a great amount of time and energy analyzing, synthesizing, and interpreting the past, and the result of their work is an almost staggering quantity of material to choose from. We often do not know where to start. The idea behind *Shaping North America: From Exploration to the American Revolution* is to present a sound starting point from which to investigate any number of topics, questions, and issues related to the history of the American continents, from the thousands of years of Indian nation-building; to exploration, colonization, and imperialism; and through the American War of Independence.

The three volumes of this collection contain entries on a vast array of topics, including Indian nations such as the Algonquin, Aztec, Inca, Maya, Pequot, Wampanoag, and others. The collection has entries about explorers and religions, individuals and ideas, and geographical locations and events that were incredibly important to the development of North America, both the well-known and lesser-known. The entries are listed alphabetically rather than chronologically, as many topics are impossible to relegate to a specific point in time.

In addition to a timeline of key events and issues, each entry—all of which were carefully written by scholars without whom this project would have been impossible—is followed by a list resources for further reading on the subject. Some of the sources listed may be familiar to specialists, but a number of them are among the newest contributions to historiography, including, for example, Marcus Rediker's latest book on an abolitionist Quaker who also happened to be a dwarf, Benjamin Lay.

Finally, many of the entries in this collection have primary sources directly connected to them. Readers can learn about a topic and then introduce themselves to sources created by those who lived through the times and events that are described. They can start to learn what it takes to carefully analyze documents and evaluate them for importance, accuracy, and bias. Overall, the editors hope that this collection will be a valuable, useful, and easy-to-navigate resource for those conducting research on the long development of North America and who seek to better understand the diverse plethora of experiences that went into hundreds of years of history.

Introduction

Hundreds of autonomous Indian nations inhabited the continents that eventually became known as the Americas for thousands of years prior to European exploration. Groups such as the Algonquin, Aztec, Pawnee, Apache, Pequot, Powhatan, Anishinaabe, Walla Walla, Kiowa, Inca, Wyandot, and Wampanoag created vast empires and constructed some of the most beautiful edifices the world has ever known. Their societies were as unique as their languages and traditions. Scholars in the present learn about them using careful research, as many of the records America's first nations created were either passed down orally or were destroyed by European invaders. Those same Europeans wrote extensively about the societies that they sought to colonize and conquer, but those sources must be carefully analyzed for bias.

When explorers reached the Americas, most notably with Christopher Columbus's arrival in 1492, both North and South America were inhabited by millions of people. Scholars disagree with estimates, but perhaps 75 million people lived in the Western Hemisphere, mostly north of the Rio Grande. One thing all scholars agree on is that within 100 years of first contact, approximately 90 percent of those millions had perished. They died due to diseases that they had no immunity to that had arrived due to the Columbian Exchange, and they also died at the hands of the Europeans who slaughtered them.

Explorers, colonizers, and conquistadors who followed in Columbus's wake, including Henry Hudson, Samuel de Champlain, Hernán Cortés, and Francisco Pizarro, increased everyone's knowledge about the world. They also disrupted lives in unimaginable ways. Cortés had heard rumors of a vast, wealthy civilization in the interior of Mexico and was ordered by his superior to investigate the claims. He went beyond his orders and tried to keep the spoils of the Aztec civilization to himself. His 1519 arrival in the Aztec homeland ushered in three years of turmoil that ended with the once-mighty nation in ruin. Others followed in his footsteps to find more examples like the Aztec, because there had to be more civilizations like them, each with untold riches. The search spread out over North and South America, and occasionally the Europeans were lucky, such as when Pizarro conquered the Inca in present-day Peru. More often, however, carnage and disease followed them, and the body count was the only thing that they had to show for their efforts.

Eventually, the French and the English became more involved in exploring the New World. The French made progress in Canada and in interior portions of North America, particularly along the Mississippi River. The English's first attempt at a stable and steady colony in North America failed when the colony of Roanoke, off the coast of the Carolinas, was found empty and abandoned in the 1580s. Their next serious attempt came in 1607. The year before, the Virginia Company had been established in London as a joint-stock venture so that like-minded investors could pool their money with the hope of sharing in the profits of exploration.

The first lasting colony they founded was Jamestown, established in 1607. John Smith, their leader, met with Powhatan Indians and eventually settled a foothold in Virginia. The colony nearly failed and faced unbelievable hardships, including disease and starvation. John Rolfe's realization that the "stinky weed" that Indians partook in, tobacco, had the potential to make the Virginia Company and its investors real money ultimately saved the colony. It also introduced new forms of labor, starting with indentured servitude and culminating in the slave trade, where millions of Africans were forcibly removed from their homes and crammed into the bowels of ships to cross the Atlantic Ocean during the Middle Passage.

Farther north, Puritan Separatists established the Plymouth Colony in 1620 in Massachusetts. Again, the colonists faced incredible hardships, and had it not been for the kind, timely interventions of numerous Indians, including the Wampanoag Squanto, that colony would have ended in failure. Other Puritans followed and established themselves throughout New England, including in colonies such as the Massachusetts Bay Colony. Often the theory and the reality of Puritanism clashed. They encouraged education, going so far as to establish the first college in North America, Harvard. They also encouraged their people to read, especially the Bible. This caused some, like Anne Hutchinson, to question some of the Puritan teachings based on her own reading of the Bible. She was the first of many that served as examples of intolerance to other beliefs and the rule of law.

Other colonies followed throughout the 17th century, including the Catholic colony of Maryland and the Quaker colony of Pennsylvania. Ultimately, the Middle and Southern Colonies became the destinations of choice for immigrants, due both to the increased profit-making potential of those colonies and because the intolerance of the Puritans was something of legend. The Puritans' worldview may have led to the Pequot War of 1636–1637, when they conducted a genocidal campaign and nearly exterminated an entire Indian nation. Many more conflicts between Indians and Europeans followed, including King Philip's War in New England in the 1670s and the Pueblo Revolt in the Spanish province of New Mexico in 1680.

The early years of Britain's colonization of North America were fraught with struggle and hardship. English settlers faced an unfamiliar landscape, contentious and often violent interactions with Native Americans, and the growing threat of foreign pressure along the frontiers. For the most part, the 13 separate colonies refused to even work together. They essentially functioned as independent nations under the umbrella of the British Crown. They had been settled by a variety of different populations and had begun to develop very different social and economic foundations. Even so, as the 18th century dawned, the colonies were coming into their own as stable, productive pieces of the British Empire. But their economies were deliberately limited by the British government with the application of a mercantilist system that restricted colonial manufacturing and prevented the colonies from open trade with foreign markets besides England. Despite these limitations, the American population swelled as immigrants from Britain arrived to take advantage of the relative freedom and opportunities the colonies offered. Unlike in the 17th century, many more of these new settlers were free men and women, not indentured servants.

However, at the same time, the colonies began importing a growing number of slaves. Cash crops such as tobacco and indigo were among the most profitable items produced anywhere in the colonies, and expanding labor demands, along with a move away from indentured servitude following Bacon's Rebellion in Virginia in 1676, meant that the majority of field labor in the Chesapeake and Southern Colonies was done by slaves. Although the largest slave populations were found in the Chesapeake and the Southern Colonies, in the years leading to the Revolution, every one of the 13 colonies permitted slavery. The Atlantic slave trade was also a source of great wealth for many New England merchants.

At the same time, there were social changes taking place that would have long-term consequences for American history. The Evangelical religious movement known as the Great Awakening was profoundly influential in American intellectual history. During the 1730s and 1740s, it introduced an intensely passionate Christian evangelism to American Protestantism. In addition, the revivalism associated with the movement, though centered in New England and the Middle Colonies, spread into the Southern Colonies. There, it seeped into slave cultures, creating a noticeable growth in Christianity among enslaved Africans who embraced the religion's egalitarian qualities as well as the symbolic importance of the Exodus.

In something of a paradox, the Enlightenment, an intellectual movement emphasizing reason and scientific investigation, also became one of the most powerful influences on American intellectual culture of the 1700s. Although predominantly a European development, prominent Americans such as Benjamin Franklin, Thomas Jefferson, James Madison, and George Mason considered themselves inheritors of the Enlightenment's ideals. Those ideals formed the core of the American response to British authority in the 1760s and 1770s.

As European settlement of North America expanded, Native Americans found themselves increasingly pressured to abandon their traditional lands. Individual colonies as well as the British Crown entered into treaties and alliances with various tribes and nations to try to maintain peace; however, there would be flare-ups, such as Dunmore's War in the Ohio River valley in 1774.

For much of the 18th century, the colonies were also embroiled in a constantly shifting game of North American influence being played by European powers, especially France, Britain, and Spain. More than once, these regional maneuverings erupted into outright war. At the dawn of the century, Britain and France squared off in North America in what was known to colonists as Queen Anne's War (1702–1713). Much of the fighting took place in Europe (where the conflict was known as the War of Spanish Succession). But the colonists, especially in the Northeast, experienced several violent encounters.

During the later French and Indian War, colonists aided the British army in resisting French encroachment along the western frontier. By the end of the war, in 1763, the French presence in North America was essentially eliminated. England controlled virtually all of North America east of the Mississippi River. But the cost of the war was tremendous, and efforts by the British government to pay down its debt resulted in new or renewed taxes that colonists found increasingly onerous.

By the 1760s and 1770s, Americans had thrived under a nearly 70-year period of "salutary neglect," wherein the British government treated the colonies with a sort of hands-off approach. However, Britain's enormous war debt forced Parliament and King George III to enact or restore a series of taxes on the empire. American colonists chaffed under these apparently arbitrary and excessive taxes and regulations. And so, resistance to these laws blossomed into outright rebellion and revolution. Tension between patriots and the Crown centered on the American belief that the British government was violating the colonists' traditional rights as British citizens. In fact, the beginning stages of resistance and rebellion were not intended to push the colonies toward independence from England. Instead, Americans forcefully argued that their rights as equal citizens of the empire were being trampled upon. Even by the time of the drafting of the Declaration of Independence, more than a year after the first shots of the Revolution had been fired at Lexington and Concord, Massachusetts, there was still debate over whether independence was the right choice. Some feared the consequences of a failed effort at separation. Others feared the consequences if the effort were successful!

Colonists in the 1760s and 1770s had to make tough choices about whether to remain loyal to the British government or to separate from the Crown and start a new government. Some Americans chose to remain loyal to the Crown out of a sense of obligation and genuine belief in the rightness of the Crown's rule. Others feared that an independent America would be violently democratic or that it would be overwhelmed on the world stage. Despite the arguments and efforts of the Loyalists, the patriots emerged victorious. Many of the hundreds of thousands of Loyalists in America were eventually forced from their homes at the conclusion of the war.

The war years were fraught with hardship and privation as the country struggled with the financial, diplomatic, and military challenges of fighting the most powerful empire on the planet. The Continental Army seemed to lose more battles than it won. Nevertheless, the victory at Saratoga, in New York, in the fall of 1777 convinced France to join the fight on the side of the Americans. Though the French saw this as much as a chance to hamstring their old rivals, the British, as it was in support of the American causes of "liberty" and "independence," their decision to provide financial, material, and military aid would be vital in helping the Continental Army achieve victory. Nowhere was this aid more crucial than at the Battle of the Chesapeake and the Battle of Yorktown in the fall of 1781, which together led to the ultimate surrender of British forces in North America.

Once America had gained its independence, the new nation was faced with some serious challenges. The government of the Articles of Confederation was weak and decentralized. The country struggled with crippling economic problems. Some dissatisfied Americans even resorted to rebellions against their own states. In the mid-1780s, men such as James Madison and Alexander Hamilton believed the country needed a more powerful and centralized national government. They led the push for the Constitution. And while the new government they shepherded into existence was certainly very different from the Congress of Confederation, it still faced challenges with an emerging two-party system and with the increasing division over slave and "free" states. These tensions, some dating back to the earliest settlements of Jamestown and Plymouth, would have profound consequences in the 19th century as the country came to grips with a growing sectional divide.

Chronology

1492	Christopher Columbus arrives in the Americas.
1519	Cortés lands at Vera Cruz and begins his march toward Tenochtitlán.
1520	Epidemics break out in Mesoamerica, including influenza and smallpox.
1535	Jacques Cartier explores the St. Lawrence River Valley.
1540	The Spanish continue their exploration throughout the Southeast, South, and Southwest.
1585	The Spanish settle in St. Augustine, Florida.
	The English establish a colony at Roanoke.
1598	Onate establishes a Spanish colony in New Mexico.
1607	The English establish a colony at Jamestown.
1616–1619	Epidemics sweep through New England.
1620	English Separatists establish a colony at Plymouth.
1622	Opechancanough leads the Powhatan Indians in a revolt against the English at Jamestown.
1630s	There is a "Great Migration" of 20,000 English Puritans to New England.
1636–1637	The Pequot War and the Fort Mystic Massacre take place.
1675–1676	Metacom, known as King Philip to the English, leads New England Indians in a revolt against the colonists.
	Nathanial Bacon leads Bacon's Rebellion, with the aim of destroying the Indians in Virginia.
1685	Pennsylvania is established.
1701	The Iroquois Confederacy agrees to peace with France and Great Britain.
1702	The royal colony of New Jersey is established by Queen Anne, unifying the separate provinces of East and West New Jersey.
1704	Fifty-six settlers are killed when French and Indian forces attack Deerfield, Massachusetts Bay Colony, during Queen Anne's War.
1712	More than two dozen are executed or commit suicide after a slave revolt in New York City.

1715	The Yamasee War is fought in the Carolinas.
1730	Franciscan missionaries establish their first missions in California.
1732	James Oglethorpe is granted a corporate charter to establish Georgia as a debtors' penal colony.
	Benjamin Franklin publishes the first *Poor Richard's Almanack*.
1735	John Peter Zegner is acquitted on charges of libel in New York, resulting in establishment of freedom of the press in the colonies.
1738	Anglican minister George Whitefield arrives in America for the first time; he will go on to become the preeminent preacher of the Great Awakening.
	Smallpox kills approximately half of the Cherokee population.
1741	New York City experiences its second slave uprising in a generation, resulting in 30 slaves hanged or burned alive and another 70 deported.
1752	Benjamin Franklin invents the lightning rod after his experiments with lightning prove that it is indeed electricity.
1754	Benjamin Franklin proposes the Albany Plan in the face of growing tension with the French and Indians.
	George Washington leads a failed raid against Fort Duquesne in one of the first actions of the French and Indian War.
1755	British forces relocate more than 11,000 French settlers of Acadia in Nova Scotia.
1759	Gen. James Wolfe leads British forces in the Battle of the Plains of Abraham. Despite dying in the effort, Wolfe's victory effectively ends French control of Canada and leads to the end of the Seven Years' War in 1763.
1763	The Treaty of Paris formally ends the Seven Years' War (known in the colonies as the French and Indian War) and grants England vast land concessions in North America.
	King George III issues the Proclamation of 1763, barring white settlement west of the Appalachian Mountains and creating one of the earliest colonial grievances that will lead to the Revolution.
	Pontiac's Rebellion takes place in the Great Lakes.
	British commander Jeffrey Amherst suggests the use of smallpox against Indians.
1764	Parliament passes a revised Sugar Act, taxing lumber, molasses, and rum.
1765	Parliament passes the Stamp Act, requiring that a royal stamp be affixed to all printed material in the colonies. Response to the act becomes a flash point for patriot agitation.

Delegates from nine colonies meet in New York at the Stamp Act Congress to coordinate a response to the tax.

The patriot resistance organization the Sons of Liberty is established in Boston to lead resistance to the Stamp Act. Prominent members include Samuel Adams, Paul Revere, and Benedict Arnold. It soon spreads to other colonies.

Patrick Henry proposes the Virginia Resolves in the House of Burgesses. Among the Resolves is one declaring anyone who supports Parliament's right to tax the colonies a traitor.

1766 Parliament repeals the Stamp Act in the face of mounting colonial resistance. It passes the Declaratory Act, reasserting its power to legislate the colonies "in all cases whatsoever."

1767 British chancellor of the exchequer Charles Townshend creates a series of import taxes for goods entering the American colonies. This affects tea, painter's lead, glass, and other staples of the economy. Americans respond with boycotts.

1770 Five demonstrators in Boston are killed when British army guards at the customs house open fire into a crowd. Patriots represent the killings as deliberate, despite a court acquitting all but two of the soldiers involved. The Boston Massacre adds to growing tension in the colonies over the actions of Parliament, the king and the British army.

Parliament repeals most of the Townshend Duties. The tax on tea remains and will play a role in the Tea Act and Boston Tea Party three years later.

1772 The *Gaspee* Affair occurs when patriots lure the British customs ship HMS *Gaspee* onto shoals near Warwick, Rhode Island. The following day, they burn the ship in protest of British taxes.

Samuel Adams organizes the first Committee of Correspondence. Other committees will be formed throughout the colonies to coordinate resistance to parliamentary authority. They will eventually be the forerunners of semiautonomous colonial governments.

1773 Parliament passes the Tea Act, granting the British East India Company a virtual monopoly to sell its tea in the colonies without being taxed.

In December, scores of patriots, some dressed as Mohawk Indians, board three British ships in Boston Harbor and toss nearly 350 crates of tea into the sea.

1774 Parliament, outraged by the Boston Tea Party, passes a series of laws to punish the city and extract recompense for the lost tea. These laws, known in Britain as the Coercive Acts and in

America as the Intolerable Acts, severely restrict Massachusetts' colonial government and judicial system and close Boston's port until the value of the destroyed tea is repaid.

Delegates from 12 colonies (Georgia being the lone exception) meet in Philadelphia at the First Continental Congress. Delegates pledge allegiance to the Crown and call for a general boycott of British goods if the Intolerable Acts are not repealed by the spring of 1775.

1775 The first shots of the American Revolution are fired at Lexington and Concord, Massachusetts, when colonial militia—the minutemen—exchange shots with British regulars marching toward Concord on a mission to capture weapons and gunpowder held at the magazine there.

Patrick Henry delivers his "Give Me Liberty, or Give Me Death" speech before the Virginia House of Burgesses.

British regulars win a pyrrhic victory over colonial militia at the Battle of Bunker Hill.

The Second Continental Congress appoints George Washington commander of the newly constituted Continental Army.

1776 Thomas Paine's pamphlet *Common Sense* is published and quickly sells hundreds of thousands of copies.

The Second Continental Congress declares the colonies independent and accepts a Declaration of Independence written largely by Thomas Jefferson.

The Continental Army loses New York to the British.

George Washington leads the Americans in a successful attack on the garrison at Trenton, New Jersey, on Christmas Day. A few days later, the Americans defeat Cornwallis's army at the Battle of Princeton.

1777 American forces under Horatio Gates and Benedict Arnold defeat the British at the Battle of Saratoga.

1778 In light of the American victory at Saratoga, France agrees to a Treaty of Alliance with the United States, promising money, material, and military support.

1781 A combined Franco-American force defeats Cornwallis at Yorktown, Virginia, effectively ending major military action in the Revolution.

The Articles of Confederation establish the first operating government of the United States.

1783 The Treaty of Paris ends the American Revolution and recognizes America's independence from Britain.

	George Washington quashes a potential coup in Newburgh, New York.
	Massachusetts bans slavery in the state.
1786–1787	Shays' Rebellion in Massachusetts convinces political leaders of the need for a stronger central government.
1787	Delegates to a convention in Philadelphia draft the U.S. Constitution.
1788	James Madison, John Jay, and Alexander Hamilton write the *Federalist Papers* to encourage ratification of the Constitution.
1789	New Hampshire becomes the ninth state to ratify the Constitution, officially putting it into effect.
	George Washington is unanimously elected as the first president of the United States.

A

ACADIANS, DEPORTATION OF THE

From their beginnings, the British colonies in New England frequently served as a refuge for people seeking freedom and liberty. But not all who sought refuge came from across the Atlantic. Indeed, seeking freedom from some of the same oppression that would ultimately lead the British colonies to independence, some refugees in fact came from other parts of North America. One of the last formal groups to do this was the Acadians, who, on the eve of the French and Indian War (or Seven Years' War, 1756–1763), were forced to flee their long-time home in Nova Scotia, modern Canada, when forced to declare allegiance to the British in 1755. Their flight was later immortalized in Henry Wadsworth Longfellow's 1847 poem "Evangeline."

The Acadians were a group of people of French descent who had inhabited the territory of Nova Scotia since the founding of Port Royal in 1604. They created a small but active colony around the Bay of Fundy. Constructing high dikes to combat and utilize the high tides and to irrigate the fertile fields of hay, they were allowed to go their own way with virtually no supervision or oversight by the French government. This freedom, which had given them a solid sense of independence, was compromised after the British conquered Port Royal in 1710 and took control of Acadia under the Treaty of Utrecht (1713). The Acadians initially resisted British control, but the British, who were technically in control of the area, adopted a benign approach, allowing the Acadians religious freedom and not forcing them to take up arms on behalf of the Crown. In 1730, they did seek to have the Acadians swear an oath of loyalty, but when the proposal was met with opposition, the governor accepted an oath of neutrality toward any French-British conflict, a demand that seemed innocuous at the time.

However, tensions between the countries grew with the construction of competing forts, with the French Fort Beausejour, on the Isthmus of Chignecto, being matched by Britain's Fort Lawrence, just a short distance away. Finally, in the summer of 1755, tensions had reached a point where the British governor Charles Lawrence, seeing the Acadian situation as nothing more than a military matter—albeit an important one—demanded that the Acadians take an oath of unqualified allegiance to Britain. Those who refused were imprisoned, and soon afterward, he gave the order for their deportation. The government soon undertook an effort to round up the Acadians and send them out of the area. By the fall of 1755, over 1,100 had left on transports headed for Pennsylvania, South Carolina, and Georgia.

Opposition continued, and while the British sought to continue the deportation effort, many Acadians sought to escape, often seeking to hide in the forest, only to be hunted down by government agents. The paths for their relocation were varied and often tragic. One group joined the existing community in the Cape Sable area, in part because Lawrence did not realize that an Acadian community existed in that region, and as a result they had been ignored as the government began its efforts. However, upon detection, that area was also cleared out. Meanwhile, others sought a new life in the British colonies with, by some reports, between 6,000 and 8,000 settling in the established British colonies up and down the Atlantic coast, from Massachusetts to South Carolina. Some of those who did not seek that option headed westward, looking for protection in areas still held by the French.

In the end, from 1755 until 1763, roughly 10,000 Acadians were deported, and while all were forced to leave, the differences in their experiences were often stark. As noted, thousands ended up in the English colonies, but they were not always welcomed. As French-speaking Catholics, they were often not treated well by the predominantly English Protestants, and many survived only by agreeing to serve as indentured servants.

Meanwhile, others returned to France and still others to the Caribbean, but not all of those voyages ended successfully; even when the ships survived the voyage, many individuals did not reach their hoped-for destination, instead dying of disease, starvation, or squalor on board the transport ships. Too, many were simply left to wander, especially once English colonists became aware of the diseases that many of the refugees carried.

Ultimately, the British recognized that the effort had been misguided, and in 1764, following the end of the French and Indian War and the signing of the peace treaty, Acadians were allowed to return—and many did—joining the English colonists who had flocked to the area as the Acadians were dispersed. However, in most cases, perhaps seeking to start anew and also recognizing that, for the most part, they would be unable to recover the property they had been forced to abandon when they were deported, they simply did not return to their previous homes or settlements. Rather, they tended to begin new lives in new areas—such as St. Mary's Bay, Cape Breton, and Prince Edward Island, as well as to the north and east of what is today New Brunswick. One cultural offshoot of the deportation effort was the small group that ultimately ended up in what became Louisiana, marking the beginnings of a still-thriving Acadian community in that area.

Historians now see the deportation effort as one lacking in reason or value. It was not necessary from a military perspective, and it was by all measure inhumane in its treatment of the thousands who were victimized by the order. Lawrence is faulted on many fronts. A lackluster leader, he misread the military and political situation while also demonstrating unfortunate cultural misunderstanding and serving as the point person for the nation's greed, manifested as it was in colonization and land acquisition. All these issues were embodied in the inhumane endeavor that was the Acadian deportation.

William H. Pruden III

See also: France; New France; Seven Years' War

Further Reading

"The Deportation Orders." Acadian.org. https://www.acadian.org/history/the-deportation-orders.

Faragher, John Mack. 2006. *A Great and Noble Scheme: The Tragic Story of the Expulsion of the French Acadians from Their American Homeland.* New York: W. W. Norton & Company.

Griffiths, Naomi E. S. 1992. *The Contexts of Acadian History, 1686–1784.* Montreal and Kingston: McGill-Queen's University Press.

"History." Acadian.org. https://www.acadian.org/history.

ADAMS, ABIGAIL (1744–1818)

Abigail Smith Adams, the wife of President John Adams and the mother of President John Quincy Adams, was one of the country's most important first ladies. During the prolonged periods when John was absent due to involvement in politics and diplomacy, Abigail oversaw the education of the children and was responsible for the family and finances. Abigail and John's correspondence, which stretched over four decades, is, according to historian Joseph Ellis, "a treasure trove of unexpected intimacy and candor, more revealing than any other correspondence between a prominent American husband and wife in American history" (Ellis 2010, ix). John often solicited Abigail's advice, and her letters demonstrate that she was a shrewd and capable adviser.

Abigail Adams, the wife of President John Adams and the mother of President John Quincy Adams, was a shrewd and capable advisor to her husband and an important historical figure in her own right. (National Gallery of Art)

Abigail took a variety of important stands throughout her life and argued for women's rights, equal education for boys and girls, and antislavery measures. In a famous letter, she admonished John to "remember the ladies" when the Continental Congress was creating a new government. At a time when many men resented and mocked female intrusion in the "public sphere," Abigail injected herself into the great questions of the day and proved herself more adept at navigating the treacherous shoals of politics than many of her male counterparts. Abigail, therefore, is important not simply because she was married to one president and the mother of another, but because of her keen intellect, shrewdness, and the profound impact she had on her family and the country.

Abigail Smith was born in Weymouth, Massachusetts, on November 11, 1744, to William and Elizabeth Smith. The Smiths had deep roots in New England. William was a popular Congregationalist minister, and Elizabeth was the daughter of John Quincy, a longtime Speaker of the Massachusetts House of Representatives. As a girl, Abigail was often sickly. Like many women of the time, she did not receive any formal education, although Elizabeth taught Abigail and her two sisters how to read and write. Later in life, Abigail argued that girls should receive the same education as boys. She spent much of her youth corresponding with friends and family and reading books in her father's library and the library of her grandfather, John Quincy. Her voracious reading exposed her to writers such as William Shakespeare and John Milton, among many others, and likely facilitated the development of her ideas about women's rights, government, and politics.

Abigail Smith and John Adams were third cousins. When they first met each other, in 1759, neither one was particularly impressed. Abigail was 15, and John was 24; this age difference was likely a stumbling block. As historian Joseph Ellis wryly comments, "This first meeting was an awkward occasion on which the abiding qualities of her mind and heart were obscured beneath the frozen etiquette of a pastor's parlor" (Ellis 2010, 4). Despite an unremarkable first meeting, by 1761, John had begun to take an interest in Abigail, and she reciprocated his interest. The couple was married October 25, 1764.

Abigail's mother was not pleased about the marriage at first. John, a country lawyer, did not seem urbane enough for her daughter. However, she eventually acceded, and the couple left Weymouth for a small cottage in Braintree, Massachusetts. As his law practice grew, John and Abigail moved to a series of rented houses in Boston and shuffled between Braintree and Boston. In a 10-year period, Abigail gave birth to six children: Abigail "Nabby" Amelia Adams Smith (1765–1813), John Quincy Adams (1767–1848), Grace Susannah Adams (1768–1770), Charles Adams (1770–1800), Thomas Boylston Adams (1772–1832), and Elizabeth Adams (stillborn).

The distance from Braintree to Boston was not particularly significant, but as John became more involved in the law and politics, the newly married couple spent time apart, presaging the long periods of time Abigail and John spent apart when John attended the Continental Congresses and served in Europe on several diplomatic missions. While John was away, Abigail took care of the property and the finances, supervised the education of her children, and reminded them, perhaps rather stridently, what they owed to the Adams's tradition. At this time, married women had limited property rights because of the doctrine of coverture, which dictated a woman's subordinate legal status during marriage. Abigail challenged coverture by referring to the property and possessions as "ours" rather than "yours," thus staking a claim to the couple's worldly goods in a way many women of the time did not.

When John went to Philadelphia in 1774 to serve as a delegate from Massachusetts to the First Continental Congress, Abigail remained in Massachusetts. John not only participated in the First Continental Congress but in the Second Continental Congress as well, and he also played a key role in drafting the Declaration of

See also: Adams, John; Adams, Samuel; Women

Further Reading

Ellis, Joseph J. 2010. *First Family: Abigail and John Adams.* New York: Random House, Inc.

Gelles, Edith B. 1992. *Portia: The World of Abigail Adams.* Bloomington: Indiana University Press.

Gelles, Edith B. 2002. *Abigail Adams: A Writing Life.* New York: Routledge.

Gelles, Edith B. 2009. *Abigail and John: Portrait of a Marriage.* New York, HarperCollins Publishers.

Holton, Woody. 2009. *Abigail Adams: A Life.* New York: Simon & Schuster, Inc.

PRIMARY DOCUMENT: Abigail Adams, "Remember the Ladies" Letter (1776)

Abigail Adams holds a unique place in American history as the wife of President John Adams. While her husband was in Philadelphia as a representative to the First Continental Congress, Adams wrote letters providing him with information and shrewd insights into the political situation in Boston while he was absent. The letter urged him to "remember the ladies" while obtaining independence for the men of the former colonies and warned of a possible rebellion if women continued to have no voice or representation.

Braintree, March 31, 1776

I wish you would ever write me a Letter half as long as I write you; and tell me if you may where your Fleet are gone? What sort of Defence Virginia can make against our common Enemy? Whether it is so situated as to make an able Defence? Are not the Gentery Lords and the common people vassals, are they not like the uncivilized Natives Brittain represents us to be? I hope their Riffel Men who have shewen themselves very savage and even Blood thirsty; are not a specimen of the Generality of the people.

I am willing to allow the Colony great merrit for having produced a Washington but they have been shamefully duped by a Dunmore.

I have sometimes been ready to think that the passion for Liberty cannot be Eaquelly Strong in the Breasts of those who have been accustomed to deprive their fellow Creatures of theirs. Of this I am certain that it is not founded upon that generous and christian principal of doing to others as we would that others should do unto us. . . .

I long to hear that you have declared an independancy—and by the way in the new Code of Laws which I suppose it will be necessary for you to make I desire you would Remember the Ladies, and be more generous and favourable to them than your ancestors. Do not put such unlimited power into the hands of the Husbands. Remember all Men would be tyrants if they could. If perticuliar care and attention is not paid to the Laidies we are determined to foment a Rebelion, and will not hold ourselves bound by any Laws in which we have no voice, or Representation.

That your Sex are Naturally Tyrannical is a Truth so thoroughly established as to admit of no dispute, but such of you as wish to be happy willingly give up the harsh title of Master for the more tender and endearing one of Friend. Why then, not put it out of the power of the vicious and the Lawless to use us with cruelty and indignity with impunity. Men of Sense in all Ages abhor those customs which treat us only as the vassals of your Sex. Regard us then as Beings placed by providence under your protection and in immitation of the Supreem Being make use of that power only for our happiness.

Not having an opportunity of sending this I shall add a few lines more; tho not with a heart so gay. I have been attending the sick chamber of our Neighbour Trot whose affliction I most sensibly feel but cannot discribe, striped of two lovely children in one week. Gorge the Eldest died on wednesday and Billy the youngest on fryday, with the Canker fever, a terible disorder so much like the thr[o]at distemper, that it differs but little from it. Betsy Cranch has been very bad, but upon the recovery. Becky Peck they do not expect will live out the day. Many grown person[s] are now sick with it, in this [street?] It rages much in other Towns. The Mumps too are very frequent. Isaac is now confined with it. Our own little flock are yet well. My Heart trembles with anxiety for them. God preserve them.

I want to hear much oftener from you than I do. March 8 was the last date of any that I have yet had.—You inquire of whether I am making Salt peter. I have not yet attempted it, but after Soap making believe I shall make the experiment. I find as much as I can do to manufacture cloathing for my family which would else be Naked. I know of but one person in this part of the Town who has made any, that is Mr. Tertias Bass as he is calld who has got very near an hundred weight which has been found to be very good. I have heard of some others in the other parishes. Mr. Reed of Weymouth has been applied to, to go to Andover to the mills which are now at work, and has gone. I have lately seen a small Manuscrip de[s] cribing the proportions for the various sorts of powder, fit for cannon, small arms and pistols. If it would be of any Service your way I will get it transcribed and send it to you.—Every one of your Friend[s] send their Regards, and all the little ones. Your Brothers youngest child lies bad with convulsion fitts. Adieu. I need not say how much I am Your ever faithfull Friend.

Source: Letter from Abigail Adams to John Adams, March 31, 1776. Adams, Charles Francis, ed. 1875. *Familiar Letters of John Adams and His Wife Abigail Adams, during the Revolution.* Cambridge, MA: Houghton, 149 150.

ADAMS, JOHN (1735–1826)

As a Founding Father and the second president of the United States, John Adams played an influential role in the formation and subsequent development of the American republic in the late 18th and early 19th centuries.

John Adams was born on October 30, 1735, the eldest son in a prominent family in Quincy, Massachusetts (then known as Braintree). His mother's family included a number of physicians, and his father was a Congregationalist deacon, lieutenant in the militia, and selectman (the equivalent of a town councilman.) He was classically educated until the age of 16, when he enrolled at Harvard

John Adams was a Founding Father and served as the second president of the United States. Though somewhat overshadowed by his contemporaries, Washington and Jefferson, his legacy as one of the leaders in the fight for independence from the British is significant. (National Gallery of Art)

College. As the eldest son in the family, Adams felt a keen responsibility to live up to the family's local reputation.

Adams first rose to prominence in Boston with his response to the Stamp Act in 1765. His "Braintree Instructions" were a statement of discontent with the Stamp Act as well as an outline of the rights possessed by all Englishmen, and which were supposedly being violated by Parliament. Adams first gained widespread recognition throughout the American colonies when he brought his Harvard legal training to bear as the defense attorney for the British soldiers accused of killing five people during the Boston Massacre in March 1770. Despite Adams's own grievances concerning the British military presence in Boston, he agreed to represent the accused soldiers because of his belief that "council [*sic*] ought to be the very last thing that an accused person should want in a free country" (Adams 1776). While many people at the time believed that there was no way that the soldiers would receive a fair trial in a city filled with as much anti-British sentiment as Boston, Adams proved the naysayers wrong by getting six of the eight men on trial acquitted and the remaining two found guilty of the lesser charge of manslaughter. Adams's performance during the Boston Massacre trials contributed to his rising status as a gifted orator and his subsequent election to the Massachusetts Assembly. Four years later, Adams was appointed by that same legislative body to represent Massachusetts as one of the colony's four delegates at the First Continental Congress held in Philadelphia in the fall of 1774. His journey to Philadelphia was one of the first times he had been away from his wife, Abigail, for an extended period. He and Abigail, a formidable woman and one of the most intelligent and well-informed women in America, had married in October 1764. Together, they would have six children, including future president John Quincy Adams.

The First Continental Congress was in session for only a short amount of time, convening on September 5, 1774, and disbanding on October 26, 1774, but it was just long enough for some of the other delegates' behavior to grate on Adams's nerves. While he respected his fellow delegates' talents, he believed that they were conducting the business of the congress far too slowly. In one of his many letters to Abigail, Adams quipped that "if it was moved and seconded that we should come to a resolution that three and two makes five, we should be entertained with logic and rhetoric, law, history, politics, and mathematics concerning the subject for two whole days, and then we should pass the revolution unanimously in the affirmative" (Adams 1963).

Despite the slow pace at which the congress attended to its tasks, it did accomplish the adoption of the Declaration and Resolves of the First Continental Congress, a statement written in response to British implementation of the Coercive Acts—which the colonists referred to as the Intolerable Acts. The declaration included a list of the colonists' grievances against Parliament as well as a colonial bill of rights. With their work completed, the representatives returned to their respective colonies and promised to meet again in May 1775, if their concerns went unaddressed.

The pace of proceedings at the Second Continental Congress, which convened on May 5, 1775, were greatly improved. Not only did the delegates raise an army, appoint George Washington as commander in chief, and issue the first form of continental currency within the first few months of being in session, but by early 1776, they had also begun open discussion of the colonies declaring independence from Great Britain. Adams had been contemplating the issue of independence privately for some time, as evidenced by his inclusion of a "Declaration of Independency" in a list in his diary of what needed to be accomplished during the congress's next session. Just as Adams's fine oratory skills aided him in convincing the jury in the Boston Massacre trial of the soldiers' innocence, they also served him well in his task of convincing those delegates against declaring independence—who also happened to be the majority—into changing their minds.

On July 1, 1776, with the vote regarding Richard Henry Lee's resolution for independence imminent, Adams gave one of the most important speeches of his political career. Although no transcript of Adams's speech exists, the effect of his words is hinted at in a description of Adams by his sometime friend and sometime foe Thomas Jefferson. In conversation with Daniel Webster, Jefferson stated that "John Adams was our Colossus on the floor. He was not graceful, not elegant, nor remarkably fluent but he came out occasionally with a power of thought and expression, that moved us from our seats" (Hazelton 1906). In comparing him to a Colossus, Jefferson was not referring to Adams's immense size—for he was a man of small stature—but the power of his thoughts and expressions to change the minds of those who opposed independence and to strengthen the resolve of those who had already decided upon it.

In addition to being the leading advocate in congress for independence from Britain, Adams was also concerned with what type of government the new nation would utilize. Initially written in response to some of his fellow delegates' requests for suggestion on what kind of governments to establish in their soon-to-be-independent states, Adams's *Thoughts on Government: Applicable to the Present State of the American Colonies* was eventually published as a pamphlet and would heavily influence the very structure of the federal government of the United States. Adams's

Thoughts on Government called for a mixed government, with a legislature to make laws, an executive to administer them, and a judiciary to enforce them. This division would ensure that no single branch became more powerful than another, thus essentially creating a system of checks and balances. The legislature Adams proposed was to be bicameral, with an upper house consisting of property owners and a lower house consisting of the landless majority. Lastly, Adams advocated that the executive have veto power as well as the power to appoint both judges and militia officers. Above all else, Adams believed that this form of government would provide the people with a government that would serve what he viewed the purpose of all governments to be: to ensure the happiness of the people.

Lee's resolution for independence was approved on July 2, 1776. Adams, along with Benjamin Franklin, Roger Sherman, and Robert Livingston, had been working with Thomas Jefferson to draft the Declaration of Independence for several weeks, and two days after Lee's resolution passed, Congress ratified the Declaration. Adams most likely believed his duty to the new nation was finished, but he was wrong. In November of 1777, Adams received word that he had been appointed a commissioner to the Court of France. He, along with Benjamin Franklin and Arthur Lee, were being sent abroad to negotiate an alliance with France, the one country Americans hoped they could count on to fight with them in the Revolutionary War against the British.

Adams left the United States in February of 1778 and arrived in France on April 1. However, before he had even left the port of Boston, the alliance with France had already been signed. With his original task already completed, Adams spent the following several weeks being introduced by Franklin to the movers and shakers of France with the hope of cultivating an even tighter alliance with America. He soon tired of his role in the commission, however, feeling that keeping up the French alliance could be accomplished by Franklin alone. In September 1778, Congress conceded to Adams's wishes and disbanded the commission, naming Franklin the sole minister to the Court of Louis XVI. The dispatches, which took until February 1779 to arrive, gave Lee an assignment in Spain, but Congress failed to provide Adams with any new orders. So, he took it upon himself to secure passage back to the United States.

Not long after Adams arrived home in Braintree in August 1779, he was called upon to serve yet again—this time as a delegate to the Massachusetts Constitutional Convention. Adams found himself essentially the lone author of the state's constitution. In writing "A Constitution or Form of Government for the Commonwealth of Massachusetts," Adams drew upon his previous work *Thoughts on Government*, incorporating a governmental structure divided among three branches. The state convention went on to approve most of Adams's draft, making only a few alterations in wording that did not change its essential character. Once again, believing he could now retire to his private life as an attorney, Adams was surprised to receive a letter from Congress in October of that year asking him to return to France to take part in negotiations aimed at achieving peace with the British.

Although Adams arrived in France in January 1780, he was again left adrift by Congress with no instructions. He kept himself busy by traveling to Amsterdam that July, with the idea of procuring a loan from the Dutch Republic so that the United States would be less dependent on France for the remainder of the Revolution. When word of Adams's unofficial sojourn to the Netherlands reached Congress in the summer of 1781, his role as America's sole negotiator of peace was revoked. Adams would have the last laugh, however, as his unofficial dealings with the Dutch garnered a loan of $2 million from three Dutch banks in June 1782 and the signing of a treaty of commerce with the Dutch Republic that October.

Formal negotiations for peace with the British began on October 30, but this time around Adams was not alone; he was part of a peace commission that also consisted of Benjamin Franklin, John Jay, and Henry Laurens. The elements of the negotiation that were of the utmost importance to the American diplomats were British recognition of the United States' independence and the ceding of all British territory between the Appalachian Mountains and the Mississippi River to the United States. With negotiations between enemies dragging on as they often do, the final draft of the Treaty of Paris was signed on September 3, 1783, nearly a year after the peace talks had commenced. Adams stayed in Paris until 1785, using it as his central hub from which to travel throughout Europe seeking commerce treaties between the new United States and the nations of the Old World. Joining Adams in this task was Thomas Jefferson, and it was this time spent in Europe together that would solidify a bond between the two politicians that would last throughout the rest of their lives.

Adams's final appointment before returning to the United States for good was as the American minister to the Court of St. James (the government of England), a position that he held from 1785 to 1788. In his audience with King George III in June 1785, Adams explained his desire for restoring old ties with Britain. His efforts would prove difficult, however, as Adams himself, as well as his mission to tie up the loose ends left over from the Treaty of Paris, were viewed by the majority of the British population with the utmost contempt. When John Adams departed Britain for the United States on March 30, 1788, he truly believed that his time in the political limelight was over and that he would return to a quiet life in Braintree, which he would spend farming and practicing law. Once again, however, his future lay elsewhere.

As mandated by the Constitution, the election of 1788–1789 determined the vice president of the United States as the candidate who received the second most electoral votes. This system would be changed in 1804 with the addition of the Twelfth Amendment to the Constitution, which established the modern system of allowing electors to vote for tickets consisting of two individuals. In February 1789, the second-place candidate was none other than John Adams. Despite holding the second-highest office in the land, Adams viewed the office of vice president as a poor consolation prize for losing the presidency. In a letter to Abigail at the beginning of his second term, Adams stated, "My country in its wisdom contrived for me the most insignificant office that ever the invention of man contrived or his imagination conceived" (Adams 1793). Adams received a second chance at the presidency in 1796. His odds of winning the election were much improved, considering George Washington's refusal to serve a third term, but he still had to go up against his friend and political rival Thomas Jefferson. When the votes were tallied, however, Adams had defeated Jefferson by three electoral votes, 71 to 68.

Not long after Adams assumed the office of the president on March 4, 1797, he had to deal with the consequences of an ongoing war between Britain and the French Republic. Since 1792, both France and Britain had made a habit of capturing the merchant ships of neutral nations—including the United States—which were believed to be trading with their respective enemies. During the Washington administration, Secretary of Foreign Affairs John Jay had negotiated a treaty with Britain in 1795 to bring an end to these ship seizures. Jay's Treaty had averted an outbreak of war with Britain and allowed trade between the Americans and the British to recommence, but it had also strained relations with the French Republic because they felt that many of the terms of the treaty broke promises the United States had previously made to France. The minister to France, Charles Cotesworth Pinckney, made an attempt to ease the heightening tensions by traveling to Paris to meet with members of the French Directory in November of 1796, but he was quickly rebuffed and had to flee Paris. In addition, French naval forces had begun stepping up their seizure of American merchant ships throughout the Atlantic. Despite the lack of an official declaration, France had essentially launched a naval war on the United States.

In an attempt to prevent the apparent quasi war with France from turning into an all-out war between the former allies, Adams sent a new commission, which included Pinckney, Elbridge Gerry, and John Marshall, to negotiate with the French in the summer of 1797. At the same time, however, knowledgeable of the fact that all-out war with France was indeed a possibility, the president also called on Congress to fund a buildup of America's military defenses. The meeting of the new commission with French authorities proved more successful than the last, as they were given an audience with Foreign Minister Charles Maurice de Talleyrand-Périgord, but it was very short and was soon followed by a series of visits from Talleyrand's secret agents.

The agents—whom the American diplomats referred to as "X," "Y," and "Z" in their dispatches home—informed the commission that if they wished negotiations to continue the United States would need to provide a "sweetener" (a bribe) of $250,000 for Talleyrand and a loan of $10,000,000 for the French Republic. Pinckney and his associates immediately refused to play along with Talleyrand's game, and the story of the XYZ dispatches took on a life of their own back in America. Adams's Republican rivals, including Vice President Jefferson, accused the president and his Federalists compatriots of making up the story in an effort to justify a declaration of war on France. Such a move would be very popular among the American citizenry and would almost guarantee Adams a second term in office.

Adams, however, did not ask for a declaration of war, wishing instead to avoid war at all costs. With an official declaration of war off the table for the time being, the Federalist members of Congress pushed forward measures to squelch any possible rebellion at home with the passage of the Alien and Sedition Acts of 1798. The Alien Act imbued the government with the power to deport foreign residents considered dangerous and at the same time increased the residency requirement for immigrants applying for citizenship from a period of 5 years to a period of 14 years. The Sedition Act, the more controversial of the two laws, made libelous writing against Congress or the president, as well as the attempt to stir up sedition, a crime.

Although Adams did not encourage Congress to pass the Alien and Sedition Acts, he nonetheless signed them into law because he viewed them as necessary war measures. The passage of the acts, and the black mark that they brought Adams's presidency, would prove unnecessary. In November 1799, Adams tried once more to avoid all-out war by sending William Vans Murray to France to hammer out a treaty that would bring an end to the quasi war. This time around, Adams's efforts proved successful when word arrived in February 1800 that the French Revolution was over and the new ruler, Napoleon Bonaparte, also desired a return to peaceful relations. The damage in terms of Adams's possibility of being reelected, however, had already been done.

On the morning of March 4, 1801, John Adams departed the President's House in Washington, D.C., for the last time. Despite having served only one term as president, Adams's years spent in service to his country were practically unmatched by any of his fellow Founding Fathers. He defended the right of a man in a free country to have access to counsel; led the movement for separation from Britain, earning him the nickname "Atlas of Independence"; created a government structure that would become the model for the newly independent states and eventually the federal government; served his new nation as a diplomat in Europe for more than a decade; played second fiddle to the beloved General Washington for eight years as vice president; and saved the infant republic from toppling in an all-out war with a major European power at the expense of his reelection and his friendship with Thomas Jefferson. Adams and Jefferson would rekindle their friendship in their later years, but Adams's reputation as a politician had suffered due to the ill-advised Alien and Sedition Acts and because his single-term presidency had been wedged between the presidencies of the more famous Washington and Jefferson.

Adams died on July 4, 1826.

Stephanie Jannenga

See also: Adams, Abigail; Adams, Samuel; Jefferson, Thomas

Further Reading

Adams, John. Autobiography, part 1, "John Adams," through 1776, sheet 12 of 53 [electronic edition]. *Adams Family Papers: An Electronic Archive.* Massachusetts Historical Society. http://www.masshist.org/digitaladams.

Adams, John. Letter from John Adams to Abigail Adams, December 19, 1793 [electronic edition]. *Adams Family Papers: An Electronic Archive.* Massachusetts Historical Society. http://www.masshist.org/digitaladams.

Butterfield, L.H., ed. 1963. *Adams Family Correspondence.* Vol. 1. Cambridge, MA: Harvard University Press, 166.

Ellis, Joseph J. 1993. *Passionate Sage: The Character and Legacy of John Adams.* New York: W. W. Norton & Company.

Ferling, John. 1992. *John Adams: A Life*. Knoxville: University of Tennessee Press.
Hazelton, John H. 1906. *The Declaration of Independence: Its History*. New York: Dodd, Mead, and Company.
McCullough, David. 2001. *John Adams*. New York: Simon & Schuster.

ADAMS, SAMUEL (1722–1803)

Samuel Adams was one of the most significant contributors to the patriot cause during the years leading up to, during, and following the American Revolution. He was a prominent social and political activist and agitator in Boston during the 1760s and 1770s. In addition, he was one of Massachusetts's delegates to the Continental Congress and a signer of the Declaration of Independence. After the American War for Independence (1775–1783), he served as the second governor of Massachusetts. His second cousin, John Adams, was also an important leader of the Revolutionary Period and would go on to serve as the second president of the United States, after George Washington.

Samuel Adams was born September 27, 1722, in Boston, Massachusetts, to Mary and Samuel Adams Sr. The younger Samuel Adams was 1 of 12 children; however, in line with the high infant mortality rate of the time, many of his siblings died young. In fact, only 3 of the Adams children survived past three years of age. Samuel Adams Sr. was a prosperous local merchant and a deacon in the Puritan Old South Congregational Church. His role as a church elder helped Samuel Adams Sr. become a leading figure of the Boston Caucus, a group that helped set the agenda for the more official Boston Town Meeting. The Boston Caucus also advanced the careers of many other leading political figures. From there, he rose through the ranks of local politics, becoming a Boston selectman and eventually winning a seat in the Massachusetts House of Representatives. While serving in the House, Adams Sr. became increasingly connected to the Whig party. Also known as the "popular" party, or the patriots, the Whigs resisted royal

Samuel Adams was a well-known patriot who was active in the events leading up to the American Revolution. He helped organize resistance to British taxation policies, notably the Stamp Act, and played a role in the events leading up to the Boston Tea Party of 1773. (Library of Congress)

encroachment on the legislative privileges and authority granted the House of Representatives under the Massachusetts Charter of 1691.

Although it would take the young Samuel Adams some time to find his footing, he eventually followed his father's lead and became a leading figure in patriot politics in New England, as well. As a young man, though, Samuel Adams struggled to settle on an occupation. He was certainly very well-educated. He had attended the Boston Latin School before earning his bachelor's degree from Harvard in 1740 and a master's degree in 1743. His parents hoped that Samuel's education would lead him into the ministry, like his father. However, in his culminating master's thesis, Adams argued that resistance to government authority was justified to preserve the liberties of a population. It was clear that he had made up his mind to eschew the cloth and instead pursue his father's other passion, politics.

Adams's enthusiasm for politics may have contributed to his lack of business acumen. After graduating from Harvard, he pursued a handful of different occupations, proving less than ideal at nearly every one. He was released from his position at a local counting house (the colonial equivalent of an accounting firm) because he seemed disinterested in business affairs. His father then loaned him a substantial sum to help him open his own business. But Adams squandered much of it on a bad loan to a friend. His business prospects dwindling, Adams went to work at his family's malthouse, preparing the barley malt used by local brewers. Despite some apocryphal evidence, the popular representation of Samuel Adams as a brewer is likely mistaken.

Gradually drifting toward politics during the 1750s, Adams came into his own as a political figure during the 1760s. The period of greatest tension between the American colonies and Britain came in the 1760s and 1770s; however, Adams had already begun agitating for the liberties of New England's colonists years before. As early as 1748, Adams and other patriots had printed political essays in their own newspaper, *The Independent Advertiser*. Adams based many of his arguments on the political philosophies of John Locke, including the right to revolution that Locke had defined in his *Second Treatise on Civil Government* decades earlier. Locke asserted that a government that failed to protect its subjects' civil liberties should be replaced with a government that would. Adams helped to introduce these ideas to a broader public, and these philosophical justifications for revolution remained at the heart of patriot resistance throughout the next 35 years. He was also one of the first patriot leaders to argue that citizens have natural rights that exist apart from the specific legal protections ensured by governments.

Adams was made tax collector of Boston in 1756, but he was often delinquent in collecting taxes. This made him popular with his neighbors, but he was liable for any shortage caused by his failure or refusal to collect. By the middle of the 1760s, his account was around £8,000 in arears. This debt threatened to derail his political career. However, he sued those who owed taxes, covering some of the shortage. Adams's friends helped to cover much of the remainder. And, despite the embarrassment of the situation, Adams rose steadily in the ranks of the popular party.

When Parliament passed the Sugar Act (1764) and the Stamp Act (1765) to raise revenue and pay down the debt the empire had incurred in the Seven Years'

War (1756–1763), Adams was soon at the forefront of colonial resistance. In each case, Adams emphasized that the colonists had no direct representation in Parliament, and so they were therefore not subject to its legislation. He was so outspoken in his condemnation of Parliament's actions that he gained a reputation among British officials in Massachusetts as perhaps the leading agitator in the colony. Many British colonial officials believed that the general population was being goaded into acts of rebellion by certain subversive instigators. In New England, especially, Samuel Adams's name was often at the top of those lists. While Adams did, indeed, support and sometimes organize boycotts, demonstrations, and other legal methods of resistance, he rejected mob violence and destruction of property as illegal, immoral, and counterproductive. His attitudes would change, however, as tensions increased. In 1773, Adams took a leading role in the Boston Tea Party.

Parliament repealed the Stamp Act almost exactly a year after it was enacted. The most onerous of the early taxes levied by the British government, the Stamp Act had sparked widespread colonial demonstrations, boycotts, and pamphleteering. England still needed to pay down the debt, however. So, in 1767, Parliament passed the Townshend Duties, a series of customs taxes on items exported to the colonies. Once again, colonial resistance grew. This time, Bostonians resorted to riots in response to specific incidents. As the cycle of escalating tensions increased, the British expanded their military presence in the city to restore order. Adams wrote extensively to oppose the military occupation and to extend the colonial boycott of the items taxed by the Townshend Duties. After the Boston Massacre, in March 1770, Adams and other patriot leaders met with Massachusetts governor Thomas Hutchinson and Col. William Dalrymple, the commander of British forces in Boston, to press them to remove the remaining redcoats from the city. Although not all the British soldiers were removed, there was something of a lull in tension for a few years.

In late 1772, word reached the Massachusetts House of Representatives that, thenceforth, pay for royal officials in the colony would come directly from the British treasury. This overturned a longstanding precedent that the colonial assembly controlled the purse strings. Many patriots considered this legislative control to be an essential check on the power of royal officials, keeping them in some way accountable to their subjects. Adams helped organize Committees of Correspondence to disseminate information regarding any incidents of overreach by British officials throughout the colony. These committees later extended to the other colonies, helping to develop more widespread patriot resistance outside the hotspots of New England and Virginia.

Adams had long since established himself as a central figure in Massachusetts patriot politics even before the events of December 1773. But it was his involvement in the Boston Tea Party, on December 16, that propelled him to new levels of influence. The Tea Act, passed by Parliament in May 1773, had granted British tea merchants a near monopoly over tea sales in the colonies. Patriots were outraged, and by the fall of 1773, rebels in a number of colonial port cities had developed plans to prevent British tea from being offloaded and the taxes collected. A similar plan developed in Boston as the tea ship *Dartmouth* waited in the harbor to offload its consignment of tea. By the night of December 16, the ship still had not offloaded its tea, but it was not permitted to return to Britain. Almost 7,000 people gathered at the Old South Meeting House to consider the best course of action. Ultimately, a group of 40–150 men boarded the *Dartmouth*, along with two other tea ships that had recently arrived, the *Beaver* and the *Eleanor*, and proceeded to throw approximately 350 crates of tea into the harbor. Historians still debate the precise nature of Adams's role in the meeting and subsequent mob action that night. Adams was one of the moderators of the meeting, and a popular story holds that his final announcement to the gathering was a signal to begin the destruction of the tea. But this story first appeared several decades after the fact, and contemporary accounts point out that the meeting did not disperse until 10 or 15 minutes after Adams's "signal."

Parliament responded swiftly and decisively to the Tea Party. The Coercive Acts, known in America as the Intolerable Acts, were designed to punish Boston by virtually eliminating its elected legislature and closing its port to all commerce until the value of the destroyed tea was repaid. Adams once again took a leading role in the patriots' subsequent resistance, and, in September 1774, he led the call for the creation of a colonies-wide government body to meet in Philadelphia. This was the First Continental Congress, and Adams was one of Massachusetts's first five delegates. Never a particularly fashion-conscious person, Adams had little to wear to such an august gathering, so his friends chipped in funds to help outfit him for the journey. After a brief return to Boston in early 1775, he was selected to serve as one of the colony's delegates to the newly established Second Continental Congress, to be convened in May in Philadelphia.

Before leaving for Philadelphia, Adams and John Hancock attended the Provincial Congress, which had been established in Massachusetts after the Coercive Acts had effectively ended the colony's self-government. The meeting was held in Concord in April 1775. While at the meeting, Adams and his compatriot, Hancock, decided it was too dangerous to return to Boston and chose to stay at Hancock's childhood home in Lexington. They fled the house shortly before the skirmishes at Lexington and Concord on the morning of April 19—events that effectively began the American Revolution.

Gen. Thomas Gage, the governor of Massachusetts at the time, had dispatched nearly 700 regulars to secure the arms and munitions reportedly held at a militia armory in Concord. No mention was made in his orders to the commander of the operation, Lt. Col. Francis Smith, that Hancock or Adams should be arrested. However, many patriots at the time were convinced that this was also part of the column's purpose, and the Revolutionary credentials of the two men were consequently greatly enhanced.

The proceedings of the Second Continental Congress were largely held in secret, but Adams seems to have had a significant role in the group's deliberations. He was an early advocate for a unified declaration of independence, and writing under the pseudonym "Candidus," he praised Thomas Paine's pamphlet *Common Sense*, which encouraged the colonies to break from British rule. Once the Declaration of Independence was finalized, Adams was among the 56 delegates to sign it, although this likely happened in early August and not on July 4. While in Congress, Adams also served on several committees, helping to coordinate the planning of the war, advocating harsh punishments for Loyalists, and acting as Massachusetts's voice on the committee to draft the Articles of Confederation. Although the delegates in Congress had approved the Articles of Confederation in 1778, the document was not ratified by the states until 1781, when the war was nearly over.

In 1779, Adams was in Boston, working with James Bowdoin and his second cousin, John Adams, to draft the state's new constitution. It was approved by the state's voters the following year. The document outlined a republican system of government similar to the one eventually established by the U.S. Constitution. Adams retired from the Continental Congress in 1781—partially due to health concerns—to devote more of his energy to influencing politics in his home state. The years following the end of the Revolution were fraught with difficulty as the new nation limped along under the Articles of Confederation. In addition to internecine conflict between John Hancock and Samuel Adams over the leadership of the state, Massachusetts, like many states, faced significant economic difficulties. These difficulties flared up into Shays' Rebellion at the end of 1786.

Shays' Rebellion, an uprising of former militia and Continental Army veterans upset over not being paid for their service, threatened to derail republicanism in Massachusetts. Many leading figures in America saw the rebellion as evidence that the nation needed a stronger, more centralized national government that could prevent a similar situation from developing again. This contributed directly to calls for a convention in Philadelphia in the summer of 1787 to revise, initially, the Articles of Confederation, but eventually to draft the U.S. Constitution. Though concerned at the lack of a bill of rights in the document to protect the individual liberties of American citizens, Adams ended up throwing his weight behind ratification during the state's ratification convention in January 1788. Combined with the influence of Hancock, Adams's support helped secure ratification by a very narrow margin.

Adams and Hancock had worked together throughout much of the early part of the Revolution, but Adams came to believe that Hancock's flamboyant and aristocratic behavior ill-befitted a republican leader. He also worried that Hancock too often gained political success by way of appealing to popular enthusiasms. Nonetheless, he served as Hancock's lieutenant governor and assumed the governorship of Massachusetts upon Hancock's death, in 1793. He then won the office in his own right for several more years, finally retiring in 1797. By this time, he had become one of the leading members of the Anti-Federalists (a group that would largely congeal around Thomas Jefferson into the Democratic-Republican Party). However, he was flexible in his support of the party line. He played virtually no role in politics after his retirement and passed away on October 2, 1803.

Shawn Selby

See also: Boston Tea Party; Committees of Correspondence; Hancock, John; Sons of Liberty

Further Reading

Puls, Mark. 2009. *Samuel Adams: Father of the American Revolution*. London: Palgrave Macmillan.

Stoll, Ira. 2009. *Samuel Adams: A Life*. New York: Free Press.

AGRICULTURE

It is believed that humans migrated to the North American continent via land connections at the site of the present-day Bering Strait about 15,000 years ago. From a livelihood of nomadic Stone Age hunters and gatherers in subarctic locations, prehistoric tribes changed over time to aboriginal farming practices. The spatial paradigm that identifies the North American continent's vastness, sharp contrasts, and natural resources as territorial advantages is becoming too limited to account solely for the positioning of the United States at the top of a globalized world economy.

The Amerindian presence on the landscape has lasted thousands of years. North America's different bioclimatic and major structural regions include the Great Plains, the Central Lowland, the Rocky Mountains, the Southwest deserts, the Appalachian Mountains, and the Eastern and Western Seaboards of the United States. The different biophysical conditions of the continent's environment constitute a rather multifaceted arrangement of soils, topography, rivers and estuaries, coastal regions, and vegetation and different climatic configurations of temperature and humidity levels.

The farming frontier in North America was pushed, in many cases, to its ecological limits. The evolution of human presence was influenced by existing resources and different hunting and foraging ways of life. Each region had endemic plants and animals that were perhaps not found elsewhere in North America. The Paleoindians who inhabited America ca. 12,000–9,000 BCE were highly mobile and adaptable. Household members had different roles. Women had important roles in planting and harvesting seeds, and men were skillful hunters.

The bow-and-arrow hunting technology as well as the trading of food and raw materials have influenced the evolution of occupation and the formation of the first small and very rudimentary agglomeration. Big-game hunting included bison and deer. In terms of vegetables, these Native peoples intensively foraged wild plants, berries, nuts, acorn, seeds, and starchy roots. They also harvested wild rice in alluvial regions. Aquatic resources such as fish, shellfish, and waterfowl were also consumed.

Natives began cultivating on the North American continent perhaps as early as 5000 BCE. In addition to multiple local cultigens, beans and squash were introduced from Mexico into North America around 4300 BCE, and this cultivation led to a period of rapid development. Tobacco was introduced from Mesoamerica about 200 CE. Native farmers had developed quite a productive agricultural system based on corn, beans, and squash along with a host of other crops by 1000 CE.

The Native people's environmental practices can be interpreted according to a continuum from exploitative to conservationist. Native pre-Colombian people frequently altered their environments through extensive clearing of forests, disruption of native plants, and soil disturbance. Natives preferred to rotate their fields instead of fertilizing them to increase productivity. Furthermore, they also changed their lands by clearing forests and using such traditional methods as slash-and-burn. Stubble from previous harvests was reintroduced to the land after being burned and tilled.

In this type of agriculture, farmers planted in rich ash-covered soil, which guaranteed the nutrients needed to grow the crops. Such practice has probably led to some environmental degradation. However, it is uncertain the extent to which Native peoples degraded their environments, especially the maize-based system. Ethnobotanical and archeological evidence of farming practices is relatively limited, as the introduction of new agricultural techniques has practically erased prior ancient traces on the landscape.

Natives settled relatively close to rivers and the coast. The Great Plains and Central Lowland had deposits left by retracting glaciers, and the Mississippi River system has created wide floodplains and prosperous river deltas. Agriculturally, this became one of the world's richest agricultural regions. This aquatic system drains the whole continental region from the Appalachian Mountains to the Rockies. Buffalos grazed this area for centuries before any European settlements. The area known as the Corn Belt benefited from centuries of prairie grazing, unique soil, and sparse rural settlements. The Mississippian economic network has stimulated agricultural development and village agglomerations.

On the other hand, the Hohokam Indians of the desert southwest supported large agricultural settlements around 550–700 CE. They depended on an elaborate system of irrigation to cultivate their fields. Such a system achieved its maximum development around 1400 CE. In the Salt and Gila River valleys, around modern Phoenix, Natives built canals that stretched 150 miles or more. Irrigation was essential for agriculture and has constituted a major component of the Native agriculture of this region.

Sandy areas of this arid "rain-starved" region are characterized by expansive plateaus and the immense canyons of the Colorado River. The Grand Canyon is over 5,000 feet deep. Farther north, Native tribes cultivated mountainous lands covered with volcanic ash. The Anasazi people inhabited cliff dwellings built more than 1,000 years ago. Zuni and Hopi tribes in the high country built pueblos. The lands in the immediacy of these settlements had mostly short grass and desert shrubs.

The Iroquois and the Huron tribes cultivated the region of the St. Lawrence and Mohawk Rivers in the northeastern part of the modern United States. There are high regional contrasts between the fertile coastal plains, the isolated Appalachian Mountains, and the Mississippi lowlands of the west. The Mid-Atlantic coastal region has long been used for growing tobacco and cotton. Mangrove swamps, sawgrass swamps, and islets are found in the subtropical region of the southeast.

Native North Americans developed a whole array of techniques to change their habitats while simultaneously increasing their food supplies. Digging sticks and hoes were utilized to weed and mound the fields. This primitive type of agriculture was characterized as extensive. Many inventions, such as farming, were made independent in the Old and New Worlds. However, certain discoveries (gunpowder, glass, and the plough) were introduced to the Americas by the Europeans.

Domestication resulted from a selection of seeds and the growing of animals for human consumption and to help in farming. Herbaceous, woody plants and cultigens were subjected to husbandry, which involved seed selection to improve productivity. In this sense, farming had a civilizing effect that served to affirm land rights, differentiate gender roles, and strengthen propinquity relationships.

Native agriculture was also based on group rights superseding individual claims. The sharing economy occurred prior to the creation of markets and involved mutual support, the exchange of goods, bartering, and other village activities without attributing monetary value. At a later stage, Native Americans developed trade networks based on periodic markets. These trading patterns were accentuated by the arrival of European settlers, which also led to the erosion of the Native culture.

The arrival of the European settlers introduced many changes in the territory: new farming techniques, plants, consumption habits, and living arrangements. This mostly happened on two fronts: through the South as a result of Spanish colonization and on the East Coast as a consequence of the British, Dutch, and French arrivals. In fact, the vast woodlands of the northeast constituted the core of Central European expansion. The contact between civilizations had a devastating effect on the Native populations. Especially destructive was the introduction of Old World diseases against which Native Americans had little to no immunity.

The arrival of horses introduced by the Spanish altered Indian culture greatly. During the 17th century, Native farmers acquired cattle from English colonists. Sheepherding and equestrian hunting became profitable, and the number of buffalos soon decreased sharply. The integration of raising livestock and widespread use of the plough into Indian agriculture did not happen suddenly. Anglo-Saxon colonists benefited greatly from their interactions with the Native Americans, as they often shared with them locations for bountiful harvest and techniques for crop selection and seed improvements.

Subsistence farming and limited agricultural trade on the part of Native Americans was perceived by the Europeans as resulting from an inadequate use of the land. Farming for profit soon thereafter superseded agriculture as a way of life. The search for profits required the extensive use of Native lands. European settlers in their westward movement and market economy displaced indigenous farmers by taking over their tribal bottomlands, which were still held communally, and forcing them to marginal and distant uplands.

Carlos J. L. Balsas

See also: Atlantic Slave Trade; Cacao; Frontier; Indentured Servants; Planters; Rice Cultivation; Tea; Tobacco Cultivation

Further Reading

Dandekar, Hemalata. 2010. *Michigan Family Farms and Farm Buildings: Landscapes of the Heart and Mind.* Ann Arbor: University of Michigan Press.

Diamond, Jared. 1997. *Guns, Germs, and Steel: The Fates of Human Societies.* New York: W. W. Norton & Co.

Doolittle, William. 2001. *Cultivated Landscapes of Native North America.* Oxford: Oxford University Press.
Hurt, R. 1994. *American Agriculture: A Brief History.* Ames: Iowa State University Press.
Kleppel, Gary. 2014. *The Emergent Agriculture: Farming, Sustainability and the Return of the Local Economy.* Gabriola Island, BC, Canada: New Society Publishers.
Pretty, Jules. 2002. *Agri-Culture: Reconnecting People, Land, and Nature.* London: Earthscan Publications.

ALBANY CONGRESS

The purpose of the Albany Congress, which met in June and July of 1754, was twofold. First, the British government, which called for the meeting, wanted its colonies to work together to formulate a means of united action against the French in the event that a new war broke out between the two nations. Second, it sought to reinforce the softening alliance of the English-speaking colonies with the Iroquois Confederacy, a powerful group of indigenous peoples in central New York that included the Cayuga, Mohawk, Oneida, Onondaga, and Seneca, who had traditionally been allied with the British. What emerged was a plan for a more centralized British colonial government in North America called the Albany Plan of Union, which was designed to better manage resources for mutual defense.

Between 1688 and 1763, the history of colonial North America was to a great extent the history of the continuing competition for colonial wealth between England and France. During those years, four wars erupted that pitted colonists in the English and French colonies against each other as one aspect of these worldwide wars for empire. In North America, the first three wars are known by the name of the English monarch who reigned when they occurred: King William's War (1688–1697), Queen Anne's War (1702–1713), and King George's War (1744–1748).

The 13 English colonies did not have a history of cooperation; rather, each colony viewed itself as separate and its relationship to England as one of a single colony to the home country. During the first three wars, there was very little cooperation between the colonies, even in the face of open warfare, except in New England, where the proximity to the French and the shorter distances led to occasional cooperation in expeditions against the common enemy.

By 1753, the English government had become concerned that the outbreak of another war was a distinct possibility. With this in mind, the British Board of Trade warned colonial leaders that they ought to prepare for a renewal of hostilities and suggested a joint gathering for that purpose. To this end, a meeting was planned in Albany, New York, where it was intended that representatives would discuss how best to organize for mutual defense. This location was selected because the second goal of the meeting was to negotiate with the six tribes of the Iroquois Confederacy, traditional British allies, to ensure their continuing goodwill. One of the participants was William Johnson, a British Indian agent who had learned the Mohawk language, married the sister of the prominent Mohawk leader Joseph Brant, and led war parties of Mohawk and other Iroquois against the French in earlier wars.

In June 1754, some 150 Iroquois arrived in Albany to meet with the colonial representatives. Occupying an important geographic position between the English and French possessions, they potentially held the balance of power in any warfare taking place in New York but had largely remained neutral during King George's War. The Iroquois were not inclined to quickly commit themselves to the English, as they realized that by waiting to see how the contest developed, they could later ally with whichever appeared to be the winning side and thereby gain concessions without the possibility of emerging with losses from supporting the defeated side. The most that the colonials were able to obtain from the gathering, after the commitment of a considerable amount of supplies and weapons as "presents," was an agreement for the Iroquois to essentially remain neutral.

All 13 colonies were invited to attend the Albany Congress, but only 7 of them sent representatives, a good indication of their lack of unity. In addition to the New England colonies (Connecticut, Massachusetts, New Hampshire, and Rhode Island), the only other colonies to attend were Maryland, New York, and Pennsylvania. Not coincidentally, these 7 were the very colonies that might expect the vast majority of warfare along their frontiers should a new English-French war develop. Twenty-one delegates attended, with Lt. Gov. James Delancey of New York chairing the meeting in the Stadt Huys (the original Dutch name for the city hall). Including negotiations with the Iroquois, the Congress met from June 19 to July 11. When it turned its attention to intercolonial cooperation, the discussions quickly centered on a proposed Albany Plan of Union developed by Benjamin Franklin, who envisioned a unified umbrella government that would be responsible for self-defense of all the colonies and negotiations with the indigenous peoples.

Franklin's plan was to ask Parliament to organize a general government for the colonies that could address the major goals of cooperative self-defense, including negotiating with the various Native groups, and exercise authority by enforcing trade and financial regulations. Under his plan, the Crown would appoint a president-general for the colonies who would preside over a Grand Council composed of representatives elected by the legislatures of each of the colonies. The individual colonies would otherwise retain their autonomy, their provincial constitutions, and their own legislatures. Representatives to the Grand Council would be apportioned among the colonies based on the amount of taxes assessed to each: Massachusetts Bay 7, Virginia 7, Pennsylvania 6, Connecticut 5, Maryland 4, New York 4, North Carolina 4, South Carolina 4, New Jersey 3, New Hampshire 2, and Rhode Island 2.

The plan provided that elections to the Grand Council would be held every three years, with any vacancies that occurred being replaced by the colony that the person represented. After the initial three years, the proportion of representatives would be adjusted to the proportion of taxes that each colony paid. The Grand Council would meet once each year for no more than six weeks, unless called into session more often because of some pressing need. In the latter case, the president-general would be authorized to call it into session, provided that at least seven of the colonies consented. The president-general would have veto power over acts of the Grand Council and the right, subject to approval by the Grand Council, to negotiate treaties with indigenous groups, to raise and pay troops and naval vessels to defend the colonies, and to appropriate and spend money.

After considerable debate, the seven colonies attending the meeting approved a slightly revised plan by a unanimous vote, the first such collective action during the Colonial Period. According to previous agreement, the plan was submitted to the colonies for approval, but there it ran into considerable resistance from legislatures that were not inclined to cede their own authority to a general government. Each colonial legislature voted independently of the other, with everyone rejecting the plan. As Franklin lamented, "The colonial assemblies and most of the people were narrowly provincial in outlook, mutually jealous, and suspicious of any central taxing authority" (Franklin 1964, 210–211). When the proposal was sent to England the Board of Trade rejected it, as it went far beyond the simple military alliance they had originally envisioned. Furthermore, an army under Gen. Edward Braddock that had already been sent to North America included two men to represent the Crown in negotiations with the Indians. As both of these provisions addressed the goals of the original British Board of Trade proposal—a single military command and dialogue with the indigenous people—the colonial plan was never presented to the Crown.

Franklin's famous "Join, or Die" cartoon that first appeared in his *Pennsylvania Gazette* in support of the Albany Plan of Union was later adapted to the colonial protest movements against England. The Albany Congress failed to result in any permanent organization of the colonies because, despite the obvious need for better coordination of defense activities, in the end, the British government rejected it as an unnecessary expense and dilution of its own authority, and the colonial governments also rejected it, fearing a loss of their own powers. Nevertheless, it did set a precedent as the first serious attempt by the majority of colonies to devise some form of joint action. Its formation served as a model for calling into existence the Stamp Act Congress to protest British taxation policy in 1765 and, with its success, the First Continental Congress in 1774. Years later, after subsequent events led to the American Revolution, Franklin asserted that if the Albany Plan of Union had been adopted, the Revolution might not have happened because the colonies would have had sufficient self-government to attend to their own needs.

James S. Pula

See also: Franklin, Benjamin; Seven Years' War

Further Reading

Franklin, Benjamin. 1964. *The Autobiography of Benjamin Franklin.* New Haven, CT: Yale University Press.

Labaree, Leonard W., et al., eds. 1959. *The Papers of Benjamin Franklin.* Vol. 5. New Haven, CT: Yale University Press.

McAnear, Beverly. 1953. *Personal Accounts of the Albany Congress of 1754.* Edited by Theodore Atkinson, and Thomas Pownall. Cedar Rapids, IA: Torch Press.

Newbold, Robert C. 1955. *The Albany Congress and the Plan of Union of 1754*. New York: Vantage Press.
Shannon, Timothy J. 2000. *Indians and Colonists at the Crossroads of Empire: The Albany Congress of 1754*. Ithaca, NY: Cornell University Press.

ALEUTS

Aleuts are the indigenous people of the Aleutian Islands of Alaska and Kamchatka (Russia). These people, related to those commonly referred to as Eskimo, populated the Aleutian Islands around 2000 BCE, emigrating from the Alaskan mainland.

Living in small villages, usually containing a group of related families, the Aleuts situated themselves near the seashore in an area serviced by a reliable source of freshwater. A seafaring people, the Aleuts derived much of their sustenance from the sea, the men hunting whales, seals, sea lions, walrus, and sea otters. Other seafood, such as fish, mollusks, crustaceans, and sea birds, were also gathered by the men and women. Land mammals such as bears and caribou were also hunted for meat and fur. Meat and fish could be preserved by drying. Despite access to modern convenience foods, many Aleuts still eat much of the traditional diet, both by choice and for economic reasons.

Agriculture was largely ignored, with plant food consisting largely of berries or other edible plants that could be gathered seasonally. Plants also supplied material for basket weaving and other household goods, but many of the implements

The Aleuts are the indigenous people of the Aleutian Islands, located in the Northern Pacific Ocean between the Alaska Peninsula and the Kamchatka Peninsula in Russia. As with other Native American peoples, Aleuts suffered from their interactions with Europeans, resulting in a significant decline in population. (U.S. Geological Survey)

employed by Aleuts in daily living came from the animal products harvested from hunting, such as bone, ivory, leather, fur, and sinew. Ivory and bone also supplied much of the raw material used by Aleuts for artistic and decorative purposes. Clothing was almost exclusively of animal origin. Women wore the furs of seals and otters, and men usually wore bird-skin clothing made of varieties of puffins and worn with the feathers still attached, either inside the clothing or on the outside.

Aleut houses were large, often 50 feet by 20 feet and partially dug into the ground, with driftwood making up the upper structure and roof and grass thatching finishing the roof. Dirt piled up and over the structure insulated the house against harsh weather.

Outsiders began interacting with Aleuts in a substantial way in the 18th century and were at first mostly Russians interested in the fur trade. Russian Orthodox Christian missionaries also took advantage of the potential population of converts and began their missionary work on the islands at the same time.

Russian interaction with Aleuts was not as benign as that between the French and First Nations people engaged in the fur trade on the East Coast of North America; it was more along the lines of the Spanish model, where the Russians saw the Aleuts as a resource to exploit. Russian society at the time was one in which the serf class of peasants was treated as property, and this philosophy was brought to the Aleutians. The exploitation and maltreatment of Aleuts by Russian fur traders led to a revolt against the Russians in Amchitka in 1784, when supplies and trade goods brought by the Russians had run out. The ensuing massacre of Aleuts by the Russians caused the remaining Aleuts to move to other nearby islands, and the leader of the Russian outpost was jailed.

The increase in fur taking caused friction between the Russians and Aleuts and their neighbors to the south, the Nicoleños (Native people of the San Nicolas Island area) and Spanish along the coast of California. War between the Aleuts and the Nicoleños broke out due to heavy harvesting of sea otters by the Aleuts. In fact, by 1853, the only remaining person of Nicoleño descent was a lone woman.

With the sale of Alaska to the United States by Russia in 1867, the United States took possession of most of the Aleutian Islands, and by default most of the remaining Aleuts. Some of the Aleuts remained in territory under the claim of the Russian Empire in present-day Russia.

The Aleuts suffered similar fates to other Native American peoples due to their interactions with Europeans. The faced disruptions to their lives, forced labor and religious conversion, and suffering from diseases previously unknown to the Native populations. On the reverse, the Aleuts were introduced to many of the modern conveniences and technologies of the European Americans, such as metal tools (knives, axes, fish hooks, and harpoons) and firearms.

By the dawn of the 20th century, the lives and culture of the Aleuts had been devastated by interaction with Europeans. The gold rushes of the late 19th century also brought a new influx of outsiders to Aleut lands, disrupting life even more. As few as 2,000 Aleut people had survived the 19th century, but with the eventual protection of the U.S. government, the Aleut people and other Native Americans in the United States and Canadian Northlands have made somewhat of a recovery, mixing old traditional ways with modern conveniences. Laws protecting Native American traditional hunting and practices have allowed this connection to the past.

During World War II, the Japanese invaded and occupied Attu and Kiska, removing the Aleuts from those islands, taking them as prisoners of war, and putting them to work as slave labor. Only a couple dozen Aleuts survived this Japanese imprisonment to return to their home islands.

Aside from the valuable furs and pelts taken by Aleuts, outsiders prized and continue to prize the artwork of the Aleuts, especially figurines, masks, carvings, decorated clothing, and baskets. The weapons and tools of the Aleuts are also valued as works of art as well as their boats. They also have a tradition of body piercing and tattooing. Today, Aleuts can be found hunting traditional sea mammals with a blend of old and new technology, sometimes using rifles and snowmobiles, and at times serving as guides to tourists.

Matthew D. Zarzeczny

See also: Hudson's Bay Company

Further Reading

Black, Lydia T. 2005. *Aleut Art: Unangam Aguqaadangin.* Anchorage, AK: Aleutian/Pribilof Islands Association.

Jochelson, Waldemar. 1933. *History, Ethnology, and Anthropology of the Aleut.* Washington, D.C.: Carnegie Institution of Washington.

Murray, Martha G., and Peter L. Corey. 1997. *Aleut Weavers.* Juneau: Alaska State Museums, Division of Libraries, Archives and Museums.

ALEXANDER VI (1431–1503)

After being elected in August 1492, Rodrigo Borgia, as Pope Alexander VI, helped mediate the claims of the Crown of Castile in Spain and the Crown of Portugal to sail to and occupy the Americas. Alexander VI established the precedent of dividing the globe into separate spheres of influence in his May 4, 1493, papal bull, *Inter caetera.* The monarchs of Castile and Portugal adapted this precedent in the Treaty of Tordesillas (1494) as the basis on which to extend their claims over undiscovered lands and peoples in the Americas, Africa, and Asia.

Pope Alexander VI is one of the most controversial figures among modern scholars. He was born to a noble family in Jativa, Catalonia, in present-day Spain, though it was a part of the Kingdom of Aragon in the 15th century. His uncle, Alonso Borgia (1378–1458), was an influential canon lawyer and civil servant of the king of Aragon. Due to his service both to the king as well as the Roman Catholic Church, Alonso was made Archbishop of Valencia and eventually a cardinal. In 1455, he was elected Pope and took the name Calixtus III.

Rodrigo had been earmarked for a career in the Church early in his life. He studied canon law at Bologna, and upon his uncle's ascension to the papal throne, he became both Archbishop of Valencia and a cardinal. From 1456 until his own election in 1492, Rodrigo held the important position of vice-chancellor in the papal curia. In this role, he was responsible for the day-to-day operations of the papal government and acted as president of the Sacred Rota, the highest ecclesiastical court. While proving to be an able administrator and an astute diplomat, Rodrigo used the information and influence he enjoyed as vice-chancellor to enrich himself and to promote the interests of his own family, even as he took a leading role in papal and Church politics. Rodrigo used this money to build splendid residences and to lavishly entertain. He also had numerous sexual relationships with a variety of women, including Vanozza de'Cataneis (1442–1518) and Giulia Farnese (1474–1524) and fathered at least eight children.

Controversies continued to surround Rodrigo Borgia even after he became Pope Alexander VI. The citizens of Rome as well as the predominantly Italian College of Cardinals resented him as a foreigner and opposed his attempts to appoint non-Italians to positions of importance. Thirty-six years spent playing and succeeding at Church politics also meant that Rodrigo had made many enemies, including Cardinal Giuliano della Rovere (1443–1513), who later became Pope Julius II (r. 1503–1513).

The Italian Peninsula was also divided into various territories, including the Duchy of Milan, the Republics of Venice and Florence, the Kingdom of Naples, and the Papal States. By 1492, it seemed likely that either King Charles VIII of France (1470–1498) or King Ferdinand II of Aragon (1452–1516) would intervene on the peninsula, as they both had dynastic claims to kingdoms there. Alexander VI did the best he could to deal with this difficult situation. Two underlying principles shaped his actions—to secure centralized control over the Papal States while at the same time advancing members of his family, especially his children, in an attempt to form a Borgia dynasty on the Italian Peninsula. Upholding these foundational principles led Alexander VI to form and break many alliances; to support his son Cesare Borgia's (1475–1507) attempt to turn portions of the Papal States into his own hereditary dukedom; and to seek new marriage alliances for his daughter Lucrezia (1480–1519), as political circumstances dictated.

In 1493, a request by Ferdinand of Aragon and his wife, Isabella of Castile (1451–1504), to Alexander VI to arbitrate their claims to the territory that would come to be called the Americas developed out of the papacy's role in international politics. As the head of Christendom, the Pope was the logical figure to resolve a dispute among Christian monarchs. There was also precedent for consulting the Pope in such circumstances, as various popes had previously granted the Portuguese Crown exclusive privileges to claim territory and spread Christianity in Africa.

In *Inter caetera*, Alexander created a demarcation line 100 leagues west of the Azores and Cape Verde Islands that extended from one pole of the earth to the other. Castile was given the areas west of this line as its sphere of influence, effectively leaving everything east of this line to Portugal. Castile and Portugal could only claim those lands that did not belong to another Christian kingdom and that they had discovered and occupied. Alexander's bull also required these monarchs to spread Christianity among the non-Christians they encountered in their new possessions. The monarchs of Portugal and Castile moved the demarcation line in the following year to 370 leagues west of the Cape Verde Islands in the Treaty of Tordesillas.

In addition to shaping the notion of separate spheres of influence, Alexander's decision in 1493 provided Europeans with a justification to explore, claim, and exploit lands and peoples in the Americas, Africa, and Asia, as it established the principle that non-Christian peoples did not own the lands on which they lived.

Lindsay J. Starkey

See also: Columbus, Christopher; Portugal; Spain

Further Reading

Burchard, Johann. 1963. *At the Court of the Borgia: Being an Account of the Reign of Pope Alexander VI, Written by His Master of Ceremonies, Johann Burchard.* Edited and translated by Geoffrey Parker. London: Folio Society.

Dawson, Samuel Edward. 1899. *The Lines of Demarcation of Pope Alexander VI and the Treaty of Tordesillas A.D. 1493 and 1494.* The Transactions of the Royal Society of Canada, vol. V, sec. II. Ottawa, ON, Canada: J. Hope & Sons.

Hibbert. Christopher. 2009. *The Borgias and Their Enemies 1431–1519.* Orlando, FL: Harcourt, Inc.

Machiavelli, Niccolò. 1988. *The Prince.* Edited by Quentin Skinner and Russell Price. Cambridge: Cambridge University Press.

Mallett, Michael. 1969. *The Borgias: The Rise and Fall of a Renaissance Dynasty.* New York: Barnes & Noble, Inc.

ALGONQUIN

The term *Algonquin* can refer to certain Indian groups who speak the Algonquian language as well as specific Indians who lived in present-day Ontario and Quebec, Canada, and encountered Europeans traveling those areas during their exploration of the New World.

Algonquin traditions state that they originated near the Atlantic Coast and migrated inland. One of their first major stopping points was near present-day Montreal, and they continued along the St. Lawrence River. They likely reached present-day Detroit approximately 2,000 years ago. Many of their people possibly participated in the midewiwin religion, which is also known as the Grand Medicine Society. Tracking down specific Algonquin practices and traditions is quite difficult, as most scholars look at the distribution of their language family as opposed to lumping in all groups who speak dialects of Algonquian as Algonquin peoples. Their language family was quite widespread throughout most of Canada and down through the Great Lakes and even some of the Great Plains. It encompassed dozens of separate Indian nations.

Europeans spoke about several Algonquian-speaking nations during their travels in the New World. They wrote specifically of the Algonquin, beginning in 1603. They had battled the Iroquois for over 30 years, and the French traders noted a victory celebration at Tadoussac in which the Algonquin celebrated a lasting victory.

That conflict likely started because of the presence of Europeans. The Iroquois wanted to obtain trade goods directly from the French rather than having to go through others, including the Algonquin and Huron. When they tried to fight, the French sided with the Iroquoian enemies and supplied them the arms that they needed to emerge victorious. The Algonquin continued supplying the Huron to keep the scales tipped in their favor. This was a tactic that countless Indian nations employed, and they were experts at manipulating situations in their favor, as long as competition existed.

Specific examples of Algonquin life can be found by looking at some of the evidence and sources that exist about specific groups. For example, the Nipissing lived in the area of Lake Nipissing, Ontario. The explorer Samuel Champlain likely met them during his travels, and French missionaries lived among them in the middle of the 18th century. That nation enjoyed plentiful fish and game, and their access to beaver made them strategic partners in the fur trade. Like many Indians, they traveled throughout their territory to follow game and resources. There were many regional rivalries among Algonquian speakers, and these were noticed by missionaries in the region. Like all Indians in the New World, they also experienced a rapid demographic decline after encountering Europeans. Their numbers remained small; Champlain estimated them at no more than 800 (Trigger 1978). Regardless of their size, they played roles in many imperial conflicts, including those between the French and the English.

Various groups of Algonquin played roles in the development of the New World by interacting with European colonizers, especially the English and the French. The name appears in primary sources scattered across colonial North America, but it is difficult to ascertain whether the writer is referring to a group that shared certain cultural characteristics or, more likely, simply spoke a dialect of the Algonquian language.

James E. Seelye Jr.

See also: Champlain, Samuel de; Fur Trade; Iroquois Confederacy; Jesuits; New France

Further Reading

Trafzer, Clifford. 2000. *As Long as the Grass Shall Grow and the Rivers Flow: A History of Native Americans*. Belmont, CA: Thomson/Wadsworth

Trigger, Bruce. 1978. *Northeast.* Vol. 15 of *Handbook of North American Indians.* Edited by William C. Sturtevant. Washington, D.C.: Smithsonian Institution.

White, Richard. 1991. *The Middle Ground: Indians, Empires, and Republics in the Great Lakes Region, 1650–1815.* Cambridge: Cambridge University Press.

AMERICAN ARCHITECTURE

Architecture in colonial America was influenced by both the European heritage of settlers and by the building materials available in particular locations. In some areas, colonists also adopted building techniques from Native Americans. As the colonies developed, architecture grew more elaborate, more built on texts as well as practice, and more influenced by trends among the European elite.

In the early days of European settlement in the Americas, architectural considerations took a back seat to practicality and durability in building. Early American buildings were designed for use rather than for aesthetic qualities, and the people who built them often had little experience in construction. Housing was also often thought of as temporary, as early Americans expected to move frequently. Housing provided the motivation for most building, but early American settlers also built for religious, governmental, military, and commercial use. When possible, they built in simple styles familiar to them from their homelands, which did not require much architectural or other specialized knowledge.

The availability of materials greatly shaped early American architecture. Building of all types in the Spanish North American colonies was influenced by the scarcity of wood, which in the Southwest led to the use of adobe, a form of baked clay with both Spanish and Native antecedents. Spanish Floridians used coquina, a limestone built from the accumulation of sea shells over the millennia, and tabby, a concrete formed with sand, lime, and crushed shells. The layouts of Spanish-American buildings were frequently based on Mediterranean styles, around an open courtyard.

Anglo-American and Franco-American colonies had greater access to wood, which they incorporated into a variety of styles, from New England wattle and daub construction and asymmetrically roofed "saltbox" wooden houses to the log cabins introduced by Swedish colonists on the Delaware. Stone was incorporated into buildings where building stone was available. While most of New England used wood as the primary building material, Rhode Island incorporated local stone into wood and stone "stone-enders," characterized by a massive stone chimney on one end of the house, sometimes comprising a wall by itself. The French colony at New Orleans initially built primarily in wood. Much of the evidence for architecture in French New Orleans was destroyed in the two great New Orleans fires of 1788 and 1794, and the city was rebuilt in a more fire-resistant style that incorporated other building materials by its late 18th-century Spanish rulers.

Spanish Florida contained the finest example of European military architecture in the Americas: the stone Fortress of San Marcos. Another great fortress in the European style was the French fortress of Louisbourg on Nova Scotia's Cape Breton. Some smaller fortresses were made of wood, with palisades rather than the thick stone walls of a classical early modern fortress.

As the British colonies prospered in the 18th century, rich Americans increasingly followed the latest European fashions in architecture and furnishings, as in other areas. Brick, more expensive but less vulnerable to fire and extremes of weather than wood, came into greater use as a building material, particularly in urban areas. (The heavy demands the colonists made on wood as fuel as well as for construction purposes meant that in many places wood itself was growing scarcer and more expensive.) Attempts at establishing brickmaking in the English colonies goes back to 1611, when three brickmakers were brought from England to Henricopolis, in Virginia. Philadelphia was a brick city from its founding in 1682, and both the fire that swept Boston in 1679 and the hurricane that swept through Charleston in 1713 were followed by efforts to rebuild these cities in durable brick rather than vulnerable wood.

Class distinctions also became more important as the buildings of the rich and poor diverged. The increased wealth and luxury of society affected public buildings, such as Old North Church in Boston, an Anglican church built in the style of the great English architect Sir Christopher Wren. In housing, the Georgian upper-class style of 18th-century England provided a way to distinguish between houses by style rather than by size, as had been the case in the early Colonial Period. (The Georgian style gets its name from the four successive King Georges who ruled Britain from 1714 to 1830.) American Georgian architecture began with wealthy immigrants from England, such as Peter Sergeant of Boston and Richard Whitpaine of Philadelphia. The Governor's Palace at Williamsburg, completed in 1722, provided a similar example for the houses of the Southern elite. Southern houses were adapted to the hot climate through such cooling features as high ceilings and by putting kitchens away from the main house.

Much of the expertise involved in building houses lay in the hands of professional builders. Building the Georgian house required more textual knowledge than previous housing styles. Books of patterns imported from England, where printers were skilled enough to print elaborate architectural diagrams, were commonly used. The Carpenter's Company of Philadelphia, an association of builders, founded a library of works on building design in 1734. These books were mostly printed in England, as American printers still lacked the necessary skills. Architectural books were also found in gentlemen's private libraries and academic libraries. Among the first works on building published in America (although the text itself originated in England) was Abraham Swan's *A Collection of Designs in Architecture*, which was printed in Philadelphia in 1775 and includes illustrations by the American engraver John Norman.

The Georgian style's basis in texts, rather than the experience of individual builders and the customs of local communities, meant that it had more uniformity across the colonies and between the colonies and Britain than previous American building styles. Like the homes of the English gentry on which they were modeled, American Georgian homes, often built on the top of a hill or other prominent position for lesser folk to see and admire, proclaimed both the owner's high social status and participation in an elite transatlantic culture. Sometimes a Georgian facade, visible to the public, concealed an older non-Georgian house whose owner did not have the money to fully upgrade.

The grand Georgian house of the 18th century was marked by brick construction, painted clapboards, and large symmetrically arranged sash windows with ornamental wooden frames and crown glass rather than inferior broad glass. Staircases were broad, straight, and unenclosed. The front room was transformed into a parlor given over to the best quality furniture and display items. Rooms were laid out symmetrically. The tall gables, huge central fireplaces, broad-glass windows with lead casements, and overhanging second floors of the 17th century disappeared, sometimes through the building of new houses and sometimes through the remodeling of existing structures. Although many splendid Georgian houses were on country estates, there were Georgian townhouses as well.

Some larger houses and public buildings adopted the Palladian style, named after the Italian Renaissance architect and theorist Andrea Palladio and based on the selective revival of classical elements, including columns and porticoes. The Palladian revival was based in Europe and Britain from which it spread to the colonies. Palladio's classic *Four Books on Architecture* (1570) first appeared in English in 1715 and was found in many libraries of members of the Anglo-American elite. Two works of James Gibbs, the English popularizer of Palladianism, *A Book of Architecture* (1728) and *Rules for Drawing the Several Parts of Architecture* (1732), were also widely influential in colonial building along with other Anglo-Palladian works.

Even in the 18th century, there was no organized profession of architect in the British American colonies. However, many American gentlemen, including George Washington and Thomas Jefferson, learned architecture and applied it to their own residences. Both Washington's Mount Vernon and Jefferson's Monticello are Palladian, as were numerous other Southern "big houses." The most active gentleman-architect in the 18th-century colonies was the merchant and customs officer Peter Harrison (1716–1775) of Newport, Rhode Island, whose style was heavily influenced by Palladianism. Most of the buildings Harrison is known for were public, including the Redwood Library in Newport; King's Chapel in Boston; Christ Church in Cambridge, Massachusetts; and the Touro Synagogue in Newport, the first purpose-built synagogue in the Americas. He also worked on several private residences, including New Hampshire governor John Wentworth's now-destroyed summer mansion in Wolfeborough, New Hampshire.

An adaptation of Palladianism, the Federal style, would become the dominant architectural influence on public buildings in the independent United States. The association of the classical style with the ancient republics of Greece and Rome made it particularly suited for the new republic.

William E. Burns

See also: Consumer Goods; Craftsmen/Artisans

Further Reading

Burns, William E. 2005. *Science and Technology in Colonial America.* Westport, CT: Greenwood Press.

Bushman, Richard L. 1992. *The Refinement of America: Persons, Houses, Cities.* New York: Knopf.

Donnely, Marian C. 2003. *Architecture in Colonial America.* Eugene: University of Oregon Press.

Kennedy, Roger G. 1985. *Architecture: Men, Women and Money in America, 1600–1860.* New York: Random House.

AMERICAN PHILOSOPHICAL SOCIETY

During the 18th century, scientific societies such as Britain's Royal Society and France's Royal Academy of Sciences played a leading role in international science. The growing scientific community in Britain's American colonies lacked such a group, although there had been a short-lived Boston Philosophical Society in the 1680s. In 1743, the New York botanist and natural philosopher Cadwallader Colden and Benjamin Franklin promoted the idea of a colonial scientific society. Franklin pointed out that Philadelphia, the central city of the colonies, was best suited for the new society's headquarters and offered his own services as secretary.

This first American Philosophical Society was short-lived, meeting only from 1743 to 1746. Besides Franklin, its leading members included the inventor of the octant, Thomas Godfrey (1704–1749), and the plant collector John Bartram. The group revived in 1767, still using the name American Philosophical Society, but it was now dominated by Pennsylvania members of the Church of England. On December 20, 1768, this American Philosophical Society merged with a similar Philadelphia-based group, the Quaker-dominated American Society for Promoting and Propagating Useful Knowledge. At the time of the merger, the American Society had just absorbed yet another group, the Philadelphia Medical Society founded in 1766. The new society's official name was a compromise: the American Philosophical Society for the Promotion of Useful Knowledge.

The new society's organization was modeled on the Royal Society, with a large, unpaid, and theoretically equal membership and a small body of elected officers as opposed to the state-funded Royal Academy of Sciences with its salaried members. The founding of the society was part of the process by which Philadelphia was challenging Boston as the center of intellectual life in the British American colonies. The initial effort to recruit members focused on the Middle Colonies and the South rather than New England, where intellectual life was dominated by universities and the clergy. New England's leading scientist, and the leading Anglo-American scientist next to Franklin, the astronomer, seismologist and Harvard professor John Winthrop (1714–1779), never became a member.

The most active members of the society and its leaders were Philadelphians. The aged Bartram was a member of the new society but inactive. In 1768, another founding member was the young astronomer David Rittenhouse (1732–1796), a future leader of American science after the Revolution who became the second president of the society. Members from the South included the Charleston physician and botanist Alexander Garden (1730–1791) and the Virginia landowner and pamphleteer Landon Carter (1710–1778). Like its British prototype and the majority of European scientific societies, the new society restricted its membership to men. Later, a single exception would be made for the Russian princess Ekaterina Dashkova (1743–1810), a friend of Franklin's who occupied a unique place in the scientific world as the head of the Imperial Russian Academy of Sciences.

Franklin's unquestioned stature as America's leading scientist made him the obvious choice to be elected president at the new society's first meeting on

January 2, 1769. As he was in England at the time, he was elected president in absentia. He held the office until his death and dominated the society's image outside America; Europeans called it "Franklin's Society." Like other scientific societies, the American Philosophical Society had corresponding members, and it used memberships for European correspondents to establish connections there. The new society was supposed to be supported by admission fees and annual dues, both of 10 shillings, but these often went unpaid, particularly as attendance and interest in the society waned after the excitement of its founding, a very common problem for voluntary scientific societies. In Franklin's absence, the society's leader was the vice president, the Philadelphia surgeon Thomas Bond (1713–1784), a gifted organizer adept at dealing with the prickly egos of many of the society's members. Elected vice president of the society in 1769, Bond presided over meetings and handled the society's correspondence, even through the difficult period of the American Revolution. He served until his death.

The society's first major project was the collection of astronomical observations of the transit of Venus across the face of the sun. Getting exact measurements of the time Venus first appeared to touch the solar disk and the time it took to cross the sun's face from as many places as possible were extremely important to astronomers. Transits of Venus occur in pairs, about eight years apart. Then they do not recur for over a century. There had been a transit in 1761, so the 1769 transit would be the last one anyone alive at the time would ever see. These transits, the first since the technology was devised that enabled astronomers to predict and observe them, had been keenly anticipated for years, as precise measurements from many parts of the globe offered an opportunity to figure the distance from the earth to the sun.

The transits called forth a massive coordinated effort from Europe's scientific societies, who sent expeditions to many parts of the globe, including North America, and encouraged local observers. They provided an ideal opportunity for the new society to prove its worth. The society applied for and received a grant from the Pennsylvania legislature for this purpose, and it coordinated and collected over 20 observations from astronomers throughout the British colonies in North America, although not all American observers worked through the society. (John Winthrop's observations were independent of the society's efforts.) The data gathered were printed in the first volume of the society's *Transactions*, published in 1771. Copies were sent to several other scientific societies, and Franklin distributed them in Europe, where they made a favorable impression.

Much of the society's activity was devoted, however, not to pure scientific research but to economic development and improving American technology—"useful knowledge." In this, the society was following the pattern of another London-based group, the Society of Arts, Manufactures and Commerce. (The secretary of the Society of Arts, Samuel More, was elected to the American Philosophical Society in 1774, possibly at Franklin's instigation.) Of the six original standing committees of the American Philosophical Society, two were devoted to technological improvement: the committee on mechanics and architecture and the committee on husbandry and American improvements.

The society engaged in a number of technological projects, often in alliance with the state and economic elites. It received a grant from the Pennsylvania Assembly of 1,000 pounds, matched by another 1,000 pounds raised by subscription, to start a silkworm industry in Pennsylvania—the latest in a long succession of fruitless efforts to develop a colonial silk industry. The society also received 200 pounds from local merchants to examine possible routes for a canal from the Delaware to the Chesapeake. The canal was not built until several decades later, and at the time, Franklin, among others, urged the promoters to get expert engineers from Europe. The group also requested that clays be submitted to it to determine the best deposits for different kinds of ceramics, offered premiums for rags for papermaking, and supported one of the few American glassmakers attempting to make a superior product, the German immigrant Henry William Stiegel (1729–1785).

Stiegel founded a glassworks in Manheim, Pennsylvania, in 1768, planning to manufacture the highest-quality glass, flint-glass, with the society's official approval. One important advantage of flint-glass was its superior optical qualities, which the society, as America's leading scientific organization, was in a position to certify. The society's efforts were in vain. High labor costs and foreign competition forced Stiegel to close his glassworks in 1774.

Much of the society's activity was thrown into confusion by the American Revolution. Many of its members, including Franklin and Bond, supported the cause of American independence, but not all did. Garden was a committed Loyalist who was forced to leave the country after the Revolutionary victory. In 1780, the American Philosophical Society received a charter from Pennsylvania, and in 1785, it began the building of a permanent headquarters, Philosophical Hall, on land on Independence Square, in Philadelphia, donated by the state. The society established its natural history museum, which later became the repository for the specimens collected in the Lewis and Clark expedition, in 1784.

The American Philosophical Society became the leading scientific organization of the new nation, and its membership rolls included many of the American elite, including the first four presidents of the United States. (Thomas Jefferson became the third president of the Society after Rittenhouse's death in 1796.) Foreign members included the Marquis de Lafayette.

William E. Burns

See also: Franklin, Benjamin; Lafayette, Marquis de

Further Reading

Bell, Whitfield J. 1997–2009. *Patriot-Improvers: Biographical Sketches of Members of the American Philosophical Society.* 3 vols. Philadelphia: American Philosophical Society.

Burns, William E. 2005. *Science and Technology in Colonial America.* Westport, CT: Greenwood Press.

McClellan, James E., III. 1985. *Science Reorganized: Scientific Societies in the Eighteenth Century.* New York: Columbia University Press.

ANGLICANS

Anglicans are members of the Anglican Church, which came to be more or less concurrently with the Protestant Reformation, a period in history when dissatisfaction with the Roman Catholic Church was writhing its way through the Western Christian world (the Eastern Christian world being largely Greek Orthodox). This transition to Anglicanism, with the Church of England as the archetypical variety, the state religion of England, is sometimes referred to as the English Reformation. In North America, British Anglicanism versus French and Spanish Catholicism amounted to a religious war of sorts, affecting attitudes and alliances. The transition of Britain from Catholic to Anglican is largely responsible for the Protestant nature of the United States of America and Canada (outside of Quebec) to this day.

The Anglican varieties of Christianity today represent the third-largest group of Christian religions (after Catholic and Eastern Orthodox). Britain had been exposed to Christianity through its association with the Roman Empire and had, according to legend, first been exposed to the Christian faith through Joseph of Arimathea, the man the Gospels claim was responsible for the burial of Jesus Christ after the Crucifixion. Over time, by the 12th century, Joseph of Arimathea became enmeshed in the Arthurian Cycle as the keeper of the Holy Grail. The story of Joseph of Arimathea is now largely recognized as a fable, but one fondly remembered. The first known British martyr to Christianity was St. Alban, executed in 209 CE. After the withdrawal of the Roman Empire in the 4th century CE, Christianity in Britain developed semi-independently of Christianity on mainland Europe. This distinctly British Christianity is sometimes referred to as "Celtic Christianity," with its distinctive differences from continental Christianity during the 4th and 5th centuries CE.

St. Augustine was sent by Pope Gregory I on a mission to Britain in 596 to Christianize the remaining Anglo-Saxon pagans, a task for which Augustine successfully converted King Aethelberht. Augustine's mission consolidated Christianity in Britain from the Celtic Christianity to a version more in line with the Roman Church. When William the Conqueror and the Normans invaded and conquered England in 1066, Christianity in Britain received another dose of continental influence.

By 1517, when Martin Luther produced his 95 Theses and the Protestant Reformation had begun, the Church in England was not insulated against complaints against the Catholic Church of Rome. King Henry VIII famously desired a divorce from Catherine of Aragon, his first wife, who had not produced an heir to the throne. Henry was anxious to marry Anne Boleyn and produce an heir with her, but the Catholic Church's proscription against divorce prevented the Church sanction of such a divorce. An angry Henry broke with the Church in 1534, and Parliament passed the Act of Supremacy, which renounced the authority of the Roman Catholic Church and declared Henry VIII as "Supreme Head of the Church of England." The marriage of Henry and Anne Boleyn produced a daughter, Elizabeth, who would become Elizabeth I, a powerful and significant monarch who ruled for 45 years.

Thus, by the time English explorers and colonists sailed to the New World in North America, the religion they brought with them was the Anglican form of Christianity, akin to the Catholic faith in most aspects, including the celebration of rites, but without the authority of the Pope and cardinals of Rome. The Anglican religion slowly developed its own unique brand of Christianity, including the King James Version of the Bible written (in English) between 1604 and 1611 under the auspices of King James I and Church officials. The King James Version, or KJV, was the third English version of the Bible, the first being published under Henry VIII and called the "Great Bible," in 1535, and the second called the "Bishops' Bible," which was published in 1568. Nagging differences of opinion and interpretation, especially by the Puritan wing of the Anglicans, led to the development of the King James Version of the Bible. The KJV has virtually become the standard Bible for English-speaking Protestants (non-Catholic and non-Orthodox Christians).

The Church of England became the state religion of England (and later the United Kingdom), although other similar versions of Anglicanism remained extant. The reigning monarch is the Supreme Governor of the Faith, and the Bishop of Canterbury is the highest-ranking cleric. The Church of England considers itself both *Catholic*, in its continuity with the Christian Faith with an emphasis on early teachings, and also *Reformed* along the line of the Protestant Reformation, especially in regard to the Book of Common Prayer and the Thirty-Nine Articles of Religion.

When English settlements and colonies were established in the New World of North America, the Church of England came with them. The Catholic-like reliance on liturgy and rites meant the building of churches and regular attendance at mass. Also, with a Catholic-like hierarchy of the clergy, although not with a Pope or cardinals, a certain consistency and control was maintained. Other English settlers (including those of other nationalities that joined English settlements) with disagreements with the standard Anglican model created their own colonies and enclaves, including the Puritans/Pilgrims, Quakers, and, of course, Catholics. The predominance of the Anglican faith gave the overall character of the British colonies of North America a distinct Anglican and Protestant flavor, one that has continued through the years, and the United States and Canada distinctly Protestant common values and traits.

Those organizing new settlements or colonies were often dogmatic in their insistence on following a certain form of Anglicanism without tolerance for the practice of other faiths or allowing dissension. Thus, certain colonies specifically stated that freedom of religion would be a fundamental right within that colony to attract people of other faiths. William Penn founded Pennsylvania as an answer to the intolerance experienced by Quakers, and Cecil Calvert founded Maryland as a refuge for Catholics. Roger Williams founded Providence, Rhode Island, when he was exiled from the Plymouth Colony (Massachusetts) due to religious disagreements with the ruling Puritans. Williams became a member of the Reformed Baptist Church, a Calvinist sect, and Rhode Island became a haven for religious dissenters, one of the early examples of separation of church and state. Under George Carteret, New Jersey and the Carolinas also became colonies that practiced religious freedom.

The archetypical intolerant practice of religious demands on a populace was demonstrated by the unyielding Puritans, intolerant religious extremists known in Britain as "Separatists." These self-described Puritans sought to rid the Anglican faith of its adherence to Catholic dogma and traits. Puritans in England were ostracized by the church and state, and attempts to force them into compliance with the state religion created considerable friction. The founders of Puritanism had been ejected from England by Queen Mary I, but allowed to return under Queen Elizabeth I.

Controlled and limited by law in England, Puritans sought haven at first in the Netherlands and then in New England, where they intended to found their own religious colony. Puritanism also slowly spread to Wales and Ireland, with acceptance by the business class that chafed under laws giving "royal prerogative" to those favored by the Crown. Puritans in Britain gained some influence over the years, especially during the English Civil War (1642–1646). The "purity" of the movement has been somewhat modified through the years, and its nature in England became less radical.

In North America, Puritan colonies such as Plymouth (Massachusetts and Maine) were among the least tolerant of conflicting religious beliefs of all the colonies. Forced adherence to the faith and attendance at church were mandatory, with severe penalties for noncompliance. Even non-church members were required to attend services. Working on or traveling on a Sunday was considered a crime and carried a hefty 10 shilling fine, as did missing church service. With an obsessive preoccupation with all things related to Satan, witchcraft and similar practices could get the accused executed (hanged) if found guilty. Sexual crimes such as adultery and fornication, as well as bestiality, could get one fined, censured, jailed, or even executed.

Jamestown and the Virginia Colony were founded in part because of James I's desire to spread the English form of Protestantism to the New World. Colonists in Jamestown were subject to laws forcing compliance with church laws and attendance, with noncompliance punishable by ex-communication and seizure of all the offender's property and goods. This forced conformity could be seen as a counter to the forced conformity to Catholicism found in Spanish settlements and colonies of the New World.

The Anglican nature of the Anglo-American colonies had a profound influence on the relationships between the European colonial efforts, as Britain was no longer part of the Roman Catholic family of nations to which Spain and France belonged. The religious differences affected alliances and general attitudes about one side by the other. To some extent, the struggle for control of North America became a struggle for religious dominance.

Adherence to the Anglican faith in North America, including forced compliance by non-Anglicans in those colonies that did not practice religious freedom, served to help form the English nature of Canada and America. Another result of the influence of Anglican and later religious freedom movements prevented the influence of the Roman Catholic Church on the English colonies of the New World, as had been the case with Spanish colonies. Without the hierarchy culminating in a grand and infallible leader like the Pope, the North American colonies were more likely to develop their own character with foreign influence. Thus, the Protestant Reformation and the establishment of the Church of England combined to help shape the way the United States and Canada would develop and evolve into today's nations.

Matthew D. Zarzeczny

See also: Calvinism; Catholicism

Further Reading

Carrington, Philip. 1963. *The Anglican Church in Canada.* Toronto: Collins.

MacCulloch, Diarmaid. 2003. *Reformation: Europe's House Divided 1490–1700.* London: Allen Lane.

Woolverton, John Frederick. 1984. *Colonial Anglicanism in North America.* Detroit: Wayne State University Press.

ANGLO-DUTCH WARS

A consistent theme during the 17th and 18th centuries was the commercial struggle between European nations to find lucrative trade routes to Asia and to establish colonies that would provide other economic opportunities. Aside from Spain, the two most aggressive nations in the pursuit of overseas advantage were England and the Dutch Republic. This commercial rivalry led to a series of four largely naval wars between the two nations. Beginning in 1652, the four conflicts took place over the next 132 years, with the fourth and last outbreak resulting from Dutch trade with England's rebellious colonies during the American Revolution. Although the pendulum of ascendency swung back and forth, in the end, the English emerged victorious, and the Dutch were forced to cede portions of their hard-won overseas empire and eventually lost their political and military importance in Europe.

Serious English interest in exploration began in 1496, when Henry VII engaged John Cabot to explore the North Atlantic to find a route to Asia. The beginnings of colonization began in earnest under the reign of Elizabeth I in the last two decades of the 16th century. By the mid-17th century, England had colonies in North America, the Caribbean, India, and the East Indies. If anything, the Dutch were even more vigorous in their overseas efforts. During the 17th century, the Dutch Republic was one of the most important commercial centers in Europe. Located along the coast of the English Channel, it was ideally situated to take advantage of the trade routes eastward to the Baltic region, south along the Rhine River into the German states, and southeast following the Atlantic Coast to Spain, Portugal, and the Mediterranean. Additionally, the Dutch opened trade with the East Indies—New Guinea, Borneo, Sumatra, and Java—operating the largest fleet of merchant ships of any nation on earth.

Separated only by the narrow English Channel, and with trading interests overlapping around the world, it is no wonder that the competition between England and the Republic eventually turned hostile. Once the Dutch supplanted Portugal as the most important European nation trading with Asia and opened a thriving commerce with their colony of New Amsterdam (later New York), a showdown was all but inevitable. The English lit the fuse to this powder keg when in 1651 Parliament enacted a series of Navigation Acts, the first of which required that all goods imported into England had to be shipped in English ships. To the Dutch, it was obvious that this was meant to bar their merchants from profitable trade routes. In response, the Dutch armed their merchant ships, and when a Dutch admiral failed to quickly offer a salute when he came upon an English fleet, the two sides opened fire, precipitating the First Anglo-Dutch War (May 1652–April 1654).

Despite an early victory, the English were soundly defeated in the coming months, losing control of the English Channel and the Mediterranean to Dutch fleets. With these defeats, the English reevaluated their tactics and adopted the new "line of battle" concept with great success; they eliminated the Dutch navy from the English Channel and the North Sea and killed its most successful admiral, Maarten Tromp. At this point, with both sides drained financially and feeling the economic pinch of lost commerce, negotiators drew up the Treaty of Westminster, ending hostilities without a clear victor. The Dutch remained the dominant commercial power and began a program to enlarge their navy. The English turned to a contest with Spain.

When the English Commonwealth Parliament restored Charles II to the throne in 1660, he quickly attempted to use the threat of military action to make his nephew, Prince William III of Orange, a stadtholder of the Dutch Republic. At the same time, he embarked on a series of moves, including expansion of the navy and the liberal distribution of letters of marque to privateers, designed to wrestle control of overseas trade routes from the Dutch. In 1663, the English became more aggressive and captured two Dutch trading posts in West Africa that were competing with the English for the slave trade. The following year, a small squadron of ships forced the surrender of an unsuspecting and unprepared New Amsterdam.

The Second Anglo-Dutch War (March 1665–July 1667) began with the English winning a significant victory in the naval Battle of Lowestoft, but the Dutch, under Lt. Adm. Michiel de Ruyter, more than offset this with the capture of a large merchant fleet and a drubbing of the English navy in the Four Days' Battle, in which the Dutch lost only 7 ships to 20 for the English, and their losses in personnel were roughly half that of the English.

Although the British succeeded in sacking Terschelling and the privateer Henry Morgan ran unchecked throughout the Caribbean, Charles II found his finances increasingly strained from the rising cost of the war coupled with a destructive plague in 1665 and a massive fire in London the following year. No longer able to keep his fleet in fighting trim, Charles suffered a serious setback when a Dutch fleet under de Ruyter ascended the Thames River, broke through English defenses, burned a portion of the anchored English fleet, and made off with the *Unity* and the *Royal Charles*, the latter the flagship of the English fleet. Humiliating as this

In June 1667, during the Second Anglo-Dutch War, the Battle of the Medway was a successful raid conducted by the Dutch Navy on English battleships that were largely unmanned and unarmed and anchored just offshore of the English coast near London. The raid was a disaster for the British and quickly led to an end to the war and a favorable peace for the Dutch. (Rijksmuseum, Amsterdam)

defeat was, its consequences were even more severe. The defeat and the rapid Dutch buildup left the Dutch Republic with the strongest naval force afloat. In fact, Charles found himself unable to respond as the Dutch controlled the coastal waters off southern England. The result was the Treaty of Breda, signed on July 31, 1667, in which the Dutch gained some trade concessions with England and retained Surinam and Pulau Run in the East Indies, but the English gained possession of New Netherland, which it promptly renamed New York. The treaty left other major English-Dutch differences unresolved and the commercial rivalry intact, thus setting the stage for a renewal of the hostilities.

Given the poor financial state of the English treasury and general public opposition to another war, Charles II was not in a very good position to renew hostilities. However, when Louis IV of France went to war with the Dutch Republic, the English monarch was forced to support France under the terms of the previous Treaty of Dover, thus initiating the Third Anglo-Dutch War (April 1672–January 1674). When a French invasion of the Dutch Republic ground to a halt before flooded defense lines, the two allies planned a seaborne invasion to bypass the obstacles. Once again, de Ruyter scored several notable victories over the combined Anglo-French fleet, which foiled the plan.

These defeats caused Parliament to force Charles II into peace negotiations. The result was the Second Treaty of Westminster by which New York became permanently English, Surinam was to be permanently Dutch, and the Dutch Republic paid an indemnity of 2 million guilders to England. Following the treaty, Charles made some furtive attempts to mediate peace between France and the Republic, but the war dragged on until August 1678, when the Treaty of Nijmegen awarded the Franche-Comté and much of the Spanish Netherlands to France.

In England, the Glorious Revolution of 1688 appeared to bode well for the Dutch when the new monarch, William III (William of Orange), aligned his kingdom with the Republic. Under the new rapprochement, Dutch merchants established trading bases in London, but over time, while English commercial profits increased, those of the Dutch waned, causing bitterness in the Republic. When the Dutch began to provide assistance to the American colonists in their rebellion against British control, the alliance between the two commercial powers became strained. It suffered a fatal rupture when the Dutch Republic became the second European nation after France to recognize the authority of and sign a commercial agreement with the Continental Congress. This led directly to the beginning of the Fourth Anglo-Dutch War (1780–1784).

By 1780, England had far eclipsed the Dutch in naval power. Although the Republic won a naval battle off the Dogger Bank early in the war, it was too weak to achieve much during the remainder of hostilities. Even with their commitment of forces to North America, the British were able to capture more than 200 Dutch merchant ships, force some 300 to remain in Dutch ports that the British had blockaded, and seize several Dutch colonial possessions in Africa and the West Indies. The latter included the valuable St. Eustatius, which was used for transshipping cargoes to and from the rebellious North American colonies. The Treaty of Paris finally ended the Fourth Anglo-Dutch War, and it confirmed Britain's right of free navigation in the Dutch East Indies and transferred Dutch holdings on the east coast of India to Britain.

In the end, the Fourth Anglo-Dutch War proved disastrous to Dutch interests and led to a gradual economic, naval, and political decline and the eventual demise of the Republic. Napoleon incorporated the Netherlands into his empire, giving the English an excuse for seizing several remaining Dutch colonies and further diminishing Dutch influence in the wake of Napoleon's ultimate defeat. Despite this loss, the Dutch still retained control over the Cape Colony in Africa and their profitable colonies in Ceylon, the Dutch East Indies (present-day Indonesia), Surinam, and the Dutch Antilles. Nevertheless, the war began the process that led to the demise of the Republic of the United Netherlands.

James S. Pula

See also: England; France; Netherlands

Further Reading

Barratt, John. 2006. *Cromwell's Wars at Sea.* Barnsley, U.K.: Pen & Sword Books.

Boxer, Charles Ralph. 1974. *The Anglo-Dutch Wars of the 17th Century.* London: H. M. Stationery Office.

Hainsworth, D. R., and Christine Churches. 1998. *The Anglo-Dutch Naval Wars 1652–1674.* Stroud, U.K.: Sutton Publishers.

Israel, Jonathan I. 1995. *The Dutch Republic: Its Rise, Greatness and Fall, 1477–1806*. Oxford: Clarendon Press.

Rommelse, Gijs. 2006. *The Second Anglo–Dutch War (1665–1667): Raison d'état, Mercantilism and Maritime Strife*. Hilversum, Netherlands: Uitgeverij Verloren.

ANTI-FEDERALISTS

The Anti-Federalists were a group of people who opposed the ratification of the U.S. Constitution after it was approved by members of the Philadelphia Convention in the summer of 1787. During the state conventions, where the ratification was to occur, these people stood in opposition due to a general feeling that the Constitution as written provided for a very strong central government that they felt would be prone to overreaching in its power and potentially threaten the individual rights of the people of the states. Their arguments against ratification played out in the press, in the state conventions, and in any number of written pamphlets and broadsides that were intended to reach a wide audience. Due specifically to the fact that the Philadelphia Convention was held in secret, these public debates were the first that many of the people who would decide on ratification heard about the proposed new government that they would be living under.

As the American Revolution began, the Continental Congress became the governing body of the united colonies. During the war, this body crafted the Articles of Confederation, which became the first governing document of the United States of America. It was under this document that the war was eventually won and the process of truly creating a new nation began. The Articles set forth a fairly limited central government with few powers and even fewer mechanisms for carrying out the powers that it did have. This was a problem, as true to its name it was more a way for 13 individual countries to work together than 13 states. Many men in the nation's leadership knew that the document was flawed and that if the nation were to prosper changes needed to be made. Chief among these men was James Madison (1751–1836), who with the help of a retired George Washington (1732–1799) and a number of other high-profile men of the Revolution convinced the states to call a convention with the intent of strengthening the Articles and providing a better way to govern.

Under the auspices of amending and strengthening the Articles, the states sent representatives to Philadelphia in 1787. However, Madison and his circle had a different idea. Instead of amending and strengthening the Articles, they were going to be replaced with a new government and a new document that would provide the nascent United States with the solid footing it would need to survive. The result of that convention was the U.S. Constitution. The creation of the document was sometimes tense and sometimes heated as a new form of government was created. In the end, the framework was finally decided upon and sent to the individual states for approval. The ratification conventions in each state would then take up the issue and vote on the document. For it to be placed into effect, 9 of the 13 had to ratify it, but everyone knew that, in reality, all 13 truly had to buy into it or it would not be worth the paper it was written on. By September 1788, 11 states had ratified the Constitution, and the new government was placed into effect.

The Constitution created a strong central government that would be led nominally by the president. Besides having the power to collect taxes and negotiate treaties with foreign powers, the government would also be able to create a standing army and would serve as the arbiter between the states in any disputes, among other things.

Leading the charge in the press for ratification of the Constitution were such men as Madison, Alexander Hamilton (1757–1804), and John Jay (1745–1829). Under pseudonyms, each wrote articles in various newspapers extolling the virtues of the new Constitution and trying to convince the people of the states that it was the best way to move forward. These men came to be called the Federalists, and their collected written defenses of the new Constitution would become known as the *Federalist Papers*. At a time when newspapers were mostly local and news could take days or weeks to reach people, these men found a way to explain to the people what the new governing document was all about and very methodically argued against the concerns of their opponents.

Those that argued against the Constitution were christened the Anti-Federalists, even though they were the ones arguing for a more federal form of government, where the states took the lead on the important issues. This group of luminaries consisted of men from the founding, such as Patrick Henry (1736–1799), George Mason (1725–1792), Samuel Adams (1722–1803), James Monroe (1758–1831), and Richard Henry Lee (1732–1794). These men tended to gather their support from the agricultural sections of the country, those that had a strong streak of individualism. In many ways, they saw themselves as the true Federalists, even trying to reclaim that name in the pseudonyms as they called pieces of the Constitution into question in the press. Names such as Federal Farmer, Brutus, Cato, and Centinel were used to evoke the Roman Republic and their vision of what the new government should be. They were not as well organized as the Federalists and therefore had a difficult time getting their message out. Although they produced a large amount of written material by numerous authors, none had the impact that the Federalists would have in swaying the people. Still, they were instrumental in shaping the debate and forcing the supporters of the Constitution to make their case.

The Anti-Federalists believed that the Constitution gave the central government too much power and that the term *president* was simply another word for *king*. There were no limits to the taxes that could be collected and very few ways for the people to limit what was done with the taxes. They saw the specter of a strong government that could raise an army as potentially tyrannical and a threat to the very freedoms and liberties that they had just finished fighting a revolution against. It was not that they were against a central government, but they felt a strong government would lead to corruption and that once given the reins of power there would be no way to stop the march to oppression. Even the built-in system of checks and balances did not offer up sufficient guarantees to them that the new government would be the best idea for all the people.

As the debate played out in public, the central theme of the Anti-Federalists became the lack of protections for the people, their basic rights, and their basic liberties in the proposed document. To them, not having those rights explicitly detailed only opened the way for them to be abused and for the people of the country to be abused. Many of the rights they sought to protect were the ones that had been guaranteed in many of the original charters of the colonies and that were so eloquently defined in the Declaration of Independence: the right to worship as you please, the right defend yourself, the right to a trial by jury, the right to own land, and the right to participate in the government, not be a subject of it. The Federalists argued that all the rights in question were implied in the document and were to be protected therein. Their fear was that by listing them specifically, they would leave the door open for exploitation of those rights not listed.

As the time for debate waned and the people of the states began voting on ratification, the Anti-Federalists were able to put into effect what would become their greatest legacy. Starting in Massachusetts, they were able to get the ratification bills to include a proviso that ratification would be dependent on the addition of a number of amendments to the proposed Constitution that would spell out the protections that the people would enjoy under the new government. Several other states added such provisions, and eventually the Constitution was ratified. Once the new government was called into session, the first order of business was to implement this condition. Initially, 12 amendments were proposed, but they were struck down to 10. These first 10 amendments became known as the Bill of Rights, and they are just as important as anything else in the core of the document. If not for the insistence of the Anti-Federalists, those rights would have remained unenumerated, and the Constitution may not have been ratified.

The Anti-Federalists and Their Roles

Each of the primary Anti-Federalists, Mason, Clinton, Henry, Lee, Adams, Monroe, and Mercy Otis Warren (1728–1814), had an important part, and for many, the very existence of the new country would be called into question during the ratification conventions that were held across the new nation.

George Mason may be best known for the work he did in Virginia prior to and during the Revolution. He was one of the major contributors to the Virginia Declaration of Rights, which Thomas Jefferson often referred to as he wrote another famous declaration. Mason attended the convention and worked diligently on the new constitution, but in the end, he found himself unable to support the finished document without an attached bill of rights and while it did not outright end the slave trade.

George Clinton was the governor of New York during and after the Revolution and would go on to be vice president under Jefferson and Madison. Under his guidance, New York was able to set a number of conditions for its ratification of the Constitution, the Bill of Rights being foremost among them. It is generally thought that Clinton was responsible for a number of articles printed in the *New York Journal* under the pseudonym "Cato."

Patrick Henry was chosen to attend the Constitutional Convention of 1787, but he declined. His major concern was that the newly created presidency would devolve into a position more akin to a king. Taking his argument to the people, he was a representative to the Virginia Convention of 1788, where he positioned himself against ratification. He was unable to prevent ratification from passing, but he held firm on the Bill of Rights.

Richard Henry Lee may be best known for his resolution during the Second Continental Congress that the colonies declare their independence from Great Britain. During the ratification debates, Lee sometimes wrote under the pseudonym "the Federal Farmer" and put his arguments out to the people. His arguments can be boiled down to the following quote: "It must never be forgotten . . . that the liberties of the people are not so safe under the gracious manner of government as by the limitation of power" (Lee 1914, 487). In the end, as with the others, he was not able to stop the document from being ratified, but he went on to serve as one of the first senators from Virginia and worked toward including the Bill of Rights.

Samuel Adams was one of the men who started the country on the road to revolution and was an architect of the Articles of Confederation. After the convention, he told his friend Richard Henry Lee in a letter, "I confess as I enter the Building I stumble at the Threshold. I meet with a National Government, instead of a Federal Union of States" (Alexander 2002, 203). As a member of the Massachusetts ratifying convention, he mainly listened and was not active; like the others, he would eventually ascent to the new document under the condition that certain amendments be added later.

James Monroe, a future president under the Constitution, opposed it as giving too much power to the federal government. Like many of his contemporaries, when ratification succeeded, he worked within the new government as a senator to amend the document into something more palatable.

Mercy Otis Warren was an extraordinary woman, not just for her time but for any time. As a political writer and satirist, she is truly one of the unspoken heroes of the Revolution. As the ratification debate took over national attention, she published a pamphlet titled "Observations on the New Constitution, and on the Federal and State Conventions" under the pseudonym "a Columbian Patriot." In this case, the pseudonym did its job so well that her argument against ratification and for a bill of rights was not attributed to her until 1790.

One common theme that can be seen in the actions of these men (and at least one woman) is that even when they felt they were not going to be able to prevent the new Constitution from being ratified, they all decided to work within the system to make the document more palatable to them. It would have been easy for them to stir up the feelings of their supporters and withhold their support, to continue to act from the political fringe and always eye the new government wearily from the outside. Most of these men had been on the front lines of the political front of the American Revolution, and to some, the gains they had made separating from Great Britain seemed to be slipping away.

After the ratification debates ended, the political scene under the Constitution became one that separated the people into a party system, much like the United States is still divided today. The Federalists, who were responsible for the

Constitution, became the dominant party and worked hard to strengthen the central government at a time of weakness and vulnerability for the new country. The Anti-Federalists eventually coalesced into the Democratic-Republican Party (usually referred to at the time as the Republican Party), which would be led for a while by Thomas Jefferson and James Madison. Sticking to the roots of their beliefs, this party favored a decentralized government that was more accountable to the people. It lasted as a party until the 1820s, when it further splintered and was no longer relevant.

Without a doubt, the legacy of the Anti-Federalists was the Bill of Rights. Their insistence on including the first 10 amendments was important to the ratification process, and though it is not guaranteed that they could have stopped ratification, it allowed the ratification to be unanimous among the states. A closer inspection of the Anti-Federalist arguments shows that, even 240 years later, many of their concerns are still being addressed in the government. In their actions, the legacy of the American Revolution truly remained intact and secured.

Stuart Hatfield

See also: Bill of Rights; Constitutional Convention; Federalists; Lee, Richard Henry; Mason, George

Further Reading

Alexander, John K. 2002. *Samuel Adams: America's Revolutionary Politician.* New York: Rowman & Littlefield Publishers, Inc.

Ferling, John. 2003. *A Leap in the Dark: The Struggle to Create the American Republic.* New York: Oxford University Press.

Holton, Woody. 2007. *Unruly Americans and the Origins of the Constitution.* New York: Hill and Wang.

Ketcham, Ralph, ed. 2003. *The Anti-Federalist Papers and the Constitutional Convention Debates.* New York: Signet.

Lee, Richard Henry. 1914. *The Letters of Richard Henry Lee 1779–1794.* New York: McMillian Company.

Maier, Paula. 2010. *Ratification: The People Debate the Constitution, 1787–1788.* New York: Simon & Schuster.

ANTINOMIANISM

Antinomianism refers to a system of theology that is primarily found in Protestant circles. The word *antinomianism* is derived from Greek and means "against the law." As a system of theology, antinomianism is typified by a negative view toward the law of God, or the Ten Commandments, as given in the Bible. While the majority of Protestants have rejected antinomianism, it has continuously made an impact on both Reformed and Lutheran Churches. In the Colonial Period, it had a considerable effect on the Massachusetts Bay Colony through the controversy surrounding Anne Hutchinson (1593–1641). Charges of antinomianism have been made against various groups throughout the history of Christianity in America.

Various forms of antinomianism have existed throughout Christian history. This is related to the center of the Gospel message being the forgiveness of sins, or the teaching of God's forgiveness for the breaking of divine law. This idea is drawn from several books in the New Testament. For example, the Apostle Paul writes in Romans 3:21 that "a man is justified by faith apart from the works of the law." In other words, people are made right with God by faith in Christ and not by their performance of good works ("the works of the law"). In the 16th century, Protestantism began to articulate this by teaching that people were justified by "faith alone." They taught that when someone exercised faith in the Gospel, Christ's sacrificial death completely paid for their sins because his sinless life covered their imperfections. Faith itself was not viewed as meriting this, it was merely understood to be the instrument through which God "imputed" (or transferred) Christ's righteousness to the believers account. This doctrine became known as "justification by faith alone," or "justification apart from works."

Although a right standing before God was thought to occur through faith alone, most Protestants also taught that true faith is evidenced by a desire to please God. The desire to please God was understood to be a desire to once again obey God's law. However, some Protestants understood "justification by faith alone" to mean that the law of God was no longer binding upon them in any meaningful way. Those who held this latter perspective formed various antinomian parties, which argued that their position was consistent with the Protestant position.

Antinomianism first began within Lutheran circles. Martin Luther (1483–1546) strongly emphasized a dichotomy between "the Law" and "the Gospel." For Luther, the Law merely exhibited God's standard of righteousness and was thus only capable of showing people their failure to keep it because of Original Sin. The heart of Christianity, according to Luther, was the Gospel, where God offers to make people righteous again simply by their exercising faith in Christ's death and resurrection. In Luther's understanding, the Law shows people their problem, and the Gospel offers the solution. To many people, this seemed to imply that the Law was no longer relevant for how Christians should live their lives, as it does nothing but condemn them. In response to that charge, Luther strongly emphasized the fact that the Law of God continued to guide people in how they were to live before God, even if they were unable to keep it perfectly.

In 1525, the first antinomian controversy broke out in the Lutheran Church around the teachings of a man named Johannes Agricola (1494–1566). Agricola taught that Christians were free from the Ten Commandments and were thus under no moral obligations. Both Luther and his successor, Philip Melanchthon (1497–1560), would continue to resist antinomianism in the Lutheran Church. In the centuries that followed, antinomianism continued to be a matter of controversy in Lutheran denominations.

In Calvinist circles, Antinomianism would teach similar doctrines while also adding in other details related to the Calvinist doctrine of predestination. Calvinist antinomians tended to emphasize what was called "eternal justification." Most Protestants believed that a person was justified (or made right with God) the moment he or she exercised faith in Christ. According to the tenets of Calvinism, such faith was understood to have been predestined by God from before the creation of the world. Therefore, according to Calvinism, if one truly believed in the Gospel, they were chosen by God for salvation. However, antinomians took this one step further and taught that Christians were not only eternally predestined to believe, but they were also eternally justified (or eternally right with God). The practical effect of this understanding was that having a right standing with God was divorced from the act of faith, as the act of justification was considered to be eternal. This meant that there was no outward evidence available to identify the elect.

For antinomians, both faith and good works could not be sure signs of salvation, not only because the elect are justified before they believe, but also because hypocrites are capable of performing good works or exercising faith for a time. This created a crisis in the minds of antinomian Calvinists because Calvinism was characterized by a quest for "assurance," or a search for tangible evidence that one was elect. In response to this tension, antinomians tended to extremes. Some taught that assurance could only come by passively trusting in Christ, whereas others taught that assurance could come through mystical experiences. Those who taught mysticism would often quote the Apostle Paul in Romans 8:16: "The Spirit itself beareth witness with our spirit, that we are the children of God." In other words, they understood Paul to be teaching that people could know they were the elect of God by an immediate intuition.

In response to antinomianism, many Puritans emphasized the necessity of looking for tangible evidence of grace in the soul. Certain theologians in England, such as Richard Baxter (1615–1692), responded to the antinomians by teaching that one was not actually justified by faith alone. Instead, justification was thought to be a state that one earned upon the condition of faith and good works. This was a reactionary view that became known as "neonomianism." This view differed from the standard Protestant understanding that faith was merely an instrument through which justification occurred.

Other Puritans reacted to antinomianism by seeking assurance through a detailed experience of each stage of salvation. According to Calvinism, salvation occurred in a specific order, called the "ordo salutis" (the order of salvation). It consisted of election, calling, regeneration, conversion, faith, repentance, justification, adoption, sanctification, and glorification. Most of these steps were thought to occur simultaneously at the moment of conversion, with the final two stages (sanctification and glorification) occurring throughout the Christian life and at the moment of death. Many pastors, especially in the New England Colonies, began demanding that their congregants produce a personal narrative evidencing that they had experienced all of these steps. In some cases, it was thought to take several years to experience everything necessary for a qualified conversion.

Thomas Hooker (1586–1647) and Thomas Shepard (1605–1649) were some of the strongest examples of this reaction to antinomianism in the New England Colonies. However, many Calvinists responded by simply teaching that sincere faith and Christian experience, as well as progress in good works, was sufficient evidence that one was elect.

In the Massachusetts Bay Colony, the antinomian controversy came to a head through the ministry of John Cotton (1585–1652) and one of his congregants, Anne Hutchinson (1585–1652). John Cotton taught a soft form of antinomianism that rejected good works as evidence of salvation and instead sought to find assurance through an experience of communion with Christ in the soul. One of his congregants, Anne Hutchinson, began hosting a study group in her home where these ideas were taken even further. Hutchinson taught that God could communicate directly with the human soul and that such experiences were known with more certainty than the teachings of the Bible. Other ministers in the Bay Colony confronted Cotton for encouraging such teaching, and Cotton later came to a compromise position with them. Anne Hutchinson, however, was brought up on charges and eventually banished from the colony in 1638. This effectively settled the Antinomian Controversy in the Colonies, although future controversies between Presbyterians and other Calvinists caused the accusation of antinomianism to be lodged against various parties throughout the Colonial Period.

During the controversies surrounding the First Great Awakening (ca. 1730–1743), both sides accused the other of promoting some form of antinomianism. The attraction and rejection of antinomianism greatly influenced the various forms of theology that are unique to American Evangelicalism. Antinomianism has continued to remain an abiding challenge to various Protestant groups in America.

Colin M. Samul

See also: Bradford, William; Hutchinson, Anne

Further Reading

Gonzalez, J. 2010. *The Story of Christianity: The Reformation to the Present Day.* Vol. 2. New York: HarperOne.

Holifield, E. 2003. *Theology in America: Christian Thought from the Age of the Puritans to the Civil War.* New Haven, CT: Yale University Press.

Noll, M. 2002. *The Old Religion in a New World: The History of North American Christianity.* Grand Rapids, MI: Eerdmans.

APPRENTICESHIPS

In colonial America, there were no "teenagers" in the modern sense, no generation past childhood, still in school, and not yet in the workforce. Labor was scarce in colonial America and into the 19th century, and only the fortunate few had the luxury of pursuing formal education beyond the rudiments. Most children took on adult roles and responsibilities as soon as possible, and before their teens, young colonials were already working, living with a tradesman and learning their life's work on the job. Apprenticeship helped to ameliorate the labor shortage while giving young people career skills. The apprenticeship system that gave young men (and increasingly women) a start on a career path through on-the-job training adjusted itself to industrialization and other changes in American society during the 18th and 19th centuries, but the basic concept of apprenticeship dates back millennia.

The Code of Hammurabi, 4,000 years ago, required artisans to train youth in their crafts. In Egypt, Greece, and Rome, those who mastered the skills then graduated from apprentice to craftsman, attained a respected status, and in turn handed on their craft to the following generation. Master craftsman was an honored status. According to the 14th-century Welsh Bardic manuscript the *Red Book of Hergest*, those welcome at the king's table included the sons of kings and masters of a craft.

In the English system that transplanted to America, the master craftsman hired an apprentice and trained him in return for service over a set period. Apprentices were normally 14 years old or younger. Having finished the apprenticeship term, the former apprentice worked as a journeyman for one employer after another until he finally attained the capital to open his own shop as a master. Then he was eligible to join a craft guild, the institution that gave and revoked rights and privileges and regulated competition within the craft.

But the guild structure failed to take hold in the Americas because most colonials were agriculturalists and the British mercantilist system blocked the development of manufacturing. That did not mean, however, that the colonies had no need for craftsmen and a training program for ensuring a future supply of masters. Although the largest colonial city in 1740 was Philadelphia, with a mere 13,000 inhabitants, there was still a need for such skilled tradesmen as shoemakers, barrel makers, carpenters, and the like.

With no guilds to regulate apprenticeships, the colonial governments increasingly took on the burden toward the middle of the 18th century. Training slaves or importing skilled Europeans helped, but the shortage remained acute; so, the colonies set up their own apprenticeship systems. There was no standardization from town to town or colony to colony because there was no enforcement authority at any level beyond the local jurisdiction. Enforcement was through appeal to the local magistrate, and disputes were common given the duration and the simple fact that one party was a child.

Apprenticeship was local. There was not even a mechanism to return a runaway once he had fled the jurisdiction. Benjamin Franklin was indentured, contracted to an apprenticeship, at age 12, to his older brother James. James received 10 pounds from their father in return for teaching Benjamin printing and providing food, lodging, and necessities, with a provision that during the final year of his apprenticeship, the year before he turned 21, Benjamin would be paid as a journeyman—if he remained through the life of the indenture. At age 15, Benjamin renegotiated his indenture to get cash in lieu of food; he was vegetarian and could eat more cheaply while saving the difference. Benjamin failed to complete his apprenticeship, quitting before his nine-year term was up because of difficulties with James. By moving from Philadelphia to Boston, Benjamin Franklin moved beyond the jurisdiction that would have enforced his contract. Some apprentices learned their father's craft. Paul Revere and his brother Thomas learned silversmithing from their father, and two of Paul Revere's sons were apprentices in the family shop in Boston.

Generally, the indenture contracted a boy age 14–17 to work until age 21. Sometimes the young children were too great a burden for their parents, and these youngsters, sometimes less than 10 years of age, were indentured to masters who promised to teach them a trade. The practice was legalized under the poor laws in New England. Children in this group could be indentured apprentices for a dozen years before attaining the age of 21. Official apprenticeship in Philadelphia dates to at least 1716, and by 1745, the city had 149 apprentice indentures in 33 crafts. Twenty-five years later, there were 537 indentures in the city. Philadelphia parish orphans were also indentured, but most commonly to farming, where no craft training was available. Girls were apprentices too, but less than one-fifth of the total and mostly learning housewifery.

Apprentices were more likely than other children to be literate because apprenticeship rules consistently required education in at least reading and writing. Otherwise, the training they received was variable. The children of the poor were bound out as servants, sometimes learning a trade but sometimes not, while children of the better-off middle class were apprenticed to learn a trade. The wealthy were sent to boarding school and then to such colleges as Harvard, Yale, William and Mary, or another elite institution before being apprenticed as clerks for merchants or lawyers. Parents who sought to apprentice their children to higher professionals, such as lawyers and merchants, usually paid the master in advance. Having finished the apprenticeship, they often joined the family business.

Indenture was the English practice of tearing notches or indentions in duplicate copies of apprentice forms. The ragged edge verified that the apprentice's copy was a duplicate of the master's. The original and copy were both signed by the master and the parent or guardian. Craft workers who migrated to the New world brought with them the custom of indenture or contract and the clearly defined master-apprentice relationship. Apprentice indentures usually banned behaviors such as fornication or playing dice. Masters promised to feed, clothe, lodge, educate, and train apprentices and, at the end of a term, to provide freedom dues, which were commonly clothes, tools, or money. Parents or guardians signed for children too young to contract. In Canada, the parents were financially liable to the master if the apprentice ran away.

Although indentured, apprentices were not indentured servants. Indentured servants were often the poor who traded their labor for passage. They had no right to learn a skill and commonly ended up as plantation workers in the South for the three to seven years of their contract. They left indenture with no skill, no tools, and no status as craftsmen. On the other hand, apprentices' degree of autonomy and actual practice of the craft varied widely, depending on the master. Some learned the full craft by taking on all elements, but others merely served as unskilled labor in support of the master and journeymen in the shop.

Apprentice indentures decreased in the first half of the 19th century. The American Revolution made apprenticeship more complicated. William Rorabaugh (1986) contends that the rhetorical tone of the age of independence necessarily broadened from the political to other spheres of life, including the interpersonal arena where independence meant governing oneself, an attitude that conflicted with traditional notions of social deference and status. Relationships were contractual rather than customary, and the master's authority inevitably weakened when faced with apprentices and servants who asserted their freedom, independence, and perhaps equality.

After the American Revolution came the industrial revolution. With the industrial revolution, the domestic apprenticeship largely disappeared. The parent-child relationship of the old apprenticeship system faded. No more was the apprentice a part of the master's household and recipient of the master's largesse in regard to food, shelter, and clothing. In many trades, the term *master* disappeared, but others preserved it into the 21st century.

Compounding the tendency was the increasing use by masters of unskilled or task-trained factory workers. This is the time when masters began to pay wages instead of providing support, with raises for experience. Indenture terms shortened. Apparently, the system evolved to reduce the impact of apprentices leaving for better opportunities before their term was done. Rorabaugh reports that apprenticeship of boys ages 15–20 declined from 20 percent to less than 1 percent between 1800 and 1860, but this may not be the national norm, as records are scarce and informal apprenticeship (not registered at any office) had seemingly increased.

In the first half of the 19th century, the tendency became more pronounced to not teach the entire craft but a limited set of skills that could be learned in a matter of months. Apprentices in factories had limited opportunities for advancement because it was cheaper and faster to recruit fully skilled craftsmen from abroad. Apprentices who wanted to advance had to learn on the job by observing craftsmen and by seeking advice and persisting through sustained periods of trial and error.

Apprenticeship changed over the years. In the Colonial Period, the system was adapting from the Old World pattern. The new republic brought about a clash between tradition and the growing markets and contracts. After the Civil War, organized labor and capital were in contention, and the terms of apprenticeship were one area of dispute. After World War I, the new industrial system diminished the skills needed by a worker and largely made apprenticeship moot. Schooling replaced apprenticeship as the means by which competence was acquired and the criterion for establishing journeyman status. The changes in the second half of the 19th and early 20th century were essentially begun in the era of the American Revolution and early industrial revolution.

John H. Barnhill

See also: Colonial Economy; Indentured Servants

Further Reading

Rorabaugh, W. J. 1986. *The Craft Apprentice: From Franklin to the Machine Age in America.* New York: Oxford University Press.

Washington State Department of Labor and Industries. "History of Apprenticeship." http://www.lni.wa.gov/TradesLicensing/Apprenticeship/About/History.

ARNOLD, BENEDICT (1741–1801)

Benedict Arnold was a general during the American Revolution. He served with distinction for the Continental Army and was instrumental in some of the most significant campaigns of the war. However, he is most well-known for his decision to hand over control of the West Point fortification to the British, a treasonous plot that was exposed in 1780. Arnold subsequently escaped to serve with the British army in America. As a result, his name quickly became a byword for "treason," or "traitor."

Arnold was born January 14, 1741, in Norwich, Connecticut. He was one of six children born to Benedict and Hannah Arnold, but only he and his sister Hannah survived to adulthood. Arnold's father was a successful cooper, sea captain, and selectman, rising to the upper levels of Norwich society. Benedict was enrolled in a private school in Canterbury, Connecticut, when he was 10 and was likely destined to attend Yale College. However, over the span of three years, three of Benedict's siblings died of yellow fever. His father struggled with the loss. He began drinking heavily, and the family's fortunes took a turn for the worse. By his teenage years, Benedict's family was facing financial hardship.

Arnold joined the local militia in 1757, at the age of 16. He served in upstate New York during the French and Indian War (Seven Years' War, 1756–1763), but his unit's campaign against the French position at Fort William Henry ended abruptly. Some accounts suggest that Arnold personally grew weary of discipline and orders, and so he quit the campaign and made his way through the wilderness back to his home in Connecticut. Other sources suggest that the entire effort was abandoned when word reached the unit of the atrocities committed against the fort's defenders by the French army's Indian allies.

In either case, Arnold was back in Norwich with no significant prospects of success and a growing burden to support his family. Unable to devote the time to train or become educated in the family mercantile business, Arnold was given a boost when his mother used her connections to secure an apprenticeship with Daniel and Joshua Lathrop. The Lathrops, Hannah's cousins, ran a successful apothecary and market. Benedict's apprenticeship at the shop lasted seven years and permitted him to open his own successful apothecary and book shop in New Haven in 1762.

In 1764, he entered into a partnership with Adam Babcock and was able to compile a merchant fleet of three ships and a thriving long-distance trade. Arnold's business dealings required him to travel extensively throughout New England, Quebec, and even as far afield as the West Indies, often in personal command of one of his ships. His business also put him squarely in the middle of tensions surrounding parliamentary taxes during the 1760s. Both the Sugar Act (1764) and Stamp Act (1765) affected his commercial enterprises and thus played a role in pushing the temperamental Arnold toward patriot resistance. He joined the Sons of Liberty, and while he did not initially participate in the occasionally violent protests and demonstrations organized by the secret organization, he did operate his business in direct violation of the laws, effectively becoming a smuggler. The taxes did have a growing impact on Arnold's business, though, and he was forced to rely on loans and other credit for much of his remaining business and military careers.

As tensions between the colonies and the British government increased in the late 1760s and early 1770s, Arnold continued in his resistance to parliamentary laws, but he still did his best to maintain his business interests. Events moved almost inexorably toward rebellion, though, and by the time of the skirmishes at Lexington and Concord in April 1775, Arnold had been elected a captain in his local militia. He and his company marched from Connecticut to assist in the siege of Boston. There, he met with the Massachusetts Committee of Safety and proposed to lead a force against the lightly defended Fort Ticonderoga, near Lake Champlain, in upstate New York. The committee issued him a commission as a colonel in the militia, and Arnold took his company northwest. There, he aided Ethan Allen in the successful capture of the fort.

Arnold followed up this action with an invasion of Quebec. Although the Continental Congress ordered the attack partly on Arnold's suggestion, he was passed over for command of the campaign. As a result, Arnold appealed directly to Gen. George Washington to undertake his own march into Canada. He was given a colonel's commission in the Continental Army and set off from Cambridge in September 1775 with 1,100 men. They marched 350 miles through dense Maine wilderness and arrived at Quebec City in November. However, the march had taken its toll. Nearly 300 men had deserted, and another 200 had died from exertion and the difficult conditions. His assault faltered at the city, and after a siege that lasted until April 1776, Arnold was forced to abandon the effort.

During the campaign, Arnold made a number of friends in the political and military establishment, including Washington. However, he had also made a number of enemies. Always a vain and proud man, Arnold's stubbornness and impulsiveness served him well at times on the battlefield. But they also contributed to his difficulties in navigating the upper echelons of power during the Revolution.

When Congress created five new major generalships in early 1777, Arnold's rashness, and the enmity he had fostered with influential officers and politicians meant that he was passed over for promotion. He remained at the rank of brigadier general. Only a personal appeal by Washington persuaded Arnold not to resign. After successfully repelling a British attack on Danbury, Connecticut, Arnold was promoted to major general; however, he was not restored to seniority in the chain of command. Such affronts rankled the sensitive Arnold and contributed to the growing rancor he felt toward an establishment that, at best, overlooked and, at worst, seemed to completely disregard his contributions to the patriot cause.

Arnold suffered a serious wound to his leg at the Battle of Quebec and spent nearly a year recovering. In the fall of 1777, he was ordered north to assist Gen. Horatio Gates in his defense of the Hudson Valley. At the first Battle of Saratoga, Arnold and Gates disagreed so strenuously over the order of battle that Gates placed Arnold in confinement and may have threatened him with a court-martial. Nevertheless, Arnold broke his confinement and operated against Gates's command at the second Battle of Saratoga on October 7, 1777. His aggressiveness in leading the Continental Army on the battlefield helped the Americans carry the day, although Arnold was once again severely wounded in the leg. The surrender of nearly 6,000 British soldiers under the command of Gen. John Burgoyne was enough to finally convince France to formally join the American cause, and the Treaty of Alliance was formalized shortly thereafter. Although Congress rewarded his contribution by restoring his seniority, Arnold interpreted the action as being a gesture in sympathy for his injuries and not as an overdue correction of an oversight.

While recuperating, Arnold was put in charge as the military commander of Philadelphia after the British abandoned the city in June 1778. He lived extravagantly while in Philadelphia and often participated in the city's social scene. His expenses caught up with him, however, and he became actively involved in business dealings designed to take advantage of his role as military commander. Although such manipulations and maneuverings were not uncommon in the Continental Army at the time, Arnold's efforts were sometimes a bit too flagrant. They also occasionally ran afoul of powerful congressmen and others who used their influence to scupper Arnold's efforts. Arnold eventually demanded a court-martial to clear his name. The hearing began in June 1779 and was concluded in January 1780. Although the court acquitted Arnold on all but two counts, there were still questions about missing funds and appropriations. Arnold's actions to publicize the clearing of his name struck many, including General Washington, as being imprudent. Washington issued a formal rebuke, further fanning the flames of Arnold's frustration. The matter reached a head when Arnold resigned his command of Philadelphia in late April 1780.

In Philadelphia, Arnold met, courted, and eventually married 18-year-old Peggy Shippen, the daughter of a prominent Loyalist judge. Peggy had been romantically linked with the British major John Andre while the redcoats had occupied the city, and she would eventually be the conduit by which Arnold would come into contact with the British army. Over the course of several weeks of secret and often coded communication, Arnold shared with Andre information about troop deployments and the locations of supply depots. Before Arnold was given command of West Point, he had been in conversations with Washington's staff about the possibility of overseeing the fort. Through his channels with Andre, he offered to sell the plans of the fort to the British. When he gained command of the fort in early August 1780, he soon communicated with Andre and the British general Sir Henry Clinton, demanding £20,000 in exchange for a detailed rendering of the fortification's defenses, which would allow the British to take the position "without loss."

The traitorous plot was exposed in September 1780 after John Andre visited Arnold near the fort. The ship that carried Andre to the meeting had been damaged in the journey, forcing the British major to return to New York on foot. Arnold wrote him a pass to allow him to move through the American pickets. He also provided the major with plans to the West Point fortifications. When Andre was stopped by a routine American patrol, the plans were discovered. Arnold learned of Andre's capture on September 24, and he hastily fled West Point, ordering a bargeman to row him down the Hudson River to the British sloop-of-war HMS *Vulture*.

Andre was hanged as a spy, and Arnold's treason had been exposed. However, the American turncoat managed to escape. He composed an open letter titled *To the Inhabitants of America*, in which he explained his actions, claiming that he was acting in the best interests of his country. Patriots dismissed his justifications, though, and his reputation was further tarnished when he led a campaign against Richmond, Virginia, in December 1780. By this time, Arnold had accepted a commission as a brigadier general in the British army. His Virginia campaign was stymied in early 1781, and he returned to New York to work with Sir Henry Clinton's staff. Although he proposed a number of daring and aggressive actions against colonial positions, Clinton ultimately rejected nearly every one. He did authorize Arnold to raid the port city of New London, Connecticut, however, an attack that, though successful, resulted in an outsized number of casualties for the British force. Arnold soon asked to be allowed to travel to England to advise the government on the course of the war.

When he was granted permission, in December 1781, he sailed for London. There, Arnold aligned himself with the Tory party and attempted to secure military postings in America. Failing that, he tried to gain a position with the government or with the British East India Company. He was rebuffed at every turn and eventually moved to St. John, New Brunswick, Canada, with his son, Richard, in 1785. There, he speculated in real estate and began building another trade network with suppliers in the West Indies. The rest of his family joined him in St. John in 1787.

Arnold's time in Canada was fraught with lawsuits and petty squabbles; the family left in 1792. Though he once again lived in London, he maintained his business dealings in the West Indies. After being imprisoned by a French garrison in Guadeloupe on suspicion of being a British spy, Arnold escaped and attempted to mobilize British militia on nearby islands, though the efforts did not result in another commission, as he had hoped. He spent his last days in London suffering from gout. He died on June 14, 1801.

Shawn Selby

See also: Fort Ticonderoga; Gates, Horatio; Saratoga, Battle of; Washington, George

Further Reading

Martin, James Kirby. 2000. *Benedict Arnold, Revolutionary Hero: An American Warrior Reconsidered.* New York: New York University Press.

Philbrick, Nathaniel. 2016. *Valiant Ambition: George Washington, Benedict Arnold, and the Fate of the American Revolution.* New York: Viking.

ARTICLES OF CONFEDERATION

With the adoption of the Declaration of Independence in July 1776, the 13 English colonies in North America severed their relationship with their founding nation, declaring themselves to be henceforth sovereign nations. This document was approved by the Continental Congress, which included representatives of all the signatory colonies—now calling themselves "states." Soon after, some of the representatives recognized that the Congress was temporary and that a more permanent governmental organization was needed to clearly delineate the responsibilities delegated to Congress by the states and those reserved for the individual states, if for no other reason than the effective prosecution of the Revolution.

One of the first to submit a proposal was Benjamin Franklin, whose Articles of Confederation and Perpetual Union envisioned a permanent unification under a central government. The Articles of Confederation established the first permanent

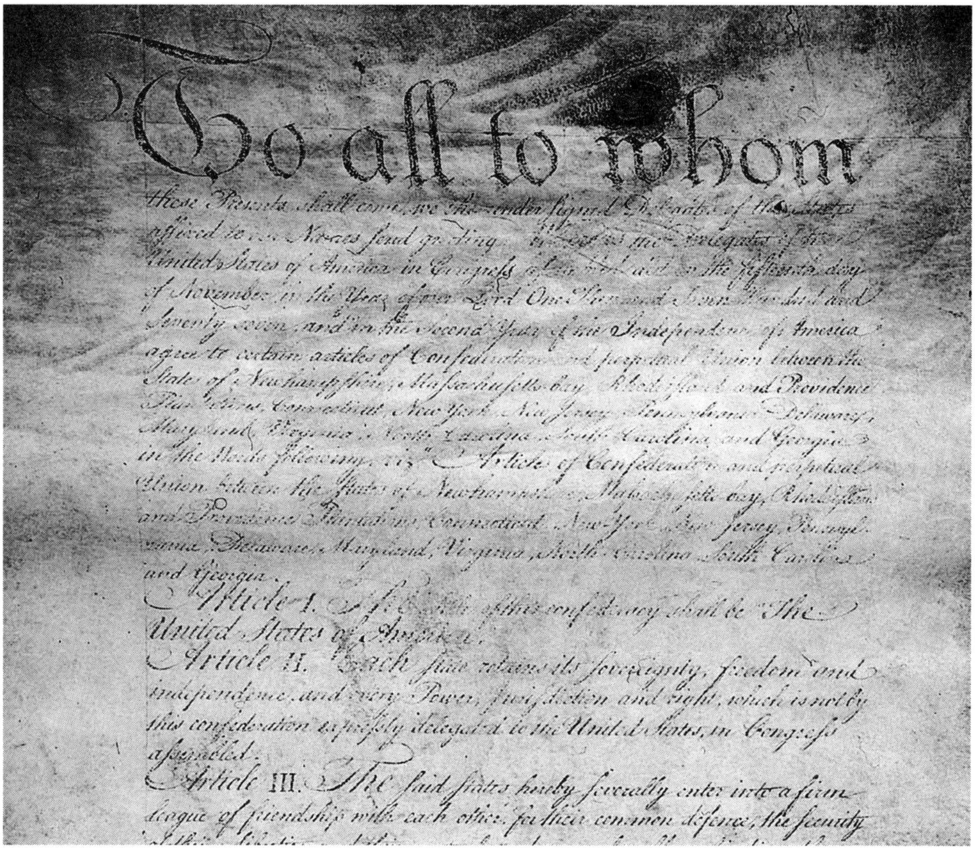

The Articles of Confederation was an agreement among the 13 states of the newly formed United States of America on a set of governing principles. It was ratified on March 1, 1781, and served as the country's first constitution. Delegates of the Continental Congress came to realize that the limits placed on the central government rendered it ineffective as a governing document, and it was replaced by the Constitution on March 4, 1789. (National Archives)

government under the name "the United States of America." However, in practice, they proved to have left too much discretion to the individual states, leaving the central government greatly handicapped, especially in financial affairs. Although states were assessed taxes for the support of the government, the lack of any enforcement mechanism meant that contributions were in practice voluntary. By the end of the American Revolution, the central government hovered on the verge of bankruptcy, threatening the existence of the new nation. The provision for unanimous consent for amendment of the Articles eventually created such a crisis that the Articles were scrapped in favor of the new U.S. Constitution.

It was not until 1777 that discussions once again began in earnest about the creation of a permanent government, with one of the major issues being whether the states ought to have equal voting rights or be proportional based on the population of each state. After considerable debate, John Dickinson of Pennsylvania submitted a proposal that, after continued debate and revision, formed the basis for the final agreement. The document was approved by Congress in November 1777 and sent to the states for approval.

Virginia became the first to ratify in December, with all but Delaware, Maryland, and New Jersey following suit during the spring of 1778. Because the Articles of Confederation required unanimous adoption to become effective, the smaller states held out for an agreement that the states with large western land claims, such as Virginia, would relinquish those to the central government. After protracted negotiations and debates, New Jersey voted in favor of adopting the Articles in November 1778, as did Delaware in February 1779. Maryland held out until Virginia agreed to give up its claims, not ratifying until March 1, 1781, when British incursions into the state prompted its representatives to accept in the hope of gaining support against the British raids.

The approved document created a "perpetual Union" between the states, with each state retaining its own "sovereignty, freedom, and independence, and every power, jurisdiction, and right, which is not by this Confederation expressly delegated to the United States, in Congress assembled." This meant that the "Confederation" was to have a central government with limited powers, and those not specifically granted to it were retained by the states that had created it. As the initial imperative for this agreement was the pressure of managing a war against the British Empire, the Articles pledged the states to "a firm league of friendship with each other, for their common defense, the security of their liberties, and their mutual and general welfare, binding themselves to assist each other, against all force offered to, or attacks made upon them, or any of them, on account of religion, sovereignty, trade, or any other pretense whatever."

To manage the new nation, each state would appoint between two and seven representatives annually in a manner to be decided by the state, with the proviso that limited the terms for delegates to no more than three years in any six-year period. Regardless of the number of representatives that a state chose to appoint, or the size of its population, each state would receive only one vote on any issue that came before Congress. To conduct meetings, Congress could appoint from among its membership a president as presiding officer, provided that no person serve in that capacity more than one year in every three years. This was not a chief executive, but only a person delegated to preside over the meetings.

When acting upon a motion, any issue regarding waging war, approving treaties, coining or regulating the value of money, approving expenses or bills, borrowing or appropriating money, regulating the military or naval forces, or appointing a commander in chief could only be approved with a majority of at least 9 of the 13 states voting in the affirmative. Motions on other issues could be decided by a majority vote. The Articles of Confederation could only be amended by a unanimous vote of all the states.

When Congress was not in session, it was authorized to appoint a Committee of the States consisting of one delegate from each state, which also appointed other committees and officers. The committee, or a committee of any nine states, could conduct normal business, but any of the enumerated powers requiring a minimum affirmative vote of nine states had to be brought before Congress.

The powers of the new government were limited. It was empowered to conduct foreign affairs, with the individual states specifically being precluded from carrying on any negotiations with other nations, from signing a treaty or forming any alliance with any other state in the union without the specific consent of the Congress, or from imposing import or export taxes that might conflict with treaties. The Congress could regulate coinage and weights and measures, establish post offices, regulate the military and naval forces, and control trade with the indigenous tribes. Congress was also to be "the last resort on appeal in all disputes and differences now subsisting or that hereafter may arise between two or more States concerning boundary, jurisdiction or any other causes whatever."

As a major reason for the new government was pursuit of the Revolution, the Articles also contained provisions regarding the military and naval forces. The central government retained the sole right to declare and prosecute war, with the individual states specifically prohibited from engaging in war without the consent of the Congress unless an invasion created such an emergency that waiting for congressional action would endanger the state. While each state was required to maintain a militia that was always ready to provide for the local public defense, they were prohibited from maintaining any navy in peacetime except such as Congress might agree was necessary for the defense of their commerce. The states were also prohibited from conferring "letters of marque or reprisal" unless authorized by Congress during a time of war. If called to national service, all officers of the rank of colonel or below were to be appointed by the legislature of the state contributing the troops, but all wartime expenses would be paid from a common treasury.

Another question was where the treasury was to obtain the money it needed to satisfy its debts. The Articles solved that with the provision that required states to contribute funds based on the value of land and buildings and improvements within each state. The central government would not tax directly but had to rely on the individual states with the proviso that their contribution to the central government was laid and levied by the direction of each state's legislature. The states, acting as individuals, would be assessed an amount based on land values that it would then be up to the state to levy, collect, and forward to the Congress.

Finally, the Articles made provision for the future entry of additional states, anticipating that Canada might wish to join if it decided to participate in the Revolution against Britain. Other than Canada, the Articles stated that no other colony would be permitted unless its entry was agreed upon by nine states.

Despite its limited authority, the new government proved workable for routine business, but it was unable to meet the economic strain of the war and the demands of the postwar years. With the arrival of peace and independence, interstate bickering and the claims of creditors constantly made demands upon the government that it found difficult to meet. Commerce became chaotic because the central government had no authority to regulate it, and Congress could not meet its financial obligations because it had no means of forcing the states to pay their assessments for the support of the government.

By 1785, imports from Britain alone reached some $6 million, while the value of exports was only $1.7 million, clearly an unsustainable imbalance. Because the United States was no longer part of the British Empire, planters no longer received the bounty on indigo, and its production collapsed. American farmers lost access to one of the largest markets for their products in the British West Indies, and Dutch and French financial firms were willing to lend money only at very high interest rates. Congress responded by printing a large quantity of paper money, which fueled inflation and further diminished confidence in the new government.

Huge debts incurred during the Revolution remained unpaid, but Congress lacked the power to tax the people directly; it could only ask the states to do so. With no money to pay the debts owed to veterans of the Continental Army, and fearing that the army might march on the government, Congress sold land to pay off some debts and gave land grants to veterans in lieu of money that it did not have. The individual states were also in debt, forcing them to raise taxes, sell land, and take other means to meet their economic responsibilities. Money was in short supply, with small farmers, debtors, and the poor suffering the most.

Some state legislatures enacted laws postponing the repayment of debts. The poor economy led to widespread unrest, especially among New England farmers. In Massachusetts, land taxes rose over 60 percent between 1783 and 1786, and the legislature failed to act on calls for relief. Farm foreclosures increased dramatically. Daniel Shays, a former Revolutionary War army captain, led a rebellion against the state government in 1786 that convinced many that fears of mob violence were justified and that a strong central government was necessary to avoid anarchy.

James Madison (1751–1836), a student of history and politics, was one of a growing number who believed the confederation form of government was simply too weak to meet the various crises. By 1783, the national debt stood at $36,500,375. Congress asked the states for $10 million to meet its obligations in 1782–1783, but the states provided only $1.5 million. At the same time, the increase in paper money led to rapid inflation. In 1778, it took 4 Continental paper dollars to equal 1 gold dollar in value. By the following year, it took 100 Continental dollars to buy the same gold dollar. Inflation proved so harmful to the economy that, in 1780, Congress legislated a legal rate of exchange of 40 paper dollars to 1 gold dollar, thereby wiping out $200 million in debt from its ledgers, but alienating those who had lost money in the process.

The ruinous economy brought increasing numbers of farm foreclosures, and in 1783, Maj. John Armstrong called for a meeting of army officers to discuss their grievances against the government. Only the personal intervention of George Washington (1732–1799) ended what might have become a revolt. Congress attempted to address the issues through an amendment to the Articles allowing the government to impose a tax on imports, but it was rejected. Another proposal for an amendment allowing taxation of the states based on their population was likewise rejected. Fearful of popular revolt and a march on Congress by disgruntled elements of the army, Congress moved from Philadelphia to Princeton, New Jersey, in 1783, and then on to Annapolis, Maryland, and eventually to New York City to escape mobs of soldiers demanding their back pay. By 1787, $3 million in interest payments on the national debt were overdue, with no money available to pay them.

Madison feared that the government was on the verge of economic collapse. Strong action was needed, and quickly, if the nation were to survive. Madison enlisted John Tyler, who was of like mind, and the two introduced a proposal into the Virginia assembly calling for an amendment of the Articles to give the central government the authority to regulate commerce. The result was a call for states to attend a convention in Annapolis, Maryland, in September 1786, to discuss the nation's commercial problems. Madison and Alexander Hamilton (1757–1804) of New York reported on the meeting, recommending that each state send delegates to another meeting for the purpose of revising the Articles of Confederation. Congress issued a call for the convention, which met in Philadelphia in the summer of 1787.

Many people brought with them complaints about the Articles of Confederation, but few agreed on the solutions. In the end, the assembled delegates far exceeded their mandate from Congress by not merely revising the Articles but discarding them entirely. What emerged was a considerably different government organization under the Constitution that provided for a stronger centralized government capable of addressing the problems that had eluded solution under the limited congressional powers of the Articles. As Gouverneur Morris explained it on May 30, 1787, during the Constitutional Convention debates, the difference was between the "federation" under the Articles, "a mere compact resting on the good faith of the parties," and a truly "national" government "having a complete and compulsive operation" (quoted in Hund 1920).

The U.S. Constitution replaced the Articles of Confederation on March 4, 1789.

James S. Pula

See also: Congress of Confederation; Constitutional Convention

Further Reading

Brown, Roger H. 2000. *Redeeming the Republic: Federalists, Taxation, and the Origins of the Constitution.* Baltimore, MD: Johns Hopkins University Press.

Hoffert, Robert W. 1992. *A Politics of Tensions: The Articles of Confederation and American Political Ideas.* Boulder: University Press of Colorado.

Hund, Gaillard, and James Brown Scott, eds. 1920. *The Debates in the Federal Convention of 1787, Which Framed the Constitution of the United States of America, Reported by James Madison, a Delegate from the State of Virginia.* Oxford: Oxford University Press. http://avalon.law.yale.edu/18th_century/debates_530.asp.

Jensen, Merrill. 1959. *The Articles of Confederation: An Interpretation of the Social-Constitutional History of the American Revolution, 1774–1781.* Madison: University of Wisconsin Press.

Jensen, Merrill. 1950. *The New Nation: A History of the United States during the Confederation, 1781–1789.* Evanston, IL: Northeastern University Press.

Morris, Richard B. 1987. *The Forging of the Union, 1781–1789.* New York: Harper & Row.

Wood, Gordon S. 1969. *The Creation of the American Republic, 1776–1787.* Chapel Hill: University of North Carolina Press.

ATAHUALPA (CA. 1502–1533)

Atahualpa was the Sapa Inca (ruler) of Tawantinsuyu (the Inca Empire) when the conquistador Francisco Pizarro (d. 1541) invaded in 1532. Atahualpa's reign as Sapa Inca was both brief and unconventional, lasting less than a year before his execution, resulting in the imposition of colonial rule over his people.

The hereditary line of rule in Tawantinsuyu followed a prescribed path. The Sapa Inca would take one of his sisters as his official wife. The next Sapa Inca was expected to come from this union. Additionally, the Sapa Inca had many other wives with whom he would bear children not destined to rule.

Huayna Capac (ca. 1488–1527), Atahualpa's father, never produced an heir through his official wife, but he succeeded in fathering 50 children. Atahualpa joined Huayna Capac on a military campaign as he marched his armies north to the region of his birthplace in Tomebamba, Ecuador. Tawantinsuyu was governed from the city of Cuzco, and Huayna Capac wanted to open another center of government in the north. His conquering armies expanded the empire to its height, and Atahualpa secured the loyalty of many of the best Incan generals. This adventure would prove costly, as Huayna Capac succumbed to a virulent illness while in Tomebamba. His passing, as well as the passing of his eldest son, Ninan Cuyochi, led to contention over who would "take the royal fringe."

Atahualpa enjoyed the loyalty of a sizable army as well as a position in the north from which to establish himself. His brother, Huascar, was in Cuzco with his finger on the pulse of the politics of the empire. Huascar was named Sapa Inca in 1527, shortly after the death of his father. However, Huascar was wary of Atahualpa's intentions and assembled an army.

Huascar's army invaded Ecuador and captured Atahualpa. It is almost certain that Atahualpa would have been put to death by his brother. The killing of claimants to the royal fringe was not unusual when the reigning Sapa Inca died. The competition between different familial lines was often brutal. However, Atahualpa managed to escape from his captivity and make his way back to Ecuador to rally his troops.

The ensuing civil war lasted for more than three years. All the people of Tawantinsuyu chose a faction to stand behind. The balance of power swung back and forth as large bloody battles whittled away at Inca forces on both sides. Eventually, realizing that he was near defeat, Huascar left Cuzco to lead his army and was captured in the ensuing battle in 1532. Atahualpa was victorious in the civil war, and he prepared to march south to Cuzco to cement his place as Sapa Inca.

In the fall of 1532, as Atahualpa proceeded south, word arrived that strangers had landed on the coast. Atahualpa was encamped at a mineral spring, just outside the town of Cajamarca when he received the news. Envoys were dispatched with gifts to greet the strangers and determine their intentions. After a brief exchange, Atahualpa agreed to a meeting in the Plaza of Cajamarca. The strangers were a group of 168 Spanish conquistadores, led by Francisco Pizarro, and they had set a trap for Atahualpa.

Cajamarca was deserted when the Spaniards and Inca converged on it, left empty after years of disease and war. The plaza was ringed on three sides with long low buildings. Pizarro hid his men, cavalry, and cannons within the buildings. When Atahualpa arrived in Cajamarca, he came born upon a gilded litter at the head of an army of around 6,000 warriors. As this was an affair of state, Atahualpa's army carried largely ceremonial weapons. They were aware of the small number of Spaniards and were not expecting a conflict. As the Inca made their way into the plaza, Pizarro's forces are said to have been terrified and to have wet themselves as they waited for the command to attack.

A Dominican priest, Vicente de Valverde, who had accompanied Pizarro on his expedition approached Atahualpa and handed him a book of Christian teachings. He told Atahualpa to submit to Spanish and Christian rule. Atahualpa must have been shocked by the audacity of these few strangers who stood before him making demands. He threw the text and refused to renounce his gods.

Under Spanish law, the *requirmiento* dictated that before "pacifying" any indigenous people, an effort must first be made to bring them into the Church. When Atahualpa cast away the religious doctrine, he essentially legitimized, in the eyes of Spanish law, military action by Pizarro. It was a calculated move, and Pizarro gave the order for his men to attack. The Spaniards burst forth from their hiding places with a roar of gunpowder and charging horses. The Inca warriors, inexperienced with these European technologies, fell into a panic. More than 2,000 were killed, and Atahualpa was captured.

Recognizing the Spaniards' lust for gold and silver, which the Inca had in abundance, Atahualpa struck a bargain with Pizarro. He offered to have his people fill one room with gold and two rooms with silver in exchange for his freedom. The Sapa Inca then commanded his men to secure his ransom, and from the end of 1532 until the spring of 1533, the treasure of the Incan Empire flowed to Cajamarca to be smelted into ingots and shipped to Spain. Having stripped Cuzco of its wealth, on July 25, 1533, Atahualpa was tried and executed by the Spanish.

Justin Power

See also: Cuzco; Pizarro, Francisco

Further Reading

Mann, Charles. 2005. *1491: New Revelations of the Americas before Columbus.* New York: Random House.

McEwan, Gordon. 2006. *The Incas: New Perspectives.* Oxford: ABC-CLIO.

Yaya, Isabel. 2012. *The Two Faces of Inca History: Dualism in the Narratives and Cosmology of Ancient Cuzco.* Boston: Brill.

ATLANTIC SLAVE TRADE

The Atlantic slave trade involved the forced transportation of Africans to the New World from 1492 until the abolition of the slave trade in different European colonies during the mid-1800s. The slave trade, which took approximately 12 million Africans, was supported by numerous European powers and African nations. Fifteen percent of Africans who were taken on the Middle Passage, the name for the maritime shipping channel between Africa and the New World, died on the journey. Those that survived the voyage faced violent forms of slavery that ruined their health and much of their sense of cultural identity. This violent and profitable Atlantic slave trade was among the first experiments in the establishment of capitalism as the dominant economic form in the modern world.

For Europeans, Sustained contact with the New World came with the voyages of Christopher Columbus (1450–1506). Spanish and Portuguese forces that followed applied a system of New World labor extraction whereby Native Americans were either forced or drafted to work for the Spanish and Portuguese during the 1500s. In the Andes, the Spanish required the Inca and other Andean nations to provide labor through the *mita* draft system, an appropriated indigenous labor arrangement that forced numerous tribes to pay tribute to Spanish leaders through providing a quota of laborers. In the Caribbean and Central America, Spanish forces applied more direct methods of forced labor, often using violent means to drive many indigenous persons to work at the end of a weapon.

During the 1500s, the Portuguese and Spanish desire for gold and silver bloodied the labor of Native Americans, many of whom lived in nations that had less violent forms of slavery prior to European contact. Many of these forced measures came to the attention of the Spanish priest Bartolome De Las Casas (1484–1566), who deemed violent forms of slavery too abusive to Native Americans, who were considered religiously innocent by most Catholic theorists. Many argued that indigenous populations should be given a chance to convert to the Church without the force of enslavement. Within the later market for slaves, Native American slavery and white indentured servitude, a form of European labor based on individual labor contracts with plantation owners, were replaced by African slavery due to the religious and royal favor provided to markets for African enslavement.

Slave systems had existed in Europe for centuries before contact with the New World. Ancient Roman slavery served as the legal basis for many of these systems prior to the Atlantic slave trade. Even the term for people from specific areas of Eastern Europe, Slavic, comes from a root word meaning slave, because for many centuries before 1492, the dominant group of people enslaved throughout Europe were Eastern Europeans. The Middle East had also enjoyed the fruits of slave systems for centuries, both before and after the introduction of Islam. Many of these earlier traditions made the introduction of slavery to the New World relatively seamless. As well, African nations had been enslaving other Africans for centuries, often through a well-defined legal system, which made it easy for Europeans to introduce larger systems of slavery into the Western Hemisphere, especially after Europeans experimented with different methods of plantation slavery on the Canary Islands, and with the early Native American slavery in the Caribbean during the 1500s that had infuriated Las Casas.

In general, the need for bodies to fill the increasing proportions of plantation slavery desired in the New World pushed many European traders to new markets along the African coast. Slavery had always been prominent in African societies. Most slaves in the African tradition were taken in warfare between African nations.

These slaves had certain informal rights and were often integrated into, rather than separated from, the rituals and customs of African nations.

When Europeans entered the fray, this system changed. Slaves were taken in more diverse forms than simply warfare, often captured merely for African nations to profit quickly from the presence of European ships. Europeans first sustained encounters with sub-Saharan Africa began in the 1400s, when Portuguese explorers funded by Henry the Navigator (1394–1460) searched for paths around the Cape of Good Hope to reach the lucrative Asian Spice Islands. These Portuguese traders found much to be gained from contacting African nations, rather than simply sailing past their shorelines. Founding significant alliances with the Kingdom of Kongo (1390–1891), the Portuguese established forts along the African coasts and created an early slave trade during the 1400s, facilitated by African middlemen, which brought many Africans to the European mainland.

For the African slave, the trade usually began deep in the African interior, an area Europeans would rarely enter due to the fear of African disease and the lack of riverine military technology. Slaves would be gathered into coffles, long walking trains, by African slave traders, who purchased groups of slaves from African leaders. The slaves were then taken on long journeys to the coast to be housed in Portuguese forts, English barracks, or Spanish *barracoons*, coastal camps that housed slaves while waiting for new ships.

The slave trade was initially facilitated by African leaders, who gained much wealth. But as time passed, through the 1600s and 1700s, Europeans were able to assert military power on interior African nations and thereafter manipulated economic arrangements to take control of the capitalist markets on which slavery depended. Still, often well into later years of the Atlantic slave trade, African influences could alter the populations available to be taken by European traders, as with the demographic fluctuations caused by jihad within the highland Futa Jallon region during the early 1700s.

During the 1600s, Europeans established a triangle trade of goods that facilitated the movement of slaves out of Africa and into the New World. These slaves were taken to plant and harvest such staple crops as tobacco, sugar, and cotton. Those crops were then shipped to European nations that had their own people complete finished products, like cotton clothing, to be sent back to the New World or to European markets for sale. On the ocean voyage, millions of slaves died horrific deaths. Slaves were usually kept below deck for most of the passage and only allowed to come up a few times a day to air out the ship's holds to prevent disease and clear the dead. Many slaves would attempt suicide, as they frequently believed their European captors to be cannibals due to the harshness of the sailors' treatment and rumors about the violence of the slave systems they were entering.

The Atlantic slave trade was first dominated by the Portuguese, who increased trade during the 1500s and shipped approximately 5 million slaves to their New World colony of Brazil in the centuries to follow. The Spanish emerged next as a leading trader. After Las Casas argued for the lack of morality in the enslavement of Native Americans, Spanish traders shifted to enslaving Africans by shipping millions of slaves to their colonies, especially to the West Indies of the 1600s and

1700s, where the sugar crop was increasingly profitable due to European cravings for sweetened drinks such as tea and coffee and an intensified desire for rum. During the late 1600s, the English arose as the next prevailing nation in the slave trade, alongside the continuing trade of the Iberians. After initial excursions by such English traders as John Hawkins (1532–1595), the Royal African Company (1660–1752) used an English monopoly over trade with West Africa to send numerous slaves to English colonies in the New World, such as Barbados, Jamaica, Virginia, and the Carolinas. Considerable slave-trading fleets were also maintained by the French and the Dutch.

Of the 12 million slaves that were taken by all European traders on the Middle Passage, only approximately 500,000 made their way to mainland North America. Most of the 12 million were taken to Brazil and the Caribbean, where slaves typically died within two years of their landing, unable to survive the seasoning afforded by the American environment and the masters' violence, though most masters used psychological manipulation, rather than simply the force of the whip, through threatening slaves with separation from their loved ones.

Much of slavery involved more obscure laboring than the common plantation agriculture associated to the memories of the slave system. Many slaves worked on ships as divers or translators, others toiled as lumberjacks in the backcountry, and still others lived alongside their masters in small-scale operations on many American frontiers. However, most slaves taken in the Atlantic slave trade, both men and women, worked on plantation fields under the eyes of overseers. These overseers were usually white men, but they were sometimes slaves themselves, employed by the plantation owner to watch slaves and guide their labor. The memory of slavery that men labored in the fields and slave women cooked in the house is a myth that describes only specific conditions of slavery that were not the most common. Most slaves toiled in fields of sugarcane, tobacco leaf, and cotton burr.

Though experiences varied due to the strictness of specific masters and the system of slavery under which Africans toiled, most slaves were able to preserve African cultures through resistance and retention of ethnic attributes. These forms of resistance could be small and include something as simple as slowing labor. Even retaining African religious traditions, such as forms of shamanism, witchcraft, and herbalism, could be understood as resistance in systems where plantation owners only wanted labor. Many historians argue slaves were usually able to retain African culture within New World slave systems. Others argue slaves combined their African beliefs with European cultures to create creolized, or mixed, identities. While some still assert that such ideals are romantically conceived and much of slave culture was only a survival mechanism, most Africans were dehumanized by the experiences of slavery.

Resistance to slavery frequently became more significant than simply slowing down labor, often through violent revolts. Many shipboard revolts occurred on the Middle Passage as slaves fought back due to their quick acknowledgment of their coming anguish. This often led to numerous maroon communities of slaves on many American coasts. At Stono, in South Carolina, in 1739, slaves also revolted against their masters, applying African military techniques to unite in the first of many slave rebellions in North America. In both 1712 and 1741, slaves in New York revolted, though many of the facts of these revolts are often disputed. In 1760, Tacky's Rebellion in Jamaica similarly involved resistance to English slave systems by a group of Africans following a famous slave healer. Similarly, the Pointe Coupee Conspiracy in Spanish Louisiana in 1795 involved the culmination of years of resistance by nonslaveholding whites, Native Americans, and Africans to various European slave systems that had controlled the area.

The Haitian Rebellion (1791–1804) was the first slave rebellion to overthrow a European colony. Led by African slaves, and later informed by free people of color who voiced concerns for liberty from the congruent French Revolution (1789–1799), the rebellion, created the first black nation in the New World in 1804 with the ascension of Jean-Jacques Dessalines (1758–1806) to the office of governor-general. Animated by the success of the Haitian Rebellion, many other Africans and free blacks resisted slavery in the years to follow. These groups included those following the artist Jose Antonio Aponte in Cuba in 1812, the slave Denmark Vesey (1767–1822) in South Carolina in 1822, and the revolutionaries who fought with Nat Turner (1800–1831) in Virginia in 1831. Nearly all slave rebellions failed, but they prove that slaves constantly resisted their masters through both subterfuge and violent means.

Abolitionism arose in the late 18th century with the goal of removing slavery from European economies in the New World. Most of the abolitionist leaders, such as English politician William Wilberforce (1759–1833) and Anglo-African writer Olaudah Equiano (1745–1797), applied religious motives to justify the end of slavery. Many other religious voices in England, especially among the Methodists, worked for the establishment of Sierra Leone in Africa as a free colony during the 1780s. They believed that the colony was a way to reintroduce New World slaves back to their homelands. Many Europeans worked heroically to defeat the slave systems their ancestors had instituted, but many historians assert that abolitionism was nothing more than a way for European nations, especially England, to switch from foreign- to domestic-focused labor economies.

These mixed sentiments were also apparent within the abolitionist movement in the United States. Though the Quakers established a moral abolitionism with the help of freed slaves in the years before the American Revolution (1775–1783), most of the abolitionists in the political realm before the 1820s focused on the end of the slave trade from Africa rather than the end of slavery itself. For many early American leaders, often slave owners like Thomas Jefferson (1743–1826) or members of the racialist American Colonization Society (1816–1919), this was because they desired profits from the slaves they already owned and hoped not to depreciate the price of their slaves by creating more supply from African coasts. The United States formally banned the slave trade in 1807, though slavery persisted in many Northern states until the 1820s and throughout the South until the Civil War (1861–1865).

Even with abolitionist efforts, moral or economic, trafficking slaves from Africa to the New World continued well into the 1800s, even rising at times due to the introduction of industrial technologies to European colonies. The slave trade was officially outlawed for most traders in 1807 by the British Abolition of the Slave

Trade Act, but slavery and illegal trading persisted to bring slaves to European colonies thereafter, especially until the General Abolition of 1833 passed by the British. In many Iberian colonies, slaves were imported well into the 1800s, and slavery persisted among slave societies either legally or illegally as late as 1888 when the last formal abolition came to Brazil.

Andrew Kettler

See also: Dutch Slave Trade; Middle Passage; Planters; Slave Religion; Slavery and Race

Further Reading

Baptist, Edward. 2014. *The Half Has Never Been Told: Slavery and the Making of American Capitalism.* New York: Basic Books.

Brown, Christopher. 2006. *Moral Capital: Foundations of British Abolitionism.* Chapel Hill: University of North Carolina Press.

Eltis, David. 2000. *The Rise of African Slavery in the Americas.* Cambridge: Cambridge University Press.

Heywood, Linda, and John Thornton. 2007. *Central Africans, Atlantic Creoles, and the Foundation of the Americas, 1585–1660.* New York. Cambridge University Press.

Morgan, Philip. 1997. "The Cultural Implications of the Atlantic Slave Trade: African Regional Origins, American Destinations, and New World Developments." *Slavery & Abolition* 18, no. 1 (April): 122–145.

Nwokeji, Ugo. 2010. *The Slave Trade and Culture in the Bight of Biafra: An African Society in the Atlantic World.* Cambridge: Cambridge University Press.

Smallwood, Stephanie. 2007. *Saltwater Slavery: A Middle Passage from Africa to American Diaspora.* Cambridge, MA: Harvard University Press.

Thornton, John. 1998. *Africa and Africans in the Making of the Atlantic World.* New York: Cambridge University Press.

AZTEC

The Aztec Empire was the most powerful Mesoamerican kingdom in history. Flourishing from about 1345 to 1521 CE, the multiethnic, multilingual realm spanned more than 80,000 square miles from Central Mexico to present-day Guatemala. Founded by a small group of Natives that called themselves the Mexica, they rose to become the greatest power in the Americas by the time the Spanish arrived in the 16th century.

Overview

The Mexica Indians were a small, humble group of Nahuatl-speaking immigrants who traveled into the Valley of Mexico from a land they called Aztlan in the north. The valley was already occupied by about 40 small city-states, all constantly engaged in battles for supremacy in the region. As late arrivals to the fertile valley, the Mexica were forced to settle in the undesirable swampland adjoining the salty lakes in the valley. On a small island, the Mexica finally found a promised omen when they encountered an eagle eating a snake while sitting on a cactus. The Mexica priests proclaimed they had reached their promised land.

The Mexica settled on the island to found Tenochtitlán (Place of the Cactus Fruit). They rapidly developed a system of dikes and canals to control the water levels and salinity of the lakes. Dirt removed while digging the canals was piled on log rafts and planted with seeds. These raised beds, called *chinampas*, were used for growing food crops and gardens. Using canoes and small boats, the Mexica were able to trade with other cities in the valley.

Huitzilihuitl, the ruler of the Mexica from 1391 to 1415, presided over one of the most important periods in Mexica history. The Mexica became highly skilled soldiers and effective diplomats from commercial dealings with neighboring groups. Huitzilihuitl established successful marriage alliances with a number of powerful family dynasties in the region, increasing their political power and prestige.

By 1400, several small empires existed in the Valley of Mexico. Texcoco, the capital of the Acholhua region, and Azcapotzalco, the capital of the Tepanec, were the most dominant. These two city-states went head-to-head in 1428 in the Tepanec War. The Azcapotzalco forces were defeated by an alliance of Texcoco, Tenochtitlán, and several smaller cities. After the war, Itzcóatl, the ruler of Tenochtitlán from 1428 to 1440, formed the Triple Alliance with Texcoco and a rebel Tepanec city, Tlacopan, and became the dominant power in the region. The Triple Alliance began a systematic campaign of territorial expansion. The spoils of war—tributes from the conquered—were to be shared equally between the three cities. Over time, Tenochtitlán came to dominate the alliance, with its ruler becoming the supreme ruler over the entire empire.

The empire continued to expand after 1430, and its military forces grew through the conscription of adult males supplied by allied and conquered states. Battles were concentrated in or near cities. As each fell, the Aztec victors claimed the city and all the surrounding territory. Tribute was extracted, and the next territory was approached. Tribute took many forms, including textiles, foodstuffs, equipment for warriors, honey, salt, and human captives for sacrifices.

Itzcóatl died in 1440, and was succeeded by his nephew Motecuhzoma Ilhuicamina. Motecuhzoma I, as he was later called, guided Aztec expansion for the remainder of the 15th century. The empire reached its apogee under the rule of Ahuitzotl, dominating as many as 25 million people throughout the highlands. Ahuitzotl was succeeded by the doomed Motecuhzoma II, who ruled during the catastrophic Spanish invasion led by Hernán Cortés in 1519.

The empire was maintained by the appointment of officials to oversee the new territories, intermarriage with noble families in the conquered towns, gift giving, construction of monuments and buildings in the new region promoting imperial ideology, and the continuing threat of additional military intervention.

Social Classes

The Aztecs had a complex and highly structured society. There were three social classes: nobility, commoners, and slaves. Each class had strict rules of behavior, but there were means to move upward or downward in social class.

The highest class was the *pipiltin*, or nobility. This status was not originally hereditary, but it later became that way. The nobility were families of rulers, priests, and those few who earned the rank, such as those working in top army or government positions. Nobles made up less than 10 percent of the population, but they maintained firm control over society. The wealth and power of the nobility came from their hold over land, labor, and tribute. Laws determined one's rank in the hierarchy and the equivalent level of consumption allowed of designer goods, size of houses, wearing of jewelry, and more for each noble family.

The *macehualtin* were commoners—the most numerous social group. These people were engaged in agricultural activities, arts and crafts, or common trading. Commoners were organized into wards and *calpolli* groups. A calpolli was a group of families who lived close together, worked for the same lord, controlled an allotted portion of land, and often shared an occupation. In cities, a calpolli was like a neighborhood. In rural areas, a small village was a calpolli. Calpolli lands were farmed by their members. Most men were probably farmers, but in some rural calpolli, family members did additional work, such as making paper from tree bark or weaving textiles. Many macehualtin produced more goods than were needed for themselves and their tribute and led comfortable lives. Urban commoners were very similar but more likely to be craft specialists directly subject to the royal palaces.

Slaves, or *tlacotin*, were an important class. Anyone could become a slave due to debt, as punishment for a crime, or as a war captive. In Aztec society, however, slaves could have possessions, own other slaves, and purchase their freedom. Slavery was personal, not hereditary. The children of slaves were free. Slaves could be set free if they could prove they were mistreated or if they had children with or were married to their masters.

When slaves were purchased, their animals, property, and any money they had went to the purchasers. When an owner died, slaves performing outstanding service were freed, but the rest were passed on as part of the owner's inheritance. People could sell themselves as slaves if they did not have the means to support themselves. This was a common occurrence among gamblers and prostitutes. Children of poor parents could be sold for a certain number of years if the family needed money. Interestingly, any slave that escaped and reached the royal palace without being caught was instantly given his or her freedom.

Changing status from free to slave was an official act that had to be witnessed by four officials. There were merchants in city marketplaces that specialized in trading slaves. Most worked as servants in royal households. Female slaves skilled in weaving or spinning were put to work making *quachtli* for their owners. Quachtli were standardized lengths of cloth used in commercial transactions. Quachtli had various grades of quality, ranging in value from 65 to 300 cacao beans per unit. Individual cacao beans were used in the markets for small purchases. Quachtli were used for larger transactions.

Daily Life

Boys were expected to grow up to be warriors and continue their father's occupation. Girls were raised to manage the household: cooking, weaving, cleaning, raising children, and marketing. Parents trained their young children at home. By the age of 15, boys and girls went to school. Teachers were revered in Aztec society. There were two types of school, the *telpochcalli* for most commoners and the *calmecac* for nobles and high-ranking commoners. Most instruction was gender specific, and girls did not learn to read or write. But all students learned to sing, dance, and play instruments for religious rituals and celebrations. In the telpochcalli, the focus for boys was military training. The calmecac was more exclusive. Each was associated with a major temple, and the students received training for leadership positions in government, the military, and the priesthood. Marriage was arranged by parents when boys were in their late teens or early twenties and girls several years younger. Once married, young people assumed adult roles in society, determined by their class, occupation, and residence.

Most men worked outside the home, which was the domain of women. The majority of men worked in the fields all day during the growing season. During the rainy season, men were away fulfilling their service obligations to the empire as warriors or laborers on public projects. The exception was artisans, who usually worked in their home or a nearby workshop.

Women spent most of their time in traditional activities around the home. However, in the Aztec world, women provided significantly to the family economy. Textiles were needed to pay tribute to the state, and extra cloth could be traded at the market for additional household goods. The woman of the home negotiated the marketing and sold the family's surplus food or craft products. Women also carried out domestic rituals, symbolically sweeping the house and yard to purify the home, burning incense, and maintaining the household altar.

Religion

Mythology and religion were closely intertwined in Mesoamerican societies. The Aztec pantheon contained a mix of deities specific to the Mexica people and gods common to several older groups, including the Maya and Toltecs. Religion pervaded every aspect of Aztec life. The majority of gods represented the natural forces vital to an economy based on agriculture. Every Aztec city was dominated by a stone pyramid topped by temples to the highest gods, where priests conducted the human sacrifices required by their deities.

The two principal deities worshipped by the Aztec were Huitzilopochtli (the sun god and god of war), and Tlaloc (the rain god). Each had a temple at the top of the Templo Mayor pyramid in the sacred district in the heart of Tenochtitlán. Another important deity was Quetzalcoatl, the feathered serpent god found in many Mesoamerican societies. Quetzalcoatl was the creator, the god of wind, and the god of learning and knowledge. He was the patron of the calmecac school and the priesthood. Codices name at least 200 gods and goddesses associated with rain, moisture, agricultural fertility, maize, alcohol, fire, life, death, the underworld, and much more. This complex array of gods presided over every aspect of human life.

The gods were honored with festivals, banquets, music, dancing, decorated statues, processions, incense burning, voluntary bloodletting, and human and animal sacrifices. Human victims for sacrifices were usually taken from conquered regions. The most prestigious offerings were warriors who had demonstrated great bravery in battle. Human sacrifice was important to indigenous tribes in the Valley of Mexico for hundreds of years, but the Aztecs took it to an unprecedented level. Spilling human blood would pay their debt to the gods, and the sun would continue to rise, crops would grow, and life would continue.

Over time, the Mexica began to feel the gods were insatiable. From 1446 to 1453, a series of devastating natural disasters decimated the population. Waves of locusts, drought, floods, and early frosts caused the people to resort to a massive number of human sacrifices. When abundant rain and healthy crops eventually returned, the people believed their efforts were successful. Priests willingly took part in the slaughter because they believed that the gods had sacrificed themselves to make the earth fruitful and might lose their power if not sustained with blood offerings.

Priests did more than conduct sacrifices during rituals. They were well educated and served as scribes, artists, teachers, and guardians of knowledge. They watched the skies for astronomical events and kept track of a complex calendar system with two cycles: a 260-day ceremonial year and a 365-day solar year. The calendars coincided once every 52 years, which was a considered a time filled with danger. On the last night of the cycle, a crucial ceremony was conducted to ward off evil and regenerate the world.

Collapse

The most common description of the end of the Aztec Empire is that Hernán Cortés, with a small group of some 300 soldiers, managed to overpower the Natives with their superior steel weaponry, horses, and armor. However, the reality is far more complex.

The Aztec Empire, which controlled about 11 million people from dozens of cultural and language groups at its zenith, always had to deal with minor rebellions. These often happened when new rulers ascended to the throne in Tenochtitlán, but they were always rapidly crushed. The tide turned with the arrival of the Spanish. As the Spanish advanced to the capital, they collected the support of conquered states unhappy with their status, giving them tens of thousands of Native soldiers to bolster their ranks. He was able to initiate alliances with local leaders desiring rebellion. When Cortés took Tenochtitlán in 1521, he was at the head of an army estimated at 150,000–200,000 warriors. By this time, successive epidemics of smallpox, measles, and typhus brought by Europeans had further decimated Native populations. Tenochtitlán was completely destroyed after the siege of 1521, and Mesoamerica became a Spanish colony called New Spain. Its capital, Mexico City, was built on the ruins of Tenochtitlán. Boatloads of colonists arrived, and new Spanish towns and cities were constructed—often on the sites of existing Aztec towns.

Legacy

The Aztec Empire suddenly ceased to exist in 1521, with Native warfare, human sacrifice, and the tribute system immediately shut down. In rural areas, however, traditional community life remained virtually unchanged for centuries. It made little difference to peasant farmers whether they were subjects of the Aztec Empire or the Spanish Empire. They still produced goods for their households, family group, and a distant overlord.

Over time, Spanish became the dominant language, but Nahuatl was still spoken in rural villages. It is still spoken today by descendants, especially in the mountainous areas of Central Mexico. Most modern-day Mexicans are mestizos, a blend of mixed indigenous and Spanish ancestry. Many towns and landmarks retain their Nahuatl names, and Mexican cuisine is based on agricultural products contributed by the Mexica/Aztecs. The modern Mexican flag bears a design depicting the Mexica migration legend.

Jill M. Church

See also: Columbian Exchange; Cortés, Hernán; Doctrine of Discovery/Conquest; Mesoamerica; Montezuma II

Further Reading

Clendinnen, Inga. 1991. *Aztecs: An Interpretation.* Cambridge and New York: Cambridge University Press.

Gruzinski, Serge. 1992. *The Aztecs: Rise and Fall of an Empire.* New York: Harry N. Abrams, Inc.

Levy, Buddy. 2008. *Conquistador: Hernán Cortés, King Montezuma, and the Last Stand of the Aztecs.* New York: Bantam Books.

Smith, Michael E. 2012. *The Aztecs.* 3rd ed. West Sussex, U.K.: Wiley-Blackwell.

Van Tuerenhout, Dirk R. 2005. *The Aztecs: New Perspectives.* Santa Barbara, CA: ABC-CLIO, LLC.

B

BACON'S REBELLION

Bacon's Rebellion was an uprising of inland farmers who were upset over a number of different issues that affected the Colony of Virginia during the middle of the 17th century. Although much of the agitation was centered on the policies of Gov. William Berkeley, there were other broader concerns regarding the Virginia economy as well as ongoing struggles with Native Americans along the frontier. The rebellion took place in the summer and fall of 1676. Although the leader of the rebellion, Nathaniel Bacon, managed to wreak havoc on the capital at Jamestown, by the beginning of 1677, Governor Berkeley had regained power (albeit temporarily), and the colony had largely returned to the status quo.

During the third quarter of the 17th century, the divide between Virginia planters and inland farmers was growing apace. Wealth, social prestige, and political power were all largely held by the landed gentry along the Tidewater of Virginia. This region was also largely free from the threat of Indian attacks. By contrast, the farmers who had settled inland were often poor squatters or former indentured servants whose labor contracts had expired. These men were marginalized in Virginia society and politics, and they were in almost constant conflict with Doeg and Susquehannock Indians.

By the 1670s, these inland farmers were further burdened by sagging tobacco prices. In addition, Virginia's neighbors, Maryland and the Carolinas, grew increasingly competitive in the tobacco economy at the same time that English mercantilist policy became more restrictive. To make matters worse, a series of unfortunate weather-related incidents, including hurricanes, hailstorms, droughts, and floods severely damaged the colony's ability to compensate for the depression in the tobacco industry. Plantation owners were somewhat more able to weather the storm, as it were, by virtue of their scaled economy. Their counterparts along the frontier, however, looked for a scapegoat to blame for their economic woes.

In July 1675, a raid by Doeg Indians was the spark that ignited the larger uprising. The Doeg raid was a specific event against a specific farmstead. However, when the colonists retaliated, they mistakenly targeted the Susquehannock tribe, leading to an escalating series of attacks and counterattacks. Governor Berkeley attempted to negotiate a settlement for the growing crisis, but the proposed solution was unacceptable to Nathaniel Bacon. Berkeley, the longest-serving governor of the colony, was a progressive-minded man, who wanted to maintain positive relations with friendly Native Americans. Bacon, however, believed that all Indians should be expelled or exterminated.

In 1676, English colonist Nathaniel Bacon led a popular revolt of colonial Virginia's frontier settlers, known as Bacon's Rebellion, against Virginia governor William Berkeley and his allies. The revolt's alliance between slaves and indentured servants was seen as a threat to the ruling class, who responded by passing legislation intended to sow division between the races. (Library of Congress)

Nathaniel Bacon had arrived in Virginia only a year before the Doeg raid. Born in Suffolk, England, in 1647, Bacon came from a relatively wealthy merchant family and was related to Governor Berkeley by marriage. An articulate and intelligent man, Bacon was nevertheless disdainful of manual labor. His father had sent him to the colonies in the hopes that Nathaniel would mature. By contrast, Berkeley was already nearly 70 when the crisis began. He was a favorite of Charles II, having been a veteran of the English Civil War, and a veteran of fighting against the Native Americans along the Virginia frontier. But he was also a playwright and a scholar.

In 1675, Bacon was a member of the prestigious Governor's Council, an advisory body for the governor as well as a court of last resort for the colony. Bacon soon demanded that he be granted a commission from Governor Berkeley to fight the Indians along the frontier. When Berkeley refused, Bacon collected "volunteers" to wage war against all Native Americans along the frontier, whether they were friendly to the colony or not.

Bacon and his followers, numbering several hundred at their greatest strength, accused Berkeley of playing favorites. They argued that his unequal treatment of certain tribes was because he and his supporters had valuable trading connections with some Indians and not others. As Bacon was personally adversely affected by Berkeley's trade policies, his grievances with the governor were also personal, as was his anger with the Indians who enjoyed favored trading status.

Bacon was elected "general" of the militia force largely because he agreed to bear the financial burden of the campaigns. Some of Bacon's raids against the Native Americans along the frontier were especially vicious. In one instance, the rebel force marched to a fort held by the Occaneechi, a tribe generally considered friendly to the colonists, and forced them to assist with the capture of Susquehannock warriors. When the Occaneechi returned with their captives, Bacon's men promptly opened fire on all the gathered Indians, killing dozens.

Much to Berkeley's chagrin, Bacon parlayed his anti-Indian campaigns into election to a seat in the House of Burgesses in June 1676. Bacon was arrested for treason almost immediately upon his arrival in Jamestown to assume his seat in the legislature; however, Berkeley, misjudging the amount of support Bacon had among inland farmers, quickly pardoned him and allowed him to take his seat. This landmark session of the assembly enacted a number of sweeping reforms to the colony's political structure. Despite being credited by some at the time for his role in securing these reforms, the majority had already been under consideration before his arrival, and his contributions were relatively minimal.

After his election, Bacon once again demanded a commission to fight the Indians, this time bringing with him nearly 500 men to the capital at Jamestown. Berkeley again refused, even though some of Bacon's men took aim at the governor's chest with their muskets. When it became clear that the governor would not relent, the men shifted their aim to some of the assembled burgesses. Berkeley granted him the commission. To culminate his "victory," Bacon issued his "Declaration of the People" on July 30, 1676. In it, he criticized Berkeley as being corrupt and ineffective as governor, especially with regard to his Indian policy. Moreover, he demanded that all followers swear an oath directly to him. From July to September 1676, Bacon served as de facto leader of Jamestown.

Although he had been driven across the James River to his plantation in Green Spring, Berkeley continued in his efforts to regain power. While Bacon and his army were on the frontier, Berkeley managed to retake Jamestown. He fortified it and waited for Bacon to return. Bacon tried, unsuccessfully, to lay siege to the town. On September 19, 1676, he finally resorted to burning the city to the ground. This extreme act cost Bacon much of his remaining support, and his calls for Berkeley's arrest went unheeded.

Just over a month later, Nathaniel Bacon died, most likely of dysentery. The rebellion limped along under the leadership of John Ingram. But the tide had turned in the governor's favor. Berkeley oversaw a series of military campaigns against the remaining insurgents, and the rebellion had almost totally been overcome by the time an English naval squadron arrived to aid the governor's efforts. Berkeley seized rebel property, and 23 people were hanged for their roles in the rebellion. Despite having overcome the uprising, Berkeley was removed from power the following year by Charles II, when the king received the report of the committee charged with investigating the incident.

Historians still debate the short- and long-term consequences of Bacon's Rebellion. Although Berkeley was recalled to England, one of the other stated goals of Bacon and his followers, the expulsion or destruction of Indians along the frontier, was not achieved. For many years, the rebellion was seen as perhaps the first significant uprising against royal authority in the colonies. This interpretation asserted that Nathaniel Bacon, in his "Declaration of the People," had landed the first blow for colonists who were growing distrustful of royal authority and who chafed under the control of the British Crown. More recently, scholars have revised their understanding of the incident, seeing it as a struggle for local power between two leading figures in Virginia society.

In either case, there was a noticeable and profound consequence for the society of the Chesapeake colonies. Leading landowners, who were also the primary political force in the region, recognized the class sympathies evident in the rebellion. Bacon's force had included a number of African slaves, suggesting that rebellion was populated by people who had overcome racial divides and had unified by virtue of their shared marginalization in Virginia's socioeconomic structure. Within a generation, legislators in the House of Burgesses passed the Virginia Slave Codes of 1705. This law was created to strengthen the caste system in the colony. The new, more rigid application of chattel slavery was intended to prevent any similar uprisings by ensuring that racial considerations would override any class-based camaraderie.

Shawn Selby

See also: Indentured Servants; Virginia

Further Reading

Rice, James. 2012. *Tales from a Revolution: Bacon's Rebellion and the Transformation of Early America.* New York: Oxford University Press.

Tarter, Brent. 2011. "Bacon's Rebellion, the Grievances of the People, and the Political Culture of Seventeenth-Century Virginia." *Virginia Magazine of History & Biography* 119, no. 1: 1–41.

PRIMARY DOCUMENT: Nathaniel Bacon, Declaration in the Name of the People of Virginia (1676)

The unofficial leader of a group of Virginia colonists bent on quelling the Indian War of 1675–1676, Nathaniel Bacon fomented a civil revolt in Virginia that was the first serious test of British authority in the New World. Calling to his banner members of Virginia's lowest social classes with this declaration, Bacon held tremendous power in the colony during the summer of 1676. Unfortunately, he died unexpectedly of disease in October 1676, and Bacon's Rebellion quickly collapsed without its charismatic leader.

1. For having, upon specious pretenses of public works, raised great unjust taxes upon the commonalty for the advancement of private favorites and other sinister ends, but no visible effects in any measure adequate; for not having, during this long time of his government, in any measure advanced this hopeful colony either by fortifications, towns, or trade.
2. For having abused and rendered contemptible the magistrates of justice by advancing to places of judicature scandalous and ignorant favorites.
3. For having wronged his Majesty's prerogative and interest by assuming monopoly of the beaver trade and for having in it unjust gain betrayed and sold his Majesty's country and the lives of his loyal subjects to the barbarous heathen.
4. For having protected, favored, and emboldened the Indians against his Majesty's loyal subjects, never contriving, requiring, or appointing any due or proper means of satisfaction for their many invasions, robberies, and murders committed upon us.

5. For having, when the army of English was just upon the track of those Indians, who now in all places burn, spoil, murder and when we might with ease have destroyed them who then were in open hostility, for then having expressly countermanded and sent back our army by passing his word for the peaceable demeanor of the said Indians, who immediately prosecuted their evil intentions, committing horrid murders and robberies in all places, being protected by the said engagement and word past of him the said Sir William Berkeley, having ruined and laid desolate a great part of his Majesty's country, and have now drawn themselves into such obscure and remote places and are by their success so emboldened and confirmed by their confederacy so strengthened that the cries of blood are in all places, and the terror and consternation of the people so great, are now become not only difficult but a very formidable enemy who might at first with ease have been destroyed.
6. And lately, when, upon the loud outcries of blood, the assembly had, with all care, raised and framed an army for the preventing of further mischief and safeguard of this his Majesty's colony.
7. For having, with only the privacy of some few favorites without acquainting the people, only by the alteration of a figure, forged a commission, by we know not what hand, not only without but even against the consent of the people, for the raising and effecting civil war and destruction, which being happily and without bloodshed prevented; for having the second time attempted the same, thereby calling down our forces from the defense of the frontiers and most weakly exposed places.
8. For the prevention of civil mischief and ruin amongst ourselves while the barbarous enemy in all places did invade, murder, and spoil us, his Majesty's most faithful subjects.

Of this and the aforesaid articles we accuse Sir William Berkeley as guilty of each and every one of the same, and as one who has traitorously attempted, violated, and injured his Majesty's interest here by a loss of a great part of this his colony and many of his faithful loyal subjects by him betrayed and in a barbarous and shameful manner exposed to the incursions and murder of the heathen. And we do further declare these the ensuing persons in this list to have been his wicked and pernicious councilors, confederates, aiders, and assisters against the commonalty in these our civil commotions.

Sir Henry Chichley, Richard Whitacre, Lt. Col. Christopher Wormeley, Nicholas Spencer, Phillip Ludwell, Joseph Bridger, Robt. Beverley, William Claiburne Jr., Ri. Lee, Thomas Hawkins, Thomas Ballard, William Sherwood, William Cole, John Page Clerke, John Clauffe Clerk, John West, Hubert Farrell, Thomas Reade, Math. Kempe

And we do further demand that the said Sir William Berkeley with all the persons in this list be forthwith delivered up or surrender themselves within four days after the notice hereof, or otherwise we declare as follows.

That in whatsoever place, house, or ship, any of the said persons shall reside, be hid, or protected, we declare the owners, masters, or inhabitants of the said places to be confederates and traitors to the people and the estates of them is also of all the aforesaid persons to be confiscated. And this we, the commons of Virginia, do declare, desiring a firm union amongst ourselves that we may jointly and with one accord defend ourselves against the common enemy. And let not the faults of the guilty be the reproach of the innocent, or the faults or crimes of the oppressors divide and separate us who have suffered by their oppressions.

These are, therefore, in his Majesty's name, to command you forthwith to seize the persons abovementioned as traitors to the King and country and them to bring to Middle Plantation and there to secure them until further order, and, in case of opposition, if you want any further assistance you are forthwith to demand it in the name of the people in all the counties of Virginia.

Source: "Declaration of Nathaniel Bacon in the Name of the People of Virginia, July 30, 1676." Massachusetts Historical Society Collections, 4th ser., 1871, vol. 9: 184–187.

BALBOA, VASCO NÚÑEZ DE (1475–1519)

Vasco Núñez de Balboa was a Spanish conquistador who became the first European to see the Pacific Ocean as well as to cross the Isthmus of Panama. He was the founder of Darién, the first European settlement in America. Despite his decisive contribution to the expansion and consolidation of the Spanish Empire in the Americas, disagreements with the governor of the area led to his trial and subsequent execution, having been charged with treason.

Balboa was born ca. 1475 in Jerez de los Caballeros, Extremadura, in Spain. Extremadura also saw the birth of a number of Spanish conquistadors in the Americas, the most prominent of them being Hernán Cortés, who conquered Mexico, and Francisco Pizarro, who discovered the Incan Empire of Peru. Around 1500, following thousands of men seeking to make a fortune and a name for themselves in the New World, Balboa joined an expedition to Colombia led by Rodrigo de Bastidas.

After the completion of the expedition, Balboa decided to settle on the island of Hispaniola (present-day Haiti and the Dominican Republic). In the town of Salvatierra, he bought a farm, but this experience as a landowner was far from being successful. In 1510, bankrupt and besieged by his creditors, he embarked on an expedition to San Sebastián (in what is today Colombia) as a stowaway. The expedition, commandeered by Martín Fernández de Enciso, was to succor Alonso de Ojeda, who was governor of the province of New Andalucía. Balboa's presence on board was eventually discovered, and he was only allowed to stay because of the crew's support and his expertise, as he had already been to the region. Before arriving at their destination, they suffered a shipwreck, causing the loss of, among other things, Enciso's credential that allowed him to discover and explore the region in the name of the Crown. This would later allow Balboa to challenge Enciso's power.

By the time the expedition arrived in San Sebastián, the colony was barely surviving after an Indian attack that had resulted in the deaths of many Spaniards.

Balboa's suggestion of moving westward was followed, and the survivors as well as the just-arrived expedition members abandoned San Sebastián. After a skirmish between the Spaniards and a group of local Indians, the town of Santa María la Antigua del Darién (usually known as Darién) was founded in December 1510. The full name of Darién comes from the fact that before the fight with the Natives, the Spaniards called on Santa María de la Antigua for help. Santa María la Antigua was worshipped in the town of León, Spain, Balboa's parents' hometown.

Darién, in present-day Panama, would become the first permanent European settlement in North America. With the aid of a group of loyal supporters, Balboa managed to get control over Darién, thus overruling the authority of Enciso. Balboa argued that this territory was not under Ojeda's sphere of authority but under Diego de Nicuesa's. According to the 1508 *capitulación*, the region had been divided into Nueva Andalucía (present-day Colombia), governed by Ojeda, and Veragua (comprising parts of present-day Colombia and Panama), governed by Diego de Nicuesa. To govern Darién, a *cabildo* (town council) was established, and two *alcaldes* were elected, one of them Balboa.

Meanwhile, the city of Nombre de Dios, founded in 1510 by Nicuesa, was suffering from severe starvation, but it was rescued by the timely arrival of Rodrigo Colmenares, who had brought much-needed provisions. Colmenares's arrival proved to be providential not only for the supplies but because he spread the news of the foundation of Darién. Nicuesa, learning of his supposed jurisdiction over the settlement, decided to claim his authority over it. However, when his ship arrived in the port of Darién, they were not given permission to disembark, forcing their ship to sail off. They were lost at sea on March 1, 1511, which allowed Balboa to become the de facto governor of Darién and have his own authority unthreatened.

In 1511, Balboa was appointed captain and interim governor of Darién by the Spanish king, although he soon faced revolts from those defying his post. These revolts were not his only problems, for he also had to deal with the indigenous inhabitations of the area. Balboa repressed them at the same time that he tried to forge alliances by baptizing their local *caciques*, or leader. As a result, Balboa made enemies as well as friends among the Natives. Balboa enlisted the help of Anayansi, the daughter of local cacique Careta. She acted as his interpreter and intermediary as well as becoming his lover.

Rumors of a rich kingdom, full of gold, southward from Darién prompted Balboa to command an expedition to search for it. In September 1513, 190 Spaniards (among them Francisco Pizarro) and 800 Native Americans took part in an expedition led by Balboa and accompanied by his loyal dog, Leoncico (Spanish for "small lion"). Balboa failed to secure the funding he needed from the Spanish Crown, largely because of Enciso's presence in Spain, where he was giving an altogether different version of the founding of Darién and Balboa's behavior. As a result, Balboa had to finance the expedition himself.

On September 25, 1513, Balboa sighted the Pacific Ocean. The Spanish claim to the Pacific Ocean had its basis on this event, as Balboa claimed the ocean and all its shores for Spain. To mark their taking possession, they erected a Spanish banner and made a cross with a tree trunk; they also sang the *Te Deum Laudamus*, thanking God. The name then given to the ocean was the South Sea, or Mar del Sur. (In 1520, Fernando de Magellan renamed it the Pacific Ocean.) In contrast to the rampant piracy in the Atlantic, for three centuries, Dutch and English ships did not cross the Pacific for the most part, resulting in the South Sea being generally known as the Spanish Lake. During this time, the South Sea was a place of trade and peace.

The expedition made its return to Darién in 1514, and soon afterward problems arose for Balboa. Pedro Arias (usually known as Pedrarias) Dávila was appointed governor of Darién, effectively putting an end to Balboa's power. This had much to do with Enciso's serious accusations against Balboa, which included the disappearance of Nicuesa after having been refused permission to disembark. All this tarnished Balboa's reputation and raised questions of his suitability for the post of interim governor of Darién. Pedrarias arrived in Darién in mid-1514, and Balboa was appointed *Adelantado* of the South Sea and governor of the Panama and Coiba provinces, which fell under the authority of Pedrarias. As Balboa's influence threatened Pedrarias's power and authority, their relationship was, at best, fraught. Balboa especially opposed Pedrarias's Indian policy, consisting of war and looting. To secure Balboa's loyalty, Pedrarias offered him the hand of his daughter, María de Peñalosa, who was in Spain. Balboa married her by proxy in April 1516. María stayed in Spain all through their brief marriage, though, and the couple never met.

In 1517–1518, Balboa, always in search of riches, led a new expedition. It was while Balboa was away that Pedrarias learned that he was about to be recalled and his governorship investigated. Fearing that Balboa might join his detractors, Pedrarias sent Pizarro to arrest Balboa and accused him of rebellion and high treason. Pedrarias accused Balboa of conspiring against him and of trying to establish a parallel government. Balboa petitioned to be tried in Spain or in Hispaniola, as he was afraid of not having a fair trial in Darién, but his petition was turned down. He was tried and found guilty of treason, together with four accomplices. The penalty imposed on Balboa was his execution, which took place by beheading on January 12, 1519. The whereabouts of his remains are unknown.

After Balboa's execution, Gaspar de Espinosa would explore the Pacific Coast, and Pizarro would go on to lead the expedition that would discover the Inca Empire of present-day Peru. What we know about Balboa is from the historical works by Friar Bartolomé de las Casas and Gonzalo Fernández de Oviedo. Balboa's figure fell into oblivion, and it was not until the 19th century that interest in him was renewed.

M. Carmen Gómez-Galisteo

See also: Cabeza de Vaca, Alvar Núñez; Mesoamerica; New Spain; Pizarro, Francisco

Further Reading

Aram, Bethany. 2008. *Leyenda negra y leyendas doradas en la conquista de América; Pedrarias y Balboa.* Madrid, Spain: Marcial Pons Historia.

Castro Vegas, Oscar. 1996. *Pedrarías Dávila, La ira de Dios*. San José de Costa Rica: Imprenta LIL.

Harding, Robert C. 2006. *The History of Panama*. Westport, CT: Greenwood Press.

Méndez Pereira, Octavio. 1975. *Núñez de Balboa*. Madrid, Spain: Espasa Calpe.

Shore, Maxine, and M. M. Oblinger. 1941. *Hero of Darien: The Story of Vasco Nunez de Balboa*. New York and Toronto: Longmans, Green and Co.

Thomas, Hugh. 2005. *Rivers of Gold: The Rise of the Spanish Empire from Columbus to Magellan*. New York: Random House.

BANNEKER, BENJAMIN (1731–1806)

Benjamin Franklin (1706–1790) is largely considered the quintessential self-made man in American history, but Banneker is arguably the closest African American example of his day and age for his work in astronomy and mathematics. Despite having little formal education, Banneker was a prominent almanac writer, amateur astronomer, naturalist, and planter—similar to Franklin in a number of respects. Perhaps his most notable accomplishments, however, came in the area of surveying, as he was among the surveying team responsible for setting out the boundaries of the District of Columbia in the early 1790s.

Born on November 9, 1731, to an ex-slave and his wife (the daughter of a former indentured servant), Benjamin Banneker was a free black man in the state of Maryland—a state still largely swept up in the controversial tradition of chattel slavery. Because his parents were free, Banneker was also able to avoid the ills of slavery, only witnessing secondhand the harsh mistreatment that many slaves encountered under a system that deemed them property instead of men. His freedom also afforded Banneker an opportunity to receive an education, though minimal, first from his maternal grandmother—an English dairy maid named Molly Welsh—and then at a small interracial Quaker school in the region. Together, these experiences fostered his interest in mathematics, which would prove vital to his later career and to his lifelong pursuit of knowledge as a primarily self-educated man. Using the skills he had learned, even innovating an irrigation system, Banneker worked for much of his life planting tobacco on the family farm, which he later took over after his parents' deaths. Sales of tobacco enabled Banneker to avoid poverty throughout his life (until bouts of rheumatism pushed him to another career path) and to explore his other interests, particularly as an astronomer.

Though the African American people were generally considered simple-minded or savage creatures in the 1700s, Banneker challenged those notions of intellectual inferiority through his expertise in mathematics and knowledge of the stars. Having borrowed books on astronomy from his neighbors, the infamous Ellicott family, Banneker spent hours at night staring at the stars and eagerly recording notes for his future almanac. Therefore, when President George Washington (1732–1799) appointed Andrew Ellicott (1754–1820) to survey land considered for the nation's capital, Banneker was highly recommended to work in the field observation tent for a period of three months, February–April 1791.

During his time as an assistant surveyor, Banneker continued his study of astronomy and began compiling a detailed ephemeris (a tabular statement of the assigned places of a celestial body for regular intervals) for his almanac titled *Benjamin Banneker's Pennsylvania, Delaware, Maryland, and Virginia Almanack and Ephemeris for the Year of Our Lord 1792*. In total, Banneker published 6 almanacs in almost 30 editions by 1797, when his sales considerably dwindled, though he continued to record his calculations until 1802. These almanacs, which earned Banneker recognition along the East Coast, were celebrated for their computational accuracy and for their innovations in the field, providing, for example, a tide table for the Chesapeake Bay that proved essential for fisherman in the region. These works, like those of both Jupiter Hammon (1711–1806) and Phillis Wheatley (1753–1784), revealed the potential for the African American community if lifted from a tradition of racial oppression.

Hoping to use his work as a platform to engage the civil rights debate of the era, Banneker famously composed a letter to Secretary of State Thomas Jefferson (1743–1826) to challenge the pervasive stereotypes of blacks that had taken hold of the American cultural imagination. In this letter, he confronted what he considered the hypocrisy of the American people in fighting for freedom from oppressive British rule during the American Revolution while simultaneously enacting their own form of tyranny on the enslaved black race. Along with this letter, Banneker provided Jefferson a copy of his almanac, and he quickly received a response.

Writing in August 1791, Jefferson not only acknowledged the talent of Banneker's work (and his eager desire to see further proof of the talents of the black race), but he also sent the almanac to Marquis de Condorcet (1743–1794), the secretary of the French Academy of Sciences in Paris. While Banneker received no reply from de Condorcet, in part due to a political shift in France that saw him displaced, this exchange and Banneker's open commentary on the institution of slavery earned him more national attention. Both letters were eventually published in the 1793 edition of the almanac. This contribution, eventually supported by several local abolitionist organizations, was therefore one of the foremost ways in which Banneker served as an activist for racial equality across the nation.

Benjamin Banneker died on October 9, 1806—about a year before the British abolished the trans-Atlantic slave trade. Having sold his land to the Ellicott family, he had only a few possessions remaining, though most of his papers and belongings were completely destroyed when his house caught fire the day of his burial service two days later. What Banneker did leave behind, however, was the story of a man uninhibited by the color of his skin, who used his meager education and newfound opportunities as tools to train himself and to produce a body of unprecedented work.

Today, Banneker is thus remembered, in part, for his innovations, from the family irrigation system to the infamous wooden clock he constructed in his early twenties—the first produced in his community—which ran until consumed in the flames. That impact was celebrated in his obituary, published on October 28, in Philadelphia's *Federal Gazette*. The obituary called attention to the mental prowess that Banneker had demonstrated as a member of the black community, a reminder of the promise that certainly awaited the African American people like members of any other nation or race.

Christopher Allen Varlack

See also: Hammon, Jupiter; Wheatley, Phillis

Further Reading

Allen, Will W., and Daniel Murray. 1998. *Banneker, the Afro-American Astronomer.* Washington, D.C.: Black Classic Press.

Bedini, Silvio A. 1999. *The Life of Benjamin Banneker: The First African-American Man of Science.* 2nd ed. Baltimore: Maryland Historical Society.

LePhillips, Phillip. 1917. "The Negro, Benjamin Banneker; Astronomer and Mathematician, Plea for Universal Peace." *Records of the Columbia Historical Society* 20: 114–120.

BAPTISTS

Historically, English-speaking Baptists have roots in 17th-century Puritanism, a subset of Congregationalism. Theologically, Baptists trace their beginnings to early Christianity, when the church consisted of committed souls who received baptism on confessing faith as adults. Baptists were influenced by the medieval rejection of Catholic baptismal practices and by 16th-century continental Anabaptists, who also later influenced Hutterites, the Amish, and Mennonites in their belief in religious freedom and believer's baptism. Baptists shared these beliefs, but they rejected the Anabaptist commitment to communal sharing of wealth and in pacifism. English Baptists also believed that churches should have local self-government and restricted membership to believers only.

Early English Baptists came in two varieties. Particular Baptists held, with old-line Calvinists, that Christ had died only for the elect, that atonement was particular. General Baptists took the view of the deviant Calvinist Jacobus Arminius that Christ had died for all, not just an elect, as mainstream Calvinists held. Both Arminian and mainstream Baptist branches regarded the Church of England as corrupt, but General Baptists believed that Christian charity required them to maintain some degree of fellowship and communication with parishes of the Church of England. They worshiped on their own but refused to accept the Separatist argument that the churches were totally false.

Members of both groups left England and Europe to avoid religious persecution. John Smyth and his band of Arminian Separatists moved to the Netherlands, where they came under the influence of Mennonites and formed the first English Baptist congregation in 1608, with Smyth baptizing himself and the other members. In 1611, some members returned to London and established a church that became the first General Baptist congregation, believing that Jesus had died for all, not the elect, an Arminian belief.

Later, in England, Henry Jacob and a group of Puritans formed the congregation that would become Particular Baptists in 1638 under John Spilsbury. Particular Baptists began in a non-Separatist church in Southwark in 1616. Some members withdrew from that church in1638 and formed the First Particular Baptist Church. In 1644, when seven Particular Baptist churches issued a confession of faith calling for immersion, Baptist became the name for those who practiced immersion.

The colonial Baptist presence dates to the mid-17th century. Baptists in the colonies sometimes emigrated as Baptists, but they more commonly became Baptists in the colonies, as happened to Harvard College president Henry Dunster and Roger Williams.

Roger Williams established the first colonial Baptist church, at Providence, Rhode Island, in 1638, shortly after his banishment from the Massachusetts Bay Colony. Williams was generally Calvinist but moved toward Separatism shortly before his conversion to Baptist. He moved to Boston in 1631, spoke indiscreetly, and had to flee for his religious freedom. Puritans believed in religious freedom, but only for themselves, and based their law on the Old Testament. Williams founded Rhode Island in 1635 on the principles of religious freedom for all faiths, church-state separation, and democratic government. Williams rejected infant baptism and came to believe that a new apostolic dispensation was necessary to reestablish the true church because all churches, including his own, were without suitable foundation.

When Williams left his church, it reorganized under General Baptist principles in 1652. The General Baptist church was only strong in Rhode Island, as it failed to have a widespread impact. Even after General Baptist churches united in 1670, the half dozen churches survived but failed to influence mainstream Baptist development, some even becoming Particular Baptists, including Williams's church in Providence.

Newport, Rhode Island, was home to the first major Particular Baptist church of note, a congregation that between 1641 and 1648 under John Clarke became Baptist. For nearly a century, aside from a short-lived church in Kittery, Maine, the Baptist presence in New England consisted of one church in Swansea, Massachusetts, and another in Boston. Seeking more hospitable surroundings, a group of Baptists moved from Maine to Charleston, South Carolina, around 1684.

The Middle Colonies were the center of Particular Baptist activity, with five churches in Delaware, Pennsylvania, and New Jersey uniting in 1707 into the Philadelphia Baptist Association. By 1760, this association had churches in New Jersey, Pennsylvania, Delaware, Connecticut, New York, and Virginia. By 1767, growth led to the formation of two subordinate associations, the Ketochton in Virginia and the Warren in New England. The Charleston Association in the Carolinas was another Philadelphia-led development in 1751.

More important than the Philadelphia Association was the Second Great Awakening of the late 18th and early 19th centuries. The Great Awakening was characterized by revivals that created a shared experience among denominations and citizens, with calls for personal decision, weakening the idea that the state church should set beliefs. Baptists came late to the awakening and were most influential in its Southern phase. Awakened by other preachers, many flocked to "regular" Baptist churches. In New England, revivalists called themselves Separate Baptists. They soon merged with the older Baptist churches there.

Baptist opposition to infant baptism led to their persecution in the late 18th century. Shubael Stearns (sometimes Shubal) and Daniel Marshall, New England Separate Congregationalists, established the Separate Baptists in Sandy Creek, North Carolina, in 1755, with a revival that influenced the entire Piedmont. In 1758, the churches formed by Stearns united into the Sandy Creek Association. Older churches had no doctrinal difference with the new ones but found the emotionalism and ecclesiastical irregularities difficult to handle. The two groups reconciled by 1787.

General Baptist views were acceptable in the southeast, but those who migrated to the southern mountains after the Revolution preferred a stricter Calvinism, including opposition to missions. The mountain Baptists became a splinter known initially as the Anti-Mission Baptists and later as the Hard Shell or Primitive Baptists.

Seventh Day Baptists, established in the 17th century, read the fourth commandment as requiring rest and worship on Saturday. The group remained small.

The Enlightenment challenged religious authority and dogma and encouraged reasoning and toleration. Liberty of conscience had not yet arrived in the colonies. Baptists led the fight to promote freedom of religion and separation of church and state, despite or perhaps because of being one of the most heavily persecuted sects.

Baptists in several colonies endured legal disabilities, colonial religious freedom being localized mostly in Pennsylvania and Rhode Island. In Lynn, Massachusetts, Obadiah Holmes was whipped in 1651 for refusing to pay a fine for holding an unlawful meeting. In 1665, Boston Baptists were fined, jailed, and denied access to a meetinghouse they had built. In 1774, 18 Baptists were jailed in Northampton, Massachusetts, for refusing to pay taxes to support the town's congregational minister.

Baptists arrived in Virginia in the early 18th century. The first ones jailed for preaching in disturbance of the peace were at Spotsylvania in 1768. In 1774, five or six men were jailed in Virginia for publishing religious opinion. Imprisonments continued for a decade with terms of up to five months. Baptist marriages were unrecognized, and Baptist child abuse was alleged because Baptists did not practice infant baptism. Baptists were pelted, ducked to near drowning, beaten, whipped, and otherwise abused. In 1770, Baptists petitioned for removal of restrictions, and in 1775, they petitioned for abolition of the established church with support from Presbyterians and some Anglicans. In 1776, Virginia disestablished the Church of England, exempted dissenters from church attendance and taxes, and allowed public expression of religious dissent. Separation of church and state was not included.

When Thomas Jefferson wrote his Bill for Religious Freedom in 1777, Baptists were among those agitating for its adoption, particularly separation of church and state, over the next decade. Baptists dissented from the position of other outsider denominations that a general religious tax was okay. In 1786, Virginia established religious freedom, and the Baptists shifted their attention to the national scene. They backed James Madison for the Virginia constitutional ratification convention because he promised to seek a federal religious liberty amendment. In 1789, Madison fought for the amendment in Congress, and in 1791, the Bill of Rights had a religious liberty clause. Massachusetts finally became the last state to enact full religious liberty in 1833.

In the 18th century, revival of the Baptists in England influenced the Baptist churches of America and brought about missionary enthusiasm and the rapid growth of American Baptists as the frontier expanded. In the South, Baptists became the largest denomination in many states, and growth continued into the 19th century. On the eve of the American Revolution, Baptist congregations numbered an estimated 494. By 1795, the estimate of Isaac Backus was 1,152.

With Philadelphia being too far away, given slow travel, new associations independent of Philadelphia began appearing during the war, and by 1800, at least 48 local associations existed. There was need for a national organization, which was reinforced by the development of the missions movement. In 1814, the General Convention came into being, with a mandate to deal with not only foreign but home missions, education, and publications. In 1826, again restricted to foreign missions, it became the American Baptist Foreign Mission Society, with additional societies, such as the American Baptist Home Missions Society organized in 1832 and American Baptist Publication Society that developed later.

Slavery in the 1840s and 1850s split the Baptists, with the Southern Baptist Convention (SBC) forming in Augusta, Georgia, in 1845. Because the SBC focused more on foreign missions, the northern home mission and publications societies continued in the South after the war until late in the century; the Southern Baptists established their own associations. The temporary split became formal in 1907 with the creation of the Northern Baptist Convention (later the American Baptist Convention and then the American Baptist Churches USA).

John H. Barnhill

See also: Anglicans; Calvinism; Catholicism

Further Reading

Bebbington, David W. 2010. *Baptists through the Centuries: A History of a Global People.* Waco, TX: Baylor University Press.

Chute, Anthony, Nathan A. Finn, and Michael A. G. Haykin. 2015. *The Baptist Story: From English Sect to Global Movement.* Nashville, TN: B&H Academic.

Kidd, Thomas S., and Barry Hankins. 2015. *Baptists in America: A History.* New York: Oxford University Press.

BARTRAM, JOHN (1699–1777)

Pennsylvania farmer John Bartram was one of 18th-century America's leading natural historians and the founder of a dynasty of natural historians that extended into the 19th century.

Bartram's mother, Elizabeth, died when he was two years old, and his father, William, who had immigrated to North Carolina, was killed by Native Americans, perhaps contributing to John's lifelong hatred toward them. Bartram inherited enough land from an uncle to become a prosperous farmer in Pennsylvania with careful cultivation and attention to the latest developments in agricultural improvement. Beginning around 1727, Bartram became interested in botany, a subject in which he was largely self-taught. An early patron was James Logan (1674–1751), one of Philadelphia's leading savants, who lent Bartram books and guided his early explorations of learned botany. Through a London correspondent and fellow Quaker, Peter Collinson (1694–1768), Bartram joined in the international world of botanical exchange, sending seeds, bulbs, and cuttings of American plants to Europe and receiving European and other foreign specimens in exchange. This developed into a business of sending American plants and animals to European gardeners and collectors.

Bartram's skill became recognized in the learned community. Europe's leading botanist, the Swede Carl Linnaeus, was an admirer. Bartram contributed specimens to enable the English natural historian Mark Catesby (1683–1749), who lived in London, to finish his *Natural History of Carolina, Florida and the Bahama Islands* (1729–1747), one of the most sophisticated works of colonial American natural history. (Bartram received a copy of this valuable, profusely illustrated book in exchange.) Through Collinson, English patrons, including commercial nursery owners as well as aristocratic gardeners, commissioned Bartram to gather particular plant specimens or to botanically explore particular regions. They sent gifts of books, which helped Bartram stay current at a time when botanical science was rapidly developing. Collinson also bridged social as well as geographical gaps by providing introductions to members of the colonial elite, such as Thomas Penn.

In 1728, Bartram established a botanical garden that attracted many visitors. He was a founding member of the American Philosophical Society and a long-term associate of Benjamin Franklin. He corresponded with New York botanist Cadwallader Colden, Alexander Garden of Charleston, and other American natural historians. These correspondences were not always free of acrimony—Garden claimed that Bartram took credit for discovering a species of live oak when it was Garden who had sent him the specimens. When Franklin became postmaster-general in 1751, he allowed Bartram the privilege of "franking," sending his correspondence free of charge for the recipient.

Much of the American frontier was previously unexplored by botanists. Bartram engaged in several expeditions to gather plants and learn more about them. In 1738, he journeyed along the James River and into the Blue Ridge Mountains of Virginia. In 1743, he traveled to the Great Lakes region of upstate New York and into Canada. The height of Bartram's botanical career was an expedition to the southeast in 1765 after Florida had become a British colony at the end of the Seven Years' War (1756–1763). Bartram was appointed by George III as king's botanist for North America in 1765 with a small stipend, an appointment in which he took great pride. This appointment shocked some in America's scientific community, as Bartram, for all his undoubted skill in collecting, was not a learned botanist. He had little knowledge of Latin and the more theoretical branches of botany, as they had developed in the 18th century.

Regardless of this skepticism, however, Bartram's trip to Florida was a success. The results of his botanical expeditions were published in two books, *Observations on the Inhabitants, Climate, Soil, Rivers, Productions, Animals, and Other Matters Worthy of Notice Made by Mr. John Bartram, in His Travels from Pensilvania to Onondago, Oswego and the Lake Ontario, in Canada* (1751) and *A Journal, Kept by John Bartram of Philadelphia, Botanist to His Majesty for the Floridas: Upon a Journey from St. Augustine up the River St. Johns* (1767). These books were published in London and seen through the press by Collinson. Some who knew Bartram well, however, such as the Swedish natural historian Pehr Kalm (1716–1779), who visited America, said that Bartram knew far more about American plants than he ever wrote down.

Bartram's hostility to Natives was out of the Quaker mainstream. He also drifted away from Quaker beliefs in pacifism and the divinity of Christ. He did not participate in the rise of antislavery sentiment among American Quakers in the mid-18th century. He only owned one slave, Harvey, whom he bought when Harvey was a small child and freed as an adult, but he acted as an agent for his son William in transactions involving slaves and was highly suspicious of efforts to educate slaves or other African-descended people. In his travels in the American South, Bartram paid tribute to what he viewed as the central role of slavery in the region's agricultural development.

What caused his expulsion from the Quaker community, however, was not his views on Natives or slaves, but his denial of the divinity of Christ. He may have been partially inspired in this by reading Confucius in English translation from a book checked out of the Library Company of Philadelphia. He regarded Confucius as a great moral teacher, like Jesus, both of whose beliefs about God were unitarian. Bartram was expelled from membership in the Darby Meeting of Quakers in 1757 after a lengthy inquiry, but he continued to attend their meetings.

Bartram exploited his image as a simple Quaker farmer in a way similar to how his friend Franklin exploited his image as a simple homespun Philadelphian. As a self-taught rustic gentleman, he became an idealized figure in Hector St. John Crevecouer's *Letters from an American Farmer* (1782), which devoted a chapter to recounting a visit Crevecouer had made to Bartram's farm. He portrays Bartram both as a rural patriarch and as a dedicated improver, turning wilderness into highly productive agricultural land.

Unlike other colonial American researchers into nature like Franklin, Bartram was never admitted to England's Royal Society, although he did correspond with the society's president, Sir Hans Sloane, and some of his letters were read to the society. However, in addition to his membership in the American Philosophical Society, he was admitted to Sweden's Royal Academy of Sciences in 1769. Bartram died at Kingsessing, Pennsylvania, on September 22, 1777.

Bartram married twice. His first wife was Mary Maris, who died in 1727 along with one of the couple's two sons. His second wife was Anne Mendenhall, with whom he had nine children. Both marriages seem from the meager surviving evidence to have been happy. Natural history was both a culture and a business for Bartram and his extended family. Working with John Bartram helped attract his cousin Humphrey Marshall (1722–1801) to science and the trade in American natural history specimens. He supplemented Bartram's export of botanical specimens by sending small animals and insects to European collectors. Marshall, whose scientific interests were broader than Bartram's, was also a keen astronomer whose observations of sunspots were published in *Philosophical Transactions*, the prestigious journal of England's leading scientific association, the Royal Society. Marshall's catalog of American trees and shrubs, *Arbustrum Americanum* (1785), attracted considerable interest in Europe and had two reprintings.

John Bartram's son John Bartram Jr. took over the nursery business. Two other sons, Isaac (1725–1801) and Moses Bartram (1732–1809), were apothecaries and active members of the American Philosophical Society. By far the most influential scientist and writer among John Bartram's children, however, was William Bartram (1739–1823), a gifted illustrator who accompanied John on his trip to the southeastern colonies in 1765. William Bartram is best known for his narrative of a series of expeditions in southeastern North America from 1773 to 1776, *Travels through North & South Carolina, East and West Florida, the Cherokee Country, the Extensive Territories of the Muscogulges, or Creek Confederacy, and the Country of the Choctaws, Containing an Account of the Soil and Natural Productions of These Regions, Together with Observations on the Manners of the Indians* (1791). Others of Bartram's descendants involved in natural history include explorer and entomologist Thomas Say (1787–1834) and illustrator Anne Bartram Carr (1779–1858). Carr also managed the garden, which remained in the Bartram family until 1850.

William E. Burns

See also: American Philosophical Society; Franklin, Benjamin

Further Reading

Bell, Whitfield J. 1997–2009. *Patriot-Improvers: Biographical Sketches of Members of the American Philosophical Society.* 3 vols. Philadelphia: American Philosophical Society.

Burns, William E. 2005. *Science and Technology in Colonial America.* Westport, CT: Greenwood.

Earnest, Ernest. 1940. *John and William Bartram, Botanists and Explorers.* Philadelphia: University of Pennsylvania Press.

Hoffman Nancy E., and John C. Van Horne, eds. 2004. *America's Curious Botanist: A Tercentennial Reappraisal of John Bartram.* Philadelphia: American Philosophical Society.

Meyers, Amy R. W., and Margaret Beck Pritchard, eds. 1998. *Empire's Nature: Mark Catesby's New World Vision.* Chapel Hill and London: University of North Carolina Press for the Omohundro Institute of Early American History and Culture and the Colonial Williamsburg Foundation.

Slaughter, Thomas P. 1997. *The Natures of John and William Bartram.* New York: Vintage Books.

BEAVER TRADE

The beaver trade or trading of beaver pelts between Native North American people and European explorers and colonists, and later among European trappers, fur companies, and Europe, was a driving economic force in the exploration and settlement of North America by Europeans and had profound effects among the

Native American populations as they struggled for new and more productive hunting and trapping grounds and trading rights with Europeans.

The North American variety of the beaver, *Castor canadensis*, is a slightly smaller version of the Eurasian variety. In the rodent family of mammals, beavers are eclipsed in size only by the South American capybara. As a semiaquatic mammal, beavers have a dense pelt of fur that has excellent insulating properties. As a large fur-bearing animal, beavers provide more of a return in amount of fur and size of pelt per animal harvested than smaller fur bearers, such as muskrats or minks. Around 3 feet long and 60 pounds in weight, the beaver is indeed a large rodent.

Europeans originally valued the beaver pelts to make robes for cod fishermen off the Canadian and northern coast of what became New England, and it quickly developed into a money-making bonanza for European fur traders. Europeans were used to the pelts of fur-bearing mammals, especially those mammals found in or about waterways, and found ready use for those pelts in the manufacture of warm and dry clothing that was stylish as well as highly functional. The use of beaver fur in the manufacture of high-quality felt, largely used in the manufacture of fashionable and prized hats, made beaver pelts the most valuable of fur-bearing pelts.

For Native Americans, the furs and pelts of local mammals, by far the most important being that of the beaver, became the primary source of economic interaction with Europeans. Without such a valuable trade commodity, it is unlikely Europeans would have been willing, or even eager, to trade guns and ammunition (powder and ball) with Native Americans. Those tribes that could amass a considerable supply of firearms, gunpowder, and ball and shot developed a distinct advantage over their fellow tribes, an advantage later used to devastating effect in wars over territory and trading rights.

Of course, Europeans possessed other trade goods highly prized by Native Americans, such as blankets and metal implements such as knives and hatchets. The beaver trade quickly became a vital economic engine for Native Americans and, in fact, the most important economic engine for those tribes engaged in the beaver trade. While the gathering of pelts was the primary goal of Native American hunters and trappers, the capture of beavers also provided a viable source of meat for Native Americans, a meat said to be similar in taste and texture to lean beef.

The North American beaver trade began when European explorers such as Frenchmen Jacques Cartier and Samuel de Champlain ventured up the St. Lawrence River and Basque fishermen pursued cod off the East Coast of Canada and what became the northeastern United States. Cod fishermen took advantage of new technology in the preserving of fish, making such long voyages across the Atlantic to the rich fishing grounds off North America economically feasible. These fishermen and early explorers encountered Native Americans of the greater Algonquin tribes, and quickly found the beaver pelts traded by those tribes made wonderful robes to combat the miserable cold and damp North Atlantic weather while at sea. This 16th-century early trade blossomed into a purpose-oriented economic trade by the 17th century that eclipsed the incidental trade for beaver pelts of the early encounters between Europeans and Native Americans.

European fur trading companies developed into major economic forces upon the exploration and settlement of North America, including the Dutch East India Company and the Hudson's Bay Company (a consortium of English and French investors). These companies formed the European version of government in North America for much of the earliest period of settlement. The Hudson's Bay Company, founded in 1670, was at one time the largest private owner of land in the world, and it is still in business today. The Dutch East India Company was formed earlier, in 1602, and had concerns largely in Asia and the Pacific as well as in North America, where it was the driving force for Dutch exploration and settlement. The Dutch East India Company is considered by some to be the first truly great corporation, although it went out of business in 1799. The influence of these great companies led to a largely standardized system of trade with Native Americans, with standard types of blankets, firearms, and other trade goods and set standard prices for goods and pelts. Of course, as the beaver population was depleted, the value of beaver pelts went up vis-à-vis trade goods, and the price Europeans paid (in trade) for beaver pelts was usually rising, creating that much more urgency to monopolize the beaver trade for Native American tribes.

As beavers have only one litter of 2–5 kits per year, heavy predation by humans can quickly deplete the beaver population, in fact, easily eradicating them from the local area. This is what occurred in short order in the farthest eastern regions of North America, necessitating a westward movement to new hunting grounds. With a pre-European influence population of perhaps 60 million beavers in North America, a harvest of 10,000 pelts or more per year left a paltry 100,000 beavers by 1900, a number no longer viable for harvest. Conservation efforts since 1900 have allowed beaver populations to rebound and be reintroduced into areas where they had once lived but from which they had disappeared. Between 12 million and 15 million beavers live in North America today.

The westward search for richer beaver populations caused friction between Native American tribes, resulting in the Beaver Wars of the 17th century. Iroquois tribes such as the Mohawk were provided with firearms by the Dutch, and these Iroquoians usurped Algonquin and other Native American tribes allied with the French, both in displacing the other tribes and taking over trading rights by force. The spread of Iroquois tribes based on the beaver trade displaced other tribes from Virginia in the south, to Illinois and the Mississippi River in the west, and the area around the Great Lakes.

The beaver trade had become the primary occupation (along with subjugating other tribes) of the Iroquois. Outnumbered by Native Americans from other tribes, the Iroquois bolstered their own population by assimilating and adopting captured members of other tribes, especially women and children. The Iroquois sought to both gather the beaver pelts and directly sell the pelts to the Europeans, while European efforts at mollifying all groups of Indians involved designating the Iroquois as the gatherers, who would then sell their pelts to Algonquin and other tribes, who in turn would then sell the pelts to Europeans. The Iroquois were never content with this arrangement and fought to monopolize the beaver trade. Native tribes in the Niagara Region, the lower Great Lakes, Ohio, and the Illinois Territory were displaced and or assimilated into Iroquois tribes, with Shawnee and Lakota tribes forced west onto the Great Plains.

In 1701, the Great Peace of Montreal lessened but did not eliminate the beaver wars entirely, but the beaver trade had entered a new phase. Constant war, famine, and disease took their toll on the Iroquois, and while Native Americans continued to trade beaver pelts with Europeans, a new breed of hardy European explorers and adventurers went ever deeper into the North American wilderness in search of richer beaver populations to trap or trade for. Europeans in the 17th century had traveled to the area all around the Great Lakes and to the Mississippi River.

After the American Revolutionary War (1775–1783), the French and Dutch had already been evicted from most of their previous North American settlements, leaving the English to continue to exploit beaver resources in Canada while American trappers hiked west to the Rocky Mountains for fresh and teeming beaver populations. The early 19th century saw intrepid "mountain men" such as Jim Bridger and Kit Carson achieve fame and legendary status for their superhuman feats of endurance and survival. The exploration and travels of these mountain men paved the way for later travel and settlement of the American West.

In 1808, John Jacob Astor founded the American Fur Company, and by 1830, he and his company had become among the richest in the United States. Astor monopolized the beaver trade in the United States, and had companies from the Great Lakes, to the Great Plains, to the Rocky Mountains and even in the Northwest (Oregon Territory). Not only did the American Fur Company compete for the European fur market, it also largely supplied the demand for fur in the United States and was a major trader with the Orient. Despite the meteoric rise of Astor and his company, diminishing demand for beaver pelts in Europe (silk hats had become the fashion over felt hats), diminishing beaver stocks in the United States, and stiff competition from European companies caused the end of the American Fur Company in 1847. (Astor survived this setback, as he had invested his money in other ventures. He remained perhaps the richest American in his day.)

By the middle of the 19th century, the beaver trade along with other fur trading had gone into serious decline. Changing fashions and depleted beaver populations put many companies out of business and spelled financial ruin for many Native Americans. Today, fur is mainly harvested from farm-raised animals (about 85 percent), and only a small portion (15 percent) comes from wild trapped animals.

Matthew D. Zarzeczny

See also: Beaver Wars; Fur Trade

Further Reading

Berry, Don. 1961. *A Majority of Scoundrels: An Informal History of the Rocky Mountain Fur Company.* New York: Harper.

Dolan, Eric Jay. 2010. *Fur, Fortune, and Empire: The Epic History of the Fur Trade in America.* New York: W. W. Norton & Company.

Phillips, Paul, and J. W. Smurr. 1961. *The Fur Trade.* 2 vols. Norman: University of Oklahoma Press.

BEAVER WARS

Once European explorers and fishermen began to frequent the East Coast of Canada and what is now the United States, the Native Americans that encountered these Europeans found that the most valuable trade item the Indians (Native Americans) had were the rich furs from indigenous fur-bearing animals in North America, mainly the beaver. As the fur trade became the primary economic engine between Europeans (English, Dutch, French, and Basque) and the Native Americans, the individual Indian tribes jockeyed for position within the trade, resulting in wars that spanned the 17th century that were fought between the various tribes and the Europeans, with changing alliances and spheres of influence along the way. The mundane sounding Beaver Wars were brutal and bloody, among the most ferocious in the history of North America.

Initially prizing beaver pelts for their own use against the damp chill of the Atlantic, cod fishermen (largely Basque at first) were eager to trade with the local Natives for those pelts. Europeans found a ready market for animal pelts and their fur in Europe, and beaver fur was found to be ideal for the making of felt. Hats made of beaver felt became a fashion rage in Europe, increasing demand for the pelts. When the fur trade became lucrative beyond that of the fishing industry, the demand for beaver pelts grew to enormous proportions, and the fur trade remained a driving economic engine in North America through the first half of the 19th century.

As the largest North American rodent and a semiaquatic mammal, the beaver, *Castor canadensis*, has a rich fur typical of mammals that live in the water. Once numbering over 60 million animals in North America, the fur trade depleted the beaver population to minimal numbers by the end of the 19th century. A harvest of over 10,000 pelts per year in the 17th, 18th, and 19th centuries devastated the population, as beavers have only one litter per year and could not make up such heavy predation by humans. By 1900, only about 100,000 beavers remained in North America. Conservation efforts have increased beaver numbers in North America to around 12–15 million today.

Even prior to exposure to Europeans, the Native American people hunted and trapped beaver for both their fur and their meat, which is similar in taste and texture to lean beef. Once the Europeans demonstrated an insatiable demand for beaver pelts, local populations of beaver were quickly depleted, and new hunting grounds were needed, causing incursion into areas claimed by other tribes. Territory became critical, as the Indian demand for European trade goods, especially guns and metal implements such as knives and hatchets, was equally insatiable.

Early European visitors to North America encountered Native Americans of the Algonquin tribes, people of coastal Canada and New England, who first traded pelts for European goods. The Iroquois tribes lived upriver along the St. Lawrence, just inland from the Algonquins, and were encountered by French explorers (Cartier et al., 1540s) that ventured up the St. Lawrence. Iroquoians were also keen to trade beaver pelts for European goods.

The late 16th and early 17th centuries saw European wars detract from the development of the trade in beaver pelts, but such a lucrative trade could not be stifled for long. Wars between Iroquoian-speaking tribes such as the Mohawk and St. Lawrence Iroquois ca. 1580–1600 were unrelated to the beaver trade and resulted in the Mohawk displacing the St. Lawrence Iroquois and some Algonquin tribes. Thus, the stage for conflict had already been set by the time fighting over beaver-trapping territory and trading rights began.

In 1603, Samuel de Champlain allied the French with Algonquin tribes from the north and Hurons against the hated Iroquois. From 1609 through 1615, the French and their Indian allies won victories against the Iroquois until a siege of an Onondaga village along the shore of Lake Ontario failed, leaving Champlain wounded. Meanwhile, the Dutch East India Company enjoyed the explorations of Henry Hudson and sought to establish fur trading posts in North America, both on the coasts of the Hudson Bay and in the area of present-day New York and New Jersey. Dutch trading with Mohican tribes led to conflict with the Mohawk, which in turn led the Dutch to abandon their Mohican allies and make peace and trade treaties with the Mohawk in 1628. The Mohicans were forcibly displaced to the Connecticut Valley. The Dutch developed trade along the Hudson and Delaware Rivers, trading with Delaware (Lenape) and Susquehannock tribes. Although the Dutch did not trade guns with these tribes, the Dutch did supply the Mohawk and other Iroquois with guns to be used against the French and their Algonquin allies.

By 1630, the Iroquois had dominated trade with the Dutch and been well armed with firearms. The Mohawk and other Iroquois tribes became somewhat dependent on trade with the Dutch for their way of life, and the only way to increase their standard of living and make up for quickly dwindling beaver resources was to seize territory from other tribes. By 1640, the Hudson Valley had mostly been stripped bare of beaver. In response, the Algonquin, Mohican, Huron, and other tribes allied with the French to form a union against the Iroquois and the Dutch. The Iroquois were forced to look northward for new stocks of beaver to exploit, lands peopled by the Huron and Neutral tribes. As the English began to colonize North America and enter the fur trade, a loose alliance of sorts with the Dutch and those tribes allied with the Dutch against the French and Iroquois was formed.

The Iroquois (mainly Mohawk) spread north into southern Ontario and west to the Great Lakes region, eventually displacing the Lake Region tribes. As conflict heated up by 1640, the French made an attempt to negotiate a peaceful resolution among the Iroquois and tribes allied with the French (Huron) along the St. Lawrence. At first successful in ending the fighting, the Iroquois were surprised and outraged to find the French solution was to have the Iroquois gather the pelts and sell them to the Hurons, who in turn would act as middlemen and sell the pelts to the French.

The Iroquois demanded to sell directly to the French, and fighting began once again. War between the Iroquois and a confederation of Algonquin and Susquehannock tribes broke out in 1647 and included the Iroquois and Mohawk directly at war against the French by the 1650s. Iroquois control spread into New France (Montreal was blockaded) and south into Virginia. The Iroquois had occupied Ohio by defeating and displacing the Shawnee and had moved into Illinois all the way to the Mississippi River. In 1666, the French burned Iroquois crops at the Richelieu River, causing a famine. Diseases such as smallpox had also decimated Iroquois numbers. Although Iroquois tribes had largely stopped fighting among themselves, in 1701, a peace treaty known as the Great Peace (*Grande Paix*) was agreed to by 39 tribes and the French. Iroquois cooperation among their tribes continued to improve.

As the Iroquois lost people through the attrition of war, disease, and famine, they sought to increase their numbers through the assimilation of captives from defeated tribes into their own society. When conducting small raids against single European homes or small outposts, the Iroquois would usually slaughter the men but keep the women and children for adoption and assimilation into the Iroquois tribe. Despite being outnumbered by the tribes the Iroquois sought to conquer (including the Erie and Neutral tribes in the Lake Erie and Niagara regions), the use of firearms by the Iroquois often made the difference in battle. The height of Iroquois power and territory occurred during the 1660s, and by the late 1660s and early 1670s, when the Iroquois sought to invade and conquer the Susquehannock in Maryland, they were met by Susquehannock armed with guns and cannon supplied by the English. The English reconsidered their Indian alliances and, in 1674, made peace with the Iroquois and turned against their previous Susquehannock allies. In 1675, the Iroquois, with their new English allies from Virginia and Maryland, defeated the Susquehannock and executed the Susquehannock chiefs. The Iroquois were now masters of non-English Virginia and remained so until selling the land to the English in 1722.

Iroquois expansion into Ohio and westward pushed the already displaced eastern tribes into conflict with the Shawnee and Miami tribes of the region. Tribes such as the Lakota were pushed all the way west of the Mississippi to the Great Plains. Although outnumbered, the Iroquois employed raiding tactics, such as night attacks with swift retreats, and the ever important use of firearms. In 1689, the Miami sought help from tribes also fighting the Iroquois to avenge the destruction of a Miami settlement in the Illinois Territory. This time armed with guns, the Miami and their allies ambushed and defeated an Iroquois army in the area of South Bend.

Fighting among the French, English, and Indian tribes continued through the late 17th century and culminated in the Great Peace of Montreal in 1701. Throughout the 17th century, the myriad conflicts between Europeans and Native American tribes in various configurations were largely driven by the need to find new and productive hunting grounds for beaver pelts. Numerous named small conflicts occurred during this period, with the overall blanket title of the Beaver Wars.

The 18th century did not see the end of conflict between Indian tribes, between Europeans, and between Indian tribes and Europeans, as evidenced by the French and Indian Wars (1688–1763), which included the Seven Years' War (1756–1763). The Beaver Wars had profound influence on the distribution and culture of Native Americans in North America and upon the conflict between European colonial powers, both shaping what was to become the course of history in the modern countries of Canada and the United States.

Matthew D. Zarzeczny

See also: Beaver Trade; Fur Trade

Further Reading

Barr, Daniel P. 2006. *Unconquered: The Iroquois League at War in Colonial America.* Westport, CT: Greenwood Publishing Group.

Jennings, Francis. 1984. *The Ambiguous Iroquois Empire: The Covenant Chain Confederation of Indian Tribes with English Colonies from Its Beginnings to the Lancaster Treaty of 1744.* New York: Norton.

Trigger, Bruce G. 1987. *The Children of Aataentsic: A History of the Huron People to 1660.* Kingston and Montreal: McGill-Queen's University Press.

BILL OF RIGHTS

The Bill of Rights refers to the first 10 ratified amendments to the U.S. Constitution. These amendments were included to offer specific protections for individual liberties that were not explicitly stated elsewhere in the Constitution. They were written by James Madison (1751–1836) in 1789 and ratified in 1791 as part of the debates between Federalists and Anti-Federalists over the ratification of the Constitution.

When finally approved by the delegates to the Constitutional Convention in Philadelphia in the summer of 1787, the Constitution was still not officially in force. To be legally effective, it needed to be ratified by at least two-thirds (9) of the 13 states. States such as Delaware, Georgia, and New Jersey ratified the Constitution quickly and with little debate. However, others were reluctant to ratify the document for a variety of reasons. One common argument put forward by the Anti-Federalists who opposed ratifying the Constitution was that the lack of a Bill of Rights specifically protecting the liberties of individual citizens would permit the growth of a tyrannical and obtrusive national government.

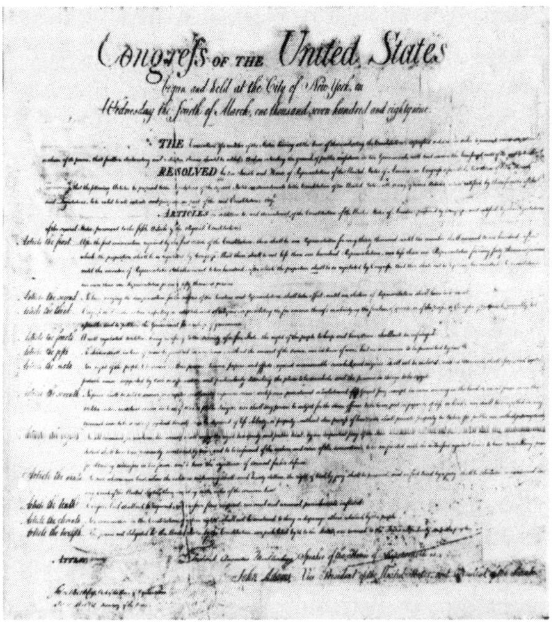

Congress of the United States

The Bill of Rights consists of the first 10 amendments to the Constitution. This crucial document outlines basic individual rights and governmental restrictions that those living in 1791, when the document was ratified, viewed as critical to freedom. The repercussions of the document, and the original intent of the amendments, is still a subject of heated debate. (National Archives)

In fact, the idea of a Bill of Rights was first proposed at the Constitutional Convention by George Mason of Virginia and Elbridge Gerry of Massachusetts. Their motion was presented shortly before the end of the convention and after virtually the entire document had been agreed upon. It recommended that the constitutional Bill of Rights should be modeled on examples from various states. The delegates defeated the motion unanimously after a short discussion. As such, when the Constitution was sent to the states for ratification, it contained no specific guarantees of personal rights.

Anti-Federalists such as Patrick Henry, Samuel Adams, and Richard Henry Lee considered the lack of a Bill of Rights to be a glaring and potentially dangerous omission, and as the Constitution came closer to ratification by the necessary two-thirds, resistance grew. Another concern for the Federalists who advocated ratification was that, by mid-1788, the two most powerful and wealthiest states, New York and Virginia, had not yet ratified. In addition, there was a growing worry that the country could potentially consist of states that had ratified the Constitution and were therefore beholden to the power of the national government it created and states that had not ratified and were thus essentially independent nation-states.

To encourage ratification, especially in New York, James Madison, John Jay, and Alexander Hamilton wrote and published essays under the single pseudonym "Publius." These 85 *Federalist Papers* offered counterarguments to satisfy Anti-Federalists and others who resisted ratification. In *Federalist* No. 84, Alexander Hamilton directly addressed the matter of whether a Bill of Rights should be included in the Constitution. Hamilton echoed other commentators who argued that any list of personal liberties that were protected by the government was problematic because of the possibility that any rights not specifically included in such a list could be claimed not to exist. Although Anti-Federalists raised legitimate concerns, they were never sufficiently organized or focused in their ideologies, or in their rhetoric, to pose a serious threat to the Federalists. Nevertheless, it became clear to the Federalists that a Bill of Rights would be necessary to ensure support from those remaining states that had not yet ratified the Constitution. This fact was emphasized in July 1788, when New York's 30 to 27 vote to ratify included a recommendation that a Bill of Rights be added.

For his part, James Madison considered the Bills of Rights to be unnecessary. He argued that the structure and limitations placed on the government by the Constitution would automatically safeguard individual liberties without the need of a separate document enumerating specific protections. Other rights were secured by the state constitutions. In essence, the Constitution's foundation on the concept of popular sovereignty meant that any rights not specifically given to the national government were implicitly reserved for the states and, ultimately, the people. The Ninth and Tenth Amendments, though, would eventually enshrine these principles into the Constitution itself.

With the ratification of the Constitution by New Hampshire in June 1788, the document became official. Yet, there was still widespread feeling that a Bill of Rights could be valuable if not necessary. After the first national elections were held from December 1788 to January 1789, the first Congress of the United States met in March 1789 in New York's Federal Hall. Although the Federalists had a sizeable majority (there were only two Anti-Federalists), James Madison worried that the lack of a Bill of Rights might result in calls for a second constitutional convention that could damage or undo the accomplishments of the Philadelphia convention barely two years earlier. And so, he began crafting almost 40 amendments that could be added to the Constitution or that would alter the existing wording of the document to more clearly enumerate the individual liberties protected by the federal government.

Based on the historical record, there is some reason to believe that Madison considered such revisions more a matter of expediency than representing any shift in his fundamental thinking on the matter. In letters and in his own drafts of the amendments, Madison pointed out that adding a Bill of Rights would likely encourage popular support for the Constitution. He also expressed his hope that the amendments would solidify the concept of free government and protect the Constitution from the threat of wholesale revision in the future.

Most Federalists in Congress continued their resistance to adding a Bill of Rights despite the reluctant change of heart of one of their prominent leaders in Madison. They pointed out that altering the Constitution so soon after its ratification might be seen as a sign of the weakness of the document and, by extension, of the system of representative government and popular sovereignty it had established. Connecticut congressman Roger Sherman suggested that the eventual amendments should be placed as a separate appendix at the end of the Constitution so that the Constitution itself would appear unchanged and inviolate. Madison initially proposed nearly 40 alterations and amendments. During extensive debate in the House of Representatives, this number was whittled down to seventeen amendments. After the Senate further edited the amendments down to twelve, it was left to a conference committee to resolve the differences in language, content, and organization. The twelve amendments were adopted by Congress and sent to the states for ratification; they needed to be approved by three-fourths of the states to become effective. Of the twelve, ten made it into the Bill of Rights as eventually ratified.

The first two proposed amendments of the twelve (known as "Articles") were not ratified at the time; however, Article II, dealing with congressional pay increases, was finally ratified to become the Twenty-Seventh Amendment in May 1997, after a delay of more than 200 years. This makes it the amendment with the longest delay between introduction and ratification. Article I deals with allocating seats in the House of Representatives based on the population figures from each decennial census. This proposed amendment is still pending before the states, as there was no time limit set for ratification when it was introduced in 1789.

Somewhat paradoxically, many Federalists who had previously objected to the Bill of Rights changed their opinions and supported the amendments during the ratification process. Some came to recognize the benefits in establishing protected individual liberties. Others believed that the revisions would help popularize the Constitution and the federal government for Americans who remembered the rhetoric of the Revolution and who were still reticent about the dangers posed by a strong central government.

By the same token, several prominent Anti-Federalists opposed the amendments. They worried that the revisions did not go far enough to address what were for them the most onerous aspects of the new federal government, including taxes and the federal judiciary. Many Anti-Federalists also desired a more democratic system of government and so held out hope that there might be a second constitutional convention to reform the government accordingly. A successful Constitution with a Bill of Rights limited the chances that another convention would be needed.

The language and content of the Bill of Rights was heavily influenced by existing bills of rights and declarations of rights in the English-speaking world, including the Magna Carta (1215), the English Bill of Rights (1689), and the Virginia Declaration of Rights (1776). The first state to ratify the Bill of Rights was New Jersey, in November 1789, and the amendments became official upon ratification by the eleventh state, Virginia, on December 15, 1791. During the initial ratification period, legislators in Georgia and Connecticut believed a Bill of Rights to be unnecessary and so refused to ratify the amendments. Massachusetts' two-house legislature could not reach a consensus on the amendments they favored and those they objected to, and so that state also failed to ratify the Bill of Rights when it was first put forward. Each of these states eventually formally ratified the amendments, even though the document was in force and applied to all the states even without their ratification.

Today, there are twenty-seven amendments to the Constitution, but only the first ten are typically referred to as the Bill of Rights.

Shawn Selby

See also: Anti-Federalists; Constitutional Convention; Federalists; Madison, James; Ratification

Further Reading

"The Bill of Rights: A Transcription." National Archives. https://www.archives.gov/founding-docs/bill-of-rights-transcript.

Maier, Pauline. 2011. *Ratification: The People Debate the Constitution.* New York: Simon & Schuster.

Rakove, Jack. 1997. *Original Meanings.* New York: Vintage.

BLACK LEGEND

The Black Legend (*La Leyenda Negra*) is a term used to identify historical writing or propaganda that condemns the conquistadors, and in particular the Spanish Empire, in a politically motivated effort to provoke animosity against Spain and damage its influence. The term originated in the 16th century, when Spain was at its height of political power, and it was initiated by propagandists from rival European powers, such as the Protestant countries of England and the Netherlands, the French Huguenots, groups in Venice, or the Protestant Walloons. The writings particularly tried to exaggerate the extent of the activities of the Inquisition or the treatment of American indigenous subjects in the territories of the Spanish Empire and non-Catholics (e.g., Protestants and Jews) in its European territories.

In the process of European colonization of the Americas, which went on over three centuries, Spain was the only colonial power to promote laws for the protection of Native Americans. As early as 1512, the Laws of Burgos regulated the behavior of Europeans in the New World, forbidding the ill-treatment of indigenous people and restricting the power of landowners. In 1542, the New Laws extended and adjusted the previous body of laws to improve their function. Although these laws were not always respected across all American territories, they indicate the will of the Spanish colonial government of the time to protect the rights of the Native population.

The colonization also led to vivid debates within Spain about the treatment and rights of indigenous peoples in the Americas. In this context, the writings of Bartolomé de las Casas, which refer to the excesses committed by landowners and some officials during the early period of colonization of New Spain, particularly in Hispaniola (today Haiti and the Dominican Republic), ignited high controversy. His work *Brevísima relación de la destrucción de las Indias* (*A Short Account of the Destruction of the Indies*), from 1552, has often been described as the first work to contribute to the Black Legend and was later reproduced by the groups and nations mentioned above. Other examples of the Black Legend are said to be the negative portrayals of the Spanish Inquisition in historiographical and artistic depictions, such as the engraved illustrations created by Theodorus de Bry. Most of De Bry's book illustrations were based on firsthand observations by explorers, even if De Bry himself, acting as a recorder of information, never visited the Americas. Today, the degree to which Las Casas's descriptions of Spanish colonization or De Bry's works can stand for a reasonable or exaggerated picture is still debated among some scholars.

The term *Black Legend* was coined relatively late, in a critique published in 1914 by Julián Juderías and titled *The Black Legend and the Historical Truth* (*La leyenda negra y la verdad histórica*). Julián Juderías was the first to describe and denounce this phenomenon and protested against the widespread perception of colonial Spanish brutality in conquering the New World. In his work, he explained how this type of tendentious historiography presented Spanish history in a deeply negative light and purposely ignored positive accomplishments or advances. Later writers have supported and developed Juderías's critique, and a more pro-Spanish historiographical school emerged as a reaction, especially within Spain but also in the Americas.

The Black Legend and the nature of Spanish colonization of the Americas, including contributions to civilization in Spain's colonies, have been discussed by Spanish writers. The Black Legend has also been used by regionalists of non-Castilian regions of Spain as a political weapon against the central government or Spanish nationalism. Some historians have argued that the historians trying to correct for anti-Spanish partiality in the description of Spanish colonialism went too far in the opposite direction and to the degree that they created a "White Legend" in describing Spain's history in an exaggeratedly positive way.

However, by the end of the 20th century, historiography turned to a more neutral depiction of the Spanish Empire, which acknowledges the positive and negative aspects of colonization without portraying the Spanish Empire as either more or less evil than other colonial empires. This modern tradition acknowledges that the Spanish Empire was the first empire to discuss and work toward the ethical treatment of its subjects and the rights of Natives, though the goals were not always put into practice.

The Black Legend remained particularly strong in the United States throughout the 19th century. It was kept alive by the Mexican War of 1846 and the consequent situation to deal with a Spanish-speaking but mixed-race population within its borders. The legend reached its peak during the Spanish-American War of 1898, when a new edition of Bartolomé de las Casas's book on the destruction of the West Indies was published. The Black Legend is considered to be the first stage of Hispanophobia (defined as a fear, distrust, aversion, dislike, or discrimination against Hispanic people, Hispanic culture, and the Spanish language) in the United States.

Inspired by the Spanish example, the term *black legend* is sometimes used in a general way to describe any form of unjustified vilification of a historical person, people, or a series of events.

Elena Popan

See also: New Spain; Spain

Further Reading

Gibson, Charles. 1971. *The Black Legend: Anti-Spanish Attitudes in the Old World and the New.* New York: Random House Inc.

Greer, Margaret R., Walter D. Mignolo, and Maureen Quilligan, eds. 2008. *Rereading the Black Legend: The Discourses of Religious and Racial Difference in the Renaissance Empires.* Chicago: University of Chicago Press.

Keen, Benjamin. 1969. "The Black Legend Revisited: Assumptions and Realities." *Hispanic American Historical Review* 49, no. 4: 703–719.

Powell, Phillip Wayne. 1971. *Tree of Hate: Propaganda and Prejudices Affecting United States Relations with the Hispanic World.* New York: Basic Books.

Sánchez, Joseph P. 1990. *The Spanish Black Legend: Origins of Anti-Hispanic Stereotypes (La Leyenda negra española: orígenes de los estereotipos antihispánicos).* Albuquerque, NM: Zimmerman Library, University of New Mexico and National Park Service, Spanish Colonial Research Center.

BOOKS AND READING

In 1607, English colonists, sponsored by the London Company, established a permanent settlement at Jamestown, Virginia. With the growth of the colonies, the need for more reading material printed in the colonies became a necessity. In 1638, the first press was established in Massachusetts, which was also the first one in English-speaking North America; one had been operating in Mexico since 1539. In 1674, a press was established in Boston. Since its founding in 1638, the press in Cambridge had exclusively enjoyed the "liberty" of printing. The growth of Boston as a commercial center with a need for printing establishments led Boston citizens to regard the Cambridge monopoly as a serious grievance.

In 1668, the General Court of Massachusetts rejected a petition for a press in Boston, but sufficient pressure was applied by Bostonians to break the monopoly in 1674, the year Marmaduke Johnson, an associate of Samuel Green's in the Cambridge press, secured official permission to establish an independent press in Boston. Johnson died before he was able to put his establishment into operation, but his press was carried on from the year 1675 by John Foster, a graduate of Harvard. By 1690, Foster had published American editions of such works as *Pilgrim's Progress*, Mary White Rowlandson's (ca. 1635–1711) *Narrative of the Captivity and Restoration of Mrs. Mary Rowlandson*, and Anne Bradstreet's poems. Other printers soon appeared in Boston and began to publish popular works of the day. Between 1682 and 1684, over 130 books and brochures, most of them religious, were issued.

By 1700, Boston was a publishing center. Measured by the number (not the quality) of imprints, Boston in 1700 was the second publishing center of the English empire, surpassing even Cambridge and Oxford. The main contribution of the presses of Cambridge and Boston was to stimulate New Englanders to write books and to afford a wider opportunity for printing them. All in all, the New Englanders, by bringing over private libraries and purchasing and printing books, created a literary atmosphere that made their educational establishments far more effective.

In the 18th century, the intellectual and cultural development of Pennsylvania reflected, in large measure, the vigorous personalities of two men: James Logan and Benjamin Franklin. Logan was secretary of the colony, and it was in his fine library that young Franklin found the latest scientific works. Later, Franklin contributed even more to the intellectual activity of Philadelphia, as he was a prime mover in the establishment of a subscription library, which he called "the mother of all North American subscription libraries."

However, literary production in the colonies was largely confined to New England. Here attention concentrated on religious subjects, and sermons were the most common products of the press. The famous Puritan minister Rev. Cotton Mather wrote some 400 works. His masterpiece, *Magnalia Christi Americana*, presented the pageant of New England's history. The most popular single work of the day was the Rev. Michael Wigglesworth's long poem, "The Day of Doom," which described the Last Judgment in terrifying terms.

Many of the British North American colonies that eventually formed the United States of America were settled in the 17th century by men and women, who, in the face of European persecution, had refused to compromise passionately held religious convictions and had fled Europe. Many brought their books with them, such as the Rev. Samuel Skelton, one of the four ministers sent to Salem by the Massachusetts Bay Company, who listed 54 doctrinal books, largely selected and purchased by him for the Bay Company, that were dispatched with the Puritans who sailed from England on six ships under a royal charter granted on March 4, 1629. He also purchased for the company 34 catechisms; presumably, these would be helpful in the conversion of the Indians (officially stated as the main objective of the settlement). Skelton's part in building the Salem Library of the Massachusetts Bay Company is one example of the role that ministers played in the later development of colonial libraries. Before the development of social libraries, ministers' libraries were a chief source of books for those wishing to read.

Beginning in 1630, as many as 20,000 Puritans immigrated to America from England for religious freedom. Most settled in New England, where the colonies were often called "Bible Commonwealths" because they sought the guidance of the Scriptures in regulating all aspects of the lives of their citizens. John Eliot was involved in the Indian translation of Book of Genesis. The Cambridge printing press, located in a room of the president's lodging from about 1646, was either given or sold to Harvard College by President Dunster before his resignation. In the inventory of 1654, it appeared as college property valued at £80. A series of books in the Algonkian language, written or translated by John Eliot (paid for by the Society for the Propagation of the Gospel in New England Amongst the Indians, known as the New England Company), was "the most notable—and least useful—production" of the first Cambridge printing press in this period. About 1654, an Indian primer was issued and in 1655 Eliot's translation of the Book of Genesis.

Three years later, Eliot requested aid for the Indian Bible Project. In 1658, he asked the London Society for the Propagation of the Gospel in New England Amongst the Indians, which had financed his early translation efforts, to print his translation of the entire Bible into Algonkian. In 1659, the London Society sent over a new press and, in 1660, employed the expert printer Marmaduke Johnson to help Samuel Green of the Cambridge Press print Eliot's Bible. An Indian convert, James Printer, was assigned to help them. The first edition of the Bible to be printed in North America, Eliot's translation into Algonkian, was published in 1663. This 1,200-page volume, a copy of which is in the possession of the American Antiquarian Society, was undoubtedly the most important production of the early press in the United States. Difficult typographical problems were surmounted, and the Indian Bible was a credit to the Cambridge Press.

An important religious text was the psalter (the Book of Psalms). Psalters were extensively printed on American presses, and they were generally published without the addition of any instructional reading material. In their religious instruction, students first studied the New Testament and then mastered the entire Bible (both Old and New Testaments). Because it was illegal to print these on American presses (John Eliot's Indian Bible was a specialized exception), English Bibles were imported until after the American Revolution.

The use of Scriptures in the reading curriculum was important. Two 17th-century instances occur in the records of New Haven. The first illustrates the 17th-century assumption that reading instruction was supposed to have begun before a child entered the town school. The job description for a New Haven schoolmaster, hired in 1651, was to "perfect male children in the English, after they can reade in their Testament or Bible, and to learn them to wright," and to bring them on to Latin, if he could. The second involved a school for girls.

In 1642, compulsory education was decreed in Massachusetts. The Puritans saw very early that their way of life could not be maintained without a high level of education. In the Colonial Period, children began attending a school to learn to read instead of learning from their mothers. Such schools were called dame schools or reading schools. The dame school is well documented in England in the 17th and 18th centuries. A woman would take small children, both boys and girls, into her own home for a few hours, usually to afford an overworked mother a few hours of respite from her small children, but many dame schools taught a substantial amount of reading.

The colonial reading curriculum was brought over to the American colonies from England. The 17th-century curriculum followed the outline sketched by John Locke, who in 1693 characterized it as the "ordinary road of the Horn-book, Primer, Psalter, Testament, and Bible." The hornbook formed the novice's introduction to reading. Its name derived from its single page, originally covered with transparent protective horn, which was tacked onto a little wooden paddle. It presented the alphabet, the first few lines of the syllabarium (ab eb ib ob ub), and the Lord's Prayer. Like primers, hornbooks appeared over the course of the 17th century, and advertisements for primers and hornbooks have been found in Philadelphia newspapers as late as 1760. The hornbook was used in dame schools, private schools for small children run by a woman in her own home, as the child's first "text."

Most hornbooks and primers, the next step in the reading curriculum, were imported, but they were a popular item in most village stores. One example of their widespread availability is documented for New Haven, in 1645, only seven years after it was founded as a separate colony. That year, a Captain Turner was accused by Mistress Stolion before the New Haven Colony Court of having reneged on a deal in which he had promised to give her two cows in exchange for six yards of cloth.

Primers were essential texts for instruction in both reading and religion, and their publication by American presses is documented early in the Colonial Period. The oldest extant American primer was composed by John Eliot as part of his efforts to convert the Massachusett Indians. Written in the Massachusetts' dialect of the Algonquian language and published in 1669 on the Cambridge, Massachusetts, press, the primer highlighted the dual role it played, like the hornbook, in both reading and religious instruction.

Primers as a genre became a publishing staple in New England and the Middle Colonies as presses increased in number. The *New England Primer*, the most famous of colonial textbooks, began publishing around 1690, when it was already in its second impression, and continued in print until long after the American Revolution. It contained several pages of instructional material, presenting the syllabarium and words of increasing length, from monosyllables to words of six syllables.

Spelling books appeared at least as early as Edmund Coote's *The English Schoole-Maister*, published in London in 1596, and reprinted 54 times by 1737. These spellers were printed very early on colonial presses: an unidentified speller came off Stephen Daye's press in Cambridge, in the Bay Colony, in about 1644, but it was not until the 18th century that the speller's ascendancy as a school text began. An important clue to its popularity is the frequency with which English spellers were reprinted on American presses, reproduced verbatim from English copies until after the American Revolution.

The greater importance placed by colonial Americans on the ability to read rather than to write is exemplified by the legislation passed in 1642 by the colony of Massachusetts. The law empowered the colony's elected representatives, the selectmen, to inquire into the "calling and implyment [employment]" of all children, "especially of their ability to read and understand the principles of religion and the capitall lawes [capital laws] of this country." Children who were not being trained to a skill or taught to read were liable to be removed from their parents and apprenticed to someone else for such instruction. While the provisions in the law for "putting out" children to apprenticeship were borrowed from English precedents, the educational provisions were unique to the colonies. The Massachusetts law that required that children be taught to read was quickly replicated by other colonies. Connecticut passed such a provision in 1650, New Haven in 1655, New York in 1665, Plymouth in 1671, and Pennsylvania in 1683. In 1660, New Haven added a writing requirement to the law.

Libraries existed along with education. Puritan ministers in early New England wanted everyone to read, the rich and the poor and men, women, and the Indians, mostly so that all could read the Bible by themselves and seek their own salvation, but these same ministers did not want everyone to write. Licensors controlled the Boston and Cambridge presses and decided what would and would not be printed. At the same time, books were scarce in the early New England Colonies. Because of the "Great Puritan Migration" of the 1630s, New England society was heavy with intellectuals by the 1640s. Out of a population of nearly 25,000, nearly 100 men had attended Oxford or Cambridge, with at least 50 holding advanced degrees. In the colonies, such men were responsible for funding Harvard College, for founding a printing press in Cambridge, and for establishing libraries, many built on the formidable collections of these learned men. By 1699, there were about 10,000 separate titles owned by individuals in New England alone.

As educational curriculums developed and settlers wrote and read their own texts, reading helped create a sense of permanence and identity in the fledgling colonies. Books were collected and housed in colonial libraries accessible to a range of reading audiences, and books written in the colonies, rather than imported from Britain, became increasingly sought after. This permanence came to its ultimate conclusion in the American War of Independence (American Revolution), when the colonies made their final break with Great Britain and created the United States of America, but the early rumblings can be found in the attempts of colonial America to establish its own customs while building on the culture brought over from England. This was especially true of educating a citizenry that could, at a minimum, read. In these early years, books were often the only connection to the wider cultures of learning and of civilization.

Martin J. Manning

See also: Literacy; Mather, Cotton; Puritanism

Further Reading

Amory, Hugh, and David D. Hall, eds. 2000. *The Colonial Book in the Atlantic World.* Cambridge, U.K., and New York: Cambridge University. Worcester, MA: American Antiquarian Society.

Casper, Scott E., Joanne D. Chaison, and Jeffrey D. Groves, eds. 2002. *Perspectives on American Book History: Artifacts and Commentary.* Amherst: University of Massachusetts, in association with the American Antiquarian Society, Worcester, MA, and the Center for the Book, Library of Congress, Washington, D.C.

Clement, Richard W. 1996. *The Book in America.* Golden, CO: Fulcrum, in cooperation with the Library of Congress.

Davidson, Cathy N. 1989. *Reading in America: Literature and Social History.* Baltimore, MD, and London: Johns Hopkins University.

Library of Congress. *Books That Shaped America.* http://www.loc.gov/exhibits/books-that-shaped-america/1750-to-1800.html.

Quay, Sara E., ed. 2009. *American Literature.* Vol. 2 of *Cultural History of Reading.* Westport, CT: Greenwood Press.

BOSTON MASSACRE

With the end of the French and Indian War in 1763, known as the Seven Years' War in Europe, the English emerged triumphant, and the French possessions in North America were transferred to British control, with the exception of the two small islands of Saint Pierre and Miquelon off the coast of Newfoundland, which France used to service its large fishing fleet. Despite the actual and potential value of the vast territory that came under British rule, the victory left the British treasury deeply in debt. In need of cash to meet its obligations, the Crown embarked on a policy of strictly enforcing commercial regulations and enacting new or increased taxes to cover the debts. These naturally stirred opposition in the North American colonies, especially in the booming seaport of Boston.

Tensions increased appreciably in 1767 when Charles Townshend, the chancellor of the exchequer, introduced into Parliament proposals for new taxes on such common commodities as glass, lead, paint, paper, and tea. Known collectively as the Townshend Acts, the colonials not only objected to the increased taxation but also to the direct imposition of these duties by Parliament. Over the course of the lengthy wars between France and England, Parliament had generally allowed the colonial assemblies to tax themselves, so by 1767, these provincial legislatures had come to believe that taxation had to be done through them and not by Parliament. As a result, they questioned Parliament's very right to impose these taxes without their consent.

To press its case, Massachusetts sent a petition to George III requesting his intercession to gain repeal of the offending acts and at the same time issued a "Circular Letter" to the other 12 colonial legislatures, asking them to join Massachusetts in a boycott of all of the items upon which the new taxes fell. In response, Lord Hillsborough, the secretary of state for the colonies, dispatched an order to each colonial governor directing them to dissolve their legislatures if the lawmakers acted favorably on Massachusetts's request. In his letter to Gov. Francis Bernard, he further demanded that the Massachusetts House of Representatives retract the Circular Letter. When the House refused to do so, and upon requests for military support from government and customs officials in Boston, Hillsborough dispatched a Royal Navy frigate to the port.

In June 1768, customs officials seized the ship *Liberty*, which belonged to John Hancock, one of the leaders of the colonial protests, on the charge of smuggling. This, together with British attempts to forcibly impress colonial men into the Royal Navy, which stirred great anger among the general populace, led to a riot that forced British officials to escape to the safety of Castle William on an island off the east coast of South Boston. In response to the unrest, Hillsborough ordered Gen. Thomas Gage, the British military commander in North America, to send troops to the city to enforce English law. The 14th and 29th Regiments of Foot began arriving on October 1, 1768, with the former housed in Faneuil Hall and the Town Hall and the latter pitching camp on the Boston Common. These were soon joined by the 64th, 65th, and a portion of the 59th Regiments of Foot and a detachment of Royal Artillery. Not to further inflame local passions, the British commander soon withdrew as many of the troops as possible to Castle William while many officers rented private accommodations about the city.

Needless to say, the arrival of troops greatly aggravated leaders of the Townshend protests, but there was no immediate violence except for a few minor individual cases of name-calling and other forms of harassment. Over the winter, the Boston boycott began to show signs of weakening, with the result that the leaders of the opposition began to pressure merchants to maintain it, going so far as to vandalize the stores of those who sold the offending goods and threatening and occasionally assaulting customs officials. Tensions rose higher toward the end of February when Ebenezer Richardson, a well-known Loyalist informer, was assailed by a mob that threatened bodily harm and began pelting him and his home with rocks, breaking windows and eventually smashing in his front door. Richardson fired a musket into the crowd, slightly wounding two people and mortally wounding a young boy named Christopher Seider. Seider's death and funeral were widely publicized by the antigovernment faction. Fistfights and other provocations aimed at soldiers increased in subsequent days.

On March 5, 1770, Pvt. Hugh White of the 29th Regiment of Foot was assigned as the lone guard in front of the Customs House on King Street (present-day State Street). During the day, a brief altercation occurred that led to a crowd beginning to form to taunt the guard. Over time, the crowd became more menacing, as some in it took to throwing snowballs. White called for assistance. Capt. Thomas Preston sent Cpl. William Wemms with 12 men to White's relief, joining them himself a few minutes later. The reinforcement was met with more taunts and a barrage of snowballs, ice, oyster shells, and rocks. Some in the crowd approached close enough to spit at the soldiers, while others dared them to fire.

At some point, an object hit Hugh Montgomery with sufficient force to jostle him. Either because of this, or in anger for it (stories vary), Montgomery fired his musket into the crowd. After a brief second or two, the other soldiers discharged their muskets. Eleven men were hit, including Crispus Attucks, James Caldwell, and Samuel Gray, who were killed outright, and Patrick Carr and Samuel Maverick, who died later of their wounds. The crowd recoiled into the surrounding streets, where it continued to grow, and Captain Preston called out the rest of his regiment as reinforcement.

Samuel Adams, John Hancock and other protest leaders immediately seized upon the incident to rouse anti-British sentiment. Paul Revere quickly circulated a drawing by Boston artist Henry Pelham of this incident graphically illustrating the troops firing into the crowd and titled "The Bloody Massacre Perpetrated in King Street Boston on March 5th 1770 by a Party of the 29th Regt." The image also appeared to show Captain Preston ordering his men to fire, along with other provocative elements. This anti-British propaganda quickly escalated ill feelings not just in Boston, or Massachusetts, but throughout the colonies. In an attempt to defuse the rising tensions, General Gage moved the 14th and 29th Regiments out of the city.

Captain Preston and eight of his men were arrested the following day. Before the end of the month, they were indicted for murder, as were four civilians accused of firing at the crowd from the Customs House. When it proved difficult to find anyone to defend the accused, John Adams, the cousin of anti-British leader Samuel Adams and himself a future president of the United States, agreed to take on the task, although he certainly risked his career by doing so in a city where the majority of residents opposed the British occupation. Adams was assisted by another noted critic of the government, Josiah Quincy II, and by Robert Auchmuty, who had Loyalist leanings. The prosecution fell to the province's solicitor general Samuel Quincy and attorney Robert Treat Paine.

Separate trials were held for Captain Preston, in October 1770; for the enlisted men, who were tried together in November; and for the four civilians, in December. Reading accounts in the local newspapers and from witnesses, it appeared that the two sides in the issue were describing completely different incidents, as their depictions were so dissimilar—one side describing a malicious planned attack on peaceful citizens and the other claiming self-defense against an out-of-control mob determined to assault the soldiers.

In the first trial, Preston argued that he had positioned himself in front of the troops, between them and the crowd, in an attempt to retain control and ease tensions. At the time, the crowd was pelting the soldiers with various objects and making threats. Some were yelling out, "Come on you rascals, you bloody backs, you lobster scoundrels, fire if you dare, G-d damn you, fire and be damned, we know you dare not." Preston testified that he did not know who fired the first shot, but he had never given the order to fire and in fact did everything he could to stop the firing once it began. The testimony of witnesses was contradictory, depending on which side they supported. Nevertheless, or perhaps *because* of the uncertainty of the conflicting testimonies, the jury deliberated only a few hours before returning a verdict of not guilty.

The trial of the soldiers was somewhat more complicated, as clearly most, if not all of them, had fired and inflicted both death and injury on civilians. Adams based his argument for acquittal on the assertion that the soldiers had acted in self-defense because the hostile assault by the mob caused them to fear for their lives. Even if they were provoked, but not to the point of a reasonable fear of life, he

Paul Revere's sensational engraving of the Boston Massacre, a skirmish on March 5, 1770, in which British soldiers fired on and killed five townspeople. Revere's historic print publicized the event and was hugely influential in stoking anti-British sentiment in the years before the American Revolution. (National Archives and Records Administration)

argued, the most they could possibly be guilty of was manslaughter, not murder. Critical to the defense was showing that ill feeling existed in the city leading to previous harassment and attacks on soldiers.

Although the prosecution presented witnesses to support its case, Adams paraded more than 40 witnesses before the jury who swore to the aggressive nature of what he portrayed as a mob. Together, their testimony supported the assertion that the soldiers had been assaulted by clubs and thrown objects so that it was reasonable they might fear for their lives. In summation, he told the jury,

> I will enlarge no more on the evidence, but submit it to you—Facts are stubborn things; and whatever may be our wishes, our inclinations, or the dictates of our passions, they cannot alter the state of facts and evidence: nor is the law less stable than the fact; if an assault was made to endanger their lives, the law is clear, they had a right to kill in their own defence; if it was not so severe as to endanger their lives, yet if they were assaulted at all, struck and abused by blows of any sort, by snow-balls, oyster-shells, cinders, clubs, or sticks of any kind; this was a provocation, for which the law reduces the offence of killing, down to manslaughter, in consideration

> of those passions in our nature, which cannot be eradicated. To your candour and justice I submit the prisoners and their cause.

The jury deliberated less than three hours before delivering a not guilty verdict for all but two of the defendants. Hugh Montgomery and Matthew Kilroy were convicted of manslaughter. The punishment was the branding of their thumbs.

The third trial, that of the four civilians, produced much less anticipation or interest. The main witness was a servant of one of the accused, whose testimony was easily refuted. The men were all determined to be not guilty, but the servant was convicted of perjury and suffered a whipping and banishment from the colony.

The Boston Massacre was used expertly by Samuel Adams, John Hancock, Paul Revere, and other leaders of the dissent in Massachusetts to mold public opinion against the British, not just in that province but to some degree throughout the other colonies as well. The anniversary of the event was cause for annual commemorations that kept anti-British feelings alive, and in this sense, it is considered by historians to be one of the more important events leading up to the Revolution.

John Adams, who went on to play a leading part in the Continental Congress and as a diplomat in Europe, was satisfied that the fairness of the trial had preserved for the colonials the moral high ground. He later wrote that his defense of the soldiers was "one of the most gallant, generous, manly and disinterested Actions of my whole Life, and one of the best Pieces of Service I ever rendered my Country. Judgment of Death against those Soldiers would have been as foul a Stain upon this Country as the Executions of the Quakers or Witches, anciently. As the Evidence was, the Verdict of the Jury was exactly right."

James S. Pula

See also: Adams, John; Adams; Samuel; Lexington and Concord

Further Reading

Adair, Douglas, and John A. Schutz, eds. 1961. *Peter Oliver's Origin and Progress of the American Rebellion.* San Mateo, CA: Huntington Library.

Allison, Robert J. 2006. *The Boston Massacre.* Beverly, MA: Commonwealth Editions.

Archer, Richard. 2010. *As if an Enemy's Country: The British Occupation of Boston and the Origins of Revolution.* New York: Oxford University Press.

Wroth, Lawrence Kevin, and Hiller B. Zobel, eds. 1965. *Legal Papers of John Adams.* Cambridge, MA: Belknap Press.

Zobel, Hiller B. 1970. *The Boston Massacre.* New York: W. W. Norton & Co.

BOSTON TEA PARTY

The Boston Tea Party took place on the night of December 16, 1773, in Boston Harbor. It is considered by many historians to be one of the most important events that led to the American Revolution. During the Boston Tea Party, several dozen members of the Sons of Liberty dumped 342 crates of tea belonging to the British East India Company into the waters of Boston Harbor in defiance of the Tea

Act of 1773. The British Parliament passed the Coercive Acts of 1774 in response. The Coercive Acts, known in the American colonies as the Intolerable Acts, were meant to punish Bostonians for the destruction of the tea and also to reverse the trend of colonial resistance to tax measures and other acts of Parliament. Neither result was achieved. Instead of isolating revolutionary sentiment in New England, the Coercive Acts actually sparked increased anti-British activity in other colonies, leading to increased agitation and, eventually, the outbreak of hostilities between Britain and its American colonies.

The Tea Act was designed to help the struggling British East India Company by allowing it to sell tea directly to the 13 British American colonies through specifically designated consignees in the colonies. It also revised the standard export taxes applied at the time. To be precise, the East India Company would either not be charged the standard export tax or it would receive a government-authorized refund for the export taxes it did pay. Although East India Company tea would still be subject to other taxes, most notably the Townsend Duties, this refund would nevertheless make the tea cheaper than the majority of tea for sale in the American colonies. In addition, the Tea Act included provisions to curtail the rampant colonial black market in smuggled (and therefore tax-free) Dutch tea. It was hoped that these measures would encourage colonists to buy tea from the East India Company, thereby helping to reduce the company's massive and potentially financially crippling surpluses. Prime Minister Lord North also meant for the Tea Act to reassert Parliament's authority over the colonies, especially its power of taxation.

On its face, the Tea Act promised to allow colonists to purchase high-quality tea direct from the East India Company for less money than tea from competitors. However, amid widespread colonial distrust of parliamentary actions, many Americans saw the act as nothing more than an attempt by Parliament to deliberately undercut colonial commerce. Patriots also argued that the Tea Act would give the East India Company a legal monopoly, making it almost impossible for American merchants to compete.

It should be noted that the protests surrounding the Tea Act were not a response to higher prices on tea. In fact, the Tea Act actually resulted in lower costs for East India Company tea. Instead, Americans who criticized the Tea Act did so for a number of other reasons. First, it seemed to be another example of Parliament overextending its authority in legislating colonial commerce. Second, it apparently limited the freedom of American merchants (who were often importing or smuggling tea from sources not subject to the Navigation Acts). Third, many patriots feared that the precedent of establishing a legal monopoly on tea could lead to monopolies being authorized on other goods. And, finally, it was seen as another example of "taxation without representation." It seemed to many Americans that Parliament was passing laws and issuing taxes without giving the colonists a voice in the legislative process.

Soon after the passage of the Tea Act, American merchants, smugglers, and patriots in several colonial port cities began agitating for it to be rescinded. Pseudoscientific treatises were published suggesting that tea was itself a poisonous substance and that it was the cause of various maladies and illnesses among European tea drinkers. Patriots also developed plans to interfere with the collection of the customs taxes. The most common way to do this was to threaten or intimidate the local consignee into resigning his post or to physically stop the tea from being offloaded in colonial harbors. Either eventuality would prevent the sale of the tea and would thus obviate the effectiveness of the Tea Act.

While these types of resistance took place in several ports throughout the colonies, the most dramatic example of such behavior was the Boston Tea Party. In the fall of 1773, seven ships loaded with East India Company tea left Britain for American ports. Four of these ships were bound for Boston Harbor, with others meant for Philadelphia, New York City, and Charleston. In each of the three cities besides Boston, patriots had forced the resignation of the local East India Company consignee prior to the ship's arrival. As such, the tea was never offloaded, and the ships returned to England with their full cargo intact and with the taxes unpaid.

In late November 1773, the first of the East India ships bound for Boston, the *Dartmouth*, arrived with its cargo of 113 chests of tea. The governor of Massachusetts, Thomas Hutchinson, was steadfast in his determination that all the tea would be offloaded and sold, and so he convinced the consignees, two of whom were his sons, to continue in their posts despite pressure from local patriots. Samuel Adams, a leader of the Sons of Liberty in Boston, called for a meeting to take place on the evening of November 23 at Faneuil Hall. According to some accounts, several thousand people came, many more than anticipated, and so the meeting was moved to the larger Old South Meeting House. During the meeting, a resolution was passed encouraging the captain of the *Dartmouth* to return to England without offloading its cargo. In addition, a guard of 25 men was assigned to stand watch over the harbor to ensure the tea did not leave the ship.

English law allowed for customs officers to forcibly remove the cargo of a ship and collect the appropriate duties if the cargo had not be offloaded within 20 days of its arrival in port. And so, the situation in Boston settled into stalemate. Customs officers and consignees failed to offload the cargo (or were prevented from doing so), and Governor Hutchinson refused to allow the *Dartmouth* to leave without paying the duty. In the meantime, two more tea ships, the *Eleanor* and the *Beaver*, arrived in Boston Harbor. The fourth ship destined for Massachusetts, the *William*, was destroyed in a storm in transit.

On December 16, 1773, the deadline for the *Dartmouth* to offload its cargo and pay the tax, Samuel Adams and a crowd of several thousand people gathered at the Old South Meeting House. When word arrived that Hutchinson had again refused the *Dartmouth* permission to leave, Adams announced his belief that "This meeting can do nothing further to save the country." Although later descriptions of the Boston Tea Party would claim that this was Adams's prearranged signal for the patriots to raid the *Dartmouth* and destroy the tea, contemporary accounts contradict this. Eyewitnesses point out that people first began leaving the meeting some 10–15 minutes after Adams's comment.

As people finally left the meeting and gathered outside the Meeting House, some 30–80 patriots walked to the docks, some of them donning Mohawk Indian costumes on the way. As many as 2,000 people followed these men on their way to

In protest against the unpopular tax on tea that Parliament levied in 1773, Bostonians boarded three ships and dumped over 300 chests of tea into Boston Harbor in what became known as the Boston Tea Party. The following year Parliament replied with the Intolerable Acts. (Library of Congress)

Griffin's Wharf, where the three tea ships were docked. Almost as soon as they arrived, they began destroying the tea on board. Using their hatchets and tomahawks to break the barrels and casks, the men threw all 342 crates of tea into Boston Harbor, destroying somewhere around £10,000 to £18,000 worth of tea (between $750,000 and $1 million in today's currency). The men then paraded through the streets of Boston while followers accompanied them on fifes and drums.

It was clear even at the time that the Boston Tea Party was not a spontaneous event but rather an organized and well-planned undertaking. The plan had been worked out some time before the 16th during a meeting at the home of Benjamin Edes, who was a part owner of the *Boston Gazette*. Thomas Hutchinson later explained that his decision not to use force to protect the tea or to punish the perpetrators was because he feared that doing so would only exacerbate the situation and potentially escalate things completely out of control.

Despite modern popular histories of the event, the immediate reaction was mixed. Some, like John Adams and his cousin Samuel Adams, felt that by this one act, the colonists had cast the die that would lead to outright rebellion instead of mere resistance to British authority. However, John Adams also recognized that the rebellion would almost certainly grow rapidly from the destruction of tea to the destruction of lives. Contrary to today's popular memory, the "Destruction of the Tea in Boston," as it was initially known, was seen by some Americans as unprovoked, unlawful, and uncharacteristically aggressive. Some worried that it would lessen the strength of colonial claims that the British were being unreasonable in their treatment of the 13 colonies. George Washington and Benjamin

Franklin, for instance, believed that the event reflected badly on colonists, who often claimed a right to property as one of the foundations of anti-British rhetoric. Franklin even expressed his desire that Bostonians should compensate the East India Company for its loss.

In Britain, though, reaction was almost unanimously furious at the wanton destruction of British property. Even those members of Parliament who had some sympathy for the American cause found it difficult to excuse or apologize for the destruction of the tea. Parliament's response was swift and punitive. Shortly after word of the event arrived in London, Parliament passed a series of laws designed to punish Boston as well as to send a message to other colonial patriots that the escalating trend of rebellion and resistance would be dealt with swiftly and harshly.

News of the Destruction of the Tea reached England in January 1774, and by the end of March, Parliament had passed the Coercive Acts. The four Coercive Acts were known in America as the Intolerable Acts. The Quartering Act mandated that British soldiers could be billeted in unoccupied public buildings (not in private homes as is often assumed). The Boston Port Act closed the port of Boston until the East India Company had been reimbursed for the cost of the destroyed tea. The Administration of Justice Act allowed British colonial officials to appeal for trials outside of Massachusetts, whether it be in Britain or elsewhere in the empire. Finally, the Massachusetts Government Act greatly altered the political structure of Massachusetts. It limited town meetings to one per year and required that nearly all political offices in the colony be appointed by the king, Parliament, or the royal governor of the colony. In addition, Thomas Gage, a general in the British army, was made governor of Massachusetts, replacing Gov. Thomas Hutchinson. Gage was relatively popular in Massachusetts, and his arrival was generally well received by Bostonians who were happy to see Hutchinson leave.

The Coercive Acts were directed almost exclusively at the Massachusetts Bay Colony, and Boston in particular. However, patriots in the rest of New England, and elsewhere, made the case that such laws could set a precedent whereby Parliament could enact similarly punitive measures against any other colony if it so chose. They also argued that such acts were examples of Parliament trampling on colonial rights. This propaganda was largely successful, and many colonists who might otherwise have been ambivalent about the matter of resistance began to see Boston as a martyr in the cause of rebellion. These attitudes were amplified when rumors spread that the British navy had bombarded Boston in retaliation for the Tea Party. Clearly, this was not the case; however, the fact that so many colonists were so willing to believe the rumor indicates how dramatically relations between the colonies and the mother country had deteriorated.

It is difficult to pinpoint a single event that was the "cause" of the American Revolution. But the Boston Tea Party and the subsequent imposition and reaction to Parliament's Coercive Acts certainly come close.

Shawn Selby

See also: Adams, Samuel; Committees of Correspondence; Sons of Liberty

Further Reading

Breen, T. H. 2011. *American Insurgents, American Patriots*. New York: Hill and Wang.

Draper, Theodore. 1997. *A Struggle for Power.* New York: Vintage.

Langguth, A. J. 1989. *Patriots*. New York: Simon & Schuster.

Middlekauf, Robert. 2007. *The Glorious Cause*. New York: Oxford University Press.

BRADDOCK, EDWARD (1695–1755)

In the colonial history of North America, British general Edward Braddock is most famous for his disastrous 1755 campaign in western Pennsylvania during the French and Indian War (1754–1763). Braddock commanded British forces sent to remove the French defenders of Fort Duquesne in the Ohio Valley, at what is today Pittsburgh, Pennsylvania. Braddock's failed mission and death on the frontier of western Pennsylvania tend to overshadow a larger point; his campaign was part of a conflict that would ultimately shift the balance of power in North America in favor of Great Britain and set the stage for the American Revolution. Furthermore, Braddock held a unique position in colonial British history because he was appointed the overall commander of British forces in North America. He was given extensive power in the British colonies. In addition to dealing with the French challenge in North America, the British Crown expected him to unify the colonists inhabiting the 13 colonies for the first time in their history. The unification that the king expected came in the decade after the French and Indian War, with the eruption of the American Revolution.

In 1754, a small engagement, where French soldiers and their Native American allies defeated an outnumbered force of Virginians led by George Washington, sparked another in a series of 18th-century conflicts between France and Great Britain. The origins of the contest, what Americans called the French and Indian War and Europeans call the Seven Years' War, was really a dispute driven by colonial expansion. Both Britain and France claimed the lands of the Ohio Valley, despite the protests of Native Americans. An influx of British traders into the region resulted in an escalation in French efforts to control access to the Ohio Valley. After French soldiers began construction of Fort Duquesne at the forks of the Ohio River in 1753, Virginia's lieutenant governor, Robert Dinwiddie, sent George Washington to convince the French to leave. Dinwiddie was determined to claim the region for Britain. The failure of this limited diplomatic mission brought battle between French forces and Virginians in 1754. The poor showing of British colonists at Fort Necessity prompted a formal military response from Britain. Gen. Edward Braddock was chosen to do what the colonists could not do: expel French forces from the Ohio Valley.

Braddock was an experienced soldier by the time he assumed command of the regiments sent to Virginia. He joined the Coldstream Guards in 1710 and was a veteran of Britain's most recent European war, the War of Austrian Succession (1740–1748), fighting in the Netherlands. Braddock appeared to be a solid choice to lead troops in North America and to direct the British effort against the French; yet, he had not commanded troops nor had he fought in North America.

He had neither experience fighting in the forests of North America nor had he faced an enemy that used the unconventional tactics of Native Americans in battle. He would be at a disadvantage in combat without reliable allies on the American frontier.

Promoted to major general, Braddock was given command of two new regiments, the 44th and 48th Foot of the Coldstream Guards. Both regiments were filled with young men pulled off farms; their military experience was limited to close-order musketry drill on the parade ground. Neither would help Braddock complete his mission on the American frontier. Braddock and his Coldstream Guards arrived in Virginia in February of 1755 fully expecting to rid the Ohio Valley of Frenchmen. Then British forces would conquer the French forts Machault, Le Boeuf, and Presque Isle, giving the British control over the waterways and lakes stretching along the northern borders of New York and Pennsylvania. The overall British strategy was to hit the key points held by the French along the frontier between Canada and the British colonies. If successful, Fort Duquesne would be isolated, an easy target for Braddock to seize for British glory.

General Braddock set his plans in motion almost immediately after reaching Virginia. He met with the governors of Virginia, Maryland, Pennsylvania, and Massachusetts in April and instructed each man in what his respective colony was expected to provide for the expeditions. He also directed the assemblies of each colony to create a common fund to pay the expenses of his army. The boldness with which he ordered colonial leaders around caught many off guard and alienated some of the powerful men in the colonies. They were unaccustomed to being ordered outright to provide men and materiel for war, and nowhere was this more evident than in Quaker-dominated Pennsylvania. Quakers steadfastly opposed allocating treasure or men for war, even if the threat was on the western doorstep of Pennsylvania. Expecting that each colony would comply without question, Braddock assembled his expedition of approximately 2,100 men at Wills Creek—Fort Cumberland (now in western Maryland).

For Braddock's plans to work, the help of Native American allies was critical in the effort. That Native warriors were essential was a consideration known too well by colonists on both sides of the war. British trader George Croghan, serving as the deputy chief to Sir William Johnson, the superintendent of northern Indian affairs, arranged a meeting between Braddock and key Indian warriors. Yet, General Braddock squandered every opportunity to enlist the help of Native Americans in the British cause against the French. One Native American, known as Moses the Song, a Mohawk, brought Braddock a copy of Fort Duquesne's layout made by Capt. Robert Stobo. The captain had been to the fort in 1754. In fact, when George Washington surrendered Fort Necessity on July 3, 1754, he had left Captain Stobo with the French as a prisoner to guarantee the safe return of 21 French prisoners. Moses had brought Braddock this gift—valuable information about his military target.

Braddock ignored the intelligence provided by Indians and proceeded to lecture them about the conduct of war. There would be no scalping in his army; those under his command would behave humanely in battle. In one of the early engagements of 1754, one of the warriors allied to George Washington's Virginia regiment tomahawked a defenseless French diplomat, Joseph Coulon de Villiers, Sieur de Jumonville, after he was wounded in a skirmish. Perhaps this episode contributed to Braddock's declarations to the warriors sitting before him. Nonetheless, it won him no admiration from Native warriors, who had not committed to either side in the conflict.

War prizes such as scalps were not the primary concern of Shingas, the Delaware leader meeting with Braddock. The principle concern of Native Americans was the status of Ohio lands after the conflict ended. Nearly 50 Indian warriors and leaders met with Braddock; they would side with whomever gave them the best chance of protecting their lands from white settlers. Braddock committed a nearly unforgivable sin when he informed Shingas that no "savage" would have the land. His war was to push the French out and claim the land solely for Britain. Braddock's inexperience with frontier diplomacy cost him dearly, as nearly all the Native Americans left. Only eight warriors joined Braddock's expedition.

Braddock launched his expedition from Fort Cumberland while cutting a road into the Ohio Valley. It was the first road across the Appalachian Mountains. Because his forces were cutting a road wide enough to move wagons and cannons, the troops moved more slowly than he had anticipated. Impatient with the pace, Braddock took 1,300 of his troops, formed them into a flying column, and forged ahead of the main army. Braddock's rush ahead cost him victory and his life. He did not have enough supplies, and his failure to secure the assistance of Native warriors became more apparent with every mile his men advanced. Without indigenous guides and scouts moving ahead of his column, British enemies easily picked off any stragglers unable to keep up with the advancing column. Nonetheless, Braddock raced ahead, and on July 9, 1755, Braddock's men crossed the Monongahela River, less than 10 miles from Fort Duquesne. General Braddock never made it any closer to the fort, as the Battle of Monongahela began.

Braddock's advancing force found itself in the center of a ferocious and deadly attack with no ability to call upon reinforcements. French attackers numbered approximately 900 warriors, mostly Indians. They unleashed a devastating assault on the British general and his men. The battle lasted a mere three hours. In that short time, French soldiers and their Indian allies demolished Braddock's army, killing or wounding more than half of his men and the camp followers accompanying them. The enemy attacked with precision and effectiveness, decimating Braddock's officers too, killing or wounding 60 of the 86 officers serving under him. Remarkably, the young lieutenant colonel George Washington escaped with several near misses; he wrote his mother that he had no less than four bullet holes in his uniform and had had two horses killed underneath him. French losses were numbered fewer than 30 men.

General Braddock was less fortunate than his aide-de-camp. Braddock commanded his men under intense fire, losing four or perhaps five horses before being shot in the arm and abdomen. Badly wounded and his army in retreat, Braddock's men withdrew as best as they could, carrying the wounded general in a wagon over the rough road. Braddock died three days later. To this day, Braddock's grave has yet to be found. His men buried him somewhere in the road and then ran wagons over it to cover the grave so Native enemies could not find his body. French victory over Braddock's army meant that the Ohio Valley remained firmly under French control for three more years.

In 1758, British forces led by Brig. Gen. John Forbes returned to the Ohio Valley. Unlike Braddock's March, Forbes constructed a new road (Forbes Road) out of the Pennsylvania colony that could be supplied more easily, and the alliance of Native Americans shifted due to the Treaty of Easton, signed in October. The treaty was immensely important in shifting the balance in the Ohio and ultimately allowing the British to take Fort Duquesne. Representatives from New Jersey and Pennsylvania, along with a representative of the Crown, met with hundreds of Native Americans at Easton. The Iroquois agreed to help the British in their relations with Delaware Indians, who had threatened any efforts against the French, and Great Britain agreed to check settlers' expansion into the region. The treaty greatly enhanced security for Forbes's army. French forces destroyed Fort Duquesne, fleeing in the night.

Although Gen. Edward Braddock failed in his mission to defeat the French in the Ohio Valley, his role in the French and Indian War had lasting implications for North America. Learning from his mistakes, later commanders succeeded in wresting control of the Ohio away from France. Unity among the colonists also came, in part as a result of the war and the changes implemented by Britain after the war ended. The colonists ultimately rallied to a common cause and followed Braddock's former aide-de-camp, George Washington, to independence.

Eugene Van Sickle

See also: Seven Years' War; Washington, George

Further Reading

Anderson, Fred. 2006. *The War That Made America: A Short History of the French and Indian War.* New York: Penguin Group.

Cassell, Frank A. 2005. "The Braddock Expedition of 1755: Catastrophe in the Wilderness." *Pennsylvania Legacies* 5, no. 1: 11–15. http://www.jstor.org/stable/27764968.

Cohen, Eliot A. 2011. *Conquered into Liberty: Two Centuries of Battles along the Great Warpath That Made the American Way of War.* New York: Free Press.

Hinderaker, Eric. 1997. *Elusive Empires Constructing Colonialism in the Ohio Valley, 1673–1800.* Cambridge: Cambridge University Press.

Keegan, John. 1997. *Fields of Battle: The Wars for North America.* New York: Vintage Books.

Preston, David L. 2007. "'Make Indians of Our White Men': British Soldiers and Indian Warriors from Braddock's to Forbes's Campaigns, 1755–1758." *Pennsylvania History: A Journal of Mid-Atlantic Studies* 74, no. 3: 280–306. http://www.jstor.org/stable/27778783.

Weidensaul, Scott. 2012. *The First Frontier: The Forgotten History of Struggle, Savagery, and Endurance in Early America.* Boston: Houghton Mifflin Harcourt.

BRADFORD, WILLIAM (1663–1752)

As a British printer, William Bradford was apprenticed to the noted Quaker printer Andrew Sowle (1628–1695) and later was recommended by William Penn (1644–1718) and George Fox (1624–1691) to the Quaker Religious Society of Friends to become the colonial publisher in Pennsylvania. In this role, Bradford's printing was restricted by the Quakers, and he was limited to the publication of approved religious texts, colonial laws, and stationary. Regardless, Bradford is recognized for publishing Samuel Atkins's *Kalendarium Pennsilvaniense*, or *America's Messenger* (1685), and Daniel Leeds's *An Almanack for the Year of the Christian Account* (1687), and the *Temple of Wisdom* (1688). Despite his success, restrictions placed on him by the Friends ultimately led to a disagreement between Bradford and the Society, which in turn led to America's first trial regarding the freedom of the press.

In 1693, Bradford left Pennsylvania after establishing America's first paper mill (1690) and became the governor's printer in New York for three decades. During this time, he published the colony's laws, pamphlets, and books as well as its first newspaper, the conservative *New York Gazette* (1725–1744). In addition to his achievements as one of the Middle Colonies' and British America's premier printers, Bradford established a printer dynasty that included his son Andrew Sowle Bradford (1686–1742), who printed the first newspaper in Pennsylvania, and his grandson William Bradford (1719–1791), who published for the Continental Congress during the American Revolution (1775–1783).

William Bradford was born in Leicester, England, on May 20, 1663. By 1685, Bradford had finished his apprenticeship with Andrew Sowle, the leading Quaker printer of London, and married Sowle's daughter, Elizabeth. Shortly thereafter, with the endorsement of William Penn and a letter of recommendation from George Fox, the founder of the Quakers, he immigrated to America and settled in Pennsylvania. Within the year, Bradford had published Samuel Atkin's *Kalendarium Pennsilvaniense* (*America's Messenger*), which was poorly received by both the Quaker Society of Friends and William Penn. As a result, in 1687, Bradford was ordered thereafter to print only material licensed by the Pennsylvania Provincial Assembly.

In the ensuing years, Bradford published, among other things, *An Almanack for the Year of the Christian Account 1687* and the *Temple of Wisdom*, which was the first full-sized book printed in the Middle Colonies. In 1689, when trouble broke out in Pennsylvania, Bradford republished Penn's original colonial charter and was reprimanded. However, Bradford was not receiving much business from the Friends and unsuccessfully argued that he was entitled to publish enough material to make a living. During this period, his mentor Andrew Sowle died, and Bradford applied to return to England to pursue his business there. However, he was convinced to stay in America, and by 1690, he and the Dutch papermaker William Rittenhouse (1644–1708) had established the first paper mill in British North America, on Wissahickon Creek outside of Philadelphia.

In 1692, a religious dispute in Pennsylvania led George Keith (1638–1716) to write a number of pieces questioning the honesty of Quaker authorities, which Bradford then published. In particular, Bradford's printing of Keith's *An Appeal from the Twenty-Eight Judges to the Spirit of Truth* (1692) was determined to be seditious, and Bradford was arrested, jailed, and had his press, type, and papers seized. Bradford argued his own case in court so skillfully that the jurors failed to reach a verdict, and he was released. Bradford's trial with the Quakers in 1682–1683 is considered to be one of the first in North America involving the freedom of the press.

In 1693, Bradford accepted Gov. Benjamin Fletcher's (1640–1703) invitation to go to New York and serve the Provincial Council as the governor's printer, producing proclamations, laws, and the journals of the assembly. There he established the colony's first press and remained the only printer in New York for 30 years. In 1710, Bradford printed the first *American Book of Common Prayer*, and by 1723, Bradford was also the royal printer in New Jersey. In 1725, Bradford began publication of New York's first newspaper, the weekly *New-York Gazette* (1725–1744), which was poorly printed, conservative, consisted mainly of foreign news, carried little advertising, and had low circulation.

During his long career, Bradford had Henry De Foreest, James Parker (1714–1770), William Weyman (d. 1768), and John Peter Zenger (1697–1746), as well as his own son Andrew Sowle Bradford, as apprentices. Each of these men would go on to have distinguished careers in the publishing field. Foreest would eventually take over Bradford's press upon his retirement and later published the *New York Evening Post*. Parker established the *Post Boy* and later *The Reflector* in New York, prior to becoming a government printer along with Weyman, who eventually also served as the publisher of the *New York Gazette*. Zenger would go on to publish the *New York Weekly Journal* and *New-York Gazette*, and he ultimately became immersed in his own trial regarding the freedom of the press after highlighting the corruption of Gov. William Cosby (1690–1736) in 1735.

William Bradford retired in 1743. He died in New York, on May 23, 1752 and was buried in Trinity Church Cemetery. Bradford was survived by his son Andrew, who was the only publisher in Philadelphia from 1712–1723 and who established Pennsylvania's first newspaper, the *American Weekly Mercury* (1719–1746). Years afterward, Bradford's grandson, William Bradford, became a noted printer for the Continental Congress during the American Revolution.

Sean Morton

See also: Penn, William; Quakers

Further Reading

Amory, H., and D. D. Hall. 2007. *A History of the Book in America: The Colonial Book in the Atlantic World.* Chapel Hill: University of North Carolina Press.

Clark, C. E. 1994. *The Public Prints: The Newspaper in Anglo-American Culture, 1665–1740.* Oxford: Oxford University Press.

McMurtrie, D. 1933. *Pioneer Printing in New York.* Springfield, MA: Private Press.

Thomas, I. 1970. *The History of Printing in America.* Edited by M. A. McCorison. New York: Weathervane Books.

PRIMARY DOCUMENT: William Bradford, *History of Plymouth Plantation* (1648)

As one of the primary leaders of the Pilgrims, William Bradford penned a history of the Pilgrims' settlement at Plymouth Plantation (in present-day Massachusetts) in 1648. The work encouraged more settlers to journey to the "New World" and served as an invaluable source of information for historians of colonial Massachusetts. An excerpt from the text, first formally published in 1856, follows.

I shall a litle returne backe and begine with a combination [the Mayflower Compact] made by them before they came a shore, being the first foundation of their governmente in this place; occasioned partly by the discontented and mutinous speeches that some of the strangers amongst them had let fall from them in the ship—That when they came a shore they would use their owne libertie; for none had power to command them, the patente they had being for Virginia, and not for New-england, which belonged to an other Government, with which the Virginia Company had nothing to doe. And partly that shuch an acte by them done (this their condition considered) might be as firme as any patent, and in some respects more sure. . . .

After this they chose, or rather confirmed, Mr. John Carver (a man godly & well approved amongst them) their Governour for that year. And after they had provided a place for their goods, or comone store, (which were long in unlading for want of boats, foulnes of winter weather, and sicknes of diverce,) and begune some small cottages for their haitation, as time would admitte, they mette and consulted of lawes & orders, both for their civill & military Governmente, as the necessitie of their condition did require, still adding therunto as urgent occasion in severall times, and as cases did require.

In these hard & difficulte beginings they found some discontents & murmurings arise amongst some, and mutinous speeches & carriags in other; but they were soone quelled & overcome by the wisdome, patience, and just & equall carrage of things by the Governor and better part, which clave faithfully togeather in the maine. But that which was most sadd & lamentable was, that in 2. or 3. moneths time halfe of their company dyed, espetialy in Jan: & February, being the depth of winter, and wanting houses & other comforts; being infected with the scurvie & other diseases, which this long vioage & their inacomodate condition had brought upon them; so as ther dyed some times 2. or 3. of a day, in the foresaid time; that of 100. & odd persons, scarce 50. remained. And of these in the time of most distres, ther was but 6. or 7. sound persons, who, to their great comendations be it spoken, spared no pains, night nor day, but with abundance of toyle and hazard of their owne health, fetched them woode, made them fires, drest them meat, made their beads, washed their lothsome cloaths, cloathed & uncloathed them; in a word, did all the homly and necessarie offices for them which dainty and quesie stomacks cannot endure to hear named; and all this willingly and cherfully, without any grudging in the least, shewing herein their true love unto their friends and bretheren. A rare example and worthy to be remembred. Tow of these 7. were Mr. William Brewster, ther reverend Elder, & Myles Standish, ther Captein & military commander, unto whom my selfe, & many others, were much beholden in our low & sicke condition. And yet the Lord so upheld these persons, as in this generall calamity they were not at all infected either with sicknes, or lamnes. And what I have said of these, I may say of many others who dyed in this generall vissitation, & others yet living, that whilst they had health, yea, or any strength continuing, they were not wanting to any that had need of them. And I doute not but their recompence is with the Lord.

But I may not hear pass by an other remarkable passage not to be forgotten. As this calamitie fell among the passengers that were to be left here to plant, and were hasted a shore and made to drinke water, that the sea-men might have the more bear, and one (which was this author himselfe) in his sicknes desiring but a small cann of beere, it was answered, that if he were their owne father he should have none; the disease begane to fall amongst them also, so as allmost halfe of their company dyed before they went away, and many of their officers and lustyest men, as the boatson, gunner, 3. quartermaisters, the cooke, & others. At which the master was something strucken and sent to the sick a shore and tould the Governor he should send for beer for them that had need of it, though he drunke water homward bound. But now amongst his company ther was farr another kind of carriage in this miserie then amongst the passengers; for they that before had been boone companions in drinking & joyllity in the time of their health & wellfare, begane now to deserte one another in this calamitie, saing they would not hasard ther lives for them, they should be infected by coming to help them in their cabins, and so, after they came to dye by it, would doe litle or nothing for them, but it they dyed let them dye. But shuch of the passengers as were yet abord shewed them what mercy they could, which made some of their harts relente, as the boatson (& some others), who was a prowd yonge man, and would often curse & scofe at the passengers; but when he grew weak, they had compassion on him and helped him; then he confessed he did not deserve it at their hands, he had abused them in word & deed. O! saith he, you, I now see, shew your love like Christians indeed one to another, but we let one another lye & dye like doggs. Another lay cursing his wife, saing if it had not ben for her he had never come this unlucky viage, and anone cursing his felows, saing he had done this & that, for some of them, he had spente so much, & so much, amongst them, and they were now weary of him, and did not help him, having need. Another gave his companion all he had, if he died, to help him in his weaknes; he went and got a litle spise & made him a mess of meat once or twise, and because he dyed not so soone as he expected, he went amongst his fellows, & swore the rogue would cousen him, he would see him choaked before he made him any more meate; and yet the pore fellow dyed before morning.

All this while the Indians came skulking about them, and would sometimes show them selves aloofe of, but when any aproached near them, they would rune away. And once they stoale away their tools wher they had been at worke, & were gone to diner. But about the 16. *of March* a certaine Indian came bouldly amongst them, and spoke to them in broken English, which they could well understand, but marvelled at it. At length they understood by discourse with him, that he was not of these parts, but belonged to the eastrene parts, wher some English-ships came to fhish, with whom he was aquainted, & could name sundrie of them by their names, amongst whom he had gott his language. He became profitable to them in aquainting them with many things concerning the state of the cuntry in the east-parts wher he live, which was afterwards profitable unto them; as also of the people hear, of their names, number, & strength; of their situation & distance from this place, and who was cheefe amongst them. His name was *Samaset;* he tould them also of another Indian whos name was *Squanto,* a native of this place, who had been in England & could speake better English then him selfe. Being, after some time of entertainmente & gifts, dismist, a while after he came againe, & 5. more with him, & they brought againe all the tooles that were stolen away before, and made way for the coming of their great Sachem, called *Massasoyt;* who, about 4. *or* 5. *days after,* came with the cheefe of his freinds & other attendance, with the aforesaid *Squanto.* With whom, after frendly entertainment, & some gifts given him, they made a peace with him (which hath now continued this 24. years) in these terms.

1. That neither he nor any of his, should injurie or doe hurte to any of their peopl.
2. That if any of his did any hurte to any of theirs, he should send the offender, that they might punish him.
3. That if any thing were taken away from any of theirs, he should cause it to be restored; and they should doe the like to his.
4. If any did unjustly warr against him, they would aide him; if any did warr against them, he should aide them.
5. He should send to his neighbours confederats, to certifie them of this, that they might not wrong them, but might be likewise comprised in the conditions of peace.
6. That when ther men came to them, they should leave their bows & arrows behind them.

Source: Bradford, William. 1856. *History of Plymouth Plantation.* Boston: Little, Brown, and Company, 89–95.

BRANDYWINE, BATTLE OF

The Battle of Brandywine was fought in southeast Pennsylvania on September 11, 1777, between American forces led by Gen. George Washington (1732–1799) and British forces under the command of Gen. William Howe. The battle was part of Howe's campaign against the colonial capital of Philadelphia. In terms of troop deployment and duration, it was one of the largest and longest battles of the entire American Revolution (1775–1783). It was a decisive victory for the British; however, due to a number of factors, Howe failed to completely destroy the Continental Army.

During his march on Philadelphia in the autumn of 1777, British general William Howe encountered George Washington and his mixed army of Continentals and militia at Brandywine Creek. Although the Americans offered a respectable degree of resistance, they suffered from a poor understanding of the local geography, which enabled Howe to outflank them. The resulting American defeat slowed, but failed to stop, the British occupation of Philadelphia, the largest city in the American colonies. (Library of Congress)

In the summer of 1777, General Howe set his sights on both the colonial capital of Philadelphia as well as on the main body of the Continental Army under George Washington. Since the British victory at Long Island, when the Americans were forced to abandon New York to British control for the remainder of the war, Howe and Washington had met in only limited engagements. Howe hoped to draw the Americans into a major battle in New Jersey, but he was unsuccessful.

At the same time, British general John Burgoyne was advancing south from Canada with a large army, hoping to gain control of the Hudson River and split New England from the rest of the colonies. Although Howe was supposed to drive north from New York to aid Burgoyne's campaign, he chose instead to remain in the Middle Colonies to destroy Washington's army. Washington's refusal to be suckered into battle forced Howe to change his tactic. He therefore resolved to sail his army of more than 16,000 out of New Jersey and north, through the Delaware Bay, to the Delaware River. This would put him in a position to directly threaten Philadelphia and, hopefully, force Washington to engage. However, after receiving false intelligence about Continental blockages along the Delaware River, Howe changed his plan. His new plan was to sail up the length of the Chesapeake Bay, reach its northernmost point, and then advance overland toward Philadelphia from there.

Howe's advance got off to a slow and difficult start. Many of his men were ill from their sea journey. A number of the army's horses died along the way. And it took several days for the entire British army to disembark. At the same time, Washington's main force was advancing south through the capital to confront the attackers. Despite initial uncertainty about Howe's plans, the American force of nearly 16,000 men ended up being well positioned to resist the British advance.

Howe began marching his column on September 3, 1777. Over the next week, the two armies maneuvered across the Pennsylvania countryside, neither side engaging the other directly. After several minor skirmishes, Howe and Washington eventually confronted each other at Chad's Ford. Chad's Ford was situated approximately 25 miles southwest of Philadelphia and was one of the few places where the Brandywine Creek could be easily crossed. The ford was commanded by heights on either side and seemed a strong position for Washington's deployment. Many of the surrounding farms were owned by prosperous—and Loyalist—Quaker families, a fact that would play a part in both armies' difficulties with gaining reliable reconnaissance throughout the battle.

The battle began near dawn on September 11, 1777. Howe divided his forces. The Hessian general Wilhelm von Knyphausen, with just under 7,000 men, attacked Washington head-on at Chad's Ford. In the meantime, Howe took his 8,000 soldiers on a flanking march, hoping to fall on the weakest part of the American line, the right flank. Howe's advance was initially covered by a dense fog. As the day wore on, however, the fog burned off, and his men were forced to finish their nearly 17-mile march in sweltering heat.

Once he became aware of Howe's divided forces, Washington knew that he had a chance to defeat Knyphausen's smaller force. However, he also knew that Howe presented a serious threat to his flank. Although the Continentals attempted an assault on Knyphausen's army, it was quickly recalled when intelligence arrived detailing Howe's movements along the right side of the American lines.

Washington swiftly ordered his army into a defensive deployment. Howe recognized his advantage and pressed his assault on the Americans' defensive lines along Birmingham Hill. The battle for the hill began around four o'clock in the afternoon. The Hessian and British advance was initially blunted by precise canister and grape shot fired from artillery that the Americans had hastily, and with great effort, dragged up the hill. The American defenses were not yet fully established, however, and the British and Hessians regrouped for another advance. After nearly two hours of intense fighting, the Americans were forced to abandon the hill, exposing Washington's flank and throwing into serious doubt any chance for a Continental victory.

At this point, Washington was forced to revise his battle plan. He abandoned any thought of success and instead tried to secure a satisfactory withdrawal. Washington's defensive positions did yeoman's work protecting the retreat, allowing the main body to escape. Nevertheless, the battle was a decisive victory for Howe and the British. Casualty estimates vary, but British sources place the number of their casualties officially at 89 dead and 488 wounded, though the number was probably somewhat higher. American figures are harder to ascertain, but they are often cited as 200 killed, 500 injured, and 400 captured, for a total of 1,100 casualties.

With the defeat of the Continentals, there was little to stand between Howe and the American capital. The British captured Philadelphia just over two weeks later, on September 26, 1777. They occupied it until the following June. Even with the substantial losses suffered by the Americans, there were reasons for Washington to be confident. His soldiers had acquitted themselves well against the British and Hessians, and Washington remarked in a letter to John Hancock later that day that, "Notwithstanding the misfortune of the day, I am happy to find the troops in good spirits; and I hope another time we shall compensate for the losses now sustained" (Washington, "Letter to Congress").

Shawn Selby

See also: Washington, George

Further Reading

Harris, Michael. 2014. *Brandywine: A Military History of the Battle That Lost Philadelphia, but Saved America, September 11, 1777.* El Dorado Hills, CA: Savas Beatie.

McGuire, Thomas. 2006. *Brandywine and the Fall of Philadelphia.* Vol. 1 of *The Philadelphia Campaign.* New York: Stackpole Books.

Washington, George. "Letter to Congress." September 11, 1777. http://www.loc.gov/teachers/classroommaterials/presentationsandactivities/presentations/timeline/amrev/turning/brandy.html.

BRANT, JOSEPH (1743–1807)

Joseph Brant, born Thayendanegea, was a Mohawk leader during the American Revolution. After developing strong ties with the British Crown during the French and Indian War (1756–1763), he remained loyal to the Crown during the American Revolution. Following the war, he devoted his life to strengthening the Iroquois and Mohawk peoples, but by remaining in Canada under British protection rather than returning to their Native lands in the newly formed United States.

Somewhere in modern Ohio, in March of 1742 or 1743, an indigenous couple had a son they named Thayendanegea. This has been translated variously as either "two sticks bound together for strength" or "he who places two bets." Not much is known about his family except that his parents were Christianized; the English records list their names as Peter and Margaret (Owandah) Tehonwaghkwangearahkwa. They were members of the Wolf Clan of the Mohawk tribe of the powerful Iroquois Confederacy that ruled over much of what is today upstate New York. Thayendanegea's father died around the time of his birth, so he grew up with his mother and a sister generally known in English as Molly in the Mohawk village of Canajoharie on the south bank of the Mohawk River, where a town by that name still exists.

In 1753 Owandah married a Mohawk leader named Kanagaradunkwa, but called Brant in English. He was a close friend of many in the English leadership—close enough that when Sir William Johnson, the superintendent for northern

Indian affairs, visited the area, he stayed with the Brants. Sir William soon became intimate with Molly, fathering eight children with her. She moved in with him as a common-law wife at Fort Johnson after it was built in 1749 and then at Johnson Hall, a Georgian-style mansion he built in 1763. As Molly's younger brother, Thayendanegea, now known as Joseph Brant, stayed with the Johnsons, and Sir William sponsored his English education at an "Indian" school operated by Eleazar Wheelock in Connecticut. There he converted to the Anglican Church.

Indian nations and individuals faced numerous difficulties at the outset of the American Revolution. Some sided with the Americans, some attempted to remain neutral, but some, such as Joseph Brant, sided with the British. In 1779, Brant was granted an officer's commission by the British military command. (Library of Congress)

During the wars between France and England, Brant fought with the Mohawk and other Iroquois tribes on the side of the British, taking part in the disaster under Gen. James Abercrombie at Ticonderoga in 1758, Sir William Johnson's battle at Fort Niagara in 1759, and Gen. Jeffrey Amherst's campaign against Montréal. He was rewarded for his services with a silver medal from an appreciative Crown. Fluent in English, Mohawk, and at least two other Iroquoian languages, perhaps more, Brant served as an interpreter for Johnson and the English government and was, by all accounts, very intelligent, perceptive, and well mannered, equally at home among the Mohawk and the English.

Brant married a woman named Peggy, whom many believe to have been captured from an English settlement in Virginia as a young girl. They lived on about 80 acres of farmland on the south shore of the Mohawk River at a place known as the Upper Mohawk Castle. After she died in 1771, he married a woman named Susanna, but she died at Niagara in 1777. Largely because of his connections with the British and his apparent skills in negotiation with and on behalf of the Mohawk, and most likely under some pressure from Johnson, the Mohawk elected Brant a chief and their primary spokesman. In 1772, he moved temporarily to Fort Hunter, where Schoharie Creek empties into the Mohawk River. There he worked with Rev. John Stuart to translate the Anglican catechism and the Gospel of Mark into Mohawk.

When the American Revolution began, Brant's long allegiance to the crown continued. The largely German and Dutch farmers in the Mohawk Valley sided with the Revolution, forcing the English leadership and its allies, including Brant and many of the Iroquois, to flee north to Canada, where they determined to raise an army to reclaim their lands. Molly Brant stayed behind; and operated an important intelligence network until increasingly suspicious locals eventually forced her out in 1777. Her husband fled to Montréal and then went with Guy Johnson to London, where Brant was received by George III, who promised the Mohawks land in Québec Province if they would fight on the side of the British. He also became a Freemason and was interviewed by James Boswell.

Brant returned to New York with Lord William Howe's invasion force in July 1776 and fought on Long Island before leaving that fall for the Iroquois territory, where he spoke at villages on the way to Fort Niagara, encouraging them to take up arms with the British. In 1777, four of the six nations of the Iroquois Confederacy decided to actively back the British, while the Oneida and Tuscarora sided with the Americans. With this, Brant linked up with a British and Indian force under Lt. Col. Barry St. Leger at Fort Oswego, where he hoped to sweep down the Mohawk Valley and crush resistance to the Crown. Brant was apparently involved in the bloody Battle of Oriskany, but when the British invasion failed, Brant traveled cross-country to join Gen. John Burgoyne's main army marching on Albany. From there, he returned to Fort Niagara, where his family joined him shortly before his wife's death. With her passing, he met Catherine Adonwentishon Croghan, the daughter of a Mohawk and the British Indian agent George Croghan They married in 1780.

Beginning in 1778, Brant led a series of raids into the Mohawk and Schoharie Valleys, burning homes, killing the inhabitants, and driving off livestock. The Americans retaliated by burning the Mohawk village at Onoquaga. Together with the partisan leader Walter Butler, Brant took part in the Cherry Valley massacre in November, although some writers claim that he had tried to curtail excesses. These raids were the beginning of five years of brutal frontier warfare in which each side conducted raids on the other with little regard for noncombatants. This led directly to the dispatch of troops from the Continental Army under Gen. John Sullivan on a scorched-earth campaign through the western Iroquois territories in 1779 that burned every village, all of the crops, and killed all the livestock they found. The devastation of these communities left the residents dependent on the British in Fort Niagara for protection and sustenance over the long winter months.

Brant was in Montréal in early 1779, where he received a commission as captain and a pledge that, following a British victory in the war, the traditional lands of the Mohawk would be restored to them. Beginning in 1780, he resumed leading attacks on settlements in the Mohawk Valley and occasional isolated American troops as well as the villages of the Oneida, who had allied themselves with the Americans, and even his former home of Canajoharie. After recovering from a wound in the foot at the Battle of Klock's Field, Brant was sent to assist in the defense of Detroit, where forces under his command defeated a portion of the American troops under George Rogers Clark, ending the threat. Wounded again in the encounter, he spent the winter recuperating.

In 1782, Brant began raiding the Mohawk Valley once again, but with the conclusion of hostilities and American independence, Iroquois claims were ignored by both sides. He was not a party to the eventual treaty with New York that ceded most of the indigenous lands to the state, but he was instrumental in obtaining a grant from the British to settle members of the Iroquois Confederacy on land along the Grand River in Ontario. In 1785, he went to London to plead with the Crown for support for his people, obtaining a pension for himself and the promise of full compensation of the Mohawks for their losses.

In 1792, Brant met President George Washington in Philadelphia, where he attempted to arrange a settlement of a war then raging between the United States and the indigenous people in the Midwest. Unsuccessful in these efforts, he rejected an offer of a reservation for the Mohawk in upstate New York, choosing to remain in Canada under British protection. He again traveled to Philadelphia in 1797 to speak before Congress to assure them of his peaceful intent. In succeeding years, he attempted to obtain land in Ohio to settle his people, but the effort was once again unsuccessful. In 1802, he retired to a mansion he had built on Burlington Bay, where he died on November 24, 1807. His remains were later reinterred in Brantford, Ontario.

Brant was a lifelong advocate for Indian rights and landownership, but his efforts largely fell victim to the international relations of Britain and America. His efforts to reestablish Iroquois solidarity following the Revolution were not successful, resulting in the dispersal of various tribes to widely separated reservations in both the United States and Canada. In Canada, a museum to him was opened, a county and city named for him, and a statue erected in Brantford in 1886. In the United States, his name remained largely associated with the terror of the ruthless frontier warfare of the Revolution.

James S. Pula

See also: Washington, George

Further Reading

Chalmers, Harvey, and Ethel Brant Monture. 1955. *Joseph Brant: Mohawk.* East Lansing: Michigan State University Press.

Graymont, Barbara. 1972. *The Iroquois in the American Revolution.* Syracuse, NY: Syracuse University Press.

Kelsay, Isabel Thompson. 1984. *Joseph Brant, 1743–1807: Man of Two Worlds.* Syracuse, NY: Syracuse University Press.

Marquis, Thomas Guthrie. 1930. *Joseph Brant.* Toronto: Ryerson Press.

Taylor, Alan. 2006. *The Divided Ground: Indians, Settlers, and the Northern Borderland of the American Revolution.* New York: Alfred A. Knopf.

BRENT, MARGARET REED (1601–1671)

Margaret Brent was one of the first American women to demand suffrage. Born in Gloucester, England, to Elizabeth Reed Brent and Richard Brent, Margaret immigrated to the colony of Maryland in 1638 with two brothers and a sister. Not much is known about her life in England. Her Catholic parents belonged to aristocracy, and she might have received a good education. Margaret had to live by herself, as her father's estate went to the eldest son. The siblings (Fulke Brent, Giles Brent, and Mary Brent) reached St. Mary's, Maryland, on November 22, 1638, aspiring for a better life and religious freedom. Her determination as well as intellect reiterated her position in a male-dominated society. The Brent family had a good rapport with their cousins, the Calverts, the proprietors of Maryland.

In 1639, Margaret's fortunes rose when the sisters established Sister's Freehold, encompassing an area of 70.5 acres. Tobacco was grown, and additional indentured servants were subsequently imported. The estate was enlarged with the addition of 50 acres called St. Andrew's. Giles Brent transferred 1,000 acres on Kent Island, as he had taken a loan from Margaret. Margaret was an excellent entrepreneur. As per the law, she allocated portions of her property to the indentured laborers of her estate. She revived an earlier law practice in England, Wales, and Ireland called *court leets*. Margaret listened to her employees' and tenants' complaints and problems annually or twice a year. She also frequently protected her interests in the court of law. Margaret appeared on her own behalf and sometimes worked as an attorney for her brothers as well as other interested parties. She had become the first female landlord in Maryland. She also adopted a Piscataway Indian named Mary Kittamaquund, who was betrothed to Giles Brent in 1644.

The English Civil War between Catholics and Protestants spread to Maryland in 1644–1646, where the majority of people were Protestants but the ruling elite were Catholic. Cecil Calvert, 2nd Lord Baltimore and proprietor of Maryland, was Catholic as well as his brother, and Maryland governor, Leonard Calvert. When the colony was invaded by the Protestant tobacco trader Richard Ingle, Margaret assisted Leonard Calvert in raising local troops and some from neighboring Virginia. After the Catholics restored order, Leonard died in 1647, leaving Margaret to administer his will. Margaret sold cattle and paid dues to the troops from Virginia, who had not been paid for their service.

The events that followed made Margaret one of the famous ladies in Maryland colonial history. On January 21, 1648, Margaret appealed to Maryland's General Assembly for "a vote and voice," as she was a landowner as well as Lord Baltimore's attorney. Her request was for two votes: one for herself as a freeholder and one as attorney for Baltimore. Her plea was turned down, and Margaret protested vehemently against this move. However, the Assembly defended her against the wrath of Lord Baltimore when he heard that his cattle had been sold without his consultation. He was suspicious that a portion of his property might have gone to the Brents. The Assembly supported Margaret in dealing with Cecil's property and told him that the colony was safe in her hands during the period of crisis as the unpaid soldiers would not have treated any man with the same respect. Margaret successfully solved the crisis relating to unpaid troops facing Maryland when she sold Cecil's cattle and liquidated Leonard Calvert's assets. This sale angered Cecil, and her relations with him deteriorated. The Brent family lost favor with Cecil, who was not well disposed toward Margaret.

Margaret's brother Giles Brent abandoned his property in Maryland and claimed land in Virginia, near Aquia Creek, in December 1648. Margaret and her sister Mary followed suit. For Margaret, the situation in Maryland was not favorable. She had lost her political influence, and there was no patronage of the Calverts. The Church of Virginia had been established, and nonconformists were barred from public offices and the task of ministering. In 1651, both the sisters left Maryland for Virginia. Margaret settled in Northumberland County in the Northern Neck. She named her plantation Peace. The refugees and servants arrived at Peace in the 1650s, and the first Roman Catholic community in Virginia was nurtured. Margaret wrote a will in 1663 leaving all her property to Giles Brent and his children. She was the mistress of approximately 10,000 acres of land at the time of her death in 1671.

Margaret was the first woman in Maryland to assert her rights and was an effective landowner and manager. She proved to be a strong advocate for herself and an astute attorney in resolving the issue of executing Leonard Calvert's will and compensating the troops raised during the Protestant attack on the colony. Her legacy remained as an attorney, land magnate, and advocate of women's rights. In 2004, the Margaret Brent Elementary School was established in Stafford to honor her memory.

Patit Paban Mishra

See also: Calvert, Leonard

Further Reading

Bernhardt, Marie Frances. 1925. *Mistress Margaret Brent.* Richmond, VA: Catholic Women's Club.

Buckley, Ann. 1990. *Mistress Margaret Brent.* Annapolis: Maryland State Archives.

Davis, David. 1981. *Margaret Brent, Gentleman.* Lexington Park, MD: St. Mary's Creative Arts Forum.

Helmes, Winifred G. 1977. *Notable Maryland Women.* Cambridge, MD: Tidewater Publishers.

Loker, Aleck. 2006. *Margaret Brent: Attorney, Adventurer, and Suffragist.* Williamsburg, VA: Solitude Press.

Masson, Margaret W. 1977. *Margaret Brent, c. 1601–c. 1671, Lawyer, Landholder, Entrepreneur.* Centreville, MD: Tidewater Press.

Riordan, Timothy B. 2004. *The Plundering Time: Maryland and the English Civil War, 1645–1646.* Baltimore: Maryland Historical Society.

Spruill, Julia Cherry. 1972. *Women's Life and Work in the Southern Colonies.* New York: W. W. Norton & Company.

BUNDLING

Bundling was a quaint practice that allowed for male and female bedmates without the possibility of sexual contact and without any negative ramifications from mixed-gender sharing of a bed. The practice started in Northern Europe, perhaps in England or the Netherlands. Bundling involved one or both of the bedmates being wrapped in blankets so that intimate sexual contact could be prevented. Another common practice was to include a bundling board between the bedmates, a wooden plank that would further preclude any erotic contact. Another physical barrier could be a bundling sack, a sleeping bag of sorts, that the female would lie inside of. The origins of bundling may be found as far back as in the Bible, in Ruth 3:6–13, where Ruth is invited by Boaz to "tarry this night," leading to an alternate term for bundling, "tarrying." Puritans likely brought the practice to the North American colonies.

During the colonial era, this practice spread to the North American colonies and was a common feature of frontier life. Distances between homes were such that it was often far more convenient for a suitor or other visitor to stay overnight rather than engage in a nighttime ride back home, a ride or walk that could easily take several hours.

Bundling is often thought of as a method of allowing some intimacy between the courted and the suitor, and that was the usual case. But bundling was also used anytime a mixed-gender couple needed to share a bed and propriety was an issue. This practice would include visitors of all types and travelers staying at someone's house or even an inn. The lack of extra beds in such situations and the nature of cold winter nights made the sharing of beds a necessity, and bundling was a method to keep that practice within the bounds of good taste. In situations where sleeping arrangements were for hire, a guest could be charged a fee for half a bed. At inns and hotels, it was not unheard of for total strangers to share a bed under such circumstances. It appears the female half of the bundle would decide whether a bundling encounter would take place and, of course, with whom she would agree to bundle.

Despite the difficulties presented by bundling, couples managed to overcome the physical barriers and often experienced intimate sexual contact, with as many as a third of colonial couples engaging in premarital sex despite strong sanctions against such behavior.

Bundling became less common throughout the 19th century and was virtually a bygone practice by the 20th century, perhaps surviving among the Amish and other sects in Ohio and Pennsylvania. Of course, not everyone thought bundling was an acceptable practice, and a certain amount of particularly prudish preachers condemned the practice. A well-known theologian that indeed condemned bundling was Jonathan Edwards (1703–1758), a Congregationalist Protestant that happened to be the grandfather of future vice president of the United States Aaron Burr. Edwards was an influential theologian of his time, and his influence continues even today; his opinion certainly held some substance. (He was eventually voted out of his position by his congregation, although it is unlikely his opinion of bundling had much to do with that.)

Another theologian that condemned the practice of bundling was Rev. James Haven, but the practice was fiercely defended by Rev. Samuel Peters, who pointed out that the practice of bundling had started in the colonies from the beginning. The attack on the practice of bundling seems to have intensified after the end of the French and Indian War in 1763.

Bundling appears in cultural references today and is often depicted in film or referred to in writing. A good example of a modern depiction of bundling is found in the 2000 major motion picture *The Patriot*, in which Heath Ledger's character, Gabriel Martin, is bundled with the girl he is courting during a visit. The HBO series *Deadwood* also depicts bundling in a scene where the characters Seth and Martha Bullock, who married for convenience, are about to go to bed with an appropriate bundling board, which Martha deems unnecessary.

Matthew D. Zarzeczny

See also: Puritanism; Women

Further Reading

Ekrich, Roger A. 2005. *At Day's Close: Night in Times Past.* New York: W. W. Norton & Company.

Shachtman, Tom. 2006. *Rumspringa: To Be or Not to Be Amish.* New York: North Point Press.

Walsh, William S. 1913. *Handy Book of Curious Information.* Philadelphia: J. B. Lippincott Company.

BUNKER HILL, BATTLE OF

On June 13, 1775, the leaders of the colonial forces besieging Boston learned that the British planned to send troops out from the city to occupy the hills surrounding the city. In response, the British in Boston welcomed the mid-June arrival of 2,000 reinforcements that would allow them to conduct offensive operations. Boston was situated on a peninsula that projected into the harbor; there were two other peninsular hills that would threaten the town if not secured. Gen. Thomas Gage intended to occupy Bunker Hill to the north, then Dorchester Heights to the south, starting on June 18. However, the British plans reached the American colonists, who quickly seized Bunker Hill on the night of June 16, 1775, and built a redoubt on the summit. They also fortified a rail fence that led down the slope on one side and secured the town of Charlestown on the other side. Separated from Boston by a quarter-mile of water, these hastily built fieldworks were an affront that the British army could not allow to stand. The result was a Pyrrhic victory for the British and the first major bloody battle of the American Revolution. They captured the hill, but they suffered over 800 wounded and 226 killed, including a notably large number of officers, while the relatively inexperienced American forces were able to retreat and regroup with few casualties.

The details of the ensuing battle are well-known: the early morning discovery by British warships, rapidly assembled British boats landing troops at the hill's base, a failed attempt by British light infantry to outflank the rail fence, the British grenadiers' frontal assault bogged down by terrain obstacles and murderous musketry, harassing American shots from Charlestown silenced by incendiary mortar shells that burned the town to ashes, and a final columnar assault on the redoubt's weak right corner that carried it at bayonet point, resulting in carnage among the defenders.

Over 1,200 colonial troops under the command of William Prescott occupied Bunker Hill and Breed's Hill and built lightly fortified lines across most of the

John Trumbull's *Death of General Warren at the Battle of Bunker's Hill, June 17, 1775* is considered an iconic work of art from the American Revolution. In the first and bloodiest battle of the Revolutionary War, British troops crossed Boston Harbor to confront a force of New England militia entrenched on a small peninsula opposite the city. General Howe's men were finally able to drive off the colonial defenders after three frontal assaults, but suffered horrific casualties—almost 40 percent of the British force—as a result. (National Archives and Records Administration)

Charlestown Peninsula. Four days later, on June 17, Gen. Artemas Ward, in Boston, ordered Bunker Hill, a quarter-mile from Breed's Hill, the actual battle site, to be fortified. From there, the British launched three frontal attacks. Historians still cannot agree on who actually said, "Don't fire 'til you see the whites of their eyes," as British redcoats marched up Breed's Hill, but a soldier who misinterpreted the command fired the first shot that started the shooting. Credit for the quote is usually given to Col. William Prescott, who was killed during the battle, but this has never been proven.

When news of the battle spread through the colonies, it was seen as a loss for the American side, as the British took the ground and there were significant casualties. But the battle report, with somewhat inaccurate casualty figures, gave George Washington, who was on his way to Boston as the new commander of the Continental Army, hope that his army might prevail in the conflict.

The Massachusetts Committee of Safety, hoping to repeat the propaganda victory it had achieved after the battles at Lexington and Concord, commissioned its own battle report to send to England, but it failed to reach England before General Gage's official account arrived on July 20, 1775. The casualty counts alarmed the British military establishment, who were forced to reevaluate colonial military capability.

The battle was reported on both sides of the Atlantic, but none of the news bearers had the clear and detailed understanding of events that evolved later in war reporting. The battle dominated colonial newspapers in late June and early July; by August, accounts began to appear in the British press. Supporters of both sides viewed the battle as a victory. London's *Monthly Magazine* published both the American and British reports. In the American version, Breed's Hill became Bunker Hill. However, it was also debated that because someone incorrectly identified the hill of the actual battle, it can logically be argued that there never was a Battle of Bunker Hill but instead the Battle of Breed's Hill. The *Edinburgh Advertiser* (August 1, 1775) filled most of its eight pages with details about what it considered the biggest and bloodiest confrontation yet experienced in the American Revolution. It published General Gage's official report on the front page and four more pages of extracts from letters by witnesses and participants.

The propaganda value of this event in the United States did much to agitate American resistance to the British occupation in New England. One common tactic was to inflate the enemy's numbers while inflating their own, as the *Pennsylvania Evening Post* (Philadelphia) did in its June 29, 1775, issue when a writer who arrived in Boston while the battle was in progress overstated by a factor of two the number of regulars engaged and indicated only a quarter of the actual colonial force. Yet, his estimate of British casualties is quite accurate, though he understated American losses.

John Trumbull's painting *The Death of General Warren at the Battle of Bunker Hill* (1786) rekindled interest in the battle, but the first memorial was not erected until 1794. The Bunker Hill Monument, completed in 1842 and dedicated a year later, is now listed as a National Historic Landmark. It is actually located on Breed's Hill, not Bunker Hill, and it remains a favorite destination in the Charlestown section of Boston. Situated on the hill, it is quite recognizable from the air on approaches to Logan Airport, and it is fairly visible from different parts of the city.

Martin J. Manning

See also: Committees of Correspondence; Gage, Thomas

Further Reading

Andrlik, Todd, comp. 2012. *Reporting the Revolutionary War: Before It Was History, It Was News.* Naperville, IL: Sourcebooks.

Farrar, Frederic B. 1975. *This Common Channel to Independence: Revolution and Newspapers, 1759–1789.* Garden City, NY: Farrar.

Kammen, Michael G. 1988. *A Season of Youth: The American Revolution and the Historical Imagination.* Ithaca, NY: Cornell University Press.

Scheer, George F., and Rankin, Hugh F., eds. 1987. *Rebels and Redcoats: The American Revolution through the Eyes of Those Who Fought and Lived It.* New York: Da Capo Press.

Stewart, Richard W., ed. 2004. *The United States Army and the Forging of a Nation, 1775–1917.* Vol. 1 of *American Military History.* Washington, D.C.: Center of Military History, U.S. Army.

BURKE, EDMUND (1729–1797)

Edmund Burke was a British statesman, philosopher, and political theorist during the period known as the Enlightenment. He was a renowned orator, especially during his time serving in Parliament. Burke is distinguished for his somewhat anti-establishment bent. Despite being an Anglican, he expressed enthusiastic support of Catholic emancipation, the movement in 18th- and 19th-century England to reduce the restrictions on Catholics that had been various English laws, such as the Act of Uniformity and the Test Act. He often considered himself an Englishman while never renouncing his Irishness. Moreover, he was one of the most outspoken of the British politicians who supported the American Revolution (1775–1783). Despite his encouragement of the American cause, he was fiercely against the later French Revolution, which swept France several years after the American Revolution had concluded.

Edmund Burke was born in Dublin, Ireland, on January 12, 1729, the son of a prominent lawyer. His initial education came at a Quaker school in County Kildare, about 40 miles from his home in Dublin. In 1744, he enrolled at Trinity College. While there, he established a collegiate debate society, Edmund Burke's Club, which would later merge with the school's Historical Club to form the College Historical Society (CHS). The CHS, also known as "The Hist," is the oldest surviving undergraduate student organization in the world. Burke graduated from Trinity in 1748 and, despite his own misgivings, traveled to London to study law at the Middle Temple. His decision was more to satisfy his father than out of his own personal desire, and he soon abandoned legal study to travel throughout Continental Europe. This seems to have caused an estrangement between Burke and his father.

He returned to England in the early 1750s, devoting much of the rest of the decade to his efforts as a writer. He published his first book, *A Vindication of Natural Society*, in the spring of 1756 to generally positive reviews, though some readers confused the satirical work as actually having been written by the target of Burke's satire, the Lord Bolingbroke. A year later, Burke's only solely philosophical treatise was released. Titled *A Philosophical Enquiry into the Origin of Our Ideas of the Sublime and Beautiful*, it was a study of aesthetics. In it, Burke argues that beauty comprises those things that are well formed and aesthetically pleasing, while "the sublime" has the capacity to compel and, potentially, to destroy us. The book was well received and came to the attention of intellectual luminaries on mainland Europe, including Denis Diderot and Immanuel Kant, although Kant's impressions were somewhat negative. In 1758, Burke founded the *Annual Register*, wherein prominent intellectuals offered interpretations of the significant international political events taking place in the preceding year. The *Register* is still published today.

Burke's political career began in December 1765. That year, he became the private secretary to Charles, Marquess of Rockingham, one of the leading members of the Whig party at the time. Such a prominent political connection helped Burke to secure election to the House of Commons as member for a small community called Wendover, in Buckinghamshire, near London. He would later represent Bristol, at the time Britain's second-largest city. Burke's first speech in Parliament immediately secured his reputation as one of the finest orators in England and, according to some observers, in all of Europe. It was this oratorical mastery that would connect Burke to the course of American history.

During the reigns of George I and George II, the monarch was somewhat less influential relative to Parliament. George III, however, worked to reassert the Crown's executive authority. This rankled the more liberal-leaning Burke, who spoke out against what he saw as antirepublican tendencies by the Crown and the ministry. His *Thoughts on the Cause of the Present Discontents*, published in April 1770, argues that vibrant and politically equal opposition parties are necessary to prevent abuses by the monarch or by factions within a government. From Burke's perspective, the dealings of the king and his ministry toward the American colonies during the 1760s and 1770s were clear evidence of such a dangerous tendency. As such, he spoke out against parliamentary laws such as the Stamp Act and the Townshend Duties as being inappropriate for the colonies.

By the 1770s, the Crown and many members of Parliament had hardened their views of the American rebellion. Burke disagreed. He believed that the colonists were expressing through their actions many of the concerns he had expressed in speeches and in writing. In March 1775, Burke delivered a speech in Parliament encouraging reconciliation with the colonies. He argued that America's growing population and economic power would be beneficial to the empire and that waging a destructive war to retain control of the colonies would make any subsequent peace even harder to manage, as the underlying objections of the patriots would not be ameliorated by the force of Britain's arms. Moreover, such a war would potentially lay waste to the natural wealth the colonies could provide the empire in peacetime. Burke's arguments and his suggested peace were rendered moot by the events at Lexington and Concord less than a month later.

Throughout the war, Burke continued to advocate for the American position to his colleagues in Parliament. The Revolution, he said, was no threat to England's government, nor was it a danger to republicanism in Britain. Indeed, Burke expressed his excitement and intellectual curiosity at the republican possibilities America's potential independence might bring. It should be noted, however, that Burke was no fan of democracy. It was this distinction that caused him to speak in favor of the American colonists but to speak out against the revolution in France.

Whereas Burke was encouraged by the republican sensibilities of the Americans, he feared the unrestricted democratic passions set loose by the French Revolution as it progressed into its middle and later stages. Moreover, the French Revolution, happening as it was on the continent of Europe, was a more proximate threat to the stability of other European states, including Britain. He expressed his views in the 1790 pamphlet *Reflections on the Revolution in France*. His work provoked a sort of war among pamphleteers, with two of the most celebrated works of the 1790s, Mary Wollstonecraft's *A Vindication of the Rights of Men* and Thomas Paine's *The Rights of Man* coming out within a year, in direct answer to Burke's piece.

Burke's political career ended with his retirement from Parliament in 1794. His positions on contemporary issues had made him a number of political enemies, and he spent his final years defending himself from his critics. Nonetheless, his speeches and publications mark him as one of the most influential figures in the British conservative political tradition. He died on July 9, 1797, at his home in Beaconsfield, Buckinghamshire, England.

Shawn Selby

See also: George III

Further Reading

Bourke, Richard. 2015. *Empire and Revolution: The Political Life of Edmund Burke*. Princeton, NJ: Princeton University Press.

Maciag, Drew. 2013. *Edmund Burke in America: The Contested Career of the Father of Modern Conservatism*. Ithaca, NY: Cornell University Press.

C

CABEZA DE VACA, ALVAR NÚÑEZ (CA. 1490–CA. 1560)

Alvar Núñez Cabeza de Vaca was a Spanish conquistador in the Americas. As a member of the ill-fated expedition of Pánfilo de Narváez in 1527, he was one of the only four survivors. In his book, *The Account*, Cabeza de Vaca recounts his travels in the Southwest of the United States, living among several Native American groups. After almost 10 years of vicissitudes in America, he was found by Spanish troops and was able to return to Spain.

Cabeza de Vaca was born in Jerez de la Frontera, Spain, ca. 1490, into a prestigious family. His maternal grandfather was Pedro de Vera, who had conquered the Canary Islands for Spain, brutally repressing the Native inhabitants in the process. Moreover, his family name, Cabeza de Vaca (meaning "cow's head"), came from the legend of a shepherd who had helped the Spaniards during the *Reconquista* by showing them a safe way, which he marked with a cow's head, thence the name.

On June 17, 1527, the expedition commanded by Pánfilo de Narváez sailed off Sanlúcar de Barrameda, Cádiz (Spain), with the goal of colonizing the territories between Río de las Palmas (eastern Mexico) and Florida. With its 400 men and 80 horses, it constituted one of the biggest and best-equipped Spanish expeditions ever. Narváez had successfully participated in the conquest of Cuba (1511–1514) and had been second in command to Velázquez, the governor of the island. For Narváez, this expedition was a decisive opportunity to regain his past military glory, which had been stained by his humiliating defeat to Hernán Cortés's troops seven years earlier. He had to prove to himself, the king, the court, and, most importantly, his own men that he represented the military glory of the old days. This, along with his emotionalism and tendency to make rushed decisions, might explain some of the desperate and risky decisions he took and that would be much questioned by Cabeza de Vaca as treasurer and second-in-command.

After two rather prolonged stops in Santo Domingo and Cuba because of storms and a series of misfortunes (including the shipwreck of two ships), they eventually landed in Florida on Maundy Thursday (the Thursday prior to Easter Sunday) 1528. Having landed in a place their pilot, Miruelo, was unable to identify, they were completely at a loss about their exact location. Nevertheless, Narváez made the decision to send the ships ahead of the terrestrial party. This, together with his decision to go farther inland to find the province of Apalachee, reported to contain gold, led to the ultimate loss of the terrestrial expedition, separated from the ships.

Conflicts with the Native Americans soon erupted, and the barges they built with the scarce materials available to them shipwrecked. Having lost contact with the ships, which eventually returned to New Spain after searching for them in vain for a year, the surviving members of the expedition scattered. With little knowledge about America and no means to return to Spain, Cabeza de Vaca and his companions had to rely on Native Americans, despite their suspicions of human sacrifices. Helpless, they became slaves to the Native Americans. Cabeza de Vaca would not return to Spain until 1537, spending the years in between living among different Native American groups, among whom he performed different roles, until he was found by Spanish troops. Cabeza de Vaca was then tempted by Viceroy Antonio de Mendoza to return to Florida with a fully equipped expedition to try to discover the fabled Native American cities made of gold about which rumors abounded. However, he turned down Mendoza's offer.

The Account (alternatively known as *La Relación* or *Naufragios*, first published in Spanish in 1542) is the chronicle of the almost decade-long wanderings of three conquistadors, Cabeza de Vaca, Andrés Dorante, and Alonso Castillo, and Estebanico, a Muslim slave. Cabeza de Vaca wrote it upon his return to Spain as part of his petition to Charles I of Spain for a royal pension and other honors in return for what he deemed a valuable contribution to the advancement of the Spanish presence in the Americas. His contribution was just from a literary point of view, as they had actually taken possession of no new territories. Cabeza de Vaca's work originally followed the formal structure of the *relación* (account). However, it soon departed from the rigid conventions of the genre to, instead, create a highly original text that not only included elements of the *relación* but also of other colonial texts, such as letters to the king, the *crónica de Indias* (chronicle of Indies), natural histories, the romance of chivalry, picaresque novels, moral novels, and pastorals. In conveying the miracles and supernatural occurrences that he claimed to have been a witness to, if not maker of, in the Southwest, his account at times reads like an adventure story, closer to such works as *The Travels of Marco Polo* or Christopher Columbus's letters.

Cabeza de Vaca was responsible for creating a vision of the Southwest that would, over the years, become deeply ingrained in the popular imagination. After failing to secure the post of *Adelantado* to Florida, Cabeza de Vaca was appointed *Adelantado* to Río de la Plata (present-day Argentina), but this second stint in America had an even worse ending: he was returned to Spain in chains and died in poverty and obscurity.

M. Carmen Gómez-Galisteo

See also: Mesoamerica; New Spain

Further Reading

Glantz, Margo, ed. 1993. *Notas y comentarios sobre Álvar Núñez Cabeza de Vaca.* México D.F.: Grijalbo.

Gomez-Galisteo, M. Carmen. 2014. *Early Visions and Representations of America: Alvar Núñez Cabeza de Vaca's* Naufragios *and William Bradford's* Of Plymouth Plantation. New York, London, New Delhi, and Sydney: Bloomsbury.

Hickerson, Nancy. 1998. "How Cabeza de Vaca Lived with, Worked among, and Finally Left the Indians of Texas." *Journal of Anthropological Research* 54: 199–218.
Maura, Juan Francisco. 2008. *El gran burlador de América: Álvar Núñez Cabeza de Vaca.* Valencia: Parnaseo.
Worth, John E., ed. 2014. *Discovering Florida: First-Contact Narratives from Spanish Expeditions along the Lower Gulf Coast.* Gainesville and others: University Press of Florida.

CABOT, JOHN (CA. 1450–CA. 1500) AND SEBASTIAN (CA. 1474–CA. 1557)

Soon after the news of the discoveries of Christopher Columbus spread through Europe, the thirst for the New World afflicted other powerful countries. Henry VII of England eagerly jumped into the exploration of the New World for possible exploitation by the English by commissioning an Italian, John Cabot, otherwise known as Giovanni Caboto, to explore what is now known as North America. John's son, Sebastian Cabot, worked primarily for the Spanish Crown in exploring the New World, establishing the first European settlements in what is now Uruguay and Argentina.

Cabot was born in Genoa and a citizen of Venice. He was a financial failure in Italy and moved to Spain to evade creditors. Spain proved no more lucrative, and Cabot headed to England to seek sponsorship for a voyage of discovery. Cabot made his first voyage in 1496, leaving from Bristol, England, with the intention of maintaining a westerly course at that higher latitude, making for a shorter voyage. Bad weather caused his single ship to turn back, and a second voyage for 1497 was planned.

This second voyage, on the ship the *Matthew*, successfully reached what is now Newfoundland, Canada, but failed to find passage to China by the rumored "Northwest Passage," the original goal. This voyage gave Cabot and his crew claim as the first Europeans to land on the North American mainland since the Viking expeditions 400 years earlier. Much of what is known about this second voyage stems from the "John Day Letter," a letter written (possibly) to Christopher Columbus by an English merchant.

Failing to meet any Native Americans, but finding traces of their existence, Cabot planted the English and Papal flags, claiming the land for the king of England and the Catholic Church. For his voyage, Cabot was paid £10. He was later granted a pension of £20 per year for his service to the Crown.

The lack of first-person accounts of the second voyage has led to debate among scholars as to where Cabot actually landed and what lands he explored. Newfoundland seems likely, but present-day Nova Scotia or Maine, among others, have also been presented as possible landing points.

In 1498, Cabot led another expedition, this time with five ships, one of which only made it to Ireland. The other four ships, laden with trinkets to trade with Native Americans, continued the voyage, but little is known of their fate. Some believe all the ships were eventually lost on the voyage, but historian Alwyn Ruddock believed Cabot explored the coast of North America from Canada south to the Chesapeake or even to the Caribbean.

Ruddock believed at least one of Cabot's ships returned to England in 1500, although no particular record of that exists. A tantalizing rumor of John Cabot having been in London in 1500 has not been corroborated. Ruddock also argued that friars with that second expedition, led by Fr. Giovanni Antonio de Carbonariis, were left in Newfoundland to form a mission. If this claim is true, this mission would have been the first Christian European settlement in North America. Likewise, if true, a church would have been built, making it the first and only medieval church in North America. Researchers Margaret Condon and Evan Jones of the University of Bristol believe they have found reason to believe Ruddock was correct in her analysis.

In any event, eager to exploit the "Isle of New Finding," as Newfoundland was being called at the time, Henry VII commissioned another explorer, Hugh Eliot, to mount an expedition, paying Eliot an unprecedented £100.

Meanwhile, John's son, Sebastian Cabot, made at least one voyage of discovery under warrant for England, searching for the Northwest Passage in 1508. Of course, like others, Sebastian did not find such a northern route to the Pacific through the Arctic Ocean, as ice prevented passage by ship. Sebastian also continued his exploration south along the North American coast, possibly nearly to Florida.

Sebastian made another voyage in 1516, this time to the West Indies and Brazil with Adm. Sir Thomas Spert. Sebastian then changed his allegiance and worked for the Spanish Crown, mounting a four-ship expedition with the overly ambitious goals of circumnavigating the globe, determining the exact location by astronomical observation of the demarcation line of the Treaty of Tordesillas (separating Spanish and Portuguese spheres of control), delivering settlers to the Molucca Islands (present-day Indonesia), "discovering" Cipango (Japan) and Eastern Cathay (China), and mapping both coasts of South America and islands in the Pacific along the way.

As it was, Sebastian abandoned these goals and searched the South American coast and up the Rio de la Plata in a vain attempt to find the riches he had heard rumors of upon landing in Brazil. While searching for riches, Cabot established the first European settlements in what is now Uruguay and Argentina. Nevertheless, Sebastian had to contend with a mutiny, for which he marooned the mutineers. Returning to Spain in 1530, Sebastian was tried and convicted for not following orders and other offenses, receiving a sentence of banishment to Oran, North Africa. Sebastian never served his exile, retaining an appointment by the Spanish king as pilot major until retiring to England in 1547. Sebastian is presumed to have died around 1557, circumstances unknown.

Unfortunately, like his father, Sebastian's accounts of his voyages have been lost, and little remains about these explorers and their voyages for scholars to study. Some people living in the 16th through 19th centuries even believed it was Sebastian, and not John, that led the Bristol expeditions, probably due to claims by Sebastian in his old age. Some have even claimed that Bristol sailors had visited the New World even before Cabot first set foot in England. Either way, these two Cabots left their mark on the European conquest of the New World.

Matthew D. Zarzeczny

See also: England; Spain; Treaty of Tordesillas

Further Reading

Croxton, Derek. 1990–1991. "The Cabot Dilemma: John Cabot's 1497 Voyage & the Limits of Historiography." *Essays in History* 33. http://www.essaysinhistory.com/articles/2012/87.

Hunter, Douglas. 2011. *The Race to the New World: Christopher Columbus, John Cabot, and a Lost History of Discovery.* New York: Macmillan.

Ruddock, Alwyn A. 1974. "The Reputation of Sebastian Cabot." *Historical Research* 42: 95–99.

CACAO

The cacao tree is indigenous to certain regions in South America. It is the source of cacao beans, from which chocolate is derived. These beans were important in many societies as a source of nutrients. More importantly, though, they came to occupy a niche as a cultural artifact that was utilized in several different ways. Ideas surrounding the beans relate to wealth, status, gender, and sacred ceremonial practices. It was given its Latin name, *Theobroma cacao* ("food of the gods") by the Swedish botanist Charles Linnaeus in the mid-18th century.

Cacao is native to the upper Amazon basin, and it also grows along the west coast of the Andes Mountains. Early Native people transplanted cacao widely, and it is grown extensively in Guatemala, the Yucatan, and Honduras. Later, in the 18th century, it was brought to West Africa as a cash crop. There are several varieties of the cacao tree, though they all seem to thrive best in lowland tropical regions. It is a cauliflory tree, meaning that flowers grow directly out of the trunk and older limbs, giving it a unique appearance. These flowers produce long pods that range in color from pink to brown and contain seeds, commonly referred to as beans, housed in a sweet white pulp.

The beans themselves are extremely bitter, and it is likely that the pulp was gathered and used before people discovered the process that renders the beans edible. The pulp is still used in juices and jellies, but the beans are the reason for cacao tree cultivation. Once harvested, the beans are fermented and then dried and roasted. The hard shells are then cracked to reach the nibs within. These nibs are still bitter, but they can now be ground into a powder to make what we have come to know as cocoa, a frothy chocolaty drink. Cacao beans contain as much as 50 percent fat, so additional processes were perfected by early cacao drinkers to make the drink more pleasant. Additions of spices as well as maize flour were common.

Known as the mother culture of Mesoamerica, the Olmecs seem to be the first people to use cacao. Their civilization flourished from around 1500 BCE to around 400 BCE, during which time they produced many beautiful objects, including pottery. In 2006, scientists from Hershey Foods analyzed scraping from an ancient Olmec vessel and confirmed the chemical signatures of cacao. This indicates that the Olmecs were the first to carry out the chocolate-making process. Because they left no decipherable written language, how they used the chocolate, aside from eating, remains unknown.

The Maya, on the other hand, left a great deal of information about the role cacao played in their society. During the long Preclassic Period, the Maya developed a

The cacao tree is indigenous to certain regions of South America and is the source of cacao beans, from which chocolate is derived. Cacao played a central role in many religious and cultural activities of the Mesoamerican civilizations and later became a popular commodity for Europeans as part of the Columbian Exchange. (Howard Sandler/Dreamstime.com)

relationship with the Olmec that, at the very least, included trade. Their use of chocolate probably dates back to these affiliations, sometime around 1000 BCE. In any case, the use of cacao was frequently recorded at their height, in what is known as the Classic Period, 250 CE–800 CE. For instance, cacao plays a role in the Maya creation story. Two attempts by the gods at creating man had failed. When it was proposed to make man from the foods that give sustenance, which included cacao, mankind came into the world, though maize was the real hero. In many of the Maya inscriptions that have survived the ravages of conquest and time, deities are represented holding cacao pods. Cacao appears most frequently as a grave good in depictions of the burials of elite members of society.

Social hierarchy was a very important element of Maya culture. Chocolate likely played a role in that system during the Classic Period. Cacao beans had value, and their uniform shape, size, and weight led to their use as a form of currency in the Maya and Aztec civilizations. In these rigidly hierarchical societies, the consumption of cacao beans was likely practiced more frequently among the wealthy elite than the laboring classes. This meant that domestic cacao consumption became a sort of decadent status symbol. However, beans could be used to purchase a variety of goods on the market. These markets were large and thriving places with wide varieties of goods available, and cacao played a central role in the commerce therein.

Both Aztec and Maya priests used cacao in religious rituals. Bloodletting and human sacrifice have long been associated with these Mesoamerican civilizations.

While these practices are based in fact, they should not be considered the central elements of these religious complexes. Cacao played a central role in many ritual activities. Marriage, birth, and coming of age were all ritual events that included the consumption of cacao. Aside from these happy instances, cacao was ritually consumed to prepare for war and was sacrificed to deities to invoke favor. In some rituals, chocolate was dyed red and used to represent blood.

When the Spanish first encountered cacao, during their exploration and conquest of Mesoamerica, they did not like it. The flavor was bitter, and the color was off-putting. Conquistadors remarked on the variety of ways the Maya consumed it, drinking it both hot and cold; powdering it and adding spices, even chilies; and serving it in a bowl as a sort of gruel. It was not until the Spaniards added sugar and vanilla to the cocoa that they found it palatable. The first commercial shipment of cacao to Spain was in 1585, where it became a favorite of the ladies at court. Soon cacao became a commodity that regularly crossed the Atlantic as part of the Columbian Exchange. Eventually, the tempering and sweetening of chocolate would become associated with places such as Belgium and Switzerland.

European transgressions in Mesoamerica had an impact on the domestic use of chocolate. By the 17th century, chocolate was being consumed more frequently by people of all social classes. It had not been relegated to a mundane food item, however, but still held ritual power for many who imbibed. The caffeine in chocolate made it an important aid during long ceremonies, such as the all-night wakes that preceded the burial of the dead. It was also believed by many to have healing powers and the ability to ward off disease. In large urban centers, a large percent of the population was ingesting chocolate in some form nearly every day.

The beliefs of the indigenous people in regard to the power of chocolate were worrying to the Spanish colonial administrators. This was a period of intense concern over traditional religious practices, which would often end up before the Inquisition. Women took care of most of the domestic duties in colonial New Spain, and as such, they were responsible for making the chocolate. This became a way for them to access certain power dynamics in society, as chocolate became a medium for their so-called witchcraft. It was widely believed that chocolate was an aphrodisiac, and women were accused of making love potions with it and otherwise preparing it in such a way as to confuse the minds of their husbands. It was a daunting prospect to accept a chocolate beverage from a woman who might hold a grudge against you.

With the demand for chocolate rising throughout Europe and the Americas, new lands were sought that could sustain the finicky cacao tree. In 1822, seeds were planted in São Tomé, off the coast of West Africa, where they flourished. From there, cacao trees became a standard cash crop in Nigeria, Ghana, Cameroon, Sierra Leone, and other West African nations. Large corporations such as Cadbury-Schweppes and Nestlé needed more beans to fill the orders of their booming industry and drove the agricultural project in West Africa. Today, nearly 70 percent of all chocolate comes from West Africa. The industry has been flagged for human rights and labor violations on several grounds. Child labor is prevalent, and many believe that the chocolate plantations are a leading factor in the kidnapping of children for the agricultural slave trade.

Cacao has been used by civilizations for millennia. While most of its utility lies in its consumption, it has represented so much more than a simple food item. Religious, economic, and gendered ideas have surrounded the bean and continue to do so. Its cultivation and use were central elements to many societies in the ancient Americas. Once encountered by Europeans, chocolate and its uses spread throughout the Atlantic World. As a decadent treat, chocolate still retains some of its power. It is a romantic gift, it is thought to bring cheer, and it is imbibed by young and old alike.

Justin Power

See also: Agriculture; Aztec; Columbian Exchange; Maya; Mesoamerica

Further Reading

Coe, Sophie D., and Michael Coe. 2000. *The True History of Chocolate.* New York: Thames and Hudson.

Few, Martha. 2005. "Chocolate, Sex, and Disorderly Women in Late-Seventeenth- and Early-Eighteenth-Century Guatemala." *Ethnohistory* 52, no. 4. 673–687.

Ryan, Orla. 2011. *Chocolate Nations: Living and Dying for Cocoa in West Africa.* London: Zed Books.

CALVERT, GEORGE (1580–1632)

George Calvert was an English statesman and colonizer who converted to Catholicism in the early 17th century, at a time when Catholics faced widespread persecution. His service for James I, however, earned him something of a reprieve from the struggles other Catholics faced, and at the end of his political service, he was granted a peerage in Ireland and given the title 1st Lord Baltimore. Calvert's dream was to establish a colony in North America where Catholics could find refuge while still maintaining their allegiance to the English Crown. His first attempt at such a colony was Avalon, a settlement on the coast of Newfoundland. When the harsh climate contributed to the collapse of Avalon, Calvert set his sights on land along the Chesapeake Bay. Although he died before the establishment of the colony, his dream would eventually be realized with the creation of the Maryland Colony in 1632.

George Calvert was born in 1580, at Kipling, North Yorkshire, to Alicia Crossland and Leonard Calvert, and he was raised as a Protestant. He graduated from Trinity College, Oxford, in 1597, and in 1603, he married Anne Mayne at St Peter's, Cornhill, in London. The couple had 11 children. The two of note were the eldest son, Cecil, who became the first lord proprietary of the Maryland Colony in New World, and the second son, Leonard, who served as the first governor of the colony. George Calvert was the private secretary to Sir Robert Cecil, one of the most powerful men in the court of James I. This position also propelled Calvert into prominence within the government. He became a clerk of the Crown for the Connaught province and was elected to Parliament from the Bossiney constituency in 1609. After four years, he was appointed as a clerk of the Privy Council. Through his service to the government, Calvert became close with James I. In 1610 and 1611, the king sent him as an emissary to European countries such as Holland and France. Two years afterward, he went to Ireland as a member of the commission to inquire about the problems faced by the Roman Catholics there.

In 1625, remarkable change occurred in his life when Calvert converted to Catholicism. Due to an English law prohibiting Catholics from holding positions in the government, he voluntarily stepped down from the position of secretary of state in February 1625. In appreciation of his loyalty to the king and for his service in royal administration, he was raised to the Irish peerage as 1st Baron Baltimore in County Longford. After the death of James I in March 1625, his successor, Charles I, wanted Calvert's services and was willing to permit him to serve without taking the mandatory oath of allegiance that recognized the king as supreme in civil and religious affairs. But Calvert declined and concentrated on colonial ventures.

Calvert was passionate about colonial affairs. In 1621, he bought a portion of land in Newfoundland from William Vaughan that had been set aside for the creation of an English colony. He paid the sum of £25,000 and founded the Colony of Avalon at Ferryland, Newfoundland. His purchase was confirmed by the king in April 1623, and Calvert became the master of the land encompassing Ferryland to Petty Harbor. The northwest and western limits were Conception Bay and Placentia Bay.

In July 1627, Calvert arrived at Ferryland accompanied by two Roman Catholic priests. By this time, the population of the colony had increased to more than 100. Soon after landing, one of the priests established the first Catholic ministry on British soil in North America. Calvert returned the next year with his new wife, Jane; several of his children; and 40 Catholic settlers. But George not only faced an inhospitable climate resulting in scurvy and food shortages, but also raids by the French privateers.

As Avalon struggled, Calvert looked for a more congenial place to set up a colony. He found it farther south, in Virginia, and appealed for a new charter for an area inside Virginia. Without waiting for the king's order, he sailed with his wife in October 1629 for Virginia. They arrived in Jamestown but were not welcomed there by the Protestants. Calvert was asked by the governor and his council to take an oath of allegiance and supremacy; otherwise, he should leave immediately for England. Calvert refused to take the oath, choosing instead to leave his wife and servants while he returned to London to petition for the charter. There was a strong lobby in England against Calvert that frustrated his efforts. The Protestant-dominated Parliament, the Virginia Company, and William Claiborne, a prominent figure in the Jamestown Colony, all tried their best to dissuade the king from granting a charter. Claiborne argued that settlers of Virginia had a right over the land, and he accused Calvert of refusing to take the Oath of Allegiance, which would obviate his right to have a colony.

Calvert's supporters argued on his behalf for a separate colony in the Chesapeake Bay area. At last, the king relented, granting an area north as well as east of the Potomac River situated on either side of Chesapeake Bay. The name Calvert desired for the colony was Crescentia, but he left the name of the colony blank while drawing up the charter. As per the wish of Charles I, the designated name was Maryland, in honor of his wife, Henrietta Maria, herself a Catholic from France. The ensuing economic benefit and a colony for the Catholics free from religious persecution in the motherland made Calvert happy. Unfortunately, Calvert was not able to see the full realization of his dream. He died of illness at Lincoln's Inn Fields, London, on April 15, 1632; the charter for Maryland was granted about five weeks after his demise.

Cecil George, the eldest son and 2nd Lord Baltimore, took necessary steps for colonization. He became the first proprietor of the province of Maryland after he was granted the charter by Charles I, on June 20, 1632. He was "Absolute Lord of Maryland and Avalon." Two ships, the *Ark* and the *Dove*, carrying immigrants and the first governor, Leonard Calvert, the second son of George and Cecil's younger brother, sailed from England in November 1633. St. Mary's City, on the Chesapeake Bay, became Maryland's first capital. The dream of George Calvert materialized as Maryland became a safe refuge for Catholic settlers.

George Calvert was an industrious, cautious, and intelligent person who performed his duties to the best of his ability. His command over languages, his inquisitive nature, and his administrative acumen resulted in his steady rise. He was a loyal servant of the king while in administration, but he showed his true mettle after resigning from service. His longing for the establishment of colonies had left a legacy of pluralism and the beginnings of rapprochement between Catholics and Protestants.

Patit Paban Mishra

See also: Calvert, Leonard; Catholicism; Maryland

Further Reading

Browne, William H. 1890. *George Calvert and Cecilius Calvert: Barons Baltimore of Baltimore.* New York: Dodd, Mead.

Codignola, Luca. 1988. *The Coldest Harbor of the Land: Simon Stock and Lord Baltimore's Colony in Newfoundland, 1621–1649.* Kingston, ON, Canada: McGill-Queen's University Press.

Foster, James W. 1983. *George Calvert: The Early Years.* Baltimore, MD: Maryland Historical Society.

Krugler, John D. 2004. *English and Catholic: The Lords Baltimore in the Seventeenth Century.* Baltimore, MD: Johns Hopkins University Press.

Land, Aubrey C. 1981. *Colonial Maryland: A History.* Millwood, NY: KTO Press.

Lough, Loree. 2000. *Lord Baltimore: English Politician and Colonist.* Philadelphia: Chelsea House Publishers. http://www.heritage.nf.ca/articles/politics/proprietary-george-calvert.php.

CALVERT, LEONARD (1606–1647)

Leonard Calvert was the first colonial governor of Maryland during the period 1633–1647. The English Civil War (1642–1651) spilled into the colony during his tenure when Richard Ingle, a supporter of the Parliamentarian forces in England, landed on the shores of Maryland with a band of armed men and the intention of capturing the colony. Ingle no doubt hoped that taking control of Maryland would be a coup for Parliament while also being a blow to the Crown. Although he was forced to flee Maryland, Calvert maintained command of the local militia and reclaimed control of the colony in 1647.

Calvert was born to Anne Mynne and George Calvert in 1606. George Calvert had been adorned with the title Baron of Baltimore by James I, and he became the 1st Lord Baltimore in February 1625. Leonard's eldest brother, Cecil Calvert, became 2nd Lord Baltimore after their father's death in April 1632. Cecil Calvert became the first proprietor of the province of Maryland after he was granted a charter by Charles I in June 1632. Thus, Maryland became a proprietary colony of the Catholic Calvert family. It was Cecil who ordered his younger brother to serve as the colony's first governor.

The Calvert family established the colony of Maryland to have a safe refuge for Catholics and to generate wealth for the family. Almost half of the immigrants were Catholics who had fled varying degrees of persecution in Great Britain. During the 17th century, England struggled with the question of religious toleration as Catholics were persecuted for not subscribing to the precepts of the Church of England. At the same time, Puritans accused the Church of England of being too Catholic in trappings and liturgy.

Many of Maryland's first settlers, including the new governor, sailed from England, in November 1633, aboard two ships, the *Ark* and the *Dove*. The ships arrived in the following spring, and the immigrants searched for a location to establish their settlement. The governor parleyed with indigenous Piscataway and Yaocomaco tribes for land acquisition. These local tribes traded land in exchange for gifts, guarantees of commerce, and also for promises of protection against rival Iroquois and Susquehannock Indians. It was on this land that the English settlement of St. Mary's City was set up along the banks of St. Mary's River, a tributary of the Potomac River. Leonard also ordered construction of a fort equipped with cannons. St. Mary's City on Chesapeake Bay became the colony's first capital.

The settlers, numbering about 140, included 20 gentlemen, 2 Catholic priests, and indentured servants, mostly Protestant. The colonists also erected a small wooden chapel. They learned farming skills from the local Native peoples. By the end of the 17th century, tobacco production had become the mainstay of the Maryland economy.

As per his elder brother's instruction, Leonard administered the colony in an almost absolutist fashion, but life was not easy for Leonard's retinue. Disease was a constant threat to the settlers, and the Piscataway Indians regularly raided English settlements. And a long-standing feud between Maryland and Virginia began almost as soon as the Maryland colony had been established. William Claiborne, a Virginia planter, contested the claims by Calvert and the Maryland colony of control over Kent Island in the Chesapeake Bay. This dispute sometimes resulted in armed action on both sides.

In addition, the religious tensions common to England at the time had also spread to the colonies. In 1635, Calvert was forced to convene the first Assembly to meet. After several years of attempting to rule the colony as a sort of petty monarch, the governor was now subordinate to the Assembly. In 1638, the Assembly brought the governor to heel by asserting that only the Assembly had the power to enact legislation and requiring that Calvert henceforth had to govern the colony in accordance with the common law of England.

During the English Civil War, the relations between Roman Catholics and Protestants in England deteriorated to a great extent, which also affected Maryland society. In the colony, the rich and ruling elite belonged to the Catholic faith, whereas the workforce was composed mainly of Protestants. The English Civil War eventually spilled over to the colony. In 1638, Leonard Calvert seized a trading post at Kent Island, in the Chesapeake Bay. The post had been established by Virginia merchant (and Protestant) William Claiborne seven years earlier. Claiborne had previously appealed to Charles I that the Calverts had no right over Maryland, but the king's directive was in favor of the Calverts.

The conflict with William Claiborne would also ensnare Calvert's extended family, the Brents. Although records are spotty, there is evidence to suggest that Leonard was married to Ann Brent, the sister of Giles Brent, a prominent member of Maryland society. What is known for certain is that Leonard had two children, a son, William, and a daughter, Anne, who grew up in England.

Leonard named Giles Brent acting governor during a visit to England in 1643–1644. Shortly after Calvert's return to Maryland in 1644, William Claiborne may have sided with another Protestant and supporter of the Parliamentarian side in the civil war, Richard Ingle, to raid the colony of Maryland. Ingle, a Protestant tobacco trader and captain of the ship *Reformation*, began plundering the property of Catholics in Maryland. Giles Brent, along with some Jesuit priests, was imprisoned and deported to England. Leonard and some other Catholics escaped to Virginia and organized a militia for a counterattack. Giles's sister, Margaret, remained in Maryland and raised a volunteer group to fight with the militia. Saint Mary's City again came under Leonard's control in 1646, restoring the Calverts to power in Maryland.

Leonard died of an illness on June 9, 1647. On his deathbed, he executed a will naming Margaret Brent the administrator of his estate. She also possessed the power of attorney of Leonard Calvert's brother and the proprietor of Maryland, Lord Baltimore. Leonard had in his possession 9,000 acres of land at the time of his death. Margaret paid the soldiers, who were on the verge of rebellion, by selling cattle and some other property that belonged to Leonard and his brother. These events made Margaret famous when she demanded a seat in the Assembly by virtue of her direct involvement in the oversight of economic and political affairs of the colony. Her request was denied. Thomas Greene, named in the will, succeeded Leonard as the governor of Maryland.

Patit Paban Mishra

See also: Brent, Margaret Reed; Calvert, George; Catholicism; Maryland; Tobacco Cultivation; Toleration Acts

Further Reading

Doak, Robin S. 2007. *Maryland, 1634–1776*. Washington, D.C.: National Geographic.

Jensen, Ann, and Marcy Dunn Ramsey. 1998. *Leonard Calvert and the Maryland Adventure*. Centreville, MD: Tidewater Publishers.

Krugler, John D. 2004. *English and Catholic: The Lords Baltimore in the Seventeenth Century.* Baltimore, MD: Johns Hopkins University Press.
Land, Aubrey C. 1981. *Colonial Maryland: A History*. Millwood, NY: KTO Press.
Liston, Paul F. 1993. *The Plundering Time: The Hardships of Southern Maryland Catholics in Colonial Times.* Berwyn, IL: Abbeyfeale Press.
Middleton, Richard. 2002. *Colonial America: A History, 1565–1776.* 3rd ed. Malden, MA: Blackwell Publishers.
Riordan, Timothy B. 2004. *The Plundering Time: Maryland and the English Civil War, 1645–1646.* Baltimore: Maryland Historical Society.

CALVINISM

Calvinism (also known as "Reformed Theology") is a branch of Protestantism that developed from the theology and practices of John Calvin (1509–1564) and other Reformation theologians. As a system of theology, Calvinism is an attempt to thoroughly interpret and apply the teachings of the Bible to all aspects of life, functioning as much as a worldview as it does a branch of Christianity. Calvinism was the theology of both the Puritans and Separatists who sought refuge in North America. Most early New England settlements were formed and occupied by adherents of the Reformed faith, and throughout the Colonial Period, it was the dominant religious influence. Churches of Congregational, Presbyterian, Baptist, and Anglican persuasion were all influenced by Reformed Theology. Controversies related to antinomianism, "the Half-Way Covenant," and the Great Awakening were all related to the doctrines of Reformed Theology in the American colonies.

Historical Background

Calvinism arose in the Protestant Reformation of the 16th century, although its adherents trace their theology back to the North African theologian Augustine of Hippo (354–480 CE) as well as to teachings of the Bible. As a distinct branch of Protestantism, Calvinism is distinguished from Lutheranism and Zwinglianism, which preceded it. John Calvin's initial conversion to the Protestant cause was influenced by the followers of Martin Luther while he was studying at the University of Paris in the early 1530s. The most prominent aspects of the Lutheranism that Calvin encountered were that man is "justified," or made righteous by God, by faith alone and that the Bible is the final authority, rather than church tradition or authority. Both of these teachings would become central to Calvin and his followers.

Another branch of early Protestantism that would influence Calvin and Calvinism was the Swiss Reformation under Ulrich Zwingli (1484–1531). After Calvin's death, the Reformed movement would actually merge with Zwinglianism and be heavily influenced by Zwingli's followers. In a very similar fashion to Luther, Zwingli taught that man was justified by faith alone. Zwingli even made the claim that he preached the doctrine of "justification by faith alone" a full year before Martin Luther (1483–1546) delivered his 95 Theses, making Zwinglianism a distinct and original branch of Protestantism that possesses its own characteristics.

One distinguishing feature of Zwinglianism was an emphasis on the doctrine of the covenant. Zwingli taught that God saved people by means of a covenant, or a contract, which he offered to them in Christ. God agreed to forgive sinners and reconcile them to himself, if they exercised faith in the death and resurrection of Christ for their sins. This understanding was drawn from the word *covenant*, which appears in both the Old and New Testaments of the Christian Bible. Zwingli taught that the entire church was to be understood as a covenant community, which one entered into through baptism.

This covenantal relationship was understood to place both privileges and responsibilities upon members of the church. In response to some who said that only adult believers were to be baptized (known as Anabaptists), Zwingli taught that children of believers were also considered to be members of the church covenant. Because of this, infant children of believers were also to be baptized and their parents were obligated by the covenant to raise them in the faith. The covenant concept would end up strongly influencing Calvin and his followers, especially the English Puritans.

Like Luther, Zwingli also taught that the Bible alone was to guide the church in doctrine and in practice. However, the application and extent of this dogma was where Zwingli and Luther would differ. While Luther taught that anything not specifically forbidden in Scripture was acceptable in the worship of the church, Zwingli taught that only those things that were *commanded* in Scripture were acceptable in worship. This led Zwingli to forbid all musical instruments in worship and, at times, to forbid all music in general.

This was diametrically opposed to Lutheran worship, which continued to mirror the format of the Roman Catholic mass. Zwingli would also have strong disagreements with Luther on the nature of the sacraments, such as the Lord's Supper, or Holy Communion. Luther's position was that in the bread and wine of Communion, believers had access to the real body and blood of Jesus by their faith. Zwingli's position denied any real access and instead affirmed that it was merely a memorial service that symbolically presented the reality of Christ's sacrifice to the faith of the believer. This precipitated an official separation between the churches of Luther and Zwingli in 1529, when they were unable to reconcile their views on Communion at the Colloquy of Marburg. A permanent split was then formed in the Reformation between churches that would later be called Lutheran and churches that would later be called Reformed.

After being converted to Protestantism in Paris, John Calvin sought refuge from persecution in the Swiss canton of Geneva in 1535. This would put Calvin in close proximity to the Swiss churches of the recently deceased Zwingli, while also maintaining a close personal relationship to Martin Luther and his followers. Calvinism would thus become a mediating theology between Zwinglianism and Lutheranism. While John Calvin himself expressed stronger sympathies with Luther, his followers would drift closer to Zwingli.

In 1537, Calvin was called by the city council to serve as the chief pastor and teacher of the churches in Geneva, a position that he would hold until 1538 and then later from 1541 until his death in 1564. Unlike Luther, the content of

Calvin's theology remained unchanged throughout his ministry, although he was constantly elaborating upon it. His influential work, the *Institutes of the Christian Religion*, went through five different editions, expanding to eventually become a two-volume work. This, along with the confession and catechisms that he wrote for the city of Geneva, would lay the groundwork for what would be known as Calvinism, or Reformed Theology. Calvinism would become an influential force in France, the Netherlands, parts of Germany, and the British Isles. Both the English Puritans and the Scottish Presbyterians who immigrated to America were considered heirs of Calvin's theology.

Theology

Calvin's system of theology had several distinguishing features. Most significant was his understanding of salvation and predestination. Like Luther and Zwingli, Calvin held to justification by faith alone as being the fundamental teaching of the Christian faith. The only way that a soul could find salvation was by placing one's trust in the death, burial, and resurrection of Jesus. He denied that one could not rely on one's own righteousness in any way to get into heaven. This was because, like his predecessors, John Calvin had a strong view of original sin and human depravity.

In Protestant theology, human works were considered too impure for heaven. Furthermore, because of sin, no human being had the ability to truly repent of their sins or exercise faith of their own free will. Like most of the reformers, Calvin taught what later theologians would call *monergism*, or the belief that only God's power could create true faith and virtue in the human heart. This was contrasted with the *synergism* of medieval Catholicism, where salvation was conceived of by cooperation between human free will and divine grace.

This naturally led Calvin to emphasize predestination and election, or the belief that from eternity God had chosen certain individuals to be saved through faith. In this system, only those who were of the "elect" were given the grace to believe and obey. This teaching was recognized throughout Church history as *Augustinianism*, after its originator, Augustine of Hippo (354–430). While Augustinianism was also the doctrine of both Luther and Zwingli, Calvin was unique in emphasizing a larger purpose in election: the glory of God. In Calvin's understanding, the purpose of God's predestination was primarily to manifest his own glory, rather than to provide human salvation. God predestined some to receive his grace and find salvation (the elect), while everyone else was predestined to be left alone in their sins to perish (the reprobate). According to Calvin, both groups were a part of God's single decree to manifest his own glory, either for his love and grace or for his justice and wrath.

What this meant in everyday life was that Christians were to examine their lives for evidence of their election in the form of faith and good works. Furthermore, because God predestined all things to manifest his glory, all of life was to be lived for God's glory. This meant that Christians could serve God in any legitimate career and were not limited to the walls of a church. Calvin also emphasized that

Christians could appreciate the contributions of pagan philosophers and artists because even their gifts come from God to reveal his glory.

The emphasis on the glory of God would be recognized as a distinguishing characteristic of Calvinism. This was so central to Calvin's understanding that the second answer in his own catechism states that God "created us and placed us in this world to be glorified in us. And it is indeed right that our life, of which himself is the beginning, should be devoted to his glory." More than just a system of theology, Calvinism was understood to be an entire worldview. This would strongly influence the Puritans and Separatists who sought to form "little commonwealths" that adhered to the tenets of Calvinism in every facet of life.

Another characteristic of Calvin's theology was his emphasis on the work of the Holy Spirit. This was an outgrowth of his emphasis on human depravity and the necessity of divine grace. Calvin held to the standard Protestant teaching of scriptural authority, but he also placed a strong emphasis on the work of the Holy Spirit in understanding the word of God. It is only by the illuminating work of the Holy Spirit that people can truly believe and know the teachings of Scripture, according to Calvin. While other reformers certainly believed in the work of God's Spirit, Calvin's emphasis on the Spirit working in parallel with the words of Scripture was unique. People could only truly know God if he moved in them by his Spirit. This emphasis would also strongly influence the colonial understanding of revival in the form of the Great Awakening, which occurred in the 1730s and 1740s.

The emphasis on the Holy Spirit and the Word would also draw Calvin closer to Zwingli than Luther on matters of worship. Calvin taught that only those things that were commanded in Scripture were permissible in Christian worship. Calvinistic worship was known for its simplicity, usually including the simple elements of prayer, a capella singing, the reading of Scripture, alms giving, and preaching. This principle of simplicity would eventually be known as "The Regulative Principle of Worship," and it would be referred to as "Puritanism" when it arrived on English soil, as the English Calvinists sought to "purify" the worship of the Anglican Church from its Roman Catholic influences.

Calvin's emphasis on the work of the Holy Spirit was also apparent in his theology of the sacraments. He developed a mediating position on the Lord's Supper that was between the views of Zwingli and Luther. Calvin taught that the Holy Spirit presented the body and blood of Christ to the believer when the bread and wine were received in true faith. This view would become known as "the spiritual presence" view of the Lord's Supper. Like Luther, Calvin wanted to emphasize that real union and communion with Christ occurred through the sacraments. Luther even commended some of Calvin's treatises on the sacraments to other Protestants. However, like Zwingli, Calvin also sought to emphasize the memorial nature of Communion and denied that any substantial change occurred to the bread and wine itself. Variations of this doctrine would become the understanding of Reformed churches, although over time the majority would drift closer to the views of Zwingli. By the Colonial Period, the majority of Calvinists were closer to Zwingli's perspective than Calvin's.

A final area of significance in the theology of John Calvin was the role of the covenant. Like Zwingli, Calvin taught that man's salvation was to be understood in terms of a covenant. Following in the train of Zwingli and Calvin, Calvinists thought of the church as a covenant community that included privileges and responsibilities for its members. The privileges of church membership were the ability to partake in the sacrament of Communion and the ability to vote in church elections. The ability to choose leaders, or "elders," was a distinguishing feature of Calvinism. Elders and deacons were to be elected from individual congregations to oversee the spiritual and material welfare of the members. Elders in particular were responsible for representing their individual churches, and they were also expected to attend regional meetings with other elders, often referred to as presbyteries or synods. This created a democratic or parliamentary form of rule in the Reformed churches, as the leaders were chosen by, and responsible to, the churches that had elected them.

In New England, the election of government officials would also be considered a privilege of church membership. The covenant idea also placed responsibilities on the members of the church. Church members were expected to attend church and tithe regularly, live holy lives, raise their children in the faith, and submit to church discipline if they consistently failed in these requirements. Discipline usually took the form confrontation, restriction from the sacraments, and finally excommunication. The church usually considered physical punishment off limits. However, in New England, where church and state were tightly bound together, physical punishment could follow. The emphasis on the "covenant community" would be a consistent theme in various Calvinistic, or Reformed, movements, but this would especially be evident in New England Puritanism.

Social Theory

Related to the doctrine of the covenant, Calvinism also included an elaborate social theory that was favorable to a republican form of government and a limitation of governmental power. Calvin himself wrote in his *Institutes* that something between democracy and an aristocracy was to be preferred in the realm of government. This can be conceived of as an espousal of republican ideals. The followers of Calvin would elaborate on this idea and develop it further. Calvinists conceived all of society as being contractual, or covenantal, in nature. Men such as Johannes Althusius in Germany (1563–1638) and Samuel Rutherford in Scotland (1600–1661) promoted ideas of federalism, parliamentary rule, and freedom of conscience within the Calvinistic tradition. Rutherford's work *Lex Rex* was influential on the Continental Congress through the mediation of John Witherspoon and others who were influenced by the Presbyterian tradition. The ideas of republicanism and freedom of conscience, which were incipient in Calvinism, would come to full fruition in the Colonial Period.

Calvinism also espoused a political theory known as "the doctrine of the lesser magistrate," which held that revolution could be appropriate in certain circumstances if led by a government official labeled "the lesser magistrate." Calvin first articulated this doctrine in book 4 of his *Institutes*, and it was also developed further by his followers. Revolution was conceived of as being appropriate in situations where ruling officials had broken their covenantal obligations by becoming corrupt, abusive, or treasonous. The reason why Calvin and his followers stressed the necessity of a lesser magistrate leading the rebellion was to avoid the threat of anarchy in the case of a successful overthrow. These ideas were manifested in the English Civil War (1642–1651) and would carry over into the colonies through the influence of Calvinism and work to justify the actions of the Continental Congress in the minds of the populace.

The religion and worldview of Calvinism strongly influenced colonial culture and politics. The early colonies were founded upon the tenets of Calvinism, which continued to manifest themselves throughout colonial and early American history. Calvinism would continue as an influential force in American religious life through the influence of Presbyterian, Congregational, and Baptist churches.

Colin M. Samul

See also: Congregational Church; Presbyterianism; Puritanism

Further Reading

Calvin, J., and H. Beveridge. 2002. *Treatises on the Sacraments, Catechism of the Church of Geneva, Forms of Prayer, and Confessions of Faith.* Fearn, Scotland: Christian Heritage.

Calvin, J., and H. Kerr. 1989. *Calvin's Institutes: A New Compend.* Louisville, KY: Westminster/John Knox Press.

Gonzalez, J. 2010. *The Story of Christianity: The Reformation to the Present Day.* Vol. 2. New York: HarperOne.

Holifield, E. 2003. *Theology in America: Christian Thought from the Age of the Puritans to the Civil War.* New Haven, CT: Yale University Press.

Noll, M. 2002. *The Old Religion in a New World: The History of North American Christianity.* Grand Rapids, MI: Eerdmans.

Singer, C. 1964. *A Theological Interpretation of American History*. Philadelphia: Presbyterian and Reformed Pub.

CAMDEN, BATTLE OF

The Battle of Camden was fought on August 16, 1780, between the Continental Army, led by Gen. Horatio Gates and the British army led by Gen. John Burgoyne. The battle was fought just outside the town of Camden, South Carolina. The result was a stunning defeat of the Continentals that allowed the British to consolidate their hold on the former colony after the capture of Charleston earlier in the year.

In the wake of the loss at Saratoga in late 1777, the war changed for the British during the American Revolution. An entire army under Gen. John Burgoyne was lost, France was now an active combatant in the war, and the northern theater was in an effective stalemate. A new strategy was needed, and most of the eyes looked to the south. The Southern Colonies were seen in Britain as more loyal and more dependent on the empire and thus more easily swayed to come back into the fold.

The Battle of Camden, fought on August 16, 1780, was a major victory for the British in the American Revolutionary War and served to solidify British control of the Carolinas, following the capture of Charleston. (National Archives)

This new "Southern Strategy" would shift the focus of the war in that direction and allow the British forces to more easily support the Caribbean islands threatened by the French and Spanish.

The campaign started in late 1778 when the British captured Savannah and thus effectively returned the colony of Georgia under Crown control. Then, in 1780, Gen. Henry Clinton, the British commander-in-chief, led a large force from New York to capture Charleston in spectacular fashion. Besides the city, they also managed to capture the bulk of the Continental Army in the Southern Colonies, which had been under the command of Gen. Benjamin Lincoln. In a few skirmishes after the fall of the city, the Continentals were effectively driven out of South Carolina.

This left the primary defense of South Carolina to the roving bands of partisan militia that made up the bulk of the fighting forces. Many of these men had accepted a general pardon issued by Clinton after the fall of Charleston and their "surrender." The conditions of the pardon were simple: if they no longer took up arms against the British and forwent partisan activities, they would be allowed to live in peace. On June 3, 1778, General Clinton issued a new edict. Any man considered a prisoner of war (which included most of the militia) would have two choices: either fight alongside the British army against the patriot forces or be considered traitors themselves. Faced with such a choice, many of these men decided that if they were going to be forced to fight, they would do so under their own terms. While the Continental Army was rebuilding, these would be the men to face the British.

Meanwhile, the remnants of the Continental Army in the South gathered in North Carolina, lacking supplies, leadership, and a plan. To fill the leadership role, Congress appointed Gen. Horatio Gates to take command of the Southern army. Viewed by many of his supporters in Congress as the architect of the stunning victory at Saratoga, Gates was chosen for the command against the wishes of Gen. George Washington, who would have preferred most anyone else.

In July 1789, Gates arrived in Charlotte, North Carolina, and took stock of his forces. Out of approximately 4,000 troops available, less than 1,500 were Continental Army regulars; the rest were local militia, many of which were going to see battle for the first time. The army was badly in need of supplies. The local population had not been very willing to provide for the army due to the long string of losses. Aware of the supply situation, Gates still ordered the army to march almost immediately to Camden, an important crossroads in South Carolina, where approximately 1,000 British troops were garrisoned. Gen. Baron Johann de Kalb, who had been commanding the army, suggested that they take a less direct route to gather supplies in the towns of Charlotte and Salisbury. Gates rejected this idea, suggesting that speed and surprise would be the most effective weapon against the enemy. The small army moved south through the relatively barren pine forests of North Carolina and were left to eat whatever they could scavenge. Along the march, many took to eating green corn and unripe peaches, which led to a lot of sick soldiers. The heat also took its toll on many of the men. With new militia units joining him en route, by the time he arrived at what would be the site of the battle, Gates had approximately 3,700 men under his command.

When the British commander, Gen. Charles Cornwallis, heard that the American army was moving, he marched from Charleston with a small force to help defend Camden, arriving on August 13. Cornwallis had just over 2,000 men at his disposal, approximately a third of which were Loyalist militia. The remaining troops were British regulars and the British Legion, a mixed force of infantry and cavalry led by the already infamous Banastre Tarleton.

Both sides made the decision to move in for the attack, with the initial fighting occurring in the dark as the two armies attempted night marches to catch the other by surprise. The morning of August 16 found the Americans arrayed for a full-on battle. On the right side of his line, Gates placed the Continentals of the 2nd Maryland and the 1st Delaware. On the left, he placed the Virginia militia, and the North Carolina militia took the center. The right side of Cornwallis's line (directly across from the Virginia militia) would be anchored by the 23rd Regiment of Foot (Royal Welch Fusiliers) and the 33rd Foot. The left would be the Loyalist militias, the Volunteers of Ireland, and the British Legion. Gates had the numerical advantage, almost two to one, but it would make little difference.

The battle kicked off as the British right advanced against the Virginia militia with a bayonet charge. The Virginians did not have bayonets, and the idea of facing the oncoming British regulars proved too much. Before the British were even close enough to spit at them, the Virginians and a number of the North Carolina militia broke and ran. Accounts state that only one militia unit fired off a volley before running and that the Virginians left the field so quickly they only suffered three casualties. One unit of North Carolina militia, the one deployed closest to the Continentals in line, held their ground.

General Gates watched as his left flank collapsed and ordered his right flank, under Maj. Gen. Baron de Kalb to attack. Having given the order, Gates then decided to join the militia on their flight and left the field, leaving Kalb in command. Meanwhile the British continued a general advance with their left under the command of Lord Francis Rawdon, who slammed his forces into the waiting Continentals.

Twice the Americans repulsed the charges by the British troops, and eventually they were even able to counterattack, which succeeded in pushing Rawdon and his forces back. They even captured some prisoners in the process. General Cornwallis himself rode to the scene and rallied the troops, urging them forward. Meanwhile, as the American militia was no longer a factor, the British right found themselves in a position to flank the remaining Continentals, tearing through the one unit of North Carolina militia that stayed. By this time, less than 800 Continental troops were facing over 2,000 British regulars. They fought well until Cornwallis ordered Tarleton's cavalry to charge the American rear. This finally broke the Continentals, and they scattered, General Kalb fell, having been wounded 11 times. The British dogged the fleeing Americans for 20 miles before finally breaking off the pursuit. The entire battle took less than an hour. By later that evening, Gates had made his way all the way back to Charlotte, over 60 miles away.

The British losses, killed, wounded, and missing, were approximately 324. American casualties included almost 900 killed and wounded and around 1,000 men taken as prisoners. The army had lost all its cannon and most all of its baggage. The Southern army was shattered, and the British were now firmly in control of South Carolina and in a position to threaten the remaining Southern Colonies. In the aftermath of the battle, Gates was removed from command. Congress passed a resolution calling for an inquiry, but his allies in Congress would not allow him to be held accountable for the loss. The matter was eventually dropped, and Gates would never hold a field assignment again. Later in the war, he found himself serving as a member of Washington's staff, where he may have had a hand in an attempted coup of Congress. Soon after, he retired from public life.

Not being willing to surrender the South without a fight, General Washington demanded his original choice for the command be given the task of rebuilding the army. Congress acquiesced, and Maj. Gen. Nathanael Greene was given the herculean task of rebuilding the army and retaking the South. The Battle of Camden was over, but the war for the South had just begun.

Stuart Hatfield

See also: Cornwallis, Lord Charles; Gates, Horatio

Further Reading

Babits, Lawrence. 2001. *A Devil of a Whipping: The Battle of Cowpens.* Chapel Hill: University of North Carolina Press.

Bobrick, Benson. 1997. *Angel in the Whirlwind.* New York: Penguin Books.

Buchanan, John. 1999. *The Road to Guilford Courthouse.* New York: Wiley & Sons.

Hibbert, Christopher. 1990. *Redcoats and Rebels.* New York: Norton Books.

CAROLINA CONSTITUTION

The Carolina Constitution is the more familiar name for the documents formally known as the Fundamental Constitutions of Carolina. Developed under the direction of the lords proprietors who oversaw the organization and the development of the Carolina colony, an area that would subsequently be divided into the colonies, and ultimately the states, of North Carolina and South Carolina. The documents are also sometimes referred to as the "Grand Model" and are viewed by historians as one of the earliest efforts to set up a state in which there was at least limited self-government.

In 1663, Charles II issued a charter for the land that is presently the states of North Carolina and South Carolina and was then called the Province of Carolina. That charter was granted to eight men: George Monck, 1st Duke of Albemarle; Edward Hyde, 1st Earl of Clarendon; John Berkeley, 1st Baron Berkeley of Stratton; William Craven, 1st Earl of Craven; Sir George Carteret; Sir William Berkeley; Sir John Colleton, 1st Baronet; and Anthony Ashley Cooper, 1st Earl of Shaftesbury. They were known as the lords proprietors, a title not of nobility but one that reflected their roles as overseers of a territory. The grant itself was a reward for the support and assistance the group had given Charles in his effort to be restored to the throne in 1660.

The Carolina Constitution represented a revision and a change from the Concessions and Agreements that the lords proprietors had given to colonists in 1665. That document, aimed in no small part at potential new settlers, provided Carolina's colonists with a substantial amount of influence in their own government. In contrast, the purpose of the Fundamental Constitutions was to protect the basic interests of the overseeing lord proprietors, and in so doing prevent the exercise of any widespread democracy. Indeed, with a goal of creating a feudal society, the resulting society created by the Carolina Constitution was to be led by nobles.

At the same time, while the locus of authority remained firmly with the lords in terms of developing the colony, the Fundamental Constitutions of Carolina offered something distinctive and attractive to prospective settlers, and that was not an accident. Indeed, the lords proprietors were particularly concerned about protecting the Carolinas against attacks from Spanish forces in Florida, and, as a result, they aggressively pursued new settlers. In addition to the benefits of their religious toleration policy, the lords proprietors also offered a generous headright system. In fact, with policies such as religious toleration, Carolina represented a departure from most other colonies and in that way was intended to attract new inhabitants. In addition, with the proprietors dealing with class distinctions in the developing feudal system based on the ability of the lords to grant titles to large landholders, they were able to go beyond the standard land rewards central to the headright system, as generous as it was, and offer a heightened social status that would set an individual apart.

In the end, the Carolina Constitution had a substantive impact on the development of the Carolinas, because with the promise of religious choice, Carolina became more attractive to settlers from different religious backgrounds, ranging from French Huguenots to Jewish settlers. While the Carolina Constitution made no pretense of being a democratic document, in practice, while the lords proprietors controlled the government through a governor and Grand Council, those bodies included representatives of the proprietors that could be seen as the region's elite, as well as a smaller, but significant (if only symbolically), representation of the common people of the colony. In this way, elements of democracy unseen in Britain were emerging. At the same time, its nod toward democracy had its limits, for while freemen were allowed a nominal say in the new governments, slaves and those (usually indentured servants) who were bound to others were not.

Early historians tended to credit John Locke as a major author of the Fundamental Constitutions, but more recent work views him more as the scribe than the author, an interpretation buttressed by his official role as the secretary to Lord Anthony Ashley Cooper, Earl of Shaftesbury, who is now seen as the major author of the Carolina Constitution. At the same time, there is an increased recognition that, in fact, all eight of the lords proprietors had a hand in the Grand Model, which is generally seen as a template for and forerunner of the Fundamental Constitutions.

The basic governmental structure laid out under the Carolina Constitution made it possible for the lords to exercise that feudal powers that were already granted in their charters. Under the Carolina Constitution, local nobility, including the manors and manorial courts, could be created by the lords. At the same time, Carolina was exempted from additional subinfeudation—thus keeping real power in the hands of the lords—as well as adherence to the Bishop of Durham clause, which technically might have reduced the lords' authority, but given the authority they had received in their original charters, the clause would have been rendered pretty much obsolete. In the end, all of these provisions left the lords possessing almost regal authority over the Carolina colony, including the power to enact laws, levy taxes, raise troops, impress ships, and so on. While many of those powers were included in their previous charters, the Fundamental Constitutions served to further reinforce their powers while also enhancing the overall impression of authority that the lords sought to leave with the settlers of the Carolina colony.

Under the system set up by the Carolina Constitution, the lords could establish titles of nobility below their own stage and then below them were the freemen. These men could own land and were allowed a minimal say in the workings of their local government. Below them were "leet-men," who were tenants of the nobles and the lords of the manor. Bound to the land where they resided, they were essentially indentured servants. In addition to the creation of these social classes, the Carolina Constitution also provided for the growth and development of the land and community. Counties could also be created as population increases warranted, with each new county being divided in such a way as to add to the holdings of the lords and to a lesser extent the freemen. In the end, all landowners benefited from the ongoing growth.

The government structure was headed by the top agency, the Palatine's Court, which was made up of the 8 lords proprietors, with the eldest lord being called the *palatine*. The Palatine's Court was only the top level of a multitiered governmental structure. Below it were seven more courts, each of which consisted of a proprietor and 6 councillors, who were chosen through a complicated process that guaranteed that at least half of the councillors on each court were either members of the local nobility, sons of the proprietors, or sons of local noblemen. This makeup ensured that power was not widely disbursed. In addition, a Grand Council, which was invested with executive, judicial, and legislative powers, was also established. This body consisted of the 8 lords proprietors and 42 councillors of the Proprietors Courts. Central to the council's powers was the determination of which matters would go before the Parliament, the primary representative body of the colony and one whose makeup included representatives ranging from the lords proprietors down to local freeholders. Its recommendations had to be ratified by the palatine and three other lords proprietors. Reflective of its position as the ultimate authority in the colony, any actions of the Parliament or the Executive Council could be nullified by the Palatine's Court.

Finally, the Carolina Constitution made provisions for local courts and officials, including municipal officers. Under its terms, freemen were to be guaranteed basic individual rights, including trial by jury and protection against double jeopardy. As noted, they were also given considerable freedom of religion.

Given all their efforts and the detailed and thoughtful governmental structure created, the lords proprietors had every expectation that the Grand Model would be implemented. In reality, it was hamstrung from the beginning. Central to its difficulty was the fact that it was not introduced until six years after settlers had first arrived in the colony, and the challenge inherent in the effort to impose a new set of structures on a people who had by that point developed a distinctive way of life could not be overcome. As a result, they were never able to make it a reality. While local governors were sent directives to implement the Fundamental Constitutions, the fact that revisions and changes were undertaken very soon afterward offers all the evidence needed of the many problems that dogged the effort; revisions became the norm. A society run according to the dictates of the Fundamental Constitutions never became a reality, and by 1700, the lords proprietors, now the heirs of the founding lords, allowed for the Carolina Constitution to be ignored. The experiment was over.

William H. Pruden III

See also: Carteret, Sir George; Headrights; Hyde, Edward, Viscount Cornbury; North Carolina; South Carolina

Further Reading

Armitage, David. 2004. "John Locke, Carolina, and the 'Two Treatises of Government.'" *Political Theory* 32: 602–627. https://scholar.harvard.edu/files/armitage/files/armitage-locke.pdf.

Lewis, J. D. "Fundamental Constitutions." Carolana.com. http://www.carolana.com/Carolina/Documents/fundamental_constitutions_overview.html.

Parker, Mattie Erma E. Parker. 1970. "The First Fundamental Constitutions of Carolina." *South Carolina Historical Magazine* 71: 78–85. https://www.jstor.org/stable/27566981?seq=1#page_scan_tab_contents.

CARTERET, PHILIP (1639–1682)

Philip Carteret (also spelled Cartaret) was a cousin of George Carteret and the first governor of New Jersey. New Jersey had been a Dutch colony known as New Netherland when it was surrendered to the English in 1664 after a fleet of four British frigates sent to seize the colony were unopposed by the Dutch colonists.

George Carteret and John Berkeley were appointed proprietors of the colony by the Duke of York under the authority of Charles II, and the British colony was renamed New Jersey after the home island of the Carteret family. New Netherland had been established as a colony by the Dutch West India Company for the purpose of exploiting the fur resources found in North America.

John Cabot and Henry Hudson explored the New Jersey area, the first Europeans to do so, and the first attempt at a European colony was actually a Swedish encampment on the Delaware River in 1640, although a permanent European settlement was not be established until 1660 at Bergen. A lack of coherent purpose and ineffective management coupled with friction from hostile Native Americans to prevent rapid growth and settlement by Europeans under Dutch control. The colony was underpopulated and undefended when the English decided to annex the Dutch colonies for their own, including New Amsterdam (renamed New York).

Philip Carteret was appointed by his cousin George and John Berkeley as the first governor of New Jersey and served in that capacity from 1665 to 1673. Born on the island of Jersey in 1639, Phillip Carteret was only 26 years old when appointed governor, certainly a tender age for such an office.

Philip was involved in the drafting of the Concession and Agreement of the Proprietors of New Jersey along with George Carteret and Berkeley, a document issued as a proclamation laying out the form of government for the New Jersey colony and stipulating a freedom of religion clause. Considered an extremely liberal framework for governing a colony at the time, the Concession and Agreement and the stewardship of Philip Carteret called for political privilege for colonists and liberal handing out of land grants. The idea of political and religious freedom was calculated to attract settlers and quickly develop the colony, in turn making the landholdings of the Carteret families and Berkeley rapidly increase in value, which created a valuable source of revenue when sold to new colonists. The sale of these landholdings was indeed profitable to the founding families. The government of New Jersey was to consist of a governor, a council, and representatives chosen by each town to meet in an assembly.

Carteret established Elizabethtown (named in honor of George Carteret's wife) as the capital of New Jersey, and it was there that an assembly representing the several towns met in 1668 under the auspices of Governor Carteret. Unfortunately, not all the towns of New Jersey were compliant, and two of those towns, Shrewsbury Township and Middletown Township, refused to send representatives or participate in the assembly. In fact, those two towns declared their independence from the New Jersey colony and elected James Carteret as their leader (James Carteret was the second son of George Carteret).

When the English first took possession of New Amsterdam from the Dutch, the territory included what is now New Jersey. Col. Richard Nicolls had taken physical and military control of the land now called New York and was taken aback when he learned of the grant to George Carteret and John Berkeley of the New Netherland area. This confused establishment of British rule in New York/New Jersey resulted in competing and overlapping grants made under the authority of each of the colonies. Land titles, land patents, borders, and ownership of property as well as religious differences (early New Jersey was largely Puritan) led to the conflict and James Carteret's rebellion.

Philip Carteret sailed for London to resolve the colonial dispute, and on his return, he levied a form of tax known as *quitrents* on the colonists, an obviously unpopular move. The New Jersey colony was split in 1674 (officially 1676) into East Jersey and West Jersey, and Phillip became the governor of East Jersey in 1674 until 1682.

Upon the death of George Carteret in 1680, New York governor Edmund Andros made a power grab for East Jersey, an attempt to seize the colony and repatriate it to New York. A precipitating cause of the conflict was over which colony possessed the right to collect customs and duties. Philip Carteret refused to resign his office as governor and cede East Jersey to New York, causing Andros to mount a raiding party to arrest (kidnap) Philip Carteret and return him to New York to stand trial. When the raiding party arrived at Carteret's home, Philip was forcibly taken and administered a severe beating in the process. Delivered back to Andros in New York, Carteret was jailed and tried, although he was acquitted. The Duke of York, the future King James II, restored Carteret to his office as governor of East Jersey. In 1682, disgusted with the trials and tribulations of running the colony, Philip Carteret sold his interest in East Jersey to William Penn and other Quakers, continuing a strong Quaker presence in New Jersey. In 1702, the people of both East and West Jersey were discontented with their governments, and under the auspices of the Crown, they were reunited as one entity, New Jersey, once again, and this time with a royal governor appointed by the Crown instead of proprietors.

Unfortunately for Philip Carteret, the severe beating he had taken at the hands of Edmund Andros's raiding party and his harsh incarceration had ruined his health. He died in 1682, only 43 years old.

Philip Carteret governed New Jersey for 17 years, and it was a time during which growth and development took place at a more rapid pace than prior to his stewardship. The political and religious freedoms espoused by Carteret contributed to the emigration of settlers from other colonies to New Jersey and, for the most part, a higher level of satisfaction of the colonists than in other colonies. Political friction with the governors of New York and mixed loyalties of the New Jersey colonists combined to adversely affect the last few years of Philip's time as governor. Philip Carteret's legacy was a viable and growing colony that would continue to grow in population and importance to the current state of New Jersey today.

Matthew D. Zarzeczny

See also: Carteret, Sir George; New Jersey

Further Reading

Brogan, Hugh. 1985. *The Longman History of the United States of America.* Harlow, U.K.: Longman Group Ltd.

Ferrell, Robert H., with Richard Natkiel. 1987. *Atlas of American History.* London: Bison Books Ltd.

Morison, Samuel Eliot. 1965 and 1972. *The Oxford History of the American People.* Vol. 1. Oxford: Oxford University Press.

CARTERET, SIR GEORGE (1610–1680)

George Carteret, known more formally as Vice Adm. Sir George Carteret, 1st Baronet, was a fundamental figure in the founding of both the British colonies of New Jersey and of the Province of Carolina. Carteret's legacy includes the naming of Carteret County, North Carolina, in his honor as well as the city of Carteret, New Jersey. Not to be left out, the name of his wife, Elizabeth, was bestowed on Elizabeth City, North Carolina.

Carteret was born in Jersey, England, around 1610, to Elias de Carteret and Elizabeth Dumaresq (both of Carteret's parents died in 1640), obviously of some sort of French heritage, which George Carteret eschewed by dropping the "de" in his last name when joining the British Navy so as to sound less French and more English.

In 1640, George Carteret married his own cousin, Elizabeth de Carteret, the daughter of an Oxford professor and bailiff of Jersey. They had three sons and five daughters. Among Carteret's sons-in-law were the 1st Earl of Norwich, a 1st Baronet of Maristow (and MP), and the Lord Chief Baron of the Exchequer. Carteret's eldest son married the daughter of the 1st Earl of Sandwich (Montagu), and another son was a captain in the Royal Navy.

Carteret served as an officer in the British navy throughout the 1630s, on various ships and in various capacities. He seemed destined to a naval life and commanded the HMS *Mary Rose* prior to being appointed comptroller of the navy in 1641. Carteret's naval career seemed to be progressing well, although he was hampered throughout his life by a lack of formal education due to his joining the navy at a young age and spending his youth at sea. The politician and poet, as well as a friend of John Milton, Andrew Marvel, a satirist with a barbed tongue, was known to make fun of Carteret's less than formal command of the English language. Samuel Pepys, a member of Parliament and, despite no seagoing experience, a career admiralty man, rising to the post of chief secretary of the admiralty, was another of Carteret's critics, bemoaning Carteret's lack of knowledge of Latin. Somehow, despite a lack of linguistic expertise, George Carteret managed his naval career with some distinction, as evidenced by his promotions.

The English Civil War (1642–1651) overshadowed virtually all other political developments of the time, and Carteret left the navy in 1642 to withdraw to his estate on Jersey. There he worked for Royalist causes and even gave sanctuary to the Prince of Wales, Charles Stuart. Carteret served as bailiff of Jersey (1643–1651) and governor of the island and as such defended the island against Parliamentarians while proclaiming Charles Stuart as Charles II (1649), King of England.

Carteret defended Jersey from Elizabeth Castle, but after a 7-week siege in 1651, he was forced to surrender to the Parliamentarians. After the defeat, Carteret was obliged to seek exile in France, where he found himself jailed in 1657 before being exiled again, this time to Venice. When the monarchy was restored in 1660, George Carteret had earned himself favor in the eyes of Charles II for the previous support of the monarchy and protection of Charles. Carteret had also earned the gratitude of other English expatriates while in exile due to his kindness and consideration he had shown them.

The goodwill earned by Carteret garnered him a position on the Privy Council (advisers to the king) and Vice-Chamberlain of the Household, placing him in the inner circle of power in England. From 1660 to 1667, Carteret also served as treasurer of the navy, a high office in the premier military service of Britain. Carteret advanced his political career by leaving his job as Vice-Chamberlain of the Household and assuming the role as vice-treasurer of Ireland in 1667. The 1660s were heady times for Carteret, who bragged of his influence on the king. The naval battles and wars of the time made the job of treasurer of the navy a target for critics, and Carteret looked outside England for new horizons in the American colonies.

Charles II rewarded Carteret's loyalty by giving him a charter for the New Netherland colony, which Carteret promptly named New Jersey after his home island. With influential contacts such as John Berkeley, the Earl of Sandwich (Montagu), and Edward Hyde, Carteret also became a proprietor of the Province of Carolina.

Carteret is notable in his administration of New Jersey in that he, along with Lord Berkeley, authored Concession and Agreement, a proclamation establishing the governmental structure of New Jersey and a guarantee of freedom of religion in the colony. This sort of attitude of tolerance would later find its way into the U.S. Constitution and was a fundamental part of the country the English colonies in America would become.

In 1669, Carteret found himself once more beset by enemies that accused him of embezzlement from his time as Vice-Chamberlain of the Household. Carteret was dismissed from his seat in Parliament (House of Commons), where he had represented Portsmouth since 1661. Still enjoying the support of a grateful king, Carteret was acquitted by the House of Lords, and the charges against him were dropped.

Carteret continued in the government service, serving as a lord of the admiralty with the rank of vice admiral from 1673 until his death in 1680 at the age of 70. His patron, Charles II, had intended to grant Carteret the title of baron, and upon news of Carteret's death, he granted the title to the Carteret's grandson, also named George Carteret.

George Carteret had a long and multifaceted career in the service of his government and king, and he and his wife raised a family of some accomplishment. Carteret accomplished these things without the benefit of a formal education, but he managed to leave a legacy on both sides of the Atlantic that is in evidence even today.

Matthew D. Zarzeczny

See also: Carteret, Philip; English Civil War

Further Reading

Henning, Basil Duke. 1983. *The House of Commons, 1660–1690*. III. London: Secker & Warburg.

Marvell, Andrew. 1971. *The Poems and Letters of Andrew Marvell*. Edited by H. M. Margoliouth. 3d ed. rev. by Pierre Legouis with the collaboration of E. E. Duncan-Jones. Oxford: Clarendon Press.

Whitehead, William Adee. 1846. *East Jersey under the Proprietary Governments*. New York: New-Jersey Historical Society.

CATHOLICISM

Catholicism, or the practice of the Catholic faith, is the Christian religion of the Roman Catholic Church (also referred to as the Latin Church) and the 23 variations of Eastern Catholic Churches, those Churches submitting to the Holy See in Rome and adhering to the "Four Marks of the Church." (Those four marks are encompassed in the four words "one," "holy," "catholic" and "apostolic.") At times, the Eastern Orthodox Church and others, including Anglican and similar religions, are considered within the family of "Catholic" Churches. The name *catholic* derives from the Greek meaning of "universal," thus the Catholic Church is the Universal Church in Christianity. Just as Catholicism is critical to understanding European life and history, it is also critical to understanding the development of North America.

At the beginning of the Colonial Period, or the Age of Discovery, Catholicism was the Christian religion and creed of the Spanish that monopolized the early exploration and colonization of the New World. Spanish explorers and colonists, starting with Christopher Columbus in 1493, brought Catholic priests (and friars or monks, especially Franciscan friars) with them as an integral part of their mission to the New World. Far from merely administering to the European flock on hand, these priests were missionaries sent to convert mass numbers of Native Americans to the Catholic faith. The formation of various Catholic religious orders, notably the Jesuits (Society of Jesus) and the Franciscans, provided a cast of zealous missionaries eager to spread their religion and their specific philosophies among settlers and the Native peoples.

Christianity, the following of the teachings of Jesus Christ, slowly spread from Israel to Africa, the Middle East, and Europe in the first three centuries CE. Basically synonymous with Catholicism in the early days, Christianity, was embraced by Roman emperor Constantine in 313 CE, and it became the state religion of the Roman Empire in 380 CE. The Roman Empire spread the acceptance of Christianity throughout the European world and the breadth of the empire, while in the East the Orthodox version of Christianity developed with relatively minor differences, largely by not submitting to the authority of the Pope (also known as the bishop of Rome). The split between Roman Catholic and Orthodox, called the Great Schism, occurred in 1054 and has remained, although efforts at reconciliation and recognition of each other as legitimate heirs to the Church of St. Peter are occasionally made, albeit in somewhat lukewarm fashion.

A significant feature of Catholicism is the clerical hierarchy that culminates in the College of Cardinals at the Vatican in Rome, with the Pope as leader of the Church. In the past, between the third and fifteenth centuries, there have been serious rifts among Catholics, to the point that rival popes and antipopes existed, each with major factions of Catholics supporting their separate legitimacy. The First Vatican Council of 1869–1870 authoritatively stated as a matter of dogma that the Pope was infallible in his decisions and opinions concerning the faith and free from the possibility of error by virtue of the promise of Jesus to St. Peter. Prior to this pronouncement, papal infallibility was more or less assumed, but the First Vatican Council removed any doubt. Papal infallibility has been a contentious issue throughout history and is ridiculed at times by Christians outside the Catholic Church.

Papal rule and infallibility is fundamental to understanding the dynamic that developed between the colonizing countries, with Catholic Spain, Portugal, and France being relentlessly opposed by the Protestant English and Dutch, often on largely religious grounds. Friction among Christians was as fierce as it was between Europeans and the Native peoples. Non-Catholic Christians feared and resented the Catholic "papists" that were presumably under the thrall of the Pope and eager to do his bidding before any duty to country and king. The Pope became a hated figure among Protestants, and by association, hatred of Catholics followed. Catholics in the New World were seen by Protestants as a threat, puppets that had their strings pulled by the Pope/puppet master that was thought of by Protestants to be in league with the Devil or perhaps even the Devil incarnate.

A factor in allowing the practice of Catholicism to spread easily around the world during the Age of Discovery and the subsequent European colonization of much of the world was the use of Latin as the language of the Church, a common language that all priests must be fluent in, and that the Mass was celebrated in standard fashion from 1570 to 1962. Thus, Catholics of any language group could find Mass celebrated in familiar fashion anywhere in the world. The Second Vatican Council of 1962–1965 proclaimed that Mass would be celebrated in the local vernacular. (Certain Slavic churches had long celebrated Mass in the Slavic language of the local parish, an exception to the normal rule.) The common language of Latin allowed for easy transition from a particular Catholic sect to another and facilitated communication between Europeans on the frontier.

Yet another defining feature of Catholicism is an all-male clergy. Although other Christian religions around the world have often allowed women to become priests and rise in the clerical hierarchy, the Catholic Church has resisted this concession to women's equality as spiritual beings. Hand in hand with the all-male priesthood has been a proscription against the marriage of priests as early as 305 CE. The celibacy of priests made the inclusion of priests on wilderness expeditions that much easier, as these holy men were not concerned with obtaining riches or looking after the legacy of their families, nor would they be likely to pine for home and a wife left behind, often allowing them to stay in remote areas to do their work unencumbered by familial ties.

After being basically a monopoly authority on Christian religion for 1,500 years, the Reformation in 1517 led to a major split of Christian religions into Catholic (including Orthodox) and Protestant. In Europe, these two main sects of Christianity (there are and have been other, non-Protestant rivals to the Catholic Church within Christianity) in turn led to religious wars within countries as the state struggled with a national religion to go with a national identity, which was particularly important as the reigning monarch (king or queen) was claimed to be ordained by God to rule the people. In England, Henry VIII made the decision to split from the Catholic Church when he was denied permission to divorce for the purpose of remarrying to produce a male heir. This request was denied by Pope Clement VII in 1527 and led to a series of Acts of Parliament, culminating in the 1534 Act of Supremacy, which established Henry VIII (or the reigning English monarch) as the "Supreme Head on Earth of the Church of England."

Mary I, a Catholic, renounced that title in 1553 and conducted a campaign of retribution against Protestants, especially those that had persecuted the Catholic Church. Mary was usurped by Elizabeth I in 1559, and the Church of England was reinstated as the state religion of England. This monopoly of the religion of the English enjoyed by the Church of England ended with the defeat of the Royalists in the English Civil War (1642–1651) and the rule of Oliver Cromwell (1649–1658) until the monarchy was reinstated in 1660.

Catholicism in England, Scotland, Wales, and Ireland languished after the reinstatement of the monarchy, with outright persecution leading to the hanging, drawing, and quartering of those clerics who dared to celebrate Catholic mass, a fate normally reserved for traitors. When North America was being colonized by England, Catholics were a minority and forbidden to practice their faith in many of the settlements, which in turn led to the establishment of certain colonies that practiced religious freedom attracting many of the Catholic colonists. These colonies included Maryland, Pennsylvania, the Carolinas, New Jersey, and Rhode Island. As Catholicism was the religion of the hated enemies of England, the French and Spanish, English authorities often looked at Catholics as a threat to the authority of the Church of England and the legitimacy of the monarchy. Catholics were often portrayed as loyal to the Pope instead of the king. For most of the Colonial Period, the English people and their governments were stridently anti-Catholic, a situation that contributed to relations with other countries in the New World and patterns of colonization. Catholics within the English zone of influence were compelled to settle together in clusters of Catholics, rather than be treated like pariahs in Protestant communities or forced by law to attend Protestant church services.

In the United States, the influence of the Catholic Church has been enormous, with major colleges and universities (at least 261 total) found throughout the states. This influence on education in North America is directly linked to the propagation of Catholic missions throughout North America during the Colonial Period, when Jesuit and Franciscan friars established schools for the children of both European settlers and Native peoples. The practice of tying education to the Catholic faith has greatly influenced education in North America and has continued to resonate through the centuries since those missionary days.

Spanish settlements in the New World had a strong Catholic flavor, with forcibly converting Native Americans to Catholicism being a primary stated goal of the

Spanish Crown. From Mexico to the southern tip of Argentina, the New World retains this influence as a predominantly Catholic region, including Portuguese Brazil. Within these Spanish territories, the brand of Catholicism practiced often contained elements of the Native religion and traditions and is more an amalgamation of Catholicism and Native religions than standard Catholicism. Spanish explorers and conquistadors seldom ventured far without a representative of the clergy with them. Native Americans were usually given the unhappy choice of conversion to Catholicism and becoming Spanish slaves or death, a blatantly un-Christian policy that seems to have been lost on these Spanish adventurers. Towering above Rio de Janeiro, Brazil, is the giant Art Deco statue of Christ the Redeemer by the French Polish sculptor Paul Landowski. This testament to the Christian/Catholic heritage is 98 feet tall atop a 26-foot-high pedestal. The statue's loving arms span 92 feet, embracing all of Rio. Weighing 700 tons and made of soapstone and reinforced concrete, Christ the Redeemer is listed as one of the New 7 Wonders of the World and serves as a highly visible symbol of the legacy of those Catholic missionaries that were ever-present with Spanish and Portuguese explorers and colonizers. In Latin America, about 84 percent of the population reports being Catholic today. The Catholic legacy of the Colonial Period continues to cast a long shadow over all of Latin America, from Mexico and the Caribbean through Central and South America.

The Native religions across the New World at the time of the arrival of Europeans have been all but erased, in large part due to Catholic missionary work, although often from somewhat involuntary conversions of Native people. The French brought their Catholicism to the New World, especially North America and particularly Canada, where the French Catholic efforts at missionary and conversion work were somewhat less brutal than that of the Spanish. This effort to convert Native Americans to Catholicism was nonetheless enthusiastic and in direct competition with English efforts to convert Native Americans to the Anglican faith. The legacy of this religious influence is seen today in Quebec, the largely French-speaking province of modern Canada that retains its Catholic nature, unlike the rest of Canada, which is overwhelmingly Protestant. Catholic religious orders prominent in missionary work in New France included Jesuits, Sulpician Fathers, Augustinians, Ursulines, Recollect Franciscans, and the Hospitallers of Saint-Joseph. These orders founded churches, schools, hospitals, and seminaries. Two notable orders of nuns were also founded in Canada/New France, the Sisters of the Congregation of Notre Dame and the Grey Nuns.

The first Catholic bishop in North America was Bishop Francois de Laval, Apostolic Vicar of Canada. Laval had responsibility for Catholic interests in most of Canada and what would become the United States. Laval's New World mission began in 1658. The Catholic Church in New France enjoyed regular growth from the establishment of New France in 1534, until New France was ceded to the English in 1763 after the Seven Years' War. Once the Restoration of Rights in Britain in 1829 had made it feasible to expand the Catholic Church into English Canada, and the 1841 Act of Union had given Canadian Catholics full rights, the Catholic Church established dioceses in major settlements of British Canada, such as

Kingston, Toronto, and Ottawa. Today, almost 39 percent of Canadians are Catholic, about 12.73 million people. This number makes Catholicism the largest Christian denomination and the largest religion in Canada. Over 8,000 priests tend to parishes in 52 dioceses.

Catholicism has had a profound effect on the settlement of the New World and the development of history in North and South America. The forces of religious differences and impetus to spread one's particular brand of Christianity gave much energy to the desire to gain more territory and convert as many Native people as possible. Catholicism shaped the history of Europe and thus the course of events in the history of the New World. This influence continues today, and its legacy is obvious in the many churches, cathedrals, schools, and universities that can be found throughout the world and notably in the United States.

Matthew D. Zarzeczny

See also: Alexander VI; Black Legend; Columbus, Christopher; Coronado, Francisco Vasquez de; Cortés, Hernán; Doctrine of Discovery/Conquest; Dominicans; Franciscans; New Spain; Portugal; Spain

Further Reading

Curran, Robert Emmett. 2014. *Papist Devils: Catholics in British America, 1574–1783*. Washington, D.C.: The Catholic University of America Press.

O'Toole, James M. 2008. *The Faithful: A History of Catholics in America.* Cambridge, MA: Harvard University Press.

Schroth, Raymond A. 2007. *The American Jesuits: A History.* New York: New York University Press.

CHAMPLAIN, SAMUEL DE (1574–1635)

Samuel de Champlain was a noted French explorer, cartographer, author, founder of Quebec City (1608), and French colonial leader in North America. He is considered the "Father of New France," he encouraged colonial settlement, oversaw development of the region, improved relations with aboriginals, and established trading routes. Throughout his career, Champlain traversed the Atlantic numerous times and explored the Ottawa River, the St. Lawrence Seaway, parts of the eastern Great Lakes, and New England, and he discovered Lake Champlain (1609). He is considered seminal to French Canadian and Canadian national history for his roles in establishing early European settlements along the St. Lawrence River, mapping the region, humanely treating and making alliances with regional aboriginal tribes, and writing accounts of Native culture and his own explorations.

Champlain was born in 1574 in Brouage, Saintonge, France, and little is known of his early life. In particular, his family's religious affiliation is unknown at the time of Champlain's birth, though he is speculated to have been Protestant. Prior to traveling to what is now Canada, he was a renowned navigator who participated in expeditions to the West Indies and Central America (1598–1600). From 1601 until 1603, Champlain was a cartographer for Henry IV (1553–1610), during which time he studied previous accounts of exploration in North America.

In 1603, Champlain accepted an invitation to join François Gravé Du Pont's (1560–1629) exploration of Canada and published an account of his first voyage to North America later that same year. In 1604, Champlain was chosen as the cartographer by Pierre Du Gua de Mons (1558–1628) for a voyage to Acadia, now Nova Scotia, where he wintered in Saint-Croix, now Maine, and aided in the colonial settlement of Port-Royal (1605), now Annapolis, on the coast of the Bay of Fundy. Along with the crew, Champlain spent three winters in the Saint-Croix region surveying potential settlement sites. Throughout this period, in addition to establishing Port Royal, Champlain also explored the Bay of Fundy, the Annapolis Basin, the Gaspé Peninsula, and the St. John and St. Croix River systems, and he extensively surveyed and mapped parts of Acadia along the Atlantic Coast, including Maine and Massachusetts.

Champlain subsequently participated in an expedition up the St. Lawrence River and, at the behest of Du Gua, founded a trading fort on July 3, 1608, which later became known as Quebec City. Now a lieutenant, it was under Champlain's leadership that the outpost survived its first winter season. During this period, Champlain directed not only the construction of the settlement and establishment of arable farmland, but also colonial defenses, which included a moat and stockade. With the fort established, Champlain built upon relations and earlier French ties with regional aboriginal tribes, such as the Huron-Wendat and Algonquin, and established a sizable system of trade. As a result of their alliance with Champlain and the French government, regional aboriginals became involved in the battle along Lake Champlain (1609–1610). With their help, Champlain aided in the defeat of the Iroquois at Ticonderoga in New York. While this encounter fostered animosity between the Iroquois and French for the coming century, its success also ensured increasing cooperation and trade between Champlain, the Huron-Wendat, and the Algonquin. As always, despite Champlain's military success and the establishment of the fur trade, exploration of the region remained his priority.

In 1610, Champlain returned to France and married the young Hélène Boullé (1598–1654), whose family had strong connections to the imperial court, now controlled by Marie de Medici (1575–1642), the Catholic regent to her son Louis XIII (1601–1643). Amid Champlain's absence from New France in North America, the fur trade suffered from consistent problems and financial losses (1611), which ultimately led to the collapse of colonial investment and sponsorship by French businessmen. However, given Champlain's influence and political connections, Louis XIII interceded and allowed the colonial enterprise to continue. As such, in 1613, Champlain was named commandant of New France by Louis XIII and received finances to continue exploring the region. Given the French monarch's support, Champlain soon reestablished his authority in Quebec, New France's fur trade along the Ottawa River, and regional exploration. As a result, by 1614, Champlain was able to convince French merchants and businessmen to again invest in Quebec's fur trade, regional colonization, and the French exploration of North America.

In 1615, Champlain voyaged farther into the Canadian interior, along the Ottawa River, into Lake Nipissing, and along the French River to Lake Huron, where he was convinced by his Native allies, the Hurons, to attack an Iroquois village near Lake Ontario. During the assault, Champlain was injured, and the French forces, along with their Huron and Algonquin allies, were repulsed. Despite these setbacks, Champlain was saved by his Native allies and spent a winter in the region of Georgian Bay, where he wrote a comprehensive account of Native life and culture before returning first to Quebec City and later to France in 1616.

Upon returning to France, Champlain discovered that events in French national politics had begun to undermine colonial support. In the coming four years, along with reestablishing his political connections, Champlain dedicated himself to writing accounts of his voyages. By 1620, after several tumultuous years, Champlain's authority in Quebec was reaffirmed by Louis XIII; yet, on this occasion, he was directed to return as an administrator and forbidden from being an explorer in his own right. In addition, in 1627, Cardinal de Richelieu (1585–1642) placed Champlain in charge of the newly established the Compagnie des Cent-Associés, or the Company of the Hundred Associates. However, despite his previous achievements and his ongoing work fortifying Quebec City, Champlain was a poor administrator, and the colony soon struggled to survive. In addition, New France, the center of a profitable trade network in North America, soon became the target of the English government during the Anglo-French War (1627–1629).

In 1628, David Kirke (1597–1654) and his brother, under commission from Charles I of England, besieged Champlain's settlement at Quebec City. Along with his sustained assault on the colony, Kirke systematically cut it off from French supply ships, depriving the settlement of basic necessities. After several months, though Champlain himself defended the settlement, Quebec City's military garrison had exhausted its supply of gunpowder, and the French population lacked for food. As a result, Champlain surrendered the colony on July 19, 1629, and soon after returned to Europe. New France would subsequently remain under English control from 1629 until 1632, when the Treaty of Saint-Germain-en-Laye (1632) was signed. On May 22, 1633, Champlain returned to New France, now the colonial commander, and once in Quebec City began its reconstruction. By 1634, the reconstruction, fortification, and prosperity of Quebec City were assured, but Champlain's declining health led him to retire by the end of 1633. In October 1635, still living in Quebec City, Champlain had a stroke, leaving him largely incapacitated until his death on Christmas Day 1635.

At the time of his passing, Samuel de Champlain was a noted French explorer, cartographer, colonial leader, and founder of Quebec City. In addition, he is noted for having published a considerable range of texts detailing his life, voyages, exploration, and experiences in New France, each of which provide invaluable insight into the period and aboriginal culture. He is considered seminal to French colonial and Canadian national history for his roles in establishing early European settlements along the St. Lawrence River; asserting France's control of regional waterways; mapping the region; humanely treating and establishing alliances with regional aboriginal tribes, which led to the development of Métis culture; establishing the fur trade; and provoking enduring hostility between the Iroquois nation and the French.

Sean Morton

See also: Algonquin; New France

Further Reading

Biggar, H. eds. 1922–1936. *The Works of Samuel de Champlain.* 6 vols. Toronto: Champlain Society.

Dionne, N. 1963. *The Makers of Canada: Champlain.* Toronto: Morang & Co. Ltd.

Eccles, W. 1983. *The Canadian Frontier: 1534–1760.* Albuquerque: University of New Mexico Press.

Morison, S. 1972. *Samuel de Champlain: Father of New France.* Boston: Little Brown Press.

CHARLESTON

When Charles II was restored to the English throne following the Lord Protectorship of Oliver Cromwell, he rewarded eight of his supporters with a grant of land in North America. Dated 1663, the charter for the land called Carolina (based on *Carolus*, the Latin form of "Charles") gave the group, styled lords proprietors, title to everything south of the Virginia colony down to what is today Georgia. Several years elapsed before a concerted effort was made to populate the area. It was not until 1670 that the first permanent settlement was founded by English colonists from Barbados under William Sayle. They chose a site along the western bank of the Ashley River, which they named Charles Town, further honoring the monarch who had issued the charter.

Almost from the beginning, one of the proprietors, Anthony Ashley Cooper, envisioned the new settlement as a commercial port, but its early years were tenuous. Located in the ambiguous border area, where the claims between England and Spain often overlapped, the colony, or its commerce, was periodically attacked by Spain, France, assorted pirates, and indigenous people dispossessed as the colony expanded. Despite these hazards, the early settlement grew with periodic arrivals from Barbados and England and of colonists moving south from Virginia. By 1680, a plan called the "Grand Model" was adopted for the organized development of the city. It was based on a central square around which civic and religious buildings were to be erected.

The colony's initial government was detailed in the Fundamental Constitutions of Carolina, written by the celebrated Enlightenment philosopher John Locke in 1669. The government included a governor and a parliament of 20 representatives elected by the colony's freeholders. It also allowed the lords proprietors to appoint 5 deputies to oversee their interests. Any legislation adopted by the parliament was only to become law when approved by the governor and 3 of the 5 deputies. In the early years, when the population was still quite small, the freemen of the colony were allowed to elect 5 deputies, who, together with the 5 appointed by

Charleston, South Carolina, was a major port city in the American colonies. During the American Revolution, the Continental Army suffered a major defeat when the British captured the city. (Library of Congress)

the lords proprietors, would form an executive council. Anyone holding any of these appointive or elective positions was required to swear an oath of allegiance to the lords proprietors and the effective instruments of governance. Most historians believe that, at that time, acceptance of the Fundamental Constitutions was required for anyone wishing to settle in the colony. This led to some early dissent as freemen asserted their right to elect an assembly, as originally envisioned in Locke's document.

By 1742, the city's population had reached 6,800. Although the large majority of white residents were of English ancestry, from an early date, the settlement attracted a diverse population, including French Huguenots, Scottish religious dissidents, Scots-Irish, Irish, Germans, Dutch colonists from New York, and Sephardic Jews. These groups brought with them a variety of Protestant religious practices as well as Catholics and Jews. Sir John Yeamans brought the first 200 African slaves to the colony in 1671. Within a few years, they formed the numerical majority of the population.

Initially, the colony's economy was based on agriculture and trading for furs with the local indigenous people. This was supplemented with the production of naval stores based on the plentiful forests. By 1700, commercial agriculture centered on the cultivation of rice from seeds imported from Madagascar, which proved profitable. By 1750, indigo had joined rice as a lucrative commercial crop, especially when the English government began paying a bounty for its production. Both of these crops were labor-intensive, and rice also required large tracts of flooded land that proved to be breeding grounds for disease-carrying mosquitoes. The need for a large amount of inexpensive labor led to the proliferation of slavery, especially along the coastal lands, where the larger commercial plantations were located at the time. In the mid-1700s, cotton production expanded and joined rice and indigo as the main commercial crops produced in the immediate area of Charleston at the time of the Revolution.

A turning point in the history of the city occurred in 1715, when the Spanish instigated an attack on the English colony by a coalition of indigenous tribes led by the Yamassee. In this brutal contest along the frontier areas, an estimated 400 English were killed. But the power of the tribes was completely broken, and their remnants driven from the colony. The expense of the war was crippling, leading the colonists to request financial assistance from the lords proprietors. When they refused, and also vetoed the colonial suggestions for instituting import or export duties or selling off the lands previously occupied by the Yamassee, the people petitioned the Crown to convert South Carolina into a royal colony, a request that was granted in 1719. The result for Charleston was a flourishing of trade and a rapid influx of new settlers.

Bermuda and various ports in the Caribbean were closely tied to the city's growing commercial network, but its major partner in North America was Boston. Given the differentials in climate, wealthy people from the two cities often spent time during the winter months in warmer Charleston and during the hot summer in cooler Boston. By 1750, Charleston was the largest and wealthiest city in the Southern Colonies. Twenty years later, its population topped 11,000, making it the fourth-largest city in the English colonies after Boston, New York, and Philadelphia. Over half that number were slaves.

With its growth in population and wealth, Charleston became the social, cultural, and political capital of the South. It was the center of business life and the seat of political influence. In addition to the prosperous merchants who made their living in the city, wealthy plantation owners resided there, hiring overseers to manage their property so they could enjoy the benefits of society and the somewhat more moderate climate tempered by ocean breezes. Those whose level of wealth did not permit this often spent the hot summer months in Charleston while residing on their estates the balance of the year. Among the benefits of Charleston were the first publicly supported library, established in 1700; the first theater built in America, in 1736; the College of Charleston, founded in 1770; the nation's first museum, in 1773; literary societies; horse racing venues; social functions; and, of course, meetings of the colonial legislature. Charleston was *the* place to be for anyone with sufficient income to enjoy the finer things in life.

In the years following the end of the French and Indian War in 1763, as the differences between the North American colonies and England widened, the city's population began to divide between the Loyalists and those who favored protest, and eventually independence. The colony sent a delegation to the Stamp Act Congress, and later, in response to the Tea Act of 1773 and the ensuing call for colonial boycotts, Charleston voted to confiscate tea shipped into the port and impound it in the customs building so that it could not be sold and the tax collected. In the following year, the colony sent a delegation of five Charlestonians to the First Continental Congress, where Henry Middleton, of the city, was elected the first president of the assembly. Throughout the war, British strategy in the South assumed that

Loyalists in Charleston would rise up to support them with the arrival of British troops. Some did, but the majority of the population did not.

Following the Revolution, the South Carolina delegation to the Constitutional Convention supported a stronger national government, a powerful chief executive, and the Virginia Plan for legislative, executive, and judiciary branches. Four Charlestonians served as the state's delegation to the Constitutional Convention: Pierce Butler, Charles Pinckney, Charles Cotesworth Pinckney, and John Rutledge. All four played prominent roles in the discussions where they all, to one degree or another, favored a stronger central government. Butler was also a vocal advocate for the slave-owning class, joining Rutledge, who continually defended South Carolina's interests. Charles Pinckney played an influential role crafting some of the compromise language on controversial issues, and Charles Cotesworth Pinckney is credited with effectively arguing for granting the Senate the authority to ratify treaties and also for a conspicuous role in formulating the compromise concerning the international slave trade that granted Congress the authority to regulate commerce.

The state convention that was called to vote on ratification of the Constitution met in Charleston. It became the eighth state to ratify the Constitution when it voted in favor, 149–73, on May 23, 1788.

James S. Pula

See also: Atlantic Slave Trade; Carolina Constitution; Rice Cultivation; South Carolina

Further Reading

Salley, Alexander Samuel. 1911. *Narratives of Early Carolina, 1650–1708*. New York: Charles Scribner's Sons.

Sellers, Leila. 1970. *Charleston Business on the Eve of the American Revolution*. New York: Arno Press.

Waring, Joseph I. 1970. *The First Voyage and Settlement at Charles Town, 1670–1680*. Columbia: University of South Carolina Press.

CHESAPEAKE, BATTLE OF THE

The Battle of the Chesapeake (sometimes known as the Battle of the Capes or the Battle of the Virginia Capes) was a naval battle that took place off the coast of Virginia on September 5, 1781. Although it did not involve any Americans, it was one of the most decisive events of the American Revolution. The French navy defeated the British Royal Navy, ending any chance for Lord Charles Cornwallis to be rescued or resupplied during the Siege of Yorktown and essentially sealing Gen. George Washington's victory there a little over a month later.

In September 1781, General Washington was camped near New York City. He hoped to use his army, recently reinforced with nearly 5,500 French soldiers under the Comte de Rochambeau, to dislodge the British forces occupying the city. While developing his plan of attack, Washington learned that a fleet of French warships under Rear Adm. François-Joseph Paul, marquis de Grasse Tilly, was sailing from

The Battle of the Chesapeake was a significant naval battle that took place on September 5, 1781. The result of the battle was the defeat of the British by a French fleet under the command of Comte de Grasse, a loss that prevented the British fleet from assisting General Charles Cornwallis, who was under siege at Yorktown. The British surrender at Yorktown prompted the British government to negotiate the end of the Revolutionary War. (Naval Historical Society)

the West Indies to aid the American campaign. However, de Grasse worried that sailing to America would leave French interests in the Caribbean dangerously exposed, and so the French fleet would only be available to Washington for a brief time. Rochambeau believed that the American effort should be directed at Lord Cornwallis's force at Yorktown instead of against Sir Henry Clinton's force in New York, as Washington favored. The French officer believed that Virginia offered a greater chance of success because the British in New York had had several years to fortify their position. In addition, Virginia was a shorter sail for de Grasse, and the waters surrounding Yorktown were more navigable than New York Harbor.

Cornwallis's army had established its position at Yorktown, Virginia, in the summer of 1781. After a series of running battles across the Carolinas and Virginia, Cornwallis expected that a fortified position at Yorktown would draw the Americans into a direct confrontation. Yorktown was a deepwater port on the York River and would allow the British army to be resupplied, and even evacuated if need be, by the Royal Navy. This plan depended on the Royal Navy's mastery of the sea-lanes, something that had not been a concern throughout the war to that point.

From his base in Santo Domingo, de Grasse collected 3,000 French soldiers and 1.2 million livres (approximately $6 million in today's money) and sailed north. His fleet of 37 ships included 28 ships of the line, 7 frigates, and 2 cutters. Setting sail on August 5, 1781, de Grasse took a potentially dangerous route through the Bahamas to avoid British patrols in the region. Washington received word on August 14 that de Grasse was sailing for Virginia. He therefore abandoned his plan to attack New York and quickly made preparations to march south, 400 miles, to attack Cornwallis at Yorktown. Washington and Rochambeau's plan was a risky one and depended entirely on the French fleet gaining control of the Chesapeake Bay.

Upon learning of de Grasse's fleet sailing north, British admiral Samuel Hood raced to catch up. Hood took a more direct path to the Chesapeake and actually passed the French without seeing them. Hood arrived at the Chesapeake Bay on August 25, but not seeing any French fleet, he immediately sailed north to New York City. In the meantime, de Grasse arrived off the coast of Virginia near Jamestown and began offloading men and supplies to join up with the Continental Army in Williamsburg, under the command of the Marquis de Lafayette.

In New York City, Admiral Hood and the commander-in-chief of the British North American fleet, Adm. Thomas Graves, combined their fleets. They sailed south to Virginia on August 31, with 19 ships of the line, under the unified command of Admiral Graves. Graves's fleet arrived near the mouth of the Chesapeake on the morning of September 5, and he soon got word that one of his scouting frigates had located the French fleet. He began arranging his ships into battle formation. Unaware that the British had arrived, de Grasse was still in the process of offloading his ships; many of his officers were still ashore. When they saw the British fleet, the French assumed it was a second French fleet under the command of Adm. Comte de Barras that had sailed from Newport, Rhode Island, a few days earlier. Upon realizing that it was actually a British fleet, de Grasse hastily organized his ships into formation. The British failed to take advantage of the French fleet's disorder, however, and the lines of battle were formed.

The British were hampered by the wind direction as well as by a series of confusing flag signals sent by Admiral Graves. As such, almost half of the British warships were unable to get into firing position. The battle lasted little more than two hours. Graves's fleet suffered 6 ships damaged and 90 sailors killed. Another 246 were wounded. The French suffered damage to only 2 ships, with some 220 French sailors wounded.

Over the next few days, both admirals waited to see what the other would do, their fleets drifting south out of the Bay, often within sight of each other. Graves was reluctant to resume fighting, especially since Admiral de Barras's ships had arrived during the battle, bringing the total number of French ships of the line to 36. He sailed north to New York on September 10, hoping to repair his ships, resupply, and return to Virginia to relieve Cornwallis's forces at the Siege of Yorktown. However, due to difficulty securing replacement parts, slow repairs, and contrary winds, Graves was unable to sail from New York until October 19, 1781, the very day that Cornwallis surrendered to Washington's forces, essentially ending the American Revolution and securing the colonies their independence.

The French victory at the Battle of the Chesapeake was decisive in securing Washington's victory over Cornwallis and thereby winning the Revolution. French control over the sea-lanes prevented the Royal Navy from resupplying or evacuating Cornwallis's besieged troops and rendered his position untenable. After

Cornwallis's surrender, the British decided to pursue a negotiated peace rather than continue fighting. Independence for the colonies would officially come less than two years later with the Peace of Paris.

Shawn Selby

See also: Chesapeake Bay; Comte de Grasse, François-Joseph Paul; Yorktown, Battle of

Further Reading

Ketchum, Richard. 2004. *Victory at Yorktown: The Campaign That Won the Revolution.* New York: Henry Holt & Co.

Nelson, James. 2010. *George Washington's Great Gamble: And the Sea Battle That Won the American Revolution.* New York: Ragged Mountain Press.

CHESAPEAKE BAY

An incredibly important historical watershed and the largest estuary in the United States, the Chesapeake Bay and its environs have provided a rich fishery, an excellent refuge for ships, and the site of the first English colonies in North America. Draining parts of Maryland, Virginia, West Virginia, Pennsylvania, Delaware, New York, and Washington, D.C. (64,000 square miles), the seven rivers and other minor tributaries of the estuary dump an average of 78,300 cubic feet per second of water into the bay. The bay stretches about 200 miles north-south and is about 21 miles wide (east-west). The average depth is 21 feet, with 174 feet the maximum depth. Maryland surrounds the northern portion of the bay, and Virginia surrounds the southern part. Native Americans first settled the area as long ago as 12,000 years and had well-established communities and societies when Europeans arrived.

Important modern and colonial cities on or near the bay include Washington, D.C., Norfolk-Virginia Beach, Baltimore, Annapolis, Yorktown, Newport News, and Williamsburg. The bay is the critical geographic feature of both Maryland and Virginia, with Baltimore the main port of Maryland and Norfolk the main port of Virginia. The estuaries emptying into the Chesapeake Bay provided access to the interior of those colonies for early European settlers, with protected entrances away from the open ocean.

The Chesapeake name comes from the Algonquin *Cheseplooc* and is one of the oldest surviving English place names in the United States. The name was first applied by the Roanoke settlers in 1585, the failed expedition by Sir Walter Raleigh to colonize Roanoke Island in North Carolina's Outer Banks, just south of the Chesapeake Bay. In 1587, Raleigh had sent a second group of settlers to colonize the Chesapeake, but when they found the Roanoke Colony abandoned, the colonists were instead ordered to reestablish the Roanoke Colony by the fleet commander, Simon Fernandez. (This group of settlers also went missing with hardly a clue in 1590.)

European explorers first came to Chesapeake Bay in 1524, when Giovanni de Verrazzano (of the Verrazzano-Narrows Bridge fame) sailed to the entrance to the bay while in service to France, although he did not explore inside the entrance. In 1525, Lucas Vásquez de Ayllón, a Spaniard, sailed from Hispaniola to the mouth of the Chesapeake Bay and the nearby Delaware Bay, although it is unknown whether he actually sailed into the bay itself. The Spanish briefly established a mission in Virginia, but it remained for the English to make the first serious effort at colonizing the bay area.

In 1585, the first English colony in America was landed at Roanoke Island in the colony named Virginia in honor of Queen Elizabeth I, known as the "Virgin Queen." This colony quickly failed and was rescued by Sir Francis Drake, abandoning the settlement. A second attempt was mounted in 1587, a sad affair that resulted in the colonists disappearing with no evidence of where they had gone or exactly what had happened, giving Roanoke the name "The Lost Colony."

The first permanent English colony in the Chesapeake was attempted in 1607, when a group of settlers led by Capt. John Smith formed the Jamestown Colony, the first permanent English colony on mainland America. After an abortive attempt to evacuate the colony in 1610, Jamestown, originally named James Fort, became the capital of the Virginia colony in 1616 and remained the capital until 1699, when the capital was moved to Williamsburg, another Chesapeake area settlement.

The Jamestown site was selected by Capt. Edward Wingfield, about 40 miles from the Atlantic, the site having the desirable traits of allowing for ships to dock and easily defensible terrain on a river bend (the James River) comprising a peninsula. Another key factor in this choice of location was that it was not inhabited by Native Americans. Unfortunately, the reason Native Americans had not settled this location was because of the swampy ground found there, making the site a virtual island beset by mosquitoes, unsuitable for agriculture, and provided with brackish river water not well suited for drinking. Compounding the problems the first settlers faced was that the expedition arrived too late for the planting of crops that could be harvested the same year. Obviously, this problem would have catastrophic consequences for the English settlers, a group not renowned for careful planning for the establishment of colonies.

The settlers themselves were also not particularly well suited for the rugged physical demands of building a settlement, as many came from the gentrified class unaccustomed to doing manual labor. The area's Native Americans numbered around 14,000 and had initially welcomed the English settlers. By the first spring, 80 percent of the English settlers were already dead, and some of the survivors had gone off to live with Native Americans as the surest way to continue to survive. In 1608, a relief expedition brought German, Slovak, and Polish settlers, tradesmen and laborers used to hard work and capable of starting the basic industries needed to survive.

Continued hardships and problems with the timely arrival of supply ships from England led to a harrowing period in 1609–1610 known as the "Starving Time," a self-explanatory time of starvation and death, which by the spring of 1610 left only 60 of the 214 settlers alive, some of the survivors having resorted to cannibalism to remain so. In June 1610, with the survivors themselves near death, relief ships embarked the colonists and set sail for England, giving up on Jamestown. Before the ships carrying the evacuees could clear the James River, another relief expedition arrived, and the survivors along with additional colonists were returned to the settlement, although life remained hard in the colony.

When the capital of Virginia was moved to Middle Plantation (later named Williamsburg) in 1699, Jamestown began to wither away as a town and fell into private hands, never to regain civic importance. Williamsburg, founded in 1632, was located on much better (higher) ground and started as a fortified settlement, serving as Virginia's capital until 1780. Aside from the modern-day Colonial Williamsburg theme park, Williamsburg is distinguished by hosting the College of William and Mary.

The third part of the "Historic Triangle," along with Jamestown and Williamsburg, is Yorktown, Virginia, a port that figured prominently during the American Civil War (1861–1865) and was the site of the decisive battle of the American Revolution (1775–1783). Yorktown was established in 1682.

Norfolk (founded 1682) is an important port and home to the largest naval base on earth, but the area first hosted English settlers in 1634. Norfolk quickly became a fortified center of commerce and industry in Virginia, growing in population and importance throughout the Colonial Period. In 1776, fighting in the American Revolution resulted in a massive fire that destroyed two-thirds of the buildings in Norfolk. Recovery from the Revolution was hampered by another great fire in 1804, but the city and the area gradually regained its prominence. The area containing Norfolk, Virginia Beach, Newport News, Yorktown, Jamestown, and the environs is called Hampton Roads and often referred to as the "Tidewater" area. This region is the original foundation of English settlement in what is now the United States, and it is called "America's First Region" for this reason. Year-round ice-free harbors made the Chesapeake and Hampton Roads an especially attractive place to form the basis for settlement on the East Coast. The importance of the Chesapeake during the American Civil War resulted in one of history's most pivotal naval engagements, the Battle of Hampton Roads, between the USS *Monitor* and the CSS *Virginia* (formerly the USS *Merrimack*), history's first battle between ironclad warships.

In Maryland, major settlements include Annapolis (founded 1649), the state capital and home of the U.S. Naval Academy, and Baltimore (founded 1729, although individual buildings and settlements came earlier), the largest city in the state and second-largest seaport on the U.S. Atlantic Coast. Baltimore was also home to Fort McHenry during the War of 1812, and its defense against British bombardment spurred the writing of "The Star-Spangled Banner," the Francis Scott Key composition that became the U.S. national anthem.

With the mass importation and exploitation of African slaves prior to the American Civil War, the Chesapeake was and continues to be home to millions of African Americans. African slaves were first brought to the region in 1619, and Virginia and Maryland were slave states. As well as being the gateway to America for African slaves, the Chesapeake Bay region was also important as a route along the Underground Railroad for slaves escaping to the North. The Chesapeake was at least somewhat unique with the large number of African Americans that found work in the fishing and shellfish industries.

Today, more than 17 million people live in the Chesapeake Bay region, and the area continues to play an important role in American life, including bordering the urban sprawl from Washington, D.C. George Washington and Robert E. Lee called the area home, and the area abounds with historic sites, recreational opportunities, military bases, fishing and marine-related industry, cultural and educational centers, and 18 trillion gallons of water that is home to myriad fish, shellfish, birds, and other wildlife.

Matthew D. Zarzeczny

See also: Chesapeake, Battle of the; Jamestown; Virginia; Yorktown, Battle of

Further Reading

Brewington, M. V. 1988. *Chesapeake Bay: A Pictorial Maritime History.* New York: Random House Value Publishing.

Mills, Eric. 1996. *Chesapeake Bay in the Civil War.* Atglen, PA: Cornell Maritime Pr/Tidewater Pub.

Shomette, Donald G. 2008. *Pirates on the Chesapeake: Being a True History of Pirates, Picaroons, and Raiders on Chesapeake Bay, 1610–1807.* Atglen, PA: Tidewater Publishers.

CHURCH, BENJAMIN (1734–1778)

Dr. Benjamin Church would have easily been considered one of the Founding Fathers if not for questionable episodes later in his life. To those that thought they knew him, the years prior to the Revolution saw him as a strong patriot and active in the Sons of Liberty. He graduated from Harvard in 1754 and studied in medicine near home and in London. His talent and skills as a physician and surgeon were only surpassed by his ardor for the cause of the struggle against Britain.

Church's skill with a pen and from the pulpit was second only to his skill as a doctor. In the aftermath of the Boston Massacre, he tended the American wounded, and as the conflict with England grew more likely, he served in the Massachusetts Provincial Congress in 1774. He served on the Committee of Public Safety that was tasked with preparing Massachusetts for war, and in 1775, he was appointed alongside Dr. Joseph Warren to inventory and supply the medical needs of what would become the provincial army.

When war finally came in April 1775, Church was tasked with supplying surgeons and medical supplies to the military hospitals. As his star rose, he found himself in front of the Continental Congress in July, where he was appointed as the first director general and chief physician of the Medical Department of the Continental Army. That appointment would prove to be the apex of his career and his reputation.

While Church may have been an excellent doctor, he left much to be desired as an administrator. Conditions in his hospital were terrible. He did not get along with the staff and proved to be a magnet for controversy in his post, so much so that Gen. George Washington eventually had to order an investigation into his department, but that was not the last bit of bad news that Dr. Church would have to face.

In September 1775, a letter found its way to General Washington that had been intercepted by the lover of a woman who had been a former paramour of Dr. Church. The letter was written in cipher and was addressed to a Major Kane, a British officer in Boston. Washington immediately set a team to work breaking the cipher, and they soon learned that Dr. Church was the author. In the letter, he not only shared information about the disposition of the American forces, but he strongly stated his loyalty to the Crown and his willingness to continue sending information.

Caught red-handed, Church was brought before a board of inquiry led by Washington himself. In his defense, Church admitted to writing the letter, but he claimed he was trying to bluff the British into thinking the Americans were more prepared for a fight than they really were. It was all meant to bring the British to the negotiation table. His attempt at defense failed, and his case was sent to the Continental Congress.

Up to this point, the Congress had been so worried about building an army that they had no provisions to cover what Church had done and no method of dealing with traitors. While they worked to decide what to do with him, Church was kicked out of the Massachusetts Provincial Congress, and in October 1775, he was confined to imprisonment in Norwich, Connecticut; banned from having pen and paper; forbidden to speak to anyone without a magistrate or sheriff present; and forbidden any communication in any language other than English. His punishment would last until further orders or until another Congress figured out what to do with him.

In effect, Dr. Church was branded the first traitor to the American cause and removed from society. In 1776, due to bad health, he was allowed to leave his confinement, and in 1778, he was released but banished from the country. He left Boston on a ship for the Caribbean, but he and the ship he had sailed on were never seen again.

The question of whether Church was a true traitor was one of some discussion for many years until the papers of Gen. Thomas Gage, the British commander in Boston early in the conflict, were finally opened for study. In those documents, they found a number of letters written to him by Church, including documents that Church had been tasked with taking in and out of Boston during the siege. The documented portion of his spy career stretched back to early 1775 according to these papers. In recent years, it is thought that his Loyalist life may have stretched back as far as 1772 and may have included his writing pro-British articles in local publications under a pseudonym. He was well-known as a heavy spender, but he somehow always seemed to have a supply of money well beyond what would be considered within his means. No clear answer as to where the money came from can be located.

While Dr. Church was one of the first traitors of the American Revolution, his story is not told very often. It is possible that is because his most grievous acts happened in the early years of the conflict, before the idea of "us vs. them" had truly had the chance to solidify. It is hard to say whether the intelligence he provided was useful to the British. The one solid thing that can be said, his major contribution to the cause may be that he forced the Congress to confront the issue of what to do with those who committed treason. Dr. Church may have avoided hanging for his crimes, but he ensured that any who followed in his stead would meet that fate.

Stuart Hatfield

See also: Sons of Liberty; Washington, George

Further Reading

Lockhart, Paul. 2011. *The Whites of Their Eyes.* New York: Harper Collins.

Nagy, John A. 2013. *Dr. Benjamin Church, Spy: A Case of Espionage on the Eve of the American Revolution.* Yardley, PA: Westholme Publishing

Philbrick, Nathaniel. 2013. *Bunker Hill: A City, a Siege, a Revolution.* New York: Penguin Group.

CLARK, GEORGE ROGERS (1752–1818)

George Rogers Clark was an American soldier who played a major role in the opening of the North American frontier. As a surveyor and soldier, he contributed greatly to the effort by first the colonies, and then the young nation, to expand westward.

George Rogers Clark was born on November 19, 1752, in Charlottesville, Virginia. He was the second son and one of the ten children born to John and Ann Rogers Clark, both of whose families were Virginia landowners. He may have briefly attended a small private school on the Mattaponi River, but that experience would represent the only formal education Clark ever received. The rest of his education came at home from a range of relatives. In addition and most importantly, when Clark was a teenager, his grandfather taught him how to survey the local land, training he would use to good effect for the rest of his life.

Despite the British-imposed ban on settlement west of the Appalachian Mountains following the French and Indian War (Seven Years' War, 1756–1763), many Virginians headed west into Kentucky. In 1772, Clark joined their numbers and spent much of the next four years securing land for himself and his family while also serving as a guide for others looking to settle in the area. In 1774, Clark played a role in Lord Dunmore's War, and as a member of the Virginia militia, he was involved with the Battle of Point Pleasant. The military experience enhanced his reputation as frontiersman and Indian fighter. Leaving the militia following that conflict, he surveyed land in Kentucky while working for the Ohio Company. Increased tensions with the Indians led to efforts by the developing Kentucky populace to secure a more formal and productive relationship with Virginia, and despite his youth, in June 1776, Clark was selected to be part of a delegation that sought to pursue this goal. Meeting with Gov. Patrick Henry and members of his executive council, the group secured both a substantive supply of gunpowder to facilitate their defense against the continuing Indian harassment as well as recognition by Virginia of Kentucky as a formal county, a relationship that represented a step toward statehood. In the end, both developments did much to enhance both Kentucky's stature and its security.

When the Revolution started, Clark rejoined the Virginia militia, and with his previous experience, he was commissioned a major. After playing an important role in protecting Kentucky and the western frontier of Virginia from attacks by both the British and their Native American allies, Clark was promoted to lieutenant colonel. During the winter of 1778–1779, he led an army through the difficult terrain against British and Native American positions throughout Indiana and Illinois, a campaign that was highlighted by their capture of British commander Henry Hamilton and the outpost at Vincennes. Clark was unable to duplicate that success later in the year when an attempt to capture Fort Detroit was rebuffed. For the remainder of the war, Clark led forces that clashed with Indian and British forces seeking to protect their lands against American settlers trying to move west of the Appalachian Mountains.

After the surrender at Yorktown, conflict continued on the western frontier, and Clark was very much involved. He was promoted to brigadier general, and working with the Shawnee, he harassed British forces around Detroit while also leading the expedition that retook Fort Sackville near Vincennes. Soon afterward, the Confederation Congress named him the chief surveyor of the Northwest Territory and an Indian commissioner, a role in which he helped with the territory's early governance. In that role, Clark worked with Richard Butler and Samuel Parsons to negotiate the Treaty of Fort McIntosh, which required that the Native American population, not all of whom had been represented in the negotiations, leave all their lands in what is now Ohio, except for the northwest part of the state.

The treaty quickly became a source of considerable controversy, as questions abounded over the authority that many signatories had to commit their people, not to mention reports that the American team had gotten many of the Natives drunk before completing the process. Once in effect, the American government did little to protect the land that was intended as a preserve for the Native American population from encroachment by white settlers. In addition, Clark hurt both his own reputation and relations between the government and the Indians by conducting a war against tribes he claimed had violated the treaty. Finally, Clark apparently engaged in some improper dealings with Spanish merchants. All of this embarrassed the Congress, and Clark was relieved of his governmental responsibilities on the western frontier.

Freed of constraints, Clark struck out on his own, unsuccessfully approaching the Spanish government in 1788 about starting a colony on the western bank of the Mississippi River near the mouth of the Ohio River. Meanwhile, he experienced serious financial difficulties and tried to secure reimbursement from Virginia for the earlier military campaigns he had personal funded. However, these requests seldom yielded anything close to what he sought, and so he was forced to sell most of the large land grants that the government had previously awarded Clark for his services to satisfy his creditors. In 1793, a financially strapped Clark worked with controversial French ambassador Edmond Charles Genet to contrive a plan aimed at driving the Spanish from the Louisiana Territory. But after personally financing the expedition preparations, Clark had to abandon the effort when President

George Washington forbade any American citizen from violating the nation's neutrality policy with regards to France.

In 1803, Clark moved to Indiana, but then in 1809, following both a severe stroke and then an accident that resulted in burns that required the amputation of his leg, he returned to Kentucky, where lived with his sister in Louisville. It was not an easy time, but it was made more tolerable when, in 1812, Virginia finally recognized his service and granted Clark a pension and a ceremonial sword. On February 13, 1818, Clark suffered another stroke and died. He was first buried in Locus Hill Grove Cemetery, but in 1869, his body as well as those of his family were transferred to Louisville's Cave Hill Cemetery.

William H. Pruden III

See also: Dunmore's War; Frontier

Further Reading

Harrison, Lowell H. 1976. *George Rogers Clark and the War in the West.* Lexington: University Press of Kentucky.

National Historical Park Indiana. 2015. "George Rogers Clark." National Park Service. https://www.nps.gov/gero/learn/historyculture/clark.htm.

Nester, William R. 2012. *George Rogers Clark: "I Glory in War."* Norman: University of Oklahoma Press.

Ohio History Central. "George R. Clark." http://www.ohiohistorycentral.org/w/George_R._Clark.

Waller, George M. 1976. "George Rogers Clark and the American Revolution in the West." *Indiana Magazine of History* 72: 1–20. https://www.jstor.org/stable/pdf/27790085.pdf.

CLARKE, JOHN (1609–1676)

John Clarke somewhat quietly played an integral role in the establishment of Rhode Island and its status as a bastion of religions liberty. Roger Williams is rightly considered an original founder of the colony, but Clarke's work on the colony's early laws and his role in the development of Newport were essential. Williams is also considered the founder of religious liberty in Rhode Island (the colony most known for such freedom), but it was Clarke who procured the Rhode Island Royal Charter from Charles II that codified this liberty and guaranteed its protection by law. Anne Hutchinson and Samuel Gorton are better known for their religious challenges to Massachusetts Bay Colony, but Clarke also drew the ire of John Winthrop and the colony, facing severe punishment of his own for proselytizing Baptist ideas in the Puritan theocracy. He played a seminal role in the creation of the First Baptist Church of Newport (now known as United Baptist Church, John Clarke Memorial) and served as an informal spiritual leader throughout his time in one of the two oldest Baptist congregations in the country. Many of his contemporaries overshadowed him, but Clarke deserves recognition for his religious, political, and diplomatic achievements; his direct influence on Rhode Island lasted for centuries.

John Clarke was born October 3, 1609, on the manor of Westhorpe, Suffolk County, England to a modest family of Puritan leaning. One of seven children, Clarke stood out because he was trained professionally as a physician, whereas his siblings did not enjoy such formal training. He was recognized as a physician in both Old and New England, but his work as religious leader and statesman signified his primary influence.

Clarke moved to New England in 1637 with members of his family. Almost immediately, he became embroiled in the Antinomian Controversy that was sweeping the Puritan colony at the time. In November 1637, Anne Hutchinson challenged authority in Boston by criticizing some religious leadership in the town of being driven by a "covenant of works" rather than by a "covenant of grace" alone; she led meetings of fellow dissenters in her home and developed a substantial following in the area, accusing ministers other than John Cotton of espousing sanctification and promoting an individual's behavior as the sign of one's grace. For Hutchinson, the Holy Spirit spoke directly to the elect, thereby obviating the need for ministers and religious authority. Her challenge was to the heart of authority itself—an idea Clarke, a man who shunned strong central authority and espoused democratic ideals, quickly supported. The colony banished Hutchinson and her followers from Boston; according to his *Ill News from New England*, published in 1652, Clarke proposed to his fellow dissenters that they should move away from Massachusetts and settle on their own. Led by Clarke and William Coddington, the group moved to Rhode Island and, with the assistance of Roger Williams, eventually established the town of Newport.

It was in Newport that Clarke began his rise to prominence both as statesman and religious leader. He framed, codified, and executed the early laws of Rhode Island, twice served as treasurer to the colony, and represented the colony both internally as an assistant and externally as its agent in negotiations with the English government. Clarke contributed to the original charter for Rhode Island, officially adopted in 1647, incorporating the four main towns under the name Providence Plantations, in Narraganset Bay, in New England. He helped establish an antinomian church in Newport, but his ideas began to evolve with his fellow churchgoers. He leveled criticism of infant baptism, believing instead that only one who understood belief—generally an adult—could rightfully consent to and fully understand baptism. But this was only one of Clarke's differences with Puritanism.

Clarke believed all in the congregation should be free to prophesy, favored decentralized authority within the church—demonstrated by the fact that generally one-third of the men in the Newport church served as preachers—and condemned required attendance at services. He believed the state had no right to involve itself in church affairs. Scholars note Clarke openly promoted a more democratic tenor; as biographer Sydney James stated, "his church had a resolutely democratic flavor" (James 1999, 22), a claim supported by Clarke's promotion of an open, active congregation and desire to decentralize authority in the church. According to historian Albert H. Newman, Clarke's Newport church displayed more "consistent and persistent devotion . . . to Baptist principles" than any other in the colony (Newman 1898, 96).

Coddington, who helped settle Newport with Clarke, viewed things slightly differently, and in 1641, he sought division of the four towns of Rhode Island between Massachusetts, Connecticut, and Plymouth. Clarke fought against this and preserved the independence of Rhode Island. Coddington aimed to preserve his authority at any price and went to England, in 1649, to garner a patent proclaiming him governor for life of Aquidneck. This was anathema to Clarke and his antiauthoritarian nature, and he set out for England a few years later to rectify this accrual of power.

Prior to embarking for England, Clarke proselytized for the Baptist church and dissented against Puritanism in the Massachusetts Bay Colony. In the summer of 1651, Clarke and two others—Obadiah Holmes and John Crandall—traveled to Lynn, Massachusetts, to meet with William Witter and a small group who had shown an interest in Baptist tenets. The three were quickly arrested, fined, and threatened with whipping if they did not pay their fines. Friends paid Clarke's fine, but Holmes suffered a severe whipping at the hands of the Massachusetts Bay Colony authority. Clarke pleaded with the colony's leadership to allow a public disputation of the charges and, in essence, an open discussion of the beliefs of the Baptist church. The court refused, and Clarke returned to Newport. This event crystallized in his mind the importance of religious liberty, and he set out to England as an agent of Rhode Island to procure religious liberty—and more importantly protection of such liberty—from the English government.

Clarke stayed in his home country until 1664, garnering both a revocation of Coddington's commission as governor for life and, more importantly, the Rhode Island Royal Charter of 1663 from Charles II. The document guaranteed religious liberty—the first such assurance "of its kind in the world" (Asher 2004, xiii)—and state protection of this freedom, but it also included significant civil ramifications: a republican form of government was secured. This charter remained in effect for Rhode Island until 1843. Clarke thus gained legalized and state-defended liberty of conscience, actualizing the ideas Roger Williams had practiced and established as the ideological foundation for the colony. This codification of the freedoms Clarke practiced in Newport and lived throughout his life in the colonies was his crowning achievement. This idea would also establish roots for the American experiment with religious liberty, a core principle of the U.S. Constitution finalized over 100 years later. He returned to the colony with little fanfare, and in accordance with his nature, he quietly worked for Rhode Island until his death.

Physician, minister, statesman, and diplomat, John Clarke was an "initiator of democratic ideals in New England . . . and played a seminal role in establishing religious freedom in the young colony" (Asher, xi). He helped to found Newport, played an integral role in the development of its first Baptist church, and garnered freedom of religion and formal protection thereof from the English Crown. He risked life and reputation to spread the ideas of his church and promote democracy at the most basic level. He died April 20, 1676, but his work in life rendered him a founding father of Rhode Island as the first true champion of religious liberty.

Scott M. Roth

See also: Antinomianism; Baptists; Puritan Dissenters; Rhode Island; Williams, Roger

Further Reading

Asher, Louis Franklin. 2004. *John Clarke (1609–1676) Pioneer in American Medicine, Democratic Ideals, and Champion of Religious Liberty.* Paris, AR: The Baptist Standard Bearer, Inc.

Barrows, C. E. 1872. "Dr. John Clarke." *Baptist Quarterly* 6: 483–502.

Clarke, John. 1652. *Ill News from New England: Or a Narrative of New-England's Persecution. Wherein Is Declared That while old England Is Becoming New, New-England Is Become Old. Also Four Proposals to the Honoured Parliament and the Councel of State, Touching the Way to Propagate the Gospel of Christ (with Small Charge and Great Safety) Both in Old England and New. Also Four Conclusions Touching the Faith and Order of the Gospel of Christ out of His Last Will and Testament, Confirmed and Justified.* London: Henry Hills. Reprinted in Collections of the Massachusetts Historical Society, ser. 4, II. Boston: Massachusetts Historical Society, 1854.

James, Sydney, and Theodore Dwight Bozeman, eds. 1999. *John Clarke and His Legacies: Religion and Law in Colonial Rhode Island 1638–1750.* University Park, PA: Pennsylvania State University Press.

McLoughlin, William. 1986. *Rhode Island: A History.* New York: W. W. Norton & Company.

Newman, Albert Henry. 1898. *A History of the Baptist Churches in the United States.* New York: American Baptist Publication Society.

Peterson, Edward. 1853. *History of Rhode Island.* New York: J. S. Taylor.

CLINTON, SIR HENRY (CA. 1730–1795)

Sir Henry Clinton was the general in overall command of British forces at the conclusion of the American Revolution. He helped plan and execute the envelopment of the Continental Army at the Battle of Long Island in August 1776. He took charge of Britain's army in the colonies in early 1778 and achieved success at the Battle of Monmouth in June 1778 and the siege of Charleston in the fall of 1780. However, he would spend much of his later life defending his actions at the end of the war.

Unfortunately, little is known about Clinton's early life. He was the only son born to George Clinton, an admiral in the British navy and a statesman for the empire. His mother, Anne Carle, was the daughter of a general, and so Henry grew up in a family with significant ties to the British military establishment. Henry spent several years in America before his service during the Revolution. His father applied for the governorship of New York in 1741, but he was not appointed to the post until 1743. Henry traveled with him to the colonies, and in 1745, the young aristocrat became a lieutenant in a company of colonial fusiliers. George Clinton's term as governor ended in 1753, but Henry had already left. He returned to England in 1751 after deciding he was not interested in serving in a provincial regiment.

Henry rose steadily through the ranks of the British army, and by the time the Seven Years' War (1756–1763) began, he had reached the rank of lieutenant colonel in the Coldstream Guards. He saw action in Germany during the war, where he reached the level of staff officer, serving as aide-de-camp to the German prince Karl Wilhelm Ferdinand. His service during the war greatly helped his reputation and standing, and by the end of the war, he had risen to the rank of general.

Clinton benefited from the patronage of several English nobles, including Henry Pelham-Clinton, the Duke of Newcastle, and Prince William Henry, the Duke of Gloucester. However, he had a difficult personality and was characterized by a curious blend of diffidence and quarrelsomeness. Partly due to the Duke of Newcastle's influence, Henry Clinton was elected to Parliament in 1774, a position he maintained until 1784. That same year, he was promoted to major general.

In early 1775, Clinton was told to prepare to travel to America to aid Gen. Thomas Gage in putting down colonial agitation in Massachusetts. Clinton traveled with Maj. Gen. William Howe and Maj. Gen. John Burgoyne. They arrived in Boston in May–June 1775, having learned en route of the skirmishes at Lexington and Concord and the resultant start of the American Revolution. Clinton spent his first several months in Boston dealing with the Continental Army's siege of the city. When Howe replaced Gage as commander, Clinton was named second-in-command, and given command of Charleston, South Carolina.

In June 1776, Clinton traveled south with a small force of about 1,500. Despite intelligence to the contrary, the colonial defenses around Charleston were not unfinished, and his attempt to take the port city was a dismal failure. Clinton abandoned the attempt and sailed back north to aid Howe's attack on New York City in August. Clinton proposed a number of plans to Howe during the course of the campaign to capture New York, but many were rejected due to the prickly relationship between the two men. Nevertheless, Clinton did oversee a successful flanking movement against Washington's forces, contributing significantly to the British victory. In nearly every major engagement in which he was involved, Clinton proposed the right strategic approach. But in nearly every instance, he was rebuffed. This wore on Clinton, and as the conflict dragged on, he became increasingly convinced that a British victory was unlikely.

After a brief stint occupying Newport, Rhode Island, and after a period of time in England, Clinton returned to the colonies in July 1777. While in England, Clinton lobbied to be given control of the northern forces, but he was rebuffed. He threatened to resign in protest, but he was ordered to resume his role as Howe's second-in-command and was granted a knighthood in an attempt to mollify him. Upon his return to America, he attempted to support General Burgoyne's campaign in the Hudson River valley, fearing that Howe's decision to stay in New Jersey would doom the effort. His support was too little too late, however, and Burgoyne's defeat at the Battles of Saratoga in October that year would have dramatic consequences for the progress of the war, by virtue of France's decision to aid the colonies in light of the American victory.

General Howe's resignation after the failures of 1777 left Clinton in overall command of Britain's forces in America. Gen. Lord Charles Cornwallis was his second. For much of 1778 and 1779, Clinton remained in New York, facing off against Washington's army. However, there was little direct confrontation. On June 30, 1779, Clinton issued the Phillipsburg Proclamation, granting British officers the power to enlist any slave who joined the ranks of the British army.

In 1778–1779, Clinton acquiesced to the king's wishes and pursued a strategy targeting the Southern Colonies. He led the successful siege and capture of Charleston, South Carolina, in May 1780, before returning to New York to oversee the overall plan to pacify the South, leaving battlefield command to his second-in-command, Lord Cornwallis. Cornwallis moved through the Carolinas, sometimes acting on occasionally contradictory or unclear orders from Clinton. As had happened with Howe, Clinton had a prickly and mistrustful relationship with Cornwallis, even suspecting him of working to supplant him as commander-in-chief.

This tense relationship may have contributed to the concluding campaign of the war as Cornwallis chose to fortify his position along the Virginia coast at Yorktown. Acting on promises from Clinton that he would reinforce, resupply, or rescue his position as needed, Cornwallis established a defensive position that would ultimately come under siege by a combined French and American army under General Washington. The French victory at the Battle of the Chesapeake, on September 5, ended any hopes for the British navy to resupply or rescue Cornwallis's army. And Clinton chose not to immediately send a force from New York to Cornwallis's aid. As a result, the American siege was effective, and on October 19, 1781, Cornwallis was forced to surrender, the same day that Clinton finally dispatched troops to Virginia. Clinton was promoted to full general in 1793; however, he died the following year on the verge of taking up a position as governor of Gibraltar. He spent much of the last years of his life defending himself from accusations that his command decisions had cost the British the American colonies.

Shawn Selby

See also: Cornwallis, Lord Charles; Long Island, Battle of; Yorktown, Battle of

Further Reading

O'Shaughnessy, Andrew Jackson. 2014. *The Men Who Lost America: British Leadership, the American Revolution and the Fate of the Empire.* New Haven, CT: Yale University Press.

Wilcox, William Bradford. 1964. *Portrait of a General: Sir Henry Clinton in the War of Independence.* New York: Knopf.

COLLEGE OF WILLIAM AND MARY

William and Mary was the second college founded in the English colonies. Most of the colonial colleges were involved in political disputes at one time or another, and William and Mary was no exception, particularly during its first years. The original plans for the college date back to 1618 (decades before Harvard), but they were derailed by an "Indian uprising." On November 18, 1618, when the Virginia Company of London gave orders for the laying out of grounds for a university at Henrico, of which an Indian School was to be a branch, and endowed it with 10,000 acres of land, Henrico was on the north side of the James River, 12 miles below the present city of Richmond. On May 26, 1619, Sir Edwin Sandys, the treasurer of the Virginia Company, reported that £1,500 had been collected toward the proposed college, following the authorization of James I that each bishop in England have a collection in his diocese for the purpose. That July, the General Assembly of Virginia petitioned the Company to send workmen from England for "erecting the University and College."

There were no major developments in the establishment of the college until 1661, when the General Assembly passed an act authorizing the purchase of land for a college and free school. Then, in 1690, the clergy of the Church of England in Virginia adopted "Several Propositions" for founding a college to consist of three schools: grammar, philosophy, and divinity. That July, Lt. Gov. Francis Nicholson authorized subscriptions in Virginia for the proposed college and allowed the clergy to issue an appeal for financial support to merchants in England who were trading in Virginia. In May 1691, the Rev. James Blair, a commissary or representative in Virginia of the bishop of London, was issued instructions by the General Assembly for the founding of a college. He was sent to England to present a request to the king and queen to grant a charter for a college.

Finally, on February 8, 1693, William III and Mary II granted a charter to establish the College of William and Mary in Virginia for a "perpetual College of Divinity, Philosophy, Languages, and other good Arts and Sciences" to be founded in the Virginia colony. The king provided nearly £2,000 sterling, the balance due upon quit-rents, toward the founding of the college; and toward the endowing of it, their Majesties allowed 20,000 acres of choice land, together with the revenue arising by the penny per pound on tobacco reported from Virginia and Maryland to the other plantations and to countries other than England. The Rev. James Blair was named president of the college and served until his death in 1743. As the first American college to receive its charter from the Crown under the Seal of the Privy Council in 1693, the College of William and Mary was known in the beginning as "their Majesties" Royal College of William & Mary. A year later, it became the first and only American college to receive a coat of arms from the College of Heralds (1694).

Although the charter suggested a site on the south side of the York River ("Townsend's Land"), the act that was passed on November 16, 1993, by the General Assembly, and consented to on November 18 by Governor Nicholson, established the site of the college "as near the church now standing in Middle Plantation old fields as convenience will permit" (the predecessor of the present Bruton Parish Church). That same day, the assembly voted an export duty on furs and skins for the support of the college. The name "Middle Plantation" was changed to "Williamsburg" when the colonial capital was moved there from Jamestown in 1699. On December 5, 1700, the college building became the temporary headquarters of the colonial government after it moved from Jamestown. The General Assembly met there for its first legislative session in Williamsburg on that date and continued to meet at the college until April 1704, when the capitol was sufficiently completed to permit its use.

In May 1718, the General Assembly granted £1,000 to the governors and visitors of the college "for the maintaining and educating such and so many of the ingenious scholars, natives of this colony, as they shall think fit." Five years later, the Brafferton Building was erected with funds from the estate of Robert Boyle; it housed the Indian School, founded about 1700.

Although exempt by law from military duty, a number of students and faculty of the college joined militia companies organized in the vicinity of Williamsburg in 1775. Two years later, the students formed a college company with the president, the Rev. James Madison, as captain. Classes were maintained throughout this period of the Revolution. This is depicted in an interesting short film, *Williamsburg—The Story of a Patriot* (1957), which is shown in the visitor center at Williamsburg. It is the longest-running theatrical film, having been shown daily at Colonial Williamsburg since its original 1957 release. Filmed in the spring of 1956 and photographed in the area restored by the Rockefeller Foundation, the story follows a fictional Virginia planter, John Fry (Jack Lord), who becomes a member of Virginia's House of Burgesses. Through contact with Patrick Henry, Thomas Jefferson, George Washington, and other patriots, he gradually loses his ties with the pro-British faction and casts his lot with the rebels. The story is set during the crucial period when the colonists resisted British taxation without representation, met force with force, and chose revolution.

The second part of the film deals with the events leading up to the outbreak of the American Revolution. The son, Robert, enters the College of William and Mary. Near the end of the film, Robert joins fellow students from the college as a militia that marches off to fight the British. The basic material for the film was put together by director George Seaton, producer William H. Wright, and Thad Tate, a Virginia historian and teacher at the College of William and Mary. In writing the final script, playwright Emmet Lavery frequently uses quotations from the writings and diaries of George Washington, Thomas Jefferson, and other Revolutionary figures to fashion authentic dialogue.

In real life, revolutionary activity played out in other ways on the campus. In 1775, professors Henley and Gwatkin, in addition to a number of students with Loyalist sympathies, left the college to return to England. The Rev. Samuel Henley took a leave of absence but never returned to America; the Rev. Thomas Gwatkin, the personal chaplain of Lord Dunmore, left for England in June with Lady Dunmore and the Dunmore children. In 1777, the Loyalist sympathies of the Rev. John Camm, the president, brought about his removal from the faculty.

Under the leadership of Thomas Jefferson, then governor of Virginia and a member of the board of visitors, William and Mary became a university in December 1779. The grammar and divinity schools were discontinued, and a professorship of anatomy and medicine and the first American chairs of law and police and modern languages were established. The elective system of studies was introduced at this time, the first such program in the United States. George Wythe, a signer of the Declaration of Independence, became the first professor of law and police, the first chair of law in North America. John Marshall, later chief justice of the United States, was briefly one of George Wythe's early students.

In 1781, during the last weeks of the American Revolution, General Cornwallis and his British forces evicted college president James Madison (cousin of the future American president) and his family from the house, set up headquarters there, and even refused the college president the courtesy of drawing water from his own well. Fire destroyed the interior of the structure a few weeks after Cornwallis departed, while the house was being used as a hospital for French officers wounded at the Battle of Yorktown. President Madison wrote, "I have not a book left since the conflagration of the house in which I lived." In that same year, college classes were suspended when the British army invaded Virginia. They did not resume until the fall of 1782.

By 1786, the President's House had been rebuilt with funds allocated by the French government, but other less destructive fires in 1879, 1916, and 1922, as well as various renovations, took their toll on the 18th-century interior of the building. However, little of the exterior has changed in the past 250 years, and some of the framing, interior molding, and flooring date from the 18th century. The house was restored to its colonial appearance in 1931 as part of the Rockefeller Restoration of Williamsburg. Since then, further changes to the interior have been made in the interest of comfort and convenience, including the addition of closets and bathrooms, an updated kitchen, and a modern heating and air conditioning system.

The College of William and Mary, often called the "Alma Mater of a Nation" because of its close ties to America's Founding Fathers, is an institution rich in colonial history, but one that is often overlooked by more well-known colleges farther north. Yet, the College of William and Mary can lay claim, like its sister school, Harvard, as the cradle of the early presidency. A 17-year-old George Washington received his surveyor's license through the college and would return as its first American chancellor. The third president, Thomas Jefferson, received his undergraduate education there, but he is better known for his design of the University of Virginia. The college also educated the nation's fourth and fifth presidents, James Madison and John Tyler.

Martin J. Manning

See also: Harvard College; Jefferson, Thomas; Madison, James; Washington, George

Further Reading

Dickon, Chris. 2007. *College of William and Mary.* Charleston, SC: Arcadia Pub.

Garrett, John H. 2005. *Colonial Well of Knowledge: Roots and Founders of the College of William and Mary in Virginia.* Philadelphia: Xlibris.

Godson, Susan H., et al. 1993. *The College of William & Mary: A History.* Williamsburg: King and Queen Press, Society of the Alumni, College of William and Mary in Virginia.

Morpurgo, J. E. 1976. *Their Majesties' Royall Colledge: William and Mary in the Seventeenth and Eighteenth Centuries.* Williamsburg: College of William and Mary in Virginia.

COLONIAL CHARTERS

Each of the original 13 colonies was governed by a colonial charter. This charter was the legal document that gave the colonies the right to exist and laid out the rules by which they were governed. In the case of the English colonies in the New World, the document also defined the relationship between the people of the colony and the home islands. These charters were often granted with the permission of the Crown, but only certain kinds gave the Crown a say in their makeup or governance. Several kinds of charters existed: company or stock, proprietary, and royal. Each of the three overlapped and bled into each other in numerous ways, and due to policies, they often transformed and mutated.

A company or stock charter was granted to a company and created a self-governing colony, most often either one centered on trade or settlement. Once the company was created and the charter issued, the way a colony was to be run was decided by the officers of the corporation. Much like a corporation, stock would be issued in the colony, and people would buy shares. Each share would entitle a shareholder to a portion of the profits of the colony. If things went well and the colony prospered, the shareholders had potential to recoup their initial investments. The original charters of Virginia and Massachusetts were such. Eventually, the charter company for Virginia went bankrupt, and after several attempts to turn a profit, it ended up becoming a royal colony. In 1684, the Massachusetts charter was voided by the courts, turning it into a royal colony as well. By the time of the Revolution, only Rhode Island and Connecticut maintained their status as charter colonies.

As charter colonies had the greatest amount of leeway in their governance, it should be no surprise that Rhode Island and Connecticut ended up with the most liberal of all the charters. In Rhode Island, due mainly to the circumstances of its founding, the idea of religious liberty played a central part in the colony's charter, and as such, it took in many disparate religious groups that would have not been welcomed in other colonies. The first Baptist church in the colonies was formed there in 1639, and the Quakers arrived in 1657. Over the next couple of years, Jewish and Calvinist communities found their way to the colony. All were protected under the colony's charter.

Proprietary charters were granted to individuals and allowed them to settle and profit from the land however they saw fit. The proprietor would determine the form of government, select who would be involved with the running of the colony, and decide on what the laws for the colonists would be. In effect, proprietors were granted legal kingdoms free from outside interference; though they still reported to the king, he usually did not interfere. These sorts of colonies would have their governance passed down along family lines, just like large estates. Pennsylvania, with William Penn (1644–1718) and his family as its proprietors, and Maryland, with the Lords Baltimore, are two examples of these kinds of charters. The practice of the Crown granting these kinds of charters faded after 1690, as there was a general feeling that the Crown had too little control over these colonies, and attempts were made to revoke the charters and bring those colonies under the banner of the other royal colonies. Pennsylvania and Maryland, along with Delaware, resisted the attempts, and these three colonies were the only remaining proprietary colonies in the 1770s.

With a royal charter, the Crown had direct control over the colony and how it would be governed. This allowed the Crown to appoint governors and to profit directly from the running of the colonies. Many of the colonies that started with either the company charter or the proprietary charter found themselves royal colonies after the charters were revoked, voided, or simply seized by the Crown in an attempt to bring the disparate colonies under a more central style of government. On the eve of the Revolution, New York, New Jersey, New Hampshire, Massachusetts, and the Carolinas fell under this category.

One thing that all the different forms of charters had in common was that they allowed the people that would live under them some sort of guarantee to the basic rights and privileges of Englishmen. These rights were the ones originally enshrouded in the Magna Carta in 1215 and reaffirmed much later in the Bill of Rights in 1689. Many of these "traditional" rights would later form the basis of the argument between the 13 colonies and the Crown that eventually led to the American Revolution: no imprisonment without just cause (habeas corpus); no quartering of troops among the citizenry; no martial law in times of peace; and no taxes levied with the consent of Parliament (which would eventually give rise to the American call of "no taxation without representation"). These were all implied rights that were included in most of the charters.

They also tended to hold forth the idea that all the colonists were subject to the natural rights of life, liberty, and property and that none of the colonial governments could surpass or circumspect English law. Most of the charters in the colonies set up governing bodies that held to the separation of powers, usually with an executive of some sort and an assembly or legislature. In some colonies, even the judicial systems were cast under the same net. There was the inherent belief in checks and balances, where one branch of the government could not hold too much sway over the others, and, most importantly, each charter put forth the idea of a representative government. Even the royal colonies would generally have a legislature that would be made up of landowning men working with a governor, even if he were appointed by the Crown.

A brief look at the founding of each colony shows the various methods that were instrumental in their creation as well as an idea of how they were chartered. Massachusetts was founded under a royal charter in 1691, when the Plymouth Colony and Massachusetts Bay Colony were combined. Plymouth Colony, one of the oldest, was originally governed by the Mayflower Compact. This document, which was written up and agreed upon by the original Puritan settlers, became the first governing document for the colonies and would prove to be the basis of not only the other charters but would show itself as an influence in many revolutionary documents down the line. Connecticut sprung from the Massachusetts Bay Colony in 1637 and was founded by Thomas Hooker; in 1662, it would become a royal colony. East Jersey and West Jersey were founded separately but were joined in 1702 under a royal charter, becoming New Jersey. Rhode Island was founded by refugees from Massachusetts in 1636 and became a royal colony in 1663.

Maryland was the first of the proprietary colonies, founded in 1634 by George Calvert, 1st Baron Baltimore. As a Catholic, Calvert was heavily discriminated against in England, so he sought to create a colony where that would not be the case. Virginia was founded in 1607 at Jamestown as a charter colony that had stockholders that decided that a general assembly would be its method of governance. In 1642, the charter was revoked due to poor management, and Virginia became a royal colony. New Hampshire came to life as a proprietary colony granted by the Council for New England to Capt. John Mason. Delaware was originally considered part of the Pennsylvania Colony and operated under William Penn's original proprietary charter. In 1701, it was granted its own assembly, but it did not completely separate from Pennsylvania until 1776. Carolina was originally founded as a proprietary colony, but a small rebellion ensued as North and South Carolina split. In 1719, South Carolina had sloughed off its proprietary governor, and by 1721, it had successfully petitioned to become a royal colony. Several years later, the remaining proprietors sold their interests in North Carolina, and in 1729, it became a royal colony.

Pennsylvania, a proprietary colony founded by William Penn, was given a charter in 1681, and it pretty much stayed that way despite an attempted "coup." In 1764, the Quakers who had been the major political power in the colony for some time tried to get the Crown to revoke the charter and declare Pennsylvania a royal colony. Their efforts failed, and the colony remained as it was until the Revolution. Georgia was established as a proprietary colony (under the same proprietors as the Carolina charter), having been given to a group of 21 trustees by George II to act as a buffer colony between the Spanish in Florida and British in the other colonies. In 1753, it transitioned to a royal colony. New York was originally a proprietary colony, given to the Duke of York, who seized New Amsterdam (New York City) and gave the citizens a limited form of self-government. In 1685, it became a royal colony.

In April 1775, the actual fighting began between the colonies and Great Britain, mainly because of the feeling that Britain had violated the spirit, if not the actual law, of the colonial charters. In May of that year, as the Continental Congress was charged with creating an army and a national government capable of coordinating a war, Congress advised all the colonies to set up new governments. These new governments would be tasked with creating new constitutions under which they would be governed. It should be no surprise that many of these constitutions were heavily based on their original charters and contained many of the same protections and responsibilities listed in the original documents. Rhode Island and Connecticut, of course, opted to keep their charters that had served them well to this point as their governing documents.

As each charter evolved into constitutions, they would play another important role in the creation of the country. Many of the ideas that were encapsulated in them that transferred to the state constitutions acted as way to grease the wheels for the Declaration of Independence. When Thomas Jefferson, and his committee, wrote the document, he borrowed heavily from the Virginia Constitution that he had helped write. These were not new ideas, as many colonists felt that they had been living under those concepts from the founding of the colonies.

In effect, each colonial charter, regardless of the type, not only created governing bodies for each colony but also, in many cases, bestowed on them the rights that their fathers and forefathers had been granted as subjects of the Crown. These rights were the ones that they felt came not from the Crown or Parliament but from on high. As generations passed, and the charters were transformed and changed, these basic liberties stayed intact, and when the people started to believe that they were not being honored by Parliament and the Crown, they decided that the only way to keep the spirit of those charters alive was to rise up and enforce them themselves.

The seeds of the American Revolution were without a doubt planted in each of the colonial charters. Regardless of which kind of charter that the colony could claim, their purpose was organization and protection of the people and their rights. It is doubtful that when the charters where granted it was known where they would eventually lead, but many of the protections are ones that are still enjoyed today.

Stuart Hatfield

See also: Carolina Constitution; Colonial Government and Politics; Connecticut; Delaware; Georgia; Maryland; Massachusetts Bay; New Hampshire; New Jersey; New York; North Carolina; Pennsylvania; Rhode Island; South Carolina; Virginia

Further Reading

Bridenbaugh, Carl. 1981. *Early Americans.* New York: Oxford University Press.
Ernst, Joseph Albert. 1970. *The Forming of a Nation, 1607–1781.* New York: Random House.
Middleton, Richard. 1996. *Colonial America: A History, 1585–1776.* Cambridge, MA: Blackwell.

COLONIAL ECONOMY

The colonial economy of British North America entailed a mix of several modes of production. As a preindustrial colonial extension of England, the American economy primarily relied on farming based on barter and export and a global mercantile trade based on staple products produced by African American slaves on plantations. Over time, the colonial economy became more diversified, though dependence on a few important staple products for export dominated the local economy of farmers, planters, and urban workers across the Eastern Seaboard until the market revolution of the 1830s.

In the Southern Colonies, the plantation system developed as an extension of the sugar plantation complex in Barbados and Jamaica in the British West Indies. In the early 17th century, white planters from these islands migrated with their slaves to the Carolinas to find more prosperous conditions. The plantation system in America relied on slavery as its major economic support. White owners held large landholdings, where slaves cultivated staple crops that brought a large return in markets throughout the Atlantic region. Tobacco from Virginia, rice and indigo from the Carolinas, and sugar from Brazil and the West Indies formed the backbone of the Atlantic economy.

American colonies specialized in various staple crops and engaged in a triangular trade between the West Indies, Africa, and England. Whites expanded slavery to meet the growing needs and profitability of the plantation system by tapping into an existing slave trade between the west coast of Africa and the British West Indies in the mid-17th century. Elite white planters, some of them nobility, dominated the Southern economy and society. Many were absentee owners who lived thousands of miles away in England and the West Indies.

A focus on the colony of South Carolina reveals the economic dependence on monocrop agriculture and slavery by white Southern farmers during the Colonial

Period. In South Carolina, the slave trade had become the economic basis of the colony by the early 18th century. The sale of people represented the most lucrative economic transaction due to recurrent ethnic violence and the lack of laborers. South Carolinians at first used Native Americans as slave laborers because of their abundance. Whites practiced a strategy of divide and conquer by encouraging Native Americans to fight one another. The losers were sold by whites into slavery, though Indians made poor slaves due to their knowledge of local geography and political connections to local Indian peoples. Nevertheless, by 1730, tens of thousands of Indians had been enslaved in the region, some of whom were transported as plantation workers to the British West Indies.

The development of rice cultivation in South Carolina in 1715 led to the widespread use of blacks as slave laborers. West Africans became essential to this Southern industry due to their experience with rice cultivation in Africa. In addition to serving as herders, blacks also processed indigo. A young white South Carolina woman named Elizabeth Lucas Pickney had adapted indigo from the West Indies to the moist lowland climate of South Carolina in the 1740s. Rice and indigo production grew rapidly over the next three decades due to the increasing presence of African slaves as agricultural workers. By the 1770s, both products had earned some of the highest returns of any staple export.

The growth of the plantation system in the Southern Colonies stimulated the rural economy of the northern colonies. The plantations of the sugar islands influenced northern people by providing a convenient market for such American products as lumber, bread, fish, and meat. The near-total dependence on the export of staple crops by Southern plantation owners led to the need for imports from northern farms. By the 1720s, farmers, merchants, and other producers in New York, New Jersey, and Pennsylvania were making a comfortable living by exporting wheat, corn, and bread to Southern Colonies and the West Indies.

Trade with the West Indies created the first American merchant elite, who founded major urban economic institutions and businesses in northern cities during the 18th century. Global traders in New England constructed factories in Boston, Newport, and Providence to process raw sugar imported from the West Indies into granulated sugar to be exported to England and Europe. These merchants also created alcohol distilleries to process molasses into rum for the foreign and domestic alcohol trade. Rum was a popular processing method for sugar because it could be more easily transported and stored for longer periods of time than in other forms. Some shipbuilders and merchants in the New England Colonies also invested in building vessels to transport slaves from Africa to America.

Economic development in colonial cities in the 18th century led to a population explosion and the growth of local economic enterprise. Although colonial American cities accounted for only 5 percent of the total colonial population, their share of the export trade, both local and global, was much higher. Trade represented the single most important facet of the urban economy. Merchants ran the local commerce in farm products and also facilitated the importation of such luxury items as furniture, art, and perfume from Europe. In Philadelphia, for example, 150 merchants controlled 70 percent of the city's booming trade. Baltimore mushroomed from a small village into a major metropolis in a few decades in the 17th century due to the wheat trade with Southern plantations. As the only Southern seaport of any size, the city of Charleston represented an important center of Southern trade, particularly in deerskins, indigo, Indian slaves, and rice.

In addition, a major fishing industry grew from the efforts of Boston, Salem, and other New England–based shipowners and fishermen. They exported barreled and salted fish to Southern plantations to feed African American slaves. By the mid-18th century, English fishing fleets based in colonial cities counted more than 600 vessels, providing employment to more than 4,000 black and white sailors. This sector of the colonial economy represented some of the only work available to free blacks living in urban areas.

Smaller cities with a less-developed connection to the global Atlantic-based economy relied more on local trade networks. People in towns depended on such local resources as trees, fish, and the soil to make ends meet. They also worked in the shipbuilding and lumber industries, two of the most important aspects of the colonial economy that affected smaller towns. In New Hampshire in the 1740s, for instance, 70 sawmills could be seen scattered along the Piscataqua River. The mills provided cheap lumber for housing and ship construction in the burgeoning local area. Artisans took advantage of a strong labor market to construct large ships for the export trade and smaller boats for river and coastal traffic. Shipyards in major East Coast cities produced more than 15,000 tons of freighters each year. Colonial ships became so popular and profitable that by the end of the Colonial Period, more than one-third of England's merchant fleet was made in America.

Most colonial cities contained a vibrant working class. Small-scale artisan production dominated all major colonial cities, and artisans comprised half the population. A variety of craftsmen, from silversmiths like Paul Revere to coopers, tailors, and hatmakers, could be found working in every major city. Lancaster, Pennsylvania, for example, possessed more than 200 German and English craftsmen who anchored the town's economic and social life. Many of these workers sought the benefits of craft guilds and early labor unions to protect their economic rights. Frequent layoffs and downturns in the economy resulted from larger conflicts affecting the Atlantic trade network. Strikes and work slowdowns occurred, and women sometimes engaged in bread riots to protest high prices on needed goods.

Less-skilled laborers also formed an important sector of the economy. The lack of technology beyond wind- and waterpower meant that the movement of goods necessitated human and animal labor. In colonial New York, for example, hundreds of stevedores, some of them free black men, unloaded goods at the wharves. The New York economy also depended on black slave laborers, who were 20 percent of the city's residents during the 18th century. Thousands of white men and women found work as artisan assistants, road builders, and farmhands. Integral in many ways to the "underground" colonial economy, women worked as washers, wet nurses, midwives, and prostitutes.

Indentured servants made up a large segment of the workforce that facilitated the colonial economy in the 17th and 18th centuries. In Philadelphia, for example, indentured servants and slaves were 25 percent of the city's residents and held half of the laboring jobs in the 1700s. After working for seven years to pay off their passage, indentured servants were free to enter the colonial economy as free wage laborers. Because most were unskilled (though some servants indentured to artisans and other skilled craftsmen learned a trade), they often became farm workers and casual laborers until they had earned enough income to purchase land, usually in the interior, where land prices were cheaper than in coastal areas.

Native Americans represented a crucial labor and transportation link between rural and urban colonial economies. Indians, such as the Hurons and Iroquois, provided the animal skins that were traded by white middlemen and shipped to coastal markets and finally to Europe. In return for the goods, Indians received processed materials that they could not make themselves, such as iron, guns, and whiskey. Transportation of goods in the trade network between small interior towns and major coastal cities was facilitated by droves of teamsters and draymen who used boats and livestock to transport the lucrative staples.

Average colonial Americans in rural areas relied on barter and trade to run the local economy. Because cash (coins were used much more than paper currency) was always in short supply in colonial America, and great distances and poor transportation plagued the colonial infrastructure, average men and women exchanged labor and goods to make ends meet. For example, a surplus of young farm women in the New England colonies in the 18th century led to agreements between rural farm families to exchange the services of their daughters as textile and farm workers in exchange for their board. Cooperative labor arrangements suffused all aspects of the colonial economy. A farmer might help his neighbor harvest a wheat crop in exchange for his neighbor's help in laying in wood supplies for winter.

Life during the Colonial Period was precarious, however, as no safety net existed if people became too sick or injured to work. Children were often sent out to work at an early age, a common labor arrangement both in Europe and America during this time. Periods of economic stagnation forced many adults into poverty, thievery, and dependence on almshouses, local places where the poor could get a meal in exchange for work. The unpredictability of global trade that depended on the relative value of various staples made colonial life uncertain for most common people.

In contrast to most American colonists, merchants continued to attract a larger share of colonial wealth over time during the Colonial Period. By the 1770s, the poorest 60 percent of the taxable inhabitants of Boston, New York, and Philadelphia owned less than 5 percent of the taxable wealth. The top 10 percent of the population comprised merchants and other elites, who controlled more than 65 percent of the wealth.

The colonial economy depended on slave labor, rural farming families, and the plantation complex to provide stability and prosperity to colonial society and politics. To a significant extent, the inability of colonial white Americans to earn steady profits from the mercantile trade by the mid-18th century led them to protest British taxes and control of the colonial economy. This agitation ultimately led to victory in the American Revolution, which enabled the American people to engage in commerce free from the restraints of the British monarchy.

Jason Newman

See also: Atlantic-Slave Trade; Indentured Servants; Mercantilism; Rice Cultivation; Tobacco Cultivation

Further Reading

Craton, Michael. 1974. *Sinews of Empire: A Short History of British Slavery.* Garden City, NY: Anchor Press.

Heyrman, Christine L. 1984. *Commerce and Culture: The Maritime Communities of Colonial Massachusetts, 1690–1750.* New York: W. W. Norton & Co., Inc.

Kulikoff, Allan. 1986. *Tobacco and Slaves: The Development of Southern Cultures in the Chesapeake, 1680–1800.* Chapel Hill: University of North Carolina Press.

Salisbury, Neal. 1982. *Manitou and Providence: Indians, Europeans, and the Making of New England.* Sharon, MA: Big Hearted Books.

Walton, Gary M., and James F. Shepherd. 1979. *The Economic Rise of Early America.* New York: Cambridge University Press.

COLONIAL GOVERNMENT AND POLITICS

The establishment of colonial governments dominated the political development of British North America in the 17th century. Although each colony in the British Empire in North America developed independent political and governing structures, all were closely tied to the Crown, which attempted to exert political and economic authority over the colonies until the American Revolution. The most powerful influence on the colonial governments was a rebellion against the divine right of kings and a move toward a limited government with a branch that represented the people.

The first iteration of the idea of limited government in England was the Magna Carta (1215), which stated that the king was subject to the law and could not change the law without parliamentary consent. Further victories for limiting the power of the monarch and increasing the power of Parliament occurred during the English Civil War of 1642–1651 and with passage of the English Bill of Rights (1689).

Movements toward a limited government were inspired in part by the writings of English philosophers. Thomas Hobbes thought society was unruly and needed to be ruled by an absolute monarch, but he was a founder of the social contract theory, the belief that a contract exists between government and the governed. In John Locke's *Second Treatise of Government*, published in 1690, Locke differed from Hobbes in that he believed people establish societies and enter into a contractual relationship with a government for convenience and "the preservation of their property." His views of a contract with the consent of the governed greatly influenced colonial leaders in British North America and the development of capitalism.

In 1620, more than 100 Pilgrims, including women and children, had sailed on the *Mayflower* from Plymouth, England. After arrival in New England, they selected a site for a town and drafted a charter of government, the first in British North America. According to William Bradford, the Pilgrims' leader, the men of the colony agreed to "covenant and combine [themselves] together into a civil body politic." The Mayflower Compact was signed to promise "due submission and obedience" to "such just and equal Laws." The compact was primarily a religious document, but it was an early example of the contractual self-government of the later colonial constitutions.

The Massachusetts Bay Colony began in 1629 when a royal charter was granted to a group of leading Puritans who protested the corruption and ceremony of the established Church of England. They had been attacked for their beliefs and wanted to remove their congregations to a place where they could freely practice their faith. Naming their enterprise the Massachusetts Bay Company, the Puritan leaders accompanied 200 settlers and their families to the Indian fishing town of Naumkeag, in Massachusetts Bay. They renamed the town Salem. In a great migration, more than 20,000 people immigrated to New England from 1629 to 1643. Like the Pilgrims of the Plymouth Colony, Massachusetts Bay residents organized local governments based on the English model of virtual representation.

Throughout the 17th century, colonial governments developed on Hobbes's idea of a social contract. The Exeter Compact (1639), signed in Exeter, New Hampshire (then Massachusetts), was an extension of the principles of self-government and the spread of democratic ideals throughout New England. Also in 1639, a few Connecticut towns adopted the Fundamental Orders of Connecticut (1639), which called for a representative assembly and the popular election of a governor and judges. In 1641, Massachusetts adopted the Massachusetts Body of Liberties (1641) to limit the powers of the colonial governor and his magistrates. The document relied on both English common law and the Ten Commandments in its support for protection of individual rights.

In the New England Colonies, colonial government at the local level reflected a nascent democracy. The General Courts of Massachusetts Bay and Connecticut bestowed townships, areas of land measuring 6 miles by 10 miles, on groups of settlers who petitioned the General Assembly and obtained permission to settle new lands. The settlers, known collectively as proprietors, decided who got the lands. Most of the available lands went to the richest men, while middling colonials received a lesser share. The lands were granted in fee simple, a relatively new concept that entailed the ownership of land without encumbrances from feudal obligations.

The male heads of families ran the local town governments through town meetings. Each year, proprietors chose selectmen to orchestrate and manage the affairs of the town. Town meetings witnessed the passage of local laws levying taxes, building fences, administering the common fields, and deciding the size of new town lots. However, voting was limited only to men who held a certain level of property. Women and white men of lesser means did not participate. Although many groups were excluded from civic participation, the New England form of government was more democratic than any other political institution then existing in Europe.

Other colonies received their governing charters in an alternate form. The creation of proprietary colonies from grants of land to noblemen served as the foundation of governments in the Carolinas, Maryland, and Pennsylvania. In 1681, Charles II gave land to William Penn in payment for a large debt owed Penn's father, the admiral Sir William Penn. The younger Penn was a defender of the Quaker religion. As a result, he established Pennsylvania as a land of free worship. Penn's Pennsylvania Frame of Government (1682) was designed to provide government support for religious diversity. His plan of government did not create an established church, levied no taxes on religion, and allowed Christians of all faiths to hold office.

Penn also established the colony of Delaware along similar lines. Formerly a colony of Sweden, Delaware had passed through the Dutch and English before becoming part of Penn's plan to give more religious and political freedom to British colonists. Penn made Delaware the Lower Counties of Pennsylvania but allowed them to select their own representative assembly in 1703.

The foundation of Georgia developed in a pattern different from other English colonies in America. Established much later than other colonies, Georgia began in the early 18th century as a colony of the poor envisioned by Gen. James Oglethorpe and a group of social reformers influenced by the Enlightenment. To further the class equality that lay at the heart of the colony's distribution of political power, Oglethorpe forbade slavery in Georgia, limited land grants to small holdings of 500 acres, and encouraged indentured servants to migrate to provide a labor force for the development of small farms. The colony of Georgia embraced slavery in the 1750s, however, when cheap slave labor became irresistible for white landowners.

The creation of the Virginia colony was also unique, as it proceeded along strictly capitalistic lines. In 1607, a group of London bankers and investors organized themselves as the Virginia Company of London (a joint-stock company) and sent ships to establish the colony of Virginia on the Chesapeake Bay. They had been granted a royal charter by James I to colonize the mid-Atlantic region. The English investors sold shares to other wealthy merchants and royal elite to pay the expenses to start the colony. The government established by the 100 male settlers in Jamestown, the Virginia capital, was based on strict adherence to company rule. Men caught stealing pigs or running away, for example, had their ears, noses, or tongues split.

During their first years of the colonies' existence, the English settlers depended heavily on forming political alliances with local Indians for survival. Virginia colonists attempted to orchestrate peaceful and pragmatic relationships with the estimated 20,000 Algonquin people in the region. The generosity of the Algonquin was remarkable given the challenge the English presented to their political domination of the Chesapeake Bay region. When the Virginia colonists began to starve, they received assistance from local Native Americans who brought the colonists corn.

In 1619, the Virginia Company created the Virginia House of Burgesses, the first elected legislature in Britain's colonial empire, to make laws "for the good and welfare" of the colony. Virginia governor George Yeardley presided over the assembly with a group of 22 elected officials, two from each of the 11 settlements in Virginia. As the population of Virginia grew, the representative assembly grew as well, reaching a total of 100 seats by 1750.

The House of Burgesses lasted until 1776, when Virginia declared independence from Great Britain with the Virginia Declaration of Rights (1776) and established the Virginia General Assembly. The House of Burgesses proved to be the school for many who developed the American government. Four of the first five presidents of the United States were from Virginia. George Washington, Thomas Jefferson, James Madison, and James Monroe constituted the "Virginia dynasty," which continued to influence the development of the U.S. government well after the American Revolution.

Warfare in the 17th and 18th centuries was a constant part of colonial politics, and it contributed to the increasing need for independence. Colonists fought beside the British in King William's War, Queen Anne's War, and the War of Jenkins' Ear. In 1754, at the beginning of the French and Indian War, the English Board of Trade convened the Albany Congress to develop a plan to strengthen ties with the Iroquois Confederacy and develop a common defense of the colonies. The colonial assemblies rejected the plan, the Albany Plan of Union (1754), because it gave too much power to the Albany Congress.

The American Revolution represented the last chapter in British colonial politics. The war grew from political disagreements between the philosophy of Parliament and George III and a large segment of American elites who wanted a greater say in how the colonies supported the Crown. Although the Treaty of Paris ended the French and Indian War in 1763, the war had bankrupted British royal coffers, compelling the king to tap the colonies for greater sums to support the empire. When colonists protested higher taxes, the English government responded with increasing autocracy, which further alienated colonial Americans.

Parliament enacted the Stamp Act of 1765, the first direct tax ever laid on its colonies in North America, on March 22, 1765. Passed to raise money for the British government, the tax caused protests throughout the colonies. The Virginia House of Burgesses led the way in the protest, as Patrick Henry proposed the Virginia Stamp Act Resolutions in May 1765. The House of Burgesses broke into factions but remained efficient, proving the success of elected legislatures in the colonies.

Under the protest of "no taxation without representation," the colonial legislatures sent delegates to the Stamp Act Congress, which drew up 13 resolutions that opposed the British actions and petitioned the king and Parliament to repeal the Stamp Act. Although unsuccessful in stopping future British taxation, the Stamp Act Congress was the first time the 13 separate colonial governments worked together toward a single goal.

That unity continued as the Crown continued to levy taxes and limit colonial freedoms. The Coercive Acts of 1774, passed in response to the Boston Tea Party, led to the creation of the First Continental Congress, which was intended to organize the 13 colonies in support of protests to British actions. The First Continental Congress aimed to limit the power of Parliament and bring more autonomy to the colonies.

The prosecution of the American Revolution and the creation of a centralized government were difficult due to the political heterogeneity of the 13 colonies. To overcome that problem, Committees of Correspondence were formed in each colony. They acted as Revolutionary governments to help unite the colonies against England. The Sons of Liberty and other ad hoc political protest groups made England more aware of colonial distaste for its mercantile policies. Thomas Paine's *Common Sense* was reproduced into a half-million copies read in America and abroad. In brilliant and compelling prose, it called attention to the economic slavery imposed on the colonies by the English monarchy.

Strapped for funds, American colonials formed the Second Continental Congress in 1776 that attempted, over seven years, to unite the colonies and win the conflict. Washington was given command of the Continental Army, and various Virginia planters, such as Jefferson, George Mason, and Madison (all slave owners), assumed important roles in the new government. While Benjamin Franklin attempted the difficult task in England of persuading the British to cease war against the American colonies, Jefferson drafted the Declaration of Independence (1776), the blueprint for freedom from colonial rule. Although colonial governments in North America operated differently, they established the need for a written constitution, an elected legislature, and the separation of powers between the executive and the legislature. John Dickinson of Pennsylvania wrote the Articles of Confederation, which called for a loose organization of states with a weak central authority. The Second Continental Congress adopted the Articles on November 15, 1777. The Articles required unanimous approval from the states, however, and did not go into effect until Maryland finally granted approval on March 2, 1781.

Because of the inefficiency of the confederate government, leaders called for a convention to revise the Articles of Confederation in 1787. However, the Constitutional Convention decided to establish a new government on republican principles. The resulting U.S. Constitution outlines the checks and balances between the three branches of government and suggests a federalist relationship between the national and state governments. The Constitution required three-fourths of the states' approval.

Ratification was met with controversy. Anti-Federalists opposed the Constitution and the strong central government that it created, fearing that the new government would simply replace the old tyrant in England with a new one at home and deprive the people of liberties. From October 1787 to August 1788, Alexander Hamilton, Madison, and John Jay published the *Federalist Papers* to influence state ratification conventions in support of the Constitution. In an act of compromise, Congress passed the Bill of Rights (1791) to guarantee citizens fundamental liberties, reassuring the Anti-Federalists, who thought the Constitution gave too much power to the national government.

With ratification of the Constitution by New Hampshire in June 1788, the new form of government had the necessary support of three-fourths of the states to go into effect. The U.S. government under the Articles of Confederation, given birth to over time by the various colonial governments, came to an end.

Jason Newman

See also: Articles of Confederation; Bill of Rights; Colonial Charters; Constitutional Convention; New Jersey Plan; Ratification; Virginia Plan

Further Reading

Carr, Lois Green, and David W. Jordan. 1974. *Maryland's Revolution of Government, 1689–1692.* Ithaca, NY: Cornell University Press.

Kammen, Michael. 1970. *Empire and Interest: The American Colonies and the Politics of Mercantilism.* Philadelphia: J. B. Lippincott, Co.

Olson, Allison G. 1973. *Anglo-American Politics, 1660–1775.* New York: Oxford University Press.

COLONIAL SPORTS

There is much debate over how the colonists viewed sports, games, recreation, and leisure. The idea of modern sports was a long way from appearing. There were few team sports, and athletes were only known locally. There were no professional athletes and no organized leagues with national champions or governing agencies. Few had written rules that everyone needed to follow. Play, sport, games, and leisure were terms often used interchangeably. Play or sport was more often associated with tasks that needed to be accomplished or skills a person needed to practice or perfect. Games often needed to have a practical component or they were not encouraged. Sport needed a purpose or it was just idleness, and that would lead to a person's or community's downfall.

Play and leisure implied idleness and a lack of productivity. There are a number of examples of sporting activity being actively discouraged because many believed play or sport took away from the work that had to be done. For example, hunting brought home dinner, but football just distracted men and boys. Target practice would make someone a better hunter, but wrestling just led to further fighting. Honor and prestige were not a large concern as sports first developed in the colonies. Sports of the colonial era looked more like what might be considered games today because they lacked the professionalism and competition of the modern era. Leisure activities gave people a chance to escape from the daily struggles of survival and have some fun.

Another difference in early sport was the inclusion of or influence by Native sports, such as lacrosse. Sharing between colonists and Native peoples did occur, and sporting habits were affected. Nancy Struna, in *People of Prowess*, argues that the influence has been exaggerated by many. Her argument focuses more on the influence, both positive and negative, of England on colonial habits.

Most of the focus by historians has been on English settlers. The Dutch colonists brought their own sports to the New World, such as kolven, which was a mix of golf and hockey. German settlers brought drinking games and sports of skill and dexterity, such as hand-to-hand fighting and gymnastics. The Swiss loved target shooting and card games. While there were some unique sports practiced, many were similar and still governed by local attitudes of survival and moderation.

The greatest factor that influenced attitudes and understandings of play in the New World was religion. Whether in the north or south, religious attitudes affected what people did on a daily basis. In the Puritan New England Colonies, observance of the Sabbath prevented play on Sundays. That idea came to be reflected in the blue laws that became so popular across the colonies. Blue laws prohibited play, drinking, and even some work being done on the Sabbath. Fines from 5 to 20 shillings were levied for sports, with the higher amounts reserved for those activities deemed most sinful. Ice-skating and dancing were acceptable, but fighting and card playing were not because of gambling and drinking. These activities centered on the local taverns as well.

In 1621, William Bradford made an exception on Christmas Day, excusing non-Pilgrims from having to work in the fields so they could celebrate Jesus's birthday. When he came back from the fields and found the men and boys playing stoolball, Bradford took all their equipment and sent them back to their homes. As some pastors pointed out, people had six days for themselves, so one day should be kept for the Lord. Court records show young people being fined, whipped, and put in the stocks for gambling, playing cards, and drinking.

The Sabbath was not the only element of concern. There were many debates over when to allow play and what kind of play to allow. Much of this debate could be traced back to England and the writings of James I. He recognized the necessity of leisure and sport to keep people happy and productive, but he did not think all sports were acceptable. Some sports took people away from productive behavior. King James issued a Declaration on Lawful Sports in 1618. The purpose of the Declaration was to identify those sports that would not lead a person down a bad path. If people did not have leisure time, they would become angry and turn to other less desirable activities, such as drinking and gambling. King James also acknowledged that Sundays and holidays needed to be opened to sports because people worked every other day.

Religious attitudes against drinking and gambling made many sporting activities suspect or prohibited. For example, card playing was prohibited in many areas, but walking and skating were allowed. Religious restrictions hindered early sporting traditions in the New England Colonies, but it did not stop them. In 1707, the Rev. Benjamin Coleman preached on the idea of "sober mirth." He thought activities that focused on rest and restoration rather than more competitive games were acceptable. Fishing came to be an acceptable idea for sport. Sports should not be all-consuming. Life was too difficult and harsh to spend time playing.

In the Southern Colonies, the situation was different, with restrictions being less severe, and those that did exist declined more quickly. Religious attitudes were not as strong due to the greater variety of religions and countries represented by those who settled in the south. Plantation owners came to have more wealth and leisure time to pursue activities of amusement, much like their aristocratic counterparts in England and Europe. In contrast to the larger plantation owners were the slaves and indentured servants who had little time or opportunity for games but found amusement in songs, dancing, and storytelling. Small farmers did not have free time to spare but still managed to mix work and play.

Tying work and play together was normal practice for many throughout the South. Gander pulling would be a good example. Participants got to practice their horseback riding skills and develop their strength when they yanked down the gander from where it was tied to a branch as they rode past. As historian Elliott Gorn points out, because of the settlement patterns in the South, their sports were often more violent and bloody. Southern colonists needed to show they could take care of themselves when there were no neighbors to help out. Eye gouging and rough and tumble brawling were more common among the poor and middling sorts, as they used these sports to show off their strength and manliness.

From the early 1600s through the end of the American Revolution (1775–1783), restrictions lessened, making play and sporting practices more acceptable, common, and organized. Religious influences from England declined, and the hard work required for day-to-day survival gradually lessened. As social classes developed, life became more structured and defined. People were able to separate work from leisure or play by the mid-18th century. Defined times and places were created for sports, and rules were developed. The appearance of sporting goods on individual inventories and in advertisements by the 1750s also revealed the growth in sport as a business. The sporting practices of this time still did not begin to take on the characteristics we associate with modern sports. The emergence of urban centers, more leisure time, new technologies, and social classes helped transform colonial sporting practices into more modern and professional sports.

As the colonists first arrived in the New World, life was difficult, and daily survival dominated people's actions. Work needed to come first. Even under such dire conditions as those that existed in Jamestown during those first few years the colonists played, there are stories of stoolball games and bowling taking men from their daily chores. For example, Sir Thomas Dale had to create a series of rules when he came to Virginia to make colonists work, only allowing play after all work had been completed. As an example, Dale forbid bowling in Jamestown. That approach did not work out well and led to Dale's eventual return to England. The Protestant work ethic came to dominate New England, but people also recognized they could not work all the time. It was important to find a balance in their lives between the serious and the frivolous.

Records indicate that these early Virginians included card games, such as loo and whist; dice games, such as Hazard; board games, such as goose; running races; wrestling matches; and even hunting contests in their ideas of play. Horses were brought to the colonies as early as 1610. Most of these activities were also accompanied by gambling and drinking, which continued to be a source of contention, as most viewed these traits as less than desirable. As late as 1786, *Boston Magazine* published a story claiming, "Few vices are more prevalent in our days than gaming" ("Fatal Effects" 1786, 3). The story went on to tell of a duel that took place as a result of gambling, and two sons died in the event. Gambling was seen, as many sports were, fine in moderation but dangerously addicting and likely to lead to ruin. The contrast lay in sports such as wrestling or target shooting that one could easily argue prepared one for warfare and fighting. The Pennsylvania walking purchase in the 1680s provided exercise and new land by walking around the perimeter of an area before your opponent. Over two days, people walked a giant circle claiming the land they walked as belonging to the colonists and not the Natives.

Native Americans worked, lived, and played as the colonists did. One of their most common sports was lacrosse. It could be played by 100s or 1000s on a single field or between communities. The games had both social and religious significance. Like the colonists, games and sports were rarely played without a larger purpose. Games taught skills and strength or reinforced religious and social attitudes. Lacrosse played well gave credit to the Creator who gave them the game. However, by the 18th century, lacrosse became a sport played more for its grace and beauty.

Other games and sports brought people together, gave participants and winners greater social status, and passed on traditions. Target practice, dice games, and bull roarers provided both fun and skills for those taking part. Bull roarers were used mainly by children; they found common objects, tied them to sinew or string, and twirled them for speed and sound. Stick catching and ring and pin games were played for bragging rights and skills. Balancing sticks on the back of one's hand and being able to toss them in the air and catch them developed eye-hand coordination and speed. Ring and pin games did the same, as did tossing spears at chunkee stones. Double ball games were generally played by Native women; they used sticks and a double ball to traverse fields that could be up to a mile long. The goal was to pass the ball without it ever dropping or being stolen by the opponent. Tug-of-war pitted tribes against one another or could be used as a test of manhood. Wrestling matches were often associated with other special occasions. One example found by researchers came after the death of a tribal leader. The hopeful successor held a stick that others tried to wrestle from him. When they failed, he became the new tribal leader.

Even with all of the restrictions and concerns, early colonists found time to amuse themselves and create simple competitions. Many of these early activities were often associated with other festivities. Harvest festivals and church celebrations combined work and play. Walking and swimming were common activities throughout the colonies. Children could be seen playing leap frog, blind man's bluff, hunt the slipper, charades, hopscotch, and pick-up sticks. Their sports tended to make do with what they could easily find or what they could make up. At the same time, children also interacted daily with adults, and so their activities were often not all that different. For example, fencing was carried out by two boys with sticks instead of swords, or quoits just had a shorter distance. One exception to the shared sports was horse racing, which was definitely an adult-only sport.

Life was tough for everyone, and sporting time was limited. For adults, hunting, fishing and target shooting combined work and play. Lawn bowling, badminton without a net, stoolball, and other ball games combined fun and competition with outcomes being wagered on. Many of these activities centered around the local taverns, as did cribbage, backgammon and quoits (later replaced by horseshoes). Cockfighting and bear or bull baits were more common the farther you moved south. In some colonies in the early years, baits were actually illegal because they were back in England. Boys and young men played football and other ball games in the streets of Boston and Philadelphia. Sporting games such as dances, ball tosses, lawn bowling, and quoits often accompanied festivals and celebrations, such as barn raisings, sheep shearing, and corn husking. Election days and militia days brought out men for target practice, wrestling, drilling and cudgels, where two men confronted each other with sticks that they used to attack and parry each other's advances.

Some sports were judged to be a nuisance that needed regulation. For example, sledding throughout New England was considered a nuisance as early as the 1630s. In Massachusetts, a law was passed in 1633 making sledding a crime because it was considered loafing. Natives and Southerners found sledding to be acceptable only if it helped develop skills in guidance and control as they raced their sleighs across the ice.

Religious restrictions did not just exist in the New England Colonies but also in the South. Virginians could be fined for missing church. Gambling, dancing, and card playing were forbidden on the Sabbath. Restrictions did decline more quickly in the South, and plantation owners had more leisure time because they had indentured servants and slaves doing most of their work. They had money and resources to devote to sports, holding large and lavish events to show off their wealth and their skills. Fox hunting, fishing contests, horse races, and boating were not uncommon activities across the Southern Colonies. In the backcountry, sports tended to be more violent and bloody, ranging from eye gouging to rough and tumble fighting, a no-holds-barred version of boxing. Manliness and honor were often at stake. Losing an eye was actually seen as a sign of strength because it meant your opponent had survived, but you did not want to be the first one to lose an eye. Some competitors were so serious they grew and filed their nails to make it easier to gouge out their opponents' eyes.

In contrast to the plantation owners were the lives of the slaves. With little free time and few resources, their activities were severely limited but not completely without fun. Dancing, music, and storytelling played important roles, as did games of chance. Most owners exercised strict control over what their slaves could do and kept their free time minimal. Slave children, until the age of seven or eight, often played simple games with the white children on the plantation, until work separated them. On a bright sunny day, seeing groups of black and white children playing with a hoop and stick or tossing a ball was not an unusual sight. Jump rope and tag kept children busy and out of harm's way.

As the colonies grew and life became a bit more stable, play and sport took on greater importance, especially for the upper classes. For those with means, work and sport began to separate. For example, games did not have to just take place with festivals and celebrations. Horse racing did not just take place on the plantation or in the town, but on separate tracks if you were wealthy. Horse racing was often prohibited for the working class. For example, Virginia had a law in the

1670s that charged a fine up to 100 pounds of tobacco if a working man tried to enter a race. Horses were even purchased simply for their potential to win a race and not to perform any other work. As early as the 1660s, Long Island had horse racing taking place at New Market, a straight-lane track modeled after the original track in England. Maryland had their first jockey club formed in 1743 to establish more formal rules and prizes to be won. Racing grew so significant that, in 1774, a single race advertised a prize of 200 pounds of tobacco. Lesser races typically awarded saddles and bridles to the winner. Researchers have found advertisements for horse racing events appearing in 1690s newspapers.

For children in the early 1700s, their sports and games began to change, and more things were available for them to use to create opportunities. In addition to the games of imagination, they added things such as marbles, yo-yos, slingshots, seesaws and whirligigs. Tabletop Ninepins, cup and ball, jump rope, and the hoop and stick allowed for more competition and rules. Nine Men's Morris was one of the most popular board games. Children's sports and games were still governed by the attitudes of the time, as they were also expected to keep the Sabbath, to work before playing, and to keep things in moderation. Toy fiddles, toy soldiers, and puzzles fit the idea of sports in moderation, as they did not require complete dedication. Puzzles could be started and left at any time to be finished another day. Fiddles provided evening entertainment and let children interact with the adults.

By 1709, a good example of the changes in sports was found with the listing of a billiards table in the inventory of Virginia planter William Byrd II. Byrd learned the game while at school in England and bought a table when he inherited Westover plantation from his father. Having a billiard table was a way of showing off wealth and status. According to some inventories, a billiard table was among the most expensive furniture one could buy. Byrd played year-round but rarely at night, as there was limited lighting available for any type of activity. Most of Byrd's opponents were members of the local elite, establishing the idea of billiards as a game of status, whereas pool was played in the local taverns. Further reinforcement of the idea that billiards was an exclusive game came when the House of Burgesses of Virginia installed a table in 1720 for the elected members, and some taverns set up private rooms with billiard tables where one paid a fee to play. A Massachusetts tavern advertised tables in 1722, providing tables for all who wanted to have some sport with a game of billiards. In other northern colonies, billiards were banned for their association with gambling.

By the mid-18th century, sports were still not organized with regular leagues, commonly accepted rules, championships, and such, but there was much greater variety and acceptance. Taverns still served as a central place for sports, both indoor and outdoor, but the venues were expanding. One of the biggest changes was venues specifically created for sports. Race tracks were appearing from Long Island to the Carolinas. Horse racing gave the owners bragging rights, but also communities and regions. There were some big purses given out for north versus south races. Shuffleboard courts, lawn bowling, and croquet required more dedicated spaces. Even badminton and shuttlecock now had nets. Fishing clubs even appeared, with the earliest being Schuykill Colony near Philadelphia in the 1730s.

Membership fees could be charged to promote the sport and control who was able to participate.

Colonists continued to play games with English origins, such as cricket and billiards, but they also began to develop their own sporting habits. Tomahawk throwing would be an example, as was pitching the bar or jumping the broom. Lacrosse, played by Native Americans for centuries along with other games, such as shinny and chunkee stones, continued to be played all over. Women also began to expand their sporting habits. Adding to long walks, dances, singing, and charades were spinning contests, sleigh riding, skating, and horse racing. Shorter tracks and smaller purses were awarded, but women found their way onto the track.

Even during the American Revolution, George Washington recognized the need for games of exercise to stay alert and fit. Games of catch, wrestling, and fencing were often common scenes in Revolutionary camps. Some activities were also directly related to the war, such as chasing and capturing cannonballs after they had been fired. Men were given a reward for each one they collected. They also bowled with cannon balls. Nathan Hale talked about playing football in 1775, and Sgt. Simon Griffin said his regiment had nothing to do but play ball (Ledbetter 1979). Snowball fights and horse races continued; but wrestling was outlawed, and swimming was discouraged. Swimming was not encouraged for fear of getting sick from the water, and wrestling led to greater injuries. Wicket (a form of cricket), shinny, and base (a ball game) continued, as did cards, chess, and backgammon. Soldiers and militia men had a lot of free time to fill, and sports kept them active and involved in positive pursuits. Even General Burgoyne brought his fishing gear with him to keep himself occupied between all the fighting.

By the 1750s, sports in the colonies became more divided and tied to class. Jockey clubs provided rules but also charged membership as a way to control who joined. By its nature, horse racing divided people who owned the horses from those who worked with and rode the horses. Races also divided those who attended with fences and social attitudes that said women of higher class should not be mixing with the regular crowds. Cockfighting and bear or bull baiting attracted the working class or the middling sort because of the gambling and drinking as well as the violence. Private lotteries were illegal, but public lotteries were fine because they benefited society.

Sports during the Colonial Period were varied and widespread. The New England colonists played more than history has acknowledged, but with many restrictions, as they were expected to avoid drinking and gambling while keeping the Sabbath holy. While restrictions seemed more lax in the South, colonists still tried to encourage moderation and usefulness in their leisure pursuits. Life was too hard to afford spending time on activities that were not productive.

By the middle of the 18th century, restrictions seemed to be loosening up but were not abandoned. Sports might have been more organized, but they were still not modern. Games such as shuttlecock, lawn bowling, and sledding did not have national rules, professional athletes, or championships. These games gave people a release from all the hard work and worry of daily survival but had not yet become a profession. Sports were useful, but they were expected to complement colonial life and not transform daily chores and tasks. That attitude held true for all participants, regardless of their place in colonial life.

Leslie Heaphy

See also: Drinking and Tavern Culture

Further Reading

Borish, Linda. 1992. "The Sporting Past in American History." *OAH Magazine of History* (Summer): 3–5.

Brailsford, D. n.d. "Puritanism and Sport in 17th Century America." *Stadion* 1, no. 2: 316–330.

Breen, Timothy H. 1977. "Horses and Gentlemen: The Cultural Significance of Gambling among the Gentry of Virginia." *William and Mary Quarterly* (April): 239–257.

Carson, Jane. 1965. *Colonial Virginians at Play.* Charlottesville: University of Virginia Press.

Culin, Stuart. 1975. *Games of North American Indians.* Vols. 1 and 2. New York: Dover Publications.

Daniels, Bruce C. 1993. "Sober Mirth and Pleasant Poisons: Puritan Ambivalence towards Leisure and Recreation in Colonial New England." *American Studies* 34 (Spring): 121–137.

"The Fatal Effects of Gaming." 1786. *Boston Magazine* (May): 3.

Geist, Christopher. 2008. "The Emergence of Popular Culture in Colonial America." *Colonial Williamsburg Journal* (Spring).

Gorn, Elliott. 1985. "'Gouge and Bite, Pull Hair and Scratch': The Social Significance of Fighting in the Back Country." *American Historical Review* 90 (February): 18–43.

Jable, Thomas. 1974. "Pennsylvania's Early Blue Laws: A Quaker Experiment in the Suppression of Sport and Amusements, 1682–1740." *Journal of Sport History* 1 (Spring): 107–122.

Ledbetter, Bonnie S. 1979. "Sports and Games of the American Revolution." *Journal of Sport History* (Winter): 2940.

Struna, Nancy L. 1996. *People of Prowess: Sport, Leisure and Labor in Early Anglo-America.* Chicago: University of Illinois Press.

COLUMBIAN EXCHANGE

The Columbian Exchange is a phrase that describes the exchanges of plants, animals, microorganisms, and human beings between the Eastern and the Western Hemispheres that have taken place since the first voyage of Christopher Columbus in 1492–1493. Though this exchange of biological organisms affected all the world's continents, it especially altered the ecology of the Americas, bringing new crops, new plants, distant peoples, and diseases that killed up to an estimated 90 percent of American Indians.

The ecology of the Eastern and Western Hemispheres gradually became different after the end of the last ice age, around 10,000 years ago, when water submerged the land bridge between Asia and North America. After the extinction of large mammals, such as horses, in the Americas around 8,000 years ago, the only remaining domestic animals in the Western Hemisphere were dogs, llamas, alpacas, guinea pigs, turkeys, the Muscovy duck, and perhaps something similar to a chicken. Peoples of the Americas also cultivated many crops that peoples in the Eastern Hemisphere did not, such as corn, various species of beans, peanuts, potatoes, sweet potatoes, manioc, squash, pumpkins, papayas, guavas, avocados, pineapples, tomatoes, chili peppers, tobacco, and cacao. The cold climate of the ice age as well as the relative lack of concentrated populations living near large numbers of livestock meant that only certain diseases existed in the Americas, such as tuberculosis, histoplasmosis, amoebic dysentery, intestinal worms, rickettsial fevers, endemic syphilis, salmonella, and other bacterial pathogens. Leishmaniasis and Chagas disease also flourished in certain niches, and it is possible that forms of influenza, malaria, and yellow fever were present in the Americas prior to sustained contact between the Western and Eastern Hemispheres.

Many different biological organisms lived in the Eastern Hemisphere prior to Columbus's first voyage. Peoples in Europe, Asia, Africa, and Oceania cultivated grains, such as wheat, rice, barley, and oats; other plants, such as sugarcane, bananas, grapes, citrus fruits, onions, olives, turnips, peaches, pears, and coffee beans; and livestock, such as cattle, sheep, pigs, and horses. They also experienced diseases such as smallpox, influenza, typhus, measles, bubonic plague, malaria, yellow fever, and whooping cough.

The sustained contact between the Eastern and Western Hemispheres that developed after 1492 caused the biological organisms of both hemispheres to interact with each other. This interaction had a number of different effects on the Eastern Hemisphere. The introduction of sweet potatoes into the agricultural practices of China solved the immediate problem of food shortages and provided a food source, which continued to fuel the growth of China's large population. Peoples of sub-Saharan Africa began to cultivate corn and turned it into a basic food source for those Africans enslaved during the Atlantic slave trade as well as one of the most important crops in sub-Saharan Africa today. Though most Europeans were slow to cultivate crops from the Americas, there is a debate about whether the endemic syphilis present in the Americas prior to sustained contact with Europeans resulted in the development of venereal syphilis, which first made its presence felt in Europe in the Italian Peninsula in 1494.

Though the changes biological organisms from the Americas helped encourage in the Eastern Hemisphere were significant, the Americas experienced many more effects from this biological exchange due to human choices as well as the immunities American peoples lacked to the diseases of the Eastern Hemisphere. When they came to the Americas, most Europeans were unwilling to abandon their traditional diets. They consciously brought with them both crops and livestock that were staples of typical European cuisines, such as wheat, olives, pigs, and cattle as well as those crops, such as sugar, that had started to emerge as significant commodities in world trade to cultivate in the Americas. The tens of millions of Africans whom Europeans enslaved and forced to travel to the Americas also brought African crops with them, such as certain species of rice. In addition to these consciously transported plants and animals, many more stowed away in ships' holds, such as rats and other vermin as well as the seeds of plants that most Europeans considered to be weeds.

The introduction of these new crops and animals would likely have changed the ecology of the Americas on their own. Yet, the ways in which both settlers as well as American Indians decided to cultivate these plants and animals helped shape the environment of the Americas after 1492. Beginning with the earliest voyages that Iberian sailors made to the Caribbean islands, Mesoamerica, and northern portions of South America, these sailors purposely let pigs, cattle, and horses run loose across various islands and landscapes to provide explorers and settlers with ready food supplies. Some attempts were made to contain these livestock populations, but pigs, cattle, and horses bred more quickly than people could control, and pigs' willingness to eat almost anything meant that wild bands of pigs roamed many portions of the Americas. These animal bands were both a blessing and a curse. Though they provided European settlers and American Indians with food, and some American Indian groups began to domesticate horses in an effort to help themselves resist European incursions, wild animal bands also rampaged through both European settlers' and American Indians' cultivated fields, ruining crops and causing famine.

The crops grown in American fields as well as the type of farming done in the Americas also began to change after 1492. Prior to contact with Europeans, many American Indians outside of Mesoamerica and the Andes Mountains combined farming with hunting and gathering. These American Indian villages tended to migrate among a variety of locations, meaning that these villagers would plant crops in different places in different years, thus saving their farming locations from soil exhaustion. Europeans, in contrast, believed in settling in one place and continually cultivating the same land. Mostly rejecting the notion of crop rotation, European settlers grew wheat and other such crops on the same piece of land year after year, draining that land of its nutrients and lowering the possible crop yield of such land.

The focus on growing cash crops encouraged the growth of farm size, as tobacco and sugar required a great deal of cultivated land to produce a profitable crop. Many European settlers, and eventually American Indians, began to fence in their fields to keep roaming bands of pigs and cattle away from their crops. New agricultural techniques also changed landscapes. In the area of present-day South Carolina, African slaves taught European settlers irrigation techniques for the cultivation of rice. Though the species of rice eventually grown here came from Asia, the knowledge of rice irrigation African slaves brought proved crucial for local subsistence as well as for the cultivation of the cash crop rice eventually became.

As plants, animals, and agricultural techniques from the Eastern Hemisphere began to change the economic and social structures of the Americas, the introduction of diseases from the Eastern Hemisphere proved to be disastrous for American Indian peoples. Living in relatively high population concentrations and in close contact with livestock, peoples from the Eastern Hemisphere had experiences with many different diseases that American Indians did not. As this experience had occurred generation after generation, many of those people living in the Eastern Hemisphere had developed genetic immunities to these diseases or they had acquired such immunities after experiencing diseases as children.

American Indians had no such disease experience, and when Europeans and Africans carried diseases from the Eastern Hemisphere with them to the Americas, these diseases caused very high mortality rates among American Indians. The effects of diseases from the Eastern Hemisphere on Mesoamerica and South America are easier to trace because more evidence for their impacts exist. For example, there is a lot of evidence to suggest that the vast majority of the Native peoples living on Caribbean islands who had had contact with Europeans were dead by 1542. Epidemics of smallpox struck both Mesoamerica as well as South America from 1518, killing as many as a third of the American Indian populations there. An epidemic of measles occurred in the 1530s; an epidemic of another disease, probably typhus, occurred in 1546; and a worldwide influenza outbreak in the 1550s followed quickly thereafter. By the beginning of the 17th century, these diseases along with malaria and the bubonic plague had become endemic to the Americas. Yellow fever also had also become endemic to tropical regions by the 1640s. The result of these repeated waves of epidemic diseases coupled with European policies of conquest and enslavement was a catastrophic reduction in American Indian populations in the Caribbean, Mesoamerica, and South America as well as the enslavement of Africans to meet the perceived labor shortages.

The effects of these diseases on North America are harder to know for certain. There is evidence of cycles of epidemics, probably including at least smallpox and influenza, in the early 17th century in both Lower California and in New England. It is also highly likely that those diseases that struck the Caribbean, Mesoamerica, and South America in the 16th century killed many American Indians in North America, as the spread of disease far outpaced European exploration and expansion, often following traditional trade routes. The best evidence for the decimation of the peoples of North America by these diseases is that many pieces of land American Indians had cleared and cultivated were empty when European settlers arrived in New England. These seemingly abandoned sites quickly became the centers of new European settlements.

The exchange of animals, plants, microorganisms, and human beings between the Eastern and Western Hemispheres since 1492 had profound effects on the world. Whereas American plants and animals helped diversify diets and sustain large populations in the Eastern Hemisphere, the deliberate cultivation of crops and animals from the Eastern Hemisphere in the Western Hemisphere completely changed the ecology of the Americas— a change that the deaths of American Indians from diseases native to the Eastern Hemisphere further encouraged. These changes to the ecology of the Western Hemisphere enabled Europeans to conquer much of the Americas, promoting the expansion as well as the economic and military hegemony of Europeans and the disappearance of entire peoples from the Americas. This so-called Columbian Exchange has continued into our modern world, decreasing biodiversity around the globe at a very high rate.

Lindsay J. Starkey

See also: Columbus, Christopher; Disease; Mesoamerica

Further Reading

Cook, Noble David. 1998. *Born to Die: Disease and New World Conquest, 1492–1650*. Cambridge: Cambridge University Press.

Cronon, William. 2003. *Changes in the Land: Indians, Colonists, and the Ecology of New England*. Rev. ed. New York: Hill & Wang.

Crosby, Alfred W., Jr. 2004. *Ecological Imperialism: The Biological Expansion of Europe, 900–1900*. 2nd ed. Cambridge: Cambridge University Press.

Crosby, Alfred W., Jr. 2003. *The Columbian Exchange: Biological and Cultural Consequences of 1492*. 30th anniversary ed. Westport, CT: Praeger.

Diamond, Jared. 1999. *Guns, Germs, and Steel: The Fates of Human Societies*. New York: W. W. Norton & Company.

McNeill, William H. 1976. *Plagues and Peoples*. Garden City, NY: Anchor Press/Doubleday.

Silver, Timothy. 1990. *A New Face on the Countryside: Indians, Colonists, and Slaves in South Atlantic Forests, 1500–1800*. Cambridge: Cambridge University Press.

COLUMBUS, CHRISTOPHER (1451–1506)

Christopher Columbus was an Italian navigator and explorer who led the first recorded European expedition to cross the Atlantic Ocean in 1492. Although Columbus searched for the elusive westward route to Asia, he landed instead on islands in the Caribbean Sea. His voyage, which was well publicized in Europe, stimulated exploration of what was for 15th-century Europeans an undiscovered world, the Americas. Although Columbus's discovery of the Americas presented undreamed of opportunities for Europeans, it also marked the beginning of several centuries of famine, disease, dislocation, and violence for the Native American peoples already living in the Western Hemisphere.

Early Life and Education

Columbus was born Cristoforo Columbo in Genoa, Italy, in 1451, to Domenico Columbo, a master weaver and part-time wine shop owner, and Suzanna Fontanarossa. He received little or no formal education in his youth. He never wrote in Italian, but he did learn to read and write in Spanish and Portuguese. Columbus spent much of his youth working as an apprentice to his father's trade, but by his own account, he took to the sea at a "tender age." His earliest trading voyages were likely to have been to collect supplies of wool or wine.

At the age of 19, Columbus made his first trading voyage in the Aegean Sea. In his early twenties, he began to make longer voyages to Marseilles, Tunis, and the Greek island of Chios (then a Genoese colony). In 1476, Columbus set out for Flanders and England, but his vessel was sunk by French privateers. He landed penniless in Portugal and was taken in by one of many Genoese living in Lisbon, which was then the principal European center of overseas exploration. In Lisbon, Columbus acquired most of his knowledge of navigation.

In 1479, Columbus married Felipa Perestrello e Moniz, the daughter of a widow of a distinguished family who had inherited property in Madeira and an interest in the hereditary captaincy of the island of Porto Santo. By this marriage, he had a son,

In this engraving by Theodor de Bry, Christopher Columbus is shown receiving ritual gifts from the Cacique Guacanagarí on the island of Hispaniola. Columbus arrived in the Americas in 1492, and his landing in the Caribbean instigated a monumental change in global events. His reputation and his role in the treatment of the natives he encountered continue to be debated by scholars. (Library of Congress)

Diego, who was born in 1480. In Madeira, Columbus learned about island discovery and settlement and caught the optimistic enthusiasm for charting new islands that was characteristic of the time.

Exploring the New World

Columbus's idea of sailing west to the Indies seems to have been inspired by three sources: Florentine cosmographer Paolo Toscanelli, Cardinal Pierre d'Ailly's *Image of the World*, and Marco Polo's account of the Far East. Columbus theorized that the world was predominately covered in land and that the distance to Asia was much shorter than previously thought. Although he clearly sought adventure, his primary motivations were most likely the pursuit of honor and wealth. When the king of Portugal rejected Columbus's proposal to finance the voyage, he turned to Spain, where he received high praise and royal patronage for his proposed adventure.

In April 1492, Ferdinand V and Isabella I of Spain agreed to sponsor the expedition. On the first voyage, Columbus commanded three ships: the *Santa Maria*, the *Pinta*, and the *Niña*. The fleet departed on August 3, 1492, from Palos, Spain. The length of the voyage tested the will of the new explorers, but on October 12, the expedition sighted Guanahaní, an island in the Bahamas. Columbus renamed the island San Salvador and claimed it for Spain. The expedition also landed on Cuba and Española (later called Hispaniola, which is now the Dominican Republic and Haiti), where Columbus left 40 men before returning to Spain to an enthusiastic welcome in 1493.

On his return, Isabella commanded Columbus to sail again immediately. He embarked on a second expedition with 17 ships and 1,000 colonists in September 1493. Upon returning to Española, he discovered that the men he had left behind had been killed by the Natives. On this second voyage, Columbus landed on the islands of Dominica, Guadeloupe, and Antigua and established the first European settlement in the Americas—the colony of Isabella, near what is now Cape Isabella, in the Dominican Republic. He explored the coast of Cuba in the spring of 1494, and before returning to Spain in June 1496, he established a new capital on Española that he called Santo Domingo. It was at the end of this second voyage that many colonists who had sailed with him and then returned to Spain began to express criticism of Columbus and his ventures, but the queen continued to support him.

Columbus Loses Status

In May 1498, Columbus set out on his third expedition. He landed on the island of Trinidad and sighted what is now Venezuela, discovering South America. When he arrived in Santo Domingo, Columbus found the colony of Española in revolt. Across the Atlantic, in Spain, discontented colonists finally managed to persuade the reigning monarchs that Española demanded a new governor. The king and queen removed Columbus in May 1499 and appointed Francisco de Bobadilla to establish order in the colony. Columbus was subsequently arrested and sent back to Spain in chains. On his return, the queen pardoned Columbus but refused to restore his office as governor of Española.

In May 1502, Columbus ventured on his fourth and final expedition. Hampered by hurricane damage to the fleet, he managed to reach Honduras and searched in vain for nearly six months along the Central American coast for the passage across the continent to Asia. In January 1503, Columbus landed at Panama and established a colony. In June of that same year, his fleet became marooned near Jamaica. Columbus summoned help from Española, but the stranded expedition waited nearly one year for rescue.

After returning to Spain in 1504, Columbus found he had lost not only his title as governor of the Indies but his chief support in the person of Isabella, who had died earlier that year, on November 26. Suffering from arthritis and humiliated and frustrated by the elusive fame and wealth that he so fiercely sought through his discoveries, Columbus died in Valladolid on May 20, 1506. His remains were ultimately laid to rest, alongside his son Diego, at the cathedral of Santo Domingo in 1542.

Legacy

Columbus was not the first European to land in the Americas. Navigators from Norway, Iceland, or Greenland had briefly settled in Newfoundland in the late 10th or early 11th century. Evidence also exists to suggest that English fishermen may have sighted some part of North America prior to Columbus's first voyage. Columbus's discovery, however, is distinguished from that of other adventurers by its consequences, mainly that Columbus's discoveries in the Western Hemisphere were followed by rapid, widespread, and permanent European settlement.

ABC-CLIO

See also: Columbian Exchange; Spain

Further Reading

Bedini, Silvio A., and David Buisseret. 1992. *The Christopher Columbus Encyclopedia.* New York: Simon & Schuster.

Davidson, Miles H. 1997. *Columbus Then and Now: A Life Reexamined.* Norman: University of Oklahoma Press.

Di, Giovanni M. 1991. *Christopher Columbus: His Life and Discoveries.* San Gabriel, CA: Columbus Explorers, Inc.

COMMITTEE OF DETAIL

The Committee of Detail played a vital role in the creation of the U.S. Constitution: it produced the first complete draft of the Constitution from the disparate resolutions adopted by the Constitutional Convention during the summer of 1787. Proposed on July 23, 1787, the committee commenced its work three days later, charged with organizing what the convention had decided thus far. Nineteen adopted resolutions or statements of principle had to be filled in and tied together as a coherent charter for the new national government. Over the course of its work, the Committee of Detail transformed the 1,200 words of adopted resolutions into 3,600 words succinctly organized into 23 articles. The committee was carefully selected to represent a balance of large and small states as well as northern and southern interests with five seasoned statesmen, all members of the Confederation Congress and thereby familiar with the weaknesses of the existing national government.

All five committee members were frequent contributors during the convention debates and displayed the ability to forge solutions. All but one member practiced law, and once the Constitution was adopted, three of them would serve as justices on the initial Supreme Court. Oliver Ellsworth of Connecticut helped lead the push for vote by state in the Senate during the convention debates; he would later serve on the first Supreme Court. Nathaniel Gorham of Massachusetts was the only non-lawyer on the committee, although he would later serve as a state court judge; during the convention, he chaired the Committee of the Whole. Edmund Randolph of Virginia presented James Madison's Virginia Plan to convention delegates during the early days of the convention; he would later serve as the first U.S. attorney general. John Rutledge, an influential lawyer and former governor of South Carolina, served as chairman of the committee; in fact, he served on a total of five committees during the convention, and he would go on to serve on the first Supreme Court. The fifth committee member was James Wilson of Pennsylvania, who along with Rutledge proposed the three-fifths clause in the convention's debate over slavery and how to determine representation in the House. Wilson later served on the Supreme Court with both Rutledge and Ellsworth.

The first outline of the committee's work is in Randolph's handwriting with edits written by Rutledge, and it notes two rules for the committee's work to draft the Constitution: to include "essential principles only" in "simple and precise language." A second draft appears to have been written by Wilson with edits by Rutledge, who presented a final draft to the delegates. The committee worked through a 10-day recess granted to the rest of the delegates. They inserted provisions that were never considered by the whole convention. Most of these insertions were not likely to be controversial, for some had been debated by the convention, and while changed by the committee, the intent remained in important ways. For example, the committee inserted that the Senate would negotiate foreign treaties and name ambassadors, and in final form, the Senate was given the power to provide the president with advice and consent on treaties and ambassadors. Meanwhile, the committee's other insertions did not survive, including a provision that the president of the Senate replace a president who dies in office.

In his first draft, Randolph replaced the vague language approved by the convention regarding the powers granted to the legislative branch with 18 enumerated powers. Many of the listed powers came from the Articles of Confederation, but by specifically naming those powers granted to Congress, the committee defined the power of the new government as limited in a way the convention had not discussed. Wilson favored a stronger central government than Randolph, and in his draft, Wilson added an important catchall phrase after the enumerated powers—today it is known as the necessary and proper clause. Wilson also included eight limits on the states, which denied them power to sign foreign treaties, issue currency, declare war, or tax imports. He also expanded the supremacy clause to specifically declare national law supreme not only to state law but also to state constitutions.

The committee inserted three provisions that were desired by the Southern states but raised fierce objections on the convention floor. The first was to protect the importation of slaves in perpetuity. The second banned taxes on any exports, including the Southern staple crops of cotton and tobacco. The third was a requirement of a two-thirds vote in both legislative houses to approve any act concerning interstate or foreign trade. The same day the convention created the Committee of Detail, Charles Cotesworth Pinckney of South Carolina had called for such provisions, warning that he would be "bound by duty" to vote against the committee's report if it did not include some security against the emancipation of slaves and taxes on exports. Pinckney proved lucky that none of the three northerners on the Committee were abolitionists. Besides the fact that none of the committee members moved to block the protections provided for the South, those Northern states that would have most strongly objected to the two economic provisions were not represented at the convention by the end of July. Of the states largely dependent on shipping, Rhode Island never sent delegates, New York's delegates had returned home, and Massachusetts's Gorham apparently chose not to oppose Southern demands.

The committee's draft included a general framework for the executive branch: one person elected by both houses of the legislative branch for a single seven-year term. He could be removed from office once impeached by the House of Representatives and then tried and found guilty by the Supreme Court. He could veto legislation, but such a veto could be overridden by a two-thirds vote in the legislature. The executive had power to appoint all government officials, except those specifically named for selection by other branches. The committee added the title president of the United States of America, to be addressed as "Your Excellency."

When the convention reconvened in early August and the secretary read aloud the Committee of Detail's seven-page report, the convention took a major step forward. While the delegates had largely debated the 19 provisions in the Virginia Plan, which contained general concepts of the new government but few details, the committee's report was more specific. Furthermore, its format was familiar to many of the delegates who had experience with the Articles of Confederation and state constitutions.

More than once in August, Rutledge expressed dismay with the tediousness of the debates, and Ellsworth expressed that the longer they debated, the less likely it became that the delegates would ever reach consensus. Still, the Committee of Detail continued to meet into early September to resolve new issues. While a series of new committees would be tasked with many details, the Committee of Detail left an indelible mark on the Constitutional Convention's proceedings by providing a new starting point for debates and for including many specific details about the executive and legislative branches.

Kathleen A. Gronnerud

See also: Committee of Style and Arrangement; Constitutional Convention

Further Reading

Beeman, Richard. 2009. *Plain, Honest Men: The Making of the American Constitution.* New York: Random House.

Berkin, Carol. 2002. *A Brilliant Solution: Inventing the American Constitution.* Orlando, FL: Harcourt, Inc.

Collier, Christopher, and James Lincoln Collier. 1986. *Decision in Philadelphia: The Constitutional Convention of 1787.* New York: Ballantine Books.

Drinker Bowen, Catherine. 1986. *Miracle at Philadelphia: The Story of the Constitutional Convention, May to September 1787.* New York: Back Bay Books.

Stewart, David O. 2007. *The Men Who Invented the Constitution: The Summer of 1787.* New York: Simon & Schuster Paperbacks, Inc.

COMMITTEE OF STYLE AND ARRANGEMENT

The Committee of Style and Arrangement was charged to produce a final version of the plan for a new national government conceived at the Constitutional Convention. The document produced by the committee bore the mark of Chairman Gouverneur Morris of Pennsylvania, a man widely respected for his command of the English language. Under Morris's guidance, the committee of largely strong nationalists strove for clarity—eliminating vague and redundant wording wherever they found it—and instilled in the Constitution, especially the preamble, a sense of pride and national purpose in the new central government. Morris restructured 23 articles into 7 and grouped together those provisions that dealt with each branch of government. He then reordered the text to clearly represent the hierarchy of power within the government, with the legislative branch first, then the executive, and, finally, the judicial branch. His choice of words in the eloquent preamble made clear the source of power in the new government—the people—as opposed to the individual states under the flawed Articles of Confederation.

Perhaps most markedly, the Committee of Style revised the language of the various approved provisions to convey a confidence and unity in the delegates' work that masked the months of disagreement and wrangling that had marked the convention's debates. For example, while the language in both Article I pertaining to the powers of Congress and Article II pertaining to the powers of the executive are concise and straightforward, it is nevertheless vague in ways that reflect the divisions within the convention as to the appropriate balance of powers between the two branches.

The five committee members were all experienced politicians representing some of the largest states. Alexander Hamilton of New York (1755–1804) was a strong nationalist who helped create momentum for the Constitutional Convention; during ratification proceedings after the convention, he wrote the majority of the *Federalist Papers*, and after adoption of the Constitution, he served as the first secretary of the treasury. Dr. William Samuel Johnson of Connecticut (1727–1819) was the only member from a small state. Johnson later served in the first Senate and then went on to become president of Columbia College. Rufus King of Massachusetts (1755–1827) was a strong nationalist born into a wealthy family who considered high public service an important responsibility; he would go on to play a key role in the ratification effort in Massachusetts. James Madison of Virginia (1751–1836) gave the convention its guiding framework from the beginning with his Virginia Plan; he was also the main architect of the convention, as he had lobbied Washington to attend, knowing that the general's presence would lend weight to the proceedings and spur other distinguished men to attend. Madison would later serve as first Speaker of the House, as secretary of state under President Thomas Jefferson, and then two terms as the fourth U.S. president. Chairman Gouvernour Morris of Pennsylvania (1752–1816) had served as one of youngest members of the Continental Congress. Once the Constitution was adopted, President Washington appointed Morris minister to France.

Proposed and appointed on September 8, 1787, the members of the Committee of Style and Arrangement worked double-duty for the next several days, attending the convention debates by day and working during their "off hours" to edit and polish an ever-changing document. For example, by September 10, after nearly two months of deliberations, the delegates had reached only tentative agreement on how the Constitution might be amended. In Article V, the Committee of Style allowed for several paths for proposal of possible amendments, including two-thirds of the state legislatures, a convention of the states, or Congress; however, the mechanism for ratification stayed the same as approved by the convention: approval by three-fourths of the state legislatures. On September 11, the delegates took a temporary recess to await the committee's report. The committee presented its draft known as "the plan" the next day. Delegates worked through the plan, making minor changes and turning down a few suggestions. They finished their review on September 15, and Gouverneur Morris went to work polishing the amended language.

Along with its final draft of the Constitution, the Committee of Style included a cover letter of sorts, drafted by Chairman Morris. The masterful letter meant to address three audiences at the same time. First, the letter addressed the delegates of the Constitutional Convention who had spent their summer in heated, secretive debates about the best form of a new democratic government. For these delegates, the letter was an attempt to justify their work. Second, for the members of the Continental Congress convened in New York, the letter was an appeal for support in the effort ahead for constitutional reform. Lastly, the letter addressed the anticipated public surprise at the scope of change proposed in the new Constitution. The delegates knew that some people would accuse them of going too far. The letter was an attempt to explain the work of the convention and its recognition of the need for an altogether different system of government than the loose affiliation of sovereign states under the Articles of Confederation. Morris acknowledged the difficulty in determining a firm line between those powers best granted to the states versus those best surrendered to a central government; he then argued for the necessity of "consolidation of our nation" to ensure its very existence.

Kathleen A. Gronnerud

See also: Committee of Detail; Constitutional Convention; Madison, James

Further Reading

Beeman, Richard. 2009. *Plain, Honest Men: The Making of the American Constitution.* New York: Random House.

Berkin, Carol. 2002. *A Brilliant Solution: Inventing the American Constitution.* Orlando, FL: Harcourt, Inc.

Collier, Christopher, and James Lincoln Collier. 1986. *Decision in Philadelphia: The Constitutional Convention of 1787.* New York: Ballantine Books.

Drinker Bowen, Catherine. 1986. *Miracle at Philadelphia: The Story of the Constitutional Convention, May to September 1787.* New York: Back Bay Books.

Stewart, David O. 2007. *The Men Who Invented the Constitution: The Summer of 1787.* New York: Simon & Schuster Paperbacks, Inc.

COMMITTEES OF CORRESPONDENCE

There have been several types of committees that have been designated Committees of Correspondence, including committees appointed by colonial legislatures to correspond with colonial agents in England. During the Revolutionary period, local Committees of Correspondence, Safety and Inspection became the vehicles of colonial protest, primarily in America's port cities, where committees were formed to oppose British taxation and legislation. They would then designate a few of their number to correspond with committees that were engaged in similar activities in other cities, especially during the Stamp Act Crisis (1765–1766) and the extended resistance to the Townshend duties (1768–1770). During these landmark events, these correspondents played an important role in coordinating the nonimportation movement among the major cities.

At the provincial level, several colonial assemblies created standing Committees of Correspondence well before the beginning of the imperial crisis. Their main function was to write to the legislature's agent in London, directing him to lobby British officials concerning issues of importance to the lawmakers and to receive the agent's reports. On one occasion, in Massachusetts in 1768, a standing legislative Committee of Correspondence wrote not to its agent but to other colonial legislatures to oppose British policy. This circular letter was supported by strong resistance from the Massachusetts Assembly, which refused to rescind it under orders from the British government, and from the South Carolina Assembly, which voted over the governor's objection to receive it.

Certain policies remained a source of trouble. The enforcement of trade laws was a constant irritant, and Americans in colony after colony made it difficult for customs officers to carry out their duties. A second source of opposition was the presence of British troops, particularly in Boston. The populace of Boston kept the troops under continuous attack in newspapers and poured abuse upon them in the streets of the town. This action, on March 5, 1770, culminated in what has been famously designated as the Boston Massacre. Although the officers and soldiers involved were acquitted, the "massacre" provided the popular leaders with a rich source of anti-British propaganda and helped them to keep party spirit alive.

The American Revolution was the work of a small group of dedicated persuaders who created the first American propaganda and agitation campaign to overthrow a monarchial government. Relations with Great Britain remained tense but relatively calm for most Americans in the years after the massacre of 1770. However, many colonists believed the fight was not over and sought ways to be prepared for future conflicts. During a three-year interval of calm, a relatively small number of radicals strove energetically to keep the controversy alive. They contended that payment of the taxes imposed by the British government constituted an acceptance of the principle that Parliament had the right to rule over the colonies. These radicals feared that at any time in the future, the principle of parliamentary rule might be applied with devastating effect on all colonial liberties.

Opposition to the various taxes imposed by the king and his ministers started as the work of James Otis, Samuel Adams, Patrick Henry, Benjamin Franklin, and Thomas Paine, radical pamphleteers who realized that effective propaganda requires organization (the Sons of Liberty and Committees of Correspondence acted as propaganda conduits throughout the colonies); creative and identifiable emotive symbols (the Liberty Tree) and slogans ("Don't tread on me" and "Taxation without representation is tyranny") to simplify issues and arouse emotions; utilization of publicity and staged events (the Boston Tea Party) to attract media attention and to enlist key supporters (religious leaders whose sermons were widely published and distributed); and exploitation of differences rather than similarities among targeted groups on a sustained, unrelenting basis through control of key public opinion tools (press, pamphlets, broadsides, and songs).

The radicals' most effective leader was Samuel Adams of Massachusetts, who toiled tirelessly toward one goal: independence. Adams wanted to free people from their awe of social and political superiors, make them aware of their own power and importance, and thus arouse them to action. Toward these objectives, he published articles in newspapers and made speeches in town meetings, instigating resolutions that appealed to the colonists' democratic impulses.

In November 1772, Adams, along with other patriot leaders in Boston, established a Committee of Correspondence to provide an organized mechanism for communication and protest when needed. The occasion was the news that certain royal officials, including judges of the Superior Court, were to be paid from British funds rather than by grant from the legislature. The Boston town meeting demanded a special session of the legislature, and when this was refused by Governor Hutchinson, Samuel Adams proposed the establishment of the Committee of Correspondence. The men on this committee were soon communicating with like-minded men in other Massachusetts towns. The committee functioned as a clearinghouse for news and propaganda and built up an effective organization within the colony and kept in touch with popular leaders. In the resolution, Adams requested that a "committee of correspondence be appointed to consist of twenty-one persons: to state the rights of the colonists, and of this province in particular, as men, as Christians, and as subjects" and "to communicate and publish the same to the several towns in the provinces and to the world as the sense of this town [Boston]" as well as "requesting of each town a free communication of their sentiments."

The committee opposed a British decision to pay the salaries of judges from customs revenues. It feared that the judges would no longer be dependent on the legislature for their incomes and thus no longer accountable to it. This would lead to the emergence of "a despotic form of government." The committee communicated with other towns on this matter and requested them to draft replies. Committees were set up in virtually all the colonies, and out of them grew a base of effective Revolutionary organizations.

Such committees had been used on a random and ad hoc basis since 1764 to deal with specific issues, but people such as Adams and Joseph Warren wanted to develop a more standardized system by tying the committees directly to the existing town meeting structure to provide official standing for the committee in the community and regular meetings to deal with ongoing concerns. Over the next 14 months, up until the Boston Tea Party, this committee sent out carefully crafted letters; received replies; sent out fresh responses; persuaded nearly 60 Massachusetts towns, and even a few Connecticut towns, to create their own Committees of Correspondence; and endorsed Boston's view that Britain was engaged in a vast conspiracy to undermine American liberties.

The complete plan for unifying the action of these colonial assemblies came from Thomas Jefferson and Richard Henry Lee, who, in March 1773, secured the appointment of a standing committee of 11 members, all anti-British Whigs, by the Virginia House of Burgess. By 1774, every assembly except Pennsylvania had established a standing Committee of Correspondence that was supposed to be free from decisions of the royal governors. An example of this was when bitterness over the Tea Act and passage of the Intolerable Acts required united action. The Massachusetts Assembly ordered the Boston Committee of Correspondence to draft a pamphlet stating the rights of the colonists and their grievances and to send copies of the Boston Port Act to other assemblies with requests for support. These letters contained the basics of propaganda for stirring up public opinion for the "insulted, besieged capital of Massachusetts Bay."

When Parliament passed the Coercive Acts (or Intolerable Acts) in the spring of 1774, the Massachusetts countryside was already substantially radicalized and ready to create a provincial government that was not based on British authority. The first, the Boston Port Bill, closed the port of Boston until the tea was paid for.

A Quartering Act required local authorities to find suitable quarters for British troops, in private homes if necessary. The Quebec Act, passed at nearly the same time, extended the boundaries of the province of Quebec south to the Ohio River. Though the Quebec Act had not been passed as a punitive measure, Americans associated it with the Coercive Acts, and all became known as the "Five Intolerable Acts."

As soon as Britain closed the port of Boston as punishment for the Boston Tea Party, the town's Committee of Correspondence and its neighboring committees were ready to form similar committees in communities extending hundreds of miles down the Atlantic Seaboard. By June, in response to the closing of the port of Boston, every major seaport had chosen its committee, and by July, many inland towns and rural counties had created their own committees. These bodies stood ready to endorse two moves: the calling of an intercolonial congress to determine the best means to meet the crisis and the initiation of a more tightly coordinated nonimportation movement in all of Britain's North American colonies.

At the suggestion of the Virginia House of Burgesses, colonial representatives met in Philadelphia on September 5, 1774, "to consult upon the present unhappy state of the Colonies." Delegates to this meeting, known as the First Continental Congress, were chosen by provincial congresses or popular conventions. The division of opinion in the colonies posed a genuine dilemma for the delegates. They would have to give an appearance of firm unanimity to induce the British government to make concessions. But they also would have to avoid any show of radicalism or spirit of independence that would alarm more moderate Americans. A cautious keynote speech, followed by a "resolve" that no obedience was due the Coercive Acts, ended with adoption of a set of resolutions affirming the right of the colonists to "life, liberty, and property" and the right of provincial legislatures to set "all cases of taxation and internal polity." The most important action taken by the Congress, however, was the formation of a "Continental Association" to reestablish the trade boycott. It set up a system of committees to inspect customs entries, publish the names of merchants who violated the agreements, confiscate their imports, and encourage frugality, economy, and industry.

Both legislative Committees of Correspondence and local Committees of Observation, Inspection, and Correspondence remained essential Revolutionary institutions until independence was finally achieved. After this, new challenges were met by local officials and institutions who were appointed by the new state governments that were operating under new constitutions. The Committees of Correspondence dominated Revolutionary commercial regulation and political mobilization in America, and they played a central role in recruiting a new Revolutionary leadership.

Martin J. Manning

See also: Adams, Samuel; Continental Congresses; Franklin, Benjamin; George III; Henry, Patrick; Paine, Thomas; Sons of Liberty; Stamp Act Congress

Further Reading

Andrlik, Todd, comp. 2012. *Reporting the Revolutionary War: Before It Was History, It Was News*. Naperville, IL: Sourcebooks.

Collins, Edward D. 1902. "Committees of Correspondence of the American Revolution." Annual Report of the American Historical Association: 243–271.

Davidson, Philip. 1941. *Propaganda and the American Revolution, 1763–1783*. New York: Norton.

Greene, Jack P., ed. 1975. *Colonies to Nation, 1763–1789: A Documentary History of the American Revolution*. New York: Norton.

Ryerson, Richard A. 1978. *The Revolution Is Now Begun: The Radical Committees of Philadelphia, 1765–1776*. Philadelphia: University of Pennsylvania Press.

COMPANY OF ONE HUNDRED ASSOCIATES

The Company of One Hundred Associates, colloquially known as the Company of New France, was a trading and colonization company. It was created to provide capital funds to develop and expand French merchant opportunities in North America, most notably the Canadian fur trade. The company was chartered under the control of Cardinal Richelieu in 1627, it and was formally approved by Louis XIII the following year. It oversaw a vast amount of land that encompassed French-controlled Canada (including Acadia and Newfoundland) as well as French Louisiana. It ceased operations in 1663.

In the 17th century, each of the European colonial powers approached developing their overseas possessions in a different manner. French fishermen had been active off the Grand Banks of modern Newfoundland even before Jacques Cartier explored the St. Lawrence River and its approaches, planted a cross on the Gaspé Peninsula, and claimed the territory for the French Crown in 1534. Despite this, and the abundant riches of the land, few settlers were willing to move to the cold, remote place. Not until the 1580s were commercial companies established to systematically organize the lucrative fur trade thus far carried on by a small number of hardy individuals. Still, early attempts to found permanent trading posts failed. Not until the dawn of the 17th century did a sufficient number of French arrive in Canada to allow for the establishment of successful settlements in Acadia and, in 1608, what became Québec City.

Samuel de Champlain, who arrived in 1608 with only 28 men, was prominent in the founding of the city. The task was not easy. Disease, hunger, and the severe winter took its toll. In addition, few new settlers arrived to bolster the tenuous colony. By 1630, Quebec City's European population stood at only 103, increasing to just 355 during the entire following decade. Largely through Champlain's favorable treatment of the indigenous Algonquin and Montagnais people, the fledgling outpost survived these lean early years and even managed to expand French influence through the "coureurs de bois" (runners of the woods). These were French settlers who Champlain encouraged to learn the language and culture of the indigenous people so they could move freely among them and further develop the fur trade.

Recognizing the potential economic benefit of New France (Nouvelle-France), Armand Jean de Vignerot du Plessis, better known to history as Cardinal Richelieu, a prominent adviser and chief minister to Louis XIII, determined to expand the French presence in the hopes of rivaling the economic benefits the English colonies were returning to their home country. Richelieu appointed Champlain governor of New France and, in line with the religious tensions of the day, prohibited non-Catholics from moving to the colony. When he further required any European already in the colony who was not Catholic to renounce their religion in favor of Catholicism, some chose instead to leave for the English colonies to the south. Despite this initial minor loss, Richelieu encouraged Recollet and Jesuit missionaries to establish a permanent presence in the region and also undertook to encourage new settlers to make the perilous voyage across the North Atlantic. Although his efforts did not result in an immediate large-scale increase in the French population in North America, they did provide the groundwork for future development.

Richelieu's major success to this end was the establishment of the Compagnie de la Nouvelle France, better known as the Company of One Hundred Associates (Compagnie des Cent-Associés). Founded in 1627, and officially approved by Louis XIII in the following year, the new organization negated all previous claims in New France, thus consolidating development efforts into a single company, under the direct approval of the Crown, and with authority in perpetuity over the vast tracts of North American land claimed by France. These claims stretched from Florida in the south, north to the Arctic circle, and from Acadia in the east to Lake Huron and as far west as French claims might reach. Within this area, the company received a permanent monopoly on the fur trade, and all commerce was to enjoy tax-free status for 15 years. The company was authorized to make land grants and, with the approval of the Crown, to issue titles of nobility.

The popular name for the new company derives from the fact that investment was divided into 100 shares that were distributed to Richelieu, Champlain, and a number of merchants and government officials who invested in the project. In return for this effective monopoly, the company agreed to recruit and provide transportation for 4,000 people to settle in New France at the rate of 300 per year, beginning in 1628. The company was to provide for the colonists' upkeep during the first three years following their arrival, including providing them with cleared farmland. Only French Catholics were eligible to migrate, and the company was obliged to provide support for Catholic priests to minister to settlers' religious needs as well as to construct a church for each new community.

Day-to-day management of the company was entrusted to a group of 12 directors. Jean de Lauzon, a founding member, was named "intendant," or director. From the beginning, plans went awry in 1628, when the initial group of settlers and supplies, sailing in four ships under the leadership of Robert Giffard, were intercepted and captured by the British. In the following year, a second attempt by a much larger fleet under Adm. Roquement de Brison similarly ended in disaster when a severe storm and British naval forces decimated it, capturing the admiral and most of the ships. Later that same year, the British even succeeded in seizing the most important French settlement at Quebec City. These catastrophes cost the company an estimated 90 percent of its investment, leaving it on very perilous footing and forcing it to seek new investors.

Champlain returned to Quebec in 1632, when Britain restored the settlement to France. Most of it had been razed during the occupation, but Champlain's efforts to restore it ended with his death, in 1635. With the company on the verge of bankruptcy, it was forced to cede a portion of its trade monopoly to the newly formed Compagnie des Habitants in return for an annual subsidy. To attract new settlers, the company began awarding large land grants with seigniorial rights, essentially creating the equivalent of feudal manors. Under this system, Montréal and Trois-Rivières grew, and the number of upper-class seigniors increased. But fewer new settlers immigrated and less than desired.

Meanwhile, calamity piled upon misfortune. A long-standing legal action ended in a verdict against the company to pay compensation to the Compagnie de Montmorency, which had lost its earlier rights to develop New France when the Company of One Hundred Associates had received its monopoly. In 1648, a renewal of warfare between the Iroquois and the French-allied Hurons resulted in the decimation of the Hurons and the loss of most of the valuable western fur trade, which was redirected to the English and Dutch traders to the south. In the early 1650s, Iroquois war parties even blockaded Montréal for a time. Under these conditions, the outpost shrunk to a few dozen residents, the original 100 shareholders in the company shrank to 36, and appeals to the Crown went unanswered because of the ongoing civil wars in France between 1648 and 1653.

By 1663, with total collapse on the horizon, the French population of New France was only about 2,500, far short of the 4,000 required in the initial monopoly granted to the Company of One Hundred Associates. Given the company's total failure to even protect New France, much less develop its potential, Jean-Baptiste Colbert, an economic adviser to the young Louis XIV, convinced the Crown to revoke the company's charter. With this, New France became a province directly responsible to the French government, regular troops were sent to protect it, and the provincial government was reorganized according to that of France.

The company later claimed that it had spent 905,084 livres on the development of New France while realizing only 242,301 livres. For several years, the remaining shareholders attempted to gain reimbursement from the Crown in the amount of 1,200,000 livres, plus interest and reimbursement for lost fur trading. In 1687, the king reduced the claim to only 103,000 livres, and the books were officially closed on the Company of One Hundred Associates.

James S. Pula

See also: Fur Trade; New France

Further Reading

Costain, Thomas B. 1960. *The White and the Gold, The French Regime in Canada.* Garden City, NY: Doubleday & Co., Inc.

Eccles, William John. 1998. *The French in North America.* Markham, ON, Canada: Fitzhenry & Whiteside.

Fischer, David Hackett. 2008. *Champlain's Dream: The European Founding of North America.* New York: Simon & Schuster.

Levi, Anthony. 2000. *Cardinal Richelieu: And the Making of France.* New York: Carroll & Graf Publishers.

McCusker, John J., and Kenneth Morgan. 2000. *The Early Modern Atlantic Economy.* New York: Cambridge University Press.

COMTE DE GRASSE, FRANÇOIS-JOSEPH PAUL (1722–1788)

Francois-Joseph Paul comte de Grasse was the French admiral who defeated the British fleet at the decisive Battle of the Chesapeake, which led directly to the British surrender at Yorktown. Scion of a noble Provençal family, de Grasse was the son of François de Grasse-Rouville, marquess de Grasse, a nobleman and captain in the French army. De Grasse entered the French navy in 1740, shortly before the outbreak of the War of the Austrian Succession. He was promoted to ensign in 1743 and participated in major naval actions against the British, including the Battle of Toulon (Lewis 1980, 22). Seriously wounded and captured at the Battle of Cape Finisterre, in May 1747, de Grasse remained in England for three months before his return to France (Lewis 1980, 25–26, 30). In 1754, he was promoted to lieutenant, and by 1762, he had risen to the rank of captain, during which time he served effectively in India, the West Indies, and the Mediterranean.

Following the British defeat at Saratoga in 1777, France signed a Treaty of Alliance on February 6, 1778, recognizing American independence and agreeing to provide financial, logistical, and military support for the American war effort. The treaty also essentially opened hostilities between France and Britain once again. Shortly thereafter, de Grasse fought in the indecisive Battle of Ushant off the Breton coast, in July 1778, solidifying his reputation as a capable naval commander (Weigley 1991, 241). Promoted to rear admiral, de Grasse distinguished himself in the Battles of Dominica, Saint Lucia, and Martinique in 1780.

In February 1780, Louis XVI approved an *Expedition Particulière* to dispatch French troops and supplies to North America. After much delay, the commander of French ground forces in the colonies, Comte de Rochambeau, sailed for Rhode Island with 450 officers and 5,300 men, arriving in July 1780. Remaining in camp for almost a year, Rochambeau marched south in April 1781 to rendezvous with George Washington for the planned assault on New York City.

Meeting at Wethersfield, Connecticut, on May 21, 1781, Washington and Rochambeau abandoned the planned attack on New York, deciding instead to encircle British forces operating in Virginia in cooperation with de Grasse and the French fleet, which had sailed from the Caribbean to aid the campaign. Changing British strategy made a southern campaign a viable option for the allies. Rather haphazardly, Sir Henry Clinton, the British commander in North America, had ordered Lord Charles Cornwallis to join with a British army marching south and begin combined operations against patriot forces in Virginia. After the conjuncture of British forces in May 1781, Cornwallis began building fortifications. The presence of British troops on the James River made control of the Chesapeake Bay an essential naval objective for both sides (Weigley 1991, 239).

De Grasse agreed to the plan, setting sail with 3,500 troops from Cap-Français in August 1781. Rochambeau's army had previously departed New York on June 18, 1781, while the French feet commanded by Adm. Comte de Barras awaited orders in Newport. Leaving the Franco-Spanish merchant fleet unprotected, the decision to sail the French fleet to Virginia involved risk. However, a disparity in the size of the opposing fleets had greatly improved French prospects for success. In a serious miscalculation, Adm. Sir George Rodney had sent half his fleet home at the start of 1781 hurricane season, assuming de Grasse would do the same. Thereafter, the movement of the French fleet to the Chesapeake created a local balance of naval forces in favor of the French.

Bad timing bedeviled British operations off the Chesapeake. On August 25, 1781, Adm. Sir Samuel Hood found no French ships upon his arrival in the Chesapeake and returned to New York. Heeding Rochambeau's request, the Comte de Barras's squadron at Newport set sail for the planned rendezvous with de Grasse on August 24, 1781. News of de Barras's departure soon led the British to realize that the Chesapeake was indeed the likely French objective. Sailing south from New York, a British force under Adm. Sir Thomas Graves arrived at the mouth of the Chesapeake on September 4, 1781, only to discover that de Grasse's fleet had already arrived.

Sighting the approaching British fleet, on September 4, 1781, de Grasse sailed out to meet Graves. In the pivotal Battle of the Chesapeake that followed on September 5, 1781, de Grasse defeated the British fleet in an imperfectly executed tactical contest. French naval supremacy in the waters off the Chesapeake completed the encirclement of the British at Yorktown and forced the surrender of Lord Cornwallis on October 19, 1781.

Although tactically indecisive, the Battle of the Chesapeake prevented the reinforcement or evacuation of British forces in Virginia. "[The] Battle of the Chesapeake was a tactical victory for the French by no clear-cut margin," *Russell Weigley argues*, "but it was a strategic victory for the French and Americans that sealed the principal outcome of the war." (Weigley 1991, 240)

Despite his victory on the Virginia Capes, de Grasse's naval career ended in disaster. De Grasse proceeded with the Franco-Spanish plan for the conquest of Jamaica, sailing to Saint Domingue in November 1781 to await the arrival of 15,000 French troops. On April 12, 1782, the British defeated de Grasse in the disastrous Battle of the Saintes, effectively ending French naval operations in the West Indies (Weigley 1991, 248–250). The British captured de Grasse's flagship, *Ville de Paris*, and imprisoned the admiral in Britain.

The British paroled de Grasse in August 1782, and he returned to France to defend himself against charges of incompetence. Although acquitted by court-martial in 1784, the indignant de Grasse continued to blame his subordinates for the defeat. Banished from the court of Louis XVI, de Grasse died in disgrace in Paris on January 14, 1788. Despite his heroic service during the American Revolution, French revolutionaries ransacked his estate at Tilly.

Brian W. Refford

See also: Chesapeake, Battle of the; Comte de Rochambeau; Yorktown, Battle of

Further Reading

Lewis, Charles Lee. 1980. *Admiral de Grasse and American Independence.* Annapolis, MD: Naval Institute Press.

Weigley, Russell. 1991. *The Age of Battles: The Quest for Decisive Warfare from Breitenfeld to Waterloo.* Bloomington: Indiana University Press.

COMTE DE ROCHAMBEAU (1725–1807)

In 2016, at the Fifth Annual Conference of the American Revolution, the Comte de Rochambeau was proposed as one of the most important military figures of the American War of Independence for his pivotal role in ensuring the success of the French alliance with America and his contributions to the Continental Army's victory at Yorktown. The gathering of historians did not reach a consensus, as the word *important* has a multitude of meanings, ranging from having a major impact on the outcome of the war, to being important to the legacy of the Revolution. Arguably, Rochambeau fits both ends of the spectrum: his name, once the watchword for advancing the attack on a British redoubt at Yorktown in 1781, lived on during the 20th century as an alternative name for the children's game rock-paper-scissors.

Born July 1, 1725, Jean-Baptiste-Donatien de Vimeur de Rochambeau was destined for priesthood until the death of his older brother in 1740 launched him into a career in the military. He won the favor of Louis XV for his valor at the Battle of Laufeldt, in the War of Austrian Succession, in 1747. Rochambeau remained markedly indifferent to court politics and this distinction early in his career helped place him in a position for greater honors later on in life. After further distinguishing himself during the French and Indian War (1754–1763), in March 1780, he was hand selected by Louis XVI to command the French army in America.

In conflicts against Frederick the Great (1712–1786) and on islands such as Minorca in the 1750s, Rochambeau gained valuable tactical and strategic experience, particularly in coordinating transportation of artillery materiel over water and land routes. This experience influenced Rochambeau's strategic vision during the American Revolution and was particularly evident in his insistence on the Chesapeake campaign and the coordinated attack by land and naval forces that led to the British surrender at Yorktown. His 1761 dissertations on discipline and military order, *Mémoire sur l'infanterie* and *Mémoires sur recrues et la desertion*, illustrate the general's philosophy of war, which he would enact with success in the

American Revolution. For Rochambeau, the 18th century was no longer an age of glorious military spectacle. Rather, wars were won only through considering the long view of the conflict, careful preparations, and well-trained, disciplined troops. Rochambeau had participated in the reorganization of the French military in the 1760s; his position as inspector of the infantry allowed him to implement some reforms and organize training camps to help improve and expand the French army along these lines.

With a pension, governorship, advantageous marriage, and solid career record, Rochambeau could easily have retired in comfort. Indeed, in 1780, he was en route to his château to recuperate from a spell of rheumatism when he was suddenly recalled to Versailles, where the king informed him he would lead the French forces in the American campaign.

French aid was instrumental in the favorable outcome of the war for the Americans, and Rochambeau played a crucial part in the success of the alliance between the two countries. Whereas previous French commanders, such as Admiral d'Estaing, were neither very flexible nor very amenable to American leadership, Rochambeau followed orders in regard to Washington as his military superior, which led to a fruitful collaboration between the two distinguished generals. This was all the more remarkable because Rochambeau was seven years Washington's senior and had over a decade more military experience than the American commander-in-chief. Rochambeau had a history of deferring to his commander even when he disagreed with his strategy. In 1778, for example, when training troops for a potential invasion of England, Rochambeau went along with the tactical decision made by Victor Francois, 2nd duc de Broglie, rather than be at odds with his commanding officer.

Thanks to his years of experience and strategic intelligence, Rochambeau also knew when and how to intervene in a situation he felt was fraught and to tactfully introduce his point of view. In 1780, Washington wanted to launch an offensive on New York. He felt that the combined American and French forces would be enough to take the city, as British commander Henry Clinton had sent many of his forces to fight in the south. Rochambeau thought this course of action would still be too perilous given the number of troops at their disposition and the inability of low-riding French ships to enter the shallower waters of New York Harbor to reinforce the landing. The French general thought a southern campaign would be more advantageous, though Washington, a Southerner himself, was leery of marching the army southward in the heat of the summer.

Rather than dismiss Washington's concerns, Rochambeau agreed to meet up with Washington and the American troops at New Windsor to revisit the New York offensive. Their prolific correspondence reveals the Frenchman's subtle hints of the benefits of a southern campaign and the possible dangers and difficulties presented by a northern one. The decision of Admiral de Grasse to land the French fleet in the Chesapeake would ultimately be the deciding factor, but while Washington and Rochambeau were each trying to persuade the French admiral of their own point of view, they worked together to scout the defenses of New York: Rochambeau's cavalry supported Washington's troops in a night attack on British outposts north of Manhattan. The attack was a failure, but it did succeed in increasing the French and American generals' mutual admiration and in weakening Washington's resolve to launch an offensive against New York. Rochambeau's logical arguments and the movements of Admiral de Grasse convinced Washington that victory in the southern theater was more feasible. He made the decision to march south on August 14, 1780.

Almost two months to the day after this change in strategy, after the Franco-American siege and storming of the British redoubts, Gen. Charles Cornwallis capitulated at Yorktown, Virginia. Washington wrote of his "infinite obligations . . . to His Excellency the Count de Rochambeau" for this momentous event (Washington 1781, 213). Rochambeau's troops stayed in Virginia through the winter, and the French general would not depart for home until January 1783. In a farewell letter to Rochambeau, Washington writes "of the happiness I have enjoyed in our private friendship. The remembrance of which will be one of the most pleasing Circumstances of my life" (Washington 1782, 428). Rochambeau replied with affirmations of his friendship and respect.

As with his other French friend, the Marquis de Lafayette, Washington kept up a cordial correspondence with Rochambeau for a few years following the American Revolution, but the outbreak of revolution in France made it hard for Washington to diplomatically retain his warm ties to his French acquaintances. Reform minded and ever disdainful of court politics, Rochambeau supported the French Revolution in 1789. But by 1790, he worried about the escalating political situation, writing in English to Washington on April 11, 1790:

> Do you remember, my Dear general, of the first repast that we have made together at Rod island. I did you remark from the Soup the difference of the character of our two nations, the french in burning their throat, and all the americans waiting wisely of the time that it was cooled. I believe, my dear general, you have Seen Since a year that our nation has not change of character. We go very fast—God will that we come at our aims. (Rochambeau 1790)

This letter would be his last to the American president, but the Frenchman was not to perish at the guillotine like so many of his peers, including de Broglie and d'Estaing. Legend has it that he could not fit onto the already crowded cart that transported the condemned to the scaffold and was reprieved by the arrest of Robespierre the next day. He outlived his American friend, passing away at his family château in 1807 at the age of 82.

Rochambeau's important place in American history, forging a strong Franco-American alliance that led to American victory, was memorialized with the Washington-Rochambeau Revolutionary Route, which was designated a National Historic Trail in 2009.

Kelsey Brow

See also: Comte de Grasse, François-Joseph Paul; Washington, George; Yorktown, Battle of

Further Reading

Borkow, Richard. 2011. *George Washington's Westchester Gamble: The Encampment on the Hudson and the Trapping of Cornwallis.* Charleston, SC: The History Press.

Fleming, Thomas. 1963. *Beat the Last Drum: The Siege of Yorktown.* New York: St. Martin's Press.

Rochambeau, Jean-Baptiste, comte de. 1790. "To George Washington from Rochambeau, 11 April 1790." *Founders Online.* National Archives. http://founders.archives.gov/documents/Washington/05-05-02-0213.

Vail, Jini Jones. 2011. *Rochambeau, Washington's Ideal Lieutenant: A French General's Role in the American Revolution.* Tarentum, PA: Word Association Publishers.

Washington, George. 1781–1782. *The Writings of George Washington from the Original Sources.* Vols 23–25. Edited by John C. Fitzpatrick. Washington, D.C.: U.S. Government Printing Office.

CONGREGATIONAL CHURCH

Congregational churches are churches that subscribe to a Congregationalist form of church government and also broadly subscribe to the doctrines of Calvinism. The Congregational model of church government is the understanding that individual congregations exist independent of one another, while also remaining united under the headship of Jesus Christ and the indwelling of the Holy Spirit. Congregational churches are generally run democratically; church officers are elected by church members who are eligible to vote. Unlike Presbyterianism, Congregationalist churches do not answer to any higher governing authorities or church courts and are thus viewed as being autonomous. However, because Congregational churches acknowledge the spiritual unity of all Christians, they also seek wisdom in corresponding and becoming voluntarily accountable to one another. In Congregational churches, the reception and ordination of new ministers is often overseen by other regional churches. Congregationalism generally seeks to maintain a pure church by voluntary consent, while avoiding the trappings of ecclesiastical hierarchies and bureaucracies. Historically, the Congregational Church has also held to the tenets of Calvinism; however, in the colonies, many Congregational churches strayed from their Calvinist background and embraced various forms of rationalism.

The Congregational Church can be traced to the earliest years of the Puritan movement in England. As a form of Calvinism, Puritanism often favored a Presbyterian form of church government, which sought to bind congregations together through regional meetings of elders known as *presbyteries*. Because the Puritans generally sought to "purify" the Church of England, such an arrangement was preferred because it allowed for democratic control of the churches while also ensuring a level of uniformity and control over them. However, very early on in the Puritan movement, groups of nonconformists became disillusioned with any hope of reforming the state religion. Instead, they sought to form independent churches that were free from interference and were thus labeled Separatists.

One of the earliest Separatist groups were the Brownists, named after their founder, Robert Browne (1550s–1633). Browne was active as a Puritan Separatist between the years 1579 and 1585 and was later reconciled to the Church of

England. In 1582, Browne published a work titled *A Booke Which Sheweth the Life and Manners of All True Christians* that set forth a congregational model of church order. Those who followed Brown were labeled Brownists, Separatists, or simply Independents. These labels were meant to distinguish them from the majority of Puritans, who favored Presbyterianism or episcopacy in their form of church government. Other leaders who followed Browne in his Separatist views were Henry Barrowe (1550–1593) and John Penry (1559–1593), who were both executed for their views under Elizabeth I.

When James I (1566–1625) came to the throne in 1603, many Puritans hoped to achieve some level of reformation in the established church. However, by 1604, James had begun to eject Puritan pastors from their pulpit ministries. This renewed the vigor of the Brownists and inspired many of them to seek asylum in the Netherlands. In 1620, the *Mayflower* departed for the New World with 35 of the 102 passengers being from the Brownist movement. When the Plymouth Colony was established in the years that followed, Congregationalism became the official religion under Separatist leaders such as William Brewster (1566–1644), John Robinson (1576–1625), and William Bradford (1590–1657). When Charles I (1600–1649) and Archbishop William Laud (1573–1649) began to persecute the Puritans in 1629, more Puritans began to seek refuge among the Separatists in the colonies. Influential ministers such as John Cotton (1585–1652) and Thomas Shepard (1605–1649) as well as controversial figures like Anne Hutchinson (1591–1643) arrived in the Massachusetts Bay Colony during this period. Congregationalism became so pronounced in New England that the Great and General Court organized New College, later named Harvard, to train Congregational ministers.

Back in England, independency would continue to grow in popularity among the Puritans. During the English Civil War (1642–1651), Parliament called the Westminster Assembly (1643–1653), which was charged with reforming the church during the war. Several of the most influential theologians at the Assembly were Independents. These included prominent voices in the Assembly, such as Thomas Goodwin (1600–1680), Philip Nye (1595–1672), and Jeremiah Burroughs (1600–1646). Their influence was so pronounced that key elements of Presbyterian Church government were left out of the Westminster Confession to please the Independent delegates.

There were other examples of Congregationalism's rising influence in this period. Oliver Cromwell's (1599–1658) chaplain was the highly respected Puritan theologian John Owen (1616–1683), who was also a committed Congregationalist. In fact, Owen came to Congregational convictions through correspondence with the New England pastor John Cotton, which was a testimony to not only the firm commitment but also the growing influence of colonial Separatism. With the victory of Cromwell and Parliament over Charles I, freedom of religion was declared throughout the United Kingdom. In 1658, the Independents amended the Westminster Confession to fit the Congregational model, in what has been labeled the Savoy Declaration. The Savoy Declaration would be the doctrinal standard to which most Congregational churches would subscribe.

In the colonies, the Congregational churches were officially unified by the Cambridge Platform in 1648. The Cambridge Platform set the boundaries and limits upon the Congregational churches in both Massachusetts and Connecticut and provided them with a Synod in which doctrinal and administrative matters could be settled. While the formation of the Synod had similarities with the Presbyterian form of church government, it also affirmed the independence of each congregation and rejected the Presbyterian implications of the Westminster Standards.

In 1662, the Synod would enact the Half-Way Covenant, which was an attempt to boost church membership by extending the right of baptism beyond the third generation of communicant church members. From the beginning of the Massachusetts Bay Colony, church and state were so intimately related that only those who were communicant members in the Congregational Church, known as freemen, had the right to vote in civil elections. By the second half of the 17th century, it was recognized that the children of the original Separatists were not as zealous for Puritanism as their parents. Many of the second generation had failed to profess faith and thus become communicant church members with voting rights. According to Calvinism, this meant that their children would not be eligible for baptism or noncommunicant church membership, as baptism was understood to be only for believers and their immediate children. The Half-Way Covenant was an attempt to extend this privilege to the third generation and beyond, in hopes that exposure to the church would encourage future generations to profess faith in the Congregational churches and therefore boost the godly electorate.

However, in 1664, Charles II ended the policy of freemen voting, making the Half-Way Covenant politically irrelevant. The Half-Way Covenant would remain in force in the Congregational churches until the Great Awakening (1730s–1743) and would remain a subject of theological controversy. Solomon Stoddard (1643–1729), the pastor of the Congregationalist Church in Northampton, remained a firm supporter of the covenant and even liberalized it further. Stoddard considered the Lord's Supper to be a converting ordinance, and he allowed noncommunicant baptized members to partake in the sacrament. This unique position by Stoddard would lead to the ejection of his successor, Jonathan Edwards (1703–1758), who rejected the practice. In opposition to Stoddard, theologians such as Increase Mather (1639–1723) and Charles Chauncy (1592–1671) sought to undermine the theological foundations of the Half-Way Covenant in the Congregational churches.

By the late 17th century, as the Half-Way Covenant failed to create more communicants in the Congregational Church, various forms of rationalism began to spread among the clergy and laity who were apathetic about Puritanism. In 1701, Yale College was founded as a response to the prevalence of Enlightenment skepticism in the colonies. Increase Mather, who served as the president of Harvard from 1685 to 1701, was concerned with the views being espoused at his own institution and hoped that Yale College would perpetuate the legacy of Puritan orthodoxy.

The growth of Enlightenment skepticism was recognized by many as a growing influence in the colonies. The superstition that was manifested in the Salem witch trials in 1692 and 1693 made rationalism and deism all the more attractive to many within the Congregational establishment. Rationalism was an epistemology that viewed human reason as being more authoritative and reliable than the teachings of Scripture. Without denying the faith in total, rationalism allowed one to reject those portions of Scripture that seemed difficult or fantastic while maintaining a form of piety. Deism, which was rooted in rationalism and Newtonian physics, taught that God had created the world but left it to run as a mechanism under the control of natural laws. Deists taught that supernatural forces never, or at least rarely, intervened in human history. Many Congregationalists saw this as a progressive modification to Christian theology, which so often seemed to tend toward dangerous forms of superstition. Because Congregational churches were democratic and independent, as the majority of congregants began to embrace liberal views, the church as an institution became liberalized. Many conservative Congregational theologians sought to refute rationalism, while also demonstrating the compatibility of Puritan theology with the new sciences.

Both Increase Mather and his son Cotton Mather (1663–1728) produced treatises that sought to engage with the new sciences while also producing evidence for supernatural events. Both men also sought to exhibit temperance in the face of fanaticism. Increase Mather stood firmly against the Salem witch trials, whereas Cotton supported them under the condition that the courts refuse "spectral evidence" (or witness testimony that is based upon seeing the accused person's spirit). Cotton Mather's book *The Wonders of the Invisible World* defended the Salem witch trials by presenting anecdotal evidence and eyewitness accounts of witchcraft and supernatural events. Despite the compromise of the Half-Way Covenant and the efforts of the Congregational Church's best apologists, the Puritan faith of the original Separatists continued to wane.

In the mid-1730s, religious revivals began to spread throughout the American colonies in virtually every Christian denomination. Revival in the Congregational Church was experienced most significantly under the preaching Jonathan Edwards, at Solomon Stoddard's former church in Northampton. Like his predecessors, Jonathan Edwards was known for incorporating the advances of modern science and philosophy into his articulation of the Christian faith. Edwards exhibited not only intelligence but also poetic imagery in his preaching, which grabbed the attention of his listeners. His most famous sermon was *Sinners in the Hands of an Angry God*, which was preached at his church in Northampton and then later in Enfield, Connecticut. The spread of the Awakening under the ministries of Edwards and others inspired both a desire for sincere love and charity as well as a renewed interest in Calvinist theology and learning. These tendencies in the Great Awakening undermined some of the trends in Congregationalism toward rationalism and skepticism.

The Awakening likewise rendered the Half-Way Covenant irrelevant. Due to the commonality of conversion experiences, the compromise of the Half-Way Covenant was no longer necessary, as the churches were flooded with individuals who professed a sincere faith. At the church in Northampton, Jonathan Edwards once again required a sincere conversion to partake in the Lord's Supper. This contradicted the policy of the late Solomon Stoddard and would eventually lead to Edwards' dismissal from the pastorate in Northampton. His pupil Joseph Bellamy

(1719–1790) would effectively spread Edwards's views in the church, that they would become the majority report in Congregational churches again.

Even though the Great Awakening grounded much of the Congregational Church in its Puritan heritage, by 1750, several Congregational preachers began teaching a doctrine of universal salvation. As early as 1752, Charles Chauncy (1705–1787) was considering the doctrine of universal salvation. After the Revolutionary War, he would publish several treatises promoting the doctrine, which would lead to the formation of Universalist Church of America in 1793. Jonathan Mayhew (1720–1766) had also begun to question the doctrine of the Trinity and espoused the belief that only God the Father was properly God, a doctrine known as Unitarianism. Mayhew's influence would spread through the Revolutionary era as he publicly opposed the Stamp Act and promoted the cause of liberty from his pulpit in Boston. By the 19th century, all but one Congregational Church in Boston was teaching Unitarianism. In 1825, the American Unitarian Association was formed to promote Unitarianism in Congregational churches.

Despite the new ideas that were becoming prevalent, conservative Congregationalism continued to exert a lasting influence in the late 18th and early 19th centuries. However, with Yale College sliding into liberalism, Congregational churches struggled to maintain doctrinal purity in their ranks. Many conservative Congregational churches began to send their ministerial candidates to Presbyterian colleges, such as the College of New Jersey, which was later known as Princeton. In fact, Jonathan Edwards was asked to serve as president of the college, a post that he filled for only a month before his death.

Many Congregational churches also sought to form alliances, and even to merge, with Presbyterian churches. Due to this, the scope and influence of the Congregational Church continued to wane, and the baton of Puritanism was in many ways passed on to the Presbyterian Church. However, while Congregationalism would decrease in influence, the Congregational model of church government would slowly become the majority report in American Evangelicalism, as it was adopted by the Baptist churches, which experienced exponential growth in the 19th century.

Colin M. Samul

See also: Calvinism; Great Awakening; Half-Way Covenant; Mather, Cotton; Mather, Increase; Plymouth; Puritanism

Further Reading

Holifield, E. 2003. *Theology in America: Christian Thought from the Age of the Puritans to the Civil War.* New Haven, CT: Yale University Press.

Noll, M. 2002. *The Old Religion in a New World: The History of North American Christianity.* Grand Rapids, MI: Eerdmans.

Singer, C. 1964. *A Theological Interpretation of American History.* Philadelphia: Presbyterian and Reformed Pub.

CONGRESS OF CONFEDERATION

Starting with the Stamp Act Congress of 1765, the 13 colonies recognized the need for cooperation to confront the growing British challenge to American rights. The culmination of these efforts were the First and Second Continental Congresses of 1774 and 1775, respectively. After declaring independence in July 1776, Congress spent more than a year drafting a framework of government for the new country, the Articles of Confederation. The Articles were approved by Congress in November 1777 and ratified in March 1781. The confederation government consisted of Congress and three civil officers appointed by Congress to oversee the country's finances, military establishment, and foreign relations. Congress was in large measure a continuation of the Second Continental Congress. With the notable exception of the Northwest Ordinance of 1787, Congress was largely defined by its inability to deal with the challenges of governing 13 independent states.

Each state annually appointed between two and seven delegates to Congress (the exact number was left up to the state) by whatever method it chose and could recall those delegates at any time. Delegates were only allowed to serve for three years out of any six-year period. Each state, regardless of size, population, or the number of delegates it sent, had one vote in Congress. Equal representation of the states was an essential principle in the Confederation, as it was the states, and not the people, that were represented in Congress. A quorum of seven states was necessary for Congress to conduct business, and most legislation required the votes of at least that many states to pass; votes related to war and peace, treaties, loans, and the raising of armies and navies required the approval of nine states.

By design, Congress had limited powers and limited responsibilities. In the midst of a Revolution fought to defend American rights against British abuses, the delegates who drafted the Articles of Confederation, and the state legislatures that ratified them, were not interested in replacing the arbitrary power exercised by Parliament with arbitrary power exercised by a new central government. Instead, the plan was to leave most power in the hands of the states and to allocate very limited power—primarily over foreign policy and national defense—to Congress. More specifically, Congress could declare war and peace, enter into treaties and alliances, borrow money, and appoint civil officers to assist with governing the United States.

What mattered more than the power Congress did have was the power that it did not: the power to tax. Without the power to tax, Congress's expenses (paying for the war or paying down the principal and interest on foreign and domestic loans) were to be paid out of a common treasury funded by the states. The amount each state had to contribute to the treasury was proportional to the periodically assessed value of all land within the state (with land serving as a proxy for the relative wealth of each state). Congress annually determined how much money it would need to meet its financial obligations and would requisition the states for their respective contributions. It was up to the states to determine their own methods of raising the requested funds, and Congress was powerless to enforce compliance.

From the very beginning, this created tension between Congress and the states. During the Revolution, some states faced heavy burdens in contributing men and supplies to the Continental Army and militias. As a result, many states were unable or unwilling to also pay money to Congress. After the war, the tension between meeting state and federal obligations only grew worse, as many states had significant debts of their own and other spending priorities beyond supporting Congress. This led to widespread nonpayment of congressional requisitions and left Congress unable pay its debts and in a precarious financial situation.

Several failed attempts were made to amend the Articles of Confederation to provide Congress with an independent revenue. The most promising effort was the 5 percent impost of 1781, which called for a 5 percent duty, or tax, on all goods imported into the United States, the revenue from which Congress would use to pay the country's war debts. Amendments to the Articles required the unanimous consent of all 13 states, but only 12 states ratified the impost; Rhode Island was the lone dissenter. Congress proposed a more limited impost in 1783; but once again, 12 states ratified, and Rhode Island said no. Other amendments were offered to address the revenue problem, including a proposal by James Madison in 1781 that Congress be authorized to use the military and naval forces of the United States to compel the individual states to comply with congressional requisitions, but the Articles were never amended.

Aside from taxes and revenues, the greatest challenge faced by Congress was the degree to which the states did not respect its authority or necessity. This went beyond states not paying their congressional requisitions. States consistently prioritized local or regional interests over the country's interests. The impost was an exception where most states were willing to act in unison, recognizing a common interest, but Rhode Island's refusal was motivated by local economic concerns.

The confederation nearly broke apart due to regional disputes over negotiations with Spain from 1784–1786 regarding American use of the Mississippi River. The Southern states viewed western expansion and use of the Mississippi to transport their agricultural products to foreign markets as essential to America's future prosperity. Spain's closure of the mouth of the river to U.S. traffic in 1784 put that future in jeopardy. Congress authorized the secretary of foreign affairs, John Jay, to negotiate a treaty that would reopen the river to American traffic, but Spain countered by offering access to the Spanish West Indies in exchange for the United States formally giving up use of the river for 20 or more years. Northerners saw Spain's offer as an excellent compromise that would benefit all parts of the country (Northern merchants would profit from increased trade, and Southern farmers would gain another outlet for their produce), but Southerners refused to concede the river. The impasse between north and south prevented the treaty from being passed, led to public speculation that the United States could split into smaller confederacies, and spurred reform movements in 1786–1787.

The best demonstration of the degree to which the states did not give much weight to congressional affairs was how frequently Congress could not act because it lacked a quorum. At least seven states had to be present for Congress to conduct business, and each state had to have at least two delegates seated for it to be counted as present. During the war, quorum was generally not a problem, but after the ratification of the Treaty of Paris in 1783, achieving a quorum became more problematic. It did not help matters that term limits caused many congressmen who were at least somewhat nationalistic in their outlook to be replaced in 1783 by delegates who were far more parochial in their views. The opening of congressional sessions was regularly delayed by weeks as Congress waited for seven states to arrive; and even when quorum was achieved, Congress was often limited in what it could vote on because nine states were not present. Perhaps even more frustrating was the fact that even if Congress reached quorum, there was no guarantee that it would last because delegates came and went almost continuously throughout a congressional session.

Despite all of these challenges, the Confederation Congress did experience several important successes, including ratification of the Articles of Confederation in 1781 and the Treaty of Paris in 1783. Endorsing the Annapolis and Constitutional Conventions in 1786 and 1787, respectively, and sending the Constitution to the states in September 1787 were also important achievements. Unquestionably, though, Congress's signature accomplishments were the Northwest Ordinances of 1784, 1785, and 1787. These ordinances determined the procedures for organizing western territories, provided them with a path to statehood, guaranteed new states equal status with the original states, and, with the 1787 ordinance's prohibition on slavery in the Northwest Territory, established a precedent that Congress could regulate slavery in federally controlled territories. The Confederation Congress thus shaped the United States in fundamental ways even after the Constitution replaced the Articles of Confederation in 1789.

Jeffrey J. Malanson

See also: Constitutional Convention; Treaty of Paris, 1783

Further Reading

Ellis, Joseph J. 2015. *The Quartet: Orchestrating the Second American Revolution, 1783–1789.* New York: Knopf.

Ford, Worthington C., ed. 1904–1937. *Journals of the Continental Congress, 1774–1789.* 34 vols. Washington, D.C.: U.S. Government Printing Office.

Jensen, Merrill. 1950. *The New Nation: A History of the United States during the Confederation, 1781–1789.* New York: Alfred A. Knopf.

Middlekauff, Robert. 1982. *The Glorious Cause: The American Revolution, 1763–1789.* New York: Oxford University Press.

CONNECTICUT

The region that is the state of Connecticut today was inhabited by 16 groups of Algonquin Indians from around 500 BCE. Generally peaceful hunters, gatherers, and farmers, these tribes feared the aggressiveness of the Mohawk based in what is today upstate New York. Another hostile tribe, the Pequot, migrated into the region around 1500 and conquered large amounts of territory during a century of brutal warfare. The Indians suffered greatly in the early 17th century, not only from internecine warfare but from a massive smallpox epidemic that killed thousands.

One of the earliest Europeans to explore the area was the Dutch Adrian Block, and Dutch settlers attempted to create a presence near present-day Hartford. Most of the Native Americans welcomed the first white colonists, viewing the Europeans as potential allies against the Mohawk and the Pequot. One of Connecticut's first permanent European residents, the Rev. Thomas Hooker, along with John Haynes of the Massachusetts Bay Colony, settled in the Connecticut River valley with a small band of approximately 100 followers in 1636. A staunch Puritan, Hooker had come to Connecticut from the Massachusetts Bay Colony seeking better farming land and a less rigid form of government. Founding the town of Hartford, he quickly established a thriving community, encouraged by the rich agricultural land.

Hooker set the tone for the fledgling colony's governance in 1638 when he preached a sermon espousing the merits of a more democratic form of government than that practiced in Massachusetts. A year later, this view was encapsulated in the Fundamental Orders of Connecticut, which served as a blueprint for the colony's governance for the next century and a half. That document also included an early form of representative government. Ultimately, the colonial governor represented the English monarch and held executive power, while he appointed men to the council. Men of lower economic classes who had not acquired a certain amount of wealth were not allowed to hold office or to vote. Connecticut also had town meetings, which ultimately became a fixture of New England governance.

South of Hartford, settlers founded another colony in 1638 along the coast. Comprising mainly merchants who hoped to capitalize on trade between the Native Americans and the Dutch stationed in New Amsterdam (present-day New York), the settlers named this colony New Haven and established New England's most theocratic form of government. In addition, the governor was not allowed to serve consecutive terms, so for nearly 20 years, two Hartford men, John Haynes and Edward Hopkins, generally rotated duties.

Both of the fledgling colonies in Connecticut were challenged by the Pequot, who in 1636 launched a series of attacks against settlements in the region. The colonists banded together and, aided by their allies the Narragansetts, led a brutal counterattack against the Pequot in June 1637 at Fort Mystic. The massacre at Mystic remains one of the worst in American history, with nearly 700 Pequot men, women, and children killed. Those who survived were sold into slavery to other tribes. The Pequot War was the first in a series of genocidal Indian wars in 17th-century New England that ultimately resulted in the virtual extinction of the Native American population in the region.

Throughout its first century, Connecticut remained an essentially conservative and traditional society, despite an influx of religious dissenters, most of whom were driven out of the colony and into Rhode Island. In 1665, colonists in New Haven agreed to annex themselves to Connecticut, and the region assumed the shape that the state holds today, although border disputes with Massachusetts, Rhode Island, and New York persisted until the eve of the American Revolution. Most economic activity centered on producing goods for other markets, such as England

and English Caribbean colonies. The majority of the farming was subsistence-level due to the typical thin and rocky New England soil that did not lend itself to large-scale, cash crop agriculture. Some of the earliest products included fish and whaling, shipbuilding, maple syrup, and items associated with the fur trade.

By 1750, the population of Connecticut had grown tremendously. Soil exhaustion and land shortages had compelled many farmers to shift from farming to livestock production. Some small manufacturing enterprises also appeared around midcentury, most notably clock making, iron forging, and shipbuilding. A strong commitment to public education had also emerged as one of the foundations of the colony, as evidenced not only by the number of government-supported grammar schools but also by the founding of Yale College in 1701, which was created primarily to train members of the clergy.

Throughout the Colonial Period, Connecticut remained a fairly stable and conservative region, with one exception. In the 1730s, the Rev. Jonathan Edwards led a religious revival in Northampton, Massachusetts. Known as the Great Awakening, the revival had spread south through the Connecticut River valley by the end of the decade. The movement's intense emotionalism prompted a serious division to emerge throughout Connecticut's Congregational churches between the New Lights (those who participated in the revival) and the Old Lights (the more conservative and traditional colonists). This split had serious repercussions in the colony's government and remained an important factor in determining loyalties in the decade before the American Revolution.

In the era leading up to the Revolutionary War, Connecticut colonists were steadfast in their opposition to Britain's increasing interference in matters of trade, although they were far less flamboyant than their compatriots in Massachusetts. During the war, Connecticut became known as the "provision state," as it supplied the Continental Army with livestock, grain, guns, and gunpowder. The British conducted four devastating raids against Connecticut but never occupied any town or port in the state. Other than these four raids, little active fighting occurred in Connecticut.

At the Constitutional Convention of 1787, delegates from Connecticut played a vital role, suggesting what became known as the Connecticut Compromise, whereby representation in the Senate would be equal among the states while representation in the House of Representatives would be based on population. The people of the state were ardent champions of the new U.S. Constitution and voted overwhelmingly for its ratification in January 1788.

Elizabeth Dubrulle and James E. Seelye Jr.

See also: Great Awakening; Pequot

Further Reading

Roth, David M. 1979. *Connecticut: A Bicentennial History.* New York: W. W. Norton & Company.

State of Connecticut. http://www.state.ct.us.

Taylor, Alan. 2002. *American Colonies: The Settling of North America.* New York: Penguin.

Van Dusen, Albert E. 1961. *Connecticut.* New York: Random House.

CONNECTICUT COMPROMISE

The Connecticut Compromise (also known as the Great Compromise of 1787 or Sherman's Compromise) was an agreement during the Constitutional Convention over the structure of the legislative body of the U.S. government as well as the process by which representatives to Congress would be allotted to the states. It essentially settled the tensions that had emerged during the convention between larger states and smaller states over the relative legislative influence that states of different sizes would have in Congress. These debates included the question of counting slaves in a state's population, but this question would be settled somewhat later with the agreement of the Three-Fifths Compromise.

On May 29, 1787, just a few days after the Constitutional Convention began, Edmund Randolph (1753–1813) of the Virginia delegation proposed a plan for a bicameral legislature to replace the legislative body for the United States at the time, the Congress of the Confederation. The original mandate for the Constitutional Convention was to revise and improve on the government system that had been created by the Articles of Confederation. However, it quickly became apparent that several delegates, most notably James Madison (1751–1836) and Alexander Hamilton (1755–1804), had plans for an almost complete overhaul of the government. In fact, Randolph's proposal, known as the Virginia Plan, clearly pointed toward such a demolition of the Articles of Confederation and sparked immediate debate among the delegates over just what the mandate was for the Constitutional Convention.

The crux of the matter was whether the convention had the authority to change the system of government for the nation from being the state-dominated Congress of Confederation to being a more national system of government. This would likely dilute the power of the individual states. Once it was generally accepted that the convention in Philadelphia was going to replace the Articles of Confederation, the issue of how each state would be represented in the new government became the first, and arguably most contentious, point for the delegates.

In Randolph's proposal, the Congress would be made up of two houses. The lower house would be allocated proportionally based on a state's population. States with larger populations, such as New York and Virginia, would receive more congressional representatives. Smaller states, such as New Hampshire and New Jersey, would have fewer. The members of the upper house would be chosen by the delegates in the lower house based on lists of candidates submitted by the various state legislatures. The larger states argued their contribution to the nation's finances and defense were greater due to their larger population and tax burden, and so they favored this arrangement. As such, they claimed they should have more representation in Congress. Moreover, delegates such as James Madison believed such a proposal would more accurately establish the idea of popular sovereignty, as it would ensure that the lower house would be chosen entirely by the voting franchise.

Smaller states feared that the Virginia Plan could potentially result in their having little to no representation in the upper house because larger states could conspire to fill the upper house with people from their own states. Many delegates dismissed the possibility of such a conspiracy among the large states, claiming the interests of large states such as Virginia or New York were so different that it would make such machinations unlikely, if not impossible. For their part, small states argued that their power as separate entities within the national government would be eliminated in the Virginia Plan. This would likely end the limited sovereignty they enjoyed during and after the Revolution in both the Continental Congress and Congress of Confederation. In the Congress of Confederation, each state was granted one vote, and the states themselves also had veto power over any laws passed by the Congress. The smaller states expressed their dismay that the Virginia Plan would end this sort of political equality. Alexander Hamilton and others declared this was a fallacy. The states had never been truly sovereign, and because the power for the national government derived from the people as a whole, the states were nothing more than arbitrary political entities made up of individuals.

Despite these arguments and the fact that the committee as a whole had voted on June 11 in favor of the Virginia Plan, smaller states held their ground and even offered their own plan for the legislative branch. Known as the New Jersey Plan, it was presented by William Paterson on June 15, 1787. In the New Jersey Plan, the legislative branch would consist of a single house with each state receiving one vote. This would essentially leave the Congress of Confederation in place with some minor alterations to expand the power of the new Congress. Clearly, this would not be acceptable to the larger states, and so the convention became deadlocked over the matter. Paterson realized that his plan lacked enough support, and he chose not to present his plan for an immediate vote. Instead, he asked for the matter to be tabled.

At its most heated, the tension became so great that James Wilson, a delegate from Pennsylvania, made a somewhat veiled threat that if the larger states did not get their way, they would abandon the convention, leave the nascent United States, and form their own country. This was likely impossible, as there was little general support, even among the delegates of other larger states, for such a radical ploy. However, it indicates how charged the debate had become. And by the middle of June, there seemed a growing possibility that the convention would break apart over the question of representation.

Roger Sherman of Connecticut presented a compromise plan on June 11 that was actually similar to a plan he had proposed to the Continental Congress in 1776. Six days later, a group of delegates from smaller states caucused to discuss possible solutions to the crisis. During the meeting, they revisited a proposal that would follow many of Sherman's suggestions to blend the Randolph and Paterson plans. When Sherman had presented his ideas to the delegates on the 11th, the compromise was rejected by large states because they felt confident they could get their way. By the time the compromise was offered again, the stakes had risen, and the two sides had dug in their heels. Even Benjamin Franklin, a known deist, was so concerned that the convention could collapse that he made a motion asking the delegates to resort to prayer for heavenly guidance on the debate.

Though the idea of a bicameral legislature gained traction over the next few days, the delegates began casting their arguments further and further afield. They considered the role of the Senate, the potential membership of each house, and the division of the legislative powers for each house. On June 29, a close vote reaffirmed that the House of Representatives should be allocated proportional to the state's population. On this matter, the small states lost. Almost as soon as the vote was cast, Oliver Ellsworth from Connecticut asked to revisit his state's compromise regarding the idea of a bicameral legislature as well as the matter of an upper house with equal representation for the states. By July 2, the sides were no closer to an agreement, and the decision was made to form a Grand Committee to hopefully hammer out a solution.

The committee was composed of one delegate from each state. Somewhat surprisingly, the Grand Committee ended up being composed largely of delegates that leaned toward the small states' position, or at least were open to compromise. This was due to some serendipitous absences among the delegations that had resulted in a slightly unbalanced committee. During a short break over the July 4 holiday festivities, the committee worked out the broad strokes of what would eventually become the Connecticut Compromise. However, it included a handful of revisions intended to grease the wheels of diplomacy and secure the agreement of the larger states.

The Connecticut Compromise established a bicameral legislature with a House of Representatives and a Senate. The House would be filled by congressmen allocated according to each state's population. These legislators would be selected by the eligible voting population of each state. This would grant the larger states more power in the House. The upper house would be filled by two senators for each state. These men would be chosen by the state legislatures. This would satisfy the smaller states by maintaining state power in the government and by ensuring they had equal voice with the rest of the union. In a nod to the larger states' argument that their larger burden of the nation's costs should give them more power in government, all appropriation bills and other monetary matters would be dealt with solely in the lower house.

The final vote on the Grand Committee's suggested solution took place on July 16, 1787. By the narrowest of margins—five votes to four—the Connecticut Compromise was approved. Four states were not even present for the vote. New York's delegation had basically disintegrated. New Hampshire's delegates had still not arrived in Philadelphia at all. Massachusetts was divided, and Rhode Island had refused to even participate in the convention. With the final approval of the compromise, the delegates had finally navigated what was possibly the biggest threat to the entire convention and had established the framework of the government system still used by the country today.

Shawn Selby

See also: Constitutional Convention; New Jersey Plan; Three-Fifths Compromise; Virginia Plan

Further Reading

Beeman, Richard. 2010. *Plain, Honest Men.* New York: Random House Trade Paperbacks.
Berkin, Carol. 2003. *A Brilliant Solution.* New York: Mariner Books.
Bowen, Catherine Drinker. 1986. *Miracle at Philadelphia.* Boston: Back Bay Books.

CONNECTICUT WESTERN RESERVE

During the Colonial Period, land exploration promised tales of daring adventures but also the possibility of new opportunities. The development of the Connecticut Western Reserve demonstrated the settlement of one of countless frontiers in America's expansion narrative. Including most of northeast Ohio today, the Connecticut Western Reserve was a tract of land that was sold and distributed by the state of Connecticut after the American Revolution. The settlement of the Connecticut Western Reserve not only extended New England culture but also illustrated the larger story of American westward expansion.

Connecticut's 1662 royal charter created a basic map for the Connecticut Western Reserve. During the mid-17th century, England found itself embattled in a civil war that resulted in periods of parliamentary and military dictatorship rule. Under the leadership of Oliver Cromwell, the military rule resulted in the execution of the king; the monarchy was restored in 1660 with Charles II. With its holdings in the New World, England's colonists faced uncertain times, particularly Connecticut.

As a Puritan colony, Connecticut's colonists were part of the faction who had condemned the monarchy (Woodward). Connecticut's governor, John Winthrop Jr., traveled to England to secure the king's approval and charter. Charters are documents that granted legal existence for the colonies. These documents detailed aspects such as governing powers and land boundaries. The generous 1662 charter stated the following about Connecticut's land holdings:

> All that Part of Our Dominions in New-England in America, bounded on the East by . . . Narraganset-Bay, . . . on the North by the Line of the Massachusetts-Plantation; and on the South by the Sea, and in Longitude running from East to West. (The Avalon Project)

Connecticut's landholdings carved a path extending from the East Coast to the West Coast of the United States, including today's cities of Cleveland and Omaha (Woodward). The charter served as validation for Connecticut's people to continue to spread outward from the state. The American Revolution, though, altered and complicated these boundaries. Although the end of the American Revolution changed the terms of these charters, Connecticut, like many other former colonies, continued to look westward.

The end of the American Revolution (1775–1783) brought about more questions of land expansion. In 1783, the Treaty of Paris officially recognized the end of the war but also granted former English territory to the Americans. The fledgling government acquired these western lands from both former colonies and Native

American tribes (Hurt 1996, 144). Due to the large area, Congress enacted a series of ordinances in an attempt to exercise control over the development of these regions. These ordinances included the Land Ordinance of 1785 (developed a systematic process for conducting surveys and selling) and the Northwest Ordinance of 1787 (outlined processes for admitting new states to the union and a territorial bill of rights).

Connecticut, unlike most of the other new states, did not relinquish all of its western territory. By petitioning Congress, in 1786, Connecticut successfully retained 5,000 square miles of land: the Connecticut Western Reserve and the Firelands (Hatcher 1966, 8). Separate from the Western Reserve, the Firelands were lands sold off to Connecticut's settlers who had lost property at the hands of the British during the Revolution. For Connecticut, this reserve was to be a New Connecticut, a vision for the future.

The reserve contained more than 3 million acres of unsurveyed land. In 1795, Connecticut sold the reserve to the Connecticut Land Company for $1.2 million (Hatcher 1996, 15). Connecticut utilized this money to benefit public education. By 1796, the Connecticut Land Company had mobilized a group of surveyors to travel to the Western Reserve to survey the area. The 52-person party led by Moses Cleaveland began at the western border of Pennsylvania. The survey followed along the 41st parallel and extended 120 miles along the coastline of Lake Erie (Knepper 2002, 23). Utilizing the Cuyahoga River as a guide, Cleaveland and his group, surveyed and divided most of the land into 25-square-mile townships. During their expedition, the group founded Cleveland, Ohio, named in honor of Moses Cleaveland. The party, however, faced difficulties with unfamiliar terrain, unpredictable weather, and inadequate supplies. The Connecticut Western Reserve remained mostly an isolated reserve until the mid-19th century.

The slow immigration and settlement to the Connecticut Western Reserve halted growth in the region. With high-priced lots and limited access to eastern markets, people and ideas gradually penetrated into the reserve. Nevertheless, its immigrants brought various New England traditions with them. For example, founders of today's cities like Hudson and Medina planned the cities in the likeness of New England towns. The cities featured town commons (greens) at their centers with buildings such as churches and courthouses dotting the surrounding space. Eventually, in 1832, the completion of the Ohio and Erie Canal helped to further connect this region with markets in the Atlantic and Gulf of Mexico coasts (Knepper 2002, 24). In opening the frontier, the Connecticut Western Reserve slowly transitioned from an agricultural economy to industrial enterprises. This industrial boom of the mid to late 19th century brought with it burgeoning numbers of immigrants to the reserve. Today, the legacy of the Connecticut Western Reserve remains evident, as it transformed into a culturally diverse region built upon resources.

Megan Smeznik

See also: Land Ordinance of 1785; Northwest Ordinance

Further Reading

The Avalon Project. "Charter of Connecticut—1662." http://avalon.law.yale.edu/17th_century/ct03.asp.

Buel, Richard, Jr. 2011. *The Peopling of New Connecticut: From the Land of Steady Habits to the Western Reserve.* Hartford, CT: The Acorn Club.

Hatcher, Harlan. 1966. *The Western Reserve: The Story of New Connecticut.* Cleveland, OH: World Publishing Company.

Hurt, Douglas. 1996. *The Ohio Frontier: Crucible of the Old Northwest, 1720–1830.* Bloomington: Indiana University Press.

Knepper, George. 2002. *The Official Ohio Lands Book.* Columbus, OH: Auditor of the State.

Wheeler, Robert. 2000. *Visions of the Western Reserve: Public and Private Documents of Northeastern Ohio, 1750–1860.* Columbus: Ohio State University Press.

Woodward, Walter C. 2012. "From the State Historian: The Map That Wasn't a Map." http://connecticuthistory.org/from-the-state-historian-the-map-that-wasnt-a-map.

CONSTITUTIONAL CONVENTION

The Constitutional Convention was held at the Pennsylvania State House in Philadelphia, Pennsylvania, from May 25, 1787, to September 17, 1787. The delegates met in the same room where the Second Continental Congress had debated independence, leading to the State House being more popularly known as Independence Hall. The original purpose of the convention was to revise and improve the Articles of Confederation. However, it quickly became apparent that a number of delegates intended to completely replace the Articles of Confederation and establish a much stronger national government. On September 17, 1787, the delegates approved the final draft of the Constitution of the United States.

The convention included a total of 55 delegates from 12 of the 13 states. Only Rhode Island (then known as Rhode Island and Providence Plantations) refused to send a delegation. This was because its state government worried that the convention would result in a government that would end up limiting the powers that individual states had under the existing Congress of Confederation. Some of the most important figures in American history were in Philadelphia during the convention. And although some states' delegations changed over time or were recalled occasionally, the roster of attendees remained largely the same throughout the process. However, 19 delegates never attended a single session, either from refusal or from neglecting their responsibility. All of the delegates were chosen by their respective state legislatures. Among the most significant attendees were Benjamin Franklin (Pennsylvania), James Madison (Virginia), George Mason (Virginia), Alexander Hamilton (New York), John Routledge (South Carolina), and George Washington (Virginia). Though men such as Rufus King (Massachusetts), Roger Sherman (Connecticut), Charles Pinckney (South Carolina), and Edmund Randolph (Virginia) were important contributors to the process as well. George Washington was unanimously elected president of the convention, although he chose not to become overly involved in the proceedings. Washington was worried that his influence would lend undue support to any matter under discussion, likely

The Constitutional Convention was arguably one of the greatest meeting of minds in the history of the world. The delegates were originally sent to revise the failing Articles of Confederation but instead created a new form of government that survives into the 21st century. (Library of Congress)

resulting in his opinion carrying the day. In an effort to ensure open and unfettered debate, then, he remained taciturn for much of the convention.

Two of the most prominent Founders did not attend the proceedings. John Adams was serving as the U.S. minister to the Court of St. James in England, and Thomas Jefferson was serving in the same capacity to the court of Louis XVI in Paris. Of the 55 delegates, approximately one-third had served in the Continental Army. Forty were either current or former congressmen. The attendees ranged in age from 26 (Johnathan Dayton from New Jersey) to 81 years old (Benjamin Franklin). Most of them had some familiarity with law, having either practiced as lawyers or politicians or having read law while in college or university. In addition to the lawyers, the delegates' other occupations included farmers, merchants, ministers, and financiers. Thirty of the men at the convention had attended college, with a plurality (nine) coming from Princeton.

The fact that so many delegates were college educated speaks to the social standing of the men at the convention. Colleges and universities in the 18th century were generally reserved for the wealthy or socially prominent men in America. In addition, this college background also impacted the Constitution. The curriculum of typical 18th-century higher education affected the political philosophies many delegates brought to their ideas for the new government. For instance, the emphasis on classical history of Greece and Rome influenced several of the delegates' views on the benefits of a republican form of government as well as the possibility (and desirability) of popular participation in the political process.

The question of how much democracy the young United States should allow was at the center of events leading up to the convention, as was a growing realization that the government established under the Articles of Confederation was not sufficient to meet the needs of the nation. The Articles of Confederation had been adopted in 1777 by the Second Continental Congress. It established a "league of friendship" among the 13 colonies/states that were waging the American War of Independence. The government system created by the Articles went into effect on March 1, 1781, after it was finally ratified by Maryland, the last of the states to approve of the plan.

Under the Articles, the government consisted almost entirely of a single house of Congress, wherein each state had a single vote. There was no executive or judicial branch, and all laws needed unanimous approval of all the states. This allowed any state almost complete veto power over any law proposed to Congress. In addition, each law passed by Congress had to be ratified by the state legislatures. In many respects, then, the states operated as almost completely sovereign entities.

It soon became apparent that the weak, largely decentralized government the Articles had created was not sufficient for the problems the country faced as it grew during the 1780s. Among other things, disputes arose over state boundaries and taxation of one state by another. One of the primary limitations under the Articles of Confederation was that the national government had no power to tax and no ability to establish a national currency. As such, international and interstate trade was practiced with an almost dizzying variety of currencies. The Congress and the tiny American military were also subject to the whims of the various states for funding. And Congress had no recourse to force delinquent states to fulfill their tax obligations.

These limitations on the national government were understandable given the political climate in America at the time of the Articles' creation. Few people in America during the Revolution would have approved of replacing the apparently oppressive and tyrannical British Empire with an American government equipped to violate citizens' liberties in the same way. However, after independence, circumstances, both domestic and foreign, convinced many Americans that the "league of friendship" needed to at least be strengthened. Others, such as James Madison and Alexander Hamilton, though, believed that the foundations laid by the Articles of Confederation were not strong enough to support the kind of centralized government America needed. They led the push for a complete overhaul of American politics, resulting in the Constitution. In September 1786, delegates from five states (Virginia, Delaware, New York, New Jersey, and Pennsylvania) met in Annapolis, Maryland, to discuss revising the Articles of Confederation. The debates at the Annapolis Convention resulted in a recommendation to the Congress that a broader constitutional convention be held the following May in Philadelphia. However, many Americans still harbored a deep-seated mistrust of centralized government.

If any single event convinced Americans of the need for a stronger national government, it was Shays' Rebellion. Shays' Rebellion was a popular uprising in rural Massachusetts during the late fall and winter of 1786 and 1787. Revolutionary War veteran Daniel Shays organized a group of disgruntled farmers and tradesmen (many of whom were also veterans). These men, numbering almost 4,000 at their peak, were frustrated with Massachusetts' economic policy as well as what they perceived as corruption and cronyism in the state government. The rebellion was ultimately unsuccessful, having been put down by a privately raised militia; however, it helped to point out the limitations of the confederated system of government at the time. Although the rebellion was specific to Massachusetts, the economic causes that led to it were being felt by other states as well, thus leading to a more widespread concern that similar unrest could break out elsewhere in the United States.

Soon after the rebellion was put down in mid-1787, prominent figures, including James Madison, Alexander Hamilton, and George Washington, began putting out feelers in an effort to gauge the level of support for a convention to revise the Articles of Confederation. The response was encouraging, and so the Philadelphia convention recommended by the earlier Annapolis Convention went ahead. It was scheduled to begin May 14, 1787. The necessary quorum did not arrive until May 25, though. And so, with Rhode Island choosing not to send a delegation, the remaining 12 states' delegations began debating the proposed changes.

Early in the proceedings, James Madison proposed the Virginia Plan. This plan would have resulted in dispensing with the existing government and replacing it with a more powerful and centralized national government with powers that had previously been reserved to the states. It was immediately apparent that the convention was no longer going to simply "fix" the Articles of Confederation. However, not all the delegates from the other states were enthusiastic about the changes proposed by Madison and his fellow nationalists. From the very beginning of the proceedings, there were debates between larger states and smaller ones, between slaveholding states and free states, and between economically powerful states and states that were more marginal to the overall economy. In many cases, there were even debates among individual states' delegations.

The absence of more democratically minded men, such as John Hancock (Massachusetts), Patrick Henry (Virginia), and Samuel Adams (Massachusetts), contributed to the Constitution's final bent toward nationalism and a relatively strong central government. In some cases, these men were committed to their responsibilities in their respective states. In others, most notably Revolutionary firebrand Patrick Henry, they refused to attend out of concern that the convention would yield a government that was too slanted toward monarchy for their taste.

During the debates, there were several issues that occupied the delegates' time. Perhaps none was as divisive as the organization of the federal government and the role of the states within the new system. Under James Madison's Virginia Plan, the states would be expected to give up a great deal of their power, which would then be vested in the hands of a much stronger Congress. The Congress would consist of two houses. The lower house would be filled by representatives from the states and be based on the state's population of white male property owners. Convention delegates from smaller states were understandably concerned that such an arrangement would limit their voice in the national government. They proposed various changes to the plan that would level the playing field by preserving some of the structure of the existing Articles of Confederation. William Paterson's New Jersey Plan called for a single house with equal representation for all states. Delegates from larger states, such as New York, Pennsylvania, and Virginia, balked at the proposal. They argued that their larger role in the nation's finances should ensure them more influence in the legislative process. James Madison, a champion of the idea of popular sovereignty, wanted a government that would be representative to the people, broadly speaking. To his mind, the idea of a representative government meant that the Congress was an expression of the will of the voting public. The states were nothing more than politically expedient divisions. Madison explained that the greater political power of larger states simply resulted from the fact that they happened to house more voters whose voices the government was meant to represent. This debate over the structure of the legislature threatened to derail the entire convention. However, in early July, a "Grand Committee" managed to find a solution that was acceptable to most of the recalcitrant delegates. The current, two-house Congress is a result of the Grand Committee's proposal.

There were other significant areas of disagreement among the delegates, however. One was whether slaves would count in a state's population numbers for the purposes of determining representation in Congress. Southern delegates claimed that the labor and intrinsic value of slaves made them essential to their economies, and so they should be counted in population figures. Northern delegates argued that, as slaves had no legal status, including them when apportioning Congress would be disingenuous and unjustly inflate the political power of states that claimed more slaves, all while not granting those slaves any role as citizens. Delegates resolved this with the Three-Fifths Compromise, which established that 60 percent of a state's slave population would count toward congressional apportionment.

With the exception of creating the legislative branch, the most contentious issue at the convention was likely the question of just how powerful the national government would be and what protections would be provided to ensure the individual liberties of Americans. Many delegates worried that the new national government would become too powerful. In an effort to prevent this, a system of checks and balances were built into the Constitution. The Constitution also established the federalist system of dividing certain powers between the national government and the states. These provisions were meant to ensure that no one part of the government (legislative, judicial, or executive) would be able to override the others and become too powerful.

Because of the emphasis that most delegates placed on the legislative branch of government, the portions of the document dealing with Congress are more detailed and more substantial than those dealing with either of the other two. For many, the executive branch was intended to consist of little more than an individual (who would eventually be known as the president) and a limited number of advisers.

These men were responsible for executing and enforcing the acts of Congress. However, the majority of delegates assumed that the chief role in the government would always be reserved for the Congress. Alexander Hamilton argued forcefully in favor of a much stronger, more centralized government under the charge of a powerful chief executive, but he was in the minority. Most of the men at the convention worried that placing too much power in the hands of any one branch or person would lead to an oppressive system like the one they had just rebelled against in the Revolution.

Although the delegates agreed to the draft of the Constitution on September 17, 1787, it would not go into effect until it had been ratified by at least 9 of the 13 states. States such as Delaware, Georgia, and New Jersey ratified the Constitution quickly, and with little debate. However, for a variety of reasons, others were reluctant to ratify the document. Two opposing groups soon emerged. The Federalists supported the Constitution and worked hard to convince state legislatures, such as New York and Virginia, to ratify it. To this end, prominent Federalists James Madison, Alexander Hamilton, and John Jay wrote a series of 85 essays to defend the government system the convention had set up. These *Federalist Papers* were specifically in response to the Anti-Federalist essays written by New York governor George Clinton and the outspoken criticisms of James Monroe and Patrick Henry in Virginia. However, they were also meant to describe to the general public the benefits of the centralized republican government the Constitution created. Nevertheless, there was resistance to ratification in Massachusetts and North Carolina.

In response to some of the concerns of the Anti-Federalists, James Madison agreed to develop a Bill of Rights that would be added to the Constitution. The Bill of Rights satisfied some opponents of the Constitution who worried that the document did not originally include any protection of individual liberties. Included in the Bill of Rights were guarantees of free speech and due process as well as the Tenth Amendment, which guaranteed that the various states retained any powers not specifically given to the national government elsewhere in the Constitution. When New Hampshire ratified the document in June 1788, it became official. However, Rhode Island did not ratify until almost two years later, becoming the last of the original 13 states to join the constitutional union.

Shawn Selby

See also: Articles of Confederation; Bill of Rights; Committee of Detail; Committee of Style and Arrangement; Connecticut Compromise; Madison, James; New Jersey Plan; Ratification; Shays' Rebellion; Three-Fifths Compromise; Virginia Plan

Further Reading

Beeman, Richard. 2010. *Plain, Honest Men.* New York: Random House Trade Paperbacks.
Berkin, Carol. 2003. *A Brilliant Solution.* New York: Mariner Books.
Bowen, Catherine Drinker. 1986. *Miracle at Philadelphia.* Boston: Back Bay Books.

CONSUMER GOODS

In many ways, consumer goods were a major factor in the settlement of the American colonies. Europeans seeking shorter, more direct transportation routes for bringing Asian goods to local markets inadvertently stumbled upon an entire continent filled with raw materials that could be turned into products highly sought after by eager purchasers. Even before there were permanent settlements in North America, trade between European and Native peoples provided the latter with consumer goods, such as beads, copper pots, and cloth. In exchange, the holds of ships crossing the Atlantic to Europe were packed with beaver pelts destined to be transformed into stylish hats and other garments. The Dutch, English, French, and Spanish all wanted a piece of this economic pie that promised them wealth and power. Trading posts and settlements sprang up and soon cultivated crops such as tobacco and rice were also exported to the mother countries.

As Europeans began to settle in North America, they needed basic material goods to sustain life. These goods initially came from Europe. Those individuals making the trip were advised to bring with them not only food and supplies for the journey aboard ship but things for their new life. Soft goods, such as blankets, pillows, sturdy sheets, and clothing, were stowed in wooden trunks and canvas sacks along with iron pots and kettles, skillets and fry pans, ceramic dishes and drinking glasses, and guns and ammunition. Hardware, including door locks, nails, hinges, and window glass, jostled for precious space with carpentry and farming tools.

European entrepreneurs realized there was money to be made supplying settlers, and a steady flow of goods crossed the Atlantic. Members of the Van Rensselaer family of Amsterdam were early Dutch traders and land developers in the Hudson Valley of what later became New York State. In 1654, 22-year-old Jeremias Van Rensselaer came to America to oversee the family's holdings. Excited relatives, friends, and even the family maid sent him all sorts of merchandise to sell on their behalf, hoping to make small fortunes by selling at inflated prices. Candles, guns, textiles, clothing, shoes, clay pipes, and tableware all found ready buyers. Even luxury goods like silk stockings and silver spoons found a market.

Along the Eastern Seaboard, forests were plentiful, and most settlements and trading posts included men skilled in carpentry. It was significantly easier and cheaper to craft furniture on-site in America than to ship it from Europe, so from the very beginning, furniture was being made locally. Gradually, more goods began to be produced domestically to supplement the imported ones. In 1646, the first successful ironworks in North America, the Saugus Iron Works, opened near Boston and turned out nails, horseshoes, cookware, tools, and weapons. As more and more people immigrated to the colonies, they brought their skills with them. Silversmiths, weavers, potters, gunsmiths, and all sorts of other craftspeople were plying their trades in communities both large and small. Most of the goods produced reflected styles found in Europe, but adapted for local materials and conditions.

Written, pictorial, and archeological evidence shows that by the end of the 17th century, American consumers had a wide variety of goods to choose from. Whether the items were made domestically and traded between colonies or imported directly from abroad, colonists with money could fill their homes and adorn their persons with fashionable wares. Utilitarian ceramics made from local clay deposits might share cupboard space with more stylish pieces from Italy, France, Spain, Holland, England, or even China. A colonist could sleep on linen sheets produced from locally grown and woven flax and wear a suit or gown made of fine imported silk.

By the beginning of the 18th century, distinct American regional furniture styles emerged in the main urban centers. Furniture produced in Boston, New York, Philadelphia, Newport, and Baltimore, among others, all had distinct characteristics and often rivaled English goods in the mind of the consumer. Southern furniture retained essentially English characteristics.

American colonial merchants placed orders with suppliers abroad and often asked that the items being sent represent the most recent fashions. The colonial merchant might not know what fads were sweeping London, but they wanted to be able to reassure their customers that the goods being offered were the latest styles (or at least they had been when they left London months before). Wealthy Americans often wrote directly to their agents in London with their orders, thus eliminating the middleman and reducing the chance of getting inferior goods procured at inflated prices. Even so, when packages arrived, the consumer was never quite sure what they might find. In addition to ordering goods from London, purchasing them at a retail shop, or contracting directly with a craftsman, colonial consumers could always buy at auction sales, and secondhand goods found a ready market among bargain hunters and those of limited means. Sir William Johnson, the British superintendent of Indian affairs for the northern colonies in the mid-18th century, utilized all these methods to supply his vast household.

Although popular mythology often depicts the American colonist as completely self-sufficient, the reality was quite different. No individual household could possibly produce all the goods it needed. American colonial society was a complex tapestry woven from goods and services that were bought, bartered, and traded.

British legislation intended to regulate trade between England, its colonies, and the rest of the world favored England, not the colonies. It began with the late 17th-century Navigation Acts, which required goods traveling to, from, or between English colonies to be transported on British ships and reached a boiling point when the Townsend Acts of 1767 imposed taxes on certain goods imported into the colonies. So, just as consumer goods were the impetus for colonial settlement and development, they were also at the root of the American Revolution.

Robin D. Campbell

See also: Craftsmen/Artisans; Navigation Acts; Trade

Further Reading

Breen, T. H. 2004. *The Marketplace of Revolution: How Consumer Politics Shaped American Independence.* New York: Oxford University Press.

Bushman, Richard L. 1992. *The Refinement of America: Persons, Houses, Cities.* New York: Alfred A. Knopf.

Haulman, Kate. 2011. *The Politics of Fashion in Eighteenth-Century America.* Chapel Hill: University of North Carolina Press.

Shammas, Carole. 1990. *The Pre-Industrial Consumer in England and America.* Oxford: Clarendon.

CONTINENTAL CONGRESSES

The Continental Congresses, of which there were several iterations, were responsible for the government of the American colonies during and just prior to the American Revolution. The First Continental Congress served during 1774, and the Second Continental Congress served from 1775 until 1781, essentially the duration of the Revolutionary War. The Confederation Congress (also referred to as the Congress of Confederation) was created by the Articles of Confederation and is sometimes considered to be an additional variant of the Continental Congresses. It operated from 1781 until 1789, when it was replaced by the present U.S. Congress, which was established by the Constitution of the United States. Taken together, the various iterations of the Continental Congress successfully managed the difficult task of prosecuting the American War of Independence. This included coordinating diplomatic efforts with European states, including France, Spain and Britain; funding the war effort through securing foreign and domestic loans; issuing a colonial currency; and overseeing the leadership and manning of the Continental Army.

Shortly after the Boston Tea Party, in December 1773, Parliament passed a series of punitive measures known in Britain as the Coercive Acts. American patriots soon took to calling these laws the Intolerable Acts. Although they were meant to reprimand the Massachusetts colony and, more specifically, Boston, they were portrayed by patriots as evidence of the extreme measures Britain was willing to use to rein in recalcitrant colonies. As such, many patriots saw the Intolerable Acts as a worrying precedent of the way Parliament and the Crown would deal with future rebellion in the colonies. Altogether, the Intolerable Acts helped to push rebellious colonists even further toward resistance against the British government, and rather than isolating Massachusetts, as Parliament had hoped, they turned the colony into a martyr of the patriot cause.

The Intolerable Acts were passed during the spring of 1774 and were soon answered with calls for another boycott on British goods. Americans had boycotted British goods several times before, with varying degrees of success; however, the demand for boycotts that began in 1774 would lead to much larger ramifications. Merchant communities were reluctant to participate in a boycott unless the effort was widespread and coordinated. Many feared that a piecemeal effort would lack the strength to compel the British to change their policy. Others worried that communities that did not participate would reap the financial benefits of the resulting trade imbalances. In an effort to encourage participation by as many colonies as possible, Benjamin Franklin resurrected his earlier call for a colonies-wide assembly. Franklin had received little support for his plan when he had proposed it a year earlier. However, colonial resentment with the Intolerable Acts helped breathe new life into the idea. As a result, a number of colonial legislatures passed measures to send delegates to meet at Carpenter's Hall in Philadelphia, starting in September 1774.

The 56 delegates who comprised the First Continental Congress were all elected by their respective colonial legislatures, and each colony was given a single vote, regardless the number of delegates in attendance. The Congress included some of the most influential men of the day. From Massachusetts came John Adams and his cousin Samuel Adams. New York's John Jay, Connecticut's Roger Sherman, and Pennsylvania's John Dickinson also attended. From Virginia came Patrick Henry, George Washington, and Peyton Randolph, who was elected unanimously to serve as the body's first president. Delegates from 12 of the 13 colonies began their deliberations on September 5, 1774. Only Georgia failed to send delegates. The southernmost colony still needed British help to secure its frontier from the ever-present threat of Indian attack.

The First Continental Congress walked a fine line during its brief existence. Delegates hoped to convince the British Crown and Parliament that their treatment of the colonies was driving the two sides apart. However, very few were yet speaking openly about the possibility, let alone the desirability, of outright independence. Among the measures taken up during the Congress's approximately six-week term were the Articles of Association, which called for a general boycott of British goods to go into effect on December 1, 1774, if Parliament had not repealed the Intolerable Acts by that time. Furthermore, if the acts still had not been repealed by the following September (1775), the colonies would enact an embargo on all American exports, with the sole exception of rice. In addition, Congress drafted separate statements of the colonial position. These statements were addressed to the British public, the colonial public, and to the residents of Quebec, a British colony in Canada that many Americans hoped would be sympathetic to the colonial cause by virtue of their relatively recent changeover from French to British control.

The most pointed document, however, was a formal petition that listed the colonists' grievances. This was addressed to George III and not to Parliament, as many Americans believed that Parliament was responsible for their perceived mistreatment. At the time, the king was considered, if not an ally, at least a potential mediator in the crisis. Lastly, the delegates decided to return to Philadelphia for a new session of the Congress to begin May 10, 1775, unless substantial progress had been made toward resolving the crisis. Few could have anticipated the outbreak of hostilities at Lexington and Concord, Massachusetts, in April 1775, which changed the role of the Second Continental Congress so dramatically.

The First Continental Congress was called to coordinate the colonial response to the Intolerable Acts. And when delegates adjourned in late October 1774, they determined to reconvene the following May if in the meantime Parliament had failed to address the colonists' concerns. However, with the skirmish at Lexington and Concord on April 19, 1775, the issues confronting the Second Continental Congress were suddenly much larger and more complex. The First Congress had been acutely aware of the need to maintain a delicate balance with Parliament and the Crown. In the fall of 1774, few Americans seriously advocated independence for the colonies. The fighting in and around Boston in the spring and summer of 1775, however, meant that previous efforts at diplomatic solutions to the colonial crisis would no longer be sufficient. Certainly, many Americans still waffled on the matter of independence. Nevertheless, when they reconvened in May 1775, this time at the Pennsylvania State House in Philadelphia, delegates to the Second Continental Congress almost immediately began coordinating a colonial military effort against the British.

In many respects, the Second Continental Congress was largely a reconvening of the First Congress. Many of the delegates to the Second Congress were holdovers from the previous session. However, there were some important changes. George Washington accepted the Congress's appointment to command the newly constituted Continental Army, vacating his seat. Peyton Randolph, the president of the First Congress, was recalled to Virginia to preside over that colony's legislature, the House of Burgesses. Elected to replace Randolph was Thomas Jefferson. Other notable arrivals to the Second Congress included Benjamin Franklin and John Hancock, a wealthy Massachusetts merchant and prominent patriot who was soon elected president of the Congress. Although Georgia had chosen not to send a delegation to the First Congress, the colonial Provincial Congress authorized a delegation in early July 1775, and the Georgia delegates arrived in Philadelphia on July 20.

For the first few months of the American Revolution, the colonial war effort was uncoordinated and haphazard and prosecuted almost entirely by militia. On June 14, 1775, Congress established the Continental Army under the command of George Washington, and it initially consisted of the various New England militia units besieging the British garrison in Boston as well as the militia in and around New York City. Essentially, the Continental Army nationalized the militia under the control of General Washington and under the oversight of Congress. This force of approximately 27,000 was soon supplemented by a call for a colonies-wide army, to be manned by volunteers serving enlistment terms of one year. These men would form the nucleus of a Continental Army that totaled approximately 17,000 at its strongest (not including the militia and state-controlled forces that were attached to but never fully integrated with the Continental Army).

Less than a month after establishing the army, Congress approved the Declaration of the Causes and Necessities of Taking Up Arms. The Declaration of Causes was a formal statement to the British government outlining colonial grievances and explaining why Americans had at last resorted to military action. The initial draft of the declaration was written by Thomas Jefferson. However, Pennsylvania lawyer John Dickinson composed the final draft. Despite the rapidly escalating antagonism between the colonies and Britain, a final effort was made to settle the crisis diplomatically. On July 8, 1775, Congress sent the Olive Branch Petition to the British government, reassuring it of the colonists' desire to avoid further hostilities. Also penned by John Dickinson, the petition arrived in London too late to change the course of the Revolution.

The Congress had no external authority to govern (it was not authorized by Parliament or by the Crown). However, it functioned as the de facto national government for the colonies. As such, it issued a continental currency. It oversaw the appointment of staff officers in the army. It also coordinated the colonial efforts at international diplomacy, most notably the appointment of ambassadors and ministers to European governments. Among the first of these was Connecticut merchant Silas Deane, who was America's first foreign diplomat to France. Deane would eventually be joined by Benjamin Franklin and Arthur Lee. Together, the men were responsible for the greatest diplomatic coup for the young nation when they secured a Treaty of Alliance with the French government. The treaty came on the heels of the American victory at the Battle of Saratoga, and it meant that France would support the colonial war effort with men, materiel, and money. French assistance was absolutely essential to the eventual American victory in the Revolution.

The Congress relied on a small number of standing committees and a constantly shifting collection of small ad hoc committees. Although there were a number of luminaries who served as the president of the Congresses (16 presidents over the 14 years that the Congresses were in session), the office had little real power to influence the legislative agenda. Instead, presidents of Congress were responsible for more ceremonial functions and for ensuring that the reports of committees were delivered on time and that the journals and records of the daily sessions were all in order. The turnover of delegates was extremely high as well. Nearly 350 men served as delegates at one time or another, and only slightly more than half spent more than 12 months with the body.

By the summer of 1776, a number of delegates were moving toward suggesting colonial independence; however, they were beholden to the wishes of their respective colonial assemblies. And few assemblies had authorized such a drastic measure. As a result, Congress passed a number of resolutions designed to encourage colonial assemblies to take a more radical position, pressuring colonial lawmakers to give their congressional delegates authority to consider independence in Philadelphia. The first colony to expressly authorize its delegation to propose independence was Virginia, and Richard Henry Lee took the lead in drafting a congressional resolution announcing that the colonies were immediately and henceforward separated from the British Empire. At the same time, delegates from other colonies worked hard to build support for independence within Congress as well as among their own colonial assemblies.

Then, on June 7, 1776, Richard Henry Lee presented a resolution in Congress declaring that the colonies were free and independent. Delegates in Philadelphia began debating independence in earnest and charged a Committee of Five with the responsibility of drafting a formal Declaration of Independence. The committee included Robert Livingston, John Adams, Roger Sherman, Benjamin Franklin, and Thomas Jefferson, although Jefferson bears most of the credit for composing the final draft. Two days after Congress voted in favor of Lee's resolution, the draft of the Declaration of Independence was approved, on July 4, 1776.

At the same time, Congress took up consideration of a proposal for a more formal governmental structure. The Articles of Confederation would not go into effect until 1781, and its loose alliance of states cooperating in a fairly weak, decentralized national government proved unequal to the challenges facing the new nation. The Articles of Confederation were replaced by the Constitution by the end of the 1780s.

Although the colonies had declared themselves separate from Britain in 1776, the final achievement of independence only came after five more years of fighting. During that time, Congress was forced to relocate several times to avoid British military campaigns. This included a move to Baltimore in the fall and winter of 1776, when British forces under William Howe threatened Philadelphia, as well as a move to York, Pennsylvania, in September 1777, when Philadelphia was occupied by the British. Congress was able to return to Philadelphia in July 1778, when Howe's successor, Sir Henry Clinton, abandoned the city to improve his defenses in New York City against the threat of a combined French and American assault.

Even in the midst of the Revolution, Congress maintained active efforts at diplomacy, especially with France and England. The crowning achievement of negotiations with France was the Treaty of Alliance in 1778. That same year, a peace delegation from Parliament met with Congress in Philadelphia. Congressional delegates refused Britain's demands that peace could be restored through a revocation of the Declaration of Independence and instead countered with a list of demands that included full recognition of American independence, navigation rights to the Mississippi River, and complete withdrawal of British forces from America. The British delegation demurred, and Congress appointed John Adams as the American minister to the Court of St. James in Britain. Although often rebuffed in his efforts in London, Adams would be one of the most important negotiators during the peace talks in Paris at the conclusion of the war.

The Paris peace negotiations and the resultant Treaty of Paris (1783) were conducted under the auspices of the Confederation Congress (sometimes referred to as the Congress of Confederation). In March 1781, the states ratified the proposal for the Articles of Confederation. The Articles provided a more formal constitutional framework, and thereby official legal jurisdiction, for the actions of the Continental Congresses. Although the Congress of Confederation would not last the decade, it was the culminating iteration of a legislative body that overcame daunting odds and successfully guided the American colonies from being subjects of the British Empire to being an independent nation.

Shawn Selby

See also: Congress of Confederation; Hancock, John

Further Reading

Henderson, James H. 1974 *Party Politics in the Continental Congress.* New York: McGraw Hill.

Rakove, Jack. 1979. *The Beginnings of National Politics: An Interpretive History of the Continental Congress.* New York: Knopf.

CONTRACEPTION

Contraception and reproductive control has been practiced and documented as early as 1550 BCE, where abortive and contraceptive methods were detailed in ancient Egyptian papyrus (Potts and Campbell 2009). Contraceptive methods throughout history have been numerous, of varying success, and were oftentimes deadly to women because of contraceptive-induced infections and ill-practiced abortions, and it is still a topic of considerable controversy today.

So controversial was the concept of reproductive control in colonial America that very few writings, even in medical texts, exist that appropriately describe contraceptive methods used by colonists, and no laws or statutes from the time exist that "proscribed contraceptive practices" (Brodie 1994, 39). Additionally, the Puritans considered abortion an abominable sin, and records exist that indicate some women were executed for engaging in self-induced abortions or for committing infanticide during this time.

Despite the lack of documentation regarding contraception in colonial America and the harsh punishments documented for those who sought to terminate pregnancies, demographic records indicate a marked decline in birth rates beginning in the late 17th century and continuing through the 19th century. Historians believe this indicates that some contraceptive or reproductive control methods may have been used frequently by colonists, and although limited records exist, these methods may have been passed through families and within settlements, particularly from mother to daughter, during tough economic times and particularly when land acquisition was limited (Brodie 1994). Some historians have noted that reproductive control was primarily dictated by men during the time period. Being that the most common documented methods of contraception were breastfeeding and abstinence, condom usage, and withdrawal, or coitus interruptus, "all depended on the willingness of the male and did not provide women with reproductive control" (Mays 2004, 47). However, despite documented male dominance of reproductive control, journal entries and personal letters between colonial women indicate that a fair amount of female-controlled contraception was practiced by these women, which some speculate indicates a strong willingness of colonial women to be in control of their own reproduction (Mays 2004).

Average family size in colonial America was between six and eight children, but the average marrying age of women also increased over the 17th century from the late teens to the mid-twenties. Additionally, historical records indicate that young brides had the majority of their children early in their married years, while older brides tended to have their children later in married life—and both groups appear to have "managed gaps" where no children were produced. Some historians speculate that, for many colonial women, breastfeeding (which can delay the onset of renewed fertility) was used as a contraceptive method, often in tandem with abstinence and, although not very reliable, allowed some of these women to exercise a modicum of reproductive control during the breastfeeding period (Mays 2004)

Although more often related to illicit sexual encounters, medical texts also document the use of male condoms, typically made from animal intestine or skin (Mays 2004; Potts and Campbell 2009). However, it appears that condom usage was not so much a means of contraception as it was a means to limit the spread of venereal disease within the colonies, and the porous and fragile state of some often rendered condoms ineffective against disease or the prevention of pregnancy. Through medical documentation and historical records from the time, it is speculated that withdrawal was the most popular method of contraception, and, again, although not particularly effective, it was one of the least harmful methods of contraception in terms of the medical health of women (Brodie 1994; Mays 2004; Potts and Campbell 2009).

As previously stated, reproductive control appears to have officially been in the hands of men during colonial times. However, through the writings of colonial women that have survived and through other historical documentation of the period, it appears that a fair amount of female-practiced contraception did exist, with varying effectiveness. A common contraceptive practice was the use of the pessary, a sponge-like device soaked in lemon juice, honey, or other herbal mixtures that could be inserted in the vagina prior to sexual intercourse (Mays 2004). Although some degree of contraceptive success was achieved by the use of pessaries, it was also quite a dangerous practice, sometimes resulting in cervical infections or even death. However, superstition and folk wisdom in regard to women's contraceptive practices weave through the historical record, indicating to some historians that ill health and death may have been worth the risk for the women engaged in these practices.

Perhaps one of the more popular means of women-controlled contraceptive and abortive practices was the use of herbal remedies as ingestions, soaks, or poultices, as prescribed in the medical works of practitioners such as John Gerard in his influential 17th-century text, *The Herball or Generall Historie of Plantes* (Brodie 1994, 42). Herbs such as juniper, angelica, and pennyroyal were often used as both contraceptive and abortive methods, despite medical reasoning indicating that the functions required for both methods would need to be different (Mays 2004). However, the use of herbal mixtures as miscarriage-inducing remedies appears to have been relatively effective, and therefore their use and the further experimentation of self-induced reproductive control continued throughout the colonial era.

Religious opinion of "sinful abomination" and "interfering with God's will" toward contraception and reproductive control in general appear to have promulgated colonial America. However, the documented practices indicate that both colonial men and women believed such measures necessary, despite the legal and physical danger, and for a variety of reasons (particularly in the case of premarital intercourse or adultery (Brodie 1994)). These reasons increased as poverty and limited land availability increased in the 18th century and into the 19th century with the rise of the industrial revolution in the United States (Potts and Campbell 2009).

One could also surmise that the letters and journal entries from colonial women discussing contraception and reproductive control indicate a shift in female thinking from "subservience and obedience" to independence and agency. From 17th-century cow dung condoms and pennyroyal tea (Brodie 1994; Mays 2004) to 20th-century condoms and intrauterine devices (Potts and Campbell 2009), contraception has an interesting and medically astounding history. For many colonial Americans, contraception and reproductive control may have been a saving grace during a time of great uncertainty and turmoil.

Shelley Blundell

See also: Households; Midwives; Mortality Rates; Women

Further Reading

Brodie, Janet F. 1994. *Contraception and Abortion in Nineteenth-Century America.* New York: Cornell University Press.

Mays, Dorothy A. 2004. *Women in Early America: Struggle, Survival, and Freedom in a New World.* California: ABC-CLIO.

Potts, M., and M. Campbell. 2009. "History of Contraception." *Global Library of Women's Medicine.* http://www.glowm.com/section_view/item/375/recordset/71685/value/375.

CORNWALLIS, LORD CHARLES (1738–1805)

Lord Charles Cornwallis, 1st Marquess and 2nd Earl Cornwallis, was a British general and statesman, who despite having a long and successful career in the service of his country is most remembered for his surrender to the combined American and French army at the Battle of Yorktown, in October 1781. This would be the last major battle of the American Revolution (1775–1783), and his surrender essentially ended the British effort to quell the colonial rebellion.

Cornwallis was born on New Year's Eve 1738, in London, into one of the most prominent families in Britain. He studied at Eton and later at Cambridge University before choosing to enter the ranks of the British army, as did many English nobles at the time. However, unlike many of his genteel comrades, Cornwallis took his craft seriously, even going so far as to attend a well-respected military academy in Turin, Italy. His devotion to military science made him one of the most capable generals in the British army during the Revolution, and despite his infamy for losing at Yorktown, Cornwallis won more battles than he lost over a career that included campaigns in the Americas as well as in India.

Cornwallis's father purchased his son's first commission for him as an ensign in the First Foot Guards, and the young officer distinguished himself while fighting in Germany during the early stages of the Seven Years' War (1756–1763). During this time, he was elected to the House of Commons before succeeding to his father's seat in the House of Lords upon his death in 1762. Perhaps surprisingly, given his role in the Revolution in later years, Cornwallis opposed many of the parliamentary taxes and regulations that were so onerous for patriots in the colonies.

Nonetheless, when resistance turned to rebellion in America, Cornwallis accepted a general's commission from George III and traveled to Charleston in early 1776, where he supported Sir Henry Clinton in his unsuccessful siege of the port city. From there, the two generals traveled north to aid in the campaign against General Washington's Continental forces around New York. During late 1776, Cornwallis took a leading role in driving the Continental Army off Long

Island and eventually chased the Americans across New Jersey, forcing them to make camp in eastern Pennsylvania.

Cornwallis had a reputation throughout the war as being one of the more aggressive and pugnacious generals in the British army. Some English staff officers considered their American counterparts to be of inferior ability and military intelligence, dismissing them as unworthy foes and approaching engagements with less verve than they might. Though he did not overestimate his enemies' capabilities, Cornwallis was somewhat more blunt in his willingness to use the full advantages of his forces to put down the rebellion swiftly and decisively.

Throughout 1777 and 1778, Cornwallis was involved in nearly every major battle in the New Jersey theater of the war. As the British advanced on the American capitol at Philadelphia, Cornwallis often took a leading role, even though he was never in overall command.

After the British captured Philadelphia, in September 1777, Cornwallis traveled to England on leave. Upon his return to America, in early 1778, he learned that Sir Henry Clinton had replaced William Howe as overall commander of British forces, making Cornwallis the second most senior British officer in America. The entry of France into the war in the wake of the Battle of Saratoga forced the British to alter their overall strategy, and they abandoned Philadelphia. Cornwallis aided the retreat to New York and played a central role in the Battle of Monmouth in June 1778, launching a counterattack that blunted an American advance that threatened to rout the British forces. In November 1778, Cornwallis returned to England to tend to his ailing wife, Jemima. When she died a few months later, Cornwallis was beside himself with grief.

Hoping to distract himself from his suffering, Cornwallis sailed back to America, where he was put in command of the British forces in the south. During his time in England, the British overall strategy had shifted. Rather than trying to destroy Washington's army in the middle states, British forces moved to the southern theater, with some redirected to defend imperial interests against the chance of the French attack elsewhere in the empire.

Clinton and Cornwallis supposed that there were large numbers of Loyalists throughout the South who would aid the campaign with material, intelligence, or other support. In addition, as British troops were relocated elsewhere in the empire, Loyalists could fill the manpower shortages that might result. The plan was to recapture the Southern Colonies one at a time, restoring Tory governments in each one. Clinton and Cornwallis mistrusted each other and increasingly had different ideas about the future progress of the war. Clinton worried that the globalization of the war meant that success in America had become impossible, and he suspected that Cornwallis was involved in machinations to supplant him as commander of British forces in the colonies.

After working together to capture Charleston, South Carolina, in 1780, Clinton returned to New York, leaving Cornwallis in sole command of the southern forces. After soundly defeating Gen. Horatio Gates at the Battle of Camden in August 1780, Cornwallis was pitted against Gates's replacement, Nathanael Greene. Greene brilliantly avoided direct confrontation with the British, instead fighting a running campaign, skirmishing and feinting against Cornwallis's forces. The Americans also benefited from effective guerrilla tactics by commanders such as Francis Marion and Daniel Morgan. While Cornwallis resupplied his force at Wilmington, North Carolina, Greene and the Americans largely recaptured South Carolina. Seeing a chance to join up in Virginia with another British army under the joint command of Benedict Arnold and William Phillips, and believing that he could not secure North Carolina unless its supply lines from Virginia had been cut, Cornwallis moved north toward the Virginia coast.

Although he was still focused on recapturing New York, General Washington worried about the British advance in Virginia, and so he dispatched the young Marquis de Lafayette to defend the state. Lafayette had just over 3,000 soldiers in his command against Cornwallis's army of more than 7,000. Lafayette cleverly avoided direct confrontations, while gathering reinforcements as he could. As Cornwallis advanced up the Virginia coast, he received a series of confusing and sometimes contradictory letters and orders from Clinton in New York. At one point, Clinton ordered Cornwallis to locate a suitable deepwater port where he could secure and shelter ships of the line (the largest vessels in the British navy). The order was almost more of a suggestion than a decisive command, but such a move would also support Cornwallis's strategy of cutting off supplies into North Carolina.

Cornwallis almost certainly recognized that such a position would be vulnerable to an American siege. However, there is some evidence to suggest that he hoped his fortified position would force the Americans into a decisive head-to-head battle. British control of the seas provided his army with an avenue of escape and the guarantee of resupply. He therefore settled on a location along the York River, near the town of Yorktown, Virginia, and in August 1781, he began fortifying his position.

As Cornwallis's men dug their trench lines and positioned their artillery, Washington and French commander the Comte de Rochambeau received word that a squadron of French warships under the Comte de Grasse was sailing to Virginia from the West Indies. Washington was still hoping to dislodge the British from New York. However, the French commanders convinced him that the British position there was too secure and that Cornwallis was much more vulnerable.

Washington and Rochambeau marched south, arriving at Yorktown in September. Although Clinton had reassured Cornwallis that he would resupply the Yorktown position, such a possibility was rendered impossible when the British navy was defeated at the Battle of the Chesapeake on September 5, 1781. After a monthlong siege by the Franco-American army, unable to escape by land or by sea, and with Clinton refusing to reinforce or rescue his forces, Cornwallis surrendered on October 19, 1781. Although the peace was officially settled with the Treaty of Paris in 1783, Cornwallis's surrender at Yorktown essentially ended the Revolution.

Cornwallis's defeat at Yorktown could have ruined his reputation. However, the king and Parliament recognized his skills as a general and as an administrator, and he was offered the governor generalship of India in 1786. He helped to reform the civil service and judicial system there, and led British forces to victory in the Third

Anglo-Mysore War (1789–1792). Four years after returning from India, in 1798, Cornwallis was named Lord Lieutenant of Ireland. In this position, Cornwallis was instrumental in the passage of the 1800 Act of Union by the Irish Parliament, which was an essential step toward the creation of the United Kingdom of Great Britain and Ireland. His time in Ireland was difficult, marked with successes and failures, and he resigned his position in 1801. He died of a fever in India in 1805, having once again accepted appointment as governor general. He was buried near the Ganges River.

Shawn Selby

See also: Camden, Battle of; Clinton, Sir Henry; Monmouth, Battle of; Yorktown, Battle of

Further Reading

Hibbert, Christopher. 2013. *Rebels and Redcoats: The American Revolution through British Eyes.* New York: W. W. Norton & Co.

Wickwire, Franklin, and Mary Wickwire. 1971. *Cornwallis and the War of Independence.* London: Faber and Faber.

CORONADO, FRANCISCO VASQUEZ DE (CA. 1510–1554)

Francisco Vasquez de Coronado was a Spanish explorer who led an expedition through Sonoran Mexico into the territories that are now the modern U.S. states of Arizona, New Mexico, Texas, Oklahoma, and Kansas. He also served as governor of Nueva Galicia, in Western Mexico, from 1539 to 1554. He is best known for his unsuccessful search for the fabled "Seven Cities of Cibola."

Francisco Coronado was born in Salamanca, Spain, to Juan Vázquez de Coronado, a nobleman, and Isabel de Luhan. Upon the death of his father, due to primogeniture, Coronado was forced to find employment away from his boyhood home. He determined to find his fortune in New Spain, arriving in October 1535. He settled in Mexico City, where he became a city councilman. Coronado arrived in Mexico as part of Viceroy Antonio Mendoza's retinue. In 1537, Mendoza dispatched Coronado to quell a revolt by African miners in Amatepeque. Mendoza awarded Coronado a city council post at Mexico City in June 1538 after his successful completion of the task. Between his political positions and having been granted several encomiendas, Coronado became quite wealthy. He compounded his net worth by marrying heiress Beatriz de Estrada, whose father had served as New Spain's royal treasurer.

Although he was one of the richest men in the Americas, Coronado's greed was not satiated. He became obsessed with the rumored Seven Cities of Cibola, which purportedly were rich in gold, jewels, and minerals. The existence of the cities had been documented by both Álvar Núñez Cabeza de Vaca and Marcos de Niza. They in fact claimed to have seen them. In 1540, Coronado, approximately 280 conquistadors, and more than 750 Natives marched north from Culiacán, Mexico.

On July 7 of that year, the Spaniards sacked what they believed to be the first of the seven cities. It proved to be a small Zuni community with no discernable wealth. They found the same to be true in other communities that they encountered. Frustrated, they seized the leaders of some of the towns and tortured them for information. The expedition ultimately traveled more than 2,000 miles in its fruitless search and passed through the present-day states of Arizona, Kansas, New Mexico, Oklahoma, and Texas. The expedition was forced to return to Mexico City, arriving in July 1542, because Coronado had suffered a head injury after falling from his horse.

Among those documenting and mapping the trip were Juan de Jaramillo and Pedro de Castañeda. They provided the first descriptions by Europeans of such landmarks as the Rocky Mountains, the Grand Canyon, and the Rio Grande River. Also included were accounts about the different American Indian groups they had encountered. The documents inspired and enabled succeeding Spanish expeditions to colonize the region.

Information about the expedition proved extremely problematic for Coronado and his lieutenants, as they were charged with crimes and forced to face a tribunal. Some of the allegations regarded the management of the expedition, as it had failed, while others centered on the maltreatment of the Mexican Natives that had accompanied the conquistadors and the brutality exerted on the newly encountered Indians north of Mexico. The last charge was among the most significant because, in the eyes of Judge Lorenzo de Tejada, future Spanish colonization efforts had become more difficult due to the presence of justifiably hostile Native populations. Coronado's political patrons ensured that he would not be held accountable for the atrocities committed by members of his command. His chief lieutenant, Garcia López de Cárdenas, was found guilty, as he supposedly issued the relevant orders, and he was imprisoned in Spain for seven years. Coronado lived out the rest of his life as a wealthy gentleman and politician in Mexico City.

John R. Burch Jr.

See also: Cabeza de Vaca, Álvar Núñez; New Spain

Further Reading

Flint, Richard. 2002. *Great Cruelties Have Been Reported: The 1544 Investigation of the Coronado Expedition.* Dallas, TX: Southern Methodist University Press.

Flint, Richard, and Shirley Cushing Flint, eds. 2005. *Documents of the Coronado Expedition, 1539–1542: "They Were Not Familiar with His Majesty, nor Did They Wish to Be His Subjects."* Dallas, TX: Southern Methodist University Press.

Flint, Richard, and Shirley Cushing Flint, eds. 2011. *The Latest Word from 1540: People, Places, and Portrayals of the Coronado Expedition.* Albuquerque: University of New Mexico Press.

Mathers, Clay, Jeffrey M. Mitchem, and Charles M. Haecker, eds. 2013. *Native and Spanish New Worlds: Entradas in the American Southwest and Southeast.* Tucson: University of Arizona Press.

CORTÉS, HERNÁN (CA. 1485–1547)

Hernán Cortés was a conquistador known for conquering the Aztecs in modern-day Mexico; he also led expeditions to present-day Guatemala, Honduras, and Baja California. The son of a nobleman in the Spanish city of Medellin, by age 12, Cortés was engaged in studies to become a lawyer. He dropped out of school at age 17 and decided to seek his fortune in New Spain. He left Spain in 1506, bound for Santo Domingo. During the six years that he lived there, Cortés was exposed to the politics of the Indies and listened intently to stories of where wealth could be obtained farther west. He then gradually made his way in that direction.

When Diego Velázquez decided to launch an expedition to Cuba in 1511, Cortés was one of his lieutenants. Once firmly ensconced as governor, Velázquez rewarded Cortés with the post of secretary and provided him an encomienda. Despite his benefactor's generosity, Cortés made a nuisance of himself. He was removed from his post in 1514 because he had advanced a proposal from fellow owners of encomiendas asking for more Native laborers. Velázquez eventually pardoned him for that act.

In 1518, Velázquez offered Cortés a commission to go to Mexico to reinforce another Spanish expedition led by Juan de Grijalva. Arriving on the Yucatán Peninsula a year later with 550 conquistadors under his command, Cortés disobeyed Velázquez's orders and began serving his own interests. Cortés encountered the Maya, who were vassals of the Aztecs. Among the tributes they were forced to send to their masters were foods and humans to be sacrificed to the Aztec gods. Although the Spanish found some gold and silver artifacts in Maya communities, they were dissuaded from attacking these communities by tales of the vast wealth held by the Aztecs in Tenochtitlán.

Cortés and his company began marching to the Valley of Mexico, the location of the Aztec capital. Aztec scouts noticed their advance and reported their presence to Emperor Montezuma II. After consultation with priests and prominent warriors, the emperor concluded that the arrival of the Spanish was a sign that the god Quetzalcoatl had returned to the Valley of Mexico. He sent emissaries to the Spanish, bidding them to stay out of the capital city until he could personally meet with them. To encourage Spanish compliance, the emissaries were accompanied by porters bearing valuable metals for Cortés and his men.

The Spanish took the gesture as a confirmation of the information he had obtained from the Maya. Cortés also perceived weakness on the part of the Aztecs, as they preferred to send gold and silver rather than armed troops. The Spanish commander accepted the bribe and then ordered his men to continue their march to Tenochtitlán. During the advance, his force grew in size as peoples that had been subjugated by the Aztecs, including the Maya, Totonac, and Tlascala, saw an alliance with the Spanish as an opportunity to rid themselves of the Aztec yoke.

Cortés arrived at Tenochtitlán on November 8, 1519. He was greeted by Montezuma, who invited the Spanish to enter the city. It was a strategic move designed to separate the Spanish from their Native allies. What he did not anticipate was that Cortés would take him prisoner. Aztec warriors attempted to free the emperor but failed. Although a prisoner, the emperor was allowed to continue ruling his empire, provided that he ordered the Aztecs not to interfere with the activities of the Spanish. Cortés was unaware that the freedom he allowed Montezuma to communicate with his subjects also gave him the opportunity to urge his cousin, Cuauhtémoc, to lead the Aztec opposition. In response, Cuauhtémoc began organizing the Aztec military. Initially, the warriors engaged in minor skirmishing because they feared a massive assault would potentially cost the emperor his life.

Spanish politics required Cortés to leave the city, as Pánfilo de Narváez had been dispatched from Cuba by Gov. Diego Velázquez with a small army to arrest him. While Cortés worked to convince Pánfilo de Narváez to join his cause, the Aztecs launched a major assault against the small garrison he had left in the city. On July 24, 1520, Cortés returned to Tenochtitlán with reinforcements. After a brief lull, the Aztecs resumed their assault and took much of the city back. Cornered, Cortés used his trump card, the captured Montezuma. The emperor ordered his people to cease their assault on the Spanish. Disgusted with his actions, the Aztecs stoned him to death.

Emperor Cuitláhuac joined Cuauhtémoc in his effort to defeat the Spanish. Together, they raised an army of 100,000 warriors. On June 30, 1520, known as "La Noche Triste" by the Spanish, the Aztecs dealt Cortés a devastating defeat that resulted in him and his men abandoning the city. Rather than pursuing the remnants of Cortés's force, the Aztecs instead dispersed their troops to reconquer all of their subjects who had cast their lot with the Spanish.

Unbeknownst to the Aztec warriors, they had been exposed to smallpox. They carried the disease to all corners of the empire. The resulting epidemic killed a third of the Aztec population, including Emperor Cuitláhuac. For Mexico's subjugated peoples, the epidemic was proof that the Aztec gods had withdrawn their favor. They subsequently flocked to join Cortés. Recognizing that their fortunes had reversed, Emperor Cuauhtémoc sued for peace but was rebuffed. The Spanish advanced on Tenochtitlán and took the city on August 13, 1521. Among the captives they obtained was Emperor Cuauhtémoc. Believing that Cuauhtémoc held a great deal of influence in lands south of Mexico, Cortés took him to present-day Guatemala and Honduras in hopes of locating other wealthy Native cities. When the search proved fruitless, Cuauhtémoc was hanged.

Despite his successes, Cortés was viewed with disfavor by the Spanish king Charles V. Charles was particularly concerned about Cortés's disregard of orders, especially those made by Diego Velázquez. It was Velázquez that had helped finance the expedition to Mexico, only to see it usurped by Cortés. Cortés was forced to compensate Velázquez for his financial losses. Although it was Cortés that had secured much of the territory of New Spain, Charles V appointed Antonio de Mendoza to serve as the viceroy of the region. Cortés had to settle for the relatively minor post of marquis of the Valley of Oaxaca.

Despite being an extremely wealthy man, Cortés's greed could not be satiated. He personally financed five expeditions that explored the Pacific Coast. He tasked all with searching for pearls and gold. One of the expeditions landed on the southern portion of Baja California. Cortés subsequently launched another expedition to establish a settlement there. Most of the 700 settlers who made the trek died from starvation or were victims of Indian attacks. The final expedition dispatched by Cortés sailed off and was never heard from again.

Cortés returned to Spain in 1541 with his reputation in tatters. His intent was to be recognized for all that he had accomplished. He believed that such acknowledgment would allow him to regain much of the wealth he had lost financing the five expeditions along Mexico's Pacific Coast. The adulation he desired was never received. Cortés died of pleurisy in Castilleja de la Cuesta in Seville.

John R. Burch Jr.

See also: Cuauhtémoc; Mesoamerica; Montezuma II

Further Reading

Nichols, Deborah L., and Enrique Rodriguez-Alegría, eds. 2017. *The Oxford Handbook of the Aztecs.* New York: Oxford University Press.

Smith, Michael E. 2012. *The Aztecs.* 3rd ed. New York: Wiley-Blackwell.

Thomas, Hugh. 1993. *Conquest: Montezuma, Cortés, and the Fall of Old Mexico.* New York: Simon & Schuster.

Weber, David J. 2005. *Bárbaros: Spaniards and Their Savages in the Age of Enlightenment.* New Haven, CT: Yale University Press.

Weber, David J. 1992. *The Spanish Frontier in North America.* New Haven, CT: Yale University Press.

COTTON, JOHN (1585–1652)

John Cotton was a Puritan minister in New England during the formative years of the colony. He was a nonconformist in a number of respects. He was essentially driven out of the Anglican church in England for his Puritan beliefs, and he was a leading figure in the Antinomian Controversy within the Puritan community in the Massachusetts Bay Colony during the 1630s and 1640s. In the last decade of his life, Cotton worked hard to coordinate the organizational structure of the Puritan churches in New England, giving the name Congregationalism to the church polity he developed.

John Cotton was born December 4, 1585, in Derby, England. Although his father, Rowland Cotton, was a lawyer, John pursued the life of a clergyman, perhaps due to the influence of his devoutly religious mother. Cotton studied at Derby School under the tutelage of an Anglican priest before moving on to Trinity College of Cambridge University in 1598. He earned his bachelor's degree in 1603, and three years later, he received his master's degree from Emmanuel College of Cambridge University, one of the centers of Puritan dissent at the time. After completing his master's coursework, Cotton continued his studies in theology as well as Hebrew. At the same time, Cotton served as a tutor, minister, and dean. He finally earned his bachelor's of divinity in 1613, by which time he had been ordained and become the minister of Saint Botolph's Church in Boston, Lincolnshire, England.

Cotton was a renowned preacher and scholar within the Anglican Church. However, he initially worked hard to walk a fine line between dissent and at least the appearance of conformity. While in England, Cotton's sermons grew more plain and direct, as a personal expression of his rejection of the Anglican Church's overly Catholic trappings and liturgy. In the first decades of the 17th century, Cotton and other leading Puritan dissenters faced increasing antagonism and prejudice in England. Escape to the newly formed colonies in North America was one of the few options available. As such, in 1629, Cotton joined John Winthrop, Roger Williams, and others in a conference to plan a large Puritan migration to New England.

Cotton and his wife, Elizabeth, did not join the group, however, and both contracted malaria shortly after seeing off the emigres. Elizabeth quickly succumbed to her illness. As John traveled England during his recuperation, he became increasingly aware of the prejudice the Puritan community faced. When he was summoned to court for his nonconformism, he resolved to flee to New England with his new wife, Sarah Story, a widow, and her daughter. They sailed aboard the *Griffin* in the summer of 1633. While at sea, Sarah gave birth to their first child together, a son named Seaborn.

Cotton's arrival in Boston in September caused a sensation. He was the most intellectually and oratorically gifted Puritan minister to reach the colony. His fervor resulted in a spate of conversions, and he introduced the spiritual concept of millennialism to New England. However, he quickly became embroiled in a battle of wills with Roger Williams, the leading nonconformist at the Salem church. Salem was a Separatist church even within the Puritan community, calling for a complete and total break with the Anglican Church. His more radical Separatism drew the ire of Puritan leaders in Plymouth and in Boston, who ordered him to be returned to England. Cotton supported the decision, blaming Williams for forcing the hand of church leadership. Williams escaped his deportation, fled into the New England backcountry, and eventually formed a new colony at Providence Plantations. He would go on to blame Cotton for being the person most responsible for his exile.

For his part, Cotton traveled to Salem in 1636 to deliver a sermon that he hoped would mend fences while simultaneously warning the congregation of the dangers of Separatist activities. The Cotton-Williams debate points out the hypocrisy of Separatist Puritans who sought sanctuary from religious persecution in England, only to demand rigid conformity to the dominant strain of Puritanism in New England.

This orthodoxy would result in another dispute in the colony, this time in what is known as the Antinomian Controversy. Cotton's sophisticated theological philosophy considered the believer to be passive in his or her personal religious experience. The Holy Spirit would provide spiritual regeneration with little to no effort needed on the part of the recipient. As a result, an individual had virtually no control over his or her own salvation and was wholly dependent on God's grace. In contrast, many of Cotton's New England colleagues were "preparationists," who believed that good works and righteousness were necessary preconditions to generate the spiritual activity that would lead to salvation.

The theological dispute grew as Cotton's followers, including Anne Hutchison, espoused his philosophy in opposition to mainstream Puritan dogma. Hutchinson and Cotton had met at St. Botolph's and had begun a mentor-mentee relationship there. In New England, Hutchinson was one of Cotton's most outspoken supporters. Together, these free-grace advocates directly challenged the orthodox ministers in the colony. In late October 1636, a group of ministers met Cotton and other free-grace proponents at Cotton's home, hoping to address the growing crisis. They left with Cotton's assurance that he would work to temper his message and bring it more in line with mainstream Puritan theology. The armistice was short-lived. Cotton and other free-grace advocates were accused of antinomianism (in essence, believing that one is not bound by any spiritual or moral law).

By the spring of 1637, what little support Cotton and other free-grace proponents enjoyed was rapidly being eroded. The new governor, John Winthrop, pursued more vigorous punishment for dissenters. John Wheelwright, a free-grace minister who was sometimes more outspoken than even Cotton, was convicted of antinomianism and banished from the colony. Anne Hutchinson was brought to the meetinghouse in Boston on March 15, 1638, and presented with a series of accusations in a session lasting more than nine hours. Cotton was forced to admonish his follower for her antinomianism, suggesting that she had taken the concept further than Cotton and others deemed reasonable. At the end of the hearing, Cotton was permitted to take Hutchinson to his home. After a week of ministration, Hutchinson seemed to have come to a more centrist understanding. However, at a subsequent hearing, her devotion to her new orthodoxy unraveled, and she was sentenced to excommunication. Cotton struggled over the next few years to downplay the depth of the controversy, hoping that his assurances would be enough to restore confidence in the righteousness of the colony.

With the Antinomian Controversy largely behind him, Cotton devoted his later career to establishing a governmental system for New England Puritanism. He espoused what he called Congregationalism, whereby each church would be largely self-governing. This was in contrast to Presbyterianism, whereby churches would be joined under the umbrella of a hierarchical polity. Presbyterianism was a more popular approach among Puritans in England. However, Cotton argued strongly in favor of Congregationalism, despite wanting to maintain ties with the Anglican church in England. Most mainstream Puritans, Cotton included, believed that the Anglican church was inauthentic. However, they believed it needed reform from within. This, and not complete separation, was the responsibility of Puritans in New England.

The debate over church polity was yet another schism within New England Puritanism. And it was another chance for Cotton to take a leading role in defining Puritan theology. In this case, he had to balance the Presbyterians who wanted the church to be more open to prospective members. At the other end of the spectrum were the Separatists, including Roger Williams, who believed that the Puritans in New England needed to break ties completely with not only the Anglican Church in England but also with any and all New England Puritans who argued in favor of maintaining a connection with England.

At the same time, Cotton was once again embroiled in a dispute over maintaining Puritan orthodoxy. This time, it centered on the sectarianism of Samuel Gorton. Gorton and his small band of followers believed that all people were imbued with the Holy Spirit, rendering the distinction between saints and sinners moot. Moreover, Gorton's theology eliminated the need for any external religious authority, as all that was required for salvation was for a person to willingly follow the dictates of this internal spirituality. He even went so far as to consider the organization of religion (ministers, churches, and the institutional structures of religion) to be a form of Antichrist. Gorton's ideas were so radical that Cotton was even willing to advocate in favor of the death penalty, believing that Gortonism represented a threat to the stability of New England and would be a black mark on the reputation of the New England colonies back in England. Despite Cotton's recommendation, Gorton was ultimately returned to his Separatist settlement in Warwick, Rhode Island.

In the autumn of 1652, Cotton became ill while traveling to deliver a sermon at Harvard. He died in mid to late December 1652, leaving behind a legacy of theological, doctrinal, and organizational influence on New England Puritanism that may be unmatched in colonial history. In addition, he grandson, Cotton Mather, would also distinguish himself as one of the most influential figures in Massachusetts' history.

Shawn Selby

See also: Anglicans; Antinomianism; Congregational Church; Gorton, Samuel; Hutchinson, Anne; Presbyterianism; Puritan Dissenters; Williams, Roger; Winthrop, John

Further Reading

Everett, Emerson. 1990. *John Cotton.* New York: Twayne.

Winship, Michael Paul. 2002. *Making Heretics: Militant Protestantism and Free Grace in Massachusetts, 1636–1641.* Princeton, NJ: Princeton University Press.

Ziff, Larzer. 1962. *The Career of John Cotton: Puritanism and the American Experience.* Princeton, NJ: Princeton University Press.

PRIMARY DOCUMENT: John Cotton, "God's Promise to His Plantation" (1630)

In England, during the early 1600s, a group of Christians called Puritans sought to purify the Church of England (Anglican Church). The Puritans also believed that individual churches should have the power to control their own membership and that the members, in turn, should control their local leaders. In this way, the Puritan church could dominate local government and society as a whole. After the Separatist Pilgrims founded a colony at Plymouth, Massachusetts, in 1620, a mix of Puritans and non-Puritans from England founded settlements along the New England coast.

King Charles I granted the Massachusetts Bay Company a charter for a New England colony in 1629. The following year, John Winthrop and a group of Puritans prepared to depart for Massachusetts. Before their departure, John Cotton preached a sermon, excerpted here, in which he asserted that it was God's will that the Puritans spread their way of life throughout the world. Cotton argued that they had a right to occupy land by casting out the previous occupants, living peacefully among them, or by finding the land vacant. The Massachusetts Bay colonists could find justification in this sermon for any action they might take regarding the Native peoples of America. Facing prosecution in England for his religious practices, Cotton immigrated to Massachusetts in 1633.

"Moreover I will appoint a place for my People Israel, and I will plant them, that they may dwell in a place of their Own, and Move No More" [II Sam. 7:10]

The placing of a people in this or that Countrey is from the Appointment of the Lord

Quest. Wherein doth this work of God stand in appointing a place for a people.

1. When God espies or discovers a Land for a people, as in Ezek 20:6. He brought them into a land that He had espied for them: And, that is, when either he gives them to discover it themselves, or hears of it discovered by others, and fitting them.
2. After he hath espied it, when he carries them along to it, so that they plainly see a providence of God leading them from one Countrey to another, as in Exod. 19:4: *You have seen how I have borne you as on Eagles wings, and brought you unto myself*. So that though they met with many difficulties, yet he carried them high above them all, like an Eagle, flying over Seas and Rocks, and all hindrances.
3. When he makes room for a People to dwell there, as in Psal. 80.9: *Thou preparest room for them.*

. . .

Now, God makes room for a People three wayes.

1. When he casts out the Enemies of a people before them by lawful War with the Inhabitants, which God calls them unto, as in Psal. 44:2: *Thou didst drive out the Heathen before them*. But this course of Warring against others and driving them out without provocation depends upon special Commission from God; or else it is not imitable.
2. When he gives a *foreign* People favour in the eyes of any *native* People to come and sit down with them; either by way of purchase, as Abraham did obtain the field of Machpelah; or else when they give it in courtesy, as Pharaoh did the land of Goshen unto the sons of Jacob.
3. When he makes a Countrey, though not altogether void of Inhabitants, yet void in that place where they reside. Where there is a vacant place, there is liberty for the sons of Adam or Noah to come and inhabit, though they neither buy it nor ask their leaves. . . . So that it is free from that common Grant for any to take possession of vacant Countries. Indeed, no Nation is to drive out another without special Commission from Heaven, such as the Israelites had; unless the Natives do unjustly wrong them, and will not recompence the wrongs done in a peaceable fort, and then they may right themselves by lawful War and subdue the country unto themselves.

. . .

This may teach us all where we now dwell, or where after we may dwell. *Be sure you look at every place appointed to you from the hand of God.* We may not rush into any place and never say to God, *By Your leave*; but we must discern how God appoints us this place. There is poor comfort in sitting down in any place that you cannot say, *This place is appointed me of God.* Canst thou say, that God spied out this place for thee, and there hath settled thee above all hindrances? Didst thou find that God made room for thee, either by lawful Descent, or Purchase, or gift, or other warrantable Right? Why, then this is the place God hath appointed thee; here He hath made room for thee. He hath placed thee in Rehoboth, in a peaceable place. This we must discern or else we are but intruders upon God. And when we do withal discern, that God give the us these outward Blessings from his Love in Christ; and maketh comfortable provision as well for our Souls as for our Bodies by the means of Grace; then do we enjoy our present possessions as well by gracious promise as by the common, and just, and bountiful providence of the Lord. Or, if a man do remove, he must see that God hath espied out such a Countrey for him.

Though there be many difficulties, yet he hath given us hearts to overlook them all, as if we were carried upon Eagles wings.

See God making room for us by some lawful means.

Quest. But how shall I know whether God hath appointed me such a place? If I be well where I am, what may warrant my removal?

Answ. There be four or five good things, for procurement of any of which, I may remove. Secondly, There be some evil things, for avoiding of any of which we may transplant ourselves. Thirdly, if withal we find some special providence of God concurring in either of both concerning our selves, and applying general grounds of removal to personal estate.

1. We may remove for the gaining knowledge. . . .
2. Some remove and travil for Merchandise and Gainsake: *Daily bread may be sought from far*: Prov. 31:14). . . .

   . . .

4. God alloweth a man to remove *When he may employ his Talents and Gifts better elsewhere*, especially when where he is, he is not bound by any special engagement. . . .
5. For the liberty of the ordinances. . . . This case was of seasonable use to our fathers in the day of Queen Mary, who removed to France and Germany as the beginning of her reign, upon proclamation of alteration of religion, before any persecution began.

Secondly, There be Evils to be avoided, that may warrant Removal.

1. When some grievous sins overspread a country that threaten desolation. . . .
2. If men be overburdened with Debts and Miseries. . . .
3. In case of persecution. . . .

Thirdly, As these general cases, where any of them do fall out, do warrant removal in general; so there be come special Providences or particular Cases which may give warrant unto such or such a person to transplant himself, and which apply the former general grounds to particular persons.

1. If sovereign authority command and encourage such plantations, by giving way to subjects to transplant themselves and set up a new Commonwealth. This is a lawful and expedient case for such particular persons as He designed and sent; Mat. 8:9: and for such as they who are sent have power to command.
2. When some special providence of God leads a man unto such a course.

Source: Cotton, John. 1686. *God's Promise to His Plantations.* Boston: Samuel Green.

COWPENS, BATTLE OF

The Battle of Cowpens was fought on January 17, 1781, between the patriot forces of Gen. Daniel Morgan and the British forces under Banastre Tarleton. The battle was fought in an area of South Carolina known as Hannah's Cowpens and ended in a dramatic victory for the patriot forces. The surprising result left the British forces in the colony severely depleted, including the loss of almost all of the light infantry. This would put them on the path to leaving the colony, eventually ending up in Yorktown at the end of the war. For the patriots, the victory served as a rally point for their flagging morale and showed that the British regulars could be beaten in the field. The year 1780 was not a good one for the Continental Army. The British had taken Charleston and the bulk of the southern Continental Army earlier in the year. Georgia had been back under British control for a while and remained so. An attempt by Gen. Horatio Gates to lead a reconstituted American army from North Carolina to face the British in South Carolina had ended in complete disaster at Camden in August. The battle in the South now would be carried out by the roving bands of patriot militia until help could arrive.

On October 12, 1780, Gen. Nathanael Greene was appointed as Gates's successor and immediately set out to rebuild the shattered army. Earlier that month, a band of patriot militia had destroyed the left wing of the British army, mostly Loyalist militia at the battle of Kings Mountain, which relieved some of the pressure on Greene's efforts. On paper, Greene's army was a respectable 2,300 men. Furloughs, desertions, and illness, however, brought that number down to around 1,500, of which less than 1,000 were Continental regulars. In December, Greene was given the secret weapon that would help him in his task. Brig. Gen. Daniel Morgan reported for duty at the headquarters in Charlotte.

Morgan was a fighter who made his reputation early in the war during the failed 1775 invasion of Quebec. He was captured and released in 1777, just in time to take part in the Battle of Saratoga. The next few years saw Morgan's health decline, and conflicts with Congress put his future in doubt until he was ordered south.

The Battle of Cowpens was fought on January 17, 1781, between colonial and British forces, as part of the campaign in the Carolinas. The result was an overwhelming and surprising victory for the Americans and a turning point in the Revolutionary War. (MPI/Getty Images)

Knowing that his army needed time and supplies, Greene did the unthinkable. He divided his small force and gave half to Morgan with the task of moving west of the Catawba River to gather supplies and to raise the morale of the patriots in the area. Morgan would bolster his force with whatever militia would join him. His initial force would number close to 600 men, 400 Continentals and the rest Virginia militia that were mostly former Continentals who had served their time. Soon Morgan was joined by militia from South Carolina, North Carolina, and Georgia.

The British general Charles Cornwallis was looking to invade North Carolina, a plan that he had to delay in the wake of the loss at Kings Mountain. Reports of Morgan threatened the left flank of the army and forced Cornwallis to send Lt. Col. Banastre Tarleton and his British legion on a mission to destroy Morgan's force. Tarleton had made his name in a number of campaigns since the war started. His troops had captured American general Charles Lee in New Jersey and participated in the conquest of Charleston and at Camden, Fishing Creek, and Waxhaws. He had a reputation for viciousness and showing little mercy to the enemy.

Following rumors, Tarleton arrived at the British outpost of Ninety-Six with Morgan nowhere to be found. He then moved farther west, looking to draw Morgan out. For his part, Morgan avoided battle until he found the right place to make a stand at a place called the Cowpens.

One of the reasons that Morgan chose this particular area had to do with the militia. Up to this point, the record of the militia in open battle had been spotty at best. Reports of militia breaking in the face of the enemy began as soon as the first battle started and were exemplified in the Battle of Camden, when the entire militia ran before even fighting. Morgan knew that a large portion of his force would be made of militia, and by picking Cowpens as the location for the fight, he basically put his men in a box where even if they ran they had nowhere to go. The field was bordered in the rear by the Broad River and along the sides by thick forest and ravines. He hoped this would encourage them to stand a little stronger.

On the morning of January 17, 1781, General Morgan received word that Tarleton's force was on the way and deployed his troops. With the local militias swelling his ranks, he had somewhere between 800 to about 2,000 men, but accounts differ. He set up his men in three lines. The first line would be militia, approximately 150 men from North Carolina and Georgia. The center line would be the South Carolina militia under Andrew Pickens. The final line, on a low hill at the back of the battlefield, would be his Continentals from Maryland and Delaware as well as the best of the militia units. From an outside perspective, it would appear that the bulk of the troops in the formation would be the weak militia, a target too good for a man like Tarleton to pass up.

Morgan's plan was to have the first line of militia engage the British in a skirmish formation and fall back to join the second line. When the British closed in, the militia of the second line were to fire two volleys and then fall back behind the Continental line. From the night before the battle, stories abound of Morgan extolling his militia to give him two shots and fall back. He knew what to expect and would ask no more of them. The British would then find themselves facing the third line, supplemented by the militia that would reform to continue fighting.

Just before sunrise, Tarleton attacked with just over 1,100 tired and hungry men. Thinking he was facing mostly militia, he saw no need to survey the field or come up with an elaborate plan, he simply ordered his men to advance. The first wave of dragoons reached the skirmish line and took fire and continued their advance. Upon coming within range of the second line they were met with a withering volley, and then another, losing almost 40 percent of their officers at one time. The British regrouped and continued forward as the militia pulled back behind the Continental line, as planned. Thinking the American army had broken, the British charged the trained and disciplined Continental soldiers of the third line. The fighting was fierce and bloody.

Meanwhile, the British reserve force, the 71st Highlanders, were ordered to move against the right flank of the Americans. The American commander of the forces on that side saw the attack and ordered his troops to turn to meet it. The order was misheard and taken as an order to retreat. The units, in good order, turned from the advancing enemy and moved toward the rear. Thinking the retreat was real, the British charged. Morgan saw what was happening and ordered the men to turn and fire. At less than 30 yards' distance, the Americans fired a volley that simply knocked the Highlanders to a complete stop. The Americans charged with their bayonets with devastating effect.

A number of Highlanders surrendered on the spot; others kept fighting. The militia under Pickens had reformed by this point and began firing into the British flanks. All up and down the line, the British surrendered. Tarleton looked on in horror as his army was torn to pieces; falling back to his cavalry, he ordered them to charge and was refused. In one last desperate attempt, Tarleton gathered about 40 men and led them into the fight, only to find himself facing Lt. Col. William Washington and his light dragoons. After a brief skirmish, Tarleton managed to leave the field intact, unlike his army.

A little after an hour from when it began, the battle was over. Morgan's troops had suffered around 150 killed and wounded. The British had suffered almost 350 killed or wounded and over 800 men taken prisoner. For the Americans, the victory was a welcome one in the South after a long string of defeats. Morgan proved that, when used properly, the militia would fight well. In winning, he was also able to rouse the countryside that had been dubious before. For Cornwallis, the loss of Tarleton's force was a mighty blow. The best part of his army had been mauled and taken prisoner. He had lost his militia units at Kings Mountain, at Cowpens his light troops, and now had to change all his plans. These changes would eventually lead to a confrontation with Greene at Guilford Courthouse and from there a journey for Cornwallis to Yorktown.

It would be easy to say that this American victory set the stage for the endgame of the Revolution. Had Morgan not won and not won as convincingly as he did, the war may have continued. As it was, Cornwallis would be started on a path that would end in America winning the war.

Stuart Hatfield

See also: Cornwallis, Lord Charles; Greene, Nathanael

Further Reading

Babits, Lawrence. 2001. *A Devil of a Whipping: The Battle of Cowpens.* Chapel Hill: University of North Carolina Press.

Bobrick, Benson. 1997. *Angel in the Whirlwind.* New York: Penguin Books.

Buchanan, John. 1999. *The Road to Guilford Courthouse.* New York: Wiley & Sons.

Hibbert, Christopher. 1990. *Redcoats and Rebels.* New York: Norton Books.

CRAFTSMEN/ARTISANS

Craftsmen or artisans were central to the political and economic life of colonial America. From the beginning, production in North America was organized on a basis fundamentally different from that in England. It operated within a space opened up by the conquest of an indigenous civilization, that of North American Indians, and was entirely outside the constraints of a feudal past. For these reasons, the guild system, for example, was never transposed to the colonies, and shipbuilding, one of colonial America's most successful manufacturing enterprises that relied heavily on craftwork, developed little or no formal craft organization. The few guilds that did form in the colonies were generally unable to maintain their unity against the pressures of unrelenting immigration, the relatively smooth upward mobility from journeyman (a person who has served an apprenticeship at a trade or handicraft and is certified to work at it assisting or under another person, usually for a day at a time) to master, and the high wages dictated by almost all types of labor.

The division of craft labor firmly increased over time, and considerable cooperation existed among different craft workers, especially after 1750, despite the efforts by Britain to confine the colonial capacity to produce craft goods. For most of the Colonial Period, craft labor was organized in a fluid mode, allowing considerable horizontal mobility from one craft to another, and substantial vertical movement from journeyman to master and beyond. Even more, master-journeyman relations were less antagonistic than in England—which helps to explain the unity of these groups in their anti-British protests in the 1760s and 1770s—and this relative harmony lasted until the 1780s, when journeymen engaged in independent organization. Given the relative absence of guilds and the persistent shortage of skilled labor, colonial workmen often developed multiple skills and talents.

Found throughout the colonies, artisans were most heavily concentrated in towns and cities, especially the major seaports, although crafts were also practiced in rural areas by settled or tramping artisans. Craftsmen worked in a multitude of trades, ranging from goldsmithing, silversmithing, and cabinetmaking at the top; to butchering, baking, and carpentry in the middle; and tailoring or shoemaking at the bottom. The trades with the largest numbers of artisans were the building crafts, particularly carpentry and masonry, which might employ almost half of craftsmen during construction season; tailoring and shoemaking followed in size.

Mid-18th-century artisans could be classified as either wage earners, the beginning of a working class, or as master craftsmen, emerging bourgeois entrepreneurs, as in the course of a colonial career they were often both. Normally, a young man of 13 or 14 would contract with a master craftsman to learn a trade as an apprentice. He made an agreement with his master, who was responsible for his rudimentary education and clothing as well as teaching him the secrets of the trade. Initiating in the secrets of the most demanding trades, such as cabinetmaking or watchmaking, took many hours at the hands of the ablest craftsmen, who passed down knowledge accumulated over centuries of craftsmanship. The more rudimentary trades, such as shoemaking, which required awl and hammer skills, took less time to master.

Following release from agreement at the age of 21, the apprentice would become a wage earner, or journeyman, often working in various cities for master craftsmen. While the vast majority of artisans in colonial America remained craftsmen throughout their lives, upward mobility was possible within the middling or lower-middling ranks of society. If able and savvy, the journeyman would open his own business and buy a master's dwelling, which commonly included a lower-story shop and an upper floor where his family lived. In fact, many of these master tradesmen later became wealthy merchants, business owners, and, in some cases, the political leaders of the young country. Expert cabinetmakers, for example, participated directly in colonial trade, shipping thousands of Windsor chairs. Other highly skilled artisans worked closely with merchants in a developing capitalist economy operating under the rules of British mercantilism.

However, within the poorest trades, notably, shoemaking and tailoring, mobility to master craftsman status was not the rule. Moreover, even masters owning small shoemaker or tailoring shops often earned a subsistence living, with little security in times of personal crisis or economic recession. This was particularly true of Boston, a city impoverished by wars for the empire, where many craftsmen declined to subsistence levels. A notable case was the one of shoemaker George Robert Twelves Hewes, the last survivor of the Boston Tea Party (1773), who was imprisoned early in his career for small debts. Poorer artisans, like other economically weak city inhabitants, were also prey to the terror of epidemics, especially smallpox and yellow fever, that decimated the nation's seaports.

One important facet of America's early development of craftwork was the role played by slave artisans. Having its origins on the West Coast of Africa, slave art was an art of anonymity influenced by African imagery and later rechanneled as a functional aesthetic, with some famous examples being the iron balconies of New Orleans; the magnificent mansions of Charleston, South Carolina; or the delicate furnishings and implements at Jefferson's Monticello in Virginia. Receiving little credit for their labor, the slave artisans and craftsmen, through their artistic skills, provided the necessary workmanship of preindustrial America and became the first class of "technocrats" (technical experts) in the New World. Capable slaves were employed to meet the demands of emerging industrialism. The diversity of skills and occupations held by black slave artisans are clear examples of why the skilled slaves became the most important agents in the rise of plantation manufacturers. Each plantation became a more or less self-sufficient economy and required slaves with numerous skills necessary to maintain the community.

In the early 19th century, it became popular for middle-class rural Americans of modest means to take the decoration of their homes and furniture into their own hands. In 1825, Rufus Porter, an artist and early proponent of the American craft movement, published *A Select Collection of Valuable and Curious Arts, and Interesting Experiments Which Are Well Explained, and Warranted Genuine, and May Be Prepared, Safely and at Little Expense*, which is a book of instructions for domestic decorative arts, including wall, floor, and furniture painting. However, by the end of the 19th century, the preindustrial craft trades had almost disappeared, as industrial expansion and westward movement had largely severed American culture from early colonial American and Native American craft roots. Against this backdrop, the Arts and Crafts movement emerged during the late Victorian period in England, the most industrialized country in the world at that time. Louis Comfort Tiffany was a pioneer of the American craft movement, arguing for the placement of well-designed and crafted objects in the American home. Tiffany's elegant stained glass creations were influenced by the values of William Morris (textile designer, socialist activist, and leader of the British Arts and Crafts movement) and became America's leading embodiment of Art Nouveau.

Uneasiness about industrial life fueled a positive revaluation of handcraftsmanship and precapitalist forms of culture and society. Arts and Crafts designers sought to improve standards of decorative design, believed to have been devalued by mechanization, and to create environments in which beautiful and fine workmanship was put forward. The Arts and Crafts movement did not promote a particular style, but it did support reform as part of its philosophy and initiated a critique of industrial labor. As modern machines replaced workers, Arts and Crafts proponents called for an end to the division of labor and advanced the designer as craftsman. Nonetheless, the rise of urban centers and the inevitability of technology eventually brought the end of the Arts and Crafts movement. The search for nature and an idealist medieval era no longer represented a valid approach to living, and by the 1920s, machine-age modernity and the search for a national identity had captured the attention of designers and consumers, bringing an end to the handcrafted nature of the Arts and Crafts movement in America.

Craftsmen and artisans, white and black, slave and free, made significant contributions to the social, political, and economic landscape of colonial America, shaping the economy and contributing to the success of the American Revolution and 19th-century working-class politics. Although the importance of craftsmanship gradually diminished, its preservation remains of great relevance, not only for historical and practical reasons, but also for artistic and educational purposes.

Elena Popan

See also: Apprenticeships; Limners

Further Reading

Hume, Ivor Noel. 2001. *A Guide to the Artifacts of Colonial America.* Philadelphia: University of Pennsylvania Press.

Newton, James E. 1977. "Slave Artisans and Craftsmen: The Roots of Afro-American Art." *Black Scholar* 9, no. 3: 35–42.

Rediker, Marcus. 1982. "Good Hands, Stout Heart, and Fast Feet: The History and Culture of Working People in Early America." *Labur/Le Travail* 10: 123–144.

Rorabaugh, William J. 1988. *The Craft Apprentice: From Franklin to the Machine Age in America.* Oxford: Oxford University Press.

CUAUHTÉMOC (CA. 1494–1522)

Although Cuauhtémoc was the last emperor of the Aztec Empire, little is known about his early years. Although sources show a consensus that he was the son of Ahuitzótl, his mother's identity is shrouded in mystery. He was raised in Tenochtitlán as a scion of the ruling family. As a young man, he distinguished himself as both a warrior and leader, as evidenced by his assumption of the lordship of Tlatelolco around 1515. This post meant that he had achieved a position in the line of secession for the emperorship, which was held by his relative Montezuma II. His place in the Aztec hierarchy was enhanced through his marriage to the emperor's daughter, Tecuichpo.

As Hernán Cortés and his Spanish force approached Tenochtitlán during November 1519, Cuauhtémoc joined Cuitláhuac, Montezuma II's brother, in counseling the emperor to defend the city against possible invasion. Their advice went unheeded, as Montezuma II opted to be diplomatic and welcomed the Spaniards as visitors. Cortés promptly imprisoned him and seized control of the city. Cuauhtémoc responded by mobilizing the Aztec military. Initially, the warriors only engaged in minor skirmishing, as they did not want harm to befall their leader. In May 1520, Cortés left the city to confront Pánfilo de Narváez and his troops, who had been dispatched by Diego Velázquez, Spain's *adelantado* in Cuba, to arrest him. During his absence, conquistadors under the command of Capt. Pedro de Alvarado attacked a gathering of Aztecs engaged in a religious ceremony, killing many. Enraged by the affront to their spiritual lives, Cuauhtémoc led a major uprising in the city to challenge Spanish authority. The fighting temporarily ceased on June 24, 1520, as Cortés returned with reinforcements. When conflict resumed, the Aztecs were able to push the Spaniards to defensive positions at the emperor's palace. To placate the Aztecs, Cortés allowed Montezuma II to address the populace. Enraged by what they perceived as accommodation of the Spaniards, the Aztecs stoned their leader to death.

Cuitláhuac was selected to succeed his brother. Staunchly anti-Spanish, he joined with Cuauhtémoc in leading the Aztec resistance. They built a force of approximately 100,000 warriors, and on June 30, 1520, in a battle known by the Spanish as La Noche Triste, or the Sad Night, dealt a severe defeat to Cortés and his conquistadors that forced them to abandon Tenochtitlán. Rather than pursuing the remnant of Cortés's force and destroying it, Cuitláhuac instead turned his attention to tributary communities that had failed to meet their commitments. He subdivided his army and launched attacks on those locales, which resulted in the loss of warriors. The Aztec military capability was further diminished by a smallpox outbreak that included Cuitláhuac among its victims.

Cuauhtémoc was named emperor, and among his first acts was to order that Tenochtitlán be prepared for a siege that was eminent by Cortés and his Tlascala allies. Since the city was built on an island, all of the bridges and causeways to the mainland were destroyed. Provisions were brought in as more than 200,000 Aztec and allied warriors prepared for war. Cortés and his Tlascala allies constructed eight ships for waterborne assaults. Despite the efforts of the Aztecs to prevent access to the city by destroying the bridges, Spanish cavalry was still able to make attacks on Tenochtitlán. The use of cannon on ships and the cavalry forced Cuauhtémoc to abandon efforts to prevent the landing of the Spanish and their Native allies into the city.

The Aztecs then turned to guerrilla warfare. Rather than massing in large groups, which would make them susceptible to slaughter by cannon fire, the Aztecs instead relied on sneak attacks from roofs or in alleys. Since their tactics relied on buildings, the Spanish responded by tearing down buildings in an orderly fashion and dumping them into the water. The net effect was that the Aztec city, and places to hide, rapidly disappeared. The combination of heavy casualties, starvation, and rampant disease, caused the Aztec cause to fail. In an effort to gain reinforcements and food, Cuauhtémoc attempted to leave Tenochtitlán, but he was captured on August 13, 1521. Cortés, convinced there was gold and jewels in the city but finding none, tortured Cuauhtémoc to discover where the Aztec wealth was hidden. Cuauhtémoc refused to divulge the information.

In 1522, Cortés left Tenochtitlán to address issues in Honduras. He took Cuauhtémoc with him to ensure that the Aztec would not rise in rebellion to free their emperor. Over the course of the trip, Cortés received a tip that Cuauhtémoc and other Aztec nobles were planning to kill Cortés and rid all of Mexico of Spanish forces. Cortés accused Cuauhtémoc and those nobles of treason and hanged them on February 26, 1522.

John R. Burch Jr.

See also: Aztec; Cortés, Hernán; Mesoamerica; Montezuma II

Further Reading

Gillespie, Susan D. 1992. *The Aztec Kings: The Construction of Rulership in Mexica History.* Tucson: University of Arizona Press.

Gillingham, Paul. 2011. *Cuauhtémoc's Bones: Forging National Identity in Modern Mexico.* Albuquerque: University of New Mexico Press.

Hassig, Ross. *Aztec Warfare: Imperial Expansion and Political Control.* Norman: University of Oklahoma Press.

Smith, Michael E. 2011. *The Aztecs.* 3rd ed. New York: Wiley-Blackwell.

CULPEPER'S REBELLION

Culpeper's Rebellion was a 1677 revolt of the Carolina colonists against British overlords known as the lords proprietors in response to the British Navigation Acts that stifled free trade among the colonies. The rebellion was named for John Culpeper, the leader of the rebellion in Albemarle County of the Carolina Province, what is now the area of Elizabeth City, North Carolina. Success for Culpeper and his allies was brief, as British authorities quickly put down the rebellion.

Apparently, a root cause for unrest in Carolina was the lack of effective governing by the lords proprietors. These so-called lords proprietors were not necessarily persons of noble birth, but they were rich or powerful people appointed to govern the colony. The position of a lord proprietor was one of overseeing the colony, similar to a landlord or a supervisor. In Carolina, there were eight such men appointed to this position. The original lords proprietors were all at minimum knights. Their task was to establish laws and a proper governing order in the colony as well as to protect the settlers from French and Spanish raiders, pirates, and hostile Native Americans. Either their indifference or incompetence led to a failure to accomplish these goals.

One thing the lords proprietors did successfully was to attract colonists, which they did by offering 150 acres of land to each settler, allowing freedom of religion, and delaying tax collection until 1670. This effort resulted in an influx of settlers that reached a population of 6,600 by 1700 (compared to a quarter that number in Spanish Florida). Indentured servants were granted 100 acres upon completion of their term, and slave owners were given an additional 150 per slave imported to the colony.

A contributing factor in the difficulty of administering the governance of the Carolina colony was the physical geography of coastal Carolina, where overland travel between settlements was made difficult by various streams, inlets, and swamps. Shallow water along the coast made visits by oceangoing ships difficult.

An inherent point of contention between the colonists and their British overlords was the mercantile system, a colonial scheme by which the mother country would export as many goods as possible and import only the raw materials to make those goods to create an imbalance of trade that would enrich the mother country. This desire to capitalize on the opportunity to enrich Britain also led to the taxation of goods and services along each step of the production of raw materials and manufacturing and sale of finished goods. Colonists were allowed to harvest and cut lumber, but not to build furniture and other finished pieces from the wood they cut. That lumber would be sent to England for manufacture into finished products. Even essential tools such as shovels were forbidden to be manufactured in the colony. This resulting inefficiency of economic fairness and the taxes levied on goods made the price of goods available to the colonists prohibitively expensive, eventually reaching a point deemed intolerable by the settlers. (This problem would again crop up in the mid-18th century and lead to the America Revolution.)

Into this already contentious situation came a customs collector, Thomas Miller, appointed to a job he performed with a bit more zeal than appreciated by the colonists. Miller was made interim governor while the governor was away, and he used his authority to imprison rivals and advance his own agenda. Miller traveled with an entourage of armed men, either by necessity for his own protection or for the intimidating value of the show of force.

Unhappy colonists resisted the oppression by Miller, and about 40 leading colonists, including John Culpeper, a man with a reputation for willingness to engage in confrontation, sought to have Miller removed from office. Earlier attempts to have those taxes required by the Navigation Acts not collected by the lords proprietors were refused, as the lords proprietors feared losing their charter if they failed to collect the taxes.

The conspirators met and held their own elections and also tried and imprisoned Thomas Miller. The elusive Miller escaped to England, as he had once before when revolt threatened, and Culpeper followed him there to make the case of the colonists. Unfortunately for John Culpeper, the English government unsurprisingly sided with the lords proprietors and tried Culpeper for treason. With the support of some of the court against the haphazard rule by the lords proprietors, Culpeper was acquitted of the charges and returned home a hero.

Despite the moral victory in court, the status quo in Carolina did not actually change, but the attention to proper governance by the lords proprietors did. One of their members, Seth Sothel, was appointed governor. Sothel was abducted by pirates on his way to Carolina, and in his absence, George Durant, a co-conspirator of Culpeper, acted as governor and restored order until Sothel finally arrived in 1683. Sothel turned out to be corrupt and ineffective, and he was banished from the colony by the Assembly. A new governor, Phillip Ludwell, was appointed after another revolt in 1691 and ran a simplified government that allowed for good order and the growth of the colony. Ludwell accomplished this feat in part by appointing appropriate leading citizens of Albemarle County as his underlings instead of engaging in nepotism.

In 1719, the southern Carolina colony revolted against the lords proprietors, and by 1729, the Carolina province had been split into North Carolina and South Carolina. The tradition of revolt started by the Culpeper Rebellion would come to maturity a century later when all the colonies would rebel and form the United States of America.

Matthew D. Zarzeczny

See also: Navigation Acts

Further Reading

McIlvenna, Noeleen. 2009. *A Very Mutinous People: The Struggle for North Carolina, 1660–1713.* Chapel Hill: University of North Carolina Press.

Rankin, Hugh F. 2011. *Upheaval in Albemarle: The Story of Culpeper's Rebellion, 1675–1689.* Whitefish: Literary Licensing, LLC.

CUZCO

Cuzco, Peru (also spelled Cusco or Kosko, Qosqo or Qusqu in Quechua), was the administrative, geographical, and spiritual capital of the extensive Inca Empire, which flourished from about 1400 to 1534. Cuzco is considered the oldest continually inhabited city in the Western Hemisphere. The name is derived from the Quechua word for "navel" or "center." Cuzco was considered a holy city—a place of pilgrimage for the Inca. During the height of the empire, there were millions of subjects in the realm and up to 200,000 inhabitants in the city itself.

According to legend, the sun god Inti created the first Inca, Manco Capac. He was charged with finding the center of the earth—a place where he could plunge a golden rod into the ground until it disappeared. He went forth with Mama Ocllo, daughter of the moon, to establish the capital of their empire in this fertile location. They named the spot Cuzco, meaning "navel of the earth" in Quechua.

Cuzco lies in a fertile glacial basin at an elevation of 11,200 feet. Crops could be grown in the valley, and the surrounding hillsides provided excellent pasture. Cuzco is also situated where three rivers meet—the Huatanay, Tullumayo, and Chunchul—providing ample water for diversion into canals.

The Inca called their empire Tawantisuyo, which means the Land of the Four Quarters. Four principal highways radiated out from Cuzco to the four quarters of the empire. Cuzco was not simply the capital, but it was an *axis mundi*—the center of existence—and a reflection of Incan power. The city was divided into two sections, upper and lower, which paralleled the upper and lower social stratifications of the residents. Cuzco was further divided into quarters that represented the four quarters of the empire, and people from those regions inhabited their representative sections of the city. Forty-one sacred sight lines (*ceques*) and well-paved roads radiated out from the central plaza, dividing space and time as a further reminder that Cuzco was the center of the world.

Cuzco was initially laid out in the form of a puma, though some scholars dispute this and take the description metaphorically. The area between the Huatanay and Tullumayo Rivers is described as the body of the puma; the imperial metropolis of Pumachupan forms the tail, and the temple complex of Sacsahuaman on a rise overlooking the city serves as the head. The upper section of the city, the *hanan*, was higher in elevation and more prestigious than the *hurin*, its lower, southern counterpart. The center of the city was dominated by the double plazas of Haucaypata (Terrace of Repose) and Cusipata (Fortune Terrace) divided by the Saphy River, where state and religious ceremonies were held. The most important and splendid building in Cuzco was the Coricancha, also called the Golden Enclosure or Temple of the Sun. According to legend, the Coricancha was built by the first Inca emperor and was expanded in 1438 by Pachacuti (1438–1471/72), who also built Machu Picchu. It was the most sacred of all Inca sites and considered to be the very center of the world. Inside, individual temples (*wasi*) were built in honor of the sun god Inti, the moon goddess Mama Kilya, the creator god Viracocha, the god of thunder Illapa, and the rainbow god Cuichu. The walls of the Coricancha were covered with sheets of gold, which invading Spaniards stripped and sent back to Spain in the 16th century.

Royal palaces and religious compounds dominated the center of the city. Each reigning Inca built a new palace complex to house his family and retainers. A series of sacred agricultural fields, parklands, fountains and canals were scattered among the buildings. The outskirts of the city had vast storehouses that held provisions distributed to city residents. Streets were narrow and stepped because the Inca did not have wheeled vehicles. Occupation within the city itself was primarily for administrators, nobility, and priests. The farming and artisan communities sprawled into the valley beyond the city walls. At the time of the Spanish conquest, approximately 40,000 people lived in the city proper and another 200,000 in the surrounding area.

During the reign of Pachacuti, the empire reached its pinnacle. He directed extensive building projects. He also completely reorganized society, creating a unified social system to absorb the dozens of ethnic and political groups that the Inca conquered. Religion was another unifying force. The Inca adopted the gods of the peoples they conquered, building and maintaining shrines and temples in Cuzco for them. The calendar was packed with public festivals linked to plowing, planting, and harvesting.

Conquest

Huayna Capac, the 11th Inca, was the last to rule over a united empire—the largest ever seen in the Americas. After ascending to the throne in 1493, he gathered his forces and headed to the northern limits of his empire, along the border of present-day Ecuador, where he fought a long series of battles. He was away for so long that the stability of the court in Cuzco and the empire itself began to unravel. Administrative decisions took a long time to reach the capital, and controlling the empire became difficult.

Simultaneously, Europeans swept into the New World, bringing Old World diseases along. Epidemics, including smallpox and the common cold, ravaged Native populations. Shortly before dying in a wave of one epidemic, Huayna Capac divided the empire between his two sons. Both wanted to rule over all, and a bloody civil war ensued.

Francisco Pizarro (ca. 1471–1541), a Spanish conquistador, marched southward in the wake of the destruction, killing thousands of unarmed Natives with a few dozen armed soldiers. Pizarro entered Cuzco in 1533 and claimed the city for King Charles V. After stripping the gold, silver, and jewels from the buildings and shipping the riches back to Spain, many structures were razed, and Spanish churches and houses were built on the foundations. The city declined in importance after Pizarro moved his capital to the coastal site of Lima in 1535. Few significant events have impacted Cuzco since the Spanish conquest, except for strong earthquakes in 1650 and 1950. The "rediscovery" of Machu Picchu in 1911 returned Cuzco to prominence as a tourist hub from the small, provincial city it remained for almost 400 years.

Jill M. Church

See also: Columbian Exchange; Inca; Pizarro, Francisco

Further Reading

Bauer, Brian S. 2004. *Ancient Cuzco: Heartland of the Inca.* Austin: University of Texas Press.

D'Altroy, Terence N. 2002. *The Incas.* Malden, MA: Blackwell Publishers, Inc.

Davies, Nigel. 1997. *The Ancient Kingdoms of Peru.* London: Penguin Books.

Farrington, Ian. 2013. *Cusco: Urbanism and Archaeology in the Inka World.* Ancient Cities of the New World Series. Gainesville: University Press of Florida.

D

DECLARATION OF INDEPENDENCE

The Declaration of Independence is the document in which the 13 British colonies in North America formally and officially cut all political ties and allegiance with the government of Great Britain. It is widely considered one of—if not *the*—founding document of the United States of America. The Declaration of Independence was written between June 11 and June 28, 1776, in Philadelphia, Pennsylvania, and the final draft was accepted by the Second Continental Congress on July 4, 1776, as they met in the Pennsylvania State House in Philadelphia. The State House soon became known as Independence Hall because of its connection with both the Declaration of Independence and the U.S. Constitution, which was also debated and composed there, 11 years after the Declaration of Independence was adopted.

John Trumbull's *The Declaration of Independence* depicts the Committee of Five submitting their draft of the document to the Second Continental Congress on June 28, 1776, one week prior to the actual signing. The painting, which has been displayed in the Capitol Rotunda since 1826, shows 42 of the 56 signers of the declaration, including John Adams, Benjamin Franklin, John Hancock, and Thomas Jefferson. (Corel)

Although modern independence celebrations take place on July 4 each year, John Adams famously predicted that Americans would henceforward celebrate July 2 as the true date of independence, as that was the date of Congress's vote in favor of the resolution dissolving ties to Great Britain. On July 1 and 2, 1776, the Congress voted in favor of a motion by Virginia delegate Richard Henry Lee to declare all 13 colonies completely separated from the British Empire and united in their resistance to British colonial authority.

Prior to this, there had been separate "declarations of independence" in several colonies, most notably North Carolina. Many of these were issued in response to the Coercive Acts of 1774, known in America as the Intolerable Acts. However, these statements—like the Fairfax Resolves, Suffolk Resolves, and Fincastle Resolutions—varied in terms of their scope, authority, and jurisdiction. Many were little more than denunciations of the Coercive Acts or statements in support of colonial boycotts of British goods. Even the most substantial of these resolutions, the Halifax Resolves of April 1776, were not a formal declaration of independence or separation but rather a series of instructions sent by the legislature of North Carolina to its delegates at the Second Continental Congress, authorizing them to encourage Congress to consider declaring the colonies independent. Despite the limited nature of the Halifax Resolves, they were nevertheless the first time a colony had authorized their delegates to encourage a general vote on independence for the 13 colonies.

Although fighting between the colonies and the British Empire had begun some 15 months before the creation of the Declaration of Independence, in April 1775, there was still widespread debate over the goals of the Revolution as well as the efficacy and legality of independence. As such, the Declaration of Independence adopted by the Second Continental Congress was the first document to officially declare that all 13 colonies were separated from English rule, and it is the first official document to define the colonies as the United States of America. The task of writing the Declaration of Independence was given to Virginia delegate Thomas Jefferson and four other delegates who made up the "Committee of Five." Congress had selected committee members from the most prominent colonies, and although the majority of the document was written by Jefferson, the committee included other luminaries of the Revolution. Benjamin Franklin of Pennsylvania, Roger Sherman of Connecticut, John Adams of Massachusetts, and Robert Livingston of New York all contributed to the final document. In an interesting historical irony, Robert Livingston was recalled by the New York colonial legislature and so was not one of the signers of the Declaration of Independence, despite being one of the men tasked with creating the document.

In later years, John Adams claimed that the Congress—and even Thomas Jefferson himself—had originally intended for Adams to write the Declaration of Independence. By Adams's own account, however, he had deferred in favor of Jefferson. This was partly because of Jefferson's recognized skill as a writer and partly because Adams feared that his irascible nature would cause some delegates to reject the document if he wrote it. As there are no official minutes of the committee's proceedings, the only insight into the drafting process comes from later accounts and recollections from Adams and Jefferson. Unfortunately, these accounts are incomplete and occasionally contradictory. The contributions made by Roger Sherman and Robert Livingston seem to have been minimal and mostly editorial in nature, while Adams's and Franklin's impact on the finished document were more substantive.

In the process of editing the final document, approximately one-fourth of Thomas Jefferson's original text was removed or substantially revised by either the Committee of Five or by the Congress as a whole. Some of these changes were done for purely stylistic reasons, while other changes were made to satisfy the demands of specific congressional delegates. In one significant instance, Southern delegates removed passages that were critical of the slave trade. Jefferson's intended draft included a large section in the list of grievances against the English Crown, wherein he blamed King George III for forcing the American colonies to participate in the African slave trade. This section was rejected by many of the delegates from slaveholding colonies because it was too inflammatory and implicitly condemned the institution of slavery itself. Additionally, there was some concern that such accusations would alienate those few prominent Britons who supported the colonies' push for independence.

The Declaration of Independence is not formally divided. Rather, it consists of five commonly agreed-upon sections: the introduction, the preamble, the list of grievances against the English Crown, the denunciation of King George III, and the conclusion, which contains the official declaration of colonial independence. The preamble is three paragraphs in length and outlines the reason for the document's creation. It also includes the broadly humanistic ideas that informed Jefferson's worldview, which he claimed were essential responsibilities of all governments to ensure the happiness of all people. These portions of the Declaration of Independence are among the most famous lines in the English language and have been quoted or paraphrased countless times since Jefferson wrote them. Many of the ideas and language found in the preamble were drawn from the earlier political theories of English philosopher John Locke as well as from the Virginia Declaration of Rights penned by George Mason in June 1776.

The list of grievances contains 27 specific and general accusations against the English government, including that the king had illegally dissolved colonial legislatures, interfered or otherwise limited the colonies' overseas commerce, forced colonists to quarter British soldiers, and issued taxes without the consent of colonists or their elected representatives. Jefferson intentionally targeted the reigning monarch, King George III, and made only veiled reference to Parliament, the English legislative body. Again, this was done partially to avoid upsetting members of Parliament who supported the colonies. It was not until the last few sentences of the Declaration of Independence that the official announcement of separation is made. Even here, Jefferson borrowed liberally from existing writings. In this case, the terminology of the actual declaration of colonial separation came in large part from the Lee Resolution of July 2, whereby Congress announced the dissolution of all political ties between the colonies and Great Britain.

A total of 56 men signed the Declaration of Independence. However, there is uncertainty about when all 56 signatures were actually added to the document. Some accounts claim that everyone signed the Declaration of Independence on July 4, 1776, when it was accepted by the Second Continental Congress. Others point out that several of the signers had not even been elected to Congress on July 4. Most historians today accept accounts saying the Declaration of Independence was signed in several stages, starting on July 4, 1776, with another group of signings on or shortly after August 2, 1776. The document went into effect when it was accepted by Congress on July 4, and so the signatures were not necessary to make the Declaration of Independence official.

Copies of the Declaration of Independence were distributed throughout the colonies, reprinted in newspapers, and read aloud at public gatherings. Reaction in the colonies was mostly positive (i.e., in favor of independence). However, Loyalists rejected the right of rebellion described in the Declaration of Independence, and other commentators pointed out the hypocrisy of claiming universal rights while ignoring the plight of African American slaves. Congress sent copies to European capitals, including Florence, Warsaw, and Paris. British officials in America sent copies to England, where they first appeared in August 1776. Interestingly, England's prime minister, Lord Frederick North, issued no official response at the time.

Although Americans celebrate July 4 as Independence Day, the United States was not officially independent until the agreement on the Treaty of Paris of 1783 and its subsequent ratification by the American Congress of Confederation on January 14, 1784. Today, the Declaration of Independence is displayed at the National Archives building in Washington, D.C.; however, that version is not the original document created in Philadelphia. Rather, it is the engrossed version that was printed later and which includes the 56 signatures. Of the original 200 broadsheets printed in Philadelphia on July 4, 1776, approximately two dozen are thought to remain.

Shawn Selby

See also: Continental Congresses; Independence Hall; Jefferson, Thomas; Locke, John

Further Reading

Maier, Pauline. 1998. *American Scripture.* New York: Vintage.
McCullough, David. 2006. *1776.* New York: Simon & Schuster.
Wills, Garry. 2002. *Inventing America.* New York: Mariner Books.

DEERFIELD MASSACRE

When the settlers in the small frontier community of Deerfield, Massachusetts, went to sleep on the evening of February 28, 1704, they expected no change from their normal daily routine the following day. Before dawn, the quiet of the New England night was shattered by shouting men bursting into the village to bring unexpected death and destruction. Violent raids along the amorphous border between the French and English colonies in North America were nothing new during the vicious series of conflicts known as the French and Indian Wars that raged on an off between 1688 and 1763. In this case, the victims were English and their attackers a mixed force of French and their indigenous allies from several tribes. By late morning, the village lay in ruins, most of its inhabitants were dead, the attackers were already retracing their path to safety. As one of the more famous of these deadly clashes, the Deerfield Massacre has come to symbolize the savage nature of warfare as practiced on the North American frontier.

The competition for wealth through overseas trade and colonization led to a series of four wars between England and France between 1688 and 1763. Known in American history collectively as the French and Indian Wars, a name derived from the perspective of British colonists, each had its counterpart in the global conflicts between the two nations: the War of the League of Augsburg (1688–1697), the War of Spanish Succession (1702–1713), the War of Austrian Succession (1744–1748), and the Seven Years' War (1756–1763). The second of these, known to the colonists as Queen Anne's War, was fought mainly in Europe, but, as with prior and later conflicts, it also spread in varying degrees to the colonial empires of the contending powers.

In North America, there were three general areas of conflict. The first of these was along the disputed border between the English colonies in the Carolinas and the Spanish possessions in Florida. Spain was an ally of France in this conflict, and therefore an enemy of England, which led each side to launch raids into the territory claimed by the other or in the disputed areas where land claims of the two European powers overlapped. Tensions were heightened by the religious differences between Catholic Spain and Protestant England and were further inflamed in the English colonies by Spanish incitement of the indigenous people to raid the English frontier settlements. Far to the north, the war pitted English settlers in Newfoundland against the French in Plaisance with the same religious divisions and the same form of warfare—intermittent raids by one side upon the other. Although the French briefly occupied St. John's, the English soon reclaimed it, and there was little general effect except damage to the economies of each side.

The third area of conflict, and the one in which the more significant action took place, set colonists in New England against their French counterparts in Acadia and Canada. Again, border disagreements were inflamed by religious differences and, among the English, by the French use of indigenous allies to carry our terror raids among the English frontier settlements. The indigenous French allies were mainly members of the Algonquin-speaking Wabanaki Confederacy—the Abenaki, Maliseet, Mi'kmaq, Passamaquoddy, and Penobscot. Some of these groups had originally inhabited portions of present-day Maine and New England, so at the time, their alliance with France also posed the opportunity of halting further English encroachments on their lands and perhaps even rolling back the frontier. These warriors, ideally suited for the hit-and-run tactics that were predominantly used on the frontier, together with their French allies, many of whom had lived among the indigenous peoples and were familiar with this type of warfare, formed a potent force that could suddenly attack isolated forts and settlements and then disappear back into the wilderness.

English use of indigenous people during Queen Anne's War was limited because their usual allies, the nations of the Iroquois Confederacy in central New York, remained mostly neutral, despite persistent British entreaties. Thus, when the war began, most of the frontier raids were those of the French and their allies into English territory, principally a series led by Michel Leneuf de la Vallière de Beaubassin against outposts from Wells to Falmouth (modern Portland), in Maine, which killed or captured some 300 settlers and caused others to abandon vulnerable frontier settlements for larger, more secure locations closer to the coast.

Of the remaining outposts, perhaps the largest was Deerfield, Massachusetts, which had originally been settled in the Connecticut River valley in 1673 on land occupied by the Algonquin-speaking Pocumtuck tribe. The English had attempted to purchase the land, but the transaction was suspect. Eventually, the remaining Pocumtuck were forced out, and they moved north to seek protection from the French and other Algonquin-speaking peoples in Canada, from which they launched an unsuccessful attempt to retake their land in 1675–1676. Thus, in addition to the French-English animosity, there was a specific history of hostility between the colonists in Deerfield and the previous inhabitants who had been forced out.

With the outbreak of war and the raids along the Maine frontier, tensions among the Massachusetts settlements were high. Rumors of attacks on the colonies were rampant through 1703, causing settlers in Deerfield to repair the wooden stockade protecting their town. It was a small settlement consisting of a meetinghouse and perhaps 40-odd cabins housing approximately 271 people, nearly all subsistence farmers and their families, and 20 soldiers. On at least two occasions, the militia was called out under threats of attack, but nothing materialized. With the onset of winter, villagers began to relax, as the threat of attack appeared to diminish with the arrival of less hospitable weather. Unknown to them, mortal danger wax approaching.

During the summer and early fall of 1703, plans matured in Canada for a raid into the Connecticut Valley. By the beginning of 1704, Jean-Baptiste Hertel de Rouville had gathered a force in Chambly, south of Montréal. Born in nearby Trois-Rivières, he was a veteran of King William's War (1688–1697), in which he had taken part in raids into the Seneca territories in western New York and in the defense of Québec. Among his force were 48 French, including four of his brothers, and approximately 240 Indians, including some Pocumtuck, whose motive for revenge was evident. Despite security, word reached the frontier settlements of a possible raid, so the residents of Deerfield all retired into their stockade for protection during the night.

Arriving on February 28, 1704, Hertel de Rouville kept his men hidden while he observed the activities of the residents. One of the things he noticed was that high snowbanks had been allowed to accumulate against at least one of the stockade walls meant to protect those inside. After dark, he sent several men up the snow, where they were able to gain entry and open the front gate. The French and their allies swept inside. The first warning most residents received was the smashing in of their doors or the wild shouting and firing from outside their cabins, if they had been lucky enough to avoid the initial onslaught. In a few of the cabins, the residents were able to hold out until morning, but in the rest of the settlement, doors were smashed and people killed or hustled outside into captivity. As the raiders left in the early morning, they set fire to the settlement, burning some 17 of the 41 homes. Estimates on the casualties vary, but the most reliable appear to be that 11 raiders were killed and 22 wounded, including Hertel de Rouville. Among the English, 49 died, including 5 soldiers, 10 men, 9 women, and 25 children. An additional 7 men from Hadley died after blundering into an ambush while pursuing the attackers. The raiders took 109 prisoners, about 40 percent of the population, along with 3 French traders who had been in the settlement when it was attacked.

The raiders retreated quickly to avoid pursuing English militia. Because of this, they hurried their captives along, and those who could not maintain the pace through the roughly 300 miles of brutal winter weather on the way back to Canada were killed, usually the very young and the old because they were the weakest. Estimates again vary, but it appears that 89 survived the journey, which would leave 20 to have died or been killed during the trek to Montréal. Once there, most of the younger children were taken to the villages of their captors, where they were adopted into indigenous families. The most celebrated of these was perhaps Eunice Williams, the eight-year-old daughter of Rev. John Williams, who wrote a detailed account of his experience during his own captivity. Eunice was adopted into a Mohawk family, where she became completely assimilated, marrying a Mohawk man in 1713 at age 16. Although she visited her original family years later, she lived the rest of her life as a Mohawk.

When word spread of the plight of the captives' families, surrounding communities took up collections in an attempt to purchase the prisoners' freedom. In the meantime, the French also worked to acquire the freedom of many of the people through negotiations with their captors. Between 1704 and 1706, about 60 of the survivors were thus returned to New England. At least 36 survivors chose to remain in the indigenous or French communities where they had been taken or bartered.

In the wake of the raid, Massachusetts governor Joseph Dudley dispatched some 2,000 troops to its frontier, and the colony increased its bounty on indigenous scalps from £40 to £100, an increase of 250 percent. Mounting calls for retribution throughout New England led to a series of raids on Acadian villages, one for the purpose of capturing prisoners who might be exchanged for the Deerfield captives. The raid—the memory of which was kept alive by the publication of John Williams's narrative of his captivity, *The Redeemed Captive Returning to Zion*—also heightened the religious animosity between New England Protestants and French Catholics and provided popular support for the removal of indigenous people from within the English colonial borders.

James S. Pula

See also: Frontier; Massachusetts Bay

Further Reading

Demos, John. 1994. *The Unredeemed Captive: A Family Story from Early America.* New York: Knopf.

Haefeli, Evan, and Kevin Sweeney. 2003. *Captors and Captives: The 1704 French and Indian Raid on Deerfield.* Amherst: University of Massachusetts Press.

Melvoin, Richard I. 1988. *New England Outpost: War and Society in Colonial Deerfield.* New York: Norton.

Smith, Mary. 1991. *Boy Captive of Old Deerfield.* Deerfield, MA: Pocumtuck Valley Memorial Association.

Taylor, John. 1969. *The Redeemed Captive Returning to Zion: Or, the Captivity and Deliverance of Rev. John Williams of Deerfield.* New York: Kraus.

DEFERENCE

Deference was one of the many ways in which people of different levels of social, economic, and political power interacted with one another in colonial America. Poor white men, African American slaves, and women sometimes deferred, either willingly or unwillingly, to the authority of elite white males in government and society. The elite, in turn, often relied on their personal respectability and influence as well as legal and physical coercion to compel the obedience of poorer white males, women, and slaves. In reality, deference was part of a complex series of negotiations that occurred daily among people of different classes, genders, and races in colonial America to determine the locus of power within their relationships.

The elite certainly expected lower classes, genders, and races to demonstrate deference. Because they were better educated, more worldly, and wealthier, elite white men believed that they were the most virtuous (for colonial Americans, virtue meant placing the interests of the entire community above your self-interest) citizens and therefore could govern in the best interests of everyone. In the words of one Bostonian in 1749, "A Man of Reading, Observation, and daily conversant with Affairs of Police and Commerce, is certainly better qualified for a Legislator, than a Retailer of Rum and small Beer called a Tavern-keeper" (Smith 2005, 341). George Washington revealed his expectation of deference when he referred to colonial Virginia voters as "plebians whose unstable minds are agitated by every breath of novelty . . . and nonsense" (Beeman 2004, 42).

At times, common people of various classes, genders, and races reciprocated the elite's expectation of deference. Confronted by discriminatory colonial legal codes and the threat of physical punishment, slaves and women particularly recognized the negative consequences that could result from a lack of deference to their masters or husbands. Common white male voters throughout the colonies consistently elected their wealthy neighbors with whom they shared economic and social connections as well as a belief in virtue and disinterestedness to local and colonial government offices. Wealthy Virginia planters' common practice of treating their neighbors to food and drink before and during elections best illustrates the deferential relationship between elite officeholders and common voters in colonial America.

At other times, however, women, slaves, and poorer white men ignored and even defied the elite's expectation of authority. The elite may have considered the common people to be their inferiors, but ordinary men and women did not consider every wealthy white man as their social and political superior. In the eyes of many common people, authority had to be proven and earned, not granted simply on the basis of wealth or status. Many women, such as female indentured servants in the unhealthy and labor-starved 17th-century Chesapeake, took advantage of social and economic conditions to flout patriarchal legal restrictions. African slaves throughout the colonies retained aspects of their African identities and ran away from their masters. Common white male voters counterbalanced their deference to the elite in elections by voicing their views and protecting their interests as members of county juries and political crowds. When common white men believed that the elite acted without regard to the interests of the entire community, they frequently formed crowds of ordinary people to voice their displeasure. These popular protests were particularly prevalent on colonial America's frontier, erupting in incidents such as the Paxton Boys in Pennsylvania, in 1764, and the Regulator Movements in North and South Carolina from 1765 to 1771.

The rise of popular protest movements on the frontier and the emergence of class politics in such urban areas as Philadelphia and Boston suggest that the nature of deference in colonial America changed over the course of the 18th century. As increasing numbers of poorer white males rejected deference to their wealthy male neighbors, they altered the criteria for deference. Where before they had given respect to men who demonstrated virtue, they now increasingly gave authority to men who displayed virulent autonomy based on manly prowess and economic success. This renegotiation of power relations among white men, however, required greater deference based on gender and race. As deference among white men broke down and transformed, white males of all classes demanded greater deference from those who in their view lacked this autonomy—women, African American slaves, and Native Americans.

Life in colonial America was a constant negotiation of power within the myriad relationships in which colonial Americans engaged. Whether they were in the bedroom, the kitchen, the slave quarter, the polling place, the public streets, or the shop or tavern, individuals chose from a wide array of means of negotiating their own power and place within a group. Deference was one such method that some colonial Americans used to negotiate their place among the people around them. At times, they chose (or were forced) to defer to those they viewed (or had to view) as their social and political betters. At other times, ordinary Americans rejected the elite's expectation of deference and asserted their own interests.

Kevin Yeager

See also: Republicanism

Further Reading

Beeman, Richard. 2004. *The Varieties of Political Experience in Eighteenth-Century America.* Philadelphia: University of Pennsylvania Press.

Brown, Kathleen M. 1998. "Antiauthoritarianism and Freedom in Early America." *Journal of American History* 85: 77–85.

Nobles, Gregory. 2005. "A Class Act: Redefining Deference in Early American History." *Early American Studies* 3: 286–302.

Smith, Barbara Clark. 2005. "Beyond the Vote: The Limits of Deference in Colonial Politics." *Early American Studies* 3: 341–362.

Smolenksi, John. 2005. "From Men of Property to Just Men: Deference, Masculinity, and the Evolution of Political Discourse in Early America." *Early American Studies* 3: 253–285.

Wood, Gordon S. 1992. *The Radicalism of the American Revolution*. New York, Knopf.

Zuckerman, Michael. "Endangered Deference, Imperiled Patriarchy: Tales from the Marchlands." *Early American Studies* 3: 232–252.

DELAWARE

Delaware, the second-smallest state in the United States, was one of the 13 original colonies and states. The state's name comes from the English nobleman Thomas West, the 3rd Baron De La Warr, who was also the first colonial governor of Virginia.

Consisting of only 1,982 square miles, Delaware is located in the mid-Atlantic region of the United States and is bordered by Maryland to the south and west, New Jersey to the northeast, and Pennsylvania to the north. Having long had to battle for respect because of its diminutive geographic stature, when the time came, it seized the honor of becoming the first state in the union, happily ratifying the newly established Constitution less than three months after its adoption. And yet that was only one way in which, despite its small size, Delaware made an outsized impact on the early history of the United States.

Prior to its initial colonization by the Dutch, who landed in Zwaanendael, near present-day Lewes, in 1631, the area was inhabited by a number of different Native American groups, most prominently the Lenape in the northern part and the Nanticoke in the south. Indeed, they did not greet the arrival of the Dutch with any great joy. In fact, efforts by the Europeans to colonize Delaware got off to a rather inauspicious start, as within a year of its settlement, all the residents of the community in Zwaanendael were killed in a dispute with local Native American tribes.

In 1638, a second effort was undertaken when a group of Swedish, Dutch, and Finnish explorers, headed by Peter Minuit, established a trading post and colony called New Sweden in an area known as Fort Christina (now Wilmington). That colony lasted until 1655, when it fell victim to a Dutch force led by Peter Stuyvesant, who established a fort at what is today New Castle before conquering and then annexing New Sweden. The next move in colonial musical chairs came in 1664, when an English fleet headed by Sir Robert Carr and backed by James, the Duke of York, conquered the Dutch in 1664.

Part of the reason for this back and forth was the fact that Delaware was in the middle of the ongoing trade and colonizing competition between the British and the Dutch. This competition led to a number of low-level wars that in turn shifted control of the colony. Finally, in 1682, control of most of what is now Delaware was vested in William Penn when James passed his ownership to the Quaker leader. Penn sought an access route from his Pennsylvania colony to the sea, a role that Delaware, which became known as the Lower Counties on the Delaware, fit nicely.

This did not completely settle the ownership disputes, however, for Charles Calvert (Lord Baltimore) contested William Penn's claim to Delaware. But England ultimately ruled for Penn, although disputes over the Maryland-Delaware border continued until 1769, with the establishment of the Mason-Dixon Line.

By 1704, Pennsylvania had grown tremendously, and the colony's leaders did not want to have to worry about input or assent from the lower Delaware counties. At the same time, the inhabitants of the lower counties wanted freedom from the overriding Quaker influence in Pennsylvania. Consequently, the two areas began to meet separately, and a separate assembly was granted to Delaware in 1704, with New Castle serving as host of the first assembly meeting. That body operated as an independent governing body, making decisions about the government and the economy while also passing laws. Delaware was still technically under the authority of Pennsylvania's governor, but its operations essentially established its independent authority, despite the fact that both Pennsylvania and Delaware operated under the same Crown-based colonial government—but similar shared executive oversight also existed in New Jersey and New York as well as Massachusetts and New Hampshire during the same basic period.

As the colony developed its economy, it came to increasingly rely on tobacco as its primary cash crop. In addition, its labor force, which had initially been based in indentured servants, turned to slaves, and in the pre-Revolutionary period, Delaware became a major slave importer. Slavery would continue to be a major part of the labor force until after the Revolution, when slavery in Delaware diminished in part because of a change in the state's economy. Indeed, with mixed farming coming to the fore and tobacco growing losing its luster, there was less need for the slave labor that had supported it.

As tensions with Great Britain increased in the aftermath of the French and Indian War, Delaware warily watched the developing movement. The colony's relations with the British governing forces were generally congenial, and the Colonial Assembly was allowed more independence than many of the other colonial bodies. And yet, New Castle lawyer Thomas Kean was an early and vocal opponent of the Stamp Act. Too, Kent County's John Dickinson—who was an influential figure in the governments of both Pennsylvania and Delaware during the Revolutionary and early federal periods—was also one of the most influential authors of the Revolutionary era.

Indeed, as the movement toward independence grew stronger, McKean and Caesar Rodney convinced the Colonial Assembly to declare itself separate from the rule of both Great Britain and Pennsylvania on June 15, 1776, only days after the formal resolution for independence had been introduced in the Continental Congress. However, when it came time for the vote to be taken in Philadelphia, despite the state's expressed intentions, George Read could not bring himself to vote to break away from the Mother Country, leaving him and McKean at odds. Happily, for a Continental Congress that had agreed that a vote for independence had to be unanimous, an ill Caesar Rodney, who had returned to Delaware to serve as a general in the colony's militia, rode through the night and arrived in Philadelphia on July 2 in time to break the state's deadlock and rescue the cause.

During the Revolutionary War, the state was more of a thoroughfare and occupied territory than a battle site. Although the Delaware Blue, led by John Haslet (who would later die at the Battle of Princeton), was an early and well-regarded regiment that did good work outside the state, Gen. Sir William Howe marched right through the state in August 1777 on his way to a victory at the Battle of Brandywine and the subsequent capture of Philadelphia. The only real military engagement of the effort came at the Battle of Cooch's Bridge in New Castle County. Following the victory at Brandywine, the British occupied Wilmington for most of the rest of the war, promising freedom for any slaves that joined their forces, encouraging the substantive local Loyalist population, and disrupting trade and commerce.

In the aftermath of the war, Delaware's leaders were in the forefront of those calling for a strong central government. Indeed, they had been one of the handful of states that had sent representatives to the September 1786 Annapolis Convention, and it was Delaware's John Dickinson who presented to the Congress that convention's recommendation that a new convention be held in May 1787 to revise the Articles of Confederation. When that recommendation was accepted and the Constitutional Convention convened, Delaware was represented by Richard Bassett, Gunning Bedford Jr., Jacob Broom, John Dickinson, and George Read. Having gotten over the fear that had gripped him over the vote for independence, Read emerged as a leader of Delaware's delegation as well as its subsequent ratification effort. The delegation was strongly opposed to the original Virginia Plan, with its population-based representation plans, but it did support the strong central government. However, the Delaware delegation readily supported the ultimate Great Compromise with its guarantee of equal representation for states in the Senate. In addition, Dickinson played an important role in developing the all-important, if controversial, compromise on the slavery issue—the Three-Fifths Compromise—as well as the limits on the slave trade. In the end, the delegation strongly supported the final document.

Indeed, once the convention had adjourned, Delaware quickly demonstrated its support for the new governmental framework when the state legislature, convening in October, issued a call for elections to be held on November 9 and 10 to select delegates to a convention to consider ratification of the new document. It was decided that there would be 10 delegates from each of the state's three counties—Sussex, Kent, and New Castle—for a total of 30 delegates, a number that matched the number of representatives in the Delaware legislature's lower house. A strong effort was made to elect pro-Constitution delegates, and in fact there were no Antifederalist candidates. No less importantly, the voters selected Constitutional Convention delegates Bedford and Bassett, who were able to translate their firsthand observations into compelling arguments in support of ratification. In the end, by a vote of 30 to 0, on December 7, 1787, Delaware opened the door to the future when it became the first state to ratify the U.S. Constitution.

William H. Pruden III

See also: Netherlands; Penn, William

Further Reading

"Caesar Rodney." Society of the Descendants of the Signers of the Declaration of Independence. http://www.dsdi1776.com/signers-by-state/caesar-rodney.
Dano, Gardell. 1974. *Colonial Delaware.* Nashville, TN: Thomas Nelson.
Federal Writers' Project. 1938. *Delaware: A Guide to the First State.* New York: Viking Press.
Munroe, John A. 2003. *Colonial Delaware.* Dover: Delaware Heritage Press.

DISEASE

Disease has shaped world history in innumerable ways. Epidemics and outbreaks have stunted economic growth, halted cities, taken governmental authority, and brought armies to their knees. Though disease has played a crucial role in the shaping of world history, it has especially altered America's history. European colonists brought animals, money, and economic development as the New World had never seen. Those beneficial things, however, came with the death and destruction of Old World diseases: smallpox, measles, typhoid, dysentery, and countless others.

The foremost historian about disease and European biological exchange is Alfred Crosby. According to Crosby, Native Americans had lived their lives in "nearly complete isolation" (Crosby 1972, 30). After living alone for thousands of years, Old World diseases found new strength inside of the New World because no one carried any kind of resistance to them. To be fair, Crosby states that disease alone did not bring the Native Americans to their knees. They also lacked recent technologies. Firearms won over bows, steel over stone, and horses over foot soldiers. Yet, in this environment, eruptive fevers tore through small populations and caused just as much carnage and destruction; smallpox, typhus, and measles were three of those destructors.

Of the Old World diseases, smallpox was the most efficient killer. According to Crosby, the Arawaks of the Greater Antilles and Bahamas had numbered somewhere around 1 million before Columbus arrived. Afterward, their numbers had dropped to approximately 500 (Crosby 1972, 40). Though Crosby blames Columbus's actions, "disease would seem to be a more logical explanation" (Crosby 1972, 45). Further research has shown that smallpox was also deadly on the opposite side of the Americas, in the areas around Mexico. In the epidemic of 1520–1521, smallpox, known as "viruelas" by the local populations, hit before explorers ever arrived; deciphering how this happened is nearly impossible, for historians can only conjecture that some 50 percent of the population was taken by the disease (Cook and Lovell 1991, 24–27). Scholars are also unsure how smallpox was dispersed over such a massive landmass with few carriers in between populations. Yet, this is one of the confounding aspects of studying disease; it is uncontrollable and had uncontrollable effects on history. However, the disease tore through Central Mexico, the Andes, and South America with devastating, destabilizing power, which also happened on other parts of the continent.

Moving to the Atlantic Coast, where the English sent their first colonists, there was a similar story of disease, conquest, and death, beginning with Roanoke Colony of North Carolina. Now considered to be the "Lost Colony," Roanoke was the first settlement established by the English. Many scholars will give this credit to Jamestown, but both settlements "failed" in their attempts to create something permanent and lasting. However, scholars know little about what happened with Sir Walter Raleigh and the Roanoke colonists. Yet, they did bring Old World plagues with them.

In 1586, Thomas Harriot, an English explorer and translator, noted that after meeting with Native American groups, they began to die rapidly. On the one hand, their relationship with the Algonquin people was friendly; the disease was not. He noted, "Within a few days after our departure . . . the people began to die very fast" (Quinn 1985, 228). Unlike other areas in the colony, smallpox was not the killer here; with such a short incubation period, it had to have been influenza or another fever-driven sickness. The Native Americans of the region attributed this to the work of the English God, and the colonists did not resist that notion. Though the disease did affect Harriot and his fellow explorers, it did not kill them like the vulnerable Indians, making the English look like gods. Old World disease, then, gave the early waves of colonists a power advantage over local populations as well as cleared the area for them.

Jamestown was the second and more successful of the two ventures, but it was immersed in disease and violence. The most recent archeological studies of Jamestown, done over many years, culminated in the 2006 publication of *Jamestown: The Buried Truth*. The archeologists had unearthed a vast array of new cultural material: flintlock handles, pottery, everyday items, and much more. The most significant findings, however, revolved around the 73 individuals identified in various types of graves. These were colonists who had lived at the time of Jamestown, somewhere between 1607 and 1614, and their remains revealed the ways in which they had left this life; some had been shot, some had died of old age, and some had died from disease. The author states that finding bodies with shards of clothing still attached, and finding multiple bodies like this in the same grave, suggests that the graves were dug quickly in "an effort to minimize contact with the bodies of the deceased" (Kelso 2006, 164).

Smallpox was not the cause of their deaths, but dysentery and typhus more than likely took their lives. At first, the colony was healthy, which led to overstatements in England about the fertility of the land and people in the New World. According to Carville Earle, an early American geographic historian, the colonists of Jamestown were in fact healthy. However, after only one month of living in an area of swamps and stagnant water, 21 colonists had died (Earle 1979, 367). George Percy, one of the leaders of the new colony, reported that there was a vast food shortage. John Smith, a fellow leader and enemy of Percy, recorded there was more than enough rations for the colony to survive. However, even if Percy's political motivations are questionable, his diary does reveal the possible causes of the high rate of mortality: typhoid, dysentery, and salt poisoning (Earle 1979, 367).

A few years after the Jamestown community was established, the Pequot people of southern New England experienced the death toll of a plague. Pequot culture was militaristic and involved reciprocal acts of violence, including fighting mourning wars and other blood feuds and territorial disputes. Their numbers dropped naturally due to those facts. However, disease was a significant factor in the decline of Native American populations, as well. Thomas Morton, a founding settler of Massachusetts, walked into a plague-stricken southern New England in 1633. The devastation that had fallen on the Pequot of the region horrified him: "The bones and skulls upon the several places of their habitations made such a spectacle. . . . It seemed to me a new found Golgotha" (Morton 1637). Pequot numbers before the plague were around 16,000. At the beginning of the Pequot War, in 1636, that number had dropped to a dismal 3,000. Sickness, along with English colonialism, had prevailed over the Pequot of southern New England. Arguably, without the effect of disease, the colonials may not have won the short-lived Pequot War. Throughout the 17th century, disease continued to make a dark impression on the landscape.

In the mid-1600s, Charleston, South Carolina, became known for its disease and unhealthy living conditions. Being a hub for the Atlantic slave trade, diseases were constantly coming in and out of the area, and the diseases along with poor living conditions destroyed the local populations. Many of these tropical diseases—malaria, smallpox, and yellow fever—came from slave ports in the Caribbean. They thrived in the low country of South Carolina because the environment was similar to the tropics of Barbados and other Atlantic points. Smallpox was always a concern for colonists because it could evolve into an epidemic quickly. Malaria, however, was more endemic, constantly infecting and killing colonists throughout the year. From 1698 to 1700, yellow fever and smallpox burned through Charleston.

One cause for tropical diseases in the area was the rice cultivation methods, which left water stagnant—a perfect breeding ground for infectious disease. Other sickness resulted from the vagaries of the slave trade in and around the city. Slave trading and buying was seasonal. If markets were not open, or no one was buying, slaves were forced to wait on the boats they were traveling on until something opened up. With dysentery and yellow fever rampant on board, hundreds died. Not willing to bury the bodies, shipman simply threw them overboard into the Carolinians' water; the same water was used for drinking and as a source for fish. Sources called the problem a "nuisance" and worried that the local people would eat fish "that had fattened on the carcasses of dead negroes" (McCandless 2011, 50). Disease was a constant problem and cause of death in Charleston up until the 1750s, when colonists began to develop resistance to them. Yet, they were not always safe.

The Revolutionary War (1775–1783), which smallpox played a large part in, provides evidence of how disease has altered American history. Despite smallpox being an Old World disease, more devastating to Native Americans than militia or British troops, no one was completely immune. Between 1775 and 1782, smallpox spread rapidly through the colonies and Native American populations. The fight for independence was never an easy one for the colonial army. Elizabeth Fenn, a scholar of the War of Independence, concluded that if George Washington had not had his troops inoculated in 1777—a process which involved placing live *Variola* strains into an incision on the patient's arm—the war could have been lost. However primitive and controversial the method, the decision was an important factor in helping the Continental Army survive one of the deadlier threats of the war. Thus, Washington "outflanked *Variola*," the scientific name for the strain roaring through the colonies (Fenn 2001, 134). However, it did not stop in the colonies.

Alfred Crosby theorized that the European introduction of the horse in battle, pigs in husbandry, and plants for food sources contributed to the destabilization of the New World by introducing a variety of infectious diseases that indigenous populations were biologically ill-equipped to deal with (Crosby 1972, 102–111). For example, by way of a horse, Southwestern Indians were able to move freely. Along with that movement came goods, services, and, of course, disease. Fenn argues that it was a continental epidemic; people as far as Mexico, Texas, and even north into Canada were affected from 1775 to 1782. Disease thus created havoc throughout continental North America, not just in a centralized geographic location.

Theaters of conflict, such as the Anglo-Powhatan Wars (1610–1646) or King Philip's War (1675–1676), brought massive causalities to combatants as well as surrounding populations. However, disease was a constant, ever-present threat that affected entire continents. Battles ended, and conflicts were resolved; disease, however, never went away. With European immigration to the New World, Old World diseases gained a new vitality in the bodies of Native Americans and English colonists. Smallpox, malaria, typhoid, dysentery, and yellow fever were the deadliest killers. Disease destroyed entire Native groups in New England. It brought the colonists of Jamestown almost to their knees. Disease prevention possibly altered the entire outcome of the Revolutionary War. The power of disease during European contact in North America cannot be overstated; yet, there is still much that remains unknown.

Seth Harden

See also: Columbian Exchange; Trade

Further Reading

Bailyn, Bernard. 2012. *The Barbarous Years: The Peopling of British North America: The Conflict of Civilizations, 1600–1675.* New York: Vintage Books.

Confer, Clarissa W. 2011. *Daily Life during the Indian Wars.* Santa Barbara, CA: Greenwood.

Cook, Noble David, and W. George Lovell. 1991. *Secret Judgments of God: Old World Disease in Colonial Spanish America.* Norman: University of Oklahoma Press.

Crosby, Alfred W., Jr. 1972. *The Columbian Exchange: Biological and Cultural Consequences of 1492.* Westport, CT: Greenwood Press.

Earle, Carville. 1979. "Environment, Disease and Mortality in Early Virginia." *Journal of Historical Geography* 5, no. 4: 365–390.

Fenn, Elizabeth A. 2001. *Pox Americana: The Great Smallpox Epidemic of 1775–82.* New York: Hill and Wang.

Kelso, William M. 2006. *Jamestown, the Buried Truth.* Charlottesville: University of Virginia Press.

Mason, John. 1966. *A Brief History of the Pequot War.* Ann Arbor: University Microfilms, Inc.

McCandless, Peter. 2011. *Slavery, Disease, and Suffering in the Southern Low Country.* New York: Cambridge University Press.

Morton, Thomas. 1637. *New English Canaan.* http://www.swarthmore.edu/SocSci/bdorsey1/41docs/08-mor.html.

Quinn, David B. 1985. *Set Fair for Roanoke: Voyages and Colonies, 1584–1606.* Chapel Hill: Published for America's Four Hundredth Anniversary Committee by the University of North Carolina Press.

DOCTRINE OF DISCOVERY/CONQUEST

The Doctrine of Discovery is a concept of public international law that was defined and expanded by the U.S. Supreme Court in a series of decisions, most notably *Johnson v. M'Intosh* in 1823. In this famous case, Chief Justice John Marshall tried to justify the power of colonial entities to claim lands "conquered" by foreign nations during the Age of Discovery who claimed authority for territories explored by their subjects who occupied a territory whose inhabitants were not subjects of any European monarch.

The Doctrine of Discovery was first expounded in the United States in 1792 by Secretary of State Thomas Jefferson, who declared that the doctrine would extend from European countries to the infant U.S. government. The 1823 case evolved after the plaintiff, Thomas Johnson, inherited land that had originally been purchased from the Piankeshaw tribes. The defendant, William McIntosh, of Vincennes, Indiana, counterclaimed the same land, which he stated he had purchased under a grant from the United States. The case started in 1775 when members of the Pankeshaw tribe sold certain land in the Indiana Territory to Lord Dunmore, the royal governor of Virginia, and others. But in1805, the Piankeshaw sold much of the same land to William Henry Harrison, the governor of the Indiana Territory and a future U.S. president, which gave rise to the conflicting claims of title.

In reviewing whether the courts of the United States had the authority to recognize land titles obtained from Native Americans prior to American independence, Marshall decided that they should not; he found that ownership of land only came into existence by virtue of discovery of that land, a rule that had been observed by most European countries with settlements in the New World. Legally, the United States owned the land because it had inherited that ownership upon its break from Great Britain. The argument was this: if the Piankeshaw tribe sold the property in 1775, the tribe had nothing left to cede to the United States in 1805; therefore, the government had nothing to sell to William McIntosh. Faced with these facts, the attorneys representing McIntosh argued that the 1775 purchase was invalid on the ground that Indian tribes lacked the legal capacity to sell land to private individuals.

In Marshall's opinion, the issues to be decided in *Johnson v. M'Intosh* were whether the Indians had the power to give away titles and whether private individuals had the right to receive a title that could be further sustained by other courts in the country.

In an effort to increase their political and economic power, both the British and the French competed to acquire more of the available land and control over the new trading opportunities that the New World presented. At the same time, the European colonial governments tried to find ways to coexist with the original inhabitants of North America, often by making alliances with some tribes while alienating others. Along with the problems in the northern American colonies, the British adopted a policy of control of the Indian trade and of western expansion, two related matters that had always been the province of the individual colonial governments. It was a vacillating policy, but one that strengthened royal control, something else the colonies looked upon as an infringement of their charter rights.

During each of their conflicts, Great Britain and France enlisted the aid of the indigenous peoples of North America; the French solicited the Algonquians, and the British courted the Iroquois. The various Indian tribes played roles of enormous significance in the conflict between Great Britain and France for control of North America. In many ways, they were intermediaries in this conflict because, as allies of the two powers, the Indians carried on much of the frontier warfare in which the conflict was waged. Then there was the economic role of the Indians, which was very great, as the struggle to secure the Indian market and fur trade was one of the chief causes of British-French bitterness.

Exploitation of the Indians began with the most famous diplomatic and trade mission, and still one of the most controversial in history: Christopher Columbus's "Enterprise of the Indies" (Voyage of Discovery) to reach Asia by sailing west. The success of the Columbian enterprise initiated a flurry of Spanish exploration to the New World. Consequently, Spaniards were the first Europeans to map the Atlantic and Pacific Coasts and contributed greatly to the knowledge of the interior of North America. Armed with a 15th-century sense of right and wrong and secure in their identity as Christians, the Spanish set out to Christianize and conquer the newly discovered lands. They were required to follow certain procedures before they could begin hostilities. Some indigenous peoples in America peacefully accepted these conditions and became subjects of Spain. Spanish rulers thus succeeded in transplanting their language, culture, religion, and legal system to a large part of the Americas.

For many years following Ponce de León's discovery of Florida in 1513, the Spanish believed the new land was only an uninteresting island and unworthy of further exploration. It was the exploration voyages initiated by Lucas Vásquez de Ayllón that turned Spain's attention to the Eastern Seaboard of North America, and it was the glowing and widely distributed reports of Ayllón's explorations published by Peter Martyr d'Anghiera and Francisco López de Gómara and distributed throughout Europe that encouraged France and England to initiate the conquest of Canada and the land that would become the 13 colonies and later the United States of America.

More than 40 years passed before the Spanish undertook a serious attempt to settle the vast territories that Francisco Vásquez de Coronado (1510–1554) had explored. In April 1598, Juan de Oñate (ca. 1549–1624), a wealthy mine owner, led a large expedition northward from Mexico. Funded by Oñate, Viceroy Luís de Velasco, and King Philip II, the expedition was to ford the Rio Bravo, the present-day Rio Grande.

King Philip II (1527–1598) was a masterful manager of Spain's overseas empire. He commissioned Pedro Menéndez de Avilés (1519–1574), who was already responsible for the security of treasure fleets returning to Spain from the Indies, to establish a colony in Florida. Menéndez de Avilés founded St. Augustine, the first permanent European settlement located on the territory of the present-day United States. Other imperial powers repeatedly destroyed the town, but the Spaniards always rebuilt it.

Permanence finally came with the English. The first exploration sponsored by the English Crown began in 1527, when the ship *Mary Guildford* explored the North American coast, from Labrador to Florida, and reached the West Indies. In 1606, merchants of London and Plymouth formed two joint-stock companies and received Crown patents for the settlement of "Virginia." The London, or South Virginia, Company was given rights to settle an area that is now between Washington, D.C., and New York City, while the Plymouth, or North Virginia, Company could settle in New England, but neither could settle within 100 miles of the other. In 1607, English colonists, sponsored by the London Company, established a permanent settlement at Jamestown, Virginia, at head of James River, Virginia. With this first successful English colony, the English hoped to find the rich natural resources similar to those discovered by the earlier Spanish explorers.

After sailing along the coast, the Pilgrims decided to settle because of the lateness of the season, but as this region was outside the territory for which their charter was valid, they had no legal basis for a government. While still on shipboard, the Pilgrims bound themselves together in a "civil body politick" (the Mayflower Compact), which was signed by all adult males, except one invalid and eight servants, on November 11, 1620 (Old Style date in text). On the day after Christmas, Plymouth Plantation was established under the first governor, John Carver. By 1629, there were settlements in Portsmouth, New Hampshire; in Saco Bay, Maine; and in Salem, Massachusetts. In 1630, the Massachusetts Bay Colony was established along the Massachusetts coast north of Plymouth under the leadership of Gov. John Winthrop.

The original case that became the basis of the Doctrine of Discovery started when Roger and Mary Williams came to Massachusetts in February 1631. The Pilgrims had established their settlement in a location beyond the domain of the Virginia Company, but they came to an agreement with the Plymouth Council for New England, which had been granted a charter on November 3, 1620, by King James I. Without any mention of Indians or Indian land rights, James granted to the council exclusive rights to all territories and waterways.

In 1629, Williams became acquainted with John Winthrop, who in that year had been elected the colony's governor while still in England. On March 4, 1629, the grant of land in Massachusetts was confirmed by a royal charter by King Charles I, who without mention of Indians or Indian land rights, granted to the Massachusetts Bay Company similar exclusive rights that his father, James I, had granted to the Plymouth Council in 1620, including "all that Parte of Newe England" described in the charter.

Although the 1620 and 1629 royal charters made no mention of the Indians who occupied the lands granted, John Winthrop and other Puritans were aware of the Native presence. In a 1621 tract defending "the Lawfulness of Removing out of England into the Parts of America," Pilgrim apologist Robert Cushman declared Indian lands to be "'spacious and void,'" and thus available to Englishmen.

Yet, prior to Williams's arrival in 1631, the English had transacted with the Indians in both public and private capacities. In 1625, New England colonists had asked the Pemaquid tribe to give them 12,000 acres of Pemaquid land, which the tribe did in the first deed of Indian land to English colonists. A month later (May 1629), John Whelewright and others, by private purchase, were deeded lands in upper New England by the Pisquataqua Indians, although the Indian title was never officially acknowledged as equivalent or superior to title to lands held under royal patent.

Marshall's pronouncement in *Johnson v. M'Intosh* that Indian tribes were not capable or able to transfer absolute title of their land to others was not universally accepted before the Supreme Court's 1823 decision. But today, the Doctrine of Discovery continues to be a legal milestone that has been cited in many U.S. Supreme Court cases, most recently in 2005, in *City of Sherrill, NY v. Oneida Nation*: "Under the 'doctrine of discovery' . . . fee title (ownership) to the lands occupied by Indians when the colonists arrived became vested in the sovereign-first the discovering European nation and later the original states and the United States."

Martin J. Manning

See also: Cabeza de Vaca, Alvar Núñez; Cabot, John and Sebastian; Columbus, Christopher; Coronado, Francisco Vasquez de; Massachusetts Bay; Soto, Hernando de

Further Reading

Miller, Robert J. 2008. *Native America, Discovered and Conquered: Thomas Jefferson, Lewis and Clark, and Manifest Destiny.* Lincoln: University of Nebraska Press.

Miller, Robert J., Jacinta Ruru, Larissa Behrendt, and Tracey Lindberg. 2010. *Discovering Indigenous Lands: The Doctrine of Discovery in the English Colonies.* Oxford, UK: Oxford University Press.

Washburn, Wilcomb E. 1988. *History of Indian-White Relations.* Vol. 4 of *Handbook of North American Indians.* Edited by William C. Sturtevant. Washington, D.C.: Smithsonian Institution.

Watson, Blake A. 2012. *Buying America from the Indians:* Johnson v. McIntosh *and the History of Native Land Rights.* Norman: University of Oklahoma Press.

DOMINICANS

Domingo de Guzman, or Saint Dominic, established the Order of Preachers, the Dominicans, in Toulouse, France, in 1214, and Pope Honorius III recognized the order in 1216. The Dominicans came into being to preach the Gospel and fight heresy with learning and logic. The English call them the "Black Friars" because of the black cloaks they wear over their white habits. Among other nicknames, they are the Hounds of God, indicative of their obedience to the faith and, negatively, to their role as church inquisitors against heresy. Like the Franciscans, they were mendicants, theoretically earning their way through begging. Although they had houses, they were not monastic, their mission being to travel, educate, and convert. Dominicans are noted for an outstanding intellectual tradition with a long line of theologians and philosophers. As well as Dominic, the order produced Saint Thomas Aquinas, Albertus Magnus, Girolamo Savonarola, and Saint Catherine of Siena, as well as four popes.

The 17th century was the peak period for the order numerically. The Dominicans had lost ground with the growth of Protestantism, but they regrouped and began growing anew in the New World. With the state and the military, the church was integral to the three-part system for establishing order and allowing exploitation of the minerals and other wealth of the New World. Pope Alexander VI, in the papal bull *Inter Caetera*, mandated that Spanish kings had the responsibility for evangelizing the New World. The discovery and conquest were to be religious.

Initially, the conquistadores brought clergy as chaplains for themselves, but no notable Dominicans. The first friars in New Spain were the Franciscans, who arrived in Santo Domingo in 1500. Nevertheless, Diego de Deza, a Dominican bishop, was Christopher Columbus's first sponsor at the court of Ferdinand and Isabella. He would later take credit for giving Spain the opportunity to claim the West Indies. In 1508, the master of the Order of Preachers, Thomas de Vio (also known as Thomas Cajetan), called for 15 Dominican friars to go to Hispaniola from the University of Salamanca, Spain.

In 1510, the first four friars arrived at Santa Domingo and settled in. Seemingly all the friars, regardless of order, were young, mostly under the age of 30. Dominicans were trained in the New World and in Europe. They mastered the indigenous language and began a ministry to both the local people and the Spaniards. Quite soon, they began to criticize the European treatment of the Natives.

Friars, unlike parish clergy, were largely autonomous, subject only to the pope, and frequently came into conflict with the church hierarchy. The friars rejected the comforts offered by the local Spaniards, moving instead into a simple hut where they shared a communal life and common prayer, supporting one another's preaching ministry. They also preached sermons critical of the way the Spanish representatives of the Crown, soldiers, and colonists were working Natives in the mines and on the colonial estates. Dominicans took their criticism of the encomendero system and human rights abuses to King Ferdinand V in 1512. The Crown enacted modified laws that provided Natives some protection, ended child labor, and banned the exploitation of Native women.

Most notable of the Dominicans was Bartolomé de Las Casas (1484–1566), who came to America in 1502 as a large landholder and major beneficiary of the fruits of forced labor and exploitation of the Natives. He surrendered his Cuban estates when he became a Dominican in 1524. As a preacher, minister, and writer, he advocated justice for the Natives.

Francisco de Vitoria (1485–1546) was among the Dominican theologians at Salamanca who used Thomistic principles to support human dignity and deny the rightness of slavery. Another notable Dominican was the bishop of Traxcala, in

New Spain, who with Las Casas and other friars petitioned Pope Paul III to defend the Natives, which Paul III did in *Sublimis Deus* in 1537. Because the papal bull acknowledged the capacity and desire of the Natives for the Catholic faith, missionary activity in Central and South America and the Caribbean expanded.

Luis Cancer, with over two decades of experience in Hispaniola and Puerto Rico, joined Las Casas among the Maya of Guatemala in 1542. The two learned the native language and attempted through cooperation and preaching to bring Christianity to the Maya in La Tierra de la Guerra, so named because the Maya continued to fight the Spanish presence. Cancer translated parts of the Bible into Mayan song and traveled unescorted through Mayan lands. He left for Florida in 1548 with another friar and a Native woman convert, Magdalena, who served as translator. On the west coast of Florida, the Dominicans were killed by Natives hostile to his message, and Magdalena vanished.

The Gulf Coast mission was difficult. Previously, in 1539, Hernando de Soto and Natives had fought near Mobile. Among the 500 Spanish were three Dominican chaplains. The de Soto exploration of the Gulf Coast ended in 1543, with only one Dominican friar surviving of the three. The Dominicans went to Florida again in 1559 and the early 1560s. Success was limited.

The missionaries were often first into a new territory, with the others following and establishing settlements and mining operations. Each order had a distinctive approach to evangelization. Franciscans worked from love and charity, while Dominicans were more theoretical and judicial. According to Edmundo O'Gorman, cited by Paz Haro in reference to the Franciscan Motolinia and Dominican Las Casas, "Motolinia was a father to the Indians, Las Casas was their lawyer" (Haro 1992).

Not all Dominicans defended the Indians. The indigenous people of the New World were something totally unfamiliar, not biblical or historical by Spanish lights. Antonio de Montesinos, in a Lenten sermon in Española in 1511, questioned whether Indians truly had souls or were even human. He and another Dominican, Friar Domingo de Betanzos, suggested to the Spanish king that Indians were not suited for conversion or marriage, but rather were beasts best suited for the mines until their eventual extinction. In 1525, Friar Tomas Ortiz told the Council of the Indies that Indians lacked the ability to learn and rejected progress; he called them donkeys. And Friar Pedro de Betanzos told the council that Indians were not competent to comprehend Christianity.

Support for the idea that Indians were capable of receiving the faith and had human rights tended to come more from the Franciscans than the Dominicans until the 1540s. Franciscans required less preparation before conversion than Dominicans. By the time Dominicans arrived in Mexico in 1526, less than a decade after Hernán Cortés had landed in Mexico, one Franciscan friar claimed to have converted 200,000 Indians, baptizing 14,000 in a single day.

From the early 17th to the early 19th centuries, the three preaching orders built missions in Northern Mexico and the American Southwest. Later, the friars established missions with Christian Indian communities. Dominicans were especially adept at operating schools and universities. Lima and Mexico City had universities in the 16th century, San Carlos, Guatemala, in the 17th. The 17th century also saw establishment of universities in Bogotá, Quito, and Santiago, and fields of study included not only philosophy and religion but also logic, history, mathematics, and physics. The Dominicans faced competition from Jesuit universities in Bogotá and Santiago as well as Bolivia, but they continued to expand, establishing a university in Havana in 1728.

Dominicans began establishing houses and convents for women in Mexico in the 17th century. The convents offered education for Spanish, Creole, and indigenous women. Separate convents taught the daughters of caciques, Native chiefs. The Dominicans rarely turned away Native women. And expansion of convents continued through the 18th century. Dominicans hesitated to accept mixed blood or Native recruits into the order, however.

Hundreds of missions dotted New Spain, many simple churches but some elaborate cathedrals. The Jesuits were organized militarily and established their churches in marginal frontier areas before their expulsion. The Franciscans were first in California, New Mexico, Chihuahua, and Baja California, respectively. But the Jesuits were the strongest in Brazil and Paraguay, governing Paraguay as a virtually independent state until Portugal expelled the Jesuits from Brazil in 1759. Spain expelled them from its American viceroyalties in 1767.

With the Franciscans, the Dominicans reaped the benefits of Jesuit expulsion, taking over the abandoned Jesuit missions. The Dominicans worked primarily in Baja California until 1772, when mission emphasis shifted to Upper California. That year, the Franciscans and Dominicans divided the territory with a cross about 50 miles east of present-day San Diego. Dominicans took over Franciscan missions in their part of Upper California.

The Dominicans had a mandate to build five missions between San Fernando and San Diego. Despite drought and starvation in the region, they built three. Two relocated because of an absence of water. The third came under Indian attack, but it mostly suffered from a smallpox epidemic that spread to the other two and delayed building of the final two until 1787 and 1791.

After Mexican independence in 1821, the missions with other Spanish institutions became disfavored. As towns and communities grew, they sometimes absorbed mission buildings for other uses. But the Dominicans left a legacy as part of the religious heritage of New Spain.

John H. Barnhill

See also: Franciscans; Jesuits; New Spain

Further Reading

Cutter, Donald, and Iris Engstrand. 1996. *Quest for Empire: Spanish Settlement in the Southwest.* Golden, CO: Fulcrum Publishing.

Haro, Maria Paz. 1992. "Religious Orders, the Indian, and the Conquest: Fifty Years of Dispute and Contradiction." *Encounters*, issue 9 (Summer). Translated by James Dunlap. http://www.shc.edu/theolibrary/resources/harodunlap.htm.

Lippy, Charles H., Robert Choquette, and Stafford Poole. 1992. *Christianity Comes to the Americas, 1492–1776.* New York: Paragon House.

Orique, David, O.P. *Bartolome de Las Casa: A Brief Outline of His Life and Labor.* http://www.lascasas.org/manissues.htm.
University of Arizona Mission Initiative. History of Spanish Colonial Missions. http://missions.arizona.edu/en/history.

DRAKE, FRANCIS (CA. 1540–1596)

As one of the great heroes of English seafaring lore, Francis Drake was many things to many people while becoming the first English captain to circumnavigate the globe. In fact, Drake was the first captain to lead his expedition on the entire voyage, from start to finish. Contrary to popular misconception, Drake did not lead the English fleet against the Spanish Armada of 1588, but he was second in command of that momentous campaign. To the Spanish, Drake was "El Draque," or simply "Draco" (the Dragon), a ruthless pirate with a price on his head of 20,000 ducats ($6.5 million in modern U.S. dollars).

The son of a farmer turned church vicar, Drake was apprenticed to the owner of a barque (a square-rigged medium-sized ship of three or four masts), taking to a life at sea so well that the master and owner of the barque left it to Drake upon his death.

Drake married twice, but he had no children from either marriage. He made his first of several voyages to the New World at the age of 23. On one of these voyages, Drake got a taste of the Spanish when the small fleet he was part of was trapped at San Juan de Ulua, instilling in him an avowed thirst for revenge. Spain had made a formidable enemy.

In 1572, Drake commanded his first independent foray against Spain in the New World, leading two small ships on successful raids, one of which included the capture of a mule train bearing 20 tons of silver and gold. This sort of success gained the attention of both the English (Queen Elizabeth I) and Spanish (King Phillip II) crowns.

Having returned to England a celebrity and hero, Drake was outfitted for another expedition in 1577. This voyage would end up including his famous circumnavigation of the globe. Setting out with five ships, Drake added a sixth, but upon reaching South America, attrition from disease and rotting timbers caused him to abandon three of his ships. Spending the winter in what is now modern Argentina, 1578 saw another of Drake's ships lost in the perilous crossing to the Pacific and another of the fleet turning for home, leaving only Drake and his ship, the *Pelican*.

Renaming the *Pelican* as *The Golden Hind*, Drake proceeded to raise havoc up the Pacific Coast of the Americas, pillaging Spanish settlements and capturing treasure ships along the way. Drake made his way north to California and may have established a small colony there, although the location is lost to history.

Drake then sailed his treasure-laden *Golden Hind* across the Pacific, making his way home to Plymouth in September 1580, with only his one ship and 59 crewmen left, but with a heavy cargo of riches and accounts of many victories against Spain. Enjoying his fame, Drake was knighted and became the mayor of Plymouth as well as a Member of Parliament.

In 1585, Drake led other expeditions, this time in command of 21 ships and 1,800 soldiers. Attacking targets in Spain, the Cape Verde Islands, and the

Caribbean, Drake added to his fame and fortune. On this voyage, Drake landed at the infamous Roanoke Colony established by Sir Walter Raleigh and evacuated all the surviving colonists. The colony was later repopulated by a separate fleet, only to vanish later in mysterious circumstances.

Anticipating an invasion of England by Spain, Drake was sent by his queen on a preemptive raid of Cadiz and Corunna, destroying at least 37 Spanish ships in the harbors and interdicting numerous Spanish vessels on his predatory voyage. Perhaps the most significant accomplishment of this voyage was the capture of 1,600–1,700 tons of barrel staves, seasoned wood that would have been used to construct water barrels for the Spanish fleet being assembled for the invasion of England. The Spanish were forced to use green wood for their water barrels, with catastrophic consequences for their sailors.

Drake's raids caused the delay of the Spanish invasion for an entire year, allowing the English time to prepare their defenses. For his efforts, Drake was appointed vice admiral, second in charge of the naval defense of the country.

When the expected attack came, Drake employed his 197 vessels and fireships (34 warships, the rest armed merchant ships) to attack and scatter the Spanish Armada, eventually sinking or capturing 5 ships, with another 30 Spanish vessels (of an original total of about 22 war galleons and 108 armed merchant ships) lost for various reasons, a catastrophe for Spain and its allies and an enormous victory for England. Drake's only losses were the 8 fireships burned on purpose, along with about 100 men killed and 400 wounded. The Spanish suffered 600 dead, 800 wounded, and almost 400 captured. These numbers refer only to battle losses. The English lost another 6,000–8,000 to disease and accidents, while the Spanish lost a staggering 20,000 men to miscellaneous reasons. Adding insult to injury, Drake captured the Spanish admiral Pedro de Valdés and his flagship, the *Rosario*.

A year later, in 1589, the Admiralty sent Drake on an expedition (the Drake-Norreys Expedition) against Spain with his own "armada," a voyage of limited success that lost 20 ships and 12,000 men.

In the ensuing years, Drake had little success against Spain, failing to conquer Las Palmas and mounting unsuccessful raids in the Caribbean. At San Juan de Puerto Rico in 1595, Drake suffered another defeat, and the ignominy of having a cannon ball fired from El Morro Castle smash right through his stateroom on his flagship.

Drake died from dysentery in 1596 while off the coast of Panama. At his request, Drake was buried at sea dressed in his full armor and placed inside a lead coffin. Researchers and treasure hunters have yet to locate his remains, despite continuous efforts to do so.

Francis Drake remains a legend in the seagoing traditions of England and the United Kingdom, with numerous places named in his honor, statues, paintings, and cultural references. Nevertheless, his reputation is besmirched by his participation as a young man on slave-trading voyages in the 1550s and 1560s, a lucrative business. Either way, Francis Drake left an indelible imprint on history.

Matthew D. Zarzeczny

See also: Cabot, John and Sebastian; Doctrine of Discovery/Conquest

Further Reading

Mattingly, Garret. 1959. *The Defeat of the Spanish Armada.* Boston: Houghton-Mifflin.
Sugden, John. 2006. *Sir Francis Drake.* New York: Simon and Schuster.
Wilson, Derek. 1977. *The World Encompassed: Drake's Great Voyage, 1577–1580.* New York: Harper & Row.

DRINKING AND TAVERN CULTURE

Drinking and tavern culture played a large role in the society of early colonial North America. Drinking traditions were common practice throughout early modern Europe, and the colonists emigrating from European countries brought their drinking habits and tavern culture with them. Drinking and tavern culture may have shared a common origin in early modern Europe, but they looked different in the various colonial settings. The colonists participated in the consumption of alcohol for many reasons, and drinking was promoted among men and women from diverse classes and racial backgrounds. Alcohol in various forms was consumed in large quantities in private and public venues, urban centers, and rural regions.

By the beginning of the 18th century, liquors such as brandy, rum, gin, and whiskey were the most common forms of distilled alcohol consumed (Salinger 2002, 2). According to one study, per capita, nearly four gallons of rum was consumed per person annually (Salinger 2002, 2). Beer and wine were less popular; however, they made the growing of grapes and grain profitable. In contrast to rum, wine was least popular in pre-Revolutionary America. Colonists consumed roughly a tenth of a gallon of wine a year. Hard ciders, containing nearly 10 percent alcohol, were generally the most popular drink among the colonists (Salinger 2002, 2).

A large majority of colonial society, from laborers to gentile elite, participated in the drinking of alcohol. Men, women, and children all consumed alcohol for various reasons. Water was often seen as unsafe to drink in colonial society because of the threat of waterborne illnesses. Alcohol provided a means to hydrate and not become ill. Alcohol was also thought to have medicinal attributes. Many colonists found that alcohol could prevent illnesses such as scurvy and dysentery (Salinger 2002, 3). Alcohol was thought to hold relaxing effects to help lesson tension and depression. Further, alcohol was a means to supplement the poor diets of lower classes when meals were few. Drinking provided brief moments of reprieve and enjoyment for laborers from long days of work.

Some of the Founding Fathers commented on the vice associated with drinking, but George Washington made sure a barrel of the best rum from the West Indies was available at his presidential inaugural party (Salinger 2002, 2). Benjamin Franklin once stated, "Drinking does not improve our faculties but it enables us to use them" (Salinger 2002, 2). Drinking was more than tolerated; it was part of the daily experiences for most men and women, poor and elite, in colonial North America.

Taverns

The popularity of drinking during the 17th and 18th centuries provided the impetus for the creation of taverns. Taverns played a large role in the consumption of alcohol by colonists in the North American colonies. According to Sharon Salinger, the role of taverns was to "provide a place where individuals or groups could gather to eat and drink, talk, sing, argue, conduct business, play games of chance, or while away the hours" (Salinger 2002, 7). Taverns often provided lodging for the poor and travelers. In colonial North America, churches and taverns were often the only public buildings in many communities, the latter being more prominent (Salinger 2002, 4).

Taverns were commonplace in early modern European society, and like the consumption of alcohol, taverns came to early colonial North America across the Atlantic Ocean with the colonists. Peter Clark's seminal work on the English alehouse provides insight into the role drinking venues played in early modern English society. The study demonstrates that English alehouses during this period grew in importance for various classes, but especially the lower classes. A growing rate of poverty in England in the 16th century fueled a rise in alehouses as more people relied on cheap options for nutrition, lodging, and entertainment; necessities alehouses could provide (Clark 1983, 48).

Providing multiple services and opportunities for the poor, alehouses were also perceived as threats to public order. Crime and disorder were associated with alcohol consumption. The alehouse was denounced by respectable society as a space for a growing alternative society, and alternative society was a threat against the established social order. The communal nature of the alehouse bringing the poor together for entertainment, lodging, and nutrition challenged the restrictive social and familial ideals of Puritans during this period (Clark 1983, 61). While crimes were committed in alehouses, they were not conducive to popular radicalism. Many alehouse keepers and their patrons were more concerned with trying to survive than creating disorder. Therefore, following public opinion and the law was more imperative.

The Puritans from England brought their traditions of drinking and tavern going to colonial New England. One study suggests that drinking and tavern culture in colonial Massachusetts was the catalyst for the development of republican ideals from 1680 to 1776 (Conroy 1995, 11). Drinking and tavern culture were at odds with Puritan ideals in the Colonial Period. Puritan leaders often attempted to control and suppress the vices associated with drinking and tavern culture (Conroy 1995, 11). Members of Puritan society used taverns as forums to resist political power and authority in colonial Massachusetts. Sharon Salinger states, "Men drank and conversed only with those from the same socioeconomic stratum; particular taverns became associated with specific political values, which in turn informed the revolutionary politics in the city" (Salinger 2002, 5).

Taverns provided more than lodging and the opportunity to drink. Taverns in colonial Virginia were places where people, primarily men, connected to discuss crop prices and find business opportunities (Meacham 2005, 140). Virginia taverns provided a direct link to the European tobacco markets of the time. While men were the predominant patrons of taverns, as one study of colonial Virginia suggests, women were most often the tavern proprietors in colonial Virginia. Nearly two-thirds of all taverns in the colony during the 17th and 18th centuries were operated by women (Meacham 2005, 140).

In opposition to gender roles held by women in similar colonial settings, women in colonial Virginia participated outside of the traditional roles of domesticity. Women were preferred by local magistrates to operate taverns. While the male head of the family was often the tavern license holder, the tavern itself was typically run by women and passed down from mother to daughter. Studies suggest that elsewhere in colonial North America, tavern proprietors came from diverse social and class backgrounds, but Virginian magistrates preferred tavern proprietors from middle- and upper-class families (Meacham 2005, 143). Colonial magistrates felt that women with families from such backgrounds often upheld proper financial and social responsibilities that would demonstrate and encourage appropriate behavior from their diverse colonial patrons (Meacham 2005, 142). This was a form of monitoring taverns and tavern culture at that time.

Drinking and tavern culture was indulged by a diverse enclave of patrons from varying social classes and racial backgrounds. Drinking in the Southern colonies during the period was no different. One study found that the Southern urban environment of Charleston provided access to taverns to enslaved Africans. In 1702, the Grand Council of South Carolina reprimanded Charleston's constables for not maintaining laws restricting enslaved populations from drinking and participating in tavern culture (Salinger 2002, 236). Colonial officials feared rumors of enslaved African cabals meeting in city taverns and resisting white owners. Further, slave owners felt drunkenness decreased a slave's productivity (Salinger 2002, 236). This evidence suggests that enslaved Africans in 18-century Charleston also enjoyed drinking and tavern culture.

The consumption of alcohol played a large role in 17th- and 18th-century society of early colonial North America. Drinking and tavern traditions in early modern European countries were brought across the Atlantic Ocean and developed in the early North American colonies. Drinking was part of the daily experience for many colonists during the period, but tavern culture looked different in the various colonial settings. Drinking alcohol provided a leisure opportunity for both the poor and elite, dietary supplement and nourishment for the less fortunate, medicinal properties for the sick, and an escape from hard labor. Taverns also provided lodging for the poor and weary travelers.

As evidence suggests, men and women both participated in drinking and tavern culture. Taverns allowed women to reject traditional gender roles in colonial Virginia to become tavern proprietors. Enslaved Africans presumably enjoyed moments of reprieve from exploitation. And in colonial Massachusetts, Puritans rejected restrictive social norms by developing republican ideals.

Nathan Allison

See also: Colonial Sports; Fraunces Tavern

Further Reading

Clark, Peter. 1983. *The English Alehouse: A Social History, 1200–1830*. London: Longman.

Conroy, David W. 1995. *In Public Houses: Drink and the Revolution of Authority in Colonial Massachusetts*. Chapel Hill: University of North Carolina Press.

Meacham, Sarah. 2005 "Keeping the Trade: The Persistence of Tavernkeeping among Middling Women in Colonial Virginia." *Early American Studies* 3, no. 1: 140–163.
Salinger, Sharon V. 2004. *Taverns and Drinking in Early America.* Baltimore, MD: Johns Hopkins University Press.
Thompson, Peter. 1999. *Rum Punch and Revolution: Taverngoing and Public Life in Eighteenth Century Philadelphia.* Philadelphia: University of Pennsylvania Press.

DUNMORE'S WAR

Dunmore's War, also known as Lord Dunmore's War, was a conflict between the Virginia Colony and the Shawnee and Seneca-Cayuga American Indian nations in the Ohio Country during the spring of 1774. It was one of the last major conflicts of the pre-Revolutionary era. The fighting was concentrated in the Ohio River valley in Pennsylvania and what is today West Virginia, and it essentially ended as a result of the colonial militia's victory at the decisive Battle of Point Pleasant on October 10, 1774.

The tensions that led to the war had been steadily escalating between the colonists and Native Americans since the late 1760s. In 1768, the Iroquois and the British signed the Treaty of Fort Stanwix, granting colonists the right to settle in areas east and south of the Ohio River. This land had been established by the Proclamation of 1763 as Indian territory, and so the new treaty was popular among the colonists, who had long seen the Ohio Valley as a prime location for settlement. As such, settlers immediately began moving into the region.

Unfortunately, however, while the Iroquois had ceded their claims to the land, many other nations had not. Although the Iroquois were the most powerful group in the trans-Appalachian region, they were not the only nation to claim land in the Ohio Valley. The Delaware, the Shawnee, and the Seneca-Cayuga all had traditional claims to the Ohio Country. None of these nations were officially part of the Iroquois Confederacy, and so they neither recognized nor were parties to the Treaty of Fort Stanwix. They considered the white settlers as infringing on their lands in a direct violation of the 1763 Proclamation.

The various American Indian nations tried to drive colonial settlers out of the Ohio Valley and back east, across the Appalachian Mountains. In April 1774, several skirmishes resulted from the appearance of a military surveying team near the mouth of the Kanawha River in present-day West Virginia. But the catalyst for open warfare was the treacherous murder, in early May, of several family members of Seneca-Cayuga chief Logan. The Seneca-Cayuga had heretofore remained neutral in the conflict. However, the murders made a negotiated settlement difficult to achieve. Shawnee chief Cornstalk urged a moderate course, despite the growing calls for retribution among the Indian population. He offered protection to white fur traders in the valley, pointing out that the murders had been committed by British colonists, not traders. His efforts came to naught, however. Logan, demanding some measure of personal revenge, led a force of about two dozen warriors into western Pennsylvania. There, they killed a number of white settlers before returning back across the Ohio River. The possibility of a negotiated peace evaporated. Most of the Ohio tribes declared open war on the settlers and, by extension, the Virginia Colony.

The royal governor of Virginia, John Murray, 4th Earl Dunmore (Lord Dunmore), called for the creation of a militia army to aid Pennsylvania's efforts to defeat the Indian warriors. Dunmore's actions were likely also an effort to reassert the colony's interest in some of the land in the Ohio Valley that Virginia and Pennsylvania both claimed. Pennsylvania militia captain John Connolly, the commander of Fort Pitt, began preparations to invade Seneca-Cayuga country. In August 1774, the Pennsylvania militia descended on Indian settlements in the upper Ohio River valley and quickly destroyed several Seneca-Cayuga villages. Fortunately for the men and women living there, the villages were abandoned, as they had received news of the advancing militia force.

At about the same time, Lord Dunmore gathered an army of nearly 2,500 men to march on the Native Americans in the Ohio Valley. Dunmore himself took a force of nearly 1,700 from Fort Pitt down the Ohio River. He met a second army of 800, under the command of Col. Andrew Lewis, at the mouth of the Kanawha River. There, the armies built a fort from which they could subdue the Shawnee and also establish their claims to the area of what is today West Virginia and Kentucky. Dunmore continued his advance into Ohio, however, and shortly after his arrival at the mouth of the Kanawha, Lewis received orders from Dunmore to cross the Ohio River and march to meet him along the Scioto River, where they would attack the Shawnee settlements in central Ohio.

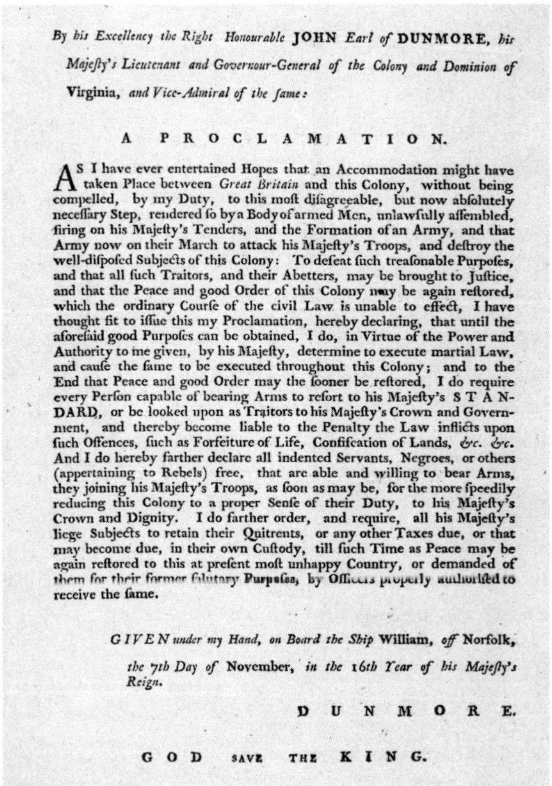

By his Excellency the Right Honourable **JOHN** *Earl of* **DUNMORE,** *his Majeſty's Lieutenant and Governour-General of the Colony and Dominion of* **Virginia,** *and Vice-Admiral of the ſame:*

A PROCLAMATION.

AS I have ever entertained Hopes that an Accommodation might have taken Place between *Great Britain* and this Colony, without being compelled, by my Duty, to this moſt diſagreeable, but now abſolutely neceſſary Step, rendered ſo by a Body of armed Men, unlawfully aſſembled, firing on his Majeſty's Tenders, and the Formation of an Army, and that Army now on their March to attack his Majeſty's Troops, and deſtroy the well-diſpoſed Subjects of this Colony: To defeat ſuch treaſonable Purpoſes, and that all ſuch Traitors, and their Abetters, may be brought to Juſtice, and that the Peace and good Order of this Colony may be again reſtored, which the ordinary Courſe of the civil Law is unable to effect, I have thought fit to iſſue this my Proclamation, hereby declaring, that until the aforeſaid good Purpoſes can be obtained, I do, in Virtue of the Power and Authority to me given, by his Majeſty, determine to execute martial Law, and cauſe the ſame to be executed throughout this Colony; and to the End that Peace and good Order may the ſooner be reſtored, I do require every Perſon capable of bearing Arms to reſort to his Majeſty's STANDARD, or be looked upon as Traitors to his Majeſty's Crown and Government, and thereby become liable to the Penalty the Law inflicts upon ſuch Offences, ſuch as Forfeiture of Life, Confiſcation of Lands, *&c. &c.* And I do hereby farther declare all indented Servants, Negroes, or others (appertaining to Rebels) free, that are able and willing to bear Arms, they joining his Majeſty's Troops, as ſoon as may be, for the more ſpeedily reducing this Colony to a proper Senſe of their Duty, to his Majeſty's Crown and Dignity. I do farther order, and require, all his Majeſty's liege Subjects to retain their Quitrents, or any other Taxes due, or that may become due, in their own Cuſtody, till ſuch Time as Peace may be again reſtored to this at preſent moſt unhappy Country, or demanded of them for their former ſalutary Purpoſes, by Officers properly authoriſed to receive the ſame.

GIVEN under my Hand, on Board the Ship William, *off* Norfolk, *the 7th Day of* November, *in the 16th Year of his Majeſty's Reign.*

DUNMORE.

GOD SAVE THE KING.

Lord Dunmore was named governor of Virginia in 1771 and instigated a series of military campaigns against the Shawnee and Mingo American Indian nations, which came to be known as "Dunmore's War." More famously, he issued a document in 1775 offering freedom to any slave who agreed to take up arms with the British against the rebelling Americans. (Library of Congress)

On October 10, 1774, before he could cross the Ohio, Lewis was surprised to find a large Shawnee force blocking his way. Chief Cornstalk's view of the white settlers had changed dramatically as a result of the escalating violence. As such, he had mustered an army of 400–1,000 Shawnee warriors to stop the militia's advance and to drive the Virginians out of Shawnee territory. The resulting Battle of Point Pleasant was a bloody and often hand-to-hand affair that largely ended Shawnee resistance to the provisions of the Treaty of Fort

Stanwix. Approximately 75 Virginians were killed, and a further 140 were injured. As the Shawnee either carried their dead and wounded away from the battlefield or put their dead in the Ohio and Kanawha Rivers, their casualty numbers are unknown.

Since the French and Indian War (Seven Years' War, 1756–1763), the Shawnee had positioned themselves in opposition to the Iroquois Confederacy. As a result, the Shawnee faced a concerted effort at diplomatic and military isolation by the Iroquois and their British allies. By the outbreak of Dunmore's War, then, Cornstalk would have to face the Virginians with little or no aid from the powerful Iroquois nation or any of the other nations that were nominally allied to it. They thus faced both the Virginia militia and the subsequent negotiations essentially alone.

Cornstalk signed the Treaty of Camp Charlotte without the help of the Iroquois Confederacy's significantly more substantial influence and leverage. The Treaty of Camp Charlotte ceded to Virginia all Shawnee claims to the land south of the Ohio River, territory that would eventually become Kentucky and West Virginia. In addition, the Shawnee promised to give free and unmolested passage to barges on the Ohio River. The peace was not long-lasting, however. With the outbreak of the American Revolution, just over six months later, the Native American nations of the Ohio Valley once again found themselves enmeshed in a complex military and diplomatic situation. Some nations chose to aid the British, while others supported the colonials. Still others fought against any Anglo-Americans to secure or restore their traditional claims.

Shawn Selby

See also: Ohio Country; Treaty of Fort Stanwix

Further Reading

Dowd, Gregory Evans. 1993. *A Spirited Resistance: The North American Indian Struggle for Unity, 1745–1815.* Baltimore, MD: Johns Hopkins University Press.

Hinderaker, Eric, and Peter Mancall. 2003. *At the Edge of Empire: The Backcountry in British North America.* Baltimore, MD: Johns Hopkins University Press.

DUTCH SLAVE TRADE

Although the slave presence in the Netherlands was minimal, the slave trade was a significant component of the Dutch economy from the early 17th century until the mid-19th century. The slave trade made Holland the richest country in the world during its 17th-century "Golden Age."

The Netherlands is a small country with few natural resources. Nevertheless, in the 17th century, it became the center of European overseas trade, including the slave trade. Due to the congruence of innovations in finance, manufacturing, and navigation at this particular time, the cost of transporting slave-produced goods and the slaves themselves dropped drastically, making both more profitable. The Dutch had the most sophisticated insurance and banking systems in the world, and as shipbuilders and designers, they had no equal. They provided ships to much of the continent while also building a domestic fleet larger than the combined fleets of England, Scotland, France, Spain, Portugal, and Germany. The Dutch West-Indische Compagnie (also known as the Dutch West India Company, or the WIC), formed in 1621, included the West African slave trade as an integral element of its business.

The WIC, headquartered in Amsterdam, established a monopoly on the African slave trade from its 1621 incorporation until 1730. The Dutch West India Company also had a board of governors and shareholders—and a trade in slaves that counted 550,000 souls during a time when the world population was only 500 million. The first slaves came to Jamestown in 1619 on a Dutch vessel, but the Dutch trade was minor until the 1630s, after the Netherlands had conquered Brazil and encountered a shortage of labor there.

The Portuguese arrived in Africa ahead of the Dutch, and the Dutch explorations in search of gold led to conflict. Between 1620 and 1655, the Netherlands contested Portugal in Africa and won many slave depots on the west coast, primarily in the Gold Coast (present-day Ghana). The Dutch took the Gold Coast headquarters of the Portuguese in 1637 and moved quickly to more suitable sections of Africa, expanding the slave trade as they expanded the area of Brazil. By 1650, Brazil had received 30,000 slaves from Ghana alone. In 1654, the Dutch ceded Brazil to the Portuguese, but by then the Dutch network was strong enough that it could become a major provider to other European states. In this way, the Dutch dominated the slave trade to Spain's Caribbean holdings during the growth of the region's sugar economy, at least until the 1690s.

Trading in slaves required the establishment of a major network of ports, shipping, finance, and other supporting elements. Slaves were a key commodity, and the WIC developed a triangular trade route that began with Dutch ships sailing from the Netherlands with cheap trade goods and weapons for the west coast of Africa. At one point, the WIC was the second-largest trader from Africa to the Americas and West Indies, the "Middle Passage." Slavers traded goods and weapons for slaves and then transported the cargo to the West Indies or the Americas. The sale of slaves there would give the traders money to purchase luxury goods for sale in Europe, financing yet another voyage from the Netherlands to Africa with trade goods and weapons.

The trip typically took 81 days, and a shipload was 500 souls. Slavers with light cargos sometimes spent months patrolling the African coast and picking up slaves until the ship was finally full. The company attempted to minimize slave mortality during these extended trips and the dangerous passage by paying a bounty to the captain for each slave he brought to the Americas alive.

As a general rule, only the captain and other officers of a slaver were Dutch. The sailors were of other nationalities. Half the crews of Dutch slavers were German and Scandinavian. The Dutch were too well off to be interested in sailing on unpleasant and difficult voyages with human cargo.

By the middle of the 17th century, Amsterdam was the principal trading center in the world and a vital cog in the Caribbean slave system. It was also home to the large warehouses that held the products of the New World's slaves. Sugar, cotton, and tobacco were principal products. The Amsterdam Commodity Exchange was a center for all of Europe for commodity traders speculating on newly arrived Caribbean goods. Prices at the Beurs (commodity exchange) influenced the demand for slaves in America. Amsterdam also processed just about all the sugar the Portuguese colonies produced and bankrolled slave traders from Sweden, Denmark, and Brandenburg.

When the WIC received permission to establish New Netherlands (present-day New York) in 1623, the new colony held little appeal for the Dutch, who were comfortably well off at home. Instead, immigrants came from modern-day Belgium, England, and Germany. Initially, too few came to permit profitable large-scale agriculture on the Hudson River valley farms, so the colonists quickly turned to slavery in 1624, the first group, 11 male Africans, arriving in Manhattan in 1625.

With the 1654 loss of Brazil, New Netherlands became the center of WIC activity in the Americas, trading around 2,500 slaves a year, and by the 1660s, the WIC was the largest slaveholder in New Amsterdam (New York City). Its slaves built roads, houses, and fortifications. Until the British took New Netherlands in 1664, immigrant whites worked in the fields in sufficient numbers, and slaves tended to be urban, particularly those with skills. It was possible for them to buy their freedom. Also, they were allowed to participate in festivals and other activities that preserved African heritage. New Amsterdam slavery was significantly easier than Caribbean slavery, but it was slavery just the same. Dutch law failed to recognize slaves as humans until late in the 17th century. The Dutch were no exception to the widespread administration of such cruel punishments as branding and whipping, another indicator that the slaves were treated as animals, not humans.

The Dutch were not the only traders. English, French, and Portuguese traders dominated the overall trade, with the Dutch transporting only 5 percent of the total slaves brought to the New World. Of the 550,000 the Dutch transported, only half were brought by the WIC, the rest being the work of independent Dutch companies.

Independent traders sailed from slaver ports such as the Zeeland towns of Vlissingen and Middleburg. Amsterdam recorded 173 voyages and 73,476 souls transported, and the Zeeland ports recorded 672 voyages to Africa and 278,476 souls transported. By 1750, the only recorded commercial activity in Vlissingen was the slave trade. The Middleburg Commercial Company, the largest independent Dutch slave trading company, shipped 31,095 Africans between 1732 and 1803, of whom 27,344 survived to reach America.

The amount of money earned in the slave trade is in dispute among historians, but general agreement is that the spice trade was more lucrative (but the spice trade still rested on slavery). The spice trade was the province of the Verenigde Ooostindische Gompagnie (VOC), or Dutch East India Company. The VOC was founded in 1602 as a multinational corporation complete with a board of governors, shareholders, and a monopoly on the East Indian trade, including the trade in slaves. Although the presence of slaves enabled a vast, complex, and highly profitable web of trading networks in Africa, Asia, and Europe, the VOC did not in fact engage in the slave trade itself. The WIC and VOC had overlapping boards, with 21 people being members of both. The slave economy of the east and slave trade of the west were integral to the wealth and power of the elites of North Holland in the 17th century.

The VOC combined Dutch companies to defend their trading posts from the Spanish, English, and Portuguese as well as local Asian rivals. Dutch traders in the region routinely had up to 200 slaves in and around the household as well as Asian wives, many of whom were slaves who might gain their freedom on the death of their husband if specified in his will. In Batavia (present-day Jakarta), the craft export business employed some Dutch, but mostly slaves from Sulawesi (Indonesia), India, Sri Lanka, and Madagascar. The first Dutch slave ship reached the Cape of Good Hope from Angola in 1658. Slavery became the major VOC labor system in the Cape by 1717.

The rise of abolitionism in the late 18th century led the WIC to discontinue trading in 1790. The VOC dissolved in 1799 because of financial and political matters that resulted in share values approaching zero. By 1838, most countries had abolished slavery, with Indonesia continuing "indentured service" in some form into the early 20th century. By 1790, the WIC had discontinued trading because by then slave trading was unacceptable. The VOC failed in 1799 in the face of English competition.

Because the Netherlands was almost continuously at war with one European rival or another—Great Britain, Spain, France—the Dutch slave trade declined in the 18th century and for all practical purposes ended in 1795. By the time of the formal abolition of the trade in 1863, Dutch traders had supplied the Western Hemisphere with 540,000 souls and established a slave-based economy from the Cape of Good Hope to Indonesia.

John H. Barnhill

See also: Atlantic Slave Trade; Middle Passage

Further Reading

Emmer, Pieter. 2005. *The Dutch Slave Trade, 1500–1850.* Translated by Chris Emery. New York: Berghahn Books.

Postma, Johannes. 2008. *The Dutch in the Atlantic Slave Trade, 1600–1815.* New York: Cambridge University Press.

DUTCH-INDIAN WARS

The Dutch-Indian Wars refer to a series on conflicts that took place in the middle of the 17th century between Dutch colonists and fur traders and some of the Indians that they interacted with, especially the Esophus. The three more well-known colonial powers in North America—the English, French, and Spanish—sometimes received opposition to their endeavors from other sources. The Dutch challenged them, particularly the French, as the settlement patterns moved further westward. Dutch powers hired the explorer Henry Hudson to find the long-sought-after Northwest Passage (a water passage through the interior of North America that connected the Atlantic to Asia, which never existed) in their efforts to claim a piece of imperialism. Hudson never found what he sought, but his explorations helped the Dutch in attempts to claim an area from the St. Lawrence River down to present-day Delaware.

Of course, those lands were inhabited by numerous Indian nations, including the Lenape, Mohicans, Munsee, Manhattans, and Esopus, the latter of which would be critical in the forthcoming Dutch-Indian Wars. The Dutch also interacted with the Pequot, who, along with the Mohicans, were critical to their expansionist goals. The other nation that the Dutch depended on was the Lenape, whose intimate knowledge of inland waterways was vital, especially as they took a larger role in the developing fur trade.

The Dutch fur trade started with a company known as the United New Netherlands Company, although independent traders soon took over. By the 1620s, the Dutch West India Company had taken a larger role in the fur trade and had also attempted to establish guidelines in which the Dutch traders were required to maintain peaceful and honest relations with the Indians with whom they worked. However, reality worked different than theory, and many regulations were ignored. Like many Europeans, the majority of the Dutch viewed Indians as subhuman and in league with, if not completely controlled by, the devil. Therefore, firearm sales to Indians were frowned upon, although other trade goods, including alcohol, were allowed.

The Dutch realized and understood the vast differences that existed among Indian nations, even those who neighbored each other. As such, they worked to cultivate relationships with many of them, at least until their usefulness ran out. The relationships that they developed with many Iroquoian nations were pleasant and cooperative throughout most of the history of New Netherland. Their relationships with Algonquin nations, however, were more tenuous, especially as the Dutch decided to dispose of their good relationships with them once they felt that their usefulness had run its course. Both vast groups of nations—Iroquoian and Algonquin—watched cautiously as the Dutch continued to penetrate farther into their lands. They viewed their arrival with caution and delight as they received a plethora of new trade goods, including mirrors, hatchets, and metal farming implements. They also received wampum, which, though not often used as a currency for nations farther inland, were enjoyed as fashion accessories. Furthermore, some Indians married Dutch men, which established new kinship networks. However, as the supply of fur-bearing animals became depleted and the Dutch were forced to move farther into neighboring lands, often aggressively, resistance increased.

Some of the measures that the Dutch took in the early days of increasing tensions certainly could have led to the eventual outcomes of the Dutch-Indian Wars. Due in large part to increased Dutch encroachments onto their lands, the Mohican and Mohawk Indians squared off in 1626–1627. Dutch officials realized the importance of the Mohawk cooperation and decided to permit the sale of firearms, shot, and powder to them, while still forbidding it to others, including the Mohicans. This led to an expanding arms trade, as the Mohawk quickly moved to arm their allies, which led to greater conflicts between Indian nations overall.

The actions that led directly to the Dutch-Indian Wars started over land and expansion. Dutch settlers coveted land that Indians, for generations, had adapted environmentally for their purposes, including the clearing of large trees for increased agricultural possibilities. Through a variety of measures, the Dutch tried to buy, squat, or swindle their ways onto those lands. In 1639, the standing, yet tenuous, policy of Dutch cooperation with Indians ended with the arrival of a new governor, William Kieft. Kieft was an ethnocentric, racist man who had no use nor respect for Indians. He immediately levied taxes on the Indians, including tributes of food, to help support the Dutch who had invaded their lands.

As can be expected, the Indians did not take kindly to those demands. Many refused to pay any sort of tax, and they refused to back down from farmers and traders who literally stole their lands and let their livestock graze on Indian holdings. In response, Governor Kieft encouraged his Indian allies, the Mohawk, to attack the Indians, as he refused to do the dirty work himself. That happened in 1643. Mohawk war parties killed numerous Mohicans and enslaved women and children. Afterward, Kieft sent a contingent of his own soldiers to attack a Lenape village, which they did so with vengeance, sparing no one, including women, children, and other noncombatants. They returned with trophies, which included 80 severed heads for display. This genocidal act spurred other Indians to randomly attack others, including the Dutch and the English throughout the region. A 1644 attempt at peace initiated by the Indians was not totally embraced, and tensions remained high for over 20 years.

By around 1657, the Esopus Indians who lived in the heart of New Netherland were tired. They were tired of Dutch encroachments on their lands, and they were weary of Dutch interference in their lifestyle and culture. Their warriors assaulted Dutch farms. On the night before a parlay with Dutch officials, Dutch soldiers murdered the Esopus officials who had captured and burned alive the Dutch soldiers. The Dutch retaliated with a full-scale attack against the Esopus. In addition, a number of them were sold into slavery in the Dutch West Indies. The state of war lasted for years, and by 1664, a treaty was reluctantly agreed to by the Esopus, in which they gave up all the land that the Dutch claimed by right of conquest. Ironically, that same year saw the English take over New Netherland, and the Esopus remained a defiant, yet defeated, people.

James E. Seelye Jr.

See also: England; Fur Trade; Pequot

Further Reading

Soderlund, Jean. 2016. *Lenape Country: Delaware Valley Society before William Penn.* Philadelphia: University of Pennsylvania Press.

Taylor, Alan. 2002. *American Colonies: The Settling of North America.* New York: Penguin.

Trafzer, Clifford. 2000. *As Long As the Grass Shall Grow and the Rivers Flow: A History of Native Americans.* Belmont, CA: Thomson/Wadsworth.

DYER, MARY (CA. 1611–1660)

Both as a participant in the antinomian controversy alongside Anne Hutchinson and as a Quaker martyr, Mary Dyer was one of the foremost thorns in the side of the New England Puritan establishment. She was born Mary Barrett in England, possibly around 1611, and married a Puritan merchant named William Dyer (1609–1677) at the Church of St. Martins-in-the-Fields, in London, on October 27, 1633 (the name was also spelled Dyre). Mary and William immigrated to Massachusetts in 1635 and were admitted to the Boston church on December 13, 1635. Shortly after that, Mary became friends with Anne Hutchinson.

Dyer was one of the "antinomians" exiled from Boston with Hutchinson in 1637. Antinomianism was a belief that the truly saved could commit any action, however sinful by conventional standards, and not offend God. Dyer was particularly prominent among Hutchinson's followers for her personal qualities and for the story of a dead and deformed infant, or "monster," she had given birth to on October 17, 1737. Hutchinson was one of the attending midwives, and Dyer and Hutchinson were close enough that when Hutchinson was excommunicated, Dyer walked out of the church beside her.

The Puritan leader who led the attack on the antinomians, the governor of Massachusetts, John Winthrop, had the dead baby exhumed after the Dyers had left Massachusetts and examined it to certify its deformities. He interpreted Dyer's monstrous infant (and another monstrous delivery by Hutchinson) as divine punishment of the women's "monstrous" opinions. He published the story in England as part of his pamphlet *A Short Story of the Rise, Raigne and Ruine of the Antinomians, Familists, and Libertines That Infected the Churches of New-England* (1645). Counting the stillbirth, William and Mary Dyer would have eight children, six of whom lived to adulthood. The last, Charles, was born in 1650.

Like many other religious exiles from Massachusetts, the Dyers went to Roger Williams's colony of Rhode Island, where religious liberty was practiced. They first settled in the community of Portsmouth, where William Dyer was one of the signers of the Portsmouth Compact, and then moved to the southern part of Aqidneck Island, where they were among the founders of Newport. A successful businessman and landowner, William held several important positions in Rhode Island, including being its first attorney general. Late in 1651, he was sent on an embassy to represent the colony to Parliament. Mary had gone to England earlier in the year for unknown reasons. William returned soon after accomplishing his mission, but Mary remained until 1657. William would become the admiral of New England during the First Dutch War, and he faced some controversy for the eagerness of the captains under his command to plunder vessels, including English vessels, suspected of trading with the Dutch.

While in England, Mary Dyer followed the opposite path of her warlike husband, converting to the recently founded pacifist religious movement, the Society of Friends, commonly known as the Quakers. Quakers were anticlerical religious radicals who denied the authority, and even the necessity, of the professional clergy that dominated Protestantism in Old and New England. While not opposed to the Bible, they also emphasized the inward light of the spirit over the written authority of the law. For these reasons, Quakers were strongly opposed by the Puritan religious authorities of New England, who saw them as heretics and a threat to the domination of religious life by educated ministers.

Dyer returned to America in 1657, possibly as part of a Quaker missionary effort. The Quakers were one of the few Christian sects of the time to encourage women to be missionaries. Although Dyer, unlike some other Quaker women, was not a public preacher or published author, her witnessing of the truth was fundamental to her identity as a Quaker.

Puritan authorities in Massachusetts reacted to the influx of Quakers with particular vigor. Even though she planned to journey on to Rhode Island, upon landing in Boston, Dyer was briefly imprisoned solely on the charge of being a Quaker. She was released only when William (who had not become a Quaker) paid a heavy bond to guarantee that Dyer would leave Massachusetts immediately, without attempting to spread her opinions. Although Rhode Island leaders, including Roger Williams, vehemently opposed Quakerism, the religious toleration enshrined there made the colony a relatively safe haven for Quakers, including Dyer.

In the summer of 1659, Dyer returned to Boston to visit four imprisoned Quakers; she was again arrested and jailed. Dyer was banished in September, but she returned in October to visit another imprisoned Quaker. For a banished Quaker to return to Massachusetts was a capital offense, and along with two male Quakers, William Robinson and Marmaduke Stevenson, Dyer was tried for sedition (merely holding Quaker beliefs was not a crime), condemned to death, and led to the gallows in Boston on October 27, 1659. Although Dyer witnessed the hangings of Robinson and Stevenson, she was reprieved at the last minute, literally with the rope around her neck, on condition that she return to Rhode Island and never come back to Massachusetts.

The Massachusetts authorities, led by the stern opponent of Quakerism, Gov. John Endicott, were influenced in their mercy by the intervention of two other colonial governors, Thomas Temple, of Nova Scotia and Acadia, and John Winthrop Jr., of Connecticut, the son of Dyer's persecutor in the antinomian case. William Dyer's political prominence may have played a role, as well. The sentence had also aroused popular opposition from the people of Boston, who compared the magistrates to the persecutors in England from whom the Puritan founders of New England had originally fled.

Mary Dyer was again briefly imprisoned on a visit to Plymouth Colony, where Quakerism was punished less harshly than in Massachusetts, in late 1659. She returned to Boston in the late spring of 1660. She was deliberately seeking to "bear witness" to the Quaker truth through martyrdom. The Massachusetts authorities again imprisoned, tried, and condemned her to death. Dyer refused to secure clemency by publicly repenting, instead calling on her persecutors to repent and abolish the laws against Quakers. William sent a letter to the court denouncing the conditions under which she was being held and begging for her life, but this time she found no mercy. She was hanged on June 1, 1660. The place of her execution is disputed. It is often said to be Boston Common, but this is unlikely, as the usual custom of the time was to erect gallows outside the city.

Along with Robinson, Stevenson, and William Leddra, a Barbadian Quaker missionary hanged at Boston the following year, Dyer is one of the "Boston Martyrs," or "Four Martyrs" of New England Quakerism, and their deaths were extensively publicized by Quakers. The executions of Robinson and Stevenson were defended by Rev. John Norton in his pamphlet *The Heart of New England Rent* (1659). Quaker advocate George Bishop portrayed Dyer as a steadfast and calm martyr for the truth, while simultaneously denouncing Endicott and the colony's repression of Quakerism, in his pamphlet *New England Judged* (1661). Shortly after the last of the executions, Massachusetts was forced by the English government to abandon its laws providing for the death penalty for Quakers, although Quakers continued to be publicly whipped.

A statue honoring Dyer by Quaker sculptor Sylvia Shaw Judson was placed on the grounds of the Massachusetts State House in Boston in 1959. Dyer is represented in a seated position, with eyes downcast. The inscription on the pedestal reads "Mary Dyer Quaker Witness for Religious Freedom Hanged on Boston Common 1660." Other castings of the statue can be seen at the Friends Center in Philadelphia and at the Quaker college of Earlham in Indiana.

William Dyer remarried after Mary's death, to a woman named Catherine, of whom little is known. William and Mary's son, William, became mayor of New York City, 1680–1681. Another son, Samuel, lived until 1740.

William E. Burns

See also: Antinomianism; Quakers

Further Reading

Pestana, Carla Gardina. 1991. *Quakers and Baptists in Colonial Massachusetts.* Cambridge, UK, and New York: Cambridge University Press.

Plimpton, Ruth Talbot. 1994. *Mary Dyer: Biography of a Rebel Quaker.* Boston: Branden Pub.

Robinson, Christy K. 2014. *The Dyers of London, Boston and Newport.* Createspace.

Worrall, Arthur J. 1980. *Quakers in the Colonial Northeast.* Hanover, N H: University Press of New England.

E

ENCOMIENDA

When Spain began following its explorations with the establishment of colonies in the New World during the 16th century, it quickly became important that some administrative organization be devised to control the newly acquired lands. At the head of the administrative structure was a viceroy who was appointed by the Crown to govern the colonies in its name. The viceroyalty was divided into provinces headed by governors, with the added oversight of a system of high courts called *audiencias*. On a local level, the Crown fell back on a system that had emerged in the Iberian Peninsula during its control by the Roman Empire, when more powerful individuals would offer protection to weaker people in return for service. This same system was used by the Spanish during the "Reconquista" (the expulsion of the Moors), when Christian leaders were given the right to demand tribute from Moors and peasants in the lands that they had reconquered. This system was called the *encomienda*, derived from the Spanish verb *encomendar*, meaning "to entrust."

As implemented in the American colonies by Christopher Columbus, beginning in 1503, the purpose of the system was essentially to control the labor of the indigenous peoples for the benefit of the Europeans. The Crown would issue a grant to an *encomendero*, in the early years often a conquistador, which gave him the right of oversight of a number of indigenous people or *Indios* (Indians), but it did not include the direct right of landownership. Originally, the granting of encomiendas was not supposed to be a permanently hereditary right, although in practice this often came to be the case. Nor were they restricted to males. Some were granted to women or accrued to them through family heredity. An example is Doña Maria Jaramillo, who received the income from her parents' encomienda after their deaths. Similarly, indigenous people, particularly group leaders, could also be granted encomiendas. Perhaps the most prominent of these were Doña Isabel Montezuma and Doña Leonor Montezuma, the children of the murdered Aztec ruler Montezuma II, who obtained their own encomiendas.

The encomendero was authorized to require a tax from the people included in the grant. The tax could be paid in commodities (gold, silver, agricultural products, meat, etc.), or labor, or often both. In return for the payments, the encomendero was supposed to offer the Indians protection from other tribes and to Christianize them. This would presumably have some advantages in insulating them against the worst excesses meted out to non-Christian Natives. Within the encomienda, there was usually an indigenous head responsible for maintaining records of the workers and ensuring that they fulfilled their obligations. Yet, in reality, the encomienda system was merely a thinly disguised means of appropriating the economic benefit of Indian lands and forcing Native Americans into a state of near slavery.

Although Queen Isabella I of Castile (1451–1504) forbade the enslavement of the indigenous peoples, whom she considered to be crown vassals, under the royal governor Fray Nicolás de Ovando (1460–1511), the treatment of Indians was often brutal, including death sentences if they resisted Spanish efforts to extract the tribute demanded from them. In these early years, the creation of profitable encomiendas often required the uprooting of Indians and their movement to other geographical areas. This led to the fragmentation of some traditional indigenous communities, and in extreme cases even family separation. The first serious effort to address these abuses came at the instigation of Dominican friars on the island of Hispaniola, whose efforts to oppose the mistreatment of Indians resulted in the Laws of Burgos, enacted in December 1512. While the laws formally sanctioned the establishment of the encomiendas, they also provided a code of behavior that prohibited abuse of the indigenous people, placed limitations on the work and tribute that could be required, and contained stipulations on the food, housing, and other maintenance provided to the laborers. Additionally, they removed the authority to punish from the encomenderos, instead placing it in the hands of local legal authorities.

Despite the codification of rights, responsibilities, and conduct, abuses continued in the years following the 1512 laws. Perhaps the strongest voice for further reform was a former encomendero named Bartolomé de Las Casas (1784–1566), a priest in Cuba who became disgusted with the abuses he had witnessed in the New World. Believing that serious reform of the system was not possible, Las Casas championed the elimination of the entire arrangement, arguing that, in addition to its excesses, the Indians were dying at such an alarming rate that the regions would soon suffer serious depopulation. The contemporary expression "*sin indios no hay Indias*" (without Indians there are no Indies) no doubt derives from the importance of labor to the economy of the Spanish holdings in the Western Hemisphere. Las Casas was not the only voice arguing for change, as periodic rebellions added Native expression to the protests. The most serious of these was led by the Taíno "*cacique*" (an indigenous leader), an acquaintance of Las Casas known as Enriquillo, on Hispaniola (present-day Dominican Republic) between 1519 and 1533. Such rebellions brought home to Spain the reality and immediacy of growing opposition to the excesses of the encomienda system in the New World.

The result of these protests and rebellions—and particularly the excessively abusive conditions in Peru—was another attempt by Spain to reform the administration of the encomiendas with the "New Laws of the Indies for the Good Treatment and Preservation of the Indians" (or simply, "New Laws") enacted under King Carlos I (1500–1558) in 1542. Under the provisions of these laws, the indigenous population was proclaimed to be free, and encomenderos were denied the right to require labor or other services from them. While a reasonable amount of tribute remained, any work that the Indians did had to be compensated. Particularly galling to the encomenderos were provisions that canceled all encomiendas owned by government bureaucrats, the clergy, or anyone who had rebelled against Spanish authority.

They also removed the hereditary nature of the remaining grants. In practice, once the current owners of remaining encomiendas died, all of the encomiendas that existed in 1542 would have been eliminated and the rights returned to the Crown.

If the Crown believed these provisions would solve the problem, they were greatly mistaken. They only replaced indigenous rebellion with encomendero rebellion. Don Antonio de Mendoza, the viceroy of Mexico, simply chose not to enforce the new laws when the extent of dissatisfaction became obvious. In Peru, where the laws were enforced, Gonzalo Pizarro raised an army that defeated and killed the Spanish viceroy Blasco Núñez Vela at the Battle of Añaquito, in January 1546. The rebellion was not put down until April 1548. The seriousness of dissatisfaction in the Americas, especially Peru, caused the Crown to fear a possible independence movement that would fracture the Spanish Empire. As a result, in 1545, the Crown announced the repeal of the provisions the encomenderos found most objectionable, thereby effectively ending efforts to eliminate the exploitation of the indigenous people.

Over time, many indigenous people sought marriage with Spaniards, Creoles (people of European/African ancestry), or Mestizos (mixed-race individuals) because they were exempt from the encomienda system. This led to a weakening of tribal communities and identity, while also reducing the overall population subject to the encomienda system. The encomienda system was officially eliminated in 1730, but it had ceased to be used in many areas long before that time.

James S. Pula

See also: Las Casas, Bartolomé de; Mesoamerica; New Spain; Repartimiento

Further Reading

Burkholder, Mark, and Lyman L. Johnson. 2001. *Colonial Latin America.* New York: Oxford University Press.

Himmerich y Valencia, Robert. 1991. *The Encomenderos of New Spain, 1521–1555.* Austin: University of Texas Press.

Lockhart, James. 1969. "Encomienda and Hacienda: The Evolution of the Great Estate in the Spanish Indies." *Hispanic American Historical Review* 49, no. 3 (August): 411–429.

Simpson, Lesley Byrd. 1950. *The Encomienda in New Spain: The Beginning of Spanish Mexico.* Berkeley: University of California Press.

Yeager, Timothy J. 1995. "Encomienda or Slavery? The Spanish Crown's Choice of Labor Organization in the Sixteenth-Century Spanish America." *Journal of Economic History* 55, no. 4 (December): 842–859.

ENGLAND

England played a profound role in settling the New World, specifically the North American continent. Although Spain had pioneered explorations and exploitation of the New World in the late 15th century and during the 16th century, its sphere of influence was largely South America, Central America, and the southern parts of North America. The legacy of English influence on North America is in evidence today by the Anglophone countries of Canada (with a minority French-speaking population) and the United States of America. After the Acts of Union in 1707, England became part of the United Kingdom of Great Britain, though the term "England" is often used to refer to the United Kingdom.

Henry VII became the first Tudor king in 1485 and reigned until 1509, a reign that saw the discovery of the New World by the Italian Christopher Columbus in 1492. With the news of a New World discovered by Columbus sailing on behalf of the Spanish Crown, Henry VII belatedly joined the rush to discovery and hopeful exploitation of these new lands by appointing another Italian sailor, John Cabot (ca. 1450–ca. 1498 or 1500), to sail west and north (avoiding Spanish and Portuguese claims), with the provision that Cabot turn over one-fifth of his profits to the Crown.

In 1497, Cabot sailed for the New World in a single ship, the *Mathew,* with a crew of only 18 men. Having settled in Bristol, Cabot was aware of tales of Bristol sailors having reached the New World as early as 1470. In 1496, the first voyage attempted by Cabot was abortive, having turned back shortly after it began. Cabot's 1497 voyage is the first documented landing of an English expedition to North America, although the actual point of landing is unknown, anywhere from Maine, to Nova Scotia, to Newfoundland or Labrador. Cabot did not venture far from the coast, and he met no Native people. The Venetian and Papal banners were left, and the land was claimed in the name of the king of England and under the authority of the Roman Catholic Church. Despite the lack of detailed information, treasure, or contact with Native people, Cabot was hailed as a hero upon his return to England.

In 1498, Cabot mounted a second expedition, this time with five ships and a cargo of trinkets to be used as trade goods with Native Americans. One ship was forced to cancel its voyage and stopped in Ireland, but the other four ships sailed on. This second English attempt at contact with the New World has no known resolution, as nothing has been heard of Cabot or the four ships ever since. The little fleet disappeared without a trace, although rumors and speculation that Cabot returned to England in 1500 exist without proof.

The Age of Discovery had begun, and the English joined the land rush. With the Iberians having a near monopoly on the South, the English competed with the French and Dutch for new lands in North America and the Caribbean. Notable English explorers included Henry Hudson (who sailed on behalf of the Dutch) and Francis Drake, who in 1577–1580 completed just the second circumnavigation of the earth during the reign of Elizabeth I (r. 1558–1603). Elizabeth's father, Henry VIII (r. 1509–1547) had taken England out of the galaxy of Catholic nations in 1534, adding a new factor to the competition among nations. Internal strife in England and Britain delayed the English from seeking new lands during the time of Henry VIII. The Elizabethan era brought renewed interest in establishing colonies and influence in North America and is referred to as England's Golden Era, a time when the power and influence of England rose dramatically, largely due to naval superiority. English preoccupation with pressing domestic issues, such as the English Civil War (1642–1651), served as a distraction from such faraway concerns as the American colonies, leaving the colonies to secondary status at various times throughout the Colonial Period.

During the 16th century, the ascendancy of the English Royal Navy began with the construction of purpose-built warships powered by sails only (as opposed to galleys that also offered rows of oars for propulsion) to go along with a merchant fleet. The advent of the "race-built galleon," or "razee," was an advance in ship design around 1570 that gave the English an advantage over their French and Spanish foes. The razee had fewer decks and a "cut-down" profile that made for better seakeeping qualities than the towering but unwieldy galleons of France and Spain. The English ships were longer compared to their beam, making them sleeker and faster than their continental counterparts. The reduction in gun decks and the number of guns may have lowered the firepower somewhat, but the decrease in weight and lowering of the ships' center of gravity made for more maneuverable fighting ships. Improved gun drills and training maximized the effect of the British cannons, making up for their decrease in number. Of course, other countries eventually followed suit and modified their own ships to the English standard. Drake's circumnavigation and naval derring-do, followed by the catastrophe of the Spanish Armada in 1588, when it was virtually destroyed during an attempt to invade England, marked a serious decline in Spanish mastery of the seas.

England's early North American forays were mainly related to fishing and fur trading expeditions, with the first attempted general permanent settlement established at Roanoke, Virginia, in 1585, an effort at colonization that saw the first English baby born on North American soil (Virginia Dare in 1587). Roanoke Colony failed, and by 1590, the colonists had disappeared, with no definitive explanation of what had happened to them, leaving one of the great mysteries of history. Early English efforts at establishing colonies were marked by a distinct lack of preparedness for such an arduous undertaking. The selection of colonists rarely reflected the skills needed to survive in an uncivilized setting, seeds for crops were often inappropriate for the new land, and supplies were insufficient to maintain a viable existence while building a new colony and waiting for crops to mature. One look at the inappropriate clothing of early English colonists is testament to the poor choices made. English interactions with Native Americans were not as friendly as that of the French nor as antagonistic as that of the Spanish. Like the French and Dutch, the English sought to trade with Native Americans, mostly for furs and pelts, while getting caught up in conflicts between Native tribes.

Meanwhile, back in England, Elizabeth died having never married and without an heir. She was thus succeeded by her first cousin, twice removed, the then reigning king of Scotland, James VI (r. 1567–1625), who now also became James I of England (r. 1603–1625), thereby unifying the island of Great Britain under a single monarch, as it remains to this day. James was the son of the infamous Mary, Queen of Scots (r. 1542–1567), a Catholic, whom Elizabeth, a Protestant, had ordered beheaded in 1587. Elizabeth reigned as the last Tudor monarch of England, and James reigned as the first Stuart. His dynasty faced a series of challenges from discontented subjects that included a brief period in which England was not even ruled by a king. From 1653 to 1658, Lord Protector Oliver Cromwell ruled

England as a virtual dictator. The Stuarts returned, however, and would rule the country until James's grandson, James II (r. 1685–1688), was overthrown during the Glorious Revolution of 1688. Despite these later problems, during James I's reign, English colonists established two lasting settlements: the aptly named Jamestown and Plymouth.

The first of these, the Jamestown Colony of 1607, became the first permanent English colony to survive, although with dire hardships and near starvation. Within the first year, 67–80 percent of the colonists died. The Jamestown Colony was in such disarray and privation that some Polish and German settlers that had been brought in to provide tradesmen in 1608 defected to the Powhatan Indians rather than remain in the colony. The colony was briefly abandoned in 1610, not surprisingly after the period known as the "Starving Time." The 1609 resupply fleet of three ships had failed to reach Jamestown because of weather, resulting in mass starvation in 1609–1610. In fact, starvation was so severe that colonists resorted to eating other dead colonists, cannibalism that has been largely glossed over by history until recently. Upon the arrival of two small relief ships in May 1610, the beleaguered colonists chose to abandon the colony and board the ships. Another fleet arrived in June 1610 and met the ships as they were still in the James River. The colonists were resupplied and returned to the colony, which then became permanent.

Relations with Native Americans had been problematic from the start, with some diplomatic success, but tempered by some conflict as well, resulting in raids against English settlements as early as 1607. In 1622, tensions between Native Americans and colonists had deteriorated to the point that the Native Powhatan Confederacy strove to eliminate the English colony altogether. Although the effort at annihilation by the Natives failed, about a third of the English and European colonists in Virginia had been killed.

Unrest among English colonists (and their European brethren) against the colonial government was always an underlying factor, and this unrest exploded in 1676 in Bacon's Rebellion, resulting in Jamestown being burned to the ground. By this time, the colony was not to be erased. Jamestown was rebuilt, and the Virginia Colony grew, largely on the cultivation of tobacco. The first African slaves arrived in Jamestown in 1619, an institution that grew throughout Virginia and other tobacco-growing colonies. The English supported the slave trade, even past the American Revolution (1775–1783), until they finally outlawed it in 1807. Slavery was completely outlawed in all English-owned lands in 1833.

The Plymouth Colony founded by the Pilgrims in 1620 became the foundation of what would become New England, eventually consisting of Massachusetts Bay, New York, New Hampshire, Connecticut, Rhode Island, and New Jersey. Like Roanoke and Jamestown before them, the settlers from the *Mayflower* were also ill-prepared to start a new life in a strange land, surviving largely due to the charity of Native Americans. Incredibly, the Pilgrims did not land until November, facing winter with no crops, dwindling supplies of food, and having to hurriedly build shelter. These colonists were fleeing religious persecution in England and Europe and were hoping to found a colony of their own to practice their separatist religion, known as Brownism or Congregationalism. Plymouth had been merged with

Massachusetts Bay. The fur trade and forestry were large parts of the economy of New England and British Canada, and the area of Plymouth and Massachusetts had already been visited for several decades by explorers, trappers, and fishermen prior to the arrival of the Pilgrims. A colony called Pophan Colony was started in 1607 in what is now Maine, but it was abandoned only a year later.

Despite the obvious lack of careful planning and preparation for establishing colonies, the bravery of English colonists and their incredible persistence resulted in the firm establishment of English colonies up and down the East Coast of North America that were protected and resupplied by the ever-present British shipping. English mastery of the sea played a major role in establishing and protecting the English colonies and was a major part of their success. The thriving British merchant fleet made trade with the colonies practical and profitable, ensuring their persistence.

As a series of civil wars and revolutions transformed England into an increasingly constitutional monarchy, the 17th and 18th centuries also saw almost continuous wars between Britain and other European colonial powers, and these wars spilled over to the North American and Caribbean regions, especially the Seven Years' War (1754–1763), which saw a victorious Britain take control of virtually all of Canada. Fought during the reigns of Britain's Hanoverian kings George II (r. 1727–1760) and George III (r. 1760–1820) and known in North America as the French and Indian War, the struggle in the New World saw large Native confederacies allied with each side and playing a key role in the fighting. The English greatly outnumbered the French in regular troops and finally conquered the fortified city of Quebec, putting an end to French Canada. New France largely became a fantasy at this point, although, on paper, a large area remained under French claim, if not control, along the Mississippi. The Seven Years' War had severely depleted the English government's funds, requiring taxes on the people, including on the colonies. The colonists had no say about these taxes, as there was no representation of the colonies in Parliament.

The effort by the English government to stifle westward expansion across the Appalachian Mountains by colonists was a failure. The government had hoped to avoid conflict with the Native tribes west of the Appalachians and with French outposts that had claimed this area for New France. After the Treaty of Paris of 1763 ended the Seven Years' War and the French had ceded the area from the Appalachians to the Mississippi River, the British government issued the Proclamation of 1763, seeking to establish a border between the lands available to colonists and the lands reserved for Native tribes. American colonists would have none of this limitation, as they considered westward expansion a sort of privilege or right to be exploited. The colonists cared little for government concerns about diplomacy with Native tribes or foreign governments. The expense of fighting even more conflicts with Native Americans created more strain on British finances, contributing to the taxes demanded by the government to provide troops to defend the colonists.

During the second half of the 18th century, the colonists in North America, south of Canada, chafed under British rule and protested being taxed without representation in Parliament. Later known as patriots, these unhappy colonists became violent in their speech and actions against British imperialism, which culminated in all-out rebellion for the purpose of seeking independence from Britain. Other Americans, known as Loyalists, or Tories, remained loyal to the Crown, but they were overwhelmed by the fervor of the revolutionaries. Despite having an enormous ocean-spanning navy and a first-class army, British imperial demands around the world were such that a maximum effort to quell the American rebellion could not be mounted. Fighting against the French, who eventually backed American independence, drained the British effort to retain the colonies to the point that, in 1783, America had won its independence.

Despite losing the American colonies to the fledgling United States, England remained a major player in North America and in the waters surrounding the continent. With a large merchant fleet and the preeminent navy of the world, England had a vested interest in all that transpired in North America and the Caribbean and in retaining control of the enormous Canadian territory. By this time, however, it is perhaps increasingly more proper to think of these territories as being under the influence of "British" rather than "English" colonization following the establishment, first, of the United Kingdom of Great Britain in 1707 that formally unified the kingdoms of England and Scotland and then of the United Kingdom of Great Britain and Ireland in 1801. In any case, the legacy of English/British involvement in North America would explode again in conflict during the War of 1812, precipitated by seagoing and naval matters.

The United States and Canada reflect the English (or "British") influence not only in their common language but also in many other aspects of society and culture, such as common law and a representative democracy. The largely Protestant nature of North American religion is owed mostly to English influence, as are many customs and notions of cultural norms. English victories over French, Dutch, and Spanish rivals in North America made the United States and Canada what they are today. The United States and Canada remain close allies with the United Kingdom today as well as major trading partners.

Matthew D. Zarzeczny

See also: Cabot, John and Sebastian; English Civil War; France; George III; Portugal; Seven Years' War; Spain

Further Reading

Black, Jeremy. 2013. *A New History of England.* Stroud, U.K.: The History Press.

Clayton, David Roberts, and Douglas R. Bisson. 2013. *A History of England.* London: Pearson Higher Ed.

Trevelyan, G. M. 1987. *Shortened History of England.* London: Penguin Books.

ENGLISH BALLADS

A ballad is a short narrative folk song with a recurrent refrain, whose distinctive style crystallized in Europe in the late Middle Ages and continues to the present day. The term *ballad* is also applied to any narrative composition suitable for singing. In England, early ballads date before 1600 and originated in different medieval sources, including metrical romances, folktales, and apocryphal gospels about the life of Jesus.

The earliest ballads were often composed for the amusement of the rich, but as printing became accessible, they were spread through printed lyrics, published on one side of a piece of paper called broadside or song sheet. Song sheets contained both lyric songs and ballads and were usually sold by street vendors at cheap prices. They typically contained only the words to the song and no musical notation. Sometimes, the name of the melody was suggested, and it was assumed that the buyer already knew it. Many vendors were also singers who could demonstrate the proper melody to a buyer. Finally, purchasers of song sheets were also free to compose their own tunes or to fit the song to any existing melody. For this reason, the same ballad text often entered the oral tradition with several different melodies attached. The most common singing style was a cappella, perhaps because common people had limited access to musical instruments.

Many early ballads from this tradition traveled to North America with the first European settlers. Most of the songs of the Colonial and Revolutionary periods originated in England, Scotland, and Ireland. Some examples include the popular traditional ballad "Barbara Allen" or the murder ballad "Pretty Polly," which is an American version of an earlier British song, "The Gosport Tragedy." "Mr. Frog," another folktale ballad about a frog who marries a mouse, derives from a ballad that was first mentioned in 1548, and for which a full text survives from 1611. "King John and the Bishop of Canterbury" tells a story about King John of England, who ruled from 1199 until 1216. Similarly, "The Death of Queen Jane" recounts the story of the birth of King Edward VI of England and the death in childbirth of his mother, Jane Seymour, the third wife of Henry VIII. Such historical ballads are often assumed to have been composed not long after the events they describe, although this is usually difficult to prove.

Some ballads traveled from country to country, translated along the way by polyglot singers. For example, "*Six ans sur mer*." or "Six Years at Sea," tells the story of a ship lost at sea, and the sailors draw lots to see which of them will be eaten. Fortunately, they are rescued in time, before implementing the decision. The ballad had a widespread international distribution, being known in Britain, Spain, Scandinavia, and other areas, but it was probably brought to America (Louisiana) from France.

The ballads sung in North America preserved many of characteristics of the songs as sung in Britain and Ireland, but they also introduced significant changes through the process of transmission from one singer to another. Although closest in form and almost indistinguishable in terms of style to British ballads, the American ballads show a particular concern with occupation and often lack the ribaldry of British broadside ballads. For example, the ballad known in England as "Young Beichan," or "Lord Bateman," became "Lloyd Bateman." As the United States does not recognize aristocratic titles, the protagonist is called "gentleman" rather than being a lord. Also, in early English versions of this ballad, the young protagonist sets sail from England for the Middle East, where he is captured and held captive for ransom. But in the American version, Bateman sets sail for Turkey from the coast of Georgia in the United States.

Another ballad, "The Farmer's Curst Wife," which reflects an Irish background, started to circulate with the alternate title "Reason Why That Women Is Wiser Than Men," showing that the ballad became more thoroughly American in some locations. However, a clear distinction is generally drawn between ballads that are of foreign origin, particularly British and Irish, and Native American ballads that developed without reference to earlier songs (e.g., "The Ballad of Davy Crockett" and "Jesse James") and followed their own trajectory. A significant development of the American ballad is, for example, the evolution of the blues ballad, which mixed the existing genre with African American music. Finally, in the late 19th century, sentimental ballads became more popular, leading to the modern use of the term *ballad* as referring to a slow love song.

Ballads became an increasing area of interest for scholars in the 19th century. Some 300 ballads sung in North America have been identified as having origins in British traditional or broadside ballads, and a further 400 have been identified as originating in North America. The first important scholar and folklorist who collected old folk songs was Francis James Child. His work *The English and Scottish Popular Ballads*, also known as Child Ballads, was published in five volumes between 1882 and 1898 and represents an important contribution to the study on English-language folk music. Child Ballads are generally heavier and darker than is usual for ballads, and many of them echoed in contemporary music recordings. The most popular motifs present in these ballads are romance, enchantment, devotion, determination, obsession, jealousy, forbidden love, insanity, and so on.

Child's efforts were continued by George Malcom Laws, author of *American Balladry from British Broadsides* (1957). Laws gave his name to a system of coding ballads that was a useful addition to the system introduced by Child. He also included many songs that Child had excluded and added some new ones that were found after Child's death.

Elena Popan

See also: Drinking and Tavern Culture; Households

Further Reading

Child, Francis James. 2003. *The English and Scottish Popular Ballads.* New York: Dover Publications.

Cohen, Norm. 2005. *Folk Music: A Regional Exploration.* Westport, CT: Greenwood Press.

Laws, G. Malcolm. 1957. *American Balladry from British Broadsides.* Philadelphia: American Folklore Society.

"Traditional Ballads." *Library of Congress Celebrates the Songs of America.* Library of Congress. https://www.loc.gov/collections/songs-of-america/articles-and-essays/musical-styles/traditional-and-ethnic/traditional-ballads.

ENGLISH CIVIL WAR

The English Civil War (1642–1651) occurred amid the tumult of what some historians refer to as the General Crisis or, less commonly, the Crisis of the Seventeenth Century. Major causes of this particular conflict included unusual weather associated with the Little Ice Age, unpopular taxes, and religious as well as political divisions within England. Impositions and Ship Money were among the unpopular taxes in 17th-century England. Impositions or customs duties became a lucrative source of income when judges ruled that the king could determine which commodities could be taxed and at what rate. Ship Money was an emergency tax on each port town to hire a merchant ship and fit it out for war. English governments seeking to raise these taxes experienced a crisis over whether England should be a constitutional or absolute monarchy.

The question of having a representative parliament and a constitution by which the government is bound would have a great influence on the New World, as colonial governments sprung up with representative legislatures and constitutions. The choice between having elected representatives or having appointed representatives of the Crown affected the development of government and cultural thought (norms and mores) about what was "right" in the colonies, helped delineate the desire for independence, and influenced the development of the form of government the United States would take. The idea of elected representatives and the people having a major say in how they are governed became a hallmark of American thought.

Constitutionalism versus absolutism refers to the two main systems of government during the global General Crisis, a period of global unrest from the early 17th century to the early 18th century. Constitutionalism is defined as the limitation of government by law. Absolutism can be described as an absolute monarch with unlimited power to declare laws by his or her own decree instead of by a consensus of the people or their representatives. This power is based on the "divine right" of kings and queens and is ordinarily conferred with the blessing of the state religion, hence titles such as "Defender of the Faith" bestowed upon the reigning monarch. In Europe, it was not uncommon for the Pope to crown monarchs, an overt display of God's hand in selecting the monarch. Some thinkers, such as Thomas Hobbes, described it in a more simplistic way: "The Nature of Absolute Monarchy is The Nature of Man." Others, such as John Locke, took the opposite side and claimed that "the natural state of man is freedom" and that no other man should rule another.

A constitutional monarchy gradually emerged in England. King John signed the Magna Carta ("More Charter") in 1215 as a contract between the people and their ruler for taxation by consent. Later, Parliament held the power of the purse. Constitutionalism emerged further during the reign of Elizabeth I (r. 1558–1603), who addressed Parliament in 1601 by giving the "Golden Speech." During the reign of James I of England (r. 1603–1625), literature and fine arts flourished, with the king himself writing many books and poems. During his rule, international trade through the British East India Company increased dramatically. James's accomplishments also include the English settlement founded at Jamestown in 1607 and the King James Bible completed in 1611. Nevertheless, his reign was marred by numerous blunders.

James's treatment of the Puritans in 1604 went against the advice of Lord Francis Bacon (attorney general and Lord Chancellor of England). Puritans fleeing James's persecution in England journeyed on the *Mayflower* for the New World in 1620, and many more followed.

In 1607, the House of Commons partly refused to support Bacon's scheme of Free Trade and Commercial Communion between England and Scotland, and the House of Lords punished Bacon, an exercise of the right of Parliament to supersede the wishes of the Crown. Moreover, the card tax, along with the fancy design and manufacturer's logo commonly displayed on the ace of spades, began under the reign of James I of England (17th century), who passed a law requiring an insignia on that card as proof of payment of a tax on local manufacture of cards. At the time of the institution of the tax, playing cards was an extremely popular activity after dinner, and so the king had taken advantage of this popularity to levy another unpopular tax, enraging his subjects. If these blunders were not bad enough, James's reign was succeeded by the even more unfortunate reign of Charles I (r. 1625–1649).

In 1629, Parliament forced Charles I to agree to a Petition of Right (1628) by which he promised not to levy taxes without Parliament's consent. From 1629 to 1640, Charles refused to call Parliament into session and sought to raise taxes via loopholes, which naturally did not sit well with the people (something akin to the use of executive orders by U.S. presidents). The final straw came with Charles I catholicizing the Anglican Church. Charles's marriage to a French Catholic named Henrietta Maria and his encouragement of Archbishop William Laud's (1573–1645) imposition of elaborate ceremonies on the Anglican Church angered the Puritans. They responded with scathing sermons and pamphlets, which in turn resulted in physical punishment of the Puritan critics. In 1637, Charles I attempted to impose a common prayer book on Scotland. Scotland rebelled and invaded northern England, thereby forcing Charles to call Parliament into session to raise funds. But the "Long" Parliament removed Laud from office, repealed recently levied taxes, and remained in session for years, meeting officially from 1640 to 1653.

Irish Catholics led by Sir Phelim O'Neil attacked Protestant centers in October 1641 and attempted to take control of the government. This assault spawned a general rebellion that resulted in the deaths of many Protestant settlers from Great Britain. Distrust and tension between Catholics and Protestants in all of Britain resulted from the alleged massacre of over 150,000 Protestants.

In November 1641, the House of Commons (the lower house of Parliament) passed the Grand Remonstrance that criticized Charles I's government. In January 1642, Charles, intending to apprehend the men he deemed responsible for Parliament's rebellion, led an armed force to Parliament House. However, the men had fled and Charles was left empty-handed. He withdrew from London and soon rejected Parliament's Nineteen Propositions for a political settlement. Thus, the royalist Cavaliers under Charles fought against the parliamentary Roundheads under Oliver Cromwell (1599–1658), a member of Parliament and leader of the rebels in the English Civil War, later Lord Protector of the Commonwealth of England, Scotland, and Ireland (1653–1658) until 1646 during the English Civil War. At Marston Moor (1644), Cromwell's Ironsides defeated the Royalists and gained the north of England for Parliament. At Naseby (1645), the New Model Army destroyed Charles's main army (as reenacted for the film *Cromwell* (1970)). Finally, in 1646, the New Model Army successfully forced Charles's surrender. The

Levellers (social reformers) insisted on increasing political participation among various social groups, as outlined in the Putney Debates (October 29, 1647). In 1646, Parliament's army was victorious and asserted their power gained by military force. Scoffing at the accusation that their army was a gang of mercenaries, Parliament portrayed their army as freedom fighters with a noble cause. Many within this army were in league with the Levellers and espoused the idea that the people were sovereign, with a right to democratic representation.

The rebellion had been led and influenced by Henry Ireton and Thomas Rainborough, both senior parliamentary army officers with divergent points of view. These examples of the gentry class were complemented by Edward Sexby, who represented the common soldiers and masses. Other prominent figures included Thomas Fairfax, Lord General of the Parliamentarians, and Maximillian Petty, a civilian rebel. This diverse group of rebels agreed the status quo must change, but they did not agree on how the change should take place. Cromwell responded to the Council of State immediately after the execution of Charles I (a line frequently invoked by communist publications, such as the International Communist Current/World Revolution on November 4, 2009): "You have no other way to deal with these men but to break them in pieces." And so the most radical notions would not be adopted. Voting rights of the kind discussed in the Putney Debates (1647) were not granted in England until the 19th century.

Thus, England remained divided among rival quarreling religious sects. In late 1648, Parliament was purged of Presbyterians, resulting in a "Rump" Parliament that created a court to try (and find guilty) Charles I. The king was beheaded on January 30, 1649. His wife fled to France and died there of natural causes in 1669. With the monarchy and House of Lords (the upper house of Parliament) abolished, Cromwell became the head of a Puritan republic before again conquering Scotland and subduing Ireland as well as suppressing Catholicism in Great Britain. In 1651, Cromwell's son-in-law, Henry Ireton, died of a fever in Ireland. Among his last words were, allegedly, "Blood! Blood! I must have more blood!" In 1653, Cromwell abolished the Rump Parliament; made himself Lord Protector of the Commonwealth of England, Scotland, and Ireland; and banned critical newspapers. Meanwhile, in Ireland, in August 1653, O'Neill was executed in accordance with the verdict of a High Court set up in Dublin by the Cromwellian government.

Cromwell later imprisoned the Leveller Edward Sexby in the Tower of London, where he developed a fever and apparently went insane before dying on January 13, 1658. After Cromwell also died in 1658, Parliament invited the son of the executed king to reclaim the English throne as Charles II (r. 1660–1685) following Gen. George Monck's military coup in support of Stuart restoration in 1660. In 1661, Cromwell's body was exhumed and his head cut off and put on public display. Although the English seized the New Netherlands in 1664, Charles II's reign was marred by the Great Plague and Great Fire of London in 1665 and 1666. In 1678, Parliament sought to prevent Charles II's Catholic brother, James, from inheriting the throne, which divided Parliament between pro-monarchy and pro-Anglican Tories and pro-Parliament and pro-religious toleration-minded Whigs. When the Roman Catholic James II (1633–1701) succeeded his brother, Charles

II, to the English throne, James proceeded to alienate virtually every politically and militarily significant segment of English society by attempting to catholicize the army and the government and to pack Parliament with his supporters. When he had a son in June 1688, fears of the establishment of a Catholic dynasty in England led prominent Protestant statesmen to invite William of Orange to assume the throne.

Both Tories and Whigs compromised in inviting James's eldest daughter, Mary, and her Dutch husband, William, to invade England. In The "Glorious English Revolution" of 1688–1689, William landed with an army in November 1688, promised to defend the liberty of England and the Protestant religion, and marched unopposed on London. James II fled to France, and Parliament then denounced James, offered the throne to William and Mary as joint sovereigns, and placed constitutionally significant legal and practical limitations on the monarchy.

After a relatively bloodless takeover, William (r. 1689–1702) and Mary (r. 1689–1694) ruled England with joint sovereignty and accepted a bill of rights guaranteeing Parliament's full partnership in a constitutional government. Monarchs would not levy taxes without Parliament's consent and would call Parliament at least every three years. It was called "glorious" because it was supposedly accomplished without bloodshed, but during the global Nine Years' War (1688–1697), also known as the War of the League of Augsburg, a rebellion of Scottish Jacobites threatened the rule of William and Mary, but the Scottish Jacobites were defeated at the battle of Dunkeld in 1689. The next year, Irish Jacobites under James II, assisted by French troops, were defeated by William III in Ireland at the Battle of the Boyne (1690), thereby ending any substantial prospect of restoration of Stuart rule. Nevertheless, William's war against Louis XIV's France continued until 1697.

The English revolutions and Civil War most significantly signaled the shift in power from the divine right of the monarchy to the democratic right of the people through an elected Parliament. This shift in power was codified by the 1689 Declaration of Rights that asserted freedom of speech, no standing army, and the right of Parliament to levy taxes. Another major result of the Civil War was the idea that a "balance of power" should exist between nations, which clashed with the attempt by France to expand their power over other countries, resulting in war between Britain and France (1689–1697). This war established England as the preeminent naval power in the world, ruling the high seas until World War II, a situation largely contributing to Britain's status as the economic giant of this time.

The English Civil War took place from 1642 to 1651, in three main periods, and although the monarchy was reinstated in 1661, the establishment of the supremacy of Parliament became final in 1688. The war cost about 50,000 Royalist lives and another 34,000 lives of the rebels. In addition to the battle casualties, perhaps another 127,000 lives were lost, as many as 40,000 of which were civilians (war-related disease). Power was largely transferred from the church and monarchy to the people, and this remains so today.

Matthew D. Zarzeczny

See also: England; Loyalists; Milton, John

Further Reading

Ashley, Maurice. 1990. *The English Civil War.* Stroud, U.K.: Sutton.

Gardiner, Samuel Rawson. 1886–1901. *History of the Great Civil War, 1642–1649*. 4 vols. London: Longmans, Green, and Co.

Scott, Jonathan. 2000. *England's Troubles: Seventeenth-Century English Political Instability in European Context.* Cambridge: Cambridge University Press.